Travelling Heroes

ROBIN LANE FOX

Travelling Heroes

*Greeks and their Myths
in the Epic Age of Homer*

ALLEN LANE
an imprint of
PENGUIN BOOKS

ALLEN LANE

Published by the Penguin Group
Penguin Books Ltd, 80 Strand, London WC2R ORL, England
Penguin Group (USA) Inc., 375 Hudson Street, New York, New York 10014, USA
Penguin Group (Canada), 90 Eglinton Avenue East, Suite 700, Toronto, Ontario, Canada M4P 2Y3
(a division of Pearson Penguin Canada Inc.)
Penguin Ireland, 25 St Stephen's Green, Dublin 2, Ireland
(a division of Penguin Books Ltd)
Penguin Group (Australia), 250 Camberwell Road, Camberwell, Victoria 3124, Australia
(a division of Pearson Australia Group Pty Ltd)
Penguin Books India Pvt Ltd, 11 Community Centre, Panchsheel Park, New Delhi – 110 017, India
Penguin Group (NZ), 67 Apollo Drive, Rosedale, North Shore 0632, New Zealand
(a division of Pearson New Zealand Ltd)
Penguin Books (South Africa) (Pty) Ltd, 24 Sturdee Avenue, Rosebank, Johannesburg 2196, South Africa

Penguin Books Ltd, Registered Offices: 80 Strand, London WC2R ORL, England

www.penguin.com

First published 2008

1

Set in 10.5/14 pt PostScript Linotype Sabon
Typeset by Rowland Phototypesetting Ltd, Bury St Edmunds, Suffolk
Printed in England by Clays Ltd, St Ives plc

A CIP catalogue record for this book is available from the British Library

ISBN: 978-0-713-99980-8

www.greenpenguin.co.uk

For: H.J.L.F.
       T.L.F.
       M.J.L.F.
       C.M.J.G.B.
       M.L.F.

ἥρωσιν ὁδηγοῦσι

Facts become art through love, which unifies them and lifts them to a higher plane of reality.

Kenneth Clark, *Landscape into Art* (1949)

I like it when somebody gets excited about something. It's nice. You just didn't know this teacher, Mr. Vinson. He could drive you crazy sometimes, him and the goddam class. I mean he'd keep telling you to unify *and* simplify *all the time. Some things you just can't do* that *to, I mean you can't hardly ever simplify and unify something just because somebody* wants *you to. You didn't know this guy, Mr. Vinson. I mean he was very intelligent and all, but you could tell he didn't have too much brains.*

J. D. Salinger, *The Catcher in the Rye* (1951)

Contents

List of Maps   ix
Preface   xi

PART ONE
Hera's Flight

1 Hera's Flight   3
2 From China to Cadiz   13
3 Travelling Heroes   30

PART TWO
East and West

4 Home and Away   45
5 Travelling Settlers   73
6 Up to Unqi   89
7 Potamoi Karon   103
8 Beyond Ithaca   121
9 Monkey Islands   138
10 Back on Euboea   162

CONTENTS

PART THREE
Travelling Myths

11 Finding Neverland   175
12 Lost in Translation   197
13 A Travelling Prophet   218
14 Travelling Lovers   240
15 A Travelling Mountain   255
16 The Great Castrator   273
17 Travelling Monsters   295
18 Base-camp to Battlefield   319

PART FOUR
Just So Stories

19 Homeric Horizons   335
20 The View from Ascra   349
21 Just So Stories   370

The Dating of Homer   381
Notes   385
Bibliography   452
List of Illustrations   502
Index   505

List of Maps

1. Khorsabad to Cadiz   14–15
2. Euboea and its neighbours   54
3. Cyprus, Cilicia and the Levant   76
4. Cyprus and the Levantine coast   90
5. North-west Greece to Sardinia   126
6. Travels of Mopsus and Adonis   223
7. Cronos' sickle, Typhon and the Giants (east)   289
8. Cronos' sickle, Typhon and the Giants (west)   290

Preface

The travelling heroes of this book are particular Greeks at a particular phase in the ancient world who travelled with mythical stories of gods and heroes in their minds. Its story is one of exploration and foreign contact, creative misunderstanding and brilliant lateral thinking. It intersects with the great masterpieces, Homer's epics, and the near-contemporary poetry of Hesiod on whose audience, sources and contacts it aims to throw new light. It also identifies an eighth-century way of thinking, active from Israel to Sicily, and credits it to particular Greeks, the first, but hitherto unrecognized, in a line which I also illuminate by their later heirs, the historian Herodotus or Alexander and his soldiers, constant companions of my mind.

The main ideas of this book have travelled with me too on journeys to almost all the places which it cites. While I have been thinking, travelling and writing, evidence has continued to be found on my main themes and I am glad not to have finished too soon. It was a special moment to stand on the beach beside Al Mina in the Hatay district of modern Turkey and to go into the Al Mina disco, hitherto unmentioned in scholarship, which stands not far from the site. On its inner walls runs a frieze of Egyptian, Greek and Levantine-style mythical figures but its Turkish owner, their painter, assured me that he had never seen any of the originals. He had made them all up, he said, because 'This is the Al Mina disco. In the Al Mina disco all the stories of the world are welcome.' This book aims to prove that they were already welcome in the proto-disco of the eighth century BC.

I have used many types of evidence and I owe a special debt to experts in particular fields. I am not an archaeologist but I am at least aware of the skill of those who are and their knowledge of a find's exact context. So much is best understood by those who excavate it and I am particularly grateful to the many who have shared their doubts and knowledge with me. I have learned much from Irene Lemos who kept me supplied with publications for many years and kindly discussed her continuing excavations at Lefkandi and invited me to visit them. She and her team exemplify the skill in the field which I had previously seen applied by their predecessor, Mervyn Popham. On Cyprus I was helped by the local knowledge of Joan B. Connelly who also put me on the track of an important item in Chapter 14. Nicola Schreiber guided my early moves through complex excavations in the Levant and has exemplified a grasp of detailed context and material in her cardinal study of Cypro-Phoenician pottery. Jan Paul Crielaard widened many horizons, both in print and in person, with a range of otherwise elusive references. Above all I was made undeservedly welcome at Eretria and shown and taught so much by the Swiss School there. Claude Léderrey transformed my faltering grasp of the shapes, styles and problems of Euboean pottery and Sylvian Fachard took me on a site-finding expedition, in my view an unusually effective one, while sharing his own exceptional knowledge of Euboea and historical study. In the north I was initially helped by the late Julia Vokotopoulou and on the crucial question of prehistoric animals by the prompt generosity of Evangelia Tsoukala in Thessaloniki, a major contributor to my knowledge in Chapter 18. Like all who write on the period I owe an immeasurable debt to the years of work in the field by Giorgio Buchner and David Ridgway on Ischia, to the many Lefkandi teams, to those who have now excavated at Oropos and to the initial work on the cemeteries at Torone completed by J. K. Papadopoulos. On Cyprus, Vassos Karageorghis and in ancient Unqi my New College forerunner Leonard Woolley are true Titans whose work underlies my sense of the subject. Across the Mediterranean and the entire period, so many objects have been interpreted and classified by two other Titans, Nicolas Coldstream and Sir John Boardman. Like everyone I owe so much to their clear judgement and I am most grateful to the latter for reading parts of my text and at once seeing weaknesses and errors.

I cite Assyrian sources and even Luwian ones but I cannot begin to read either language. I am most grateful to Stephanie Dalley for random help over many years and to the late Jeremy Black for characteristic insights and corrections, especially in Chapter 14. I owe much to a chance meeting with Ian Rutherford, a fellow library-user, whose own grasp of Hittite and related scholarship has been crucial at several points. The late O. R. Gurney gave sceptical help for many years, finally driving miles into Oxford in his advancing eighties in order to confirm that he could actually substantiate one of my most elusive ideas. H. C. Melchert gave prompt and penetrating answers on philological questions in Chapter 13. I was similarly helped by J. D. Hawkins, whose superb Corpus of Hieroglyphic Luwian Inscriptions is the supreme scholarly monument in my horizons. I have written of the 'Near East' or 'east' as a convenience to readers, not as a comment on the nature of these very varied societies.

In my own home pastures of Greek, Latin and Oxford, I gained from work kindly lent me by Nicholas Richardson and from Jane Lightfoot's masterly grasp of evidence. I have been kept up to the mark by Robert Parker, Denis Feeney, Peter Wilson, John Ma, Peter Thonemann, Angelos Chaniotis and Bryan Hainsworth. Maria Stamatopoulou has been an invaluable bridge to archaeology in northern Greece and, as ever, kind. I have gained so much from the writings of Walter Burkert, who also sent me important offprints. Above all I am indebted to M. L. West, whose brilliant commentary on Hesiod's *Theogony* inspired me to begin and whose *East Face of Helicon* is an unsurpassable work of comparison between texts which he, not I, knows in their original languages. I began simply by thinking that his literary work might gain from a fusion with John Boardman's Euboean theories. He has thought of so much else meanwhile.

Nonetheless I have retained this idea and pursued it with many other companions across the world, especially my son Henry in western Asia, my daughter Martha who uniquely had the nerve to drag me to the top of the Jebel Aqra and charm its Turkish soldiers, and Lord Michael Pratt who drove me, without killing us, through many sites and landscapes in the Colline Metallifere where, happily, his wife Janet was able to house us so well. Several sides of my life coincided on Ischia in the fine garden of Lady Walton at nightfall, so close to the Pithecussans' settlement and audibly above one of my main subjects. Lord Charles Fitzroy and Jane Rae, Caroline Badger and Aurélia Abate are among those who have caused me to stand on cardinal sites along the trail, clearer to me than to them. William Poole found books not in any British library, no less of a gain.

There would be nothing to read without the skill of pupils who typed it, above all Robert Colborn whose accuracy and grasp of the subject have made it all possible. I am also grateful to Jane Goodenough, Jane Anderson and especially Christopher Walton for their expert typing of the notes and to the generous help of Gene Ludwig. Claudia Wagner has been a patient and brilliant tracker of the illustrations which I most wanted and Alison Wilkins' expertise made the maps a reality. The title and the jacket are the publisher's choice. I am especially grateful to the firm editing and criticisms of Stuart Proffitt and Charles Elliott, masters of the art. Elizabeth Stratford has been the most acute and helpful copy-editor. Phillip Birch, in turn, gave a close editorial reading of the first chapters and made a crucial observation on them. As ever Jonathan Keates has been my literary support, this time reading the entire text. For some while it has occupied a seat or two in the Library of New College whose Librarian, Naomi van Loo, has been very kind to it and whose former Fellow Librarian, Tony Nuttall, remains a constant presence to me even in absence.

I began this study while teaching early Greek history and literature and learning Arabic as a lecturer, then Fellow, at Worcester College, Oxford. It seemed appropriate that I was making a daily journey between Asia and the world of Homer. The first person to read any of it was Martin Frederiksen, whose judgement and exceptional ability to bring texts and archaeology together left a permanent mark on me and the many whom we taught. One of the first outings for a bit of it was a lecture in Oxford to an audience which included many of the older gods. Some of them, fortunately, could not hear it. Absentees asked for the text, which did not exist, so that they could improve or, rather, dominate it. One hearer merely commented on the movements of my left hand. Another, however, asked a delicately phrased question, as if I understood it, and put the core of the book on a new track. At the time I hardly knew George Forrest but for the next twenty years in New College he taught me so much about Greek history, not least by posing clear, new questions round which evidence then clustered in unforeseen ways. I hope this book is not untrue to what he, too, loved.

PART ONE

Hera's Flight

Your letter found me, as you would wish, in the Iliad, *to which I return with ever greater pleasure, for one is always raised up above everything earthly, just as in an air balloon, and one finds oneself truly in the intermediate zone where the gods glide to and fro.*

Goethe, writing to Schiller, 12 May 1798

One measure of man's advance from his most primitive beginnings to something we call civilization is the way in which he controls his myths, his ability to distinguish between the areas of behaviour, the extent to which he can bring more and more of his activity under the rule of reason. In that advance the Greeks have been pre-eminent.

M. I. Finley, *The World of Odysseus* (1954)

I

Hera's Flight

In the fifteenth book of Homer's *Iliad*, the goddess Hera flies across to Mount Olympus and the poet compares her to a particular movement of the human mind. When a man has travelled far and wide, he tells us, his mind will sometimes leap and he will think, 'I wish I was here, or I wish I was there', as he 'longs for many different things'. Hera's sideways flight is as swift as these inconsistent thoughts as she moves from the peak of one mountain to another.[1]

Two thousand seven hundred years later we still know from inner experience what Homer meant. We do not connect such thoughts with the speed of a passing goddess, which we imagine, rather, as the invisible speed of light. Homer's imagination is so much more precise. When a goddess descends directly to earth he compares her descent to a vertical shower of hailstones.[2] When she flies sideways he refers us inwards to those lateral fancies which express our enduring sense that life does not have to be as it is.

Two thousand seven hundred years are a very long gap between Homer and ourselves and at such a distance the psychology of his heroes has been thought by some of his modern readers to be primitive. Homer's heroes think in their 'hearts', not their brains; like us, they can disown an idea or impulse, but they often disown it as if it has come from outside or from an independent source; they have no word for a decision and because they are not yet philosophers they have no word for the self. Yet, as Hera's flight reminds us, Homer's idea of the mind is not limited by the words which he happens to use.[3] Like ours, his heroes' inconsistent thoughts belong in one unifying mind; they decide on actions; like Hector outside the walls of Troy they sometimes know what is best, but fail to act on their knowledge.

Above all, they share our human hallmark, the sense that our life could be lived elsewhere and that people once loved and lost can seem in the contrasts of the present as if they were never really so.

'I wish I was here, or I wish I was there . . .' In our age of global travel we are all potential heirs to the simile of Hera's flight. Among writers it may seem most apt for novelists, the idealized heroes of our habits of reading. Novelists, surely, need to imagine, whereas earth-bound historians have only to collect such mundane information as survives. Yet novelists become constrained by their own creations and by the need for them to be coherent as they develop. Historians must amass and collect but they then have freedoms too. It is for them to assess the credentials of what survives, to pose questions which some of it helps to answer, and to check that there is not other evidence which tells against their answer and which cannot be explained. As they reconstruct a life, a practice or a social group, their sources control their image of it, but they also need to imagine what lies beyond their surface, the significant absences and the latent forces. When they imagine these absentees they need to think how life would have been beyond their own particular lives. 'I wish I was here, or I wish I was there . . .': these thoughts also flash in minds which have travelled far among evidence for other times and places.

Philosophers will continue to tell us that it is an illusion, that historians cannot be in two times at once or travel backwards while remaining themselves. Yet we 'long for many different things', to be good, perhaps, in the new age of the first Christian emperor Constantine, to be wonderfully wild with Alexander the Great, to question convention in Socrates' Athens or to uphold it on an estate of outrageous size in late Roman north Africa, with the names and pictures of the family's beloved horses on the villa's mosaic flooring, a Christian saint's shrine on the farm for the prayers of the indebted tenants and a strong sympathy with that least Christianized company of Christians, the nearby members of Augustine's congregation.

We can only wish, simulating Hera's flight, but after travelling far and wide among evidence for the years from Homer to Muhammad, I continue to wish to revisit the Greek world of the eighth century BC. It is not a world with famous names, who are exactly dated and known from biographies. It is not even known through histories or memoirs which were written in its period: history had not yet been invented. Its main sources are particularly hard to interpret: poetry and archaeological finds. From the latter, especially, modern scholars have described this period as a 'Greek renaissance', or an age of distinctive 'structural transformation', propelled, perhaps, by a newly increasing population, an increased use of cultivable land and a new willingness of its village-leaders to combine into city-states. One sign of these changes is even discerned in the use of organized burial grounds for the dead.[4] Others detect the origins of icons of our 'western world', the birth of the 'free market' after an age of exchange based on reciprocal favours, or the unencumbered ownership of small family farms, the birthright of those 'other Greeks', the small farmers whom our modern histories of warriors and lawgivers tend to pass over.[5]

It would be intriguing to test these theories by revisiting their eighth-century reality, but my own researches would be different. I would like to verify a pattern long visible to my eye, a trail of travel and myth traced by eighth-century Greeks, which stretched across the Mediterranean and is the subject of this book. Hitherto unrecognized, it bears on other great elements of ancient life to which we still respond, aspects of landscape, songs and oracles and the unsurpassed poetry of Homer and his near-contemporaries. It also points to a way of thinking and of understanding the world which is not prominent in modern histories of this early period but which was active from Israel to the furthest points of the Greeks' presence, at a time when philosophy did not yet exist and there was no separate sphere of 'western thought'.

Realists in the modern world will raise immediate objections to this wish to return to the edges of what appears to be such a dark age. Life expectancy was low in the eighth century; there was extreme exploitation of the many by the very few; there were the past's invisible companions, intense smell and pain, compounded by the absence of flushing drains and lavatories. Among Greeks there was grumbling sexism, best seen in the myth of Pandora, the origin of man's sufferings, and 'from Homer to the end of Greek literature there were no ordinary words with the specific meanings "husband" and "wife"'.[6] There was also an absence of small significant comforts, no sugar, no chocolate, no pianos. In the dry spines of a Greek landscape were there ever horses worth riding? Objects and painted pottery of the period show men naked, not clothed, and surely those Greeks who competed in sports and races had to do so in the nude? It is a mercy that our lives have moved on . . .

Such objections are not all misplaced. Excavators of two of the best-studied cemeteries in the Greek world between 1000 and 750 BC have given few grounds for optimism. At Lefkandi, on the island of Euboea, 'the most complete burials confirmed that adults tended to die quite young . . . in the prime of life, say between 17 and 40 years. The young persons recovered from all three cemeteries indicate that child mortality, too, was probably high.'[7] At San Montano on the island of Ischia, where Greeks settled from c. 770, 'the cemetery population was divided roughly into one-third adult and two-thirds pre-adult', 27 per cent of whom were babies 'often new or stillborn'.[8] Studies of bones, teeth and skeletons at these and other Greek sites in this period imply a distressing proportion of damage, decay and distortion. At Pydna, up on the coast of south-east Macedon, a sample of forty buried skeletons has shown that 'degenerative joint diseases emerge early, from 13–24, and concern both sexes . . . At least nine individuals in our sample were suffering from arthritic changes, mainly in the spinal column . . . both of the individuals over 45 years show severe arthritic changes.'[9]

For those who lived on there were no human rights, no challenge as yet to the domination of the many by the powerful ruling few. Without compunction, this 'happy few' enslaved fellow-humans, using them in households or on their farms. They might even sell tiresome dependants abroad, as the suitors in Homer's *Odyssey* acknowledged when they told Odysseus' son to pack off two troublesome beggars to 'the Sicels' (in our Sicily) in the west 'in order to fetch for yourself a worthy price'; they were unaware that one of them was noble Odysseus himself, in disguise.[10] Slavery, meanwhile, was only the most extreme form of gain. In Attica, the nobles also took one-sixth of the produce of other Attic landowners' farms. In Sparta, by the late eighth century, the Spartans were taking half of the produce of the Greek neighbours whom they had conquered and made their 'serfs'.

These obstacles will hang over my wish to revisit this era unless they are agreed on and countered at the outset, from the high mortality to the nudity in public. The one counter to an early death was a lucky draw in the lottery of life. In the eighth century such a draw was possible, although the odds against it were much higher than ours. The 'average' lengths of eighth-century life in some of our modern tables include all the unlucky others and obscure the peaks and valleys of an individual's span. Prospects were longer for those who survived the acute risk of infant mortality. Individual males who passed through this hazard and escaped death in war might go on to live for more than sixty years. Aristotle noted their political prominence in early Greek communities; a council of males over sixty had political powers in Sparta; elderly Nestor exemplified wisdom in Homer's epics. Women had to survive the further cull of giving birth, but even so there were older ones who survived: an appropriate role for them, if well born, was to be made priestesses of the gods.[11] A small minority of people, therefore, beat the index of life, propelled, in the view of one recent elderly historian of the Greeks, 'by creative activity under tension, with the rewards of achievement, honour and fame . . . tension of a different quality, so to speak, from the ceaseless tension of those who struggled daily for sheer survival, which exacerbated their anyway inferior physical conditions of life'.[12]

This 'creative activity under tension' was most evident in one particular class, the male nobles who dominated their communities. To be born male into a noble family was the defence against social exploitation. Noblemen, and especially noblewomen, were at risk to enslavement, but only if their community was invaded and conquered. Ties of friendship between families, hosts and guests helped to reduce the risks from noble outsiders. Within their own home communities nobles would not be enslaved by fellow-nobles.

As for the pain and the smell, they existed even in this small upper level of society: how could they be overcome? Here, we need to be cautious. Homer's poems describe fearful wounds in battle, 148 of them, and sometimes describe the accompanying throes of death (three-quarters of the wounds are fatal).[13] We cannot assume that Greeks' threshold of pain in the eighth century BC was higher than ours because suffering was so much more widespread or because their texts' emphasis on it is different from our own. Homer is already aware of a fact we now accept, the time lag between a serious injury and the sufferer's sensation of pain. He does not trace it to our brains, as we do: he links it to the flow of blood from the wound, as if it is the blood's flow which delays the pain's onset.[14] He says little about the prelude to a natural death: he does not show an awareness that it can be as painful as death from a wound. This silence is not evidence that the experience of pain in Homer's time was different from ours: it may be evidence only about the aspects of pain which it was conventional for poets to describe. Except, perhaps, at the margins of our modern sensibility, eighth-century Greeks acknowledged what we also feel, the 'black pain' from wounds and body-damage. The counter to it was not a difference in their sensibility: like ours, it lay in the use of palliatives. Wounds could be bound 'skilfully', although we hear only twice in Homer of specific bandages (one is called the 'sling').[15] Pain-relief in Homer's epics is also linked to the skills of women. In Nestor's tent, the captive slave-girl Hecamede (her name imples 'cleverness') offers the wounded and battle-weary wine mixed with barley and flavoured with onion and grated goat's cheese. To us it sounds like a recipe for rapid death, but the drink was assumed to relieve pain and restore strength: cheese-graters have even been found in a few pre-Homeric Greek burials, suggesting that in real life, too, rich Greeks believed in the value of mixing 'cheese and wine'.[16]

Hecamede's onion was the least of Homer's healing plants. They are the ancestors of so many of our own painkillers which are also derived from plants in nature. Soon after Hecamede we meet another Homeric lady, freeborn fair-haired Agamede ('Extremely Clever') who 'knew all the drugs which the broad earth bore'.[17] In the *Odyssey*, Helen mixes a drug into the wine of her menfolk when their storytelling causes them to shed tears: 'Whoever drinks this down', she tells them, 'would not for the course of a day let a tear run down his cheeks, not even if his mother and father were both to die.'[18] Helen's tear-stopper came, significantly, from Egypt, a recognized source of excellent medical drugs for the Greeks. It has never been found in nature, nor has the herb 'moly' which the god Hermes gave to Odysseus as an antidote, a plant with a black root and a flower like milk.[19] We know, however, that the poet was magnifying practices in the real world. There, too, plants were used as palliatives, including opium.

Pottery, shaped like the seed-heads of the opium poppy, was being made on Cyprus *c.* 850–800 BC and exported to neighbouring islands, including Crete. In the eighth century BC small handmade jugs may have transported opium to Greeks who had settled off western Italy on the faraway island of Ischia.[20]

Drugs, not a different mental threshold, were the ancients' resort against pain, but drugs did not palliate the smells of everyday life. In Homer's poems the smell of the dead on a battlefield is not unduly emphasized although people surely noticed it as exceptional: the smell of the dead, a cause of diseases, was later cited as a reason why Alexander moved so quickly off the site of Gaugamela, his great victory in Asia.[21] Unlike acute pain, smell is blurred by habituation and in lesser circumstances than a battlefield we would probably become used to it quite quickly. Homeric heroes are sensitive only to very bad smells, like the smell of slaughtered seals' skins when exposed to the sun. Lesser smells were made easier to accept by the widespread use of scents and oils. In the eighth century, as in so many pre-modern eras, scents and their making and trading were not just the means of stimulating feminine luxury and male and female desire. They were a basic sweetener of everyday life, prepared from a wide range of the Mediterranean's flora: they are known to us from the durable flasks in which these products were traded.[22] People in the eighth century knew their plants so much better than most of their modern historians. Oils from madonna lilies, roses or saffron crocuses were among their defences against invisible foes.

Scents were not an uncontested feminine charm. They might be expensive, one of the extravagances, therefore, which prompted male fear, even resentment, of idle and luxurious women. In the poetry of Homer's near-contemporary Hesiod this sexist grumbling is explicit. In one of his poems the first woman Pandora releases so many evils, the end of an all-male era in which men had lived in happy masculine company with the gods. In another poem, his Pandora is lazy and luxury-loving, the origin, he tells us, of the 'deadly race' of women, with whom, nonetheless, men must marry to breed heirs and to be sure of care in their old age.[23] Yet this grumbling is only one aspect of contemporary Greek perceptions. In Homer there may be no ordinary word with the specific meaning 'wife', but there is no such word, either, in the courteous language of French. From the absence of a word nothing follows about the absence of love between wives and husbands. Sensitive readers of the *Odyssey* know that the relations of Penelope and Odysseus are not simply those of a man and a 'bed-mate' or a man returning to an object of property or casual desire.

Other brighteners of life were available besides married love. There was no sugar, admittedly, but there was honey from the many beehives which were densely spaced in parts of the Greek landscape. There were no pianos, but the sound of music was ubiquitous, the strings of the lyre, the harvest-songs, the trumpet, even, or the box-lyre. There was also the challenge, and comfort, of horses. Horses were the beloved status symbol of the age, painted on big Greek pottery vessels of 'geometric' style, modelled on rounded pottery boxes for libations to the dead, incised on bronze belts and cast, above all, in bronze as attachments to big cauldrons and as figurines to be dedicated in sanctuaries, the most commonly found votive objects of this era which are evidence, too, of the social class and tastes of those who offered them.[24] Among high society in Greece the eighth century BC was the supreme age of the horse. Horses grazed in the pastures of horse-breeding Greek aristocrats and influenced the very names which were given to noblemen's children. We know them as horses drawn with spindly legs and schematic arching necks, but they were horses, too, for riding, something which Homer mentions only twice.[25] A fine flat-bottomed cup from Athens *c.* 740–720 BC shows four horses on its inner frieze, on each of whose hindquarters stands a rider holding the reins in his right hand. This spectacular act of balance showed up inside the cup as its owner drank the contents. It was not symbolic: it represented eighth-century horsemanship at the highest level. 'As a breeder and trainer of horses the Geometric period aristocrat embodies a new kind of master of animals. The message of the . . . cup could not be clearer.'[26]

In eighth-century Greek art and life, horses were admired and widely represented: it was even said later that one of them was responsible for the invention of drawing. When an eighth-century Greek, Saurias of Samos, saw a horse standing in the sun, he was said to have drawn the outline of its shadow and produced the first sketch ever.[27] What, though, about the nudity which seems to be so prominent in contemporary vase-painting and figurative objects? Would we have to walk, run and meet in the nude? Here, drawing is not a straightforward reflection of real life, and its scope changes, too, in the course of the century. Nakedness was a convention of the craftsmen and at first was employed for all figures, without distinctions of sex. By *c.* 750 BC, on the great pottery vessels which were made in Attica females are shown naked while mourning the dead, as never happened in everyday practice. Figurines of naked women, carved in ivory, are also known in quantity, mostly from sites in the east Mediterranean and the Levant, but they originated as stylized votive offerings to the gods.[28] By *c.* 740 BC women on Greek painted pottery are shown clothed, as are men who ride or drive chariots. The remaining male nakedness in art is not a sign that men really hunted, fought or lamented their dead in the nude.[29]

Were male athletes the exceptions? Their practice is the subject of stories set in the eighth century, the age which saw a new prominence for the Olympic Games. There are several stories of the first Greek men to compete naked, the later Greek practice, at public games, but as they survive only in texts of a later era, they are not reliable evidence of earlier custom. They are best understood as the competitive inventions of later ages. When naked exercise had become conventional, it was projected back into the eighth century and ascribed to competing champions as their invention; contenders were Athenians, Spartans or even Megarians, whose champion Orsippus was said to have first run naked at the Olympics, probably in the year 724.[30] However, long after 720 vase-paintings continue to show Greek athletes running in loincloths: Homeric heroes wear loincloths when they are boxing and they are never said to be racing in the nude. Orsippus' winning streak is perhaps a fiction, alleged by Megarians (who honoured him) in order to counter Spartan claims that they were the first to compete in the nude. Modest time-travellers need only shelter behind the great authority of the historian Thucydides in the late fifth century BC. The Spartans, he tells us, were the first to exercise naked, but nudity had replaced loincloths 'not many years ago', even at the Olympics. His dating has not persuaded everyone, but he did not believe in athletic nudity as early as the eighth century.[31]

It would take luck in the Greeks' eighth century to avoid an early male death and luck, too, to be born into the ruling noble class. Other obstacles could then be negotiated. Pain could sometimes be blunted by drugs, and scents would help to dull the smell. There was music in plenty, and a husband could certainly respond to an epic story which expressed a man's love for his wife. There were no saddles or stirrups or horseshoes but there were horses in plenty for riding; there was no need for a man to dance, run or box in the nude. Life was hard, but not unimaginable for a twenty-first-century male. I could imagine, therefore, revisiting it in pursuit of my eighth-century trail, but as an actual visit is impossible, I will have to proceed by stages, guided by surviving evidence, first on the tracks of particular travellers, then on the tracks of particular myths which travelled with them. These travellers were Greeks, but, as our age of multi-cultural history likes to reiterate, Greeks were by no means the grandest or richest of peoples on the wide canvas of their age. As the eighth century BC seems so remote from us, I shall begin by evoking points on its wide horizon, a series of new starts and famous names which stretch from China to Cadiz. They lead to particular people with whom Greeks, too, made contact and from whom they gained a new and important impetus. As Greeks, however, they had one asset which no others had then or since. The trail of their travels and its myths runs in parallel with this great Greek asset, the epic poems of Homer, and shows them off in a new, but contrasting, light. It bears on the poems' elusive origins but it also bears directly on an elusive Homeric sound, one which, as time passed, his readers in antiquity were unable to understand. It can still be heard in our world: by following the trail laid by Greek contemporaries, at last we shall grasp what Homer meant.

2

From China to Cadiz

Those who lived at the time had no idea that they were living in the eighth century BC. It is a chronology which we impose on them. They reckoned time in generations only or, if they were attentive and living at court in a monarchy, by the years of their reigning king. In the eighth century BC, nonetheless, we place so many significant dates, '776 BC' (for the Greeks), '771 BC' (for Chinese history), '753 BC' (for the Romans), '745/4' or '705 BC' (for the Assyrian kings) or '722/1' (for the kingdom of Israel). Among the Greeks '776 BC' is the date given to a distinctive cultural event: the beginning of the Olympic Games. In China or Assyria or Israel nobody sat and watched regular horse-races or the running and wrestling competitions of free-born adult males. The date '776 BC' is our modern calculation, but it is based on the researches of the Greek scholar Hippias and the list of Olympic victors which he compiled c. 400 BC. There were probably games at Olympia before the starting-point of Hippias' list, so '776' is an arbitrary date. However, it was used in later Jewish and Christian polemic to show that the Greeks' history and accurate chronology were relatively recent in world history, especially when compared with events in the Scriptures.[1]

In an eighth century marked by such dates, people were on the move at many points across the world, in China, the Middle East or the Mediterranean as far as southern Spain. The Greeks' eighth-century activities are one patch in a wider picture, much of which was set in lands unknown to them. Certainly they never knew the big event of 771 BC. In that year, after three centuries of power in northern China, the ruling Zhou were driven eastwards by invaders and eventually obliged to settle at their secondary centre, modern Luoyang on the

Lisbon

Huelva

Cadiz

Malaga

Lixus

Populonia

Vetulonia

ELBA

Rome

SARDINIA

Pithekoussai

Carthage

SICILY

MALTA

| 0 | 100 | 200 | 300 | 400 | 500 Miles |

| 0 | 100 | 200 | 300 | 400 | 500 Kms |

1. *Khorsabad to Cadiz*

Dur Sarrukin-Khorsabad

R. Euphrates

R. Tigris

Amanus Mts

Arpad

Kinalua

Hamath

Babylon

EUBOEA

Athens

Ephesus

inth

Aspendos

CYTHERA

Ialysos
Lindos

Knossos

Paphos

Kition

Amathus

Kommos

CRETE

Tyre

Sidon

SAMARIA

Jerusalem

Gaza

Hermopolis

Mersa Matruh

Memphis

Yellow River. It was a cardinal change because in their wake northern China split into small states, leaving a vacuum, crucially, into which the Qin would start to move. After taking over the Zhou's old western capital at modern Xi'an, the Qin, centuries later, would provide the first emperor of Chinese history.[2]

In India, we have no evidence which was written down in the eighth century BC. Instead we have religious texts, the Vedas, and epic poems which are older than their first written versions: they refer back to an earlier age before states began to form in the River Ganges plain. They leave us with the impression of warlike, horse-loving societies where 'leisure hours were spent mainly in playing music, singing, dancing and gambling, with chariot-racing for the more energetic ... The gamblers lamented, but played on ...'[3] No big names from India's eighth century BC are known to us and the archaeology of the sub-continent suggests a very diverse range of societies.

To the north-west, in and around modern Afghanistan, our written sources are also much later. They began life, however, as oral compositions, parts of which are as old as the eighth century: they were passed on because they were religious, the hymns and Avesta of the Zoroastrians. They refer to impressive settlements, 'beautiful' places 'with raised banners' or standards, which suggests that they were the sites of meetings, of troops, perhaps, or crowds for festivals. These 'beautiful' places are sited on either side of the Hindu Kush mountains, in Bactria, where the obvious such settlement is ancient Balkh, and in 'Arachosia' by the Helmand river, where another 'beautiful' place must be the ancient site near Kandahar, known archaeologically to us as a settlement which already occupied some two hundred acres by c. 700 BC.[4]

To the west in modern Iran we can glimpse one significant eighth-century people, the Medes, if only through the texts of their attackers from the south. These Medes, we learn, have 'towns' by the hundred, though archaeology has yet to find them: 'lords of the city' rule what we might otherwise imagine to be a nomadic, pastoral society. 'Nearer Medes' in the Zagros mountains were distinct from 'distant Medes' who were encountered as far off as 'Mount Bikni', probably the snow-capped Mount Demavend near Iran's Caspian sea. Above all, Medes were horsemen, true riders, not secondary chariot-drivers.

They were already exceptionally 'mighty', although their best-known years of conquest lay a century and a half in the future.[5]

The literate attackers through whom we know the Medes are the Assyrian kings in Mesopotamia (northern Iraq) near the Tigris river. The important eighth-century figure here was their usurping king Tiglath Pileser III. First, in 745/4 he began to re-establish Assyrian power against its enemies on the north, south and eastern borders of the kingdom. He reasserted Assyrian control over the great ancient city of Babylon; he marched armies north-west into the mountainous kingdom of Urartu up near Lake Urmia and Lake Van in modern east Turkey.[6] Here too the Assyrians found horsemen and horses which caused them to marvel: they wrote of a 'people without equal in all Urartu in their knowledge of horses for riding. For years they have been catching the young colts of wild horses. They do not saddle them [at once but when they do] . . . the horses never break away from the harness.'[7] The horses were a magnet for the Assyrians' attacks: they needed them for their own war-chariots and also, as we can see on their sculptures, for the mounted attendants who rode beside the chariots' drivers.

In 740 and 738 BC Tiglath Pileser crossed the Euphrates and drove south-west into northern Syria. He conquered the kingdom of 'Patina' in north Syria which his scribes also called 'Unqi', from the West Semitic word for a low-lying plain. Like previous kings he went up to nearby Mount Amanus, which bars this plain from the north. It was the 'Mountain of Box-trees', whose pale wood was highly appreciated by craftsmen at the Assyrian court.[8] From here he could look onto the 'Great Sea', our east Mediterranean, a landmark to the Assyrians, who were not seafarers themselves. Their conquering power surveyed the edges of a sea patterned by the travels of ships from many different ports, including ships of the Greeks.

'I am Tiglath Pileser,' runs the contemporary text on the monument which he set up in north-west Iran, 'king of Assyria who from East to West personally conquered all the lands. From the Great Sea of the East . . . to the shore of the Great Sea of the West, I marched to and fro, and I ruled the world.'[9] Tiglath Pileser's victories were more impressive than his geography. He asserted Assyrian power as far as modern Bahrain; he also saw the Mediterranean, but he was not conquering lands which had never submitted to his predecessors. In the Levant he had been preceded by Assyrian kings of the mid- and late ninth century. At the beginning of the eighth century BC local rulers in north Syria were still appealing to Assyrian officials for arbitration of their disputes.[10] It was Tiglath Pileser's achievement to turn an older Assyrian presence in north Syria into outright conquest.

At their western edge, these conquests touched on Greeks, but it is not through Greek sources that we know of them. They live on, rather, in the Hebrew Scriptures and their books of kings and prophets, reminding us that there were important religious consequences when Assyrians 'came down like the wolf on the fold'. In the Hebrew Scriptures an Assyrian envoy would warn the stubborn men of Jerusalem: 'Where are the gods of Hamath and of Arpad?'[11] In the Assyrians' eyes, the answer was that those gods had deserted their great cities in north Syria and joined the Assyrians. Arpad fell in 740 and Hamath soon afterwards. 'Five hundred and ninety-one cities of the 16 districts of Damascus', the king's annals claimed, 'I destroyed like the mounds of ruins after the Deluge.' The Assyrian conquerors then added to the region's linguistic diversity. Into their conquests they moved tens of thousands of new settlers, putting Assyrians, Babylonians and other easterners into Cilicia (our southern Turkey), Syria and northern Israel.[12]

They also brought in their own gods. Some of them can be seen on a rare memorial beside an ancient route south from Unqi through the modern Turkish borderlands with Syria. Beyond the village of Senkoy the tobacco-fields give way to a grassy valley whose ancient track runs past some unmapped walling, probably a Roman guardpost, and the façades of rock-cut tombs for Christian burials. At Karabur, steep pinnacles of rock rise sharply from the fields and on their faces Assyrian masons carved four divinities, one of whom is receiving homage from a robed dignitary. Unbearded and bareheaded, he is surely an Assyrian governor of the late eighth century, perhaps a eunuch, who is worshipping his gods here, a witness to Assyria's significance on this neglected route to the south.[13]

Further south on the road to Egypt, the city of Gaza also had to accept a newcomer into its cults: 'A statue bearing the image of the great gods my lords, and my own royal image out of gold I fashioned.

In the palace of Gaza I set it up' (probably a single statue of King Tiglath Pileser himself, with pictures of the gods on his belt and dress). 'I counted it among the gods of their land.'[14] Long before Alexander the Great, this new god of Gaza was the region's first cult of a living ruler. Its image was to leave a mark on stories which were later transposed to King Nebuchadnezzar and the worship of his 'golden image' in the biblical book of Daniel.[15]

In the kingdoms of Israel and Judah we can best follow the impact of these eighth-century upheavals. By a rare coincidence, the scriptural books of Kings and Isaiah present from one side events which Assyrian texts present from another. The Hebrew Scriptures make the Assyrians seem sacrilegious, but in the Assyrians' view, the gods of their enemies were merely joining their own conquering progress: Yahweh, the god in Israel, was no exception. Kings who submitted to Assyrian power took a routine oath of allegiance by Assyria's gods and if they broke it they were in the wrong.[16] When Hoshea king of Israel promptly broke his oath, the Assyrians considered that by attacking him they were giving him the just reward for sacrilege. They had already done the same to the ruler of Unqi. In the later 720s Hoshea's strongly walled capital of Samaria was stormed and many of his subjects were deported to northern Mesopotamia. Accepting the inevitable, charioteers and grooms of the northern Israelite kingdom entered Assyrian service. They can be traced there in contemporary texts, serving in the military hierarchy of the Assyrian conquerors' homeland.[17] In their place the Assyrians brought in new settlers from southern Babylonia who took up land in Israel and 'made Samaria greater than before'. They worshipped Yahweh, a local god, beside their own, but in due course they worshipped him as their one and only god. Here, Yahweh was to triumph in a way which the prophet Isaiah had not foreseen. The conquering gods of Assyria are long dead, but in a ghetto near Nablus the self-styled heirs of the ancient settlers, the modern Samaritans, have continued to worship Yahweh with their own traditions.[18]

Since the 920s BC the Israelites had been split between two kingdoms, Israel in the north and Judah, with Jerusalem, in the south. In 722/1 the destruction of the northern kingdom caused shock waves in Judah, the southern Israelite kingdom, and challenged its followers of Yahweh to find an explanation for the catastrophe. Prophets in Jerusalem, including Isaiah, came up with a view very different from the Assyrians' pronouncements. Yahweh had not defected to the conquerors: he was punishing, they believed, his chosen people because he had been alienated by their sins. During the next twenty years the threat of an Assyrian attack drew ever nearer to Judah too, culminating in a siege of Jerusalem. Nonetheless, the city escaped. Its king Hezekiah was merely 'cooped up like a bird', the Assyrian annals' spin for a failed attempt at a conquest.[19] These events are the setting for Isaiah's continuing prophecies of doom and punishment which include the eighth century's most influential words. As the Assyrians threatened the city, Isaiah prophesied to the king of Judah that a woman either would conceive or had conceived a child, to be called Immanuel, and that 'unto us a child is born'. The prophecies, when uttered, applied only to a contemporary child, a late eighth-century birth. Their sense and translation were then disputed and distorted many centuries later, changing them into two of the best-known prophecies of the Christian Nativity, an event to which they had never referred. As for the birth of a child from a virgin, it was not a method which Isaiah had contemplated.[20]

Despite its vivid rhetoric Assyrian power did not carry all before it. Local kings in the Levant crept back into their cities 'like a mongoose', and like the king of Jerusalem some of them survived there, albeit 'like caged birds'. The Assyrian armies also stopped on the borders of eighth-century Egypt. In the Scriptures, the hope of help from Egypt runs through the books of Kings and Isaiah, but our knowledge of the country in this period is still very sparse. Its most vivid witness is King Piye from Nubia in the south, a member of the Twenty-Fifth Dynasty who ruled in varying degrees over Egypt in the latter half of the eighth century. Piye captured Hermopolis on the Nile, probably in the 730s BC, and on entering the palace, he tells us, 'His Majesty proceeded to the stables of the horses and the quarters of the foals. When he saw they had been [left] to hunger, he said, "I swear as the god Re loves me, the fact that my horses were made to hunger pains me more than any crime you committed in your recklessness." '[21] After an attack on Memphis, horse-loving Piye returned southwards to Nubia.

In the Nile Delta of the 730s there was still an alternative dynasty (the Twenty-Fourth), but we now know from Assyrian evidence that the last of its kings was put to death by Piye's successor as early as the 720s.[22] Thereafter, eighth-century Egypt was not as fragmented as we have previously assumed: we see better why the Assyrian kings did not yet go on to capture this ultimate prize. They had difficulties enough in taking the walled cities which lay along the coast of the Levant on the approach-route to Egypt. In 701 Tyre had to be besieged again and Sidon merely came to terms. There was no prompt surrender by these two well-established kingdoms on the route south.[23]

Here, we touch on an area of direct contact between the Near East and travellers from the Greek world. Following the Greeks' example we know these coastal Levantine cities as 'Phoenician', from the Greek word *phoinix*, meaning purple-red. The name arose from the purple dye for which these Levantines were famous, but it was not a name which the 'purple people' used of themselves. They were the people of Canaan, the Scriptures' 'Canaanites', who spoke and wrote a West Semitic language and whose presence on this coastline went back long before the eighth century.[24] By *c.* 800 BC they had formed or taken over some twenty separate settlements, extending from Arwad on its island down to Acco near Mount Carmel. Many of them were independent little states with their own local kings. Close to the sea, these states were usually shut in by mountain-chains to the east, but some of them had also held significant territory inland: in the Hebrew Scriptures we learn of the gift to Phoenicians of territory near Lake Galilee.[25] It is as seafarers that we most readily imagine the 'purple-people' nowadays because it is the role which they play in Greek sources from Homer onwards. 'Phoenicians' were not limited to the production of their famous purple dye. They had many other luxurious distinctions: textiles, ivories, decorated shells, silverwork or bronzes, including their bronze candlesticks for burning incense, the heads of which were shaped like the flowers of fine Levantine lilies.[26] Above all, they shipped big cargoes of timber and wine and brought home cargoes of precious metals from their exchanges abroad. They even kept monkeys, as we can see from the records of tribute which Phoenician cities paid to the Assyrians. They were literate, too, with a Semitic script of their own, a non-syllabic script which included some, though not all, of the vowels in each word and which is attested for us at least since *c.* 1000 BC.[27]

These Phoenicians are the people through whom our notional divisions of 'east' and 'west' make contact. Since *c.* 1050 BC objects from Cyprus had been reaching Phoenician sites. Conversely, Phoenician pottery was to be found at the ancient site of Paphos on the south-west coast of the island.[28] Cyprus's population included Greeks, so the two peoples coincided here. Phoenicians then made at least one settlement on Cyprus, what they called a 'Qart Hadasht' or 'New Town': it is almost certainly Kition, the modern Larnaca, founded by *c.* 850–820 on the south-east coast.[29] Historians usually credit this settlement to Tyre, but our only contemporary Phoenician source, an inscription on a bowl found in Cyprus, implies that Kition was dependent on the king of the more northerly Sidon. Rivalry between Tyre and Sidon was intense and remained so in later centuries: perhaps Kition was indeed Sidon's foundation, but the Tyrians later claimed the credit for their rival's initiative. They may even have backed up their case by specious claims in their royal 'annals', especially in the text which was translated much later into Greek.[30]

Even before the pressure of Assyrian conquests, Phoenicians were to be found further west. Thanks to recent finds we can trace them on the south-west coast of Crete by *c.* 900 BC, another point of contact with resident Greeks.[31] They are also said to have founded towns on the coast of north Africa, the modern Tunisia, beginning with an enigmatic 'Auza' between *c.* 880 and 850 BC. Tyre then founded another 'new town', the Qart Hadasht which we know as Carthage.[32] Archaeologists have now traced evidence of occupation on the site of Carthage at least as far back as *c.* 800–760. True to its origin, its connections with Tyre remained close.

Perhaps it was their prior contact with Cypriot Greeks which encouraged Phoenicians to travel on into this westerly zone. They stopped on the coast of Crete, but although it was only a staging-point for further voyages, we should think of a real inter-relationship in which travellers from the two different cultures, Greek and Phoenician, influenced one another. We know that by the later ninth century Phoenicians were to be found on Sardinia, where Cypriots had long preceded them, and by the early eighth century archaeological finds connect them with mining activities on the north-west of the island.[33] In due course Phoenician objects also reached the 'Italian' mainland, both Campania behind the Bay of Naples and places in our modern western Tuscany. Once again metals attracted their attention here, bringing them into contact with another 'city-state culture', the Etruscan communities which were such an expanding force in Italy in the eighth century BC. Should we also think of a Phoenician or two travelling up the Tiber to eighth-century Rome? Their presence has been detected there in aspects of the cult at Rome's 'Greatest Altar', which was positioned at one of the river's main crossing-points. The connection is still controversial, but the possibility opens up another eighth-century horizon.[34] It was in 753 BC, according to later chronology, that Rome was said to have been founded by the wolf-twins Romulus and Remus. The twins are fine figures of legend and the date of Rome's 'foundation' is not historically accurate. It is the invention of later Greek chronographers who were placing the origins of Rome only in relation to Greek foundations elsewhere in the west.[35] In the eighth century BC Rome existed, but was much less momentous in reality than she was to be in subsequent legend. Any Phoenicians who came here were not witnessing the birth of the future 'eternal city'.

In the early to mid-eighth century Phoenicians were to be found 'all round Sicily', using some of its promontories, we are told, as trading posts. We may, then, be wrong in thinking of Carthage as their first western stop. They were also, surely, already on Malta, although their presence there is still hard to support archaeologically before c. 750 BC.[36] From stopping-points on Crete Phoenicians may already have been heading on past Malta and Sicily to Sardinia and even further west: this roundabout route avoided contrary currents along the rest of the north African coast. Here, they were to be originators of important eighth-century changes: they installed themselves on the southern coast of what is now Spain. From the Adra river to the bay of Algeciras, six Phoenician sites lie in a crowded row on low coastal promontories, a typical 'model' for Phoenician settlements.[37] The heavenly climate of Malaga was enjoyed by Phoenicians, while beyond, in the Atlantic, a Phoenician outpost at Cadiz dominated the river mouth of the Guadalete on the coast opposite. Even further up the Atlantic coast Phoenicians settled by the Tagus river near modern

Lisbon in Portugal. In the opposite direction, they settled southwards at points across the straits on the coast of modern Morocco.[38] In the eighth-century lifetime of the prophet Isaiah there were Phoenicians who travelled west down the full length of the Mediterranean, past Crete and Libya, Malta and Sardinia to our Straits of Gibraltar and out onto the turbulent Atlantic, a sea which lay in the legendary realms of 'encircling Ocean' in the Greeks' idea of the world. The Greek mainland was left to one side of these travellers' direct route to the west.

How far did westward-travelling Phoenicians go? From Cadiz some of them are said in due course to have gone on to the 'Tin Islands', a destination which is hard for us to locate. Might it include the tin-mines in British Cornwall whose sources were indeed exploited later, or should we think of them at Mount Batten, a possible site for metal-trading beside nearby Plymouth Sound? A Phoenician presence at either site in the eighth century is unsubstantiated, although Cornish patriots and local historians have liked to claim a Phoenician link.[39] In eighth-century Britain, however, yet another horizon opens up to modern eyes. According to the learned medieval chroniclers, the eighth century BC was the century of Britain's King Lear. He was born *c.* 820 BC and died (they reckoned) *c.* 760. Like Romulus, Lear is to be imagined in a distant eighth-century setting, touring the 'good hunting here, good fishing there' of his kingdom but perhaps not losing every-thing quite as Shakespeare later devised for him.[40]

Like Romulus and Remus, Lear and Cordelia are figures of legend who add lustre to the fictional eighth century BC. In real life, the Phoenicians' long-range travel across the entire Mediterranean is intriguing enough: should we explain it by the pressure of Assyrian conquerors on the Phoenicians' coastal cities in the Levant?[41] On this view the eighth-century changes inter-relate. Tiglath Pileser and his Assyrian successors forced Phoenicians to trade ever further afield in order to pay their demands for tribute: they caused a domino-effect which extended west across the Mediterranean as far as Spain. On the way, Phoenician goods, settlements and trading affected western societies of which Assyrians knew nothing: the Libyans, Etruscans, Iberians and some of the Greeks. If this explanation is correct, even the trail of Greeks and myths which I wish to retrace might relate to the impact of Assyrians on the Phoenician city-states.

Such an explanation is only valid if it fits with the dating and purpose of the Phoenicians' westward travels. Precious resources are the obvious reason for such long-distance voyages and no resource is more localized than metal. Phoenicians did not need to go so far west to find iron: it was available on the coast of the Levant.[42] Gold, silver and the copper and tin which made bronze were also known locally, but an easy access to such prestigious items was always attractive. Copper was known and mined prolifically on Cyprus, the 'copper island'; Sardinia was rich in copper and other metals, including silver, whereas Sicily, most of which the Phoenicians neglected, had no known source of silver at all. In Italy, however, the 'metalliferous hills' in modern south-west Tuscany were accessible from the coast. Tin, a rarity, was available on Sardinia and is also inferred by archaeologists to have been passing down established routes from southern Europe into central Italy: by barter and exchange, it perhaps reached Phoenician ships which could then carry it to supplement their sources in the Near East.[43] In north Africa we do not know whether metal-routes already ran near to Carthage and gave access to the African gold which was later to be such a bait. In south-west Spain, however, rich sources of silver existed in the Rio Tinto river-valley, while archaeological evidence for silver-working down on the coast goes back into the eighth century. It is highly likely that silver was the Phoenicians' main lure here from the start of their contact. 'Such was the greed of their traders', later Greek sources alleged of Phoenicians in Spain, 'that they replaced the lead anchors of their ships with silver ones when there was no more room for silver on board.'[44]

When did these far western ventures begin? We have the hints of Phoenicians stopping over on western Crete c. 900 BC and a possible settlement at Auza in north Africa before 850 BC. In the early eighth century we can point to archaeological evidence of settlement at Carthage in north Africa and of Phoenician goods on Sardinia. Some arguable datings by radiocarbon have suggested that Phoenician settlements on Spain's southern coast may belong as early as the ninth century BC. Later Greek texts give even earlier dates for these foundations, but they are only the calculations of later Greek scholars and are of very dubious value. Since 1998 the time-gap has begun to close with important finds at modern Huelva in south-west Spain beyond Cadiz.[45] Here, Phoenician pottery has at last been found with a small proportion of datable Greek pottery, taking its arrival back into the ninth century BC. The finds include an unworked elephant-tusk, Greek plates made on the island of Euboea and pieces of the distinctive 'black-on-red' pottery which probably derived from Cyprus. These imports were unknown previously to us in the west and may have arrived with various carriers, Greeks as well as Phoenicians. At Huelva, Phoenicians evidently settled 'specialists of all kinds, including metallurgical specialists, potters, carpenters and ivory workers', certainly by c. 850 BC.

The Huelva finds confirm a Phoenician presence in south-west Spain long before Tiglath Pileser renewed Assyrian pressure on the Phoenicians' home cities in the 730s BC. They did not go west, then, only because his Assyrians pushed them. Should we connect their voyages with the impact of Assyrian expeditions during the ninth century instead? The problem is that Phoenician goods have been found on Cyprus and western Crete in contexts which are even earlier: as for the route from 'Tyre to Huelva', it may go back further in time, too. In the book of Kings we are told of King Solomon's 'navy of Tarshish with the navy of Hiram', king of Tyre: once every three years it would arrive with 'gold, silver and ivory', though not with the 'apes and peacocks' which biblical mistranslations credited to it.[46] Faraway 'Tarshish' has remained a controversial place, but it lies in the west, most probably at or near Huelva, the future 'Tartessos' of the Greeks. Again, the finds at Huelva bring it nearer to Solomon's biblical dates c. 965–930 BC: if the biblical reference is historical, the Phoenicians' far-western ventures preceded the Assyrians' pressure on their home cities. By c. 950 the Phoenicians already had good local reasons for importing yet more gold and silver. Their own local kings and notables would already want them, as would the neighbouring kinglets (including gold-loving Solomon) who surrounded them in the Near East. When the Assyrians arrived later, they took booty and tribute but silver was not particularly emphasized in their records of what the Phoenicians were made to pay. In the sixth century BC the Hebrew prophet Ezekiel gave a brilliant survey of the goods reaching Tyre from abroad: silver was one of the goods he listed, but it was an item for 're-export' from the Phoenician city.[47]

The Assyrian conquests, then, may have given Phoenician traders a greater impetus to travel across the Mediterranean, but they did not force them westwards in the first place. By the time of Tiglath Pileser in the eighth century BC, Phoenicians in the west had come to know their western contacts' resources very well. From north Africa they were bringing the fragile eggs of the ostrich, objects which were luxury items for customers in Cyprus or Italy.[48] To south-west Spain they had brought tusks of ivory and no doubt their purple-red dye. Like the modern pirates of valued brands, they were copying goods which were known in Egypt: they gave them fake hieroglyphic inscriptions before trading them on. Phoenicians were the first people to exploit an Orientalizing style in art.[49]

They travelled eastwards, too, with their skills and luxuries, because there was a demand for them in the Assyrians' Mesopotamian homeland. Of all the eighth century's cities, the most amazing was not Carthage or even Tyre, let alone little Athens in Greece: it was the Assyrians' new Dur Sarrukin, 'Sargon's citadel', at Khorsabad in modern Iraq, to which Phoenician craftsmen came. Dur Sarrukin was built just to the north of the meeting-point of the Tigris and Greater Zab rivers and it is hard, even now, to do justice to its scale.[50] Huge walls more than 65 feet high enclosed an area of a square mile, including palaces, an artificial terrace and a multi-coloured temple-tower which was no less than 165 feet high. This enormous city was built and decorated in ten years of intense activity between 717 and 706 BC. Its demands for wood, craftsmen and precious decoration can still be traced in a variety of contemporary Assyrian letters. Vast winged bulls, bigger than ever before, were carved in order to stand guard at the city's gates and palace-entrance: made of stone, they were up to 20 feet high and 50 tons in weight. Blue-glazed bricks by the thousand were prepared and painted with animal and religious symbols. Above all there was a 'tremendous park' and a carefully landscaped garden.

At 'Sargon's citadel' a royal garden included 'all the aromatic plants of Hatti [the north-west, including Syria] and the fruit trees of every mountain'.[51] The aim was to make a garden which was a record of power and conquest. We can follow some of the pressures its making caused through letters which were sent to and from Sargon's court. They mention the problems of snow and ice and the transport of thousands of young trees, whether quinces, almonds, apples or medlars.[52] On the central canal of Sargon's garden stood a pillared pleasure-pavilion which looked up to a great topographic creation: a man-made Garden Mound. This Mound was planted with cedars and cypresses and was modelled after a foreign landscape, the Amanus mountains in north Syria, which had so amazed the Assyrian kings. In their flat palace-gardens they built a replica of what they had encountered.[53]

Craftsmen from north Syria and the Phoenician coast were brought east to decorate the palace, and in 706 BC the New Year festival was held in its splendid new setting, the climax of all eighth-century display. We can still read King Sargon's inscribed notice of the event. He invited Assur, father of the gods, and all the 'great gods who dwell in Assyria'. He gave them gifts and offerings, and 'sitting in my palace with rulers from the four quarters of the earth, with the governors of my land, with the princes, the eunuchs and the elders of Assyria I celebrated a banquet' and received gifts of gold, silver and precious materials. Sargon also believed that the gods would grant him to grow old in his newly built wonder of a city.[54]

The belief was severely mistaken. In 705 BC Sargon was killed while campaigning in Urartu. After this brutal shock to the Assyrians his new city and garden were abandoned and still await excavation of most of their surface area. Instead, the Assyrians' royal splendour moved to Nineveh where it was to last for almost another hundred years. At nearby Nimrud we can now follow a female conclusion to his reign.[55] One of Sargon's queens, Atalia, was entombed beneath the paved floor of a room in a palace which had existed already in the ninth century. Her body was placed on top of a previous queen, Yaba, the wife of Tiglath Pileser. The royal ladies had each died in their thirties and were buried with exceptional gold objects and gold jewellery, one of recent archaeology's most remarkable finds. Yaba's burial had been protected by an inscribed curse against anyone who moved her or her jewellery 'with evil intent' or who added anyone else to her tomb or 'breaks its seal'. Nonetheless, Atalia was put on top of her. In 1989 the tomb was reopened by archaeologists from the Iraqi Department of Antiquities and Heritage.

Despite Sargon's claim to influence the 'four quarters of the earth' he and Atalia knew nothing about China or Etruria or Spain. Nonetheless, there was a long western axis with which his Phoenician subjects were familiar. On it there were many lives worth living, most of them beyond the horizons of eighth-century Greeks. Lear and Romulus are legends who came to be placed in its time-zone, but in real life there were silver-traders at faraway Huelva, Israelite charioteers turned traitors in the Assyrian army, landscape gardeners of Sargon's Mound and perhaps even some ostrich-breeders in the Phoenicians' Qart Hadasht in Libya, where it had begun to be worth rearing the birds for the sake of their fragile decorative eggs. In Nubia there was King Piye, who cared more for horses than people, and in Israel there was the prophet Isaiah, whose lips, he believed, had been touched from heaven by a burning coal. In western Asia Minor (now Turkey) we even have an eighth-century face, forensically reconstructed from bones buried in the big grave-mound at the Phrygian capital of Gordion. It is the skull of a man, perhaps Gordios himself, the father of King Mita of Muski, the Greeks' King Midas with the legendary golden touch, the icon of modern investors.[56] From Khorsabad to Cadiz there were many such people worth knowing and changes worth studying, all linked by travelling Phoenicians whose routes went way beyond those of the Greeks. These Phoenicians had myths and songs but despite their literate abilities we have no direct knowledge about them, except in texts which were written many centuries later in the distorting medium of Greek. We cannot, then, attach them to their accompanying mental baggage, whereas their travelling Greek contemporaries can still be reunited with theirs. They will be my travelling heroes, whose stories relate to the great Greek poets and a particular way of thinking about the world.

3

Travelling Heroes

I

Although there was no Greek name for Tiglath Pileser or Sargon or Dur Sarrukin, the great events on the western edge of the Near East in the later eighth century BC did not altogether pass Greeks by. Greeks were living not only on the mainland of what is now Greece: they had settled on the western coast of Asia (now Turkey) at many sites since *c.* 1100–1000 and they also lived on the islands of the Aegean sea, including Cyprus. Cyprus was only some 40 miles by sea from the Mountain of Box-trees in Syria which Tiglath Pileser climbed before looking west. From the island, 'seven kings' sent gifts to his conquering successor King Sargon and went up to his palace, so his inscriptions tell us, to 'kiss my feet', at a date we can place between 709 and 707 BC. Cyprus did not become an Assyrian province with a governor, but its allegiance was marked by the erection of a big block of grey-black basalt inscribed with a text by Sargon's scribes. It was set up at non-Greek Kition, probably in the city's main sanctuary.[1] To the Assyrians, it tells us, Cyprus was Ia', a 'district of Iatnana'. In the seventh century Iatnana is the Assyrian name for Cyprus only, but here in this early use it is attractive to take it in a wider sense, the 'land of Ionian Greeks' of which Cyprus (Ia') was classed as only a part.[2] Some or all of the 'seven kings' were Greeks, but they were not a new discovery: 'Ionian Greeks' had already been encountered by Sargon's troops in another context.

'In the midst of the sea', Sargon's texts had recorded, Sargon had 'caught the "Ionians" like fish and brought peace for the land of Que (Cilicia) and the city of Tyre'.[3] The implication is that these 'Ionian'

Greeks had been harassing places on the coastline which runs south-wards from Cilicia (now southern Turkey) to the Phoenician Levant (including our Lebanon). A fragmentary entry in Sargon's royal annals puts his victory over these Greeks in 715 BC; it was won by 'sailing against them'. They had been troubling the coastline, he tells us, up to Que (Cilicia) since 'far-distant [days]'.[4] This detail from the annals connects well with parts of an earlier letter to King Tiglath Pileser which was written c. 730 BC. One of his officials, active near Tyre and Sidon, wrote to report that the 'Ionians' had appeared: they had given battle at three towns: he had gone against them with troops, but the '"Ionians" [escaped] on their boats and in the middle of the sea [disappeared]'. They took 'nothing' with them.[5] This letter's text is fragmentary, but the official appears to be reporting a known threat: these 'Ionians' were not a newly arrived menace. Their conduct fits well with what Sargon's texts describe: seaborne raiding, it seems, and piratical harassment by Greeks.

The official in question had no idea that he was dictating our first surviving mention of Greeks in an Assyrian text. The implications of this 'Greek nuisance' have also been traced in five other Assyrian texts which describe trouble in 712/11 BC. At Ashdod, on the Levantine coast towards Egypt, the Assyrians supported a king, one of two royal brothers, whom people in the city then expelled. Instead, they made a certain Iamani their king, a commoner, the Assyrian texts claimed, with 'no claim to the throne'. The approach of an Assyrian army caused this Iamani to run away to Egypt where the ruler eventually handed him over.[6]

Ionian Greeks were sometimes written in cuneiform script as *ia-am-na-a*: could this usurping Iamani be a Greek?[7] This inference, for long accepted, has been challenged recently on several grounds, but it continues to find expert support: one of the texts calls him 'Iadna', recalling the root of the word which we have seen being used for Cyprus. Although the word 'Iamani' ought to be a personal name, would Assyrian scribes be exact about the name of a lowly rebel? Perhaps he was described to them dismissively as 'the Greek'. If Iamani was Greek, he is a spectacular case of a non-royal outsider who was made the king of a non-Greek city by local acclaim. This piece of history would also make sense if the main skills of 'the Greek' were those of fighting, like those of the other Greek raiders on this coast. Unfortunately he has left no memoirs.

Whatever its local origin, the profiles of this Greek minority were raiding, war and piracy, as seen by Assyrian contemporaries on the coast of Cilicia and the Levant. They are part of the context in which Greek 'travellers' came east. To judge from the absence, as yet, of archaeological evidence, they seldom visited Egypt, but it was not completely unknown to them. Centuries later, Baken-renef of the Twenty-Fourth Dynasty was remembered in the Greek tradition as 'Bocchoris' and was credited with laws and a just reign. He was a surprising choice, the king who had ruled only briefly in a part of the Nile Delta during the 720s BC. Perhaps some Greeks, unknown to us, had had close dealings with him: from his reign we have scarab-seals bearing his Egyptian name, one of which found its way into a contemporary Greek grave on Ischia up near the Bay of Naples.[8]

Above all, there was a wider and closer Greek knowledge of Phoenicians in the eighth century, as the Greek name for them implies. It was not only the knowledge of Greeks who had met 'purple people' on the Greek mainland or on Cyprus, Crete or other islands. Phoenicians also travelled up the coast of western Asia, putting in at several Greek settlements there and establishing themselves on the metal-rich island of Thasos in the north Aegean.[9] In mainland Greece, their physical presence is much more arguable, needing to be inferred from later Greek stories of mythical Phoenician ancestors' travels or from finds of Phoenician goods. These eastern objects did indeed reach some of the Greek sites: they were most publicly seen when displayed at rich Greeks' funerals before being placed in their graves or when dedicated at sanctuaries of the gods. It is there that we, too, find them, especially in the important sanctuary of the goddess Hera on Samos where conditions for their survival have been unusually good. The most impressive items have a particular Near Eastern origin, not coastal-Phoenician but north Syrian. Bronze handles and bits of decoration survive from much bigger bronze pieces which were made there, whether cauldrons or military items. There were also finely carved ivories which had been made to be the decoration of furniture. They are wonders of Near Eastern workmanship, but they, too, are not exclusively Phoenician: many of them can be classified as north

Syrian by their distinctive style. Greeks and their sanctuaries stood on the edge, and at the end, of the great 'age of ivory' (1000–700 BC), exported across the Mediterranean from Near Eastern craftsmen.[10]

As north Syrians were not seafarers, the north Syrian objects in Greek contexts imply that others had visited their land and brought them over to the Greeks. Might these items have been carried west by Phoenicians who also brought their own luxury objects to the Greeks? The question is not uncontroversial among historians, as we shall see, but another possibility is that some, or all, were simply brought from the Near East by visiting Greeks. Phoenician burials are distinctive, but as yet not a single Phoenician-style burial from the eighth century has been discovered in Greece. The mainland of the Greeks was not rich in metals, the Phoenicians' main foreign lure.

Our best evidence for a direct contact between a Phoenician and a Greek is rather different: not bronze bowls, but the Greek alphabet, the father of the script which is still in modern Greek use. Our first inscribed examples of it are still dated c. 750 BC, but its invention had evidently occurred earlier, perhaps fifty to seventy years before these survivors.[11] For nearly four centuries Greeks had been illiterate, except on Cyprus, where a local syllabic script had persisted. The new alphabet, by contrast, was not syllabic: it was the first ever attempt to represent spoken language. It was developed by a Greek from personal study of the Phoenicians' contemporary script, although the place of its acquisition remains undecided for lack of evidence. It seems most probable that it originated outside the Greek mainland and, to judge from the particular script of its early examples, it seems most likely to have originated with a particular Greek who had travelled east to the Phoenicians' sphere. This origin would well explain how it became the most important cultural export by Greeks to lands far from Greece itself. Very quickly it reached some of the Phrygians in northern Anatolia (now Turkey), who devised a similar script, one which was later available to the court of 'Mita', King Midas.[12] Contact with literate Greek travellers and their script then caused Italy's Etruscans in the west to adopt an alphabet too.

The raiders in the Levant, the memory of Egyptian 'Bocchoris', some or all of the north Syrian bronzes and ivories at Greek sites, some (perhaps most) of the Phoenician exotica there too, the very existence of a Greek alphabet of 'Phoenician letters'; these items all point to the existence of Greeks who travelled in what we have seen to be a turbulent zone of eighth-century contact between our 'West' and 'East'. The alphabet, however, has left evidence that the context was not only one of raiding and material struggle. Our early examples of Greek writing are not letters or records of traders and transactions. Some of them are inscriptions of individuals' names on objects to mark their ownership or their personalized dedications to a god. They, and others, include lines of poetry, pointing to a social world of wit and pleasure with texts about sex and love, including sex between males. Writing eventually helped long Greek poems to survive, but it was not for the sake of writing down poetry that the alphabet was first adopted.[13] It opened up other possibilities, most of them for people who already knew how to enjoy themselves. It did not cause a dramatic change from an 'oral' to a 'literate' mentality: most Greek culture continued to be seen and heard, but not read. In the new alphabetic age, therefore, orally transmitted myths remained prominent: such myths, we can infer, had already been a prolific presence among Greeks in their pre-literate communities.

II

The Greek word *muthoi* means 'tales' and it is only we who call them more grandly 'myth', our word for tales about named individuals, distinct from 'folk tales', whose elements may contribute nonetheless to a myth's story.[14] One impetus for making and sustaining *muthoi* about named protagonists is a community's sense of a distant, more splendid past, a sense which the Greeks undoubtedly had. Unlike the Phoenicians or Israelites of the Near East, by the eighth century BC the Greeks of the mainland had lived through some four hundred years (*c.* 1180–800 BC) of social dislocation and change since a grand 'Late Bronze Age' past (*c.* 1350–1180 BC). In Greece, this age of palace-based societies is known by us as the 'Mycenaean age' after the palace, partly excavated, at Mycenae in the Greek Peloponnese. The collapse of the palace-societies then destroyed the syllabic script which their scribes had been using in Greece and in Crete. The following centuries have been traditionally called the Greek Dark Ages, dark to us (in the absence of Greek literacy) but not dark to Greeks at the time. During these centuries Greek folk tales and myths proliferated, partly round the remains and vague memories of the grand, vanished age. We can see this process in parts of the Greek mainland where big grave-mounds had survived the collapse of the Mycenaean era. In the ninth and eighth centuries BC copious new offerings were made at or beside them, although the identity of the dead persons inside the mounds had long been forgotten. To judge from the types of offering, Greeks were honouring the occupants as if they were local heroes, semi-divine figures with the continuing power to influence people's lives.[15] Old conspicuous landmarks thus took on a new significance in a creative, if distorted, view of the past. Stories began to be told to individuate the persons who were now believed to be buried in these old and imposing sites.

Muthoi, or 'myths' in the plural, were also spread by hymns or festivals for the gods in the Greek communities. Many Greeks in the eighth century BC were grouped in small 'city-states', or *poleis*, the characteristic social organization of much of the Greek world after the collapse of the ancient palaces and their world of monarchical kings. The 'origin of the *polis*' (the singular of *poleis*) remains a disputed issue among modern historians, in the absence of decisive evidence, but the extreme view is most unlikely, that it was a new creation of the eighth-century world.[16] Probably *poleis* emerged at different times in different parts of the Greek world in the years between *c.* 1050 and 750: we should not think of a single, rapid 'transformation' which spread quickly wherever Greek-speakers lived. What we can say is that there were Greek communities in the eighth century, whether in a *polis* or a 'pre-*polis*' grouping of local villages, which had clearly marked calendars of cults and festivals in honour of their gods. They sang hymns to them and told stories about them which defined the gods' personalities, especially in an age without monumental personalized sculpture. They even received their gods' words of advice, above all at oracular sites. The most famous such site, Delphi, was a new, post-Mycenaean foundation which may well have begun *c.* 825–800. Other oracular Greek cults existed already, whether of Zeus at Dodona or Apollo at Claros. The voice of Apollo at Delphi gathered credit from questions increasingly put to it by Greek communities, especially those who set out to found new settlements beyond Greece in the later eighth century.[17] In some of their oracles, the gods, too, seemed to speak in mythical terms and tell mythical stories about themselves, with the help, naturally, of their prophets, priests and priestesses.

Above all, we have an unforgettable range of myths in a source unique to the Greeks, which still captivates us and draws us back to this particular era and culture. The Greeks' eighth century was an unsurpassed age of poetry, the age of epic and (probably) of Homer himself; it was also the age of Hesiod, who is known for two shorter remarkable poems, *Theogony* and *Works and Days*, our best insights into aspects of the later eighth century's culture. Nothing in the Greeks' material evidence, the pottery, the metalwork or the rudimentary architecture prepares us for this dazzling achievement. The Greeks of the eighth century were distinguished for words rather than things.

Of course, Near Eastern societies had their own poetry too, some of which was vastly older than anything known in Greece.[18] A thousand years before any Greek poets at Mycenae, Sumerian poems were being composed and copied in Mesopotamia, *c.* 2500–2000 BC. Fragments of them have survived on clay tablets, and even in the eighth century, written versions of these old poems were being used by Assyrian scribes and singers. The great ancient poem of *Gilgamesh* was still known and copied, as was the old Babylonian *Epic of Creation*. Nothing which was sung in Greece in the eighth century was of a comparable antiquity. New poetry was also being composed at Tiglath Pileser's Assyrian court, in the kingdoms of Israel and Judah and no doubt in north Syria and the Levant. Among the Assyrians, modern scholars classify 'epic' poems, but they are only short poems which are less than a hundred lines long; we have fragments of such poems on the military exploits and virtues of the king. In tenth- to eighth-century Israel, meanwhile, the Hebrew Scriptures contain many references to songs, music and singing which show the importance of poetry in this period. Here too the indications are that the Hebrew poems were short hymns and psalms or short tales of battle. In the Levant, scenes carved on Phoenician ivories and metalware show the prominence of musicians, although no Phoenician poetry has survived. Phoenician songs and poems must have resounded on the sea-routes from Tyre to Cadiz and from Carthage to Sardinia. Their harvest-song made such an impression that Greek hearers imitated it and called it the 'Linus song'. Scenes shown on the fine silver bowls of Phoenician craftsmen seem to allude to narratives now lost to us, about sieges and hunts, battles and the courts of kings.[19] Perhaps they too were told as poems.

Among Greeks, heroic poetry had long been current in the complex hexameter metre, wholly unlike the poetic forms in the east. The absence of writing means that no Greek poetry has survived for us to read before the eighth century, but we can infer from Homer's poems that his metre, his diction and some of his stories had had a long prehistory. His predecessors' heroic stories were probably told only in short cycles, one episode after another, like the songs which Homer gives to singers in his own epics, poets whom he imagines so touchingly in an earlier heroic world. As far as we know, it was Homer who invented epic, in the sense of a long, structured poem with a single guiding plot; it is most evident in his *Odyssey*.[20] The ancients later gave various dates for Homer's lifetime because nobody knew the truth of it, but most of these dates are much earlier than those which we now prefer. Most modern scholars place Homer in the eighth century BC, in my view rightly, although a minority now champion a later date, *c.* 680–660.[21] Whereas all the known Near Eastern poems are quite short, the Homeric epics are so long that they need two or three whole days for their performance. Poetry on this grand scale occupied a different place in society to anything known in Near Eastern sources: perhaps it was performed on special days at a festival in honour of the gods, the setting, we know, for many consecutive days of poetic recitals later in Greek city-states.[22] The humble swineherd Eumaeus in Homer's *Odyssey* pays admirable tribute to it. 'As when a man gazes on a singer', the *Odyssey* makes him tell Odysseus, 'who sings lovely verses to mortal men, having learned them from the gods, and they long to hear him endlessly, whenever he sings . . .'[23] So, then and now, people longed to hear the 'endless' Homeric poems themselves, the *Iliad* with its pathos and hard irony and the *Odyssey* with its pathos, too, and courtesy, and its hero's many reversals during the plot which brings him home to his wife, his son and revenge. In the *Odyssey*, for the first time, nostalgia confronts us in world literature.

These eighth-century epics may have been orally composed poems which Homer performed without memorization or the aid of a written text.[24] If so, they may owe some of their singular style to composition in a long tradition of metrical, orally composed song near the end of Greek poetry's 'oral phase'. Alphabetic writing, a recent invention, was perhaps an aid not so much to their composition as to their preservation. As some scholars have suggested, Homer might perhaps have recited his two epics to alphabetic writers. As there was such a profit to be made from them, his family or his close associates would be keen to have a text of their performance, however laborious.

We shall probably never know where Homer performed, whether there was one Homer for the *Iliad*, and another for the *Odyssey* (certainly the later of the two epics), whether women were present in his first audience, what exactly was the scope of the poems when first sung. What we do know from his poems is that his hearers were living in a world which teemed with *muthoi* of the gods and heroes. Sometimes he refers to myths off his main storyline, but they are told in such a condensed manner that he presupposes familiarity with the tale among his hearers: the exploits of Bellerophon, perhaps, or the misconduct of Clytaemnestra or the labours of Heracles. A few, perhaps, of these myths went back, at least in outline, to the Greek-speaking Mycenaean palaces some five hundred years before Homer's time. Many more were creations of the intervening 'Dark Ages', the illiterate era when stories had multiplied, partly around relics or dim memories of the lost palace-age, partly round the gods and cults of each little Greek community, its landmarks, landscapes, water-springs or hills.

Homer could invent *muthoi* or adapt them anew: his own poems are *muthoi* themselves and sometimes they make up for gaps in the Greeks' real world. There were no landscape gardens among the self-styled 'best' Greek nobles, nothing to compare with King Sargon's Garden Mound, but this Mound disappeared without influencing posterity, bold though its scale had been. The most famous and influential garden of the eighth century was to be a Greek one, Homer's mythical garden for King Alcinous in the legendary land of Phaeacia in the *Odyssey*. It existed only in Homer's magical poetry, but poets and orators continued to imitate it.[25] Is this garden also a clue to how

Homer composed his poem? Remarkably, he describes it in the present tense, although his speaker Odysseus is narrating his former experiences and describing the rest of them in the past. Are the verbs a sign that Homer has moved these particular verses from another context, perhaps from a previous speech to Odysseus in which somebody, perhaps the fair young girl Nausicaa, described the garden to him more appropriately in the present tense? If so, Homer was already working with a written text, his own.[26] Such are the ingenuities of modern critics but more plausibly the present tenses are descriptive, making the details immediate to us still. This test-case for Homer's technique is still a garden, after all. It has an orchard and a vineyard and 'neat' beds for vegetables which are wondrously gleaming all the year round. There are fruit-trees, even pomegranates, but conspicuously there are no flowers for ornament's sake. It is not that Homer and his teachers were insensitive to flowers, to the violets round Calypso's cave or the carpet of crocus and hyacinth on which the gods Zeus and Hera made heavenly love. But flowers for their own sake were an extravagance which not even the finest imaginary Greek garden contained. Luxuriant flowers and greenery were either the luxury of gods or potentially sinister, implying that danger was imminent.[27]

Through the hazards of such landscapes, Homer tells of the return of mythical heroes from the 'great event' of the sack of Troy. Odysseus' return is the most detailed tale but even here Homer innovates and tells new *muthoi*: other poets then followed what Homer had exemplified. As a result, many of the mythical heroes are known to us after Homer's time at new addresses to which they were supposed to have come during their 'return' from Troy, settling on islands and coastlines as far away as Libya or Italy. We know of these placings thanks to later Greek poets and ethnographers, the ever-growing mass of local Greek inscriptions and even the eloquent images on cities' subsequent coins. Consequently, they have remained at the centre of modern scholarly study, mythical 'travelling heroes' who became located at real places which they connected to the prestigious currents of Homeric epic. The problem is to trace the placing of these legendary 'travelling heroes' at these faraway sites before the seventh to sixth centuries BC.[28]

The travelling heroes whom I wish to trace are different: they are particular Greeks from a particular part of Greece in the real world. They are heroic in what they actually did and encountered across much of the Mediterranean despite (no doubt) the low morals with which they sometimes raided and killed. Their travels included journeys eastwards and with them as they travelled went a baggage of specific myths which they already knew. As we shall discover, they encountered myths in foreign lands which they assimilated too. They then believed that they had found specific items in these very same myths as they continued to travel even further across the sea. Particular myths thus became located like a 'songline' across the entire span of their travels. Strikingly, their trail of myths contrasts repeatedly with the horizon of Homer's epics. It connects, unexpectedly, with other eighth-century poetry and a criss-cross pattern of travellers which brings both the myths and the poetry into a new focus.

Their trail also brings a specific gain for our understanding of Homer's horizons, the nature of that sound which perplexed the ancients too. About three hours into an oral performance of his *Iliad*, after the middle of our second book, Homer starts to describe the first advance of the Greek army across the dusty plain of Troy. He prepares us with three similes, each of which helps us to envisage an abstract quality, the sight, the multitude, and then the sound of the Greek troops on the move.[29] The Greeks' bronze armour, Homer tells us, gleamed like the glare of a 'consuming fire' in a 'boundless forest' on the mountain-peaks, the forerunner, therefore, of our modern summer forest fires. Their many peoples poured out like the 'many tribes of winged birds, geese and cranes and long-necked swans' which fly to and fro in the 'Asian meadow round the streams of Cayster' where they settle with a crash, like the echoing of the ground when struck by the Greek troops' feet. The troops were teeming in such numbers as the 'hordes of swarming flies around the herdsman's farmstead in spring when the pails are wet with milk'.

Forest fires still burn in summer in the Mediterranean, flies swarm in the dairies in spring and we know these plains of the Cayster river which still runs by the city of Ephesus, although the exact 'Asian meadow' is disputed and the swans, but not the cranes, have disappeared from the likeliest candidates for the site.[30] The *Iliad* then goes on to give us its lengthy Catalogue of the Greek ships and their heroes, a list which draws on much older traditions. When it ends Homer reverts to the qualities which he has already tried to make visible to us by similes. The advancing Greek troops, he tells us again, sweep onwards as if 'all the earth were being swept by fire': once again the ground resounds beneath them. But this time the crash is not one of geese and swans who settle in a meadow. It is like the crash of the earth beneath the 'anger of Zeus who delights in thunder, whenever he lashes the ground around Typhoeus in Arima, where they say is Typhoeus' bed . . .'[31]

Even the ancients were uncertain. Did Homer mean a place called 'Arima' or people known as the 'Arimoi'? Where was the place or people to be found? What, we might wonder, is the force of 'they say' here: did Homer mean 'so rumour has it' or 'so informed observers say' (although Homer had not seen it himself)? Is the phrase conferring authority or expressing non-committal doubt? Typhoeus was a huge snaky monster, whom we also know as Typhon, but unlike the Cayster river the exact location of Homer's comparison has never been clear. It seems to depend on the words of others, but we are not told who they are.

The din of the Greeks' first advance has thus perplexed readers ancient and modern, despite Homer's customary precision. But we can understand it if we follow my travelling Greeks to specific places and follow, too, their discoveries among the local myths which gathered round them. From their perspective as men 'who have travelled far and wide' we can then look afresh at Homer's simile and hear at last what Homer had in mind, the exact echo of the Greek army's advance across the Trojan plain. It is a discovery worth an eighth-century journey, because it is one with a resonance which the sound of King Tiglath Pileser's chariots has never been able to equal.

PART TWO

East and West

The modern tendency to identify 'Euboians' in Syria, Cyprus, Crete, Ischia, and even Euboia itself may be a mistake ... Those who initiated this network of trade and settlement were not Greek, but Levantine, and the culture they helped sponsor was too mixed to call Greek.

Sarah P. Morris,
Daidalos and the Origins of Greek Art (1992)

If the Greek pottery found in Syria in the 8th century [BC] was carried there by Easterners we await an answer to the question, often posed but not answered, why it is overwhelmingly from the Euboean straits, and none for example from Crete which we know to have been visited by Easterners, both Syrian and Phoenician. The answer can be only – Euboean carriers. But I do not wish, or need, here to argue further about the role of Euboea ... prejudice against them in the West [is] shown by some scholars and the same applies also in the East.

Sir John Boardman, 'Al Mina: Notes and Queries',
AWE 4 (2005), 286

It is a reasonable supposition that, somewhere in the soil, almost all the pottery vessels ever made survive in fragments waiting to be excavated and studied.

Bryan Ward-Perkins,
The Fall of Rome and the End of Civilization (2005)

4

Home and Away

I

The general traces of eighth-century Greek contact with the Near East need to be made much more precise, even, if possible, accurate, so that we can trace a trail of particular travellers and connect them to accompanying myths. We have two types of contemporary evidence, archaeology and poetry, including Homer, on the well-founded and widespread modern assumption that Homer, like Hesiod, was an eighth-century poet. We also have a supporting range of evidence and information, some of it the evidence of places. It helps us to identify particular sites where contacts with Greeks occurred, to reunite sites known in texts or modern archaeology with their correct ancient place names and thus to exploit, above all, a knowledge of their landscape. Not much of this landscape has changed dramatically. There were many more fine trees on Sicily or Cyprus, and there were no untidy eucalyptuses in the Mediterranean which eighth-century Greeks saw, no oranges or lemons, no maize or cotton or tomatoes. However, there were still the same mountains, bays, plains and rivers, with only some relatively minor changes to their courses.

We also have widely scattered references in texts which were written much later in Greek and Latin and which allude to events, places and people whom we would date, on reasoned grounds, back in the eighth century too. It is easy, but misguided, to dismiss all this information indiscriminately, as if it is all guesswork or invention or the tendentious creation of people with later interests to advance. Some of it goes back to earlier written sources (mostly *c.* 450 BC onwards), including the researches of Aristotle and his pupils (*c.* 330 BC) into the earlier 'constitutional' history of 158 Greek states, which they based on local oral sources, texts and even laws and inscriptions otherwise lost to us. Even when storytelling and typical motifs have elaborated what survives, a core of historical names, places and events can still be unwrapped from them: this critical rereading is quite different from misplaced attempts to find underlying factual history in purely mythical narratives about mythical people outside historical time. Ultimately the value of such later material depends on oral sources maintaining it from the eighth century to its first writer's own age. Most Greeks, like many people nowadays, tended to remember accurately back to about two generations before their own time (their great-grandfather's doings were a haze to them), but, as in many other semi-literate societies, 'great events' were sometimes passed down accurately across many more years. They might include the origin of a social group or city-state, its founders and its siting. These items in 'social memory' are particularly useful for tracing our trail of Greeks overseas.[1] They might also concern wars, civil conflicts or monuments which were still visible to posterity. Memories of such things were sometimes passed on by regular retelling at festivals or commemorations. Not every such item in our later texts is therefore true or well based: guesses, inventions or distorting bias are always possibilities. Their use rests on critical discrimination, not on a random determination to fit every surviving reference into one and the same eighth-century jigsaw puzzle.

Of the primary sources which are the main guide for our trail, the most copious, Homer's epics, are an oblique witness to his own times. They are set in a distant heroic world and their main stories are myths lying far outside any eighth-century warrior or traveller's real life. However, Homer is frequently very precise about places or points in a real landscape, known, therefore, to him or to previous poets in the hexameter tradition which had formed him. Whatever its ultimate origin, there is detail here of places known to Greeks. There are also 'tales within a tale', shorter tales of travel which Homer causes his heroes to tell, particularly in the *Odyssey*. They lie off the main lines of the plot which he inherited and when they refer to specific places and travels outside a world of fantasy, the details have to arise from Homer's own invention. He would probably draw on bits of what he had heard or known in order to make these invented stories seem convincing. They even cohere in a typical pattern which he uses in several contexts and in a general way this pattern too may tell us something about the poet's horizons. If we heard a poet nowadays telling us a story of Australians travelling abroad and of students on summer vacation in Bali or Thailand (even without telltale mobile phones), we could assess it as critical historians and see that these elements in it belong after *c.* 1790 (the mention of Australians) and after *c.* 1965 (the student-travellers, in hordes).

When Homer's epics tell tales of eastern travels they deploy similar elements and a similar pattern. They refer to Phoenicians, but only to the rich city of Sidon, not Tyre or Byblos or any of their other city-states from Arwad to Acco. Greek heroes only visit Sidon in exceptional circumstances, when eloping with fair Helen or returning home from Troy. Phoenicians, in turn, are found abroad, but mainly in Egypt and as visitors to Crete or as traders with plans to visit Libya.[2] Once they sell goods from their dark ships off the wondrous isle of 'Syrie', a fantasy island peopled by fortunate Greeks whom neither we nor Homer can place in the real world. Abroad they are imagined as faraway visitors who motivate rare travels and adventures in stories which Homer's heroes tell. They are not a presence back in the heroes' own Greek homeland. They tend to be rapacious and crooked, but there is no racial animosity, blackening all Phoenicians as deceitful non-Greeks. In one tall story, Homer's Odysseus tells of 'noble' Phoenicians who are the trusted mainstays of the tale.[3] The fact is that Homer's Phoenicians tend to be traders and in Homeric epic, traders both Greek and non-Greek tell lies and are out for gain in a most unheroic way. So is Odysseus, but his own lies, deceit and gain are not a trader's: they are nobly and heroically deployed by a king, a man of war.

At Phoenician Sidon, Homer's local king gives away cleverly worked bowls of metal and fine textiles as gifts to his noble Greek visitors. As traders, Homer's Phoenicians sell 'trinkets' and fine necklaces when they moor off a faraway Greek island.[4] The main 'triangle' of Phoenician trading is Sidon, Crete, the coast of Egypt ('Aigyptos' is Homer's name for the Nile) and an outlying point in 'Libya', our north Africa. From Crete, alternatively, they might go north-west, up the sea and islands off the north-west coast of the Greek mainland, presumably on their way to south Italy, Sardinia or Spain, lands which Homer never mentions.

Naturally, the plots of Homer's two epics do not concern the trading and travelling of real Greek traders and raiders in Homer's own (eighth-century) times. However, when Homer is most free to invent off the main lines of the plot, Egypt, Libya and Sidon are the place names which he repeatedly invokes for the trading and raiding. We shall return to the significance, even the sources, of this recurring pattern, but instead we must follow alternative evidence, real objects from the eighth century and its forerunners, the 'dark' tenth and ninth centuries, which have been unearthed and classified by archaeologists. In a more general way there is a useful Homeric contribution to their understanding, the reminder that not every person or object travelled because of trade. Homer's epics show us that Near Eastern objects could sometimes arrive as gifts, not items of trade, and then be recycled and travel as ransoms, like the Phoenician silver bowl in the *Iliad* which first stopped on Lemnos as a gift, then passed to Patroclus as a ransom and ended as a prize on offer from Achilles at the funeral-games he held in Patroclus' honour. If we found it buried with its final winner we would never give it such a complex prehistory.[5] Solid, material objects can thus be elusive evidence too. With this Homeric lesson in mind we can use them to follow Greeks in the real world, my 'travelling heroes' who knew very much more than Homer's epics of foreigners and their lands.

II

The most abundant evidence of people and objects on the move in the eighth century BC is not poetry: it is pottery, the most durable debris which archaeologists find. It has none of Homer's consummate art, and it does not address us through inscriptions or stories painted on its surface. In the eighth century BC human figures were sometimes painted on pots at particular places of production, but narrative painting of mythical stories was rare and on our surviving examples the painting of an epic scene from Homer's poems was not yet attempted.[6]

The most impressive eighth-century pieces are densely patterned with geometric designs which probably derived from the patterns of Greek textiles. Few visitors to museums still value their smaller contemporaries, the drinking-cups with handles and 'compass-drawn concentric circles' or the cups and big bowls with the most frequent types of figurative decoration, schematic birds, horses or trees. However, these same pots, even small fragments of them, are significant for historians. Archaeologists can now reconstruct a whole piece from a significant fragment and can often ascribe its manufacture to a particular Greek site. Sometimes their ascription is supported by analysis of a pot's particular clay. Each piece contributes to a complex story of the movement of goods and people, exactly what we need to retrace.

There is history in the travels of cups and bowls, although 'ceramics do not equal history'.[7] They are only one small part of history and even there, they are only part of the evidence. In the tenth to eighth centuries BC Greeks from particular places may well have travelled more widely than we can trace. The lack of finds of Greek pottery from Egypt in this period means that we cannot document Greek contacts with Egypt, not that such contacts never existed. In an illiterate age, however, pottery lays the only contemporary trails of travellers which we can still follow. Pottery's ordinariness has several advantages for such a study. Most of it is more relevant to everyday exchanges than fine jewellery or metals, which might travel only as booty or rare personal gifts. It is also a marker of other goods now lost to us which travelled in it or perhaps with it and were then consumed, wine perhaps, or grain, scent or olive oil. Here, the shapes of pottery tell a story too, whether they are big open-necked containers of bulky goods or narrow-necked slow-pouring flasks for contents which were precious, like our French scents, and were used only drop by drop.

The exact context of discovery is significant too for its social history. When pottery is found in a tomb it may have been an important part of the funerary rituals or perhaps a status symbol or a marker of the dead person's former social contacts. If it is found in a secular building or a settlement it may have been there because of the goods which it once contained. If it belongs in a set of related pieces, it may have been used socially by bigger groups of diners or drinkers. How did they acquire it, by purchase, exchange or perhaps by gift? Homer's poems show the importance of gift-giving between noble guest-friends: did some of the biggest items of pottery, far from home, travel as gifts to important people? The relations between makers, transporters and eventual users are important too. In the tenth to mid-eighth centuries pottery is more likely to have travelled with Greeks from its place of production, because trading was more localized than later and a separate class of carriers and 'international traders' had probably not formed. Even so, we need to be cautious: a Corinthian pot may mean a Corinthian Greek is present, but not necessarily. If found in a non-Greek site there is the further question of whether a Greek or a travelling non-Greek brought it there. However, the discovery of a high proportion of everyday Greek pottery among the total pottery of such a site is significant. It strongly implies, without proving, that Greeks were present.

Used in this way, pottery has corrected a popular view of Greeks' relations with their eastern neighbours. Fifty years ago they were quite widely believed to have been cut off for four 'dark' centuries. Greeks had visited Cyprus and the coast of the Levant during the age of the Mycenaean palaces (c. 1350–1180 BC), but when this palace-society collapsed, their capacity for travel was thought to have contracted. A few Greeks migrated eastwards initially, but then the eleventh and tenth centuries were believed to be a time of isolation and poverty. 'Darkness' was considered to have persisted until contact was renewed with the Levant in the late ninth century. Until then long-distance travel by sea was at most a memory from the former Mycenaean age.

Archaeology has now moderated this extreme idea of darkness. The first phase, c. 1100–1050 BC, has been recognized to be even more active, because a migration of Greeks to post-Mycenaean Cyprus has become more solidly supported by evidence.[8] Across the Aegean the continuing discovery and classification of Greek pottery then brings light to the darkness of the eleventh, tenth and ninth centuries too. The chronology of the earlier phases is much debated because pottery dated in Greek sites is also found in Near Eastern contexts. Here, archaeologists apply a separate timescale which is grounded on the local changes of style in accompanying non-Greek pottery and a few externally attested sieges and local destructions, mostly mentioned in the Hebrew Scriptures.[9] Both the Greek and the Near Eastern chronologies depend ultimately on the same fixed points: events or objects connected with Egypt's pharaohs, the rulers whose dates are deducible in a sequence with justified precision.[10] Unfortunately such connections are still rare.

Meanwhile the arguments are less about the sequence in which particular Greek styles of pottery decoration evolved than about the lengths of time and dates at which the changes in the decoration occurred. The sequence deduced from Greek sites is the most detailed and whatever absolute datings we give to its upper reaches between c. 1050 and c. 850, we can now detect Aegean Greek networks of exchange in this era. The best-represented items are pots made in the tenth century BC in Attica, which travelled across the Aegean to Crete and even Samos just off the coast of Asia.[11] Another network extended up much of the east coast of central Greece and north to the coast of what later became Macedon, through the Cycladic islands and across to the east Aegean islands of Rhodes and Cos. This Greek network was already close to the non-Greek Levant. By origin its objects link especially to the long island of Euboea off the east coast of Attica.[12]

My eighth-century Greek trail depends on the existence of close Greek contacts with particular points on the south coast of Asia Minor (now Turkey) and the Levant (now Syria and the Lebanon). It is important, therefore, to see that this trail does not mark the first renewal of a Greek presence in the east. It is important, too, to consider whether Greeks from one and the same home site take the credit both for this overture and for laying the eighth-century trail of myths which followed, and if so, why they laid that trail only then. However humble and fragmented, pottery is a contemporary clue to the answers.

Its first lesson is that mainland Greek objects in the east were preceded by goods from the island which our maps identify as the likeliest intermediary: Cyprus. Less than 50 miles of sea divide northeastern Cyprus from the coast of the Levant and during most of the sailing season the local winds blow steadily from west to east. Unsurprisingly, Cypriot pottery of the eleventh and tenth centuries is found in quantity at sites on the Levantine coastline, including the major Phoenician site of Tyre.[13] Exchanges of Cypriot metal objects were also especially active on Crete where potters later imitated the imported Cypriot shapes.[14] Cypriots are also credited with the most elegant new pottery of the tenth and ninth centuries, the 'black-on-red' style for small flasks and jugs which held precious contents, surely scents and oils. 'Black-on-red' was exported widely down the coastal sites of the Levant and travelled inland, too, to sites which are now in modern Israel.[15] As tenth-century Cyprus was populated by pre-Greeks, Greeks and Phoenicians, we cannot yet be exact about the ethnic identity of the originators of 'black-on-red' on the island. Even so, the carriers of this Cypriot pottery to the nearby Levant will have included Greek-speakers.

In the wake of such Cypriot pottery, pieces of pottery made or influenced by more distant Greeks have begun to be found very early in Near Eastern settings. The two most recent finds typify the surprises and problems. One is a big rounded vessel, a sort of pottery cauldron with Greek decoration whose pieces were found in a building, perhaps a storehouse, at Tell Hadar on the east shore of Lake Galilee, 50 miles south-east of Tyre. They were discovered with about a hundred local and Levantine Phoenician vessels and had been broken up before the building was damaged.[16] The other is a small piece of a Greek deep pottery bowl which was found in a building at Tell Afis, a major site in Syria south-west of Aleppo and well to the east of the main route south down the Orontes river.[17]

Lake Galilee and inland Syria are remarkable places in which to find early imports from the 'dark' Greek world. Their excavators have proposed dates for them which are remarkable too: *c.* 1020–1000 BC for the Galilee piece, before the building (on this view) was destroyed during the reign of King David, and *c.* 1050–1000 for the Syria piece at Tell Afis. However, the Greek style of their decoration implies a later date. The Galilee piece's style belongs *c.* 950–920, while the Syria fragment has clear parallels in Greek contexts *c.* 950 too.[18] Both pieces then fit well with other Greek finds on and near the coast from where they travelled inland. We have pieces of four big storage-jars at the Syrian coastal site of Ras el-Bassit less than 30 miles north of modern Lattakieh: from their Greek style they are dated *c.* 980–950.[19] Pieces of another such storage-jar were found a little further north in the plain near modern Antioch and a piece of a cup (whose Greek date is *c.* 950–900) was found recently on the southern sector of the coast, just south of Mount Carmel at ancient Dor.[20] Above all, Greek objects have been found in identified levels at tenth-century Tyre, a storage-jar and two cups, while four other big pieces and a cup were found in unstratified levels. All of them are datable by their style to *c.* 950–900. Importantly the cups at Tyre match three others which have been found in a coastal cemetery at Amathus (modern Limassol) on the south coast of Cyprus.[21] They suggest that the two sites shared similar contacts with travelling Greek goods in the late tenth century. The journey, with a following wind, was easy from Cyprus to Tyre.

Even the lower, Greek-based dates for these finds are surprising: so, too, are their non-Greek contexts, some of which lie far inland. Another surprise is their origin or likeliest Greek milieu. Almost all of them connect to the pottery known in one Greek region: the island of Euboea. From our maps we would never pick Euboea as the source of Greek objects which travelled to Tyre or Mount Carmel and even to inland Syria and Lake Galilee. However, excavations on and around Euboea itself have helped to blunt the surprise. The important exca-vated site there is Lefkandi, a settlement on the Euboean Gulf.[22] The gulf runs up the western, inner coast of Euboea's long island and divides it from the mainland coast of Attica and Boeotia opposite. This part of the Euboean coastline is characterized by beaches and natural harbours without steep cliffs behind. The settlement is beauti-fully sited on a slight hill above the sea which probably ran in on either side of it in antiquity, offering a good anchorage. Inland it looks across from its slope to the peak of Euboea's own Mount Olympus to its north-east. Lefkandi's ancient name is unknown, posing a fine challenge to modern scholars, but Old Eretria is the most attractive guess.[23] A little further up the gulf, the channel narrows and the currents become complex and very dangerous, but the great settlement of Euboean Chalcis lay here, although most of it is inaccessible to excavations as it lies under the modern town. In ancient Chalcis's absence Lefkandi is especially significant because its cemeteries have been found unplundered: they are concentrated on a separate hill and its slopes, about half a mile to the west of the settlement. It is through

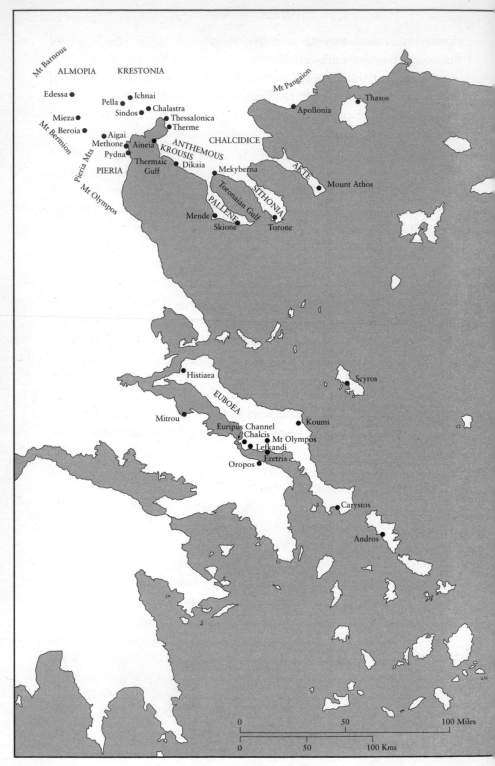

2. *Euboea and its neighbours*

pottery finds made recently at Lefkandi that we can ascribe an exact Euboean origin to tenth-century Greek pieces in the Near East.

Finds at Lefkandi also show that there was a reciprocal route from east to west.[24] In the early tenth century BC a small pottery jug of Cypriot or Near Eastern origin had already reached one of the tombs there. It was followed by faience and glass beads, also of Near Eastern origin, in another tomb and then, mid-century, by the finds which have done most to puncture ideas of an isolated Greek 'Dark Age'. On a levelled hill, separated from the nearby cemetery, archaeologists have excavated the ground-plan of a monumental building, 150 feet long, which was buried under a big mound of earth (Toumba).[25] The floor of its central area was found to contain a pit-burial of four horses, and beside them the burials of the bones of a man and the skeleton of a woman, surely the ruler and his lady, perhaps his wife. The man's bones had been cremated and then placed in a cloth in an antique bronze jar, originally made in Cyprus and decorated with scenes of hunting. Beside it lay weapons befitting a warrior. The lady's skeleton, facing west, had her arms folded and feet and hands crossed. She was buried with finger-rings, dress-pins and two big gold discs on her dress over her breasts. They were evidently the cups of an externally worn gold bra. Her necklace of gold beads included an exceptional pendant of ancient Near Eastern origin. Beside her head lay an iron knife with a choice ivory handle. One view is that the knife had been used to kill her, but it might symbolize one of her public roles, as a priestess at sacrifices of animals to the gods. On either view, the warrior-king was laid to rest and his 'wife' was buried beside him: four of his horses were killed nearby, probably from his chariot team, and so was a dog whose bones, after cremation, were found in a box with other ashes from the pyre against the wall of the section of the building in which the burials lay. After these burials the building was constructed over them, only to be destroyed soon afterwards: a large mound of earth was heaped over the site. The ground to the east of this mound then became a cemetery too, in which men, women and children were buried during the next hundred years. Many of their burials included imported objects, some of which are of Near Eastern origin. The Euboeans who were buried near the Toumba mound were therefore people of social eminence. The first such burial was placed carefully in line with the buried building's axis. Families were choosing to be buried close to the monument which covered the 'very special dead'.[26]

In several ways these remarkable Euboean burials relate to aspects of Homer's poetry. In Homer's *Iliad*, great heroes are cremated and their bones are laid in precious urns to be set beneath man-made mounds of earth. The grandest funeral is the one for Achilles' beloved Patroclus, on whose pyre are thrown various animals, including four fine horses and two of Patroclus' nine household dogs.[27] His bones are placed in a gold urn, and a man-made mound of earth is to be set above the pyre. It is a modest mound at first but it is to be enlarged when Achilles dies and is set beside him. Naturally, poetic licence enhances the memorial. For Patroclus a dozen 'sons of great-hearted Trojans' are also slaughtered. Earlier in the poem we hear about a burial mound for Andromache's father on which exquisite elm-trees (no doubt disease-resistant) were planted by the mountain-nymphs, the rural daughters of Zeus. No wife of a Homeric hero was ever killed and buried beside her husband, but Hector's bones, too, were wrapped in 'soft purple robes' inside their golden urn. The grave-mounds for Homer's heroes ensure fame in the future, fame for themselves or even for their killers. Hector imagines how a great Greek champion will be covered by a huge mound when he kills him in a duel. The mound will be so big that a future passer-by 'sailing on the wine-dark sea in his many-benched ship will say, "This is the mound of a man who died long ago whom noble Hector killed, champion though he was."' The name of Hector, not his victim, is the one to be remembered.[28]

The burials under the building covered by Lefkandi's Toumba were some two centuries older than Homer and in general terms are a source in history for what might otherwise seem to be Homer's own poetic invention. Travellers on the Euboean Gulf could look across from their 'many-benched ships' towards the man-made mound on the shore, the memorial to the very special dead beneath. There were no elm-trees by courtesy of the mountain-nymphs, but under the floor of the big building there were horses (buried, not cremated), a metal urn (bronze, not gold), cremated bones in a special cloth and even a dog cremated and deposited on site. In Homer's poems, burials were never placed inside a big building which was then destroyed, but in his heroes' world and funerals there were many antique objects, weapons, bowls or jewellery which had 'taken on a life of their own',[29] just like the antique bronze funerary urn in the Lefkandi ruler's burial which had been made on Cyprus at least a century earlier or the astonishing Near Eastern pendant on the lady's necklace whose nearest analogy lies some nine hundred years before the burial.

The big building above this couple is of uncertain purpose, and its history is much discussed.[30] It seems from its layout to have been built after the burials inside it. There are no signs of funerary cult, although one side of the site is inaccessible under a modern road. It is unlikely, then, to be a shrine in which the dead were worshipped as heroes. It cannot be the buried couple's house, as they died before it was built. Perhaps it was a funerary house in their honour which was then demolished as part of their funerary rites. Was it, perhaps, modelled on their hall elsewhere in Lefkandi where they entertained and dined with their contemporaries? They may have lived on the hill of the nearby settlement and surely such an important couple paid poets, long before Homer, to sing poems for them in hexameters.[31] These could have been short episodic songs about the heroes, like the episodic songs which Homer gives to the poets whom he imagines in a world long before his own. In the tenth century BC there were as yet no long epic poems with an overarching plot, but in nearby Thessaly there were localized myths of many great heroes, Achilles among them, of whom, at shorter length, tenth-century poets of Lefkandi may already have sung.

The funerals of major Homeric heroes are on a grand scale, extending over two or three weeks. The effort put into Lefkandi's big building, its platform and the mound above it were huge projects, implying a ruling group in the early to mid-tenth century who were far from feeble or impoverished. Burials of weapons, gold ornaments and cremated bones in bronze urns can be paralleled archaeologically, at first on Cyprus and then on Crete, suggesting that this expensive style of funerary rite may have spread through social links between leaders of these 'dark age' Greek communities. Horse-burials are also known on Cyprus in the eleventh century BC, where they resumed a practice known earlier in the second millennium. It is possible that, like the bronze urn, a knowledge of this style of death reached Lefkandi from Cyprus.[32] Like the imports in the Euboeans' graves they refute the idea that these Greeks were isolated from the world beyond. The couple who were buried under the Toumba mound were contemporary with the far-flung travels of Euboean pottery to Tyre, north Syria and the hinterland. They were contemporary, too, with Hiram king of Tyre and Israel's King Solomon, famous kings in the Near East. It is extremely important that scattered, fragmentary pottery in the Toumba mound above their building matches exactly some of the Euboean pottery which is found in the near-contemporary east.[33]

The Euboeans who were then buried beside the Toumba mound, from c. 950 to 820 BC, continued with similar contacts. More than eighty tombs and thirty funeral-pyres have been studied here and the presence of imported objects is notable throughout. In the other nearby cemeteries at Lefkandi these imports are much rarer. It seems, then, that imported objects were included here as marks of the dead's superior status. Goods of Near Eastern origin are the most conspicuous markers, including faience, glass beads, two more Syrian bronze bowls and several objects of Egyptian style and origin, including finger-rings.[34] One burial included six unusual faience vases and some Egyptian-style trinkets, so much so that intermarriage with a Levantine bride has even been suggested as an explanation: the grave, however, is more complex, as it contains two burials, one of which seems to be a child's.[35] Throughout the cemetery there is a distinctive difference between men's and women's grave-goods. The women are the people buried with the gold rings, ornaments and beads of faience necklaces: they are 'trophy wives', decorated by their husbands to look smart and showy, even in death.[36] Male burials had a different scope. One male burial of the mid-ninth century included arrows and weapons, six Euboean-style plates, some local weights, an antique north Syrian seal, a small Cypriot-style 'black-on-red' jug and others of Levantine or Cypriot origin beside a bronze cauldron for the dead man's bones. This male was not an eastern immigrant. He was a Euboean who had evidently combined warfare with Near Eastern contact and exchange. For such men the line between war and trade was blurred.[37]

The social context of the buried building and the cemetery which grew up round it is also a vexed question. The settlement at Lefkandi shows a rare continuity from the Mycenaean age into the succeeding centuries and it may be that under and around the Toumba we have evidence of a transition which has long eluded archaeologists. Perhaps the couple buried under the building's floor were the last of Lefkandi's old ruling family and those who were then buried beside their mound are the families of the upper class who followed them. If so, we see here the transition from monarchy to aristocratic rule by 'kings' in the plural, the *basileis* whom we then meet in eighth-century Greek evidence, when monarchy has largely disappeared. Certainly the objects buried with them continue to run gratifyingly in parallel to finds of Euboean pottery in the late tenth- and ninth-century Near East: any gap in the earlier ninth century is more apparent than real.[38] At Lefkandi we have the 'home' end of the connection which runs 'away' to the Levant. On ninth-century Cyprus, Euboean pots appear only in tombs and in this period only at Amathus and Kition (Larnaca) on the island's south coast.[39] In the ninth-century Levant, it is at Tyre that finds of Euboean pottery are at present most conspicuous, including a small number of Euboean plates. Others are now reported, predictably, at Sidon: further south a very few Greek pottery items continue to turn up from the same century at a distance from the coast. Here too connections with Euboea are in the majority. In the Jordan valley, on the river's west bank, we have bits of two mixing-bowls and two cups which are Euboean objects made *c.* 850–830, and an Attic storage-pot of a similar date which Euboeans probably brought to the Levant too. These objects had travelled to the big site of Tel Rehov, close to the major route for goods along the Jordan valley.[40]

The Euboean finds thus run in tandem, 'home and away', but who were their carriers and which way did the exchanges go between Euboea and the Near East? An older view was that Greek cups in the Near East always required Greeks themselves to be present, just as wineglasses later indicated the presence of Europeans in Muslim countries. However, Greek cups have now been found in several non-Greek cemeteries and this sharp distinction is no longer valid. The very few finds of Greek pottery inland behind the Levantine coast also imply that non-Greeks carried these stray objects inland, apparently from coastal points like Tyre or Ras el-Bassit. River- and land-routes run inland here and the land-bound stage of the objects' travel would probably not be in Greek hands.[41]

Were Phoenicians, then, the carriers of all the Greek bowls, jars and cups found in the tenth- and ninth-century Near East, their own home sphere? Phoenicians certainly crossed the Aegean: Phoenician pottery has been found on Cyprus (from the period *c.* 1050–950 BC) before any Greek cups and plates there: the important Cypriot centre at Old Paphos has produced Phoenician pottery, but no imported Greek pottery, in at least half of its excavated tombs of this date.[42] Phoenician pottery is present with the Greek pottery in the seven tombs which are most 'Greek' among those at Amathus; above all, a Phoenician's grave on the island was protected by a Phoenician inscription whose style is dated by its lettering to *c.* 900 BC.[43] In the ninth century Phoenicians founded their 'New Town' on Cyprus, surely at Kition.[44] Phoenicians are also said to have settled and inter-married at Ialysos on Rhodes, though admittedly only in much later Greek sources; they had contact with parts of Crete, including a stopover point at Kommos (by *c.* 900 BC) on its south-west coast, and in later Greek sources they are credited with contacts with the islands of Melos and Thera and above all Cythera off the southern tip of Greece.[45] Could they not have visited Euboea too, exchanging jewellery and trinkets (as the *Odyssey* describes elsewhere) and bringing back to the east the contents of the big Euboean jars (which the *Odyssey* never mentions) among our earliest Greek finds in settlements in the Levant? The problem is to see what could have drawn them up the Euboean Gulf to Lefkandi. Briefly, between *c.* 850 and *c.* 830 BC silver was worked from the nearby Athenian mines at Laurion, but this phase was short-lived and silver remains a notorious absentee from burials in Greece of the tenth to early eighth centuries BC.[46] Lefkandi and no doubt Chalcis had families who were honoured by a burial with horses under a big mound of earth, but in terms of Sidon, Tyre or Solomon their 'splendour' was relative and inconsiderable. Farther west, meanwhile, Phoenicians had contacts with metal-rich Sardinia and southern Spain, destinations for which the Greek islands of Crete or Cythera were stopping-points on a much more lucrative route.

Above all there are no Phoenician goods of this period on island stopovers which would lead to Euboea and the islands in its immediate sphere of influence. No Phoenician burials have been found on Euboea, either, and nothing which requires a Phoenician's prolonged presence. Nothing in the smart Toumba cemetery suggests that any Phoenician was buried here among Euboean families, the *basileis*, perhaps, of the new age.[47] If there were eastern immigrants resident on the site they would at most be craftsmen, not shippers of valuable Phoenician trinkets: in subsequent Greek history the usual transfer of such foreign craftsmen was as slaves. There is no sign, either, of any Phoenician women travelling to marry Euboean men. All the women's funerary rites are Greek and although some of them were buried with Near Eastern seals, so were men who were certainly not Near Easterners.

Should we think of Cypriots, rather, as the intermediaries between Euboea and the Levant? Some of the Near Eastern objects at Lefkandi are Cypriot by origin; Euboean objects appear at Cypriot Amathus; did Cypriots simply carry all the other Euboean objects on to the Levant? The problem is that on Cyprus there are no Cypriots' graves with the same Phoenician and Egyptianizing objects as at Lefkandi: why would they pass these luxurious objects only to Lefkandi in Euboea and not retain similar ones themselves? The obvious answer is that Euboeans brought their own goods, including pottery, to Cyprus and the coast of the Levant, even if a few pieces were then casually carried further inland by non-Greeks. The selection of Euboean-made objects as the main goods from Greece to the Levant is then most readily explained. There are no obviously 'Euboean Greek' burials in the Levant at this date, but there too we need only think of visitors, not resident settlers.

The range of the Euboeans' contacts elsewhere supports this explanation. Graves at Lefkandi which contained objects from the Near East also contained distinctive pottery from northern Greece: it points to their contact with the coastline which would later become Macedon and with the bays and promontories of the nearby Chalcidic peninsula. To reach it they passed from Lefkandi up a coastline where settlements already existed and over parts of which, even in the tenth century, their rulers may have exercised power. Across the gulf, on the Boeotian side, lay the Greek settlement later known to us as Oropos.[48] It was said in later sources to be a foundation by Eretria: it first becomes significant in the later tenth century BC when this 'Eretria' would surely be Lefkandi, whose pottery sequences precede those at Oropos. Further up this same coastline, about 40 miles north-west of Lefkandi, lies a newly located Greek settlement at Mitrou, protected for archaeologists on its islet set in a bay off the Euboean Gulf. It, too, was thriving in the early tenth century: there are then signs of destruction, perhaps because it lay within easy reach of Euboeans from the north of their island.[49]

The Euboean orbit extended even further north, as the graves at Lefkandi imply. Excavations on two of the prongs of the Chalcidic peninsula and at sites in and near modern Thessalonica, the future lands of Macedon, have greatly enriched our impressions of a Euboean northern presence.[50] At Sindos, near Thessalonica, Euboean contacts may well have begun by the time of the Lefkandi burials in the tenth century BC. The nearby river was a recognized source of gold: some of the gold for the Euboeans' jewellery at Lefkandi may have derived from the north here, including the gold for their royal lady's gold bra. At Mende, on the west side of the Chalcidic peninsula, Euboean contacts may also be contemporary with Lefkandi's main graves, just as they are at the beautiful site of Torone on the peninsula's central prong.[51] Here, a Euboean influence on the pottery of the best-excavated cemetery is more evident than actual early Euboean imports: at present there are only two Euboean cups there before 850 BC. Scarcely 3 miles to the east of Torone, however, there are signs of Euboean contact at the site of modern Koukos. Sources of copper and iron lay nearby: there is a local mould and tools for metal-working at the site dating to the mid-ninth century BC.[52]

The Euboean contacts here are signs of a new Euboean presence. They had not been preceded by an earlier, post-Mycenaean settlement of migrant Euboeans in this area:[53] during the eighth century BC these contacts then developed into a series of Euboean settlements, as never happened on Cyprus. The local ethnic structures in the north were weaker than the Cypriot kingdoms' and did not keep them out. The evidence of Euboean imports intensifies at several northern sites: the local use of the Euboeans' distinctive calendar, well attested later, goes back at least to this eighth-century phase, implying a dominant Euboean presence. The Greek historians of the fifth century BC then endorse the existence of real Euboean colonies here and attest the name of the 'Chalcidic' peninsula which derives from Euboean Chalcis.[54] As well as providing metals, the north was a fine source of timber for shipbuilding, an asset in which Euboea herself was not rich but which her naval adventurers would welcome.

Nearer home, Euboeans were also in close contact with contemporary 'Dark Age' Attica. There is a strong presence of Attic pottery in burials at Lefkandi: a huge Attic urn, about 3 feet high, was even found in pieces at the big Toumba building. One possibility is that Athenian immigrants, even brides, came over to the site.[55] Before Lefkandi's discovery much was made of the foreign elements in two mid- to late ninth-century Athenian burials, each of which included objects of Near Eastern origin. Although one was even called the 'Rich Lady' of the Areopagus hill, she now seems only modestly rich in the light of Lefkandi's contemporary residents: it is some compensation that archaeologists now recognize that she died pregnant.[56] Two other well-equipped burials at nearby Eleusis were also burials of women: one of them was buried with an Egyptian figurine, but this item is no longer so special when set beside the Lefkandiots' earlier examples.[57] Formerly, some of the techniques of these ladies' gold jewellery and earrings were suggested to be the work of 'migrant craftsmen', experts who had settled in Attica from the Levant. They were used to support arguments that Phoenicians came and even settled among 'Dark Age' Athenians.[58] However, we can now see that these Athenians' Near Eastern objects and jewellery were not innovations: they need only have come down from nearby Lefkandi where contemporary Attic pottery was being imported and similar jewellery had already long been in use.

Euboeans' close contacts with Athens, with Chalcidice and the north were matched by another of cardinal importance: Euboeans (with Cretans) are credited with settling on the favoured island of Chios in the east Aegean where the Greek presence was to be so rich for so long. Excavations here are still minimally relevant to this period, but Euboean pottery of the early to mid-ninth century has been discovered on the island.[59] The settlements go further back in time, making Chios an eastward horizon of Euboeans and their kin as early as the lifetime of the warrior-ruler who was buried beneath Lefkandi's mound. On Chios there were also Cypriots and it may well be through contacts made on this island that Euboeans were drawn to try their luck on Cyprus too and thence move on to the Levant. Phoenicians are not linked in our surviving texts with Chios, but with Chios's rival Erythrae on the mainland of Asia opposite, a stopping-point on their separate route up the Asian coastline to the north.[60]

From the south coast of Chios the Aegean coasts of south-east Euboea are surprisingly visible on a clear day: tenth-century Euboeans had an eastward horizon beckoning to them here, independent of any Phoenician contact. It built on the older Aegean Greek networks laid by their fathers and grandfathers, networks which ran already as far east as Rhodes and the islands of the Dodecanese. Like Lefkandi's burials, these contacts point to an outward-looking and enterprising group, for whom the further trip to Cyprus or even to Tyre was not such a leap into the dark.

We can therefore answer one of the puzzles of these once 'dark' centuries: why was Euboea so prominent?[61] It is not just an accident of our limited archaeology. At Lefkandi the settlement was unusual in continuing through the post-Mycenaean centuries; there was a ruler c. 950 BC who was remarkable enough to be buried and commemorated on the grand scale; the next generation of an upper class continued his outward-looking contacts, north, south and east. What was true at Lefkandi was true, surely, at nearby unexcavated Chalcis. Some of these Euboeans already had kin or compatriots on Chios and perhaps in settlements on the western coast of Asia. They carried their existing network a little further to Cyprus, then on to the Levant. No other contemporary Greek settlement is known to have had this scale, social structure and connected horizons of kinsmen and contacts. Euboeans also had the necessary sea-skills. Seamen who could cope with the complex currents of their home Euboean Gulf would be less deterred by a crossing of the Aegean from one island to the next.

There were also important riches to be brought home for local craftsmen who knew increasingly how to work their raw materials. At Lefkandi the burials included gold jewellery and evidence of local bronze-working. Gold was to be found in the north, with copper, too, near Torone on the Chalcidic peninsula. Above all, copper proliferated on Cyprus while copper and tin were available in north Syria and the Levant. One reason why Euboeans continued to spread outwards was the scope for acquiring metals to be worked at home and one reason why they began to work them so skilfully may have been their early contact with Cyprus and its skilled workers.[62] We can at least see beyond Homer's picture of heroes who travel only to Sidon in the Levant, and then only when returning home from war or as an adulterous lover, Paris, on the run with his prize Helen.

III

We are left wondering what Euboeans might have given, carried and exchanged abroad. In Homer we are especially aware of the role of splendid gifts, given by one noble hero in honour of another; everyday trade, however, is considered vulgar and ignoble. In real life the two types of exchange were not always separable. A trip eastwards was an adventure which would offer scope for raiding and fighting in self-defence. Those warriors who risked such a trip might give or exchange gifts with a social equal overseas, someone who might one day be buried with a memento of his contacts with a Greek. Those Greeks who gave such gifts could also exchange and trade perishable goods with others whom they met through their foreign guest-friends.[63] By its nature none of this perishable trade survives: how, then, should we relate it to the durable items of pottery which we still have? The big Greek mixing-vessels for wine have been explained as gifts to important people, interpreted by the sort of gift-giving which we know from Homer. Although only a few such vessels survive for us in Cyprus or Hamath or Samaria, they survive in places which were all royal centres in the ninth and eighth centuries BC.[64] Perhaps these very big vessels were grand enough to be gifts at court, but the cups, bowls and plates were not, especially in eastern cultures where the finest vessels were made of precious metals. In Homer's *Odyssey* we are told of the gifts which were considered suitable for nobles: they were 'swords and cauldrons', metal ones, not humble pots.

If the other imported Euboean pots and plates are relics of a bigger trade, they are unlikely to have been that trade's main items: the existing cultures of eating and drinking in the Levant had plenty of bowls and plates of their own. The items, however, may have acquired a symbolic value which was greater than their cheap materials. On Cyprus they are found in tombs, although they were not necessary for the funerary rites. Only a small proportion of the tombs on each Cypriot site includes them and so, despite appearances, we should perhaps understand this Greek pottery as a memento of the foreign contacts which the tombs' occupants had made. If so, even some of the simple Greek cups were unusual enough to be deposited as a social statement about the dead person's previous life.[65]

What perishable goods might have been traded beside them? In the late sixth century BC the Hebrew prophet Ezekiel imagines the far-flung trade of Tyre with foreign peoples and credits Greeks with supplying 'the souls of men', meaning slaves.[66] Raiding and plunder along the Near Eastern coastline would indeed provide Greeks with slaves for resale, but in the tenth to eighth centuries Euboeans would be unlikely to set out on a prolonged sea-journey with cargoes of Greek slaves and surplus children for exchange in a Near East which had local sources in plenty. From later Greek papyrus evidence, sheep have been suggested as an alternative cargo, but their management at sea across long distances would be even less likely in this early period.[67] Textiles are a more plausible guess, supplied by the weaving of Greek women, both slave and free: the designs of contemporary Greek pottery may give us an idea of their patterns. The Levant, however, had its own long history of fine textiles, including those with valued purple dyes, and an interest in simple Greek fabrics is unattested. The source of purple dye was a small mollusc, one of whose many homes was the Euboean Gulf: we know that the dye was extracted on a small scale at Oropos, opposite Euboea, and also at Eretria.[68] However, Phoen-icians did not need to import any more of it: they had rich local sources of their own. Much likelier exports are products of the soil. In later centuries Euboea was known for its excellent use of localized scent-plants, from which the Eretrians made a particular *chrisma*, or oil.[69] In the tenth to eighth centuries BC, however, these plants were not the source of their eastward trade: Euboean pottery in the east does not include small slow-pouring bottles and flasks for oils and scents. Vessels of that type are above all a Cypriot speciality.[70] In the big Euboean jars the likelier export is olive oil. Olives grew in the Levant too, but quality mattered and Euboean oil may have been clearer and finer.

Above all there was local Euboean wine. Vines grew well in the fertile and contested Lelantine plain around Lefkandi, as they still do in its rapidly disappearing traditional vineyards. They grew well, too, in the plain east of Eretria where some vintage personal names based on 'wine' (*oinos*) were bestowed on male children in antiquity. There was also wine from the north-west coast where Histiaea was already praised by Homer for its grapes.[71] Histiaea has a small fertile plain behind it but the supreme site for vines in Euboean history has been modern Koumi on the island's north-facing Aegean coast. In the 1830s William Leake, travelling carefully in the area, remarked how Koumi was providing a huge quantity of wine each year to contemporary Smyrna (İzmir in Turkey) and to sites on the Black Sea. The reasons lie in local conditions which the ancients, too, would have recognized.[72] The district round modern Koumi has a high rainfall, the highest in the island, while the slopes of the mountain ridge beside the modern town are made of volcanic soil. In the very distant past this ridge was volcanic and its old craters are still traceable near Mount Oxylithos, its terminal point. Blocks of its brown lava-stone have been used in the local buildings and the volcanic soil is ideally suited to vines. The wine from modern Koumi's territory grew partly in vineyards on these volcanic slopes until the vines were killed in the epidemic of the early twentieth century.

Did an ancient site called Cumae stand near modern wine-growing Koumi? It has been dismissed as an 'urban myth', because only one later Byzantine text attests it directly. However, that text used earlier Hellenistic sources and there is indirect evidence about a Cumae in the eighth century BC which is hard to evade.[73] Archaeologically, the ancient Euboean Cumae remains to be found in this very area, but for historians it is already an important missing link in our understanding of Euboeans in the tenth to eighth century. From this area they looked out onto a bay with access for ships to the nearby island of Scyros and thence to the eastern Aegean. Items in graves on Scyros of the tenth to eighth centuries are closely matched by items found on

Euboea, whether pottery or handsome gold diadem-bands which were worn on the forehead.[74] These objects came across from the Euboean coastline near modern Koumi. From Scyros, Euboean ships could then travel up to their contacts in the north or turn eastwards to go over to Chios. The northern Aegean coast of their island was important in the Euboean network.

In the tenth to eighth centuries, as in later times, volcanic vineyards near modern Koumi may have been one of the main sources of Euboeans' eastward exports. Wine from here and Lefkandi's nearby Lelantine plain could be transported more easily in skins than in breakable pots, a reason why we find only the accompanying Euboean cups and plates which were the extras and the gifts beside the main perishable cargo. Certainly, wine would find ready buyers in the Near East. In the later sixth century the prophet Ezekiel's list of Tyre's foreign imports includes wine imported from two faraway sources, one in north Mesopotamia (modern Iraq), the other 'Helbon', the district of wine-growing hills about 10 miles north of Damascus in Syria, which produced excellent wine, appreciated throughout antiquity and on into the Middle Ages.[75] Phoenicians had a taste for fine wine from far afield and also, according to Ezekiel, re-exported it. Euboean wine could fit neatly into this Levantine demand which was considerable and had a wide span.

Whatever the trade which went on beside the gifts, its total scale should not be exaggerated. Fragments of at most a hundred Greek pottery vessels dating from the period down to c. 800 BC have been found at Tyre, our most prolific source of them, and even so, they are a tiny fraction of the total pottery recovered on the site. About 140 Greek pottery vessels of the period c. 920–720 are the total so far discovered in Cyprus, all in tombs, not settlements. Even at Amathus, they occur in only about a fifth of the known tombs and usually there is non-Greek pottery with them too.[76] Finds of imported Euboean pottery are concentrated along the southern and eastern coasts of the island, where the local winds and weather help us to put them into perspective.

In the eastern Mediterranean the prevailing winds for most of the year blow from the west. From the harbour-site of Amathus on south Cyprus, ships could sail directly across to the north Syrian coast with a wind from the west, and the trip could be done in a day. North-west winds would also blow regularly here, taking ships easily down the Levantine coast to Sidon or Tyre or further south to Ascalon.[77] Our finds of Euboean pottery in the tenth and ninth centuries fit this pattern very well; they concentrate at Amathus and Tyre with outlying pieces found to the north and south of Tyre on the Levantine coast. The problem was the return voyage, especially for ships which had travelled on south to Egypt. The best evidence comes from eyewitnesses in the age of the Crusades when this region was again of major importance. 'The blowing of the winds in these parts', observed the acute Ibn Jubayr at Acre in the mid-fourteenth century, 'has a singular secret. The east wind does not blow except in spring and autumn. The spring voyages begin in the middle of April when the east wind blows until the end of May. The autumn voyages are from the middle of October when the east wind sets again . . . it blows for fifteen days. There is no other suitable time.'[78] Cargo-ships would cluster off the Holy Land in late April and early May or late September and early October, hoping to unload quickly and then return during the brief spell of easterly winds. Traders did not wish to be caught in the eastern ports all summer nor to set off to the west so late that they would hit the storms of mid-November.

There were also difficulties in the passage to and from Egypt. A trader could be helped south from Crete, Rhodes or Cyprus by a fine spell of north to north-west winds, but the return to each of these islands was more difficult across open sea. Crusaders knew they should return from Egypt up the coast of the Levant: they would then use the current which ran up to southern Asia Minor (Cilicia) as often as voyaging against the wind directly to southern Cyprus. The straight crossing from Tyre and Sidon to Rhodes was possible but not always easy: the journey of some 550 miles took Ibn Jubayr an entire month on a rough, unpleasant sea. One speech by an orator in classical Athens claims that travelling between Rhodes and Egypt's Nile Delta was easily done three times during winter.[79] Connections between Rhodes and the Delta were very important, but the orator is being tendentious here for the sake of his case, inventing this winter travelling before an ill-informed jury based in Athens.

Centuries earlier, travelling Euboeans had been subject to similar conditions. For them, cargoes had to be traded, gifts given and local contacts sought and maintained: they would usually be held up at their destination for longer than a simple unloading. Journeys to the Levant and back were thus seasonal affairs, best managed when carefully timed. As for Egypt, it was best visited when a return up the coast of the Levant was possible. Many of the Egyptian goods discovered at Lefkandi are probably to be imagined as goods acquired in the Levant from Phoenician intermediaries and then brought back to Greek waters.

In the light of these conditions, the Greek pottery found on Cyprus and the Near East down to *c.* 800 BC is not evidence of a big production for export which was transforming its producers' home economy. The underlying trade was very much smaller than the big cargoes and quantities of objects which are attested by surviving 'Mycenaean' texts and which we recover from local shipwrecks in the age of the 'Mycenaean' kingdoms (*c.* 1350–1180 BC).[80] Historically, the trade *c.* 980–800 does not matter because of its scale. It matters, rather, because it brings Greeks, especially Euboeans, across to Cyprus and the Levant when 'darkness' used to be ascribed to their Greek world. Has this renewed Greek contact *c.* 980–800 left any trace in later written texts?

There are two suggestive bits of evidence. In the Hebrew Scriptures, King David is credited four times with troops of 'Kerethites and Pelethites'. They have their own important commander and they seem to rank as the king's guards. One possible interpretation is that both groups are foreigners, the Pelethites being Philistines from the coast and the Kerethites being Cretan Greeks from across the sea.[81] Archaeologically, Crete *c.* 850–750 BC appears to be only the passive recipient of Phoenician and north Syrian objects, whether bronze, ivory, faience or glass. But Homer's Cretans are fighters and travellers and if there was any raiding to be done on the Asian coast it is hard for historians to credit that Cretans were not somehow involved. Perhaps there were Cretans who had already seen Jerusalem in the early tenth century, just when the first Euboean Greek pottery imports were travelling inland from the coast.

More solidly, we have the inscribed genealogy of a Greek on the island of Chios. Without citing any hero or mythical ancestor, one Heropythos was listed here on his gravestone with fourteen generations of his family's forebears, a remarkable chain through the generations of an orally remembered past.[82] His inscription is dated before *c.* 400 BC by the style of its lettering, perhaps *c.* 440–420, and if we allow an average of about three generations to a hundred years the fourteenth ancestor, the oldest, would have lived *c.* 870 BC. His name is none other than Kyprios, presumably a Cypriot: on Chios, Euboean settlers could indeed meet Cypriot settlers, people who could support their further travels and encourage contacts with Cyprus.

These connections are slender, for a good reason. No contemporary Cretan wrote of his service in Israel or the Levant and no ninth-century Euboean recorded his family's links with Chios or the Near East. They were illiterate, and the finest witness to Greeks' travels in this area is eventually the alphabet itself. As we have seen, our earliest alphabetic Greek inscription dates to *c.* 750 BC, but there are earlier signs of the alphabet's influence which imply that it must be an earlier innovation, arguably beginning *c.* 820–800.[83] We know one thing for sure: it arose from an individual Greek's contact and discussions with a Near Easterner, a Phoenician from the Levant, it still seems, rather than someone from the north Syrian zone of Aramaic writing. It arose, therefore, in a place where Greeks and Phoenicians had personal contact and on the evidence of its early diffusion and of the style of its earliest known examples its inventor is most likely to have been a Euboean Greek.[84] Its place of invention is still uncertain: the coast of Crete or Rhodes, perhaps, or somewhere in the Levant itself, perhaps even Tyre where Greek pots and plates had found a home. It might even have had a floating origin on board ship, when a Phoenician and a Euboean passenger had long hours to pass and writing-tablets (as we know from shipwrecks in the Aegean) might have been to hand for a lesson. My own guess is an origin on coastal Cyprus, despite the syllabic Greek script which already existed in parts of the island. An alphabet was more convenient. On the south coast at Amathus we know from tomb evidence that Euboean and Phoenician goods had coexisted from *c.* 920 BC onwards. So, no doubt, did the two peoples, and one day an alert Euboean might have learned from a neighbouring Phoenician the signs and names of his lettering. He learned them in the standard sequence of their Semitic script: alpha, beta, gamma . . .

the order which Greeks themselves then learned, taught and preserved. 'The inference is that the "inventor" who first used these letters for the notation of the Greek language had participated in at least one school lesson . . .' Crucially he misunderstood it and so introduced vowels where his Semitic prototype had none. The alphabet was the result of 'the Greek genius for creative misunderstanding'.[85] It was not, as we shall see, to be the last such result in the Near East.

Chariots decorating the neck of a Geometric amphora, c. 740 BC.

5

Travelling Settlers

The Greeks who were travelling to the Near East with these objects did not encounter a single unchanging eastern culture. On Cyprus their first ports of call were ruled by kings: Homer represents Cyprus as under kingly rule, naming a king with a fictitious Greek name and once naming Cinyras at Paphos, whose name perhaps derived from a non-Greek root.[1] In his epics Homer does not show knowledge of how many separate kings there were on the island. From Assyrian texts, however, we know that by the later eighth century Cyprus was already divided into at least seven kingdoms, the innovations, archaeology suggests, of the twelfth to eleventh centuries.[2]

On the south coast, Amathus had grown to need several cemeteries and by the mid-eighth century there was a palace for the king on its acropolis. The site had a fine hill and a natural harbour but it had no older Bronze Age past: it was settled only in the eleventh century. When Greeks from Euboea arrived in the tenth century, Amathus already had a multi-cultural tone. It was home to speakers of the distinctive non-Greek Cypriot language and it also had contacts with Phoenicians from the Levant.[3] By the later eighth century a burial ground by the coast contained a significant proportion of babies and very young children laid there by Phoenicians. Notoriously, Phoenicians would offer infants and young children to their gods, a practice which Greeks tried to explain but never imitated: we find them in the special burial grounds, or tophets, of Phoenician settlements.[4] Further east beyond Amathus, however, the history of Kition (Larnaca) was different. It had been resettled as a 'new' Phoenician foundation, although its growth after the Bronze Age went back at least into the tenth century, when its population was already distributed beside its harbour. There was presumably a tophet here too, but surprisingly we have not yet found it. A Greek's first impressions would include the brilliant glare from the site's salt flats, the assets which so often accompanied Phoenician settlements, whether in Sicily or southern Spain. Kition was a distinctive Salt Lake City to Greek eyes, with good access to the sea and a network of cults and shrines at either end of the salt plain.[5]

Back on Euboea, Lefkandi's main age of eastern imports ends *c.* 820 BC when the cemeteries decline, on our present evidence, without the settlement being wholly abandoned. However, other Euboean towns continued to look eastwards and the growth of a 'new Eretria' east of Lefkandi from *c.* 800 BC ensured that the Euboean Gulf's involvement in overseas contacts did not fade out. By *c.* 770 Greek goods were also reaching Salamis on Cyprus's east coast. Salamis, too, was on a site first occupied in the eleventh century: it was placed there because the silting of the nearby river had caused an older Bronze Age town to be re-sited. Our best idea of what Greek visitors saw here comes from the impressive tombs in which Salamis's kings and nobles were buried during the eighth century. Even though their main chambers had been looted by tomb-robbers before their rediscovery, the traces of their splendour are most remarkable, above all the tomb in whose entrance-corridor was found a silver-studded sword and a fine chariot. Horses, even, had been brought to the tomb with the chariot and killed in its corridor. When it was excavated after some 2,700 years, their bodies were found in contorted positions just as they had fallen in a great equine slaughter, one after the other.

At first the tomb's skilful excavator, Vassos Karageorghis, saw another Greek import at work here: the poems of Homer, with which some of the fine objects and parts of the funerary rite, including the horses, could be matched. Had the court at Salamis heard Homer's poems from Greek visitors and then imitated his heroes' magnificent funerals? On closer study this fine possibility has faded: better parallels for the burials and their objects lie in the real non-Homeric world of north Syria and the Levant and even in the funerals of Assyrian kings.[6] Although an export of Homer is not in evidence, the royal tombs included Greek exports of a more everyday type: the earliest Greek pottery to be found on the site. Its most impressive items are plates, drinking-vessels and a big mixing-bowl which make up a dining and drinking set. The big bowl and twenty of the cups were made in Attica, matching those in the graves of contemporary Athenians. As scenes of seafaring were painted on grand Athenians' pottery, perhaps Athenian sailors took to sea and brought these wares eastwards to this one royal site on Cyprus. However, all the plates and three of the cups have designs in the Euboean style. Their clay suggests that they originated in the Cycladic islands, also within the Euboeans' orbit. Connections between Lefkandi and Attica had been strong and like almost all other Greek pottery which was imported into Cyprus, this part of what became an exceptional set was perhaps brought by Euboeans instead. It has even been interpreted as a very special gift, a wedding present sent with a royal bride.[7] Its size and elaborate decor are impressive but pottery dowries are unattested in the eighth century, as are wedding lists. As elsewhere, the bowl may have arrived as a gift to an important guest-friend without an accompanying bride. Some of the items with it may have arrived as gifts too, whereas others may have been acquired separately through trade. All the pottery may then have been included in the tomb not for its value but once again as a symbol of the dead man's foreign contacts. Phoenician pottery was found with it, perhaps for the same reason.[8]

Throughout the eighth century the Greek pottery which reached Cyprus is our basic evidence for Greeks visiting the island. Almost all of it has been found in or near the capital sites of kingdoms on the island, although we still know it mainly from tombs rather than from the accompanying settlements, which have been much less excavated.[9] For our trail, it is significant that by origin this pottery is overwhelmingly Euboean. Its supreme monument is a tall mixing-bowl discovered in a royal tomb at Kourion and bought from its excavator in the 1870s by the Metropolitan Museum in New York, where it is prominently displayed. Its painter was probably a Euboean, perhaps from Chalcis, who excelled in depictions of horses, water-birds and a tree, probably a 'tree of life', flanked by goats on their hind legs.[10] His geometric patterns and these symbols of the natural world found imitators in and near Euboea, but the piece for Cyprus, perhaps a gift for a king, is his masterpiece. In the eighth century such Euboeans intensified the contacts begun in the long 'Lefkandi century' (c. 950–825). The total, however, of Greek pottery on eighth-century Cyprus

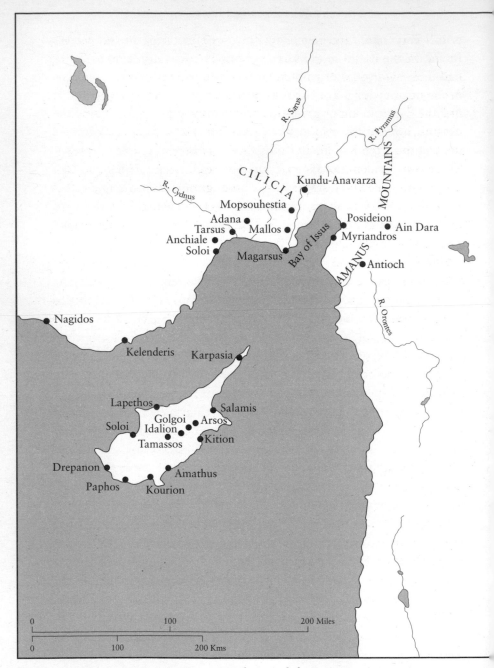

R. Sarus

R. Pyramus

R. Cydnus

C I L I C I A

AMANUS MOUNTAINS

Kundu-Anavarza

Mopsouhestia

Adana

Tarsus   Mallos

Anchiale

Soloi

Magarsus

Bay of Issus

Posideion

Myriandros

Ain Dara

Antioch

R. Orontes

Nagidos

Kelenderis   Karpasia

Lapethos   Salamis

Golgoi   Arsos

Soloi   Idalion

Tamassos   Kition

Drepanon

Amathus

Paphos   Kourion

0   100   200 Miles

0   100   200 Kms

3. *Cyprus, Cilicia and the Levant*

is still very small and remains a tiny proportion of all the pottery found on the island in the same period. The reason is that Cypriots had their own styles of painted pottery and showed minimal interest in copying the designs of Greek imports, even the best Greek pieces. At first the Euboean imports were decorated only with simple 'geometric' designs: not until *c.* 760 BC do we have a Greek piece with figured decoration, from Kition, and even then it is simple, imitative work.[11] There is no evidence of Greek craftsmen settling on Cyprus and supplying other newly resident Greek immigrants. The dominance of Euboean pottery is an important support for the idea of a Euboean trail, but there is no evidence for a Euboean settlement on the island. They visited and moved on.

From Cyprus, two 'eastern' coastlines were directly accessible, making the island one cardinal point on an interconnected triangle, the heartland of the landscapes and myths whose impact and travels we shall follow in Greek company. One of these coasts, to the east, is north Syria's, which becomes to the south the coast of the Phoenician city-kingdoms along the Levant. The other is the Cilician coast of southern Asia Minor (modern Turkey), which is even closer to Cyprus's northern shoreline. In Homer's stories of eastern travel, we have met a different 'triangle' based on Cyprus, Egypt and Crete. Homer never mentions travel from Cyprus to Cilicia, and when looking eastwards modern historians, too, have said much less about this Cilician point of contact. However, its sites, topography and underlying cultures are crucial to the contacts from which Greek travellers made the mental leaps which will concern us. Contact with Cilicia was encouraged by the sea-routes and currents which ships used when coming up from the Levant, as the later Crusaders' texts remind us. Sometimes they would prefer to put in on Cilicia's coast and only then go across to Cyprus or Rhodes. Southern Cilicia was not an out-of-the-way oddity.

This Cilician coastline is made up of two distinct sections, a well-watered plain and then, to the west, rough wooded mountain-territory. The plain is an appendage to mountains which surround it on its north-east and west, and it is only entered by narrow passes which the Greeks called 'gates'. Down from its northerly mountain barrier run three great rivers which account for its exceptional fertility.

Far into antiquity the 'abundance' of this area was personified and recognized in Greek (its *euthēnia*): it was best described by Xenophon when marching with the Ten Thousand into Asia.[12] In 401 BC he came down through the mountains' northern gates and found a 'large and beautiful plain, well watered and full of all sorts of trees and vines: it produces lots of sesame and millet . . .' Its wetlands made several valuable crops possible, including flax, which needs particularly damp soil.[13] In the plain and its defining mountains there were many localized varieties of scented and medicinal plants, as precious as silver-dust for the ancients, many of which were noted in later centuries by the botanical author Dioscorides, who was himself a man from the north-east edge of the plain.[14] Where the wetlands became marsh there were even some buffaloes and everywhere the lush pasturage sustained excellent horses. They are unmentioned by the passing horseman Xenophon, but in the Hebrew Scriptures King Solomon (*c.* 965–930 BC), we are told, imported horses from the Cilician plain into Israel for his chariots: horses continued to be paid as tribute to the later kings of Persia (*c.* 530–333 BC); the plain is still one of the few places in modern Turkey where worthwhile horses can be seen grazing.[15]

In Homer's *Iliad* this plain is mentioned once, and then only as the 'Aleian plain', site of the distressed hero Bellerophon's aimless wanderings.[16] Perhaps the name 'Aleian' derived from the salt marshes (*hals*, meaning salt in Greek) along the southern shore. Homer does not even place Cilicians here: instead, they are one of the peoples his epic transposes northwards near Troy, on whose side they fight in the war. In the Troad, his 'Cilicians' lived in cities with significant women whom the Greek heroes had captured or made widows and orphans. Poignant though Homer's use of these places is, they set a major puzzle for subsequent Greek travellers and geographers, who were inclined, like Alexander's personal historian, to site them in or near the real Cilician territory on Asia Minor's southern coast.[17] Nonetheless they are a striking anomaly in Homer's geographical consistency, and simply from our epics' text we would have to conclude that the poet and his teachers knew nothing of the details of the real Cilicia in their ninth- or eighth-century world.

It is not, then, so surprising that Homer never mentions the region's ancient cities whose pre-Greek names are known from our non-Greek texts, places like Tarzu (Tarsus, the future home of St Paul), Ingira (Anchiale, near modern Mersin), Danuna-Adana (whose name is still in modern use), Pahri (perhaps modern Misis) and the sheer cliff of Kundu (plainly the Greeks' Cyinda, site of a royal treasury even after Alexander's conquests: it then became Anazarbus, and is now Anavarza).[18] These cities and strongholds had local rulers whose names are known from some of our surviving Near Eastern texts but never from Greek ones. They were not always divided and at war with each other. From contemporary local texts we know of a single dynastic family which ruled the plain, its cities and its north-eastern mountainous fringe in the eighth century. As we shall see, this dynasty (the 'house of Muksas') may even have extended its control further westwards through the rough wooded coastline and into the next coastal plain beyond, the region which was later known to the Greeks as Pamphylia.[19] If so, a single big power had ruled far along the coastline before the 830s when Assyrian troops first attacked the Cilician plain and conquered it. Parts, at least, of its kingdom then reappeared (or survived) before Assyrian troops returned to the area in the later eighth century BC. At that date the royal 'house of Muksas' was based in Adana. In the ninth and eighth centuries Greeks who visited the Cilician plain and coastline were not entering lands without rulers who were trying to keep the peace. These local rulers' continuing impact was to be important for discoveries which Greeks made here.

West of the plain's Lamos river, the flat coastal lands narrow and the rough mountains extend much closer to the sea. Assyrian kings distinguished between the plain (Que) and this Rough Cilicia (Hilakku) which proved so hard for them to control: its reputation for piracy was to last throughout antiquity. Visitors from Cyprus were better advised to avoid it and to head north-eastwards for the mouths of the big rivers in the plain. Connections between Cyprus and this fertile area were evident in the local styles of pottery and were presupposed by later Greek stories of the ancestry of several local families.[20] Greek objects reached the plain too in the eighth century: a small quantity of Greek pottery is known from excavations at Tarsus, including Euboean pottery of the early to mid-century. Then imports arrived c. 720–700 from the nearby Greek island of Rhodes and other east Aegean Greek sources.

Any Greeks, including Euboeans, who travelled to the Cilician coast with these Greek items found themselves in a humid land which had a multi-lingual, multi-cultural texture. It is evident partly in its few known items of sculpture, partly in the scripts, cults and personal names attested by its surviving inscriptions. During the Bronze Age (until *c.* 1200 BC) Cilicia and its plain had been known as 'Kizzuwatna', an important southern part of the empire of the Hittite kings of central Asia Minor. When this big empire broke up, a 'neo-Hittite' cultural style evolved from the past and remained important for its impression on Greek visitors here. The local inhabitants' gods and personal names still reflected their Hittite past far into the second century AD, names like 'Rondas' or 'Tarkombios' and gods like the important Storm God 'Tarhunta' or the god 'Santa' who was prominently worshipped in Tarsus and later called 'Sandon' by Greek-speakers.[21] Above all, texts were inscribed in a hieroglyphic 'neo-Hittite' script whose origins trace back to the imperial Hittite era. In Cilicia, as in north Syria, this script was used to write down the 'Luwian' language, Indo-European by origin and probably the language which most people spoke in the Cilician plain.[22] In the ninth and eighth centuries BC some of the local rulers put up big bilingual inscriptions which used Phoenician too, the West Semitic language of the cities down the coast of the Levant. This second written language may not say so much about most people's everyday speech in the region, but it too was presumably spoken sometimes as well as written. Significant examples of it have been found in inscriptions on the north-east edge of the plain, where the steep range of the Amanus mountains defines its edge.[23] One was found by the Beylan pass through this range, the ancient 'Syrian Gates', where it presumably marked the boundary-limit of 'Que' under eighth-century Assyrian rule.[24] Another cluster of inscriptions lies up the most easterly of the plain's three rivers, the Pyramus (now the Ceyhan), where the fortified site of Karatepe displayed Phoenician texts about the deeds of its ruler, probably a man of the later eighth century BC.[25] They show the site's significance for Phoenician visitors, who would arrive by sea and follow the Pyramus river north into the mountains beyond. This river-route gave access to sources of metals in the interior. Karatepe and its sister-fortress Domuztepe were guard-points on this major trade-route which brought Phoenicians directly up from the Levantine coastline.[26]

At Karatepe, the surviving sculptures give us our best idea of the culture of an eighth-century Cilician court when Greek pottery and its Greek carriers were arriving in the plain round Adana which the rulers also controlled.[27] On the main gateways and some of the buildings we see scenes of drink and food being brought to the ruler, who is seated and attended by a cupbearer. A cow is being pulled towards his presence and a rabbit approaches too. There are frequent scenes of hunting involving lions or even a bear and the shooting of arrows into a deer. The gods are honoured and female dancers and musicians play their various instruments: there is even a scene of boxing. The most important occupant of the place is the Storm God who is sitting there, carved from a huge block of grey-black basalt.[28] Inscriptions proclaim the mortal ruler's self-image: 'In those places which were formerly feared, where a man fears . . . to go on the road, in my days even women walked with spindles. In my day there was feasting, luxury and good-living.' On carved funerary reliefs from adjacent north Syria we see this same imagery in art, men holding their cups as if feasting and women seated safely opposite them with their spindles.[29]

The date of Karatepe's founding ruler and its various sculptures is still controversial. A late eighth- to early seventh-century date for the ruler is most likely, although he might perhaps belong fifty years or so earlier, c. 760 BC. For our purposes it is important that he refers to the dynastic 'house of Muksas' as an earlier existing entity. It was significant, then, in the earlier eighth century: we even have a hint of its span, because the surviving sculptures are in two distinct styles, one of which is older than the other, 'so heterogeneous that one wonders how the king of Karatepe could bear looking at them in their present arrangement. One suspects that he was rather parvenu-ish in his building programme . . .'[30] It is also significant that the sculptures include scenes with an obvious Phoenician influence. The ruler's inscriptions were bilingual too, using hieroglyphic Luwian and Phoenician, suggesting that Phoenicians were indeed active in his service.

It is unlikely that any Greek came up to Karatepe itself because nothing Greek has ever been found there. However, a similar court-style surely existed in the other cities under its ruler's control, though they are as yet unexcavated in the Cilician plain. Later Greek writers place actual Greek settlements here and even claim that mythical Greek heroes in the legendary past once founded the important towns. False claims to a Greek origin became notorious in the plain in later centuries, arising when non-Greeks wished to compete for status in the later Greek-speaking age.[31] There is, then, no truth in these particular foundation-stories, but off the main plain three sites were more plausibly connected to Greek settlers. They lie on its western edge and on the narrow coastal strip of Rough Cilicia beyond it. Here Greeks from Rhodes were said to have settled the coastal site of Soloi, while to the west of them Greeks from the island of Samos were credited with settlements at Nagidos and Celenderis.[32]

These latter sites already had non-Greek names and excavations at them have not yet confirmed an early Greek presence. However, they have not refuted one either, and archaeologically, the role of Greek settlers at them is still open.[33] Historically, a Samian and a Rhodian initiative on this stretch of the coast is not unlikely, even c. 720–700 BC: it would link up with the Rhodian and east Greek pottery of this date which has been found elsewhere in the Cilician plain. There were assets nearby to attract them to these places. Soloi lay close to Ingira, which the Greeks called Anchiale, an established site which it could serve as a coastal trading post. Soloi's name was later explained as meaning 'metal ingots' and may allude to the silver and iron which were mined in the mountains inland. Iron was accessible, too, just to the west of Celenderis, but we should not think only of metals.[34] In the eighth and seventh centuries Rhodians were noted for their decorated pottery flasks which held precious scents and oils, small items which were carried as far west as Italy. Not only was the rose the symbol and namesake of their island: rose oil was a prized scent in the Greek world, having a funerary role too, as Homer reminds us in his account of the gods' protection of Hector's dead body.[35] The Aegean world already had roses, but this south Cilician coast has a particular variety, the white-flowered rose we know as *Rosa phoenicea*, characterized by its ability to flower twice in a season.[36] Twice-flowering roses doubled the scent-makers' trade: they became known in antiquity and it may be from contact with their Cilician source that growers first grafted them onto the once-flowering varieties and made this important break-through. In Cilicia, Rhodians had access to a specially productive source of rose oil, perhaps the oil which was then carried far and wide in their little decorated flasks.[37]

One particular Greek 'founder' has proved more of a problem. On the east side of the plain, a short way up the Pyramus river, the important town of Mallos in due course traced its origins to a legend-ary Argive Greek hero, Amphilochus. The town is most unlikely to have been a Greek foundation, but the claim is known to us quite early and was enough, as we shall see, to convince the conquering Alexander the Great in 333 BC.[38] Perhaps Mallos had indeed had an early Greek enclave, Rhodians perhaps who claimed a special kinship with Argos and might possibly have introduced Amphilochus here. Most importantly, this Argive Amphilochus was said in some versions of his story to have gone on east and founded a second site called 'Posideion'.[39] It has become a major battleground for excavators and historians.

Anyone who stands on the lower course of the Pyramus river and looks out across the sea will readily appreciate the eastward 'travels' of the legendary hero Amphilochus. The landscape connects regions which our texts and history books preserve in separate compartments. On the near horizon, the ancients' north Syria, our Middle East, looms large across the waters. The sea, meanwhile, forms a gulf at the eastern head of the Mediterranean, the ancient Bay of Issus. From the Cilician plain, by land or sea, the coastline of the bay was wide open for potential settlers. At modern Kinet Hüyük, on the bay's coastline, recent excavations have revealed a settlement with local pottery, copi-ous Phoenician pottery and a smaller proportion of Greek wares, including Euboean pottery of the mid- to late eighth century.[40] In antiquity the site was probably called Issus, from which the bay took its name, but the Greek finds here are few in proportion to the non-Greek and do not imply an actual Greek settlement. To locate one we must follow the shore of the bay on south through the defensible mountain-pass just north of Sariseki, a narrow point which has served as the border 'gate' of several kingdoms throughout history. In antiquity this place became the border between Cilicia and Syria, a role in which it was witnessed by Xenophon and by the troops with

Alexander the Great.[41] It allows us to place the site first described by Herodotus in the mid- to late fifth century BC. He gives a detailed list, on sound authority, of the tributes paid by peoples and districts of the contemporary Persian empire. The fifth of those districts, he tells us, began at Posideion, 'founded by Amphilochus' on the Cilician-Syrian border: he implies that this Greek town was the first settlement on the Syrian side.[42]

The name Posideion has caused frequent confusion. Greeks gave it to many places where they encountered a significant cape or an accessible beach and connected it with their sea-god Poseidon. We know of one Posideion on the coast of Rough Cilicia, while another was sited in due course on the Syrian coast just north of modern Lattakieh.[43] Herodotus' Posideion is neither of them. Unlike them it lay by the Cilician-Syrian border near modern Iskenderun (Alexandretta), whose own little bay is an important anchorage and a safe haven from storms, especially in autumn, on the open sea. A short way down this same coast lay the separate settlement of Myriandros which was frequented by Phoenician ships and traders, at least when seen by Xenophon in 401 BC.[44] We do not know when Myriandros was founded but there was a good reason why two settlements lay so close to each other on this one short stretch of coast. Immediately inland behind Iskenderun a land-route runs to the south-east up the range of the Amanus mountains, over the pass which the ancients called the Syrian Gates and down into the great plain which stretches east to Aleppo and on to the Euphrates river.[45] This was the recognized land-route into Asia. The armies of Xenophon and of Alexander the Great both headed inland by this very route. Before them, Greeks had settled Posideion on the coast, positioning themselves brilliantly for a safe haven on the difficult surrounding sea and for an easy access to the direct route into Asia's interior.

There are still big mounds near modern Iskenderun but the coastline has been heavily developed, its line has altered and an excavation of Posideion is probably now impossible. Even without it, the site must return to our histories of direct Greek contact with the Near East, a storm-centre of archaeological scholarship. Herodotus located it in a list which he based on serious evidence, although without excavation we cannot know which Greeks first settled it. By c. 450 BC it was being traced back to the legendary Amphilochus the Argive, but Argives are most unlikely to have played any part as founders: should we think here too of Rhodians as originators of this legend, people who claimed a kinship with Argos?[46] As for other participants in the settlement, there is an obvious guess: Euboean Greek pottery of eighth-century date has been found at nearby Kinet Hüyük (surely the ancient Issus): in the eighth century 'Posideion' was a name well known to Euboeans; there was a Posideion on their home island and they had sited another in their coastal settlement of Mende in northern Greece.[47] Euboean pottery had been reaching sites on the north Syrian plain from the tenth century onwards and some of it may have arrived by the inland route from the Bay of Issus which began by the future site of Posideion and crossed the Amanus mountains. Euboeans, therefore, may have founded, or co-founded, Posideion here, perhaps in the early eighth century: Rhodians may have joined them later in the century and then, in the seventh century BC, when the Euboean presence at Posideion declined as elsewhere in the Near East, Rhodians on the site may have claimed a grand Greek hero as its founder, the Argive Amphilochus, the hero who was also claimed by Mallos on the other side of the bay.

From a few pieces of Greek pottery elsewhere, Near Eastern archaeologists are reluctant to accept a Greek settlement in southern Asia, let alone a 'colony'. But Herodotus' Posideion is attested in a well-founded text and obliges them to accept such a place. The problem is simply that we have not yet found or excavated it. Its ancient existence, however, is certain, although its origins in the eighth century are necessarily a guess. They are a compelling guess because we have primary Assyrian texts which connect the Cilician coast with an established Greek presence in this century's later decades. We have seen how texts of King Sargon (721–705 BC) refer to Ionian Greeks who were bothering the coast from Que (Cilicia) as far as Tyre: Posideion, near Alexandretta, fits well as one of their bases. Assyrian texts contain evidence for yet another rebellion which troubled the plain of Que and Rough Cilicia in 696 BC.[48] At that time, one 'Kirua' gathered troops from his strongholds, including his base at 'Illubru' north of the main plain. Assyrian horses, chariots and infantry were sent against him and defeated him after heavy fighting. Kirua had been an Assyrian dependant, or 'slave', and so he was taken off to Nineveh and skinned alive by order of the king. In the plain the cities of Tarsus and 'Ingira' (the Greeks' Anchiale near the coast) were captured because they had helped the revolt.

So much we know from surviving Assyrian texts written at the court of King Sennacherib. We also have two excerpts from Berossus, a later Babylonian historian writing in Greek (*c.* 270 BC), who used old Mesopotamian records which are now lost to us. His account was then abbreviated by two later Greek authors (one using the other): their versions are preserved by a third, the Christian Eusebius, *c.* AD 320, although his account is known to us only in an Armenian translation of his original Greek.[49] The merits of the information under these multiple layers have long been recognized, but the excerpts have not been fully exploited. They refer not to one and the same battle but to two separate battles in the same campaign, fought between Assyrian troops of Sennacherib and opposing Greeks. One battle was by land, the other by sea. These two separate battles belong to the Assyrians' Cilician campaign of 696 BC. By land, they help us to see, the Assyrians won a victory against an army of (Ionian) Greeks who 'marched against Cilicia', although the Assyrians lost 'many men'. Sennacherib himself was not present, but we are told in our Greek source that he caused a 'statue' of himself to be put up on the battlefield and inscribed it in 'Chaldean script' (actually, wedge-shaped cuneiform) as a memorial of his 'bravery and heroic deeds'. We know independently of this monument, because it was seen and described by Alexander the Great and his historians when they passed later through the Cilician plain.[50] They came upon it at Anchiale, the Assyrians' 'Ingira', which had participated in the revolt in 696 BC and had been punished for its role. It stood exactly on the site of the land-battle.

The Assyrians, we learn, also 'defeated a group of Ionian warships on the coast of Cilicia'. This sea-battle was a separate engagement with a separate location, but it is said to have been marked by another memorial: Sennacherib built a 'temple of the Athenians', put up 'bronze pillars' and 'caused, he said, his great deeds to be inscribed truthfully'.[51] As he himself was absent, the truth here was questionable. 'Bronze pillars', however, are exactly right for a memorial put up by Sennacherib as he is the one and only Assyrian king who claims to have used pillars of bronze elsewhere as monuments.[52] The problem is the 'temple of the Athenians', self-evident nonsense as Athenians had no role in this area until nearly three centuries later. The Armenian translator may have slightly misunderstood the underlying Greek. If the temple was a 'temple of Athena' (not 'the Athenians') in the original Greek, it makes excellent local sense.[53]

At the mouth of the Pyramus river lay the ancient site of Magarsos (modern Karatas). The site was long famous for its temple, which was dedicated, in the Greeks' view of it, to none other than the goddess Athena. This Greek interpretation of the goddess is first known to us by chance in the 330s BC but it remained central to the site's civic history during the next two centuries.[54] Magarsos issued coins then, on which we see the statue of its goddess represented in the new Greek age after Alexander's conquests. Her pose and surrounding attributes, however, have been diagnosed as being non-Greek with clear connections to Mesopotamian culture.[55] We can now see why: her cult and temple owed their origin to an Assyrian king, to King Sennacherib who had instituted the shrine in 696 BC for the martial goddess Anat (or Ishtar), whom he credited with helping his army's victory over the Greeks. Sea-battles were not an Assyrian speciality, but his ships had beaten the Greek ships just off Magarsos, by the mouth of the Pyramus river, with the aid of the goddess whom he rewarded with a temple.

This battle of the Pyramus is thus the first full battle-encounter between the ships of Ionian Greeks and the ships of an Oriental monarch. It occurred in 696 BC off the Cilician plain, which had been receiving Greek pottery for nearly a century, and within sight of the Greek base at Posideion near Iskenderun. Like this Posideion, it deserves to return in honour to our modern histories: its monument has a further military history.

In autumn 333 BC Alexander the Great and his army passed along this same stretch of coast.[56] At Anchiale they saw Sennacherib's monument and inscription in honour of his troops' land-victory but as we shall see, they misunderstood it. They then marched to Magarsos at the mouth of the Pyramus river and sacrificed to a goddess there whom they identified as Athena. They went up the river and stopped next at the town of Mallos, which persuaded their king that it had been founded by a legendary travelling Argive, none other than the hero Amphilochus. They then marched south in late October, quite unaware that the Persian king Darius and his huge army were marching northwards and were passing them, unseen, on the other side of the Amanus mountain-chain. They halted inland by the old coastal site of Posideion, perhaps now greatly diminished as its identity escaped mention in our brief surviving summaries of their route. On hearing the news of Darius' positioning they turned round, thanks to Alexander's genius, and confronted the Persian army in the narrows south of Issus, where they won a stupendous victory in early November.

The Cilician plain was a multi-cultural area whose layers of history overlapped in its various cults and settlements. It was exactly the place for creative misunderstandings, as the Greeks on our trail of travel and myths will exemplify. Alexander the Great was mistaken there too, about Sennacherib's monument, perhaps about Mallos' 'Argive' origins and certainly about the whereabouts of an entire Persian army. Before marching back to his eventual victory he had sacrificed to 'Athena of Magarsos'. Even here he was mistaken. The goddess, we now realize, had first been honoured here by the Assyrian king Sennacherib. Alexander was hoping for victory in Asia, but the temple was Sennacherib's thanks for the first ever naval victory of an Oriental fleet against bothersome Greeks.

Compared with Cyprus, southern Cilicia has so far produced sparse evidence of travelling Greek objects in the eighth century BC. It implies, however, that a Greek trail extended here and when we move on to the separate evidence of Greeks' local discoveries of myths and place names, it too will confirm an actual Euboean presence. First, the routes south of Posideion need to be followed. They take us again into sites where Homer's poems are not a guide.

6

Up to Unqi

After Cyprus and southern Cilicia the 'triangle' of Greek contact in this east end of the Mediterranean finds its third point on the coast of the Levant. In antiquity, as nowadays, this coastline was politically and culturally very varied too, the beginnings of our Near or Middle East, but less than 50 miles by sea from the north end of Cyprus. It fell into three main sections, more diverse in their contacts with Greeks and Greek objects than we would guess from the horizons of Homeric epic, for which the one point of contact with Greeks was Sidon, a rare and random port of call.

The northern section of the three was the north Syrian plain (now in Turkey), a flat, well-watered enclave which lies between two major mountain-barriers. On the north it is blocked out by the ascending hills of the Amanus range, the boundary between the north Syrian plain and the settlements of Cilicia to the north-west. From the Syrian plain, these mountains, the Cedar or Box-tree Mountains of Assyrian texts, were crossed north-westwards by the road from 'Pahri' in Syria at their foot (the site which Greeks called Pagras).[1] This road went on up through the Syrian Gates to a height of some 6,000 feet before descending to the bay of Iskenderun near the Greek Posideion, a site chosen partly for this inland route. On a map it seems a long trail across a major mountain-barrier, but we know from early modern travellers that the journey up and over was only six to seven hours on horseback, four of them from the Syrian Gates down to Iskenderun.[2]

Later in antiquity, as nowadays, this north Syrian plain was to be best known for the great city of Antioch, founded by a Successor of Alexander the Great c. 300 BC. Because of Antioch, above all, we think of the plain as 'married to the Mediterranean' into which Antioch's

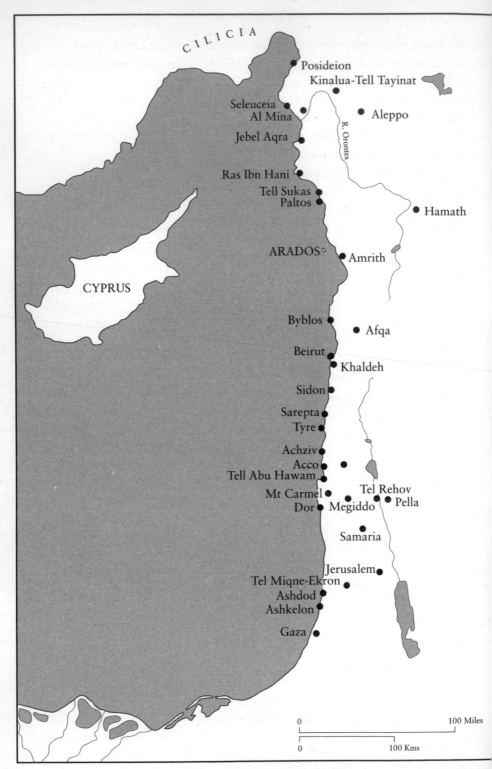

4. *Cyprus and the Levantine coast*

Orontes river runs.[3] In the ninth to mid-eighth centuries there was no royal town as close to the coast as Antioch would later be on the Orontes' course westwards. The plain's 'marriage to the Mediterranean' was thus less evident than its long-standing engagement to two land-routes, one running south down the Orontes' course into Syria, the other the route north-west to the Syrian Gates and the bay of Iskenderun beyond them.[4]

At its southern end this plain is blocked by the hills and main peak of the Jebel Aqra, the great mountain-beacon of the region. Here a second section of the coast began. Here too the settlements were no more politically coherent. The best-known were the royal city-states of the Phoenicians, which ran from the island site of Arwad (Arados, to the Greeks) as far south as Acco near Mount Carmel. Further south beyond the Phoenicians lay a third section, the settlements on the coast of ancient Palestine, those which edged the northern kingdom of Israel and those further south like Ascalon or Ekron, which were centres of Philistine culture. Here the prevailing currents would help ships to travel down from Cyprus, but so far Greek finds from the ninth and eighth centuries are minimal. However, they include Euboean cups and raise the pleasant possibility of a Euboean and a Philistine or an Israelite drinking together and using and bestowing Greek cups as mementoes.[5] Fragments of two Euboean cups survive from the coastal site of Tell abu Hawam and are arguably connected with a destruction on the site, probably in the mid- to late ninth century BC.[6] Tell abu Hawam lay near a protected bay off Mount Carmel, close to modern Haifa, which was linked in antiquity to an easy inland route to Megiddo and the Jezreel valley. It was perhaps through this port that more Greek items reached Megiddo (c. 830 BC) and then Samaria, the capital of the Israelite kings, where the few Greek pieces known include at least one tall mixing-bowl of Athenian origin, a substantial piece for an Israelite drinking-party among King Ahab's descendants, c. 780–760.[7] Further south, in the Jordan valley, two cups and two mixing-bowls of Euboean origin reached Tel Rehov, as did an Attic storage-jar which Euboeans probably brought to the Levant too, c. 850–830. The items travelled in from the coast.[8]

A Euboean presence on these three sections of the Levantine coast can be inferred in various ways and the strongest evidence of it is particularly important for the next step, their encounter with specific non-Greek, localized myths. It needs, then, to be followed piecemeal, although there is still the uncertainty of whether a Greek actually lived where a Greek object is found. Can the style of their objects help us? All down this coast the non-Greek societies already had their own style of partying, as we can see from local sculptures and above all from the Hebrew Scriptures' book of the prophet Amos. He deplored the extravagant habits of Israelites in the kingdom of Samaria c. 760 BC, who 'lie on couches of ivory and are draped on their beds ... who howl to the sound of the lute ... who drink wine from big basins and anoint themselves with the finest oils'. Amos uses strong words to intensify the excess of their noisy singing, their 'lounging' on couches, their drinking from huge bowls. It sounds riotous, but Amos predicts with a fine play on words that the 'shouting spree of these sprawlers' will be the first to go into exile.[9] The big basins have been identified as 'the beautiful ring-burnished multiple-handled ceramic bowls of Iron Age II ... the finest of all products made by the Israelite potters'.[10] We might, then, wonder why Levantine drinkers needed Greek cups, and thus infer that finds of such cups in a settlement imply that a Greek was indeed present on the site, using his own distinctive pottery.

Habits of drinking differed too. Like others in the Levant, Israelites drank their wine neat but flavoured with spices, whereas Greeks mixed it with water, a practice which the prophet Isaiah regarded as most inferior. Greeks therefore developed types of cups with handles, long stems and feet which they could hold between their fingers and move from side to side so as to mix their water and wine.[11] The earliest Greek imports, however, do not have these distinctive Greek shapes: they are thick wide cups, or *skyphoi*, with a base, not a tall foot, and a pair of small handles by the rim. They would fit quite easily into the local style of drinking from bowls which Amos exaggerates. The tall Athenian-made mixing-bowls on their pedestals and feet were a novelty in the Levant, but they too could have been used locally for wine only, not for watered wine as in Greece. They might have been regarded as a curious centrepiece at a non-Greek party. From the shapes of these Greek cups and bowls, therefore, we cannot argue that they were fit only for Greek use and thus prove a presence of actual Greek residents where we find them in a settlement's buildings. Greek pottery certainly passed into non-Greek hands. At Old Tyre, or at Khaldeh, just south of modern Beirut, a few Greek pieces ended up in the sites' non-Greek cemeteries during the eighth century. Similarly, a big Greek jar, or *pyxis*, of probable Attic origin was found intact, dating to *c.* 850–820 BC, in a tomb about 4 miles south-west of Sidon: it was found together with five big Phoenician urns, each used for a cremation, one of which had a clear Phoenician inscription.[12] These Greek pieces were placed in non-Greek tombs near examples of non-Greek writing and plainly they could only have been put there by non-Greeks. At most they imply contact with Greek visitors who brought them east to the Levantine coast and passed them on.

Even so, any such Greek presence was a tiny part of a much bigger local pattern of trade and travel. Up and down this coastline Phoenician ships were carrying anything from silver to cedarwood and were continuing to trade with Egypt quite separately from any Greek traffic. Our understanding of them has been transformed by the recovery of two Phoenician trading ships which had sunk with their cargoes on the open sea about 30 miles west of Ascalon. Located in 1997, they have now been analysed and dated to the later eighth century BC.[13] They are not unduly big, having a capacity of about 30 tons and a crew of about half a dozen, Phoenicians to judge from their accompanying cooking-pots. Each sailing ship, however, held nearly 400 big jars, evidently filled with wine, each jar holding as much as 4 gallons. At Tyre and Sarepta near Sidon, big pottery kilns have been found on the mainland, places where such transport-jars were mass produced. The wine in the two Phoenician ships was probably in this category. It was being exported down to Egypt, a land which had no grapevines, but the ships were swamped on the sea-journey and sank, preserving evidence of a big bulk trade which continued on this route into Egypt for centuries. It is quite different from the trading of trinkets and amber necklaces, the trade which Homer credits to Phoenicians.

Apart from merely visiting this coast, as the arrival of Greek cups and bowls implies, did Greeks ever reside for long or develop close social contacts? Archaeologists are rightly wary of assuming from a find of imported pottery that the makers and carriers of it lived and settled on its site for any length of time. They look for local imitations of it as stronger evidence that its carriers actually resided there for a while, but on the central and southern sections of the Levantine coast we have no such imitations in the ninth and eighth centuries. Instead, historians can only cite facts from a better-documented age and leave the earlier possibility open. During the classical period of the early fourth century BC we know, but only from texts, that there was a resident Greek community at Phoenician Carthage in the west.[14] Without these texts, archaeologists would not easily accept the existence of Greek residents from the sole evidence of the few Greek objects excavated on the site: there were no obvious Greek burials or local imitations of the Greek goods. What happened later at Carthage may have happened already in the mother-city of Tyre in the ninth and eighth centuries BC. A few Greeks, using Greek goods, might indeed have resided in Phoenician city-states. We cannot rule them out, even at this early date: our archaeology is not decisive.

What we can infer is some close contact: we can then best explain a practice which Euboeans imitated from Phoenicians. In Phoenician cities, as elsewhere in the Near East, goods were bought and sold for silver and precious metals. The metals were cut from bars and small objects and were weighed, not coined, because coinage was not yet in use. One unit of weight was the 'shekel', a word which simply meant 'weight'. In Euboean settlements we then find a unit of weight called the 'stater', also the Greek word for 'weight'. Its basic weight is almost exactly that of a shekel and like the shekel it was a fiftieth part of a bigger unit, the 'mina' which Greeks also imported from the Near East. Euboeans, therefore, had copied the Phoenician unit.[15] It became their official unit of weight and eventually of coined money, and it is known as early as the late eighth century in one of their western settlements. It was not borrowed from western Carthage. It was borrowed directly during commercial exchanges with Phoenicians so as to match their 'weight' of exchange. It was surely imitated during Euboeans' direct contact with the practices and units of Phoenicians in the Levant on something more than a casual visit.

It is consistent, at least, with this contact that, from the period between c. 850 and 750 BC, about a hundred pieces of Greek pottery have so far been recovered from Tyre, the one major Phoenician site to reveal such a quantity.[16] They are still a tiny minority among the total non-Greek pottery found there, so they are not conclusive proof of a small Greek presence. They are merely explicable by one, however short it might have been in each instance. If it existed, it is not a presence we would ever guess from Homer's epic poems. He never mentions Tyre at all.

If we move northwards from the Phoenician city-states to the next stretch of the Levantine coast, we pass out of Homeric horizons altogether. Beyond the Phoenician island-state of Arwad we enter an important chain of harbours and anchorages which Phoenicians also frequented and which Greeks and Greek objects also reached. They are not all strictly 'Phoenician' foundations and their place names and sequence need close attention, because their ancient names and significance have been confused with crucial points of Greek contact just beyond them. Exact places and landscapes are essential if we are to trace the myths which Greeks then developed, so we have to be sure of their ground. To appreciate the sites and their ancient place names we can draw on texts written later for Greek sailors here in the Greek age after Alexander. Even if they were compiled no earlier than c. 100 BC–AD 300 they are valuable evidence because the coastal conditions changed so little.

Beyond the island of Arwad the pattern remained one of anchorages by river-mouths or in bays formed by the few promontories on an otherwise exposed coast.[17] Heading north, travellers would be able to stop at Paltos (now 'Arab-al-mulk) at the mouth of the Nahr-as Siren river.[18] It was a very short trip from here up to Suksu (nowadays Tell Sukas), a well-excavated coastal site which Cypriot pottery had been reaching already in the eleventh and tenth centuries when Suksu was a settled town. It had a long history before the arrival of the three Greek cups, probably all Euboean, which are the only Greek ones found in the settlement between c. 850 and 750 BC. Another seven pieces, also in the settlement, date from c. 750–700.[19] Nonetheless the excavators suggested that these contacts grew into a resident Greek enclave. When they found a building for cult in the centre of the town which was datable c. 650 BC their first thoughts were that it was a Greek temple serving Greek residents and Greek visitors in the seventh century, a major discovery, therefore, for our trail. The building had roof-tiles (a Greek feature) but renewed study of its plan and shape has identified it, more plausibly, as non-Greek.[20] There are no early Greek burials anywhere in the settlement and given the rarity of early Greek pottery eighth-century Suksu was nothing more than an occasional port-of-call for a few Greeks.

If we go on north past a good coastal plain and the then-modest site at modern Lattakieh (which was only developed after Alexander), the next significant marker after 5 miles is the coastal promontory of Ras ibn Hani. Here, too, lay settlements with a history stretching far back into the Bronze Age.[21] The cape lies only 3 miles to the south-west of the big site of Ras Shamra (ancient Ugarit), particularly important in the years c. 1400–1200 BC, when invaluable finds of clay tablets have given us fragments of the ancient Canaanites' myths about their gods and confirmed the multi-lingual culture of their scribes. Cypriot pottery was already reaching the site in that period, as was pottery from Mycenaean Greece: Ugarit has given us about a third of all Mycenaean Greek pottery known in the Levant.[22] At the end of the Bronze Age (c. 1180 BC) Ugarit's inhabitants dispersed, but no crisis could neutralize their invaluable asset, the coast's best natural harbour on the promontory of Ras ibn Hani. It became known from its low white cliff as the 'White Harbour' in later Greek coastal guidebooks, a name which persists in modern Arabic as Minet el-Beida.[23] Cypriot pottery continued to reach Ras ibn Hani after the Bronze Age and as the previous Mycenaean Greek contacts had been important, we might expect that the excellence of the site and its harbour's long history would quickly attract other Greek travellers as they returned to the Levantine coast. However, only two cups from Greece have been found there, both of which date between c. 850 and c. 750 BC. They have the familiar Euboean decoration, but they imply visitors, not settlers.

What, then, did Greeks call the settlement which they found by this harbour? At Ras Shamra, texts and statues show the honours accorded to El, father of the gods. Ras Shamra's later small settlement and the nearby Ras ibn Hani were surely the site which Greeks later knew as 'Betyllion' (their version of the Semitic phrase 'bait-El' or 'House of El'). They noted Betyllion for its natural harbour, surely the 'White Harbour' which we can still admire and which had been the port since

Ugarit's Bronze Age. We can therefore understand why Betyllion's 'natural' harbour is described as the first staging-post for the Roman emperor Trajan when he set out from Rome to join his troops in Syria for their fateful campaign into Mesopotamia (modern Iraq) in AD 114–17.[24] He had landed at ancient Ugarit. The correct location of Betyllion is important for different reasons, not because it was a Greek settlement but because it has become involved in a major topographical puzzle about Greek contact further north and also because the name ('house of El') confirms that Canaanite-Phoenician culture never entirely died at the site.

Moving north from the White Harbour, Assyrian texts of the eighth century BC refer to a separate cape called 're'si-ṣurri', a landmark for them. It is probably to be translated as the 'Cape of the Rocks'.[25] The natural candidate for this cape is the modern Ras el-Bassit, about 15 miles to the north of Betyllion. It, too, has an attractive natural harbour and an excellent view up to the defining chain of the Jebel Aqra mountain, the next major landmark to the north. Fortunately it has been well excavated, showing that it is yet another settlement on this coast whose history extends continuously back into the Bronze Age and whose culture owes next to nothing to Greeks. Phoenician pottery was imported to it from the south in considerable quantity during the ninth and eighth centuries, while the burial customs of its well-studied cemetery connect with those of the Syrian settlements inland.[26] Once again a problem lies in its name, the source of a mistake about its eighth-century significance for Greeks. We happen to know from Greek texts of the late fourth century that Greek sailors called this promontory Posideion, that favoured name on many coastlines. In Alexander the Great's lifetime, Greek influence was extending on this coast and as a 'Posideion', Ras el-Bassit was striking coins with the god Poseidon's figure on them.[27] The modern name 'Bassit' (from the Arabic for 'flat') has even been traced, somewhat fancifully, back to the Greeks' 'Posideion' name.[28] In the ninth to eighth centuries Ras el-Bassit was not a Greek settlement or indebted to a Greek initiative. Fragments of imported Greek pottery have been found on the site, especially pieces of Euboean-style cups which date from the eighth century, but there are not more than fifty pieces in all.[29] They are never concentrated in any particular tombs and there are no local imitations. The implications of Ras el-Bassit for eighth-century Greek contact are that Greeks visited with their goods and perhaps resided briefly but never settled there in the ninth to eighth centuries. Only later was it called 'Posideion' and it was never connected with a legendary Greek hero as its founder. Ras el Bassit was not the Posideion which Herodotus credited to the travelling hero Amphilochus. He sited that one much further north.

So far, these coastal places are all sites with long non-Greek histories which extend for at least four hundred years before any Euboean cups and plates came near them. Most of them also had overland access to major royal settlements inland, Tell abu Hawam to Samaria, Ras el-Bassit by a hill-route to Syrian Hamath. Important routes ran even further into the interior, including the Jordan valley. Above all, a major route from Ras ibn Hani ran up quickly and directly to Aleppo in the north Syrian plain, linking this significant site to the southern 'Canaanite' sea-coast in a way which our local studies of the plain would never suspect.[30] When Greek pottery turns up inland it is most likely to have been carried, still, by non-Greeks. On the coast, meanwhile, the main seafarers and visitors were Phoenicians.

Beyond Ras el-Bassit a Greek maritime guidebook of the fourth century AD is explicit about the difficulties.[31] Ships had to pass the range of the towering Jebel Aqra (the modern frontier between Syria and Turkey) where they encountered severe winds from the west threatening to drive them into the mountain's base. There were islands just off it, rocky ones with names like 'Long Island' and 'Pigeon Rocks', and there was also a small bay, later 'sacred to the nymphs', immediately on the Jebel Aqra's far side.[32] Northbound ships for the south Cilician coast would be wise to stay further out to sea and miss this awkward stretch of coast. They could make one long day's journey straight up to the mouth of the Pyramus river and the edge of the Cilician plain. If necessary they could put in after about 20 miles at the last north Syrian promontory (now in Turkey) and supply themselves from the river-waters which gushed naturally from its hill, as they still do. Greeks knew this place as 'River of Waters' before Alexander's Successor Seleucus developed it into the major harbour-city of Seleuceia. It became Seleucus' first capital, housed his tomb and endured for nearly a thousand years. Significantly, his builders had to construct its harbour artificially at the end of a canal which protected it from the storms on the turbulent sea beyond.[33]

A direct sea-route from Ras el-Bassit up to Cilicia thus had its attractions and Phoenicians were the most likely users of it because of their well-attested presence in the Cilician plain. As well as the metal-resources of the mountains beyond Karatepe, there was a resource in the plain which has left no archaeological hoofprint: horses. The specific evidence of the biblical book of Kings is to be taken seriously here: horses were brought from 'Que', the Cilician plain, and taken south to Solomon's Jerusalem.[34] Some of this horse-trade may have been by land but the problems of access, horse-thieving and delays made sea-transport the obvious option. The art of shipping horses is amply attested in later Greek history, but it may already have been practised down the Levantine coast in the tenth century BC. In the later sixth century Ezekiel even credits Tyre with importing horses from central Anatolia, also, no doubt, through Cilicia and perhaps on southwards by boat.[35]

Ships which took this direct route to Cilicia missed the northern section of the coastline, the north Syrian plain which runs beyond the Jebel Aqra mountain for about 20 miles until the Amanus mountains intervene and cut it off. Like the Cilician plain, it was the fertile creation of three rivers, of which the most important is the Orontes, which snakes and twists onto it from modern Syria and then bends sharply west before running out onto the coastline. Here, the Orontes created a delta at its mouth which was about 10 miles wide.[36]

Naturally and culturally this plain was an attractive asset. Its northern limit, the Amanus mountains, had the box- and cedar-trees which were prized for buildings by the Assyrian kings. The plain had an area of wetland, valuable as always for flax (its local kings' linen robes were notable), and a significant lake. It had once been a home for elephants, as we know from an elephant's shoulder-bone found in the plain itself: there are grounds for supposing that elephants survived there into the first millennium BC.[37] There were also hippopotamuses, whose teeth were another source of ivory for the region's important ivory-carvers.[38] There were precious metals too, including copper and silver, in the Jebel Aqra mountain which formed the plain's southern boundary.[39] We can gain an idea of the riches of the royal town which was nearest to the Orontes delta from the records of the conquering Assyrian kings. From inland 'Kinalua' (the modern Tell Tayinat) on the westward bend of the Orontes river, the Assyrians' first conquest in the 870s BC took silver, gold, '100 talents of tin and 100 talents of iron, 1,000 oxen, 10,000 sheep', fine linen robes, decorated couches and beds of box-wood, '10 female singers, the king's brother's daughter with a rich dowry, a large female monkey and ducks'.[40]

Kinalua was only one royal town in a patchwork in the plain. Even more than its Cilician counterpart, this Syrian river-plain was a multi-cultural, multi-lingual tapestry which is important for the debts which Greeks will turn out to owe to it.[41] Since the ninth century BC Aramaean tribes had conquered and settled in several of north Syria's most important sites, especially Hamath (modern Hama) and Arpad (north-west of Aleppo, at Tell Rifa'at). These Aramaeans had a West Semitic speech and script (our Aramaic) and brought with them their own religious culture.[42] At particular sites inland, the Phoenicians' script and artistic styles are also visible, especially in evidence from the ninth century. Above all, as in Cilicia, the legacy of the former Hittite empire had lived on prominently, giving rise to a clear 'neo-Hittite' style.[43]

These various cultures coexisted and inter-related to an extent which we cannot unravel into neat zones and decades. At Hamath in the ninth century kings with neo-Hittite names put up hieroglyphic inscriptions in Luwian, but already worshipped a well-established non-Luwian goddess, 'Our Lady' or Ba'alati, as they knew her by her Semitic name.[44] During the later ninth century the rulers at Zincirli at the foot of the Amanus mountains changed from putting up inscriptions in Phoenician and used Aramaic instead, but continued to have neo-Hittite Luwian personal names.[45] Royal inscriptions are not even proof of a town's everyday spoken language: they may simply be statements of power and display, while ordinary people spoke something else. The patterns of speech may have been different, another cultural complication.

The neo-Hittite legacy is particularly important for discoveries which the Greeks made here and the evidence for it is strong, though individual items are not easy to date closely within the years from c. 900 to 750. Inscriptions, not only royal ones, were composed in

the Luwian language and written in 'neo-Hittite' hieroglyphic script:
styles of sculpture were distinctively neo-Hittite, whether for the big
block-sculptures in the doorways of local palaces or the smaller funerary reliefs which commemorated members of private families. This
culture is most prominent in the tenth and ninth centuries, especially
in centres like Hamath before *c.* 800 BC.[46] At Aleppo there is excellent
evidence of a temple and important cult of the neo-Hittite Storm
God;[47] at Kinalua the rulers continued to have historic Hittite royal
names in the eighth century; at Ain Dara, by the Afrin river (Chalos,
to the Greeks), there was a palace and a temple platform much of
whose style, sculptures and cults remained neo-Hittite too.[48] Even
in the eighth century BC this cultural imprint persisted, as Luwian
continued to be written in neo-Hittite hieroglyphic script and the
Storm God and other neo-Hittite deities in the area were still worshipped.[49] In the 730s the king of Zincirli by the foot of the Amanus
mountains kept a signet-ring with his name in hieroglyphic Luwian
characters as well as having another which was inscribed in Aramaic,
the language in which his family put up royal inscriptions during the
eighth century BC.[50]

This multi-cultural vigour went with a history of changing settlement. Like the towns up the Levantine coast, the towns in north Syria
had not been eclipsed by the ending of the Bronze Age. Instead,
between the tenth and the mid-eighth century many of them had
emerged as new settlements, clustering round a fort or palace and
showing no sign of a reduced population.[51] For coastal visitors the
important zone was the plain nearest the sea, part of the land which
Assyrians knew either as 'Patina' (a neo-Hittite name) or as 'Unqi'
from the Aramaic word for its low-lying plain.[52] In Patina–Unqi the
royal town of Kinalua lay inland on the far eastern bank of the
Orontes river where the river had wound north from Syria and was
about to bend sharply west towards the sea. Kinalua is the Calneh of
the Hebrew Scriptures, and its culture was still strongly marked by
a neo-Hittite style when the Assyrians in 740 BC forced its king
Tutammu to submit.[53]

Despite its position beside the Orontes' bend to the west, Kinalua
should not be assumed automatically to have had constant links with
the Orontes river-delta and the coast: its connections by land-routes

to the south along the river-valley were also very important. For travellers going north and south on the sea, meanwhile, the Orontes delta was not a self-evident attraction. Its coastline has advanced nowadays through river-silting but even today the open shore is not a safe haven for boats brought onto it.[54] Strong winds from the west interrupt the boats at anchor, while modern naval handbooks recognize the hazards of winds and currents and also the sandbanks at the river's mouth. In antiquity, as until recently, the Orontes remained navigable, but the winds, currents and probably some of the silting were present in the ninth century BC too. They may help to explain the muted presence, so far, of explicitly Phoenician goods and culture in the early eighth-century levels of sites in the delta and the coastal sector of the plain of Unqi. With the entire Syrian coast to choose from and south Cilicia ahead of them, it seems that Phoenicians may often have preferred to give this beach a miss.

The delta is crucial, however, for the Greeks' trail in the eighth century because of a much-discussed mound which has been excavated on the north-west bank of the Orontes as it approaches the sea. Far more Greek pottery has been found here than in any eighth-century level of the settlements on the Levantine coast or the Cilician plain. In 858 BC the conquering Assyrian king Shalmaneser III had recorded how 'in the wide area of the seashore I marched by right of victory. An image of my lordship, which establishes my name for all time to come, I made and set up by the sea.'[55] This monument has long disappeared from the coastline and the honours have passed instead to a site with Greek contacts, founded within a hundred years of his departure.

7

Potamoi Karon

I

Like much else in contacts between Greeks and the non-Homeric 'triangle' of Cyprus, Cilicia and the Levant, the rediscovery of the crucial mound in north Syria began from a creative mistake. In 1936, fresh from his triumphant excavations at ancient Ur, the archaeologist Leonard Woolley transferred his skills to this river-plain and chose to dig two particular mounds among scores of possible candidates. Already in his mid-fifties, Woolley had moved west from Mesopotamia (Iraq) after restrictive changes in its laws on antiquities. He returned to excavate in north Syria, then under the French Mandate, a cultural region in which he had dug some twenty years before at Carchemish near the Euphrates with the young T. E. Lawrence as a member of his team. In 1936 his aim was to find a Bronze Age site in north Syrian Unqi, the river-plain which he viewed as a 'self-contained hollow . . . from the point of view of commerce, the meeting place of the Great Powers'.[1] Instead, one of his finds was a site which had flourished in the eighth century BC, a period for which he had not been looking. It gave a precise turn to an established debate about the impact of the crafts and techniques of north Syria on eighth-century Greek craftsmen. It then generated a new debate about its own role and significance for Greeks visiting the Levant.

Woolley chose to dig a mound, or tell, just to the north-west of the Orontes river which had been cut by a small modern road leading to the nearby village of Sueidia. On the mound's northern end, as now, stood a shrine to Sheikh Yusuf, a local Muslim Alawite saint: at first Woolley called his site the 'Tell of Sheikh Yusuf'. Although it lay about a mile inland from the coastline, he inferred correctly that the plain had advanced through silting of the river and that the mound had once lain by the river-mouth. So it came to be called 'Al Mina', Arabic for 'the port' or 'the anchorage'.

Digging deep down to the ninth and tenth of its ancient levels Woolley struck virgin soil across an excavated span of about 650 yards. These levels were characterized by scattered fragments of painted Greek pottery which Woolley considered to have begun to arrive in the mid-eighth century BC. The mound produced no supporting burials and the outlines of the single-storey buildings in the lowest levels were extremely humble. At most they had pebbled floors and mud-brick walls which had collapsed inwards, leaving only their uncut bases of local stones. The near-total preponderance of Greek pottery was remarked by Woolley and led him, unsurprisingly, to the view that the site was first occupied by Greeks.[2]

In Woolley's opinion it was not a normal settlement. The floor plans of the buildings were so ordinary and the site seemed to be typified by broken bits of cups and drinking-vessels. About 3 miles up the Orontes river at Sabouni, Woolley located a second mound, which he examined but never excavated. Here he found pieces of Mycenaean Greek pottery from the Bronze Age, but Sabouni showed signs of an eighth-century presence too and so Woolley became 'fairly certain that this was the place where there lived the merchants who did business at Al Mina. Others, very likely, had villas elsewhere . . .' The social proprieties, he thought, could be resolved: at Al Mina there must have lived 'residents of the poorer sort . . . but the richer merchants lived in the healthy surroundings of Sabouni and came down to their offices every morning'. Woolley, one feels, and Mrs Woolley, would have settled with servants in a Sabouni villa: 'Sabouni was the town proper, standing to Al Mina much in the relation of Athens to the Piraeus.'[3]

For Woolley, Al Mina was the ancient Posideion of Herodotus and the legendary travelling hero Amphilochus was a memory of real Argive Greeks who had once settled at Sabouni in the Mycenaean age. On the seashore to the north of Al Mina stood a Muslim shrine to a pilgrim-saint who was known (as he still is) in Arabic as the 'lord of the Sea'. For Woolley, this shrine was a living memory of the local sea-god, a god whom the Greeks of this Posideion had once equated with Poseidon and who was still 'ignorantly worshipped', so Woolley believed, in a Muslim form.[4] In later antiquity the name Posideion, he suggested, fell out of use and the site became known as Betyllion.

We have seen that both these place names belong elsewhere on the map, but Woolley's discoveries were far more important than his attempts to link them with names in texts. Earlier in the twentieth century, without any knowledge of these sites, German archaeologists had already established the detailed impact of north Syrian skills and objects on eighth- and seventh-century craftsmen of the Greek islands and mainland.[5] Magnificently, Woolley appeared to have found the underlying point of contact: a Greek settlement at the very mouth of the Syrian river which led on up to the royal city of Kinalua (Tell Tayinat) inland. Through this 'port' (Mina), north Syrian goods were evidently channelled by Greek traders into the Greek world. In the late 1930s and early 1940s the pottery and minor objects which Woolley preserved from Al Mina were published only in part and were then dispersed to collections far and wide. However, Woolley's view of the site prevailed, and in 1957 the Oxford archaeologist John Boardman intensified its interest by arguing that much of Al Mina's earliest Greek pottery was Euboean in style or origin.[6] His brilliant hypothesis was proved correct when Lefkandi and other sites in Euboea were later excavated and revealed similar pottery of their own.

Nonetheless doubts began to be raised about Woolley's explanations. Al Mina was plainly not Posideion (as we have seen, Posideion lay further north on the Bay of Issus and the name was then given later to Ras el-Bassit, just to the south). If the place really was a Greek settlement, why did it have no known Greek name? Why were there no Greek burials and no Greek architecture or roof-tiles? Why, even, were there no Greek cooking-pots and everyday kitchenware? Where were the early Greek inscriptions? Why could not the Greek pottery have been brought here by visiting Phoenicians who might even have founded the site?

Each of these questions has been answered.[7] In the early to mid-eighth century Greeks had not yet invented roof-tiles and as elsewhere abroad they would build simple dwellings in local materials without a distinguishable Greek style.[8] The burials could have been lost to changes in the course of the Orontes nearby: whoever lived at Al Mina, some of them must have died there and yet no burials at all have been recovered from the earliest phases. There are no non-Greek inscriptions, either. The one known early inscription happens to be Greek, scratched on a piece of imported pottery which has been dated c. 700 BC.[9] The near-total absence of cooking-pots also applies to whoever lived on the site, although a few non-Greek pieces have been traced from the earliest levels. Greeks may have brought their cups here for their own favoured style of drinking, but used non-Greek ware for the common task of cooking. Allegations that Woolley threw away the non-Greek pottery are disproved by what survives and by his own field-notes.

What was the site called? Here, non-Greek evidence has made an unexpected contribution. A recently published Assyrian account of Tiglath Pileser's conquests in 738 BC lists conquered places on the north Syrian coastline from the 'Cape of the Rocks' (Ras el-Bassit) to the Jebel Aqra mountain, then 'Ahta', the 'trading post by the edge of the sea, the place of the kingship's "store"' (a storehouse?) and then the Amanus mountains on the north edge of our river-plain. Although Assyrian lists do not always follow a geographical order, this one is clearly going northwards in a correct sequence at this point. The 'trading post by the edge of the sea' belongs on the coast just north of the Jebel Aqra mountain, precisely in our river-delta. Either Ahta is itself this 'trading post by the edge of the sea', surely our Al Mina on the seashore, or Ahta is one place, possibly the still unexcavated mound at Sabouni, and the 'trading post' is Al Mina, while the 'place of the kingship's "store"' is the same or yet another site (the translation 'storehouse' is uncertain).[10]

The placing of this trading post is important for a neglected later itinerary, the progress of the fleet of Alexander's friend and Successor the historian Ptolemy, up the north Syrian coastline in 312 BC. His fleet stopped to ravage Posideion, none other than Ras el-Bassit at this date: it then went on to ravage a nearby place called 'Potamoi Karon' before heading on north to the river-mouths of the south Cilician plain.[11] 'Potamoi Karon' is a strange name for a purely Greek site. It translates as 'Rivers of the Carians', referring to a people from south-west Asia who included notable sailors and were later transplanted to the Persian Gulf as a naval contingent by the un-nautical Persian kings.[12] However, no object, text or reference connects any Carians with the mouth of the Orontes. The word-order 'Potamoi Karon' is odd for a Greek name and we should therefore consider the possibility that like other known local Greek place names it arose from an underlying non-Greek word. Just such a name confronts us now in the list of Tiglath Pileser's conquests: 'karu' or a trading post.[13] The Greek 'Karon' may have arisen from 'karu(n)': the name 'Potamoi Karon' would then mean 'River(s) of the Trading-post', referring to the mouth of the Orontes on which Al Mina stood; the uncertain 'royal storehouse' in Tiglath Pileser's list may well be the same place. On separate, secure grounds Woolley ascribed the final phase of Al Mina to a destruction datable to the late fourth century BC. He credited the damage to Seleucus during the building of his nearby port-city of Seleuceia. But we can now see the likelier culprit, not Seleucus but Ptolemy, whose fleet sailed up here in 312 BC laying waste to coastal bases and devastating Potamoi Karon.

If correct, the use of a curious name which derived orally from an ancient Assyrian word would remind us that Al Mina was not a full Greek settlement for much of its later life. However, the majority of the first settlers (before 738 BC) were Greeks and that fact about the place may have been recognized by Assyrians too. We have a recently found letter in which an Assyrian official, evidently from the Levantine coast, reports to the court at Nimrud: he describes attackers who had raided 'the town of Iauna', evidently the 'town of Greeks'. The text is fragmentary, as usual, and the siting is uncertain: the attackers fled to 'snow mountains'.[14] But a 'town of the Greeks' in the Levant is not Ras el-Bassit, a non-Greek place at this date, or any other site on its coast. Assyrian governors on this coastline were unlikely to be involved with the Greek Posideion up near Cilicia: the natural candidate is Al Mina itself, at the foot of 'snow mountains' running south.

Woolley's publication of some of the finds has been enough to show that Al Mina was indeed a fitting 'town of Iauna', a site with Greek contacts on a scale far greater than the others, excavated later, which we have followed along this coast. At Tyre or the nearby Ras el-Bassit we have been referring to Greek cups, plates or drinking-vessels only by the dozen, increasing to fifty or so in the mid to later eighth century BC on long-occupied non-Greek sites. At Al Mina, the pottery in Woolley's two lowest levels numbered pieces by the hundreds. They lay on virgin soil which had not been occupied before. Those hundreds have now been increased by yet more deposits from these same levels which were sent by Woolley to the British Museum and never published. No other site in Cilicia or the Levant, no cemetery on Cyprus has produced anything like this concentration of Greek pieces, let alone in the earliest level of a settlement. By contrast, Al Mina's two lowest levels have nothing inarguably Phoenician in either of them.[15] Even in the next level, Phoenician pottery has been correctly diagnosed only in a few instances: proportionately, the Greek pottery is still the main, dominant ware. The same arguments apply here as we have already applied in the era when Lefkandi still flourished in Euboea. Greek pottery from a single main source, once again Euboea, was not carried back to the coast of Unqi by north Syrians: they were not seafarers. Nor was it brought there by Phoenicians: they left next to no trace of their contact with the earliest settlement at Al Mina. Euboea also had little of special value to attract Phoenicians when the whole west Mediterranean stretched before them. We cannot easily explain why the pottery brought from Greek sites to the Levant was predominantly from Euboea, despite so many other attractive Greek brands across the Aegean, if the carriers were Near Easterners who had been stopping at other Greek islands with local Greek pottery of their own on their way home. The cogent answer is that it was brought by Euboeans.

The inference, then, is that Euboeans lived at Al Mina, perhaps with some east Greeks (a very small amount of pottery from Samos has been identified) and perhaps with Cypriots too.[16] Euboeans, it seems, founded the settlement, or dominated it, but was it a home for some of them year after year, or did they come to and fro for trade, spending only part of their time in this 'port'? Initially there would be no civic structures, no rules about citizenship, and we should not exclude non-Greeks even when the place began. There was a role for non-Greek women, people from the north Syrian plain, as these Euboean adventurers would not have brought their own women on journeys for trade and piracy; for sex they needed the locals. The date of the first settlement remains controversial, and suggestions still vary between *c.* 800 and 760. We must also allow for casual Greek contacts before the full settlement began, because the earliest fragments of pottery on site are classified as 'Euboean Subprotogeometric', with perhaps a piece of Athenian 'Middle Geometric' going back in origin into the mid-ninth century.[17] In the early eighth century a non-Greek piece of recently found evidence is also relevant, although its reference is still disputed.

Beside the Orontes river, about 3 miles east of the mound of Sabouni, an inscribed text on stone was discovered in 1968, but its contents were so unexpected that one response was to argue that the stone must have been carried downstream from far away up the river.[18] It recorded the awarding of the 'town of Na-ah-la-si, its fields and orchards', to the king of Arpad (inland, in north Syria) by the authority of the Assyrian king and governor: the date of this arbitrated award falls almost certainly between *c.* 805 and 795. The most attractive interpretation is that the land and town given over by this arbitration lay in our river-delta: if so, the 'orchards and gardens' should be those which stood near Sabouni where the stone was then set up to record the boundary of the arbitrated ground. Without it we would not think of Arpad as the likeliest Syrian state to control this place. Kinalua (Tell Tayinat) on the bend of the Orontes river or even Hamath further south were geographically much more likely candidates. Perhaps the award to Arpad was controversial and gave a political framework in which Greeks at Al Mina could take root. Perhaps Greeks were able to settle in the power-vacuum, or perhaps the king of Arpad may have tolerated these outsiders at the mouth of his newly confirmed river-delta as he and his subjects were not seafarers. Even after the arbitration there was a risk of attack from Arpad's rivals, especially from one or other Phoenician city, whose sailors might try to put in by sea and attack the river-delta which landlocked Arpad, their Aramaic rivals inland, could not easily defend.

By *c.* 800 BC the site was probably known already to Euboean visitors, even if they had not yet formally settled it. Since the 950s pieces of their Euboean pottery had been reaching some of the north Syrian sites which lie further inland in the plain. Some of these pieces may have come from the Bay of Issus by crossing the Amanus mountains and coming down by land through the 'Syrian Gates'. Other pieces may have come up from the mouth of the Orontes, after casual Greek visitors brought them to the river-delta. To Phoenicians, the site which became Al Mina had not hitherto been of much interest, as we have inferred from its coast's local conditions and the greater appeal of ports in Cilicia further up to the north. For Greeks, coming across from Cyprus, or down from the Bay of Issus, the weather conditions were less of a deterrent than for Phoenicians who had to come north: for Greeks, the winds and currents ran helpfully from the west off Cyprus, and the Jebel Aqra's range, to the south of Al Mina, did not have to be negotiated. There are many uncertainties, but if the recently found inscription shows that the river-delta was suddenly awarded to the king of Arpad, the new development of a Greek settlement at Al Mina would fit intelligibly just after this change in the political landscape.

A subsequent change, at least, is clear to us. After taking an oath of submission in 740 BC, King Tutammu of Kinalua broke it and in 738 BC Assyrian troops returned. 'I set up my throne inside Tutammu's palace,' Tiglath Pileser's inscriptions recalled. '[I took] 300 talents of silver, weapons, many-coloured robes, linen robes, all types of herbs and furnishings . . . I placed my eunuchs over them as governors.'[19] In the ruins of Kinalua's palace the visual images of these events survive: six panels show Assyrian soldiers holding the severed heads of their enemies by the hair and marching over naked bodies underfoot.[20] Remarkably, we can even follow Tutammu's deportation eastwards in a letter which was sent up to the coast at Nineveh by one of the governors on his route. 'Tutammu and his courtiers will come to Nineveh,' he reports, and we can assume he was cruelly executed on arrival. In this new phase of direct rule Al Mina or its neighbour became the 'trading post by the sea' in the Assyrians' list of their conquests which their scribes drew up promptly in 738/7. We cannot trace any direct Assyrian involvement in the sparse remains of the site, but by c. 710 BC a new level of settlement superseded the previous foundation-layer. As Woolley emphasized, it contained much more Cypriot pottery, and as others have analysed it since, 'Syrian' and specifically Phoenician pottery is present too. Several possible stories could explain this change, but an 'eclipse of the Greeks' is not necessarily one. Instead, more Cypriots may have joined a venture which was flourishing under Assyrian rule: some Phoenicians, too, may have started to see the place as a worthwhile stop.

In the absence of written historical sources we can only make informed guesses from the site itself, its objects and its local context.[21] At Al Mina we have imitations of pottery in a Euboean style, and although we are not sure where they were made, they suggest that some Greeks did persist on the site: as their first cups and bowls broke, they needed local replacements.[22] Some Greeks stayed on, then, but others probably went to and fro across the Aegean, like those who visited the rest of the coast. Were the Greek visitors essentially there to sell their distinctive cups and pottery to non-Greek wine-drinkers, engaging in a bulk trade whose surviving fragments represent only the bits of the stock which became broken by accident?[23] As I have argued, it seems most unlikely, because these patterned Greek cups, with no images, were such a minority interest in Near Eastern societies which had their own drinking-culture and their adequately shaped cups and bowls for local use. Although a few Greek cups occur inland, further south in the Levant, they are extremely few and when they are found in tombs they are best understood as symbolic objects, placed there as mementoes of foreign contact. Excavations inland in Unqi have turned up Greek pottery at Tell Tayinat, the ancient Kinalua, but even after many years it remains unpublished by its American excavators and so its style, dates and proportional quantities are still unclear.[24] However, as elsewhere, this pottery would have accompanied other, more important cargoes in ships from the Aegean and its presence is only indicative of other exchanges. Besides trading it, visiting Greeks may simply have retained some of it as personal items to which they were attached. Unlike most Near Eastern cups, their cups and bowls always had handles, and were therefore more familiar to them.[25]

If the first Greek settlers at Al Mina were not pottery traders, were they perhaps mercenary soldiers, maintained by the king of Arpad or Kinalua inland to defend the delta from attackers, including Phoenicians, but then prolonged as a military outpost by subsequent Assyrian conquerors?[26] No weapons have been found on site and specialized military service for regular pay over a long period is unlikely for Greeks at this date, especially at a site on the edge of their paymaster's kingdom. We should think, rather, of a range of skills and opportunities among the first settlers and visitors, as this was an age, as Woolley emphasized, when trader, warrior and pirate were not separate professions. At Al Mina, people's basic livelihood depended on working the surrounding land: nobody could live for long from casual trade only. It helped that there were natural goods worth exporting from the plain, quite apart from the items made by Syrian craftsmen which were to have such an impact on craftsmen back in Greece. There were metals, including the tin and copper which are listed in Assyrian texts about the region's assets. Exactly on the nearby Jebel Aqra, the mountain which closes the south end of Al Mina's coastline, King Sargon's texts (c. 710 BC) refer to the mining of copper as an impressive fact.[27] There was also local gold. Back in Greek communities, copper and tin would make the bronze for armour and for the ever-popular bronze cauldrons on bronze tripod stands. The gold would make jewellery: a local type of stone mould for making earrings has been found in the level at Al Mina which begins c. 710 BC.[28] Perhaps local women helped Euboeans with this craft. In return, Euboeans might sell their wine and oil and trade their own services intermittently as workers, sailors and warriors. As the Assyrians' texts remind us, there was continuing scope for Greeks to practise piracy at sea even if they were residents with the permission of one or other king inland. Al Mina may have been a base for their raids.

Uncertainties remain because the most-discussed Greek site in north Syria is only part of an incomplete study. Woolley noted, but never excavated, the nearby Sabouni, although it is the site where much complementary evidence awaits us. To Woolley the relations between Al Mina and the hinterland were primary, stretching out, he believed, down 'caravan-routes' as far as Aleppo and the Euphrates river. However, we risk overestimating this long-distance link and overplaying the centrality of inland Tell Tayinat for trade conducted down on the coast.[29] Tell Tayinat looks south at least as much as west, because it lies on the far bank of the Orontes' sharp bend southwards to Syria. When more finds are published from it and from the plain of Unqi's other inland sites, the scale, or otherwise, of the Greeks' inland connections may be clearer. The crucial point for the trail and contacts which we shall go on to follow is not whether Greeks founded Al Mina as a Greek settlement (in my view they did) nor whether non-Greeks lived in it too (in my view, non-Greek women lived there from the start, and non-Greeks joined as the Greek site flourished). What matters is that Greeks, above all Euboeans, lived there at all: the earliest pottery, found in dominant quantity on virgin soil, is clear evidence that they did and its local imitations show that their influence persisted.

Meanwhile we should allow each party to play to its attested strengths. In 738 the Assyrians listed all types of herbs together with metals and fine linen as their booty from the rebellious King Tutammu at Kinalua.[30] Greeks' words for herbs and spices are some of their clearest borrowings from Near Eastern languages, including coriander, crocuses (the source of valuable saffron) and types of incense: they go back initially to contact by Greeks in the east in the Bronze Age, but they remained to be regained by the Greek visitors who returned in the eighth century. On the Amanus mountains between Posideion and Al Mina grew the rare styrax-trees with their precious scented resin. They were to be found on the Jebal Aqra mountain too, just above Al Mina, while the humid plain of the Orontes river was an ideal site for the other great source of scented 'balsam' and amber-like resin, the eastern liquidambars.[31] In return we know that Euboeans on their home island were above all skilled as riders, men with a talent for horses. Such men were not only the Euboean nobles who rode into battle: they included the supporting grooms and attendants who looked after the mounts. From the Cilician plain, King Solomon had once imported horses, and no doubt the north Syrian kings who were so much nearer to it welcomed these imports too. The herding, let alone the shipping, of horses from place to place is not an easy business. Perhaps Al Mina's Euboeans applied their home skills to bringing in the warhorses which the inland lords of the plain required. Between their bouts of piracy one source of the Euboeans' livelihood on this coastline may have been four-legged.

II

In detail, we have followed the traces of a Greek pottery trail from the Cilician plain, on round the Bay of Issus and so to the north Syrian river-plain which is punctuated by the winding Orontes. Have we hit here on the answer to our Homeric puzzle, those 'Arimoi' or 'Arima' where Zeus's lashing of 'Typhoeus' caused the ground to resound as it once resounded beneath the advance of the Greek troops across the plain of Troy? In north Syria, from the ninth century onwards, we have evidence of 'Aramaeans' who were speaking and writing Aramaic. Even earlier, *c.* 1060 BC, texts of the ruling Assyrian king refer to the land 'A-ri-me', 'A-ri-mi' or 'A-ra-me', out east in Mesopotamia. Its people recur as 'A-ra-me' in a text from the scribes of the Assyrian king Sargon *c.* 710 BC.[32] Surely they solve the problem, making the Arima or Arimoi a distant hint (hence 'they say') in Homer's *Iliad* of the grand Syrian and Mesopotamian world known to these Greek visitors? The truth, however, is much more subtle, as we shall gradually see: it spans the world in ways which no Aramaean or Assyrian knew.

In the triangle of Cyprus, Cilicia and north Syria the local Greek contacts which answer this question will emerge. For the moment what has emerged is a crucial role for Euboean travellers and much scope for their close encounters with non-Greek people abroad. From the Cilician plain round to the plain of Unqi we should think of Euboeans as travelling from site to site, using Posideion and Al Mina as stops for their ships and their piratical raids. We can connect them through one particular class of small objects, a much-discussed type of engraved seal-stone which shows the schematic figure of a 'lyre-player' on its green or reddish surface. Such lyre-player seals are known at Al Mina, but also in the Cilician plain, and significantly, one of their sites on the other side of the Aegean is Eretria in Euboea: another is Lefkandi in its later phase (*c.* 720 BC). As we shall see, the seals had an even wider distribution, but their particular type of stone has at last been precisely located. It is at home in the hills in the central Cilician plain and on the plain's north-eastern edge beyond the Pyramus river. The seals are 'a bazaar product . . . each seal may not have taken more than about ten minutes to make and they could all be the product of a small family business within the working lifetime of one man'. Their imagery is extremely revealing.[33] Several of the types match sculptures up at Karatepe, imitating their style of dress, their musicians and tables with cups and food. They belong in this neo-Hittite milieu, one whose style was repeated on smaller sculpted reliefs and no doubt on sculptures at other royal centres like Tarsus and Adana in the Cilician plain. Such centres were visited by Greeks, including Euboeans, in the eighth century. The seals are a quick, clever adaptation of local neo-Hittite art which their cutter had observed. He may have been a local non-Greek who sold or gave a stock of these seals to a Euboean visitor or to a Greek from Posideion on the Bay of Issus, where Euboeans, in my view, and Rhodians may have met in the mid- to late eighth century. So far, none has been found in a Phoenician context. These small, prized objects link Cilicia to north Syria and gratifyingly include Euboean owners among their destinations.

In this multi-cultural zone it was not possible for Greek visitors to remain entirely monolingual, a characteristic sometimes ascribed to them by modern scholars.[34] They had to talk with their non-Greek women, with their customers and fellow-travellers and traders whom they met. Loan-words from these contacts entered Greek, although the scale and date of their adoption remain controversial in the absence of hard-and-fast philological rules about their origins. Naturally they included words for eastern luxuries, the special scents, textiles, gems and spices in which the Cypro-Levantine triangle was so rich.[35] In due course Greeks are known to have copied other Near Eastern words and ideas related to commerce besides the 'shekel': one was a 'deposit', or *arrabon*, and another, on one view, was the dreaded idea of interest-bearing debt. 'Presumably the connections reach further than can strictly be proved,' their distinguished classical champion Walter Burkert has recently concluded: a Semitic origin has even been argued for the Greek words for 'deceitful' and 'counterfeit' and their well-known word for love (*agapē*).[36] If true, these loan-words say much about Greeks' cross-cultural experiences in the Levant.

A Greek presence in north Syria also explains the imports of north Syrian objects which Greek craftsmen elsewhere in the Greek world began to imitate from *c.* 800 BC. Across the Aegean came big bronze cauldrons with animal figures on their rims and handles, small ivory figures of naked females and conspicuously, on Crete, embossed and decorated big bronze shields, which were given a ceremonial use.[37] These objects did not travel west with Aramaeans and Luwian-speakers because neither of these peoples were bold seafarers. If any of these foreigners reached Crete as craftsmen, once again we should think of them travelling not as free 'migrant entrepreneurs' but as slaves taken in war or raids. Their physical presence there is increasingly questionable, as renewed studies of the objects and their contexts now prefer to leave local Greek craftsmen on Crete to adapt their style independently without the need for foreign teachers at their side.[38]

One particular class of objects sums up the complexity of such transfers and stands as a fitting conclusion to the inter-relations we have followed: pieces of horse-harness from the Near East. As we know from north Syrian and above all Assyrian representations, Near Eastern chariot-horses wore decorated bridle-pieces, especially plaques on their foreheads and blinkers fitted to direct their eyes. From three Greek sanctuaries in the Aegean we have seven such blinkers and five front-pieces.[39] One of the blinkers and at least one of the front-pieces is inscribed with the same historically significant Aramaic words: 'that which Hadad gave to our lord Hazael from 'Umq, in the year that our lord crossed the River'.[40] The contexts in which these two inscribed pieces were found are also extremely suggestive. One was in a deposit at the temple of Hera on Samos, the other in the precinct of the temple of Apollo at Eretria, no less, on Euboea.

The front-pieces found in the Greek sanctuaries are triangular pieces of metal. They are decorated variously with sculpted figures, with groups of lions, with a male 'master of the animals' who holds sphinxes or a lion upside down in either hand and, above all, by naked deep-bosomed women who are holding their breasts with their hands and standing on lions' heads on which another naked female sometimes supports them. These figures and their accompaniments are north Syrian in design and execution. The repeated use of these themes shows that a clear meaning underlies them. The 'master of the animals' represents the ability of humans to master wild animals, a highly relevant symbol for the riders or drivers of the strong-willed horses who wore this decoration. The women are erotic, presenting their big breasts but not pressing them, and yet they also trample or triumph over lions. They are probably attendants of a warrior-goddess, the erotic and warlike Ishtar: in a fine ancient Hittite hymn to the goddess, we have names for her attendants, both the 'first' ones and the 'last' ones. They are groups of four, just as there are four ladies shown on the bronze frontlet found in Samos. These lady-attendants are said to be like 'pillars' when Ishtar goes to war. They bring love and desire to happy households and strife to unhappy marriages: they also fight in battles.[41] The harness's decoration alludes to these ancient elemental functions. Its imagery suits its use on warhorses, unruly animals when driven to the frenzy of battle.

To Greeks these Syrian meanings would be even more opaque than they are to us. The Syrian inscriptions, however, are important evidence for these pieces' origin. 'Hazael' is the notorious King Hazael of Damascus whose warfare in Syria and Israel is so brutally commemorated in the scriptural book of Kings. In the later ninth century, c. 830–815 BC, we can best locate a campaign by Hazael into ''Umq', the north Syrian river-plain. He crossed 'the River', which must be the Orontes, as he came up north to Unqi.[42] The 'Hadad' who gave him these spoils is Hadad the storm-god of Syria. These pieces, then, were booty which was taken in battle in Unqi and dedicated, most probably, in a temple of Hadad with Hazael's thanks. From a Near Eastern context we know of another such looted ornament, an ivory plaque, whose inscription refers to the help of '[H]adad of Imma' to Hazael.[43] The geography fits very well. 'Imma' is Imm, famous as the site of medieval battles because it commands the best narrow route from inland Syria across the Orontes into the plain of Unqi.[44] Its storm-god is the right divinity for Hazael to have honoured: it was he who let Hazael through safely to cross the 'River' and win battles.

These pieces for horses belong in exactly the area we have studied and their afterlife in Greek hands fits perfectly with our main Greek travelling heroes, Euboeans in the Near East. In the 730s King Tiglath Pileser and his Assyrian troops completed their conquest of Unqi and in 733/2 they took Damascus. No Greek participation is attested in this victory, and yet these bits of horse-armour, now nearly a century old, came into Greek hands. Perhaps Greeks from Al Mina, horse-experts from 'the trading post by the sea', joined in the Assyrian army's looting: several other bits of equally old horse-armour were taken off by Assyrians to new homes beyond the Euphrates. Perhaps some Greeks went as far south as Damascus but more probably some of them stopped and raided a site which had votive offerings to Hadad and lay nearer to the north Syrian plain: the obvious site is Imm, whose god Hadad had been honoured with trophies by Hazael. Once again these items of harness became trophies and were taken out of Unqi, but this time they were taken west and dedicated in Greek sanctuaries. They were not dedicated there by an Assyrian or an Aramaean. They were dedicated by Greeks who had acquired them: their Greek find-spots are extremely significant. One inscribed blinker was found in the sanctuary of Apollo at Euboean Eretria: there was another blinker there too, uninscribed but displayed on a wooden post by the temple's entrance.[45] They were two right-sided blinkers, not even a pair. A front-piece, inscribed like the Eretrian one, was found on Samos, where five other uninscribed pieces have also been discovered. In the mid- to later eighth century BC the lower levels of Al Mina coincide neatly with this human chain: they contain Euboean pottery and a few pieces of Samian pottery too. A Euboean took the blinkers, a Samian acquired the front-piece, and they returned home from Al Mina to dedicate them proudly to their Greek divinities. Horse-harness was an eminently appropriate trophy for a Euboean adventurer who was skilled with horses, who might therefore have served as a groom in the Assyrians' advancing cavalry and looted or received some valuable items for horses, quite unlike those which his horse-loving Euboeans knew at home. Perhaps a Samian, skilled with horses, had helped him, but it is possible that Euboeans, too, gave the other pieces to recognized Greek friends. A third cluster, including a front-piece, was dedicated to Athena at east Greek Miletus. We know of two special guest-friendships between Euboeans and other Greeks, one with Samians and one with Milesians.[46] The diffusion of these pieces of harness fits them beautifully. Blinkers, on present evidence, were not a Greek item, nor were metal front-pieces. They were given by Euboeans to their Greek guest-friends, like so many objects which heroes exchange in Homer's epics. The items were special, so they were then dedicated to the gods.

In Homer, we hear only of a Carian or Lydian woman from west Asia who is staining an ivory cheek-piece for a bridle for horses, a precious treasure, fit for a king which 'many horsemen prayed to wear . . . a glory for a driver'.[47] Homer never refers in any simile to bronze or ivory horse-harness from north Syria, to deep-bosomed ladies presenting their breasts or to a hero's mastery of lions by their paws or tails. However, we, too, need to take off our own blinkers and look finally beyond the Greek pottery which has led us exactly to the north Syrian coast. We can see this coast in a new way with the help of two later types of visitor.

The first is Macedonian, the cluster of settlers whom Alexander's Successors brought to live here in the new Antioch and Seleuceia *c.* 300 BC. For Macedonians, this coast had a very evocative look of their own Macedon back home. At the north end of the river-plain, they called their king Seleucus' harbour-city 'Seleuceia-in-Pieria'. Pieria was the coastal plain of their own Macedon which lay between Mount Olympus, seat of the gods, and the Haliacmon river before it bent round south-eastwards into the Thermaic Gulf. Pieria included the kings' ancient capital and burial place, the magnificent site of Aigai-Vergina, the scene of King Philip's murder and Alexander's accession in 336 BC. Behind the coast, Macedon's Pieria ran into well-watered farmland and a memorable landscape of woods and hills.

At first sight 'Pieria' sits most oddly in north Syria. All over the Near East, Macedonian kings gave Macedonian place names to towns and rivers, new and old, some of which were taken from their kings' own families and others suggested by an existing non-Greek place name.[48] No non-Greek name suggested 'Pieria' to them in Syria: it was given for quite other reasons. It marked the coast of a new 'Macedon-by-the-Mediterranean', which Alexander's settlers spattered widely with Macedonian names. The new 'Pieria' was based on their impression of the landscape: the sea, the coastline, the two defining hills at either end.[49] One was Seleuceia's hilltop (which they called the Crest, or *koryphaios*), and the other was the great Jebel Aqra, the seat, like a local Olympus, of the ruling god whom the Greeks identified as Zeus. Beside it the Orontes river spilt out onto a sandy silted plain, suggesting to Macedonian eyes their own great Axios river which also ran into a silted delta and extended the Macedonian coastline out into the sea. For a while, the Orontes was actually called 'Axios' by the nostalgic Macedonian settlers.[50] Inland in Unqi, as in Macedon, there was a swampy plain, the home for its Macedonian kings' important herds of war-elephants: after Alexander's conquests, elephants were kept in Macedon too, in the then-swampy plain below the famous capital of Pella. Above all there was the Jebel Aqra, the Greeks' 'Mount Kasios', which was as much a seat of the gods as the Macedonians' own Mount Olympus back home. What mattered to the Macedonian settlers were these individual features rather than exactly similar relationships between them. The Macedonians were not brought up on maps. They were men with an eye for landscape and its evocative similarities.

Nearly four hundred years before them, Euboeans had also known 'Macedonian' Pieria while trading and travelling on the northern Greek coast. Perhaps they too were sensitive to similarities between coastal Pieria and Unqi and their two great mountains of the gods. However, an even wider view was possible, which is best caught for us by the sharp eyes of a later traveller, Gertrude Bell. Coming to this coastal plain in 1906, she visited Seleuceia and responded to its exceptional setting. 'It was with real regret', she wrote in 1907, 'that I left Seleuceia ... Delicate bars of cloud were lying along the face of the hills and as I swam out into the warm still water the first rays of the sun struck the snowy peak of Mount Cassius [the Jebel Aqra] that closed so enchantingly the curve of the bay.' She paid it an acute tribute: 'The Bay of Seleuceia is not unlike the Bay of Naples and scarcely less beautiful ... The Orontes flows through sand and silt further to the south and the view is closed by a steep range of hills, culminating at the southern point in the lovely peak of Mount Cassius which takes the place of Vesuvius in the landscape.'[51]

When Gertrude Bell looked, swam and made her imaginative leap here, she had no idea that a buried Greek presence lay at Al Mina in her line of sight, still less that it was a Euboean presence or that Euboeans had followed the very course westwards which occurred to her mind's eye. Long before her, Euboeans had linked the two bays, those of north Syria and Naples, the next stretch of their far-flung trail.

8

Beyond Ithaca

As we turn westwards, our respect increases for the Greeks whom a trail of objects will again help us to identify in faraway waters, true travelling heroes on the eighth-century sea. Texts, at last, will help us to fix the end of their journey, strongly supporting the Euboean connection which we have so far favoured. It seems like a journey into a new 'western world', but 'east' and 'west' are relative terms and along the open axis of the Mediterranean they mark less of a cultural division than 'north' and 'south'. For a sense of the 'west' we can begin again from Homer, that elusive but contemporary witness to faraway horizons. He refers to places far west of Greece which nothing in the plot of his epics requires him to mention. Once again he leaves us to guess about the range of his understanding.

I

Four times near the end of the *Odyssey*, we meet incidental references to 'Sicania' or 'the Sicels', a land and people in the west beyond Ithaca, Odysseus' home island. They are the faraway source of a good household slave or the point of sale for slaves who are to be sent out from Ithaca itself. Odysseus' father Laertes has an elderly Sicel slave-woman among the 'slaves under compulsion', as Homer calls them, in his rustic household. They live beside his humble dwelling in a *klision* which runs 'on all sides' and in which they would 'eat and sit and sleep'.[1] The ancients themselves were puzzled by the meaning of this *klision*: should we think of a simple farm building, running round to make a courtyard so that old Laertes' house was as close to its slave-quarters as the houses of the slave-owning farmers which we can still visit in the American South? Laertes was looked after here 'with kind care' by his elderly Sicel slave-woman. She would wash him in the bath and oil him, but she was married to another of his slaves, by whom she had had sons. Her husband, too, had lived to be an elderly man whom she also looked after 'with kind care'. Laertes' nameless Sicilian is the first old-age carer known in history or literature.[2]

Elsewhere in the *Odyssey*, Sicels are plausible, faraway buyers of people whom one of Penelope's wicked suitors regards, wrongly, as potential slaves. The land of the 'Sicels' is the right sort of place in which to be rid of a pair of nuisances.[3] Conversely, in Odysseus' last lying story, he tricks his father Laertes by pretending that he is a man from 'Sicania', who has been blown off course to Ithaca by the wind at sea. He pretends to have a Greek name, although its exact meaning and spelling have been disputed ever since: a man from legendary Alybas, whose father's name perhaps means 'Unsparing' (perhaps in the sense of 'Generous'), himself the son of 'Many Possessions' (or 'Many Troubles').[4] One possible interpretation of these names means a man of riches and open-handedness who comes from a far-off family of plenty. They are fictional Greek names with nothing non-Greek or Sican about them.

For us, and surely for Homer, Sicels and Sicania were located to the west in what we now know Homerically as 'Sicily'. They were a faraway place and a faraway people and apparently they were one and the same. However, by applying Homer's two different words, the Greeks in Sicily later distinguished two separate peoples on the island: Sicels, who were encountered in the east of the island, and 'Sicans' in the centre. For Homer the words had had no such distinct precision.

Homer also names Libya. It was there that Menelaus had travelled while returning from Troy by way of Cyprus and Egypt. Menelaus had found Libya to be a land rich in sheep where the lambs grew horns, apparently soon after birth, the ewes gave birth three times a year and such was their milk and flocks that no shepherd went short of milk, meat or cheese. Again we are in a faraway land, but one which is also a place of utopian wonder. What exactly does Homer mean by Libya: is it our north Africa or a Libya more narrowly defined or is it the modern Libya, perhaps, where Greeks would eventually settle and flourish?[5] If Homer means the latter, is he betraying his own date by what he tells us? Greeks first settled permanently on modern Libya's mainland only in the 630s BC. The question, however, is more complex and will bring neglected evidence for Greek contact with north Africa to our attention.

On Odysseus' home island of Ithaca, Homer surprises us by mentioning one Eurybates, who is bent and 'rounded in his shoulders, dark skinned, woolly-haired'.[6] Woolly Eurybates is described precisely by Odysseus, who is lying but wanting to give his hearer, Penelope, an unusual and specific detail and thereby validate his account of the Odysseus of whom he deceptively speaks. This Eurybates was a herald, with a clear loud voice therefore, but he was also the man whom Odysseus honoured 'far above his other companions, because he was like-minded with himself'. Eurybates was a well-chosen man for Odysseus to specify in order to validate his story. Eurybates' skin and hair were black and woolly. Greeks specified ugliness in much more detail than beauty: Eurybates' 'bent shoulders' were not the mark of a well-born hero or one of the long-haired 'fine and fair'. His herald's voice, perhaps, was 'black' and distinctive too. The physique is meant to be odd, with a touch of prejudice which historians have tended to gloss over. But neither Homer nor Odysseus is racist. Woolly-haired, stooping Eurybates might be expected to be stupid at first sight, but Odysseus knew that, underneath, his mind belied his looks. Eurybates is therefore a doubly unusual person for lying Odysseus to describe, a firm proof of his veracity. Homer does not need to tell us where the woolly-haired Eurybates had come from. In context he needs only to make him so different that he can serve as a 'sign' of Odysseus' knowledge. Negroid features suffice for the story, reminding us that somehow, perhaps in slaves, Homer had seen them himself. Eurybates was invented to fit an improvised story which had not passed to Homer from older epic tradition.

What about Homer's hints of the western world beyond Sicily? Ocean is its boundary, as is usual in early Greek thought, but although Atlas is mentioned once, it is not clear that he is in the far west when he is said to be holding up the pillars which keep the heaven above the earth.[7] By later patriotic authors in antiquity, place names in southern Spain were connected with Ulysses–Odysseus because of their verbal likeness (Olisippo, our modern Lisbon, being one).[8] Homer shows no such precision. However, the *Odyssey* describes Odysseus' approach to the fearsome underworld at a place, as Circe has told him, by the shores of Ocean and by Persephone's grove of 'tall poplars and willows' where two great 'sounding rivers' meet at a rock. One of the rivers is 'Pyriphlegethon', or 'Flaming with Fire', the name for a red-watered river. For Homer, this site lies far away in the fabled land of the Cimmerians, but the location is given with precise details.[9] Has a real landscape guided the description? In 1920 the great local historian Adolf Schulten observed that in south-west Spain, the details of Homer's topography are conspicuously present.[10] Near Huelva two great rivers meet, the Rio di Huelva and the 'fiery' Rio Tinto with its famous red water, a true Pyriphlegethon. They collide at a conspicuous rock which is now the site of the Catholic Christian monastery of Santa Maria da Rabida. Had Homer or his fellow-poets heard of this memorable landmark which lay so far away towards Outer Ocean in the west? Had it passed into their imagined topography of the distant underworld? We now know that by the later ninth century BC Greek pottery had been carried, some of it surely by Greeks, to Huelva which lies just upriver from the rock of Santa Maria. We cannot conclude simply that 'Odysseus communed with the dead on the banks of the Rio di Huelva in Andalusia', but it may be that through rumour and second-hand reports, a touch of Spanish colour went into the first Greek description of the whereabouts of hell.[11]

II

Once again, travelling objects take us behind the allusions which Homer's epics happen to make to faraway lands. As in the east, they show that there was a long history of contact between the west and the Aegean before Greeks founded a clearly defined settlement in western territory. They also remind us that there were no empty spaces in the eighth-century Mediterranean. Greeks and Greek goods arrived from highly significant places but they did not enter a vacuum, romantic though it may be to plot them in a blank New World.

As in the east, there had been a lively history of contact between Greeks, parts of Sicily and western Italy during the previous Bronze Age of the Mycenaeans, the 'first western Greeks' (c. 1350–1180 BC). Contact was then believed to have broken down, but once again the older idea of darkness has been challenged. Evidence centres on Sardinia rather than Sicily or the Italian mainland. The big island of Sardinia stands to one side of classical Greek histories (there were never any Greek settlements on it) but c. 1100–800 BC it was still an important centre of metal-working and building skills. It also had rich resources of metals, including iron and copper and even some tin which may already have been worked in this period. Unlike Sicily it had silver too, particularly silver which could be extracted from lead.[12]

The island exemplifies the absence of a vacuum before Greeks returned to the west. In the eleventh to ninth centuries BC Sardinian bronze objects continued to reach western Italy and occasionally travelled inland beyond the Etruscan sites which had access to the coast. In the tenth to ninth centuries Sardinian pottery also reached the Lipari islands off Sicily.[13] Sardinians themselves probably shipped much of it. Sardinians dedicated model boats in bronze and clay to their gods, surely in hope or thanks for safe journeys at sea. The models take various shapes, rounded or long, and some of them have a deer's forequarters on the prow.[14] Cutting the waves, these boats took Sardinians to the river-mouths of Italy and down as far as Sicily as if on the backs of stags at sea. They were to be joined by Phoenicians, whose boats had prows shaped like horses, galloping through the water.

Sardinia also attracted foreign visitors, as we can infer from the ultimate origin of particular finds on the island. The most significant are three bronze bowls which were found in a hut at Sardara where they were deposed beneath a room used for social meeting and perhaps for feasting. The room was destroyed before the later eighth century BC but the bowls had been made much earlier, at a date between c. 1000 and 900. Their shape and the style of their handles trace back to Cyprus, their ultimate source. Other such bowl-handles have been found elsewhere on Sardinia and although they were discovered out

5. *North-west Greece to Sardinia*

of context they point to a similar Cypriot origin. The Sardara bowls are particularly important because their style was then imitated on Sardinia, implying that they are chance survivors from a type which was more widely known on the island.[15]

Who brought these foreign objects from the east Mediterranean to this island? No Cypriot pottery was found with them, but an important Cypriot imprint has been detected on the pottery of contemporary north-west Greece. Cypriots perhaps were passing regularly up its coast and then turning west for south Italy and Sardinia. Connections between objects found in Cyprus and objects in Sardinia suggest that Cypriots visited the island, bringing their bronze bowls with them for exchange. On Cyprus's south coast, at Amathus, a revolving metal spit for roasting meat was placed in a Cypriot's tomb and is itself datable to c. 1050–950 BC. It is almost certainly an import whose origins lie as far away as modern Portugal, on the Atlantic coast.[16] A Cypriot is perhaps unlikely to have gone so far west so early, but we have a similar spit in Sardinia, preserved in a hoard of bronzes where it, too, dates before 800 BC. The island of Sardinia was an intermediary for goods brought from the far west: Cypriots who visited it could then take this sort of far-western object home. In the eleventh and tenth centuries BC, while Cypriot pottery was also going east to the Levant, other Cypriots, perhaps Greek-speakers, seem to have been heading west to Sardinia. If so, they were the first post-Mycenaean Greeks to span so much of the Mediterranean world. It is sad that in their pre-alphabetic age none of these widely travelled Cypriots could leave us a memoir.

Sardinia, meanwhile, was a point of contact for objects from even further west, for bronzes which we can best match in Spain and even for bronze sickles whose style traces to types known far away in the British Isles. These objects from distant Atlantic networks had probably travelled in stages on their long journey to the island.[17] Likewise, it was probably after a stop on Sardinia that a bronze bowl of Cypriot type ended up further west, inland in the Estremadura of western Spain c. 900 BC.

The obvious human links between Sardinia and Spain are travelling Phoenicians, although evidence for Phoenicians on Sardinia in the tenth century BC is still indirect. We can follow them to the south coast of Italy where renewed study of graves at Torre Galli in Calabria has opened some fascinating horizons. A small number of Egyptian-style 'seals' were found in the graves of women and young children where they evidently served as protective charms for the dead person. Cypriots may have brought or supplied some of them, but Phoenicians were probably involved here too: a high dating for them has now been proposed in the local Iron Age c. 950–900 BC.[18] Even if this date is optimistic we must reckon with local women here who were choosing and learning to use these faraway charms as a protection against evil spirits, as in the Near East. Further on to the north, Phoenicians' skills and imports also influenced the Sardinians' own notable bronzework. It was probably c. 825–780 BC that a Phoenician visitor then put up the island's one famous early Phoenician monument, the Nora Stone, which was rediscovered at Nora on the island's south coast in 1773. Parts of its text and translation are still disputed, but it certainly refers to a traveller from 'Trss' (surely Tarshish–Tartessos in the west) who had come to 'Shrdn' (the Phoenician name for Sardinia). The text honours a god, most probably in thanks for the traveller's safe arrival after a storm.[19] It can only be dated tentatively by the style of its lettering, but after the recent Phoenician finds at Huelva (the likely site of Tartessos), a Phoenician's journey from Spain to Sardinia fits credibly at the end of the ninth century BC. The traveller may even have had links with Cyprus, suggesting that Cypriot contacts had guided Phoenicians to this island.

The next datable sign of Phoenicians is still more suggestive. On the north-west coast of the island the village of Sant' Imbenia looks over the excellent natural harbour at Porto Conte and lies conveniently on a route inland through good farmland to metal-resources in the hills behind Algero. Continuing excavations here have given an intriguing context to finds of Phoenician pottery at the site.[20] In a room of one of the huts, two amphoras, or big jars, were found packed with small copper-ingots: one of the jars was of Phoenician origin, whereas the other was probably a local copy of a Phoenician original. They are best explained as elements of a local trade. Phoenicians brought big jars filled with olive oil, nuts, spices or wine and in return the local Sardinians offered them packs of their excellent copper, returning them in the jars or copying the jars' shape when making new containers. Above all, the finds are relatively datable. Beside the big jars there were two fragments of a broken Greek cup: they join together to make a cup with telltale decoration, the painted semicircles of a Euboean Greek cup, no less, whose date is most probably *c.* 800–780 BC. In the settlement outside the hut, among other Phoenician pottery (including a cooking-pot), three more pieces of Greek pottery were found which are probably slightly later in date (perhaps *c.* 770–750 BC) but are decorated with the other two hallmark Euboean designs. In faraway north-west Sardinia, therefore, these three pieces of Euboean Greek pottery make up a 'full house' of the three typical Euboean patterns.

Perhaps the earliest of the Euboean cups was brought here by Phoenicians who exchanged it locally during their exchanges for metals. Alternatively, like one or other of the cups outside the hut, it arrived with a Euboean Greek in person, perhaps one who was travelling with Phoenicians on a Phoenician ship. To later Greek visitors by sea Sardinia was known as 'Footprint Island', because of the shape of its perimeter.[21] We cannot know, but the cup is a sign of a possible Euboean presence on 'Footprint Island' or nearby in the west in the late ninth century BC.

It is worth comparing the Euboean contacts in our 'triangle' of Cyprus, Cilicia and the Levant in the east. In the tenth and early ninth centuries a few Euboean jars and cups had been reaching Cyprus or Tyre or Ras el-Bassit in years when eastern imports had started to be deposed in the graves of Euboeans back home in Lefkandi. In the west, by contrast, nothing Euboean is known so early. The western traces begin later, surely as a result of Euboeans' contacts with Phoenicians in eastern places like Cypriot Amathus or in harbour-towns along the Levantine coast. From these practised travellers Euboeans then realized that there were things and people worth going for in the opposite western direction. By the later ninth century they had begun to go for them.

A clearer trail of Greek goods then runs westwards in the eighth century from Ithaca and the Ionian islands. In the west, its dating involves a bigger margin of uncertainty. We have no connections with the datable biblical narrative and no link to anything royal and Egyptian, and therefore datable, before the 720s BC. Sequences of dates are ascribed to objects found in the big cemeteries on the coast of Italy, but they are not yet securely correlated between all the differing sites. The Greek objects, too, are uncertain markers, partly because the absolute dates of their own sequences are not firmly fixed either, and partly because they are found so far from their origin, placed casually in tombs where they may have ended up many years after their original making at home. If our present dating turns out to be wrong, it will be because it is often too low. The effect, then, will be to mark out the first Greek phase of renewed travel to the west even more clearly from the subsequent phase of Greek settlement which followed and is more securely dated. Meanwhile the trail itself makes geographical sense, even if we know that elsewhere the furthest points on a route are not always the last to be visited.

The westward trail begins *c.* 800 BC (on the provisional, traditional dating), going up from Ithaca and the surrounding islands and then across to the 'heel' of the Italian coastline. Here, southern Italy, the island of Corcyra (Corfu) and north-west Greece are no more remote from each other than are Cilicia, Cyprus and the Near East. Sea-travellers would prefer the route up modern Ithaca's west coast, running up past Cephallenia to Corcyra (Corfu) and then to the island of Oricos in the Bay of Valona: later Greek sources connect Oricos with Euboeans who are even said to have founded a settlement there.[22] The journey across the straits to Otranto in Italy is then only some 40 miles by open sea. Already, *c.* 800 BC, the most prominent Greek pottery on Ithaca was Corinthian, not Euboean: it relates to Corinth's convenient siting on its own westward-facing gulf and the beginnings of Corinthian contact with sites like Ambracia on the Greek coastline's north-west.[23] A few Euboean pieces turn up too but they are in a minority. Archaeologists suggest that we should think here of a 'closed circuit' as the eighth century began, linking mainly Corinthian goods (and probably Corinthian travellers) to the Ionian islands and then running up the coast to the straits and over to Otranto (Hydrous, to the Greeks) just across the sea. The adjoining Salento peninsula and the coastline of Calabria (south Italy) have even been credited with an 'intensity of circulation of Greek material' in the early eighth century which is 'unparalleled elsewhere in Italy'.[24] However, there was apparently no attempt by visiting Greeks to settle at once on

Italy's pointed heel in its good farmland. The main reason was the hostility of the local Messapians, reflected in the protective stone walling around the village of I Fani, about 8 miles north-east round the cape. It was already in place by c. 750 BC. Euboean pottery is then present on the site, but not till c. 725 and then only casually.[25]

Euboean pottery, but much less Corinthian, then travels on round the south-east coast of Italy past Calabria and on to Sicily in c. 800–780 BC: why was there no immediate Greek interest in the eastern coast of Italy up the Adriatic? The main reasons were navigational: the exposed Adriatic sea, the scarcity of islands and prominent landmarks and the increasing problem of shallows.[26] Another, surely, was the example of Phoenicians and Cypriots, people whom the Euboeans had already met in Cyprus and the Levant. Such people had already made the long journey up to Sardinia on their travels to the far west and could talk knowingly about it to Euboeans. More adventurous and better informed than most of the Corinthians, Euboeans and others set off further to the west, staying close to the coastlines.

In east Sicily an evocative trace of them duly emerges: fragments of three Euboean cups at Villasmundo up the River Marcellino whose good plainland was controlled by the resident Sicels (it grows the best rare types of blood-oranges, nowadays).[27] The cups are datable to c. 800–770 BC, chance survivors but most suggestive in the light of Homer's allusions to the Sicels and to Laertes' elderly slave-woman, his Sicel carer. She makes sense as an eighth-century detail, known to Homer through Greeks' contemporary reports of this end of the island. Perhaps, as in Homer, slaves were already an attractive asset here for Greek visitors.

From Sicily, Sicel goods had already been travelling northwards up to the Salerno peninsula in Italy and the big outlying settlement at Pontecagnano just upriver from the peninsula's coast.[28] The Euboean trail edges gratifyingly northwards in this same direction on a route which others, therefore, had travelled before them. It took Euboeans up the Sicilian coast to the straits between Sicily and Italy and as they looked across them, and then ventured on the crossing, they were surely reminded vividly of the straits between their own Euboea and the mainland opposite. The line of the hills behind either shore of Sicily and Italy is strikingly similar to the view across the Euboean

Gulf from Lefkandi or Eretria. The likeness is particularly striking to an eye trained on Euboea's gulf which looks back to Sicily from the first hills in Italy above modern Reggio, a natural first point of call. The currents in both the Euboean and Sicilian straits are extremely awkward: Euboeans from Chalcis knew ways of avoiding the rapidly changing currents in their own Euripus channel, and so the challenge of crossing the currents from Sicily to Italy would not be so unfamiliar.[29] Perhaps they already knew by hearsay what lay beyond, but none of them had yet seen it. The view from the straits is one of mysterious headlands advancing northwards up the coast of what we now know to be Italy: it helps us to imagine the lure and uncertainties of a Euboean venture which was to stretch so far beyond this sightline. Like Sicels before them, Euboeans travelled up to Pontecagnano on the Salerno peninsula where early eighth-century Euboean cups were placed in graves of the non-Greek Picentines and Etruscans. Only eight cups with Euboean semi-circle decoration, the earliest pattern, have so far been found in Pontecagnano's very big non-Greek burial grounds, and in total Euboean cups are a tiny minority of the pottery found in the graves throughout the eighth century.[30] The place was never a main Euboean destination.

The same cups occur at points northwards up the coastline, including the other big outlying Etruscan settlement, Capua, which lay on the northern edge of the immensely fertile plains of Campania behind modern Naples. On the coast at the north-western end of the Bay of Naples there are also three Euboean cups in native burials, set to one side of the site which later became a Greek settlement at Cumae. Like Pontecagnano, this coast was already in active contact with Sardinian goods brought partly by Sardinians, partly perhaps by Phoenicians. Through contacts in these places we can well understand how Euboean cups then went on across to Sardinia and Sant' Imbenia, accompanied by Phoenician contemporaries. The Greek visitors had coincided with a pre-existing network.

Up the west coast of Italy the Greek trail runs on, intriguingly, to the River Tiber and its tributaries in Old Latium. Near its mouth at Ficana, five Euboean cups and twelve good imitations imply that a Euboean Greek had even settled and worked here by c. 750 BC.[31] Whereas all other such cups have been found only in tombs, these were in the settlement itself, proving that they had a daily use other than in funerary ritual. Suggestively, they were found in the area of the settlement where iron and metals were worked. On up the Tiber and to the north-west of it at least five more Euboean cups (with an early Corinthian one) are now known in tombs at Veii, a major Etruscan settlement, where they date from the period c. 800–760 BC. Here too they inspired good imitations whose clay is local but whose style is in the Euboean manner.[32] Unsurprisingly, therefore, there are Euboean traces at Veii's nearby rival on the Tiber, the fledgling settlement of Rome. Two graves on the Esquiline hill have produced two small jugs with Euboean-style decoration. A few more fragments, harder to place exactly, have been found out of context below the Palatine on the way to the Tiber's bank.[33] It may, then, be right to think of Euboean Greek visitors c. 770–750 BC rowing up to Rome on the River Tiber much as Virgil would later imagine for his travelling hero, the Trojan Aeneas, whose boats were 'overcoming the river's long bends, shaded by its varied trees, and cutting over the green woods reflected in the water's calm surface'.[34]

What might have drawn Greek visitors up the Tiber? At Veii, as elsewhere, the Euboean cups are accompanied by familiar Near Eastern trinkets, scarab-seals in Egyptian style and 'lyre-player' seals cut in stone.[35] These trinkets connect directly with the points of contact which we have credited to Euboeans in the Near East and linked with a pattern of Euboean ownership. Some of them, therefore, were brought west by the very Euboeans who had prior connections, direct or indirect, with the east: we can justly think here of travelling Greeks spanning both the eastern and western sectors of their trail. From Veii, a route follows the river's course up into central Italy to territories ruled by Etruscan leaders and where access might be given to deposits of precious metals. At second hand, perhaps, Euboean visitors might have hoped to acquire these metals through exchanges. But the Tiber had its own assets too, the great salt flats at its mouth which remained such items of conflict for centuries between Veii and Rome.[36] In Cyprus, north-west Sicily and Spain, Phoenicians were to settle conspicuously by big natural salt flats. Neither they nor the Euboean visitors would have ignored the value of these salt marshes which were so crucial for human and animal survival and for the Phoenicians' particular skills in drying and salting fish. Euboeans may have exchanged goods at Veii or even at Rome for access to the salt which they could then consume or exchange with other networks on the coast.

This trail of Euboean goods up the coast to Rome and Latium helps to answer one question while posing others. For long-distance traders the most precious resources in central and northern Italy were the metals, including silver, which occurred up the coast in the Tolfa hills (in modern Lazio) and above all in the 'metal-bearing hills' of northern Etruria just inland from the coast around Vetulonia near modern Grosseto in our south-west Tuscany.[37] Until c. 750–720 BC, however, the Greeks' trail dies out a long way to the south. To continue it we must consider a different type of evidence, Etruscan objects which were dedicated c. 800–770 BC at sanctuaries back in Greece. The most conspicuous are two crested metal helmets, Etruscan by origin, which have been found at Delphi and Olympia.[38] Although some of the Etruscans were seafarers, the dedicators of these objects at Greek sites were probably Greeks who had either acquired them as gifts, or perhaps more likely as trophies in combat. The piratical habits of Euboeans will not have been suspended in the west where Etruscan ships were raiders too, complicating our Greek visitors' progress.[39]

Why is the 'Euboean aura' not more prominent up in the metal-bearing regions themselves? At Vetulonia, in its heartland, Sardinian objects are conspicuously present, brought across by Sardinians and perhaps by Phoenicians.[40] The island of Elba, too, was an important source of iron, which was shipped across to the coastal settlement at Populonia. Etruscans dominated this port ('Fulfuna' in their language). It had been founded (according to late Graeco-Roman sources) by the inland Etruscan town of Volterra which stands on a commanding hill-site inland in the Cecina river valley.[41] There was no one dominating centre among the towns of the Etruscans' homeland, which ran in the great sweep of country between the Tiber and Arno rivers, but nonetheless the well-armed leaders of the individual centres were more than a match for visiting Greeks. Sardinians, followed perhaps by Phoenicians, may have had older and closer relations with the mainland, making a Greek penetration of its emerging Etruscan 'city-state' culture more difficult.

By *c.* 770 BC Greek visitors were still a very small minority on the coast of western Italy if we may judge from the tiny proportion of their pottery found in non-Greek tombs. What, indeed, did they have to offer which was special? Phoenicians, too, could sell Near Eastern trinkets and jewellery, true to their Homeric image. Long before the Greeks' arrival, 'Tuscany' was already growing grapes for wine. Perhaps, then, Greeks brought better wine and olive oil.[42] There may have been wild olives in Italy already, but Greeks had better varieties and so the Latin word for olive oil, *oleum*, is copied directly from Greek *elaion*: in the eighth century, as in Homer, this oil may have been used and sold by Greeks as a distinctive body-oil. Euboeans also brought their patterned cups, but these cups cannot have been their main trade: until *c.* 760 BC they were decorated only with geometric patterns, not images, whereas rich Etruscans preferred smart metal cups to such humble clay ones. As in the east, the Greek cups placed in non-Greek graves are probably only symbolic mementoes of a contact with Greeks which was based on other goods. These contacts did not mark the Etruscans' introduction to the joys of wine (they had it already) or to the etiquette, as yet, of orderly drinking-parties (none of the supporting Greek vessels for such parties is found in the west so early). Euboeans brought better olive oil and better wine, and on one view another attraction was their mixing of 'painkilling' grated cheese and onions into a wine-based drink. The Greek vessels deposed in the local tombs may sometimes refer to this new-found palliative Greek tonic.[43]

Whatever the trade, it is wrong to think of Greek visitors impinging on a primitive, dormant west. As in north Syria, so in central to southern Italy they arrived on the edge of a rapidly expanding and changing landscape of settlements. Changes were being driven above all by the Etruscans and their expanding population who were altering the simpler village-style settlements of the previous age. The Etruscans' big southern outposts at Veii or Capua or Pontecagnano stood out among the villages of the Latins and Campanians among whom they were established.[44] By Greek standards they were huge settlements, supported by wide use of the surrounding land, no doubt (as later) through forced labour. The Etruscan network also shared metal-working, distinctive funerary rites and lines of communication, enough to bring metal goods from Bologna down south to Veii or to link Pisa with goods from Volterra and Populonia. Theirs was an interconnected world into which Greeks, we imagine, had to insinuate themselves slowly by gifts and services.[45] It was not, however, as advanced a world as the 'triangle' which we outlined in the east. There was no imperial past in Italy like that of the Hittites in Cilicia and north Syria and there were no dynasties as old as the 'house of Muksas' in Cilicia or the kings of Hamath or Carchemish. Despite the Etruscans' heavy metal armour, local warfare was less developed, without such an emphasis, as yet, on horses and swift war-chariots. Above all there was no literacy, nothing to compare with the multi-lingual scripts used at Karatepe or Zincirli. If there were ever any long Etruscan poems we have no trace of them whatsoever. There was no Etruscan Homer.

In this network of contacts we can better understand the most remarkable of recent archaeological finds. Unlike the Etruscans, Euboean Greeks had developed an alphabetic system of writing after a Euboean had studied with a Phoenician and his script. This unknown Euboean devised his alphabet somewhere in the eastern 'triangle', perhaps in Cyprus, but it quickly caught on with fellow-Euboeans who then brought the new skill with them to the west. Chronologically our first surviving trace of it, so far, derives from the west, from non-Greek Gabii, a Latin settlement which lies about 11 miles east of Rome.[46] Here, a small locally made pottery flask was inscribed with five letters after firing and was later pierced with a hole, presumably so as to pour from its side. It was then placed beside an urn containing cremated bones which were probably a woman's, about sixty years old. The urn was buried in a grave-pit, part of which had already been used for the burial of a man in his thirties. This double burial is most unusual and is placed to one side of the burial ground at Gabii in a distinctive family plot. On one interpretation the five letters on the pot are Greek and seem to spell 'Eulin', a puzzling sequence which is not in itself a Greek word. Does it stand for Eulinos, 'good at spin-ning', a tribute, perhaps, to the skills of the woman (if woman she is) who was cremated in the nearby jar?

Soon after its discovery this inscription was brilliantly matched with a Greek text by the antiquarian Dionysius who wrote in Rome in the late first century BC. He described eighth-century Gabii as if it was already a centre of Greek: to Gabii, he even states, the honest, humble keeper of pigs took the two foundling 'wolf-twins', Romulus and Remus, so as to assure them an education in Greek music, Greek weaponry and, best of all, Greek letters. Have we found at Gabii a trace of the culture in which Rome's two founding twins were trained at primary school before they returned to found Rome *c.* 753 BC? The story is a superb false turning. Romulus and Remus were figures of legend and the tale of their Greek education was only a variant in their story, perhaps introduced as late as the second century BC.[47] These legendary people do not explain our first bit of alphabetic writing in Italy. We are not even sure what it says. On an alternative view the letters are Latin, running backwards from right to left as other early writing did in Italy. They then say 'Ni Lue', perhaps signifying 'do not' (*ne*) '(cause yourself) to pay a penalty' (*luas*), perhaps by breaking or taking the object.[48] Even if this reading is right it still implies contact with a Greek visitor: the Greek alphabet was the source of the Latins' own (which is using vowels here, already). A Latin reading of the letters merely puts the Greek contact back at one remove. What explains it is the trail we have been following, one of alphabetic Phoenicians going west up Italy to Sardinia, literate Euboean Greeks writing vowels in an alphabet of their own and following them round southern Italy and Sicily, up to the Bay of Naples and the River Tiber, perhaps to Rome and then on to Gabii beyond. Archaeologically, families at Gabii seem to have had links already with south Italy, as did Euboeans, and from there they came north.[49] Conceivably, a Euboean visitor to Gabii scratched a Greek word of praise for a Latin lady's wool-working on a small flask in her honour: early alphabetic inscriptions in Italy tend to occur on women's goods only. More probably, a Euboean Greek had taught a Latin to write, and here one of the Latins used the new skill. The pot was then pierced to pour an offering in the lady's honour and was left beside her funerary urn, the earliest lettering yet known in a non-Greek milieu, one of whose existence, but not message, we can make sense.

9

Monkey Islands

I

In these early Greek travels to western Italy we are close to the roots of an element which went into Homer's *Odyssey*.[1] Its hero lived on Ithaca, off the north-west coast of Greece, to which he gradually travelled home. Into Odysseus' journey Homer worked his incomparable tales of travels in the lands of the Lotus-Eaters or the Cyclops where calm and abundance were so dangerous and dreadful hazards lay. Ultimately these types of story developed from tales of seaborne Greek adventurers who were known to have set off for far-distant lands, probably in the west, away from the direction of Circe, daughter of the (rising) sun. It is tempting to identify these adventurers as Euboeans, travelling west beyond Ithaca from *c.* 800 BC onwards, but it would be excessive to make the *Odyssey* itself a Euboean creation.[2] Fabulous stories arose about such adventurers, but perhaps not directly from them, in a phase when Greeks were travelling into new landscapes, exchanging goods, making contacts with strangers but not as yet founding a new home of their own.

In due course Greeks did found such a place, the first western Greek settlement of this period, which sits very well with the contacts we have been following. They chose to settle on Ischia, the island out beyond the coast which rounds off the north-western reach of the Bay of Naples. At last we have literary texts which specify the first founders: they were written *c.* 20–10 BC but they used earlier informed Greek predecessors (above all, the scholarly Timaeus, himself a western Greek whose full text is now lost to us). Reassuringly for our trail, the most precise one names the founders as 'Chalcidians and

Eretrians', Greeks from the best-known settlements on Euboea's gulf.[3] There is no political reason in subsequent western Greek history why these founders should have been invented and read back into the past. A settlement's origins were anyway likely to be accurately preserved: they were one of the 'great events' which oral tradition tends to remember, before later writers preserve it in a text.

From finds on the Italian coast of Euboean cups, Near Eastern trinkets and Cilician 'lyre-player' seals in close proximity, we have already inferred that the first Greek travellers to eighth-century Campania included Euboeans who had prior contact with the source of these objects in the east. On their new settlement at Ischia, evidence of this link between east and west continues. Neither end of it is securely dated, but no modern scholar has yet wished to date the foundation at Al Mina after the first western settlement on Ischia. Probably Al Mina existed by c. 780 BC and the elusive first Posideion to the north of it on the Bay of Issus perhaps existed earlier still. Traces of the first Greek phase on Ischia are very few, but a date of c. 770–760 is the most likely, about ten years after the Greek settlement at what came to be known in north Syria as 'Potamoi Karon'.

Why did Euboeans ever settle on Ischia, their furthest point in the west, first of all? We should think of reports coming back to Euboea with the travellers up western Italy in the previous decade. These travellers were Euboeans from various settlements on the island, seafarers who were still acting on their own initiative. So often on our map of later Greek overseas settlements a foundation abroad was to be preceded by informal Greek contacts nearby. Although the dating of each pottery item is still disputed, some, at least, of the 'Euboean trail' up the west coast of Italy preceded the organized decision of Chalcis and Eretria to move in on Ischia. This move was not made in order to take good farmland. The island's soil was volcanic and rocky with very little level ground for ploughing and sowing. It was also not well watered. If the first Greeks had been looking for good farmland they would have stopped much earlier on the rich east coast of Sicily where the Sicels were no match for them.

Using later Greek terms, historians class Greeks' foundations either as 'trading posts' (*emporia*) or fledgling 'city-states' (*poleis*). Ischia, the first in the west, has seemed to fit neither: it was not the most fertile stopping-point for a proper *polis*, and yet it seems a cumbersome venture if all the Euboeans wished to do was trade: some of them were trading locally already.[4] Perhaps it seems perplexing because it was chosen for one purpose, but turned out to suit another too. Initially Ischia was perhaps intended to be a first stop, a vantage-point for taking in a wider plan. It was not seized as a port of trade, the sort of place which Al Mina–Potamoi Karon had become by lying on the edge of the land of Unqi and the Assyrians' conquests. Ischia was not connected politically to a state on the mainland nor was its trade to be directed or drawn from any one point. On the mainland, Euboean visitors had already seen the exceptional fertility of Campania behind the Bay of Naples. They could settle on Ischia, indulge in their usual sea-raids and piracy, continue their contacts with Etruscans and others on the coast and then eventually move to a second, richer site there when they felt secure. This two-stage pattern is frequent in later Greek settlements on other mainlands overseas, although the second stage was probably to be slow in this case.

There were no Phoenicians on Ischia, no resident Etruscans, nobody except a local population which was living quietly on the north-east coast of the island. The first Greek settlers concentrated themselves nearby. The modern harbour of Porto d'Ischia did not yet exist on the north-east. Instead, Greeks came to the north-west and settled on the high promontory of Monte Vico, which had access by sea on either side of it. On its west side lay San Montano bay, an 'attractive little cove', but one which is exposed to the strong north winds and slopes gently 'so that a sizeable vessel could get nowhere near the shore'. The beach of modern Lacco Ameno lay on the east side with its thermal sands, 'the most radioactive in Italy', but it too did not offer 'anything like complete all-weather protection. The island could hardly have met the needs of warships or sizeable merchant vessels.'[5] The hill, then, was not suited for a major trading post. Rather, it was a first stop on which settlers could support themselves from the land while looking out to the coastline on the north-west edge of the Bay of Naples where several of their typical cups had already been acquired by local non-Greeks.

The settlers named the island 'Pithekoussa(i)', a name which means 'Monkey Island(s)' in Greek: the plural perhaps referred to the two other islands near it which were thought to be fragments of the main one.[6] Zoologists deny that apes or monkeys ever lived on Ischia or in central Italy, but the Greeks did not invent the name by mistake. They learned it, we are told, from Etruscans who already called the island by their own word for monkey.[7] These informants would be Etruscans whom Euboeans met at Capua and Pontecagnano and who would know the nearby island's nature. The Etruscan monkey-name caused the Greeks to give one in their own language. The name, as we shall see, became part of an even bigger story. Meanwhile painted traces of a monkey's head and tail have been discerned, in a crouching 'monkey-position', on a broken piece of a Greek mixing-bowl, made on Pithecussae in the late eighth century BC.[8] Not everyone is convinced by this questionable reading of it, but even so there is a good case that Pithecussan painters did indeed depict monkeys: their example has been seen behind the representations of monkeys which turn up later in south Etrurian arts. The island's name also encouraged legends which confirm how Greeks understood it. In later Greek poetry (c. 200 BC), Zeus is said to have mocked some of his enemies by establishing them as monkeys on Ischia.[9] The name 'Monkey Island' was not idly bestowed, as we shall see from its use by Greeks elsewhere. Either we ascribe it to an Etruscan and Greek view of the existing non-Greek inhabitants who seemed monkey-like in their speech and demeanour, or, more simply, we disbelieve the zoologists and accept that real monkeys lived on the island.

The cemeteries and areas of settlement below Monte Vico have been excavated in the most testing conditions of soil and heat, but the first phase of the settlement is still almost totally unknown. The excavators point out that their heroic work concerns only a fraction of the entire burial ground, perhaps as little as a tenth, and that they have only found graves from c. 750 BC onwards, ten or twenty years, perhaps, after the first settlers arrived. We know far more, therefore, about some of the settlers' children and grandchildren than about the founding fathers themselves. The early evidence for them has mostly had to be sifted from a large dump of mixed pottery fragments which were discarded from the original acropolis-hill and then rediscovered on its east flank. Sixteen fragments of early Euboean cups have been detected in it, four of which can be ascribed by their style to the first phase, *c.* 770–750: 'the first fleet did not, it seems, travel without its master-potters'.[10]

This first settlement was surely not very big. We should imagine hundreds of male Euboeans, not thousands, but even so they must have had acknowledged leaders. No names have been preserved but they were probably led by members of Euboea's leading families, people who were as ready as Odysseus and his crew for raiding and long-range adventures and the prospect of settling, then moving across to a new home on the fertile Italian coast. The decision to send off settlers was nothing new for them, after (probably) their Posideion near Iskenderun, Al Mina on the Orontes river and their contacts, including settlements, in northern Greece on the prongs of the Chalcidic peninsula. A settlement on Ischia was more of the same, but in a new and even more remote direction.

Neither our texts nor the earliest bits of Ischia's pottery dump give any sign of a significant non-Greek partnership. Nonetheless, as in the east, some of the Euboean males would turn to local, non-Greek women for sex and children: Euboean women would presumably not have been sent so far at such risk and effort. Nearby Etruscans acted as informants (whence the name 'Monkey Island') but there is no hint, or need, of Phoenician partners too. The island was rocky and volcanic and Phoenicians had so far ignored it. They had Sardinia instead, and Elba offered them access further north to metals, especially iron.

Nonetheless the first Greek settlers succeeded, 'prospered', even, according to Strabo (*c.* 20 BC), who was probably drawing on Timaeus (*c.* 300–260 BC).[11] The reason, he claims, was the 'fertility' of the soil but also, more enigmatically, 'gold items'. By 'fertility' he perhaps means, as elsewhere, a volcanic soil and the island is only truly fertile for one crop: vines, the source of its long-admired wine. The first settlers probably discovered this asset only after their arrival, but we can see why Euboeans were the ideal Greeks to exploit it. At modern Koumi on Euboea's Aegean coast, we have emphasized the importance of 'volcanic vineyards' in the similar local soil. Euboeans, especially Eretrians, would know this rare asset: men from Euboean Cumae, we know, were present in the west either with the first settlers or soon afterwards. They knew exactly how to farm volcanic soil. They would also plant olives in it, a slower crop, however, to yield a return. In due course wine and olive oil were shipped over to the mainland in distinctive transport-jars (*amphorae*), mostly adapted from a Phoenician prototype, some of which hold as much as 14 gallons.[12] But neither crop was a reason for settling on Ischia in the first place. The pattern, rather, was one of farming to support the first foundation which developed a wider scope as the soil's potential was recognized. Beyond Monte Vico and the valley behind it, traces of a Greek presence have been found elsewhere on the island, but we should not overestimate them and magnify the settlement into a big, island-wide venture. On the south coast at Punta Chiarito, finds of an eighth-century site with Greek pottery and crop remains (including fishbones) may point to nothing more than a coastal look-out post or even (on one view) the lair of a well-established pirate, based on the hill above two convenient bays.[13]

The 'gold items' are at first sight more puzzling. There are no gold mines on Ischia and the island's most valuable mineral is alum, rediscovered in 1465 and retained thereafter as a papal monopoly for its value in dyeing and in medicine.[14] Alum is extracted from sulphuric, volcanic soil but, oddly, our ancient accounts of it never single out Ischia, although they praise the alum on Sardinia and emphasize its great value for the volcanic Lipari islands off Sicily.[15] Euboeans were familiar only with extinct volcanoes: did they for once miss a great natural asset? The 'gold items' (in Strabo's original text, according to five main manuscripts) can in fact be accommodated.[16] Beyond the cemetery below Monte Vico the excavators have indeed found a metal-working quarter: some iron slag traceable to Elba and some tools for heating and working it were also found up on the acropolis. The iron has proved a distraction to historians.[17] Euboeans did not choose to settle on Ischia so as to trade iron from Elba or to ship it, worked or unworked, back home. Euboea had plenty of sources nearer to hand. Rather, the iron was essential for the first settlers themselves, for ploughs, knives and weapons. Their metal-working district worked other metals too, not only bronze (from copper and tin) but also the silver which is conspicuous in the setting of Pithecussans' trinkets and finger-rings. So far, the gold-working which Strabo singles out is undiscovered, but is not so implausible, despite this gap. Since the tenth century BC Euboeans had been deftly working gold into jewellery, having found supplies of it in northern Greece. In their new western settlement they could have worked it and then traded it, making an exotic gain which was therefore remembered. Gold has been found so far in only one of the settlers' graves on Ischia, where it made up a band to be worn on the head of the dead baby boy, about nine months old.[18] In general, however, the graves are the graves of lower-class settlers who would not surrender gold to their dead. It is only an accident of survival that we do not readily find Euboean goldwork of the early to mid-eighth century in the graves or settlements of grand Etruscans on the mainland. In due course we do find goldwork there which is influenced by the Pithecussans' 'Orientalizing' style.

Goldwork and wine became important, but it was even more important that the settlement started to fit into a wider, changing context and to prosper from it. By c. 770 BC Phoenicians were trading with Sardinia and, according to the great historian Thucydides, were 'all round Sicily' on offshore islands and promontories, trading there too.[19] They then concentrated on its west and north-west coast, where we can locate them archaeologically from c. 720. Above all, Phoenicians founded a settlement with a far greater future than Ischia's: their New Town or Qart Hadasht in north Africa, which we call 'Carthage'.

In the third century BC it is Timaeus again who dates Carthage's foundation, fixing it to what we reckon as 814/13 BC. A splendid tale of its origins came to be told, including the flight of Elissa (Dido) from Tyre, her refuge at Kition on Cyprus, her arrival in Libya, the support of eighty Cypriot girls, all of them destined to be temple-prostitutes, and her trickery when offered only as much of the ground as an oxhide could cover: she cut a hide into strips and laid them end to end.[20] In its earliest known form the story spared her a disastrous contact with the legendary, taciturn Aeneas, but she was said to have killed herself on a bonfire nonetheless, if only to escape marriage to a local north African prince.

There is truth behind this fine story. Carthage was indeed founded from Tyre in the Levant; a stop by the settlers at the other 'New Town' on Cyprus is very plausible and a contact with Cyprus is proved by some of the earliest pottery found at Carthage.[21] The main story is a legend but its emphasis on Elissa–Dido happens to allow us to date its presumed foundation, *c.* 830–810 BC. Dido, we can work out, was the niece of the biblical queen Jezebel whose active life we can fix from the Scriptures to *c.* 870–850 BC. Timaeus' date of 814/13 is too precise: perhaps it was given so as to make Carthage eighty years older than its supreme Greek rival Syracuse in Sicily, which was founded in 733 BC; Carthage, therefore, could be presented as grandfather to this Greek upstart which was born two generations later. Even so, the dating is broadly consistent with the date implied in the Dido-legend: Timaeus may have based his date on discussions with a Greek-speaking Carthaginian.[22]

Renewed excavations at Carthage have increased our evidence: bones of animals killed on the site have now been dated tentatively to *c.* 800 BC but the earliest datable imports are still no earlier than *c.* 770–760.[23] Tantalizingly, they are bits of a Euboean-style cup. The earliest piece came from a tomb in one of the burial grounds (the 'Juno' necropolis), but others have been found more recently in the settlement below the main Byrsa hill.[24] From *c.* 750 seven more such pieces are known, with another twenty which are attributed to Pithecussae itself. Back on Pithecussae, seventeen of the published graves (out of 501 in this period) contain items which are traceable back to Carthage.[25]

These finds are proportionally very small and might be explained by Phoenician settlers at Carthage who came up to visit Ischia and its nearby Greek settlements and took some Greek objects home. There is, however, textual evidence which brings Euboeans (other than potters) to north Africa. It lies in a Greek description of the coastline which was composed for sailors *c.* 350 BC but which used earlier sources, among them the important *Circuit of the Earth* written by the great geographer Hecataeus of Miletus (*c.* 500 BC).[26] This text takes us along the north African coast from Utica, another early Phoenician settlement, probably founded even earlier than Carthage, from which it was a day's sea-journey. The text then specifies 'Horse's Point' (Hippou Akra) in what is now Tunisia. Behind it lay a lake with settlements all around it which the text appears to locate inland. As transmitted to us, its Greek is clearly confused: some or all of these sites must be on the coast or else 'opposite' it in the sense of islands offshore. Their names could hardly be more remarkable: 'Pithekous-sai', 'Naxos-towns' (Naxos was founded on east Sicily by Greeks, mainly Euboeans, in 734 BC) and, above all, an island 'Euboea'. Their siting has recently been clarified. 'Horse's Point' is the cape looking onto the Mediterranean, just north of Bizerta in Tunisia; the lake is the fertile Lake Ichkeul-Bizerta behind it, perhaps with 'Naxos' beside it. The 'Pithekoussai' islands are best placed on the Cani islands offshore from Bizerta. As for 'Euboea', the great historian and top-ographer Stéphane Gsell wished to place it about 80 miles west of Bizerta at modern Tabarka. He observed, correctly, that the modern promontory there had once been a small island. It would not, however, have been much of a place, whereas the home island of Euboea was so big. 'New Euboea' fits better as the modern Île de la Galite, out to sea about 15 miles off Bizerta.[27] We learn, perhaps through Hecataeus, of a 'Bay of Monkeys' in this region too. It fits very well on the coast opposite the Île de la Galite, in the modern Gulf of Stora, off which there is still an 'Îlot des Singes'. Monkeys proliferated on the Tunisian coast: in 307 BC the Greek general Eumachus marched further inland and found three local 'Pithekoussai' which show vividly what the Greek name could mean. Monkeys lived in the residents' houses; the killing of a monkey was punished with death; children were named after monkeys, receiving 'pithecophoric' names, therefore, like the 'theophoric' names which Greeks gave to children after the names of their gods (*theoi*).[28]

This 'Euboean aura' in Tunisia lay only two days distant from Carthage and it centred on the next major promontory into the Medi-terranean. The Greeks here were not naming existing African settle-ments in which they themselves played little or no part. The local monkeys suggested the name 'Pithekoussai' to them but 'Euboea' and 'Naxos' were proud Greek names and were given to new homes modelled on their counterparts on Greek Sicily.[29] To an approaching Euboean adventurer the cape at Bizerta would indeed look like a friendly horse's-head: there were monkey islands galore and there was an island big enough to be named Euboea. These names existed before 500 BC when Hecataeus wrote: surely they go back into the eighth century when Naxos was young and Euboeans were the main Greek visitors to Sicily, Italy and the West. Like the Euboean pottery in the earliest known levels of Carthage, they point to a direct Euboean presence in north Africa. There is no archaeology as yet to support them, but so far there have been no excavations on the right sites. The evidence is literary, but still strong. It implies that Euboeans had come south from Italy and across from Sicily and founded second homes among the monkeys, the lakes and the fishing of this ancient Libyan (Tunisian) coast.

When did this neglected Euboean network begin? It might even precede Pithecussae off Naples. Euboeans may have come even earlier to north Africa, following Phoenicians who were settled at Auza (by c. 850 BC), Utica and Carthage. From there they may have joined the route west to Huelva in Spain where Euboean plates and cups arrived by c. 800. The north African venture would then have developed, beginning with a local Pithecussae and spreading to a Naxos which followed the Euboean one in Sicily (734 BC). If the north African 'Monkey Islands' came first, it was from their example, perhaps, that a (second) 'Monkey Island', scarce in monkeys, was named at Ischia. The Euboeans' early African venture may also help to answer the Homeric puzzle. When Menelaus talks in the *Odyssey* about the abundant sheep and lambs which he had met in wondrous 'Libya', we can perhaps trace Homer's knowledge to early Greek reports about the coastline we now call Tunisia. It is not a sign of the *Odyssey*'s late date, as if it depended on the later Greek settlements in modern Libya, away to the east near Cyrene c. 630 BC. It may have been based on the tales of Greeks who had travelled to north Africa, going beyond Carthage and living among 'dark-skinned, woolly-haired' people like Homer's Eurybates. The travellers were Euboean Greeks, active in the mid- to later eighth century BC.[30]

The first Euboeans on Ischia's 'Monkey Island' had not known that such networks would develop. Nonetheless, they are symptomatic of others which helped the first western outpost to flourish. By c. 750 BC Phoenicians were settling at Sulcis just off the coast of south-west Sardinia. Nowadays the site of their settlement is joined to Sardinia's mainland by a narrow isthmus, but in c. 750 it was still detached as an island. Rapidly, Phoenicians expanded onto the Sardinian mainland opposite and settled in an arc from San Giorgio near the sea to Monte Sirai inland. Existing Sardinian settlements here did not deter them from taking land for themselves.[31] On our present datable evidence, this offshore settlement was followed by another in western Sicily, the flat little island of Motya, which lies just off the town of Marsala and the important local salt flats.[32] Both settlements, however, were later than the Euboeans' Ischia. If the Phoenicians needed a local western example for their new offshore ventures, they had one in their midst: it was a Greek example, the Euboeans' 'Monkey Island'. Certainly, the two peoples continued to make contact. At Sulcis, Euboean pottery appears from *c.* 725 onwards, while a little Phoenician pottery (some of which is Carthaginian) appears on Ischia too. The settlers in these two spheres interrelated. It was from such contacts that Euboean pottery continued to go west to reach sites in the Phoenician zone in southern Spain. It existed in the late eighth century at Toscanos near Malaga, where its style and shapes were then imitated, the sign of an important Euboean impact.[33]

In the years from *c.* 770 to 730 Ischia became a sustainable settlement whose Greeks planted and traded vines and olives, practised goldwork and also gained from the various settlements which had sprung up between Tunis and Sardinia. It belongs in a remarkable 'long lifetime' of Euboean settlements north, east and west of Euboea itself, hard though it is for us to give their chronology a secure sequence. In the context of all this activity, another settlement was founded on the Italian coast beyond Ischia. The heights of what would come to be called Cumae were visible across the sea from Monte Vico. They were inhabited by non-Greeks, but a few Euboean cups had already ended up in graves there and clearly there had been some contact. Nonetheless no further attempt at a Greek settlement had been made. One reason for the delay may be volcanic: a layer of volcanic dust has been found in some of Cumae's pre-Greek tombs, suggesting a local volcanic fallout.[34] Another may have been continuing Euboean caution, as the site was by no means empty. A further problem is our evidence: we cannot be sure of the date of the first settlement here, either. As on Ischia, the first settlers' graves at Cumae and their first level of habitation have not been found. In 1913 a few fragments of early Greek pottery were published from the acropolis and from some of the graves after the first Greeks' arrivals. They suggest a date *c.* 730 BC, but there were probably at least ten years of earlier occupation. Unfortunately we cannot yet know: recent researches have even located pieces of earlier Greek pottery, datable *c.* 750–740, by the line of the city's later wall. They have been disturbed from burials below which might be non-Greek, but alternatively they might be the first early signs that Greeks had moved in. If so, they would close some of the gap after the settlement on Ischia and support the view of that island as a planned first stop. But the question remains open.[35]

One fact, at least, is certain. Unlike Ischia, Cumae was on an excellent mainland site. The new arrivals found a natural acropolis-hill which stood out against the flat coastline and on either side had access to the sea, although this has nowadays silted up. The settlers appear to have been quick to make a harbour, perhaps on its south side.[36] They were quick to expand across the level coastland and were soon occupying at least 2 miles of it to the north. We also know the names of the settlement's leaders: Megasthenes of Chalcis, a Euboean, and Hippocles of Cumae, almost certainly a Euboean from that Euboean town of Cumae which lay on the island's Aegean coast beside the volcanic vineyards.[37] Their names complicate our view of the process. Were they Euboeans by birth, but living on nearby Ischia? Or were they newcomers to the west who were dispatched with volunteers from Euboea and who acquired, or encouraged, more volunteers from Ischia itself? We cannot fill in the human background: if the venture had to wait until the 730s it becomes part of yet another story, the founding of Euboean Greek settlements in east Sicily. Conditions on Euboea itself must be important to the decision, but all we can say here is that neither of Cumae's founders came from Eretria, although Eretrians had helped to found Ischia. There are signs of the tensions which were to bring settlers from Chalcis, but not Eretria, to the wave of new settlements in Sicily in the later 730s, and which were to see the expulsion of Eretrians from their previous settlement on Corcyra.

The 'Monkey Island' which settlers at Cumae left behind them was not diminished. It may even have helped the islanders that the new mainland Cumae could now supply them with more grain from its big territory, although it was not for that reason that Cumae's founders had set out. They had the men, the force and the will to found a lasting new home and they were well led. So far we have no graves on Ischia which are rich enough to be credited to the upper class. At Cumae, however, such graves are some of the first known to us, in which rich settlers, children perhaps of the founding group, have been distinctively buried and equipped. On Ischia pieces survive from some poignantly decorated big pottery mixing-bowls; they are painted with a favourite contemporary Euboean motif, horses at a manger or grazing on open land.[38] On rocky islands, as Homer makes Telemachus remark, there is no scope for using fine horses. By contrast, Cumae's flat territory is a horse-lover's dream. There are horse-bits in the earliest known Greek graves there and Cumae's cavalry were to be famous. One attraction in the move to the mainland, it has been aptly observed, was the scope for horse-breeding and for a good gallop.[39] On Cumae's acropolis one of the earliest finds was a big jug for pouring wine, decorated with a line of galloping horses. Their riders hold the reins high in their left hand beside the horse's arched neck and stretch their right hand out to its hindquarters, as if balancing themselves without stirrups. They are probably our earliest Greek representation of a horse-race: the curious placing of the right hand is a convention of artists only in the eighth to early seventh centuries BC.[40] Cumae's Greeks would also ride out for sport. On the wetlands near the city the local flax was to be famous, the finest in the Greek world for making woven hunting-nets.[41] We should think of the Greek leaders hunting and riding in their new land, our Italy.

No Phoenician is known to have been involved in this settlement but there is no reported conflict with Phoenicians in the general neighbourhood. The two peoples went their separate ways, but not to the exclusion of one another. We can thus correct a suggestion of modern scholarship and two images made famous in English poetry. Phoenicians did not begin to found settlements of their own in the west in order to defend themselves against Greek 'encroachment' on their trade.[42] Both peoples settled on new land there because there was gain to be had from taking it. At the sight of new Greek arrivals, Phoenicians did not behave like the 'grave Tyrian trader' at the end of Matthew Arnold's poem 'The Scholar Gypsy'. They did not sail 'indignantly' all day and night to a safe haven in the further west where they could trade with 'dark Iberians' far away 'where the Atlantic raves'. Nor, as John Masefield imagined, were they the graceful carriers of 'apes and peacocks' and 'sweet white wine' from these distant lands. Rather, they brought metals back from the west, cargoes of silver and 'pig-lead', much like the 'dirty British coaster' with which Masefield wrongly contrasted them.

No doubt, as in Homer, there was individual sharp practice, and not all of it will have been on the Phoenicians' side. But the authorities of the settlements allowed the two peoples to coexist, Euboeans visiting Sulcis, Phoenicians visiting Ischia. Greeks had Cumae and their Monkey Islands, and from the mid-730s a string of new settlements in east Sicily; they had even founded a new Euboea off Africa. Phoenicians, meanwhile, had Sardinia and west Sicily, Carthage and southern Spain. There was not yet a contest, one people against the other. Both wanted gains, including land, and in the eighth century BC there was more than enough in the west for them to set about getting them in peacefully separate spheres.

II

In 1717 Bishop Berkeley wrote to the poet Alexander Pope and described Ischia as the 'epitome of the whole earth' as it had every natural advantage. Even after the foundation of the new Cumae, Monkey Island continued to prosper. From the period c. 750–700 BC we have much more material evidence, most of it from the excavated graves but some, too, from outlying finds and from deposits of charred Greek pottery, including pieces of big vessels, painted with pictures of horses. These vessels were probably burned on funeral-pyres but not transferred to the cremated individual's resting place.

At first sight the ultimate origin of this evidence suggests that Bishop Berkeley's phrase might as well refer to the multiplicity of the island's settlers. There is some fine pottery in contemporary Euboean style, imported from Euboea; there are many local imitations of it; there is much in a Corinthian style, some of which may have been made in Corinthian outposts which were already in the west. Small scent- and oil-bottles become ever more numerous: Corinthian ones turn up from c. 725 BC and three separate Corinthian potters have been identified and credited with coming to work on the island.[43] There are also small flasks imported from Rhodes whose style of decoration imitated Cypriot (not Phoenician) prototypes. There are even some special little Greek pots, made carefully by hand, which held special slow-poured contents, drugs probably, including (it has been argued) opium.[44] There is Phoenician pottery too, including plates, some of which may have come from Carthage, others from their settlements on Sardinia. There is even a small perfume-vase shaped like an Oriental's face, a type which derives exactly from Cilicia and its boundary with north Syria.[45] There are a few pieces of east Aegean Greek origin: there are more of the 'lyre-player' seals whose origins we have traced to Cilicia; there are imitations of Egyptian seals shaped like scarab-beetles which were perhaps made by Rhodian Greeks; there are genuine Egyptian seals too which include a cardinal dating-point, a scarab-seal with the name of the short-lived pharaoh Baken-renef ('Bocchoris' to the Greeks), who ruled in the 720s BC.[46] Nearer home, the Italian mainland left a clear imprint too. It is clearest in the clasps with which the settlers fixed their robes and dresses. They are big rounded clasps of metal (*fibulae*) of a distinctive Italian-Etruscan style. The settlers on Ischia adopted them and even produced them on the island: most of them were used by women (who also put them as offerings in their children's graves). It is most likely that they were adopted from local women, the 'wives' of the early settlers.[47] Back in Greece these big circular metal clasps looked remarkable and so they were sometimes dedicated to the gods in sanctuaries. There were also Etruscan users of Greek pottery. On one small Corinthian Greek wine-jug, made from local Italian clay *c.* 700 BC, we find the Greek inscription 'I am Ame's', a female name which has been traced to Etruscan families on the mainland at nearby Pontecagnano. The script used is the Euboean alphabet.[48]

This diversity has suggested that Monkey Island grew into a truly international settlement. It has even been seen as a settlement abroad 'of a particular type, one which cannot be traced directly back to Greek models'. Was it more like a trading post of a Near Eastern type, perhaps, one whose ethnic structures were more mixed?[49] When the nobility moved over to Cumae, did a greater social freedom take root behind them, causing people of various talents to mix in a new sort of 'skills-centre' and even encouraging Greek craftsmen to sign their names for the first time on pottery which they decorated?[50] The first such craftsman-names in Greek are indeed all known from the west, not from the Greek homeland.

Objects found on the island are diverse, but their proportional numbers vary and their implications may be less dramatic. About a tenth of the San Montano cemetery has been excavated and we still do not know where the settlement's 'top people' were buried. Of the graves so far published and reported, almost all are simply equipped, if at all, and none is rich: nearly three-quarters of them are for children and infants. The surest sign of a non-Greek's presence is the use of a non-Greek burial rite, but the San Montano cemetery follows Greek practices in almost every case. We have no sign of the characteristic cemeteries, or tophets, of Phoenician settlements like Carthage or Sulcis or even, in part, Amathus, in which Phoenicians placed the babies and children whom, we are told, they had killed and offered to the gods. Out of the 501 published graves from eighth-century Ischia, only four have been claimed to show evidence of a non-Greek funerary rite.[51] Two of these four are indeed convincingly 'Oriental', one of them because it shows the smashing of plates at the grave itself, a practice found in the Levant, including at some recently excavated graves at Tyre.[52]

In the absence of many non-Greek burials, multi-culturalists have to reason from the non-Greek grave-goods, but the implications of these items are even more uncertain. As at Lefkandi, non-Greek objects could easily end up as personal objects in Greeks' graves. A Phoenician-style plate with a Phoenician inscription is dated c. 700 BC (perhaps from Carthage) and a much-discussed jar, reused for a child's burial, is suggestively inscribed: it shows an Aramaic sign, a Greek mark and (possibly) a Phoenician letter which was added for its final funerary use. Many of the storage-jars on the island derive from Levantine shapes and plainly there were Levantines who visited and sometimes lived on the island. But they need not have been many (they had their own settlements on south-west Sardinia). Euboean Greek pottery exists in the Phoenicians' burial ground at Sulcis on Sardinia, and at least one Euboean potter resided in Carthage.[53] Nonetheless Sulcis and Carthage were Phoenician settlements.

Only one text (Strabo) preserves anything of the settlement's history: after a while there was 'civil conflict' and some of the settlers were driven out. As elsewhere in Greek history it would probably be 'conflict' between the two founding-groups, Chalcidians and Eretrians.[54] If the Eretrians were expelled, the quarrel fits well into a wider pattern. From the mid-730s onwards, Euboeans helped to found new settlements on the east coast of Sicily and on the island's straits with Italy, but the new Euboean settlers here were mainly Chalcidians, never Eretrians. Eretrians had settled on Corcyra, probably by *c.* 750 BC, but were then driven out by Corinthians, the Chalcidians' partners in Sicily in the late 730s: Corinthian pottery appears in quantity on Ischia, continuing after the Eretrians' expulsion; up in north Greece, on the Chalcidic peninsula, Eretrians settled on the western prong, whereas Chalcidians settled on the central prong. At Cumae in Italy there were Chalcidians, but no Eretrians. The two Euboean towns did not get on, and the 'conflict' on Ischia was probably an early sign of it.

An expulsion of some of the Greek settlers was a major event, although it would never be guessed from our excavated fraction of the cemetery: no arms and weapons have been found in its lower-class graves. The settlers, however, had not settled down cosily into being Pithecussans. One group took control and maintained it so as to keep the others out. This sort of conflict becomes familiar in Greek settlements later, in places with Greek institutions. If it happened at Pithecussae, it happened because there were dominant Greeks there who could force it through in a settlement which was run by Greeks with a Greek council (no doubt), and a largely Greek population.

The cemetery, our main evidence, also shows that social conventions were organized and funerary 'rules' were observed. The graves tend to group into family plots and the Greek rites vary according to age. Adults, including women, were almost always cremated; children were usually buried and babies were slipped whole, sad little skeletons, into plain pottery storage-jars, a bit of which might be knocked out to admit them. There were shared rules of death and there would also be shared rules of ordinary living.[55] Our later authors consider the island as Greek, run by Euboeans. In the metal-working quarter we have a weight, made to what we later know as the Euboic standard, based (we have seen) on Phoenician weights in the east. It too is a hint that Euboean rules were applied.

As yet we know nothing directly of the island's cults and religious life, although shrines were built on the Greeks' acropolis, at least from c. 725 BC onwards. We also need to remember the problem of languages: not many people could communicate in Greek, Phoenician and Etruscan. A Greek may have copied a Phoenician's plate, so useful for eating, and Greeks clearly adopted their non-Greek women's chunky metal dress-clasps: there is also a hint, as we shall see, that a Greek sailor talked to a Phoenician about the guiding stars. But there is not much of a cross-cultural legacy.[56] Instead the diversity of objects in the graves makes neat sense in the light of something else, their Greeks' contacts elsewhere.

The presence of Corinthian goods is unsurprising. Corinthians had co-operated with Euboeans previously on the routes to south Italy and occasionally some of them travelled on beyond: if the Eretrians left Ischia after the quarrel, ever more Corinthians may have come in, moving on from Corcyra (which they also seized) and being welcomed by their partners in Sicily, the Chalcidians. The objects from Cilicia, north Syria and Rhodes fit neatly too.[57] It is exactly in this eastern triangle that we have traced Euboean eighth-century travellers who visited Tarsus on the Cilician plain and were followed by Rhodians who also settled by c. 700 at Soloi on the Cilician coast. Together they perhaps settled at the unexcavated Posideion across the Bay of Issus. At Pithecussae we duly find more 'lyre-player' seals than are yet known anywhere else: their stones and many of their designs were ultimately derived from south Cilicia. There is no surprise, either, in the presence of small Rhodian scent-bottles and Egyptianizing seals, probably of Rhodian origin. The likely content of the small scent-bottles is oil from the roses for which Rhodes was so famous. As we have suggested, the roses may have been improved by recent Rhodian contact with Cilicia's twice-flowering forms.[58] On Ischia, too, rose oil was surely being offered to the Greek dead. It is also less of a surprise that from the 720s onwards genuine Egyptian seals reach Ischia. The 720s are the decade in which, we now know, Pharaoh Baken-renef ruled in the Delta, the short-lived 'Bocchoris' whom Greek traditions later praised as their friend. For a brief moment, Greeks from the eastern triangle of Cyprus, Cilicia and the Levant may have had favoured access in Egypt's Delta.

The Ischian grave-goods, therefore, cannot be understood only in terms of a local Euboean-Corinthian network and a parallel presence of some Phoenicians beside it. The most exotic goods make excellent sense in terms of our wider Greek 'travelling heroes' and their simultaneous presence in the east and west. They turn the apparent multiculturalism of Pithecussae into an exact Greek connection. Euboeans and Rhodians from our eastern triangle came on west to enjoy the new opportunities by the Bay of Naples. They sold or gave away some of the typical goods which they carried with them. Not every grave which includes such goods is necessarily the grave of a Greek with eastern contacts, but some of them are. They are the graves of true Greek travelling heroes who settled on the island itself and who help to place two of the graves' most remarkable features.

The 'lyre-player' seals and the Egyptian scarabs are often set in silver, a type of setting which points to the Pithecussans' access to Etruscan silver from the mainland. Although they were often mounted locally on the island, they retained a distinctive use. They are mostly found in the graves of young children, where they are best understood as amulets to ward off evil spirits and protect the child in death. This use is known in the Levant and Egypt, and is attested for Egyptian-style scarabs at Torre Galli in south Italy, perhaps as early as c. 950–900 BC: the use had been transmitted here by visiting Cypriots and Phoenicians. Back in Greece the objects are found almost only in sanctuaries, as dedications and not as protective charms. Their use as charms on Ischia need not mean that these children and their families were non-Greek Levantines.[59] The amulets were placed with their dead bodies by their parents, perhaps especially by fond mothers. With some of our Greek contingent from the eastern triangle non-Greek women may have come west: there was also the continuing influence of their non-Greek mothers and marriages in the previous generation. These amulets point to the mind-set of non-Greek women and their continuing influence on their families when 'married' by Euboeans or Rhodians in the eastern triangle. Such Greeks with Near Eastern contacts brought the eastern practice to Pithecussae. They also brought it to their home towns in Greece: an example of such a scarab in a child's grave *c.* 700 BC is now known at Lefkandi, no less, on Euboea.[60]

The most famous object in Pithecussae's cemetery also points to Greek contacts in this same area. In the 720s a young boy, aged about ten, was cremated rather than buried, the usual rite for his age group in the cemetery. In his grave with his ashes his family placed no less than four big pottery mixing-bowls for wine (the only ones known in an Ischian grave, so far), three small jugs for pouring it and a deep drinking-cup, made on Rhodes, with a Greek inscription on its upper rim. The alphabetic lettering is in the Euboean script and two of its three lines of verse are hexameters. They begin with a statement of ownership, like other inscriptions on known cups of this period: 'I am Nestor's cup, good to drink with'. They go on with a significant 'but': 'But whoever drinks from this cup, at once the desire of fair-crowned Aphrodite will seize him.' Endlessly discussed, these verses are best understood as playing with a witty contrast.[61] In Homer's *Iliad* we know of the old hero Nestor's cup, the famous heavy cup fitted with gold in the eleventh book which befitted such a warrior. Our inscribed cup belonged to a Greek called Nestor, 'but' whoever drinks from this one will 'make love, not war'. The language draws on epic hexameter phrases, but the message is light-hearted.[62] We know of other early Greek cups inscribed with a warning curse: 'Whoever takes this one will be struck blind.' Nestor's cup has a 'curse' of a different kind, the 'curse' of being love-struck.

This drinking-cup and the accompanying bowls have been explained as items for a Greek male drinking-party of the type known later as a *symposion*. They are not the first such items found in a Greek grave: at Eretria on Euboea we have others which go back to *c.* 875 BC and in northern Greece there are others which are even earlier, long before the *symposion* existed.[63] By themselves these items do not prove that Greek drinking-parties already had their fully developed form, the one which separated the drinking from the earlier dinner and caused the male guests to recline on couches, not sit on chairs, while enjoying their watered wine. On Ischia the novelty, rather, lies in the inscribed verses' wit and their erotic reference. They suit the tone of a grown-up Greek *symposion*, as we know it later, where male love and sex were part of the atmosphere and where male guests enjoyed poetry and sometimes improvised verses of their own. On Ischia the cup and the mixing-bowls were put in the grave as a tribute to the young boy, before he himself could participate in such male party fun. The cup, then, had existed earlier: it has been well explained as the cup of a family-member who left it with the dead child as a token of the life which the young boy might have had.[64]

Above all, the verses on the cup allude knowingly to Greek heroic poetry and, for all but extreme sceptics, allude specifically to Homer's epic the *Iliad*. They are 'Europe's first literary allusion'.[65] Out here on Ischia, in a far from noble family, there were people who knew Homer. The verses are not elegantly written out: only three verses are inscribed, and already the writer's hand starts to fail. But they were written in Euboean script on a Rhodian cup which had been made *c.* 740–730 BC and used for parties by adults before being put in the boy's grave. Two other graves in the same family plot have been proposed to show 'eastern' influence. We can well see why. This family of Homer-lovers, the poet's first known fans, were surely Euboeans from the eastern 'triangle' who had had contact with Rhodians and who then came on west to another home on Ischia. With them, from east to west, they brought a love of Homer's *Iliad*.

In Ischia's cemetery, some of the cremation-burials include a small Greek wine-jug in the grave, unburnt and therefore not brought from the funeral-pyre. These have been interpreted as jugs from which wine was poured to put out the pyre's flames, copying the practice in Homeric heroes' funerals.[66] But these graves are very lowly affairs and the Homeric cause is not, unfortunately, convincing. The wine-jug may have been placed in the grave to satisfy the ever-thirsty dead: lower-class Ischians would hardly have modelled their last rites on an epic hero's. Homer's epic presence, rather, is suggested by the words on our boy's drinking-cup, a small, but vital, insight into social life on this Greek island. Unfortunately we have no such detailed excavations at Cumae on the mainland opposite. No doubt there were more verses, more parties, more witty allusions to epic in Cumae's grander houses.

Instead what we can document is a clear Greek cultural imprint on Etruscans in their own big settlements on the mainland. From *c.* 700 BC Etruscan aristocrats enter an 'Orientalizing' age of their own, absorbing foreign luxuries and styles which befit their own rich, noble standing. Some of this influence comes from their Phoenician visitors.[67] Phoenicians brought silver and silver-gilt shallow bowls, decorated with narrative scenes whose underlying story we, probably like the Etruscans, cannot decode. These bowls were fine gifts from the Levant, accompanied by the usual ostrich-eggs, shells and (no doubt) purple textiles. In return, Etruscans gave metals, especially the prized silver of their metal-bearing hills.

Greeks also gave gifts and they too brought new items for Etruscan families. From *c.* 720 onwards Greek-style pottery becomes more frequent at the non-Greek sites on the Italian mainland which earlier Greek pioneers had visited. Up near Grosseto, beside the main Etruscan metal-zone, we have a remarkable tall mixing-bowl in the Greek style: it imitates the designs of the greatest contemporary painter of pottery back on Euboea and was perhaps imported directly rather than made locally.[68] These items changed the appearance of an Etruscan party. Elsewhere Greek potters went to live in Etruscan company and caused their designs to be imitated locally. Everywhere in Etruscan company this Greek imprint is Euboean, radiating out from Euboean Cumae and Ischia. It is a further significant proof of the strength of the Euboean presence which we have tracked in the west.

From Euboeans, Etruscans adopted their form of the alphabetic script and learned to write. They already had wine and drinking-parties but they adopted Greek bowls, cups and jugs and transferred the Greek names for them directly into the Etruscan language.[69] It is still disputed whether they also took over the Greeks' word for wine, *oinos* (through Etruscan contact, it became *vinum* in Latin, whence the Italian *vino* and our 'wine').[70] They certainly took over the Greek word for olive oil.[71] These items also changed the style of Etruscans' parties. They even adopted the Greek mixing of 'cheese and wine': bronze cheese-graters are known in Etruscan graves, beginning with one *c.* 730–700 BC.[72] Perhaps, too, on seeing the Euboean Greek example around them, Etruscans increased their skills in horsemanship. Etruscans already had chariots and they were quick to adopt the latest innovations from Cypriot chariot-designers.[73] Before the Greeks arrived they had also been riding horses, but perhaps they had never ridden them quite as the cavalrymen of Greek Cumae rode and raced. It was from Greek craftsmen that Etruscans then learned the art of drawing and painting the horse.

Phoenicians never founded a town on the Italian mainland, but the Euboeans had founded Cumae, very close to Etruscan settlements. As on Ischia, some of their settlers will have married Etruscans, a channel through which their strong Greek cultural imprint could run.[74] Naturally Etruscans adapted what they received. Most of the earliest uses of Etruscan writing, unlike Greek writing, are on women's objects, not men's; at Etruscan parties, even with Greek-style pottery, Etruscan women were present, contrary to the Greek all-male custom.[75] The men of Euboean Chalcis, like the men of Corinth, were famous for a different art: they were said to be exceptionally keen on sex between males, as the Greek verb *chalkidizein* testified and later anecdotes elaborated. By the mid-fifth century BC Greeks claimed to have taught pederasty to the Persians: did male Chalcidians at Cumae enliven the sex-lives of male Etruscans and Campanians? The word *katmite* (meaning 'catamite') entered the Etruscan language from Greek, adapting the Greek 'Ganymedes' (Zeus's beloved boy). The Euboeans of Chalcis even claimed that Ganymede had been abducted from their own territory.[76]

Even so, noble Etruscans were a match for Greeks in their midst. The most famous rich burial at Cumae, *c.* 720–700 BC, is that of a man who was cremated and preserved in a silver urn, protected inside two bronze ones. The burial rite matches that of a near-contemporary Euboean who was cremated and buried back in Euboea by the West Gate of Eretria.[77] At Cumae this western Euboean was buried with fifty-two metal items, including eight silver items for a drinking-party, weaponry and two horse-bits, perhaps for horses who pulled his chariot. Some of the weapons, metal objects and the bronze shield in his grave are Etruscan, so much so that his identity has sometimes been read as Etruscan. However, his own funerary rite is decisive: he is a Euboean Greek. Near to his grave lies a woman's grave, arguably for his Etruscan wife. She was found in it with traces of a magnificent silver-threaded robe.[78] Here and elsewhere, Etruscan fashion made everyday Greek women and their homespun, criss-cross skirts seem as dowdy as Bavarian wives at a Hollywood gala evening.[79]

Spanning east and west in the eighth century, our travelling Euboean heroes had met styles and languages which their families at home had never imagined.

Alphabetic inscription on Nestor's cup, c. 740 BC, for Ischia, beginning
'I am the cup of Nestor, good to drink with . . .'

IO

Back on Euboea

The trail has been long, but from north Syria to the Bay of Naples we have followed the tracks of travelling objects which locate the movements of Euboean travelling heroes across the sea. In Homer's epics, however, we meet the Euboeans only once, in the Catalogue of the Greek ships in his *Iliad*'s second book. Seven places are mentioned on the island, homes of the swift warrior-Abantes, who 'breathe might', carry ashen spears and wear their hair long on the backs of their heads. Their leader is Elephenor, who brings 'forty black ships' to the Trojan War.[1] Homer's Catalogue probably draws on information which is much older than the rest of his *Iliad*, but in the eighth century Euboeans on the central Lelantine plain were still known as 'Abantes', men from Chalcis and Eretria. They were still keen warriors, although unlike Homer's heroes they rode into battle. They were more than able to manage 'dark ships'.

It is we, not Homer, who track Euboeans up to the Chalcidic peninsula in northern Greece, across to Chios and Cyprus and off to their settlement by the mouth of the Orontes river. It is we, too, who track them by their travelling objects to Corcyra, the west coast of Italy and to Ischia and Cumae by the Bay of Naples. The ancient Greeks themselves forgot most of this wide horizon in the Euboean eighth-century past. In the late fifth century BC when the great Athenian historian Thucydides wrote a brief outline of earlier Greek history, the first phase of this Euboean venture was one of several modern rediscoveries he omitted.

In Greek topographic texts, the Euboean settlement of Ischia and Cumae was explicitly recorded later and therefore available to be believed or contested by Thucydides' modern followers. Fifty years ago, however, a Euboean presence on tenth- to eighth-century Cyprus, in the Levant or at Al Mina, had only just begun to be suspected from a new identification of the pottery which we now know to be theirs. On Euboea, the significance of Lefkandi and its tenth-century contacts was wholly unknown. Even thirty years ago Euboeans' presence and settlements in the north of the Chalcidic peninsula were widely considered to be no earlier than the seventh century BC. Almost none of their objects in the Near East between *c.* 980 and *c.* 780 had been discovered.

As their trail began to become clearer, the first archaeologists to see it considered that Euboeans were the early to mid-eighth century's 'masters of the trade between the East Mediterranean and central Italy'.[2] From north Syria they brought back objects and skills which changed the range of archaic Greek arts and crafts; to Etruscan Italy they brought literacy and luxury-objects which changed Etruscan upper-class culture and introduced a literate and 'Orientalizing' age. This dominant role then began to be questioned from several sides, by Near Eastern archaeologists who were wary of such a prominence for Greek 'pioneers', by Italian archaeologists who emphasized the importance of existing western non-Greek networks and by scholars who simply feared that Euboean pottery was being taken uncritically to prove Euboeans' presence. Others even saw a western colonialist mirage in such an emphasis on Greek pioneers who had supposedly settled 'colonies' in the east and west, transformed their eastern borrowings and brought a new culture to 'primitive' western societies. Instead, Phoenicians were invoked as the carriers of Euboean goods eastwards, while Cypriots, Phoenicians and Etruscans were given greater emphasis in the west. Al Mina, even, was presented as a non-Greek settlement; Herodotus' Posideion was wrongly located at the non-Greek Ras el-Bassit and the Greek and Latin texts about Euboeans on Ischia were downgraded as the supposed projection of remote sources in a later Greek age.

We have followed the tracks of Euboeans and their objects so closely because the trail of myths which they also laid will depend on their contacts with exactly located sites and landscapes. No other such trail in the eighth century is discernible to my eye, but naturally in a mobile age contacts between Greeks and the entire Asian coastline cannot be limited to this one Euboean network. The ancients remembered ties of friendship between Euboeans and Ionian Greeks in western Asia Minor (now Aegean Turkey): Chalcis was linked with the island of Samos, Eretria with Miletus on the Asian mainland, and those links were still active when a major war broke out between these two Euboean settlements in the later eighth century BC. No doubt Ionians and east Greeks were already engaged with non-Greek societies in Asia: in the ninth and eighth centuries Samian pottery existed in the lowest levels at Al Mina and the dedication of horse-harness from Unqi was dedicated in sanctuaries on Samos and at Miletus. However, these pieces of harness may simply be gifts from Euboeans, an Eretrian's gift to a Milesian, a Chalcidian's to a Samian, one guest-friend to another. On present evidence, these east Greeks do not match the scale of the trail which was left by Euboeans in both the east and the west. Other Greeks had contacts, but they are not nearly so prominent nor so far-flung.

In the 730s and the next two decades Euboeans who had shown the way on Ischia, Cumae and Corcyra went on to found at least six more settlements, true *poleis*, on the east coast of Sicily and in Italy across the straits. A 'new Euboea' and other settlements on and off Tunisia existed too. While kings Tiglath Pileser, Sargon and Sennacherib were terrifying Israel and Judah and the Phoenician and Syrian cities, Euboean leaders were settling city-state after city-state, untroubled by Yahweh or the gods of Assur. Out in the west, their presence had begun in the wake of Cypriot, then Phoenician predecessors in the years before Tiglath Pileser's demands for tribute intensified pressure on the Phoenicians' cities in the Levant. In the Near East, Euboean ventures had also begun long before Assyrian pressure was a major issue. Euboeans had sustained their own mobility for more than two centuries, passing down existing Greek networks, going east for the further lure of precious metals, going west, then further west on the tracks of Cypriots and Phoenicians. In 706 BC Greeks were founding Tarentum in Italy, the offshoot of civil strife in its homeland, Sparta: the town's settlement was later blamed on the bad behaviour of Spartan women. In 706 BC, by contrast, King Sargon was holding his magnificent New Year celebrations in his great Dur Sarrukin and its landscaped garden. But the Euboeans in the west were not a side effect thrown off across the Mediterranean by the conquests of Sargon and his predecessors. They had flourished independently: as the inscribed cup on Ischia implies, they had also taken a love of Homeric epic with them to the west.

What emphasis should we give to contacts between Levantine visitors and such Greeks at home? On Euboea itself we have ruled out an important Phoenician presence: if there were Near Eastern craftsmen at Lefkandi, they may have been imported as slaves. Phoenicians were active elsewhere in the Aegean, but on trails which were distinct from the Euboeans' main lines. Phoenicians settled at Thasos in the north Aegean because the island's gold and silver mines attracted them.[3] They were present on the island of Cythera, just off southern Greece, because it was a natural stopping-point for their journeys on to the west.[4] We have seen how in later history the Crusaders' ships circled carefully round from the Levant to the Cilician coast, then on to Rhodes, then Crete on their journeys west. Many centuries earlier both Rhodes and Crete were on the line of Phoenician travellers going westwards too: away from Euboea, what evidence do we have on each island for contemporary eastern contact?

On Rhodes, the first signs of foreign contact are Cypriot, with only one tomb (near Ialysos on the north-east of the island) showing direct contact with faience objects and a seal from the Levant.[5] There is nothing to compare with the eastern goods in the contemporary cemeteries at Lefkandi: Rhodes in the ninth century is almost a blank to us. From the mid-eighth century onwards, however, the island's settlements began to form and the main sanctuaries began to attract imported dedications. Between 750 and 700 BC, Lindos's fine sanctuary of Athena then received small ivories from the Near East, a north Syrian bronze figurine and some bronze north Syrian mace-heads. At Camiros, a notable series of carved ivory figurines was also on site by c. 700 BC. However, these goods had not necessarily been brought by Phoenicians. We have followed Rhodians in the later eighth century into Cilicia and also (under the hero Amphilochus' guidance) claimed them tentatively for Posideion on the Bay of Issus. The later eighth century is exactly the time when their Rhodian compatriots were also exporting objects, and perhaps themselves too, to western Pithecussae. Most of the eastern dedications on eighth-century Rhodes could therefore be Rhodians' own trophies, acquired overseas. At Camiros a gold-equipped burial of a warrior in this period includes a (possibly) Euboean mixing-bowl: it too may be a sign of contact with travelling Greeks.[6] At Ialysos, Cypriot imports of 'black-on-red' flasks brought precious oils, a type of container which Rhodians rapidly copied.[7] The case for Phoenician residents on the island is much more localized and is ultimately based only on Greek texts written much later. Phoenicians were located at Ialysos by a local Rhodian Greek historian, one who was writing in the early second century BC. He claimed that a group of travelling Phoenicians had once been blown by a storm to Ialysos and had founded a cult of the sea-god there in thanks. They then retained its priesthood in the families which they bred by inter-marriage. Ialysos attracted other such 'Phoenician' stories: at least they make sense in terms of Phoenicians' natural sea-routes towards the west.[8] Archaeologically, at present, they have left even less of an eighth-century imprint on the island than Levantine imports have left across two centuries on Euboea.

On Crete, a crucial point for such routes, we have more solid evidence, some of it for actual visitors. At Kommos on the south-west coast, Phoenician pottery is found from c. 900 BC at a cult-site which was rebuilt and equipped, c. 800, with a small three-pillared Phoenician-style shrine. Phoenicians clearly worshipped here, but probably only when they put in briefly on sea-journeys to the further west.[9] In the eighth century Phoenician pottery on the site dies out. Even in the ninth century the main imports into Crete are Cypriot, as on Rhodes, although a few Phoenician items appear too, most famously an inscribed bronze bowl, which ended up buried in a Greek grave at Knossos.[10] Near Eastern jewellers and bronze-workers have also been proposed on the island, with varying plausibility, but only recently have we found Phoenician-style stone grave-markers. One has been detected in a tomb at Knossos where it had been reused during the later eighth century. Others appear to have marked out a small burial area in the cemetery of Eleutherna, a settlement inland in western Crete.[11]

Here, at least, it looks as if a Phoenician family came to reside, die and be buried. We would much like to know if they included craftsmen or traders because Eleutherna lies on a route to the island's most

important cult-site, one with by far the most prolific evidence of
Near Eastern imports and artistic influences in the entire ninth- and
eighth-century Aegean. High up on the peaks of Mount Ida a cave
marks the site which was linked in Greek myths to the birth and
infancy of the god Zeus. Excavations in the cave have produced
imported ivories of varied Near Eastern origin, including what may
even be pieces of a throne.[12] Among the offerings and trinkets the
most spectacular are decorated bronze shields with patterns or central
bosses which draw on Near Eastern, especially north Syrian, models.
These shields had a use in ceremonies in honour of Zeus, one which
we can infer from the cult's accompanying myths: the dancing worshippers would clash shields like the youthful attendants who had
once clashed shields, so the later Greek story said, in order to drown
the cries of the infant god Zeus in the cave. The Ida cave lies above
the snowline for much of the winter, but nonetheless it looks out
onto a wide enclosed plain which could hold a big festival crowd of
spectators. The ceremonies here drew pilgrims despite the altitude
and remoteness of the site: some of them brought very luxurious
dedications, including silver jugs and bronze bowls. They will turn
out to have had an important role for a mythical trail which reached
our Euboeans, but as yet we do not know if the worshippers up at
this cave also included visitors from the Near East. Myths about the
god developed at the cave with the help of stories ultimately acquired
by Greeks in the Levant, but its remarkable 'Oriental' range of offerings may be the exotic offerings of Cretan Greeks only. The rites in
their Zeus's honour required shields and music: the dedicated objects
include an exceptional 'gong' on which a god and his attendants are
shown in a style based firmly on Near Eastern originals. Even so, there
are Greek details in its decoration, implying that this item was adapted
from a Near Eastern object by a Greek craftsman on Crete itself.[13]

The objects at the Ida cave may not point to Near Eastern worshippers, but they are a reminder that strong currents of eastern
influence could run in the ninth and eighth centuries independently of
Euboean carriers. Cretans profited from one such current and as a
result of their contacts may even be the first Greeks to have adopted
the Near Eastern practice of drinking and reclining at parties on
comfortable 'sofa'-couches, the eventual practice of the rest of the

male Greek world.[14] Other such currents of influence may be discovered in future in the Aegean, but even so they will not dislodge the
scope of the Euboean trail which we have followed across more
than two centuries from the last days of Lefkandi's ruler, buried and
honoured with his huge building, to the Euboeans at Al Mina on the
edge of Unqi, at Mende in northern Greece or Ischia and Cumae in
Italy. This particular Euboean line and its consequences are singularly
important and inter-linked.

So far I have written only of 'Euboeans' and credited them indiscriminately with important settlements and contacts from Tunisia to
the Chalcidic north, from Syria to the Bay of Naples. Were there really
enough travelling Euboeans to man all these places? On the island
itself, between c. 950 and 730, we should not think of a 'population-
explosion' or more vaguely of sudden 'over-population'. Probably we
should think of no more than a few hundred settlers at Al Mina or in
the Chalcidic peninsula or even in the first settlement on Ischia, let
alone in north Africa. This Euboean core then took non-Greek women
and reproduced. On their home island, meanwhile, there were various
settlements which we loosely class together as Euboean. They too
provided settlers besides the two main sources, Chalcis and Eretria,
on which archaeology at present concentrates. We have noted the
importance of the other Euboean coast, which looks out onto the
island of Scyros and the Aegean with an ancient Cumae nearby and
access to volcanic vineyards. Settlers from here too went west and
other Euboeans, no doubt, joined the expeditions, whether from
Eretria's eastern dependencies on the island or places like Histiaea on
its north-west coast in good grape-growing land, or Carystos on its
opposite southern extremity. There is so much more to discover on
the island if modern development allows it.

Even the best-known sites on the gulf saw changes in the years of
the Euboeans' increasing presence abroad. In the later ninth century,
c. 820 BC, Lefkandi was not abandoned, as previously thought, but it
appears to have diminished. The obvious guess is that some of its
families moved further down the coast and joined in the settlement of
what emerges as the 'new Eretria' just to the east. Meanwhile, west
up the gulf from Lefkandi, the city-state of Chalcis persisted, although
only a few of its outlying graves are accessible to modern excavations.

It is misguided to exalt one Euboean settlement here over the others, to credit only Eretria with the alphabet or to deny Chalcis a serious naval presence down the gulf.[15] The foundation-stories of Ischia show that both sites acted together before 750 BC. Afterwards, our impression is one of growing hostility which left Chalcis and her allies dominant in the west, while Eretria settled on the Chalcidic peninsula on one prong, Chalcis on another, glowering at each other in the north. Famously, these tensions led on to the 'Lelantine War', fought for Euboea's valuable Lelantine plain, its vines, its horse-pasturage and crops. Endlessly debated, the signs of this war are late eighth century, involving other warriors from distant Greek settlements, who were drawn in by contacts made by previous Euboean networks. The outright winner of the war remains uncertain, although Chalcis is perhaps the current favourite.[16]

The two leading Euboean states thus ended by fighting each other at home. Before their war ended (perhaps c. 705 BC), can we see effects of their trail from east to west in the archaeology of their own sites? The one place, so far, which can help us is the increasingly excavated site of new Eretria.[17] Just as burials at Lefkandi have shown us the eastern contacts of the previous centuries, so Eretria in the later eighth century shows a gratifyingly clear impact of the wider Euboean trail. Western objects are not so evident, except for a notable Etruscan metal belt which was acquired on Euboea, perhaps near Eretria, by a nineteenth-century Danish visitor.[18] Eastern imports and influence are much more prominent. They are visible in small seals and Oriental objects which were deposited in a sanctuary area for worship, perhaps a sanctuary of the goddess Artemis, in Eretria's main area of settlement.[19] Eastern contacts may also underlie a personal hoard of gold which resembles the bullion-hoards of metals which are found in the Levant.[20] Above all, eastern contacts are visible in inscriptions found on items of pottery which were offered at Eretria's temple of Apollo. Recently published, these inscriptions extend through the eighth century BC and concentrate in its later decades: they are proof of the diffusion of the alphabet which had arisen from a Euboean's Near Eastern contact and then spread among these Eretrians too.[21] The forms of some of the inscribed letters bring us close to the first transmission of alphabetic writing from Levantine prototypes. They even include Semitic letters inscribed on a locally made pot. As they do not make sense as a Semitic word, they may be the work of a Greek who knew the Semitic script but not the Semitic language. At Eretria we also have a pair to the 'Nestor cup' on Ischia: it is another Rhodian cup inscribed with a similar metrical statement of ownership and some fragmentary verses, also three lines in all. It alludes to a woman in its second verse, giving us a matching 'his' and 'hers', one on Euboea, one on the Euboeans' western outpost at Ischia.[22]

In the mid- to later eighth century, as the war for the Lelantine plain loomed, Eretrians had begun to erect buildings which made up a co-ordinated settlement. They had several burial grounds, one of which lay near the seashore, others in the settlement a short distance inland. Both sites contained graves with some rich grave-goods, so we cannot infer that they were socially distinct, one cemetery for the poor, the other for the rich. Eretrians also controlled the coastal plain which ran on to the east of them, including the ancient site of Amarynthos and its important temple of Artemis, a major extramural sanctuary for Eretrian worshippers.[23] On their own site they had goldsmiths and potters. They also had access to the finest known painter of the age, the craftsman whose masterpiece is the big mixing-bowl which was exported out to Kourion on Cyprus and whose favourite patterns, the grazing horses, water-birds and symbolic trees, were copied by admiring lesser craftsmen. His style was exported to Scyros and Eretria's dependent islands, to Cyprus and even to Ischia and the west: his own home is uncertain, perhaps Chalcis with clients at Eretria.[24] With the help of his painted imagery we can imagine bold 'sons of the Abantes' on Euboea with their long hair flowing Homerically on the backs of their heads. They were armed with their famous swords and spears, and mounted on their beloved horses. They wielded one of their master-painter's favourite symbols, the double-headed axes which they used when hunting or when felling trees for their houses, ships and funeral-pyres. Metal axes were even useful when trading, because they were acknowledged as items of pre-monetary value and exchange.[25] From a funeral-pyre in the settlement of new Eretria there are newly found items which evoke such people's wit and spirited existence. They are fragments of a big painted mixing-bowl for wine, a fine centrepiece for the table of an Eretrian party *c.* 760 BC.[26] On one side, the rim is decorated with a picture of a stallion mounted on a mare and ready to penetrate her. The other side has the same image, but there is another image beside it of two figures, one bigger than the other, engaged, or about to engage, in a sexual act. They may even be a man and a younger boy. At parties the host's big bowl would amuse his guests, showing horses doing it one way, while men, it seems, do it another.

These Eretrians were credited (in later texts) with control of their nearby Aegean islands, including Scyros and Andros, sites which are archaeologically part of a similar network of styles and objects in the eighth century.[27] They also founded settlements in the north, especially the important site of Methone on the coast of what was to become Macedon. We can for once date a settlement there with more confidence, because a story of its origins presupposes a date for the foundation *c.* 733–732 BC.[28] Excavation there has begun to find evidence of the first settlers, promising us invaluable glimpses of an 'Eretria overseas' with similar pottery, imports and perhaps even eighth-century inscriptions. Nearer home, Eretrians were also credited with the important foundation at Oropos, which lies across the gulf directly opposite their own site. Already in the mid-eighth century Oropos shows the establishment of a second settled area which would become increasingly a centre of houses and public buildings. For more than a thousand years Oropos and its territory were to be contested by its three strong neighbours, Eretria, Attica and Thebes.[29]

In later texts, Oropos is located in territory called 'Graia', a district which had been mentioned by Homer on this side of the Euboean Gulf and was to be located there too by the authoritative Aristotle.[30] Our increased knowledge of eighth-century Oropos has added force to an older conjecture: it aims to answer one of the great problems of Greek 'identity'. The Euboeans who first went west came from various Euboean sites, to judge from the diversity of the pottery which we can connect to them in Italy and elsewhere in the west. Were some of them men from Eretria's Graia, from the site of Oropos which was growing so significantly in the later eighth century? Pottery found at Oropos resembles early Euboean pottery which was carried out to the west; Oropians were also sometimes buried in graves covered by heaps of stones similar to those which are found among the settlers' graves on

Euboean Ischia. If men from Oropos–Graia were among the early
Greek visitors to Capua or Veii and even early Rome, we can better
understand an age-old puzzle: why Greeks were called 'Greeks' in the
Latin west. Such people told their first contacts in the Latin region
that they were 'Graikoi', that is, people from Graia. They were thus
called 'Graeci' by the people whom they met. It was not a name which
Hellenes, back at home, used ethnically of themselves. The names
'Hellenes' and 'Graikoi' may then have attracted separate support in
statements from two oracular Greek sites. The 'Hellenes' seem to have
been at home initially in Thessaly and to have been endorsed as a
wider 'Hellenic' name by Apollo's Delphic oracle.[31] The 'Graikoi'
were later located in the north-west near Zeus's ancient oracle at
Dodona, a likely point of oracular consultation by Euboeans and
'Graians' on their way further west.[32] Perhaps the great oracle at
Dodona spoke of 'Graikoi', while its rival at Delphi talked of 'Hellenes', the name which prevailed.

'I wish I was here, or I wish I was there . . .' From Potamoi Karon
to Monkey Island, such thoughts of alternative travel could flash
readily in an eighth-century Euboean's mind. The Euboean trail is a
challenge to retrace, from the 'Lefkandi era' to the late eighth century,
but having tracked it we need to pursue an uncharted dimension, the
question of what these travelling heroes carried in their minds. It is
the dimension which marks them out among travellers in this eighth-
century world.

*Lyre-player seal, showing a standing lyre player and beneath the lyre
a six-pointed star and a small bird set to the side, c. 730 BC.*

PART THREE

Travelling Myths

Following an old underground track which often narrowed down like a tunnel, we pressed on forwards. Splendid images of calcified rock surrounded us and the white walls shimmered in the light of our lantern ... A glance at our burnt-down candle, for which we had no replacement, made clear to us the danger in which we found ourselves. In fact we lost the way and if, when the burning time of the candle had only a few minutes left, Dr Miltner had not found again, by a lucky coincidence, the little entry-hole into the gorge, in all likelihood we would have remained as prey for Typhon in his gloomy, stifling cave.

Josef Keil and the great epigrapher Adolf Wilhelm (who had transferred his researches from Euboea to Cilicia) recalling their experiences in the Corycian cave in 1925, in *Monumenta Asiae Minoris Antiqua*, vol. 3 (1931), 215, translated from their German

THE VISITOR: *One group [the 'Giants'] simply grasp rocks and oak-trees with their hands and ... insist that only what admits of contact and being touched exists, because they define 'body' and 'being' as the same. If one of the others says that something without a body exists, they totally despise him and refuse to hear anything more from him.*
THEAETETUS: *You do describe dreadful people: I, too, have met quite a few of them already.*

Plato, *The Sophist*, 246A–B (c. 355–350 BC)

11

Finding Neverland

I

As we turn to these Euboeans' minds, we need to respect their physical context. On routes from the Levant to the further west they were travelling heroes in a practical way. They coped with the hazards of winds and currents and braved storms and shallows which have defeated many more solid vessels in their wake. In calm weather they rowed, with a sail only as a back-up. Homer gives us hints of what their ships might be like, holding twenty oarsmen on a single level and 'broad-beamed and black' with a single mast like the big pole, he tells us, with which Odysseus destroyed the Cyclops' only eye.[1] Unlike a warship, they could carry water and supplies for their crew, but even so they would usually avoid long distances on open seas in unpredictable weather. They crossed from island to island and on the voyage west would prefer to keep the north-west coast of the Greek mainland in view, choosing the sheltered channel on the west side of Ithaca and making use of Corcyra (Corfu), from where the open voyage across to the tip of Italy is only some 40 miles. The uses of a single sail in contrary winds were perhaps not as limited as some have assumed but for much of the time most of the pottery and durable goods we find so far from Greece was brought by human power, pulling day after day on oars.[2]

The crews had no maps and no compasses. They did not have our cardinal points, 'north' or 'east', but to judge from Homer and the poets they were partly oriented by the rising and setting of the sun, solstitial directions which vary from our true east and west. They believed the world was flat, and if they took time from a day's navigation to wonder about the bigger picture, they would think of themselves on a flat disc, surrounded by encircling Outer Ocean. Their day-to-day world-view was shaped by local landmarks, especially promontories and distinctive white cliffs, like the White Rock which they recognized on the southern tip of the heel of Italy, White Island (Leukas) across near Ithaca, the White Cliff by Kommos on south-west Crete or White Harbour, long used beside Betyllion – Ras ibn Hani on the north Levantine coast. Their pilots were the true heroes, crew-members who were often nicknamed after words for cleverness. At night, when some of our handbooks cite 'land breezes' as an aid, the pilots would know better and fear increased unpredictability, not least because the white-capped waves, a warning of storms or shoals, would be indistinguishable. 'From the night', Odysseus' crew protest, 'the fierce winds are born, the wreckers of ships.'[3] But night-travel had the advantage of an overhead orientation, the power-points of the stars.

Homer sometimes divides the night into three watches, and when Odysseus leaves Calypso's island he steers 'skilfully', looking up at 'the Pleiades, the late-setting Ploughman and the Bear which they call the Waggon'. Eighth-century seafarers did the same. On Ischia we have a fragment of a big pottery mixing-bowl which had been scratched, perhaps after being broken off, with a Greek contemporary's 'star-map'. A letter *b* (beta) seems to indicate the Ploughman (Boötes) and implies that the rest of the map included the nearby Bear.[4] Homer, unwittingly, makes a multi-cultural observation about the star. Sometimes men called it 'the Waggon', because somebody had discovered that the star's name meant 'waggon' in Semitic languages including the speech of Phoenicians. Men also called it the Bear, because its Semitic name sounded like the Greek word for 'bear' (*arktos*).[5] These two poles of understanding characterize subsequent contacts between Greeks and non-Greeks: 'bears' predominate over well-founded 'waggons'.

Greeks steered by the Great Bear whereas Phoenicians more advisedly steered by the Little Bear: if Odysseus had been a Phoenician, his course from Calypso would have been more true. No doubt our travelling Euboeans were Great Bear navigators too, but under this friendly canopy the sea was a fickle companion. In the straits, crosswinds would spring up, and between Italy and Sicily the currents changed 'twice by night and twice by day', less frequent but more dangerous than the changes in the Chalcidian Euboeans' own narrow Euripus channel at home. Everywhere lurked the fear of big hungry fish: on the straits between Scylla and Charybdis, the monstrous Scylla, Homer tells us, hunts for 'dolphins, big dog-fish and whatever monstrous fish, even bigger than them, she may catch from the thousands which deep-sounding Amphitrite feeds'.[6] On a fragment of a mixing-bowl found at Ischia, a painter has evoked a travelling Euboean's worst fears: men swim or float away as corpses beyond their ship, while one of them is disappearing head first down a 'monstrous fish'. No Greek would swim out onto the deep from a boat for pleasure. The painter shows us twenty-one fish in this one small fragment ranging from 'maneaters to little spectators'.[7]

We have no text by any of these travellers, no source for them except landscape and analogy: how best are we to imagine them in terms of those two human constants, sex and class? When Greeks later set out to found new settlements from their homeland, they did not usually take Greek women with them. At most, a priestess or two is attested in our evidence, 'distinguished mature women' in the opinion of the modern scholar who has drawn most attention to them, who would preside over women's cults of the gods in the newly founded towns.[8] In an age before organized civic settlement, a trading-boat and a little-known sea were no places for women fellow-travellers, least of all for the distinguished and mature. At Al Mina or Pithecussae the first explorers and settlers were surely men only, able to pull their weight at sea, unless they were shipping captive women to and fro as saleable slaves, like Laertes' fair Eurycleia, whom he had brought for the price of twenty oxen in the prime of youth but 'had never yet made love to in bed, for he feared the anger of his wife',[9] or the old 'Sicilian woman' of his later years. A few non-Greek women, we have suggested, came west to Pithecussae with the influx of Greeks from Cilicia and the Levant from c. 750 onwards. These particular Greeks may have had a different motive: if they were abandoning their eastern home as the Assyrians began to conquer, they may have taken their women to the west to settle a new home with them. The women were usefully skilled, too, not just in putting amulets on their young children, but in goldwork and jewellery. They were brought west partly because they would be profitable.

The social class of the male crews is less certain. A Phaeacian onlooker, notoriously, insults Homer's Odysseus as being like a 'captain of sailors who are men of business, someone who is mindful of his cargo and watches for the goods on board and grasping gain': in short, not at all like a noble athlete. The people in Homer's world who imagine themselves on a foreign voyage for trade are usually simple people, too. Rude Melanthius, driving a herd of goats, taunts the unrecognized Odysseus, back home at last on Ithaca, and threatens to abduct his faithful swineherd Eumaeus and 'take him one day on a black-benched ship far from Ithaca [and sell him] so that he may earn me a good livelihood'.[10] Trading, therefore, was not beyond a herdsman's expectations: we can also cite the poet Hesiod's father in real life, who 'would sail in ships, lacking a noble livelihood', and was forced by poverty to make the long sea-journey to a new home in mainland Greece.[11] However, most of these humbler people would be bound by obligation to their social superiors at home. Ideals about ignoble trade were all very fine, but noblemen would be best able to provide sea-traders with a big enough boat for their bigger voyages. Long-distance trading was more adventurous than local cabotage. It shaded over into heroic raiding and fighting and so the younger sons of a nobleman, perhaps a nobleman too, might lead an expedition abroad in uncertain pursuit of gain. There was a practical reason, too, for a nobleman's presence. If the crews were his social dependants and went off unsupervised, there was the risk of their fraud and desertion as soon as they passed beyond well-known points of call. The question remains disputed without enough evidence yet to settle it, but on long-distance ventures to the east or the west a nobleman's presence is readily imaginable.[12] When Greeks sent out settlers to Cumae or to sites in Sicily from c. 740 to 710 BC, people with noble names like Hippocles or Crataimenes were chosen to lead these ventures. They are unlikely to have been novices in the long sea-voyages which were then required of them.

Other companions, at least, are certain. With the travellers went a sense of the gods and semi-divine heroes, 'evident helpers' whose

1. Face reconstruction of the skull found in the mound at Gordion, tentatively identified as Gordios, father of King Midas, and dated to the early eighth century BC.

2. Ivory Sphinx of Phoenician workmanship, eighth century BC.

3. The Garden Mound at Khorsabad, recalling the Amanus Mountains. Drawing of a bas-relief of the late eighth century BC.

4. The flight of King Luli of Tyre from the Assyrians in 701 BC. Drawing from a relief fragment from the palace of Sennacherib in Nineveh.

5. Silver-gilt Cypro-Phoenician bowl found in Praeneste, Italy, early seventh century BC.

6. Idaean cave on Crete, before the recent excavations.

7. Horses decorating the lid of an Attic geometric jar, or pyxis, eighth century BC.

8. Attic cup depicting riders on horseback, eighth century BC.

9. Ostrich-egg with incised ornaments and birds, from Montaldo di Castro, Italy, *c.* 650 BC.

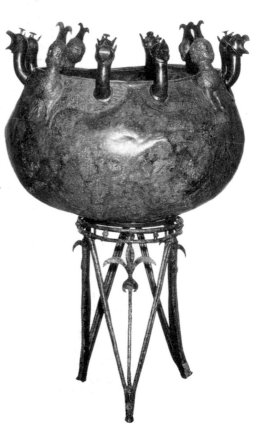

10. Bronze cauldron with griffins and sirens on an iron tripod, from a tomb in Salamis, Cyprus, late eighth century BC.

11. A statue of Herakles–Melkart, found in Idalion, Cyprus, 490–470 BC.

12. Daedalus the craftsman working on a wing. Cornelian ringstone, probably third century BC.

13. The hero Mopsus hunting a wild boar, shown on right. Silver drachma of Aspendos, Pamphylia, *c.* 400–360 BC.

14. Perseus rescuing Andromeda from the sea-monster (Ketos). Corinthian amphora, first half of the sixth century BC.

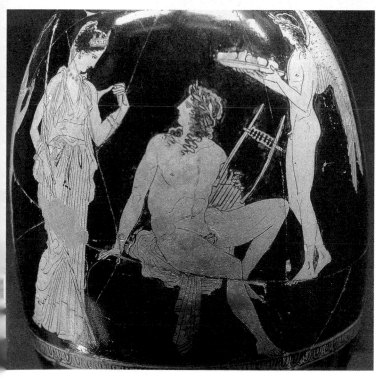

15. Aphrodite and Adonis attended by Eros. Attic red-figure squat lekythos, *c.* 410 BC.

16. Storm God from Karatepe. Basalt sculpture, *c.* 700 BC.

presence is rooted in Homer and Hesiod and in the art, inscriptions and votive monuments of subsequent centuries. They seemed to be 'manifest', above all, at moments of crisis, never more so than in storms or perils at sea, forerunners of the Christian saints of seafaring, like St Nicolas of Bari, on these same routes from Greece to Italy or Syria. The goddess Hera has been suggested as one particularly important Euboean companion, on the grounds of her later cults on Euboea, a possible cult on Ischia (only an archaeologist's guess) and her cult, eventually, at Cumae in Italy. She could protect seafarers, but the most relevant god was Poseidon, the god of the sea and of horses too, who thus united two of our Euboeans' skills. When Euboeans located the place name 'Posideion' on many sites, from northern Greece to the Bay of Issus, the places would have altars to Poseidon, landmarks by which successive travellers would steer.

With the gods and semi-divine heroes there also travelled a mental cargo, the baggage of stories (*muthoi*) which we categorize imposingly as 'myth'. They were not yet known through Greek pictures or sculptures and, despite the recent invention of the Greek alphabet, many were not yet known through texts, either. They were known orally, in the many contexts in which stories of gods and heroes circulated. One such context was religious, although cults for the gods did not require the telling of *muthoi*. The essence of worship was an offering, often an animal, and an accompanying prayer, but stories of the gods and heroes attached to these rites, if only to 'explain' what was being done, albeit for quite other reasons. On public occasions choirs of young men and girls might sing a hymn to the god of the moment, an orally learned composition which included stories, *muthoi*, of the god's exploits. There were also the social occasions, the festivals or drinking-parties, where oral poets, even the young Homer, would recite on demand a portion of their vast heroic repertoire. There was also much storytelling in families, by the old or by nurses to the young, or in public at times of leisure when the men, at least, would gather in their community's public *leschē*, a place for talk and socializing. The *leschē* was a matter of concern to Hesiod when warning his brother against idleness in their Boeotian village community.[13]

There is no such thing as a private myth, but these various contexts meant that stories of the gods were widely shared, especially the hymns or the stories attached to rituals, making them into 'traditional' tales which would pass on orally to the next generation. So, stories became myths, varying locally from one community to another, coalescing into clusters or cycles which poets would elaborate, but never becoming entirely fixed or canonical. As a result, poets, artists and others could retell their outlines and patterns in different ways. Travelling Euboeans would certainly know such stories, and as they travelled east and west there were long hours to kill, at night, in hostile weather and even on board ship. From shipwrecks off west Italy in c. 600 BC, dice survive, one way for sailors to pass their time. There were also musical instruments. It was with seafarers in the early eighth century BC that one such instrument, of Syrian-Levantine design, travelled west to Italy and ended up buried under a woman's elbow in a grave in the territory of the future city of Sybaris.[14] On their travels Euboeans would sing and make music and among their songs would be *muthoi*, or stories, of the gods and heroes.

During their first phase in the west c. 800–740, stories of mythical heroes were not already sited at points on the coasts of Italy or Sicily. It was only later that such stories became located there, as if mythical heroes had been driven westwards or fled from Asia while leaving the sack of Troy. Aeneas is only the most famous of such legendary travellers: mythical Diomede and Philoctetes later received new addresses in the west, as did the humble Epeios, who was said to have settled in south Italy with the very toolkit with which he built the Trojan Horse.[15] These legendary travellers were not a dim reflection of real history, when Greeks had been in the west during the distant Mycenaean age (c. 1350–1180 BC). The legends only became sited in the west much later so as to attach western communities (including, eventually, Rome) to a prestigious ancestry in the Greeks' mythical past. From the 730s onwards other Greek settlements in the west were maintaining festivals, cults and historical memories of the people who had been their real Greek founders. For those who did not have such memories, mythical founders were a neat alternative. They were a claim to an origin which could not be refuted: it gave their communities an even older connection with the Greek world.[16] In due course, we know of such Greek legendary travellers above all on Cyprus. The mythical Teucer was credited with founding Salamis on the island;

the Arcadian hero Agapenor was claimed by Paphos in the south-west; the citizens of Kourion on the south coast even claimed to be the 'offspring of Perseus', the supreme wanderer among noble heroes from Argos.[17] Euboeans visited these places from the tenth century onwards, but there is no evidence that any of these legendary heroes were already being claimed by kingdoms on the island, although Greek settlers had arrived there in significant numbers since c. 1125–1075. Stories of the legendary heroes' arrival were probably exploited by the epic poem the *Cypria*, which was not composed before the late eighth century BC and is known to us only in outline. They were then maintained by the separate little Greek-speaking kingdoms on the island as part of their mutual rivalries. As in the west, they had not been current when Euboeans first arrived in the east.

There was, however, one hero who was already located on the north-west edge of the established Greek world: Odysseus, king of Ithaca, the Greek outpost on the edge of the Adriatic sea. When Greeks set out for the west in the early eighth century BC, hugging the coastline of north-west Greece and picking their way through the Ionian islands, might they not have thought of him, king of the very Ithaca which lay on their route? Homer's *Odyssey* does not need to have existed for Odysseus to have been on their minds. Odysseus' connection with Ithaca was pre-Homeric and tales of him would have been known before Homer shaped his epic. Unfortunately, no literary evidence survives to ascribe this interest to westward-bound Euboeans in the early eighth century or later. On Ithaca's western coast we have something else, a variety of iron tripods set in a seaside cave at Polis Bay, which was associated with Odysseus in later centuries.[18] We need to be cautious, however, before linking them to Odysseus and early Greek travellers up and down the coast. Some of these tripods were made as early as c. 850 BC and if they were placed in the cave then, they were meant as dedications to a god or hero: Odysseus was perhaps not yet such a one. As Odysseus is connected with this cave only by a votive inscription which dates to the second century BC, people on Ithaca c. 800 may have been dedicating tripods here to another divinity. We do not even know who the dedicators of these tripods were, let alone that they had come up from other parts of the southern or eastern Greek world and had been preparing for sea-journeys to the wilder shores beyond. Homer does not help us, either. When his Odysseus returns home, he is said to deposit a treasure of tripods for safe keeping in an Ithacan cave (not, however, the one on Polis Bay). Perhaps Homer had heard that such objects were being dedicated locally on Ithaca and so he filled out his story with this transposed local detail. He, too, does not connect it with foreign sailors who were travelling on past Ithaca to the further west.[19]

The *Odyssey* itself gives no hint that Odysseus had or would become a role-model for Greek contemporaries as they travelled beyond Ithaca to Corcyra and across to Italy. Instead, the geography of its mythical plot shows very well how myths, *muthoi*, varied in their relation to real places. When the mythical Greek heroes sailed back from Troy, Homer shows them opting for itineraries which ran exactly, and correctly, from Chios back to Euboea. When Odysseus returns to Ithaca Homer describes briefly the position of the island, its features and neighbours. He is precise, and (in my view) often accurate, defying the continuing modern attempts to locate the places which he names on an Ionian island other than modern Ithaki. We have the impression of reality here, but not always the fact.[20] In his earlier wanderings, Odysseus passes out of the world of fact altogether into a memorable world of fantasy. His tales of the Cyclops and the Lotus-Eaters, the maneating Laestrygonians or the idyllic Phaeacians cannot be fixed in space. They belong in 'neverland'.

The urge, after Homer, was to fix as many Homeric items as possible at sites in the real world, and as part of the process 'neverland' became located too. The happy Phaeacians came to be sited on Corcyra; monstrous Scylla and Charybdis were placed on the dangerous Straits of Messina between Sicily and Italy; Aeolus, king of the winds, came to rest on the Lipari islands; the Laestrygonians acquired an address near Sicilian Leontini; the Sirens were sited on islands off modern Sorrento. The luxurious Baiae near Naples was even linked to a supposed steersman in Odysseus' crew, the non-Homeric 'Baios'. Circe found a home on 'Monte Circeo' midway between Rome and Cumae, although the *Odyssey* seemed to have placed her very far away, in the east.[21] The beginning of these attempts to locate Homeric items in the west is still very hard for us to date. Near the end of our texts of Hesiod's *Theogony* (the main poem dates from *c.* 710), two verses mention children whom Circe bore to patient Odysseus: Agrios ('Wild Man') and Latinos who 'ruled over the glorious Tyrrhenians [the Etruscans] very far away in a corner of the holy islands'. Here, Circe, Odysseus and their kin are sited on the western coast of Italy. Increasingly, historians have been tempted to give these verses an early date, but on stylistic grounds literary scholars judge them, rightly, to be additions to Hesiod's poem.[22] At best they may be early additions, perhaps c. 680–650, when a Greek might still refer to the Latin and Etruscan peoples rather vaguely as living inland, 'where the wild things are'. Agrios is a generic 'wild man', not a precise reference to, say, Faunus, the subject of Roman cult or myth.[23] Homer had said nothing about a pregnancy for Circe or any children by Odysseus. These fictional kin were invented later and brought peoples beyond the Greeks' western settlements into the explanatory orbit of Homeric myths.

Can we, nonetheless, take other specific locations of Homeric myth back to an earlier date? Significantly, Hesiod himself does not yet locate Scylla or Charybdis on the western seas. However, knowledge of Greek heroic poetry travelled early to the west and was not confined to the aristocracy: the proof lies in those verses which refer to 'Nestor's cup', inscribed c. 750 BC on that humble cup in the child's grave at Ischia c. 730. If people in the west were well aware of Homer, surely they would want to locate some of his spellbinding stories in the 'new world' which they had found? In due course, most of the Homeric stories came to be placed on the east coast of Sicily or up by the Bay of Naples, along the very routes taken by Euboeans who travelled there from c. 800–780 BC onwards. The problem is still how to date these myths' arrival there. Certainly Euboeans reached the west before the myths did, for although we cannot date the *Odyssey* with confidence, a date c. 760 is about as high as most scholars would readily accept for it: in the poem, the stories which duly came to be located in the west are not yet sited outside neverland. Did they perhaps come west with a second generation of Euboean travellers, after the *Odyssey* existed? Again, the problem is that Greeks continued to settle and travel on these routes in later centuries and some of the Homeric locations along them are known to have been made subsequently. The placing of 'Circeii' south of Rome implied that Circe's elusive home

Aeaea had been discovered. But this association began at the earliest in the later sixth century BC. The Etruscan king Tarquin the Proud (c. 534–510) was credited with the settlement and in due course the very 'cup' of Odysseus was shown at the site.[24] It was all a post-Homeric invention, long after our pioneering Euboean age. We cannot as yet point to other Homeric stories which travelled for certain in the earlier Euboean company and found a new home in the eighth century.

In principle, nonetheless, stories of the great legendary heroes might have found new addresses so early: we can see from other examples that stories about them were already moving around freely at that time. In Homer's *Odyssey*, we can detect that the poet has connected Odysseus with stories which others had linked to the travels of Jason and the Argonauts.[25] Outside Homer, conversely, Jason was brought over to the island of Lemnos and linked there with the myth of one of its local cults.[26] For Homer and his predecessors, stories were already movable counters on a poet's board. The changing social contexts of the eighth century were also causing stories to be re-sited. As the *poleis* or city-states of early Greece became more established, their ruling classes and the poets whom they patronized filled in their territory's missing past. This filling in is most evident to us at Corinth, perhaps already by c. 700 BC. In the *Iliad*, Homer refers to an unidentified place called 'Ephyrē' near Argos. Corinth then claimed to be the very place in question and also claimed stories to fill in the void. The sun-god and Poseidon the sea-god were said to have competed for supremacy over its land. Mythical Medea was said to have visited it, as was Nestor's brother.[27] Like *polis* territories, the family trees of local aristocracies also moved stories around: they became enriched by re-sited myths, as we know best from poems of the sixth century BC. The most spectacular enhancement occurred at Argos. Kinsmen with Oriental names were added into the family line of the mythical Argive hero Inachus and his sons, reflecting a greater Greek awareness of an eastern world, like the Orientalizing imports into Argos which are known to us archaeologically in the later eighth century.[28]

It is in this general context of mobile stories that the locations of 'neverland' belong. As people travelled or settled, they fixed mythical places and stories which had begun by being outside space and time.

They were not always being arbitrary. Nowadays we find 'paradise' more feebly with the help of advertisers, whether in Bali or the Seychelles, but the Greeks located their myths with the help of evidence. Their findings did not depend on wide learning, although educated writers later made much of them. Simple, practical men contributed too. We can best see how they contributed if we look briefly at the legacy of travellers in a later period, Macedonian Greek and Roman soldiers who also visited unfamiliar lands from *c.* 330 BC onwards. Writers embellished the stories they told, but underneath lay the reasoning of plain blunt men who were convinced they had found what had hitherto been floating in their minds. These travelling Macedonians and Romans show what was possible. Then we can look for more of the same in the earlier age when our evidence is so much scarcer, the age of travelling Euboeans, bright sparks of the 'Dark Ages' with stories, but no texts, as their companions.

II

A *muthos*, or story, is transferred most directly between two cultures when it is heard and translated in detail. It travels more obliquely when it is partially heard or misunderstood. It leaves a mark, often a distorted one, when items in it are seen, but not heard. This sliding scale of hearing, mis-hearing and seeing will be crucial for the thinking of the travelling Euboeans: we can establish its existence from excellent later evidence and then look for it more confidently in their world.

The most fertile sources for it are Alexander the Great, his historians and soldiers, who were travelling eastwards some four hundred years later, but also through cultures and languages unknown to the Greeks. It is Alexander's own 'master of ceremonies', the Greek Chares of Mitylene, who gives us our best example of a travelling myth. Unfortunately his history book is only known in a few later quotations by other authors, but one of them credits him with telling a remarkable romantic tale which was current among 'the Persians'.[29] One of two brothers, Zariadres, had loved a distant lady, the 'most beautiful woman in Asia'. He was the son of divine parents and, across a great distance, the two of them dreamed of each other as lovers do, she being 'sleepless in Scythia'. Her father then ordered her to pick a bridegroom at a festival to be held for the purpose, but Zariadres arrived just in time and the two of them rode off on his horse, last-minute lovers with a happy future. The story, so Chares tells us, was painted in many Iranians' private houses and in temples too. It is our best insight into the cultural life of Iranians in the fourth century BC, better than anything yet found by archaeologists.

Chares was very well placed to know, being the 'master of ceremonies' at a court which included many Iranians, Alexander's new friends. Evidently he was bilingual, because the story can be followed into later Iranian legend as the tale of valiant 'Zarir' in the Persian romantic epic the *Shahnameh* of Firdausi (tenth century AD): it has roots, too, in the storytelling of the intervening Sassanian age (*c.* AD 240–636).[30] We can thus picture Persians, contemporaries with Alexander, holding parties in their houses and drinking and listening to the songs of their invited expert storytellers who would enchant them with the loves of valiant Zarir while pointing to pictures of the story on the walls of their host's house. In return, we learn, Persians would sometimes name their daughters after its heroine.

Chares had a privileged position at court and a linguistic gift which befitted it, but even so he retold the story in Greek terms: 'Zariadres' is a Greek version of Zarir's name; he is said to be the son of Aphrodite and Adonis, two divine Greek figures of love and romance; the 'most beautiful woman in Asia' was an ever-expanding category for Greeks who were happily away from Greek women, and two members of it were to be lovers of Alexander the Great.[31]

No eighth-century Euboean would find himself as the privileged court butler of a Near Eastern king. Their contacts would be less formal and so language would be more of a problem. Here, too, Alexander and his soldiers illustrate the possibilities. Famously, his expedition located the mythical cave of Prometheus in the Hindu Kush, thinking that these mountains were the distant Caucasus. The 'locals' contributed, reportedly showing the cave on a high mountain-crag and the 'lair of the mythical eagle', which pecked at Prometheus' liver, and the very 'marks of his chains'.[32] In Armenia, above all, two of Alexander's officers, Thessalian Greeks, visited and reported on monuments called 'Jasonia', erected, they discovered, in honour of the Greek hero Jason. The monuments were one of several proofs that the Armenians were descendants of a Thessalian like themselves, 'Armenos', the follower of Jason. The Armenians wore cloaks and clasps like Thessalians and used similar horse-bits and saddles. Plainly they were Jason's kin.[33]

Each of these spectacular fantasies rested on local verbal evidence. The old Persian name for the region of the Hindu Kush meant 'higher than the eagles': eagles were visible, as they still are, and there was a typical confusion of the geography, causing this mountain to be seen as part of the Caucasus mountains far to the west.[34] It was in the Caucasus, previously, that Greek myths had located the eagle and Prometheus' rock. The Jason memorials have been brilliantly explained by the local word for the holy places sited on hilltops, what western Iranians called *ayezana*. To imaginative Greek ears these *ay-ez-ana* sounded just like 'Jasonia', especially when so much else in Armenia appeared to derive from Jason's visit. A Jason memorial was even located out east in what is now Tajikistan: here, too, a local *ayezana* presumably underlay it.[35]

The roots of these discoveries are important for what we, too, need to find in the eighth century BC. The historians who recorded them tend to involve local non-Greek informants, so much so that their role becomes a pattern when such a story is written up. 'The Indians say ...', or 'the people of that country say ...', yet sometimes they can have said nothing of the sort. Alexander's friend and admiral Nearchus recorded that Alexander's march into the dreaded Gedrosian desert in south-east Iran in late 325 BC was partly motivated by his rivalry with 'Queen Semiramis' and her march into this same region. The locals, he wrote, told of her exploit, but they cannot have said such a thing: Semiramis was an invention of Greek legend only, and none of the 'locals' near this remote Makran desert knew Greek.[36] At best, they had been misunderstood through a chain of interpreters in answer to questions posed by Greeks. 'A Greek inquirer in a foreign land', concluded their acute modern scholar Elias Bickerman, 'did not feel himself bound by the question of what his informant actually meant.' Not until Julius Caesar, he pointed out, do we find a classical author not just 'quoting the indigenous tradition respecting the origins of a people but . . . accepting it by virtue of its being an indigenous account'.[37]

For the mind-set of our Euboeans in the eighth century, Alexander's locations of the god Dionysus are particularly suggestive. Before his march to India, no Greek is known to have connected Dionysus with that distant land. Dionysus was imagined to have come from the east to the Greeks, but only because an 'eastern' origin fitted best with the god's luxury and his effeminate style. As the god of intoxication and altered states, he was represented as a foreign outsider, effete and Oriental. This floating legend then became fixed at points on the Greeks' eastern horizon. In Lydia, near to the Aegean, they met the Lydian personal name 'Bakivas', which sounded to them like 'Bacchios', Dionysus' name, and which they translated as 'Dionysicles'. It was one reason for siting the childhood of their Dionysus on Lydia's snow-capped Mount Tmolos; another was that vines, Dionysus' plants, grew on its lower slopes.[38] As Lydia became too familiar, Greeks looked even further afield for their god's starting point. By the late fifth century Dionysus was said to have come westwards from Bactra, out near the River Oxus at modern Balkh in Afghanistan. But was Bactra his point of origin?

There was good reason for Alexander and his officers to carry this Bactrian location in their minds: it featured memorably in words ascribed to the god himself in the prologue of Euripides' *Bacchae*, the very play which the poet had composed while staying in Macedon near the end of his life.[39] In the theatre below their royal palace at Aigai-Vergina, Macedonians had heard of Dionysus' eastern stopping-points. Perhaps Alexander and his officers had learned the play or even acted it in their youth. The notion stayed with them and out in the field they then found new evidence.

Beyond the Jaxartes river, the Syr Darya, in modern Tajikistan, Alexander's men invaded lands to the north of Euripides' furthest site for the god. Across the river they made two odd discoveries, stones which they understood to be the very 'boundary-stones' of Dionysus, and ivy, Dionysus' plant, which was growing on the tree-trunks. The stones' local purpose is unknown to us (perhaps they marked local leaders' burials) but the ivy was a clue to their interpretation.[40] For months and for miles the soldiers had not seen ivy and so they explained its reappearance by the presence of their Dionysus. The far bank of the Jaxartes was the scene of an inconclusive march by Alexander on which he fell sick and had to turn back: did poets and flatterers in his circle begin the story about Dionysus' presence in order to dignify the unhappy episode? It began, however, in a broader context of misunderstanding. Fir-trees were also visible locally, the first to be seen in the east, and the surveyors with Alexander 'inferred' that they were therefore on the borders of Asia and Europe, the ivy and fir's familiar home. If central Asia was Europe, surely Dionysus could belong there too, at the point from which he had come south to Bactra and joined Euripides' route for him? No local story is said to have helped with this conclusion, and if it began as flattery it was flattery in the context of a major geographical muddle.

Within two years Alexander's army was invading India, splitting into two to conquer the Swat Highlands east of the Kunar river and north of the Kabul river. It was here that they heard of an exciting 'Mount Meros', towering above a settlement which seemed to be called 'Nysa', the very name of Dionysus' mythical Greek home in childhood. Plainly they had half-understood these names from the replies of local people whom they questioned through interpreters: in the Greeks' own tradition, Nysa was a mountain but it was never a city.[41] Indians had also mentioned their own legendary Mount 'Meru', which Greeks understood as 'Mēros', the Greek word for a thigh: it was from the thigh of Zeus that Dionysus was said to have been born, so the implications were exciting. According to one of Alexander's historians, the place's connection with Dionysus was even explained by one of the local envoys, but his 'speech' to Alexander is only a historian's way of improving the story: in real life the envoy knew no Greek.[42] The local botany was more relevant. On 'Mount Meros', Alexander went up with his cavalry and here too found ivy in abundance, the yellow-berried Himalayan ivy which is still visible in this part of Nuristan. There were laurels and box-trees and there were also vines, another of Dionysus' plants; there were thickets fit for hunting, like the sacred groves of a Greek god. There were not, it seems, ripe grapes when Alexander visited, but his companions wreathed their heads with ivy, just as boys in the Nuristan villages still wreath themselves with trailing vine-leaves and long green stems of ivy. They even sang hymns on the hillside to the god Dionysus and called on him by his cultic names. Then there was a sacrifice and a feast in the god's honour: some said that there were Macedonians who became seized by Dionysiac frenzy, running wild after calling on the god. No doubt there was more than enough to drink.

How much of it all did Alexander believe? Three centuries later, the sceptical geographer Strabo thought Alexander had been filled with mad vanity at his successes and had not been duly critical. But the visit had a context: the mental baggage of the lines from Euripides' *Bacchae*, the previous sightings of ivy beyond the Jaxartes, the will to believe that the army was now treading in and beyond the sites of the god. The belief would encourage the troops, but it was not adopted only for that reason.[43] There was local evidence, a pre-existing context and some apparent support in what the locals seemed to be saying. For Alexander, the case was strong enough.

For Euboeans in the age of Homer there would often be as little proof, not more. For one rational mind, two millennia later, no more was needed. In the 1890s, up in the same Kunar valley, Sir Thomas Holdich helped to survey for Britain the boundaries of India and north-east Afghanistan. Two separate native sources, in two different places, told the British map-makers of a place named 'Nusa' or 'Nysa', locating it just to the south of a three-peaked hill called Koh-i-nor, 'whose outlines', Holdich reminds us, 'can be clearly distinguished from Peshawar on any clear day'. Wild vines and ivy grew on this hill, just as they grow on the west bank of the Kunar river where Holdich was 'astonished at the free growth of the wild vine and the thick masses of ivy which . . . clung to the buttresses of the rugged mountain-spurs as ivy clings to less solid ruins in England'.[44]

Like Alexander, Sir Thomas had hit on a truly Dionysiac flora and an evocative place name from local informants. He then capped them both by hitting on a local Dionysiac hymn. Two Kafirs from the Kunar valley 'submitted gracefully enough to much cross-examination and . . . sang a war-hymn to their god . . . and executed a religious dance'. Their words had to pass through two interpreters, but they confirmed that the hymn began most remarkably: 'O, thou who from Gir-Nysa's lofty heights was born . . .', an 'obvious reference', thought Holdich, to the 'mountain of Bacchus, the Meros from which he was born on the slopes of which stood the ancient Nysa'. For Holdich, the entire verse was a 'Bacchic hymn, slightly incoherent perhaps as is natural ... it only wants the accessories of vine-leaves and ivy to make it entirely classical'. It did not want them for long. West of the Kunar, Sir Thomas was offered the local wine, as Alexander perhaps had been offered wine there from a previous year's harvest. 'It is not of a high class,' he concluded. 'It reminded me of badly corked and muddied Chablis which it much resembled in appearance.'[45]

III

Alexander and Sir Thomas arrived in the region with unlocated baggage, for one the eastern travels of the god Dionysus, for the other the unsited exploits of Alexander himself. What they heard was supported by what they saw, encouraging them to 'find' stories which had long been important in their minds. The more the seeing and the less the hearing, the more imaginative the conclusions would become. We can follow them through three particular items: women on horseback, sculpted monuments and extraordinarily big bones.

A year before Alexander's death, about a hundred women rode into his camp near Babylon, armed and mounted on horseback.[46] They had been recruited in western Iran, but Greek women never rode and the soldiers could only make sense of them as Amazons, the mounted females of Greek myth. Nobody was encouraging this notion out of flattery or in order to make the troops march on. It was a spontaneous 'camp myth': word even spread that the women were exposing one of their breasts, but Alexander sent them away before his soldiers could molest them and find out. In Macedonian minds, before their arrival, the Amazons of myth were still hovering in a homeland yet to be discovered. They were widely believed to live near the Black Sea where their weapons, but not their persons, had been discovered by Greek visitors. Only with Pompey's campaigns in the area, in the 60s BC, did historians on his staff at last run them to ground, beside the marshy Thermodon river whose lower course was such a fine breeding-ground for horses, the Amazons' mounts.[47] Without this local information Alexander's soldiers had interpreted what they saw because of what they believed.

It was at ancient monuments, above all, that local details and Greek misunderstandings were particularly likely to combine. We can see this combination best in autumn 333 BC while Alexander's army was delaying in southern Asia Minor on the coast of Cilicia. While they waited, some of them encountered a big sculpted relief of the Assyrian period, the one which actually showed the Assyrian king Sennacherib's victory here in the campaigns of 696 BC. Callisthenes, kinsman of Aristotle, was one of the officers in camp who described what the monument signified. In his view it showed 'Sardanapalus', who was snapping the fingers of his right hand. It was inscribed with foreign signs which said that Sardanapalus built the nearby cities of Anchialus and Tarsus in one day: 'eat, drink and make love, for other things are not worth this' (the flick of the royal fingers).[48]

This reading by a highly educated man was a brilliant web of error and misunderstanding. Sardanapalus was an existing Greek fiction, a 'king' of ancient Assyria who was a legend in Greek for Oriental luxury and hedonism: no such king had existed in Assyrian history. An Assyrian king, Sennacherib, had indeed rebuilt Anchialus and Tarsus (he called them 'Ingira' and 'Tarzu'): about the rebuilding, at least, Callisthenes had picked up local information surviving across the centuries, although the two cities were not rebuilt in one fantastic day. He had also looked at the monument's details. On Assyrian monuments, the gesture of snapping the fingers of one hand is indeed attested, but it was meant as a gesture of prayer to the gods. The Greeks took it in our sense, as a gesture of indifference, 'not worth so much as this'. The relief which the learned Callisthenes saw is now lost to us, but other surviving Assyrian reliefs depict symbols of the gods above the sculpted ruler. They are uncaptioned, and to outside eyes the symbols resemble cups and plates and even male and female sexual parts.[49] 'Eat, drink and have sex' (or in polite versions, 'have fun') was already a sentiment of Greek popular poetry: we have recently found a text of this saying inscribed in Greek in western Asia c. 400–370 BC, before Alexander's march.[50] His historians looked at the incomprehensible wedge-shaped script and read it as supporting what they already believed.

Among the multi-cultural clamour, the strange monuments and objects of the Near East, Euboean travellers had been ripe for similar misunderstandings in the eighth century BC. There was another dimension: the animal kingdom, ancient and modern. It too was to impress Euboeans and encourage them to brilliant misinterpretation: the best evidence for its possibilities is somewhat later than Alexander. Already in the eighth century Euboean travellers had visited the coast of north Africa and the islands which they named in Greek off the coast of Tunisia. Inland lay landscapes of exceptional curiosity, half-known but never tamed, in which 'neverland' and its items might plausibly be uncovered. From *c.* 630 BC onwards Greeks also settled in Libya further east and sited some of the labours of a great and reassuring predecessor in the adjoining deserts. Heracles, their stories said, had wrestled with the giant Antaeus, the enemy of strangers and travellers: he had defeated him, and where better to locate this important victory over terror than in the north African deserts, potentially so hostile beyond the Greeks' cities?[51] Tamed by Heracles, Antaeus decomposed: in the 80s BC the remains of his body were unearthed by subsequent visitors, including Romans.

When the Roman commander Sertorius crossed from Spain into north Africa he was told by residents of Tingis (modern Tangier) that they knew the very site of Antaeus' long-lost grave. The elements for a fertile discovery were all present: information from non-Greek, non-Roman locals; famous Greek stories in the visitors' minds; scope for confirmation, even, by research. Following this lead, Sertorius had a designated grave-mound dug open and inside he found a skeleton 60 feet long, obviously the relic of a giant. In amazement he closed up his dig, made offerings and 'helped to magnify the tomb's reputation'.[52] His magnifying did not stop a subsequent dispute. Some of our sources, perhaps correctly, placed the actual find on the west coast of Morocco near Lixus. Others made Tingis the site both of the grave and the initial information. The 'Tingis version' gained a powerful, but not conclusive, champion, the learned king Juba (*c.* 47 BC–AD 23), husband of the daughter of Antony and Cleopatra. Juba traced his own ancestry back to a 'marriage' between Heracles and the wife of Antaeus, a lady called Tinga (the first known Tangerine).[53] Perhaps this ancestry inclined him to favour Tingis's role in the story.

Impressive though this find of a giant seems, it had been excelled some twenty years earlier. The Argive hero Perseus, the myths said, had confronted a fearsome Gorgon and in due course this encounter too became sited by antiquarians in the trackless deserts of north Africa. During their hard war in north Africa against the Numidian Jugurtha, troops with the Roman commander Marius are said to have met an amazing creature alive and hissing in the African dunes. They saw a Gorgon trotting towards them, though 'at first they thought it was a wild sheep because its head was bent low and it moved slowly'.[54] After a skirmish they ambushed it and their accompanying African cavalrymen shot it dead. The authority for this neglected story is a Greek, Alexander of Myndus, who wrote with knowledge on the local birds of Libya. He was prone to flights of wild fancy, but his tale of the Gorgon had some foundation: the troops flayed the animal and took its skin back to Marius in camp where the other soldiers supported its identification. According to Alexander of Myndus, the local Libyans contributed here too: they explained that they called this sort of animal the 'downward-looker', because of the way it held its head.

There was evidence, then, behind this Gorgon's sighting, the evidence of an actual animal killed in the desert: perhaps it was a mouflon, a variety of sheep with curly horns. But there was evidence, too, behind the discovery of Antaeus' skeleton. Sertorius was not fantasizing, nor were the locals in Africa who had buried the giant, they said, and enabled the Romans to locate very big bones indeed. Whatever were they? We now realize through recent researches that they were unrecognized bits of an extinct species, one of those 'Neogene elephants, early African mammoths and giant giraffids' which we, too, discover in Morocco's prehistoric soil.[55]

All around the Greek world, bones of the dinosaurs caused items from mythical 'neverland' to be discovered on the ground.[56] When found in quantity they established the sites of great battles in mythical stories. On the island of Samos, long before Sertorius' lifetime, huge bones were discovered in an area of topsoil whose colouring, too, was significant. It was so red that the place was named 'Panaima' ('Utterly Bloody') and explained as the site of a bitter ancient battle. So big were the bones that the fighters must have been the biggest of combatants, nothing less than war-elephants. In myths, the god Dionysus was said to have brought elephants to a battle against the Amazons. This story can only have blossomed after Alexander the Great's exploits had linked Dionysus with India, the supreme land of the war-elephant. On Samos, 'Panaima' and its bloodstains can still be located, on a plateau near the site of Mytilini whose 'unique red surface contrasts starkly with the surrounding hills of white sediment, containing masses of chalk-white bones'.[57] In the light of Alexander's exploits, Greeks looked down here and made sense of what they saw, big bones and blood-red topsoil which became intelligible through myth.

Five hundred years or so before these inferences were made, Euboeans had been in the east and the west, witnessing old monuments, strange places and even big bones. They too related them to stories which were already in their minds. These stories were Greek *muthoi,* or myths, many of which had formed during the illiterate 'Dark Ages'. There were also *muthoi* in the Near Eastern cultures which Euboeans encountered: there was scope for them to amplify or redirect the stories which Greeks brought with them. The study of Near Eastern 'influence' on Greek myths has been thoroughly pursued by modern scholars, most massively through lists of apparent 'parallels' between texts of the stories in Near Eastern languages and our Greek texts, whether or not a transfer from one culture to the other occurred in each particular case. Such study has been mostly concerned with early Greek poetry, not with actual Greeks and particular places: these points of contact have been left more open. Can we connect Euboeans directly or indirectly with such contacts? They had unusual scope for them. Within some twenty years of settling in the Near East at Al Mina, Euboeans and their kinsmen had travelled west to settle on Ischia. As we have seen, they found themselves in another populous world which was also, to their eyes, an unknown and uncharted wonder. With them on their travels went their gods and heroes and as they settled far from home they set up new local cults in their honour. These settlements in the west then endured as Greek settlements on the map, and from later local evidence we can sometimes work back to cults and heroes which the Euboean settlers may have brought with them to such places. The goddess Hera, Orion the hunter, the giant Briareus are among those who have been proposed, with varying degrees of uncertainty.[58]

These transfers from a home on Euboea to a new western settlement are not exceptional, because so many colonists and settlers throughout Greek history did much the same, bringing cults and heroes from their mother-cities to their new homes. However, Euboean travellers were special: they spanned not one world but three, their own home culture, the triangle round Cyprus, Cilicia and the Levant, and the west as far as the Bay of Naples. No Roman or Macedonian soldier ever found one and the same myth at either end of his world, but these Euboeans could have done so, finding an apparently familiar story among the stories and objects of their Near Eastern contacts and then going west and finding yet more of it in a second 'new world', in the west.

Such a travelling myth would be a spectacular recovery from the past, with a double scope, both east and west. 'Men celebrate most', Homer's young Telemachus tells his mother Penelope, 'the newest song which circulates for listeners.'[59] The Euboeans, however, might have 'celebrated most' the old songs, because they were made fresh and new at either end of their world. In the eighth century BC there was a time for Greeks on the move when the world could have seemed to be telling the same story towards both the rising and the setting sun. This trail is the one we can now recover for the first time since the eighth century BC, starting with mythical persons who span both east and west, moving on to channels through which such a trail could have passed, and leading, finally, to the items which demonstrably travelled along it with Euboeans in the eighth century. They are not exactly items which Homer's contemporary epics would lead us to expect.

12

Lost in Translation

There is no shortage of legendary heroes who travel far and wide in early Greek myths, but there are three who have so far been linked by modern scholars with eighth-century Euboean travellers and their journeys in the real world. One is winged Daedalus, another is labouring Heracles and the third is the unfortunate Io whom Zeus seduced and turned into a cow. We can follow Daedalus to Sicily, Heracles to southern Spain and Io to Syria, Egypt and the Adriatic sea. Each of them shows how history can be inferred from a myth's locations at particular sites, but whether that history includes early Euboeans or a fertile contact with non-Greek stories in the east and west remains to be seen.

I

In Greek myths Daedalus is not just a travelling hero: he is the greatest travelling craftsman. We meet him on Crete, although the Athenians, patrons of arts and crafts, claimed that he had originated in Athens. It was on Crete that he built wonders for mythical King Minos, the puzzling labyrinth in which the monstrous Minotaur lived, half-bull, half-man, and especially the wooden cow in which the love-crazed Pasiphaë waited on all fours for sex with her lover, a bull. King Minos was so very angry at this awful commission for his queen that he imprisoned Daedalus, at least until his prisoner built wax wings and flew to safety, followed by his son Icarus. Icarus flew too near the sun and went into 'meltdown', falling, some said later, into the Aegean near Euboea.[1] Daedalus flew on west to Sicily where the local king Kokalos received him on the island's south coast and put him to work once again with his technical skills. Minos pursued him, but without success, and Daedalus ended up working in Sicily.

This story has to be pieced together from Greek sources of varying dates and places, including images on pottery which remind us that our texts do not amount to the totality of Daedalus-stories at any one time. It is in images, not texts, that we first see Daedalus associated with wings, but images do not fix the items and stories to particular places on the map. For this fixing, we depend on surviving texts and in them the earliest location of Daedalus is indeed on Crete. Already we meet him there in Homer's *Iliad* when the lame craftsman-god Hephaestus adds a few last scenes to his wondrous shield for Achilles. He decorates it with a superb scene of the dancing of finely dressed young men and girls on a 'dancing-floor', says Homer, 'which once in broad Knossos, Daedalus crafted for fair-haired Ariadne'.[2] On his first appearance in poetry Daedalus is plainly not Homer's invention: he is a point of comparison and so he belongs in stories which Homer's audience already recognized. Grounded in Crete, he then travels in epic poetry to a western site linked to Euboeans: the sculpted doors of Apollo's temple at Cumae in Italy. They were confronted, eight centuries later, by Virgil's hero Aeneas on a terrace which looked out to Pithecussae and the Bay of Naples. It stood, Virgil tells us, on 'Euboean rock' beneath a 'Chalcidian citadel', and Daedalus had sculpted its golden doors. At Euboean Cumae, Daedalus had depicted scenes from his own life, his help for the princess Ariadne on Crete and the story, twice attempted, of his own son Icarus' fall from heaven, an event too painful, says Virgil, with typical pathos, for Daedalus' hands to succeed in carving its image.[3]

From eastern Crete to western Italy, Daedalus thus flies on the finest wings of epic poetry and with Virgil he stops at a Euboean site in the west. His myth has been upheld as the perfect story for the travelling Greek craftsmen who are attested for us in the west by archaeology at Pithecussae. Daedalus' works were precious and cleverly crafted, like the meaning of his own eloquent Greek name. In Homer's *Iliad*, objects which are called *daidala* are mostly items of armour, but they include fine bowls, furniture and, once, the 'bronze-working' (the word is used only here in Homer) of 'clasps, twisted brooches, earrings and necklaces' by the god Hephaestus while hiding with goddesses of the sea. These 'daedalic' items of bronze jewellery overlap with bronze-worked items which have been found in the metal-working zone of eighth-century Pithecussae.[4] If their workers had heard Homer's songs, Daedalus and 'daedalic objects' were allusions to which they would relate. Did these very same craftsmen, many of them Euboeans, locate Daedalus in the west, the story which Virgil later accepts?

At the other end of the flight-path, Daedalus' name has been traced, on one view, to Near Eastern inspiration as far back as the thirteenth century BC. On the north Syrian coast, just south of the future Al Mina, the Bronze Age residents at Ras Shamra had a god of craftsmanship whose connections almost certainly extended to Crete. This god, Kothar, was later identified by the Greeks with their own craft-god Hephaestus, the associate of Daedalus. Kothar's name and the epithets which attached to it had the meaning of 'Skilful and Wise, or Cunning'.[5] Was 'Daedalus', then, created from a Greek translation of these Near Eastern titles for the god of arts and crafts? In Cretan texts of the Bronze Age, we also find a *da-da-re-jo* which was a place at Knossos, evidently a place of worship.[6] Here, some seven hundred years before Homer, do we have early evidence of Daedalus' location at Knossos on Crete, exactly where Homer refers to his work? Did he, perhaps, take root here after Cretan Greeks' contact with the Near Eastern coastline and its 'crafty' Kothar, god of crafts?

These connections are not convincing. We do not know what *da-da-re-jo* meant in these early Cretan texts or even that the word was Greek: we certainly cannot say that it was a place of worship for the Daedalus known later to us. As for the suggestion of a Near Eastern origin for his name, the problem is that the supposed translation is not very clear: *daidalos* in Greek has the meaning, rather, of 'finely worked' or 'elaborate'. No Greek source ever connects Daedalus with the Levant, although such connections are sometimes credited in other Greek figures of myth. There is a simpler alternative origin. Metal-working and well-crafted objects were known in Greek for being *daidalos/daidala*. As so often, Greeks then invented a namesake for them, a 'Mr Daidalos': the proper name derived from the Greek adjective. In the tenth and ninth centuries Crete was a prominent centre of elaborate, well-crafted *daidala*. Perhaps 'Mr Daidalos' was invented there, a mythical master of craftsmanship.

If he was, his name soon spread more widely and he became connected with Athens too, like the craft-god Hephaestus whose role in the city and its festivals was old and deep-rooted. By the eighth century Daedalus was probably at home already in Athens and in Crete.[7] We then find him in the west in early Etruscan company, thanks to a recent find of their grey-black figured pottery at Cerveteri on the west coast of Italy, nearly 300 miles north of ancient Cumae. A winged figure, captioned 'Taitale', is shown on one side of a jug, and on another, a figure who is captioned 'Metaia' (the Greek Medea). This find has put the Greek Daedalus securely on the Italic map and its linking of these two mythical figures is unparalleled.[8] The link was probably based on their wondrous, miraculous art. Magically, Daedalus could fly and, magically, Medea was able to rejuvenate the old (the scene on the jug seems to show her doing just this). The imagery is datable to c. 630 BC, and implies that stories about Daedalus were already well known locally. The jug is an Etruscan one.

Even without this Etruscan image, there were Greek texts which fixed him quite early to specific western sites in Sicily. In the 680s Greeks began their important settlement of Gela on Sicily's south-east coast: we are told, but only centuries later, that their heirs then seized statues sculpted by Daedalus from a nearby settlement of the non-Greek Sicans, the Greeks' predecessors in this part of the island.[9] To the west of them lived the Sicels, also non-Greeks, whose king, the famous Kokalos, was celebrated at the ancient capital of Kamikos. By c. 560 BC, yet another work by Daedalus was believed to have been found there too.

The evidence for this daedalic object lies in one of antiquity's most beguiling sources, the chronicle of the temple of Athena at Lindos on Rhodes. It was composed c. 100 BC and was prefaced with a list of ancient gifts to the temple's treasury. According to the chronicle, the Greek tyrant Phalaris had donated a sculpted mixing-bowl (presumably of bronze) whose earliest inscription described it as 'Daedalus' gift of hospitality for King Kokalos': on one side it showed the 'battles of the Titans', on the other 'Cronos taking his children from their mother Rhea and swallowing them'.[10] Phalaris ruled Acragas (Agrigento) in the 560s and 550s, and some of Acragas' Greek colonists could claim a kinship with Lindos, the site of the temple. There were good reasons why Phalaris believed in this well-contrived fake: Kokalos' non-Greek capital, Kamikos, lay in territory controlled by his city-state of Acragas. Evidently an ingenious Greek had inscribed an archaic metal bowl with just the sort of pedigree and ancient imagery which Phalaris of Acragas would like to discover. Perhaps the forger sold it for money: Phalaris then presented it to his sister-shrine at Lindos, presumably in good faith. Whatever the object's origin, it traded on the belief that Daedalus was located in the pre-Greek past on Sicily's southern coast.

In the 480s BC, as Persian invaders threatened the Greeks, we have solid evidence that the story of Daedalus' westward migration had become widely credited. In Herodotus' *Histories*, the Cretans consulted the oracle at Delphi about whether to fight the Persians, but were reminded by the Delphic priestess of the wrath of their ancestral king Minos: he was angry because they had never avenged his untimely death in Sicily. Minos, Herodotus explains, 'is said' to have travelled to pre-Greek Sicily in pursuit of the fugitive Daedalus.[11] The Delphic oracle cited this 'wrath' as a solid reason why the Cretans should not join the other Greeks in fighting against the Persian invaders. To us, the oracle is fascinating evidence of the living power of myth and divine anger among Greeks in their early classical age: it is also a proof of Daedalus' Sicilian location which the Delphic oracle's verses took for granted.

Daedalus' role as a Greek craftsman in the west then grew in subsequent stories. All around them Greek settlers in Sicily encountered old or natural non-Greek wonders, marvels like the great temple-terrace at the non-Greek site of Eryx (a few stones are still visible), hot springs on the southern coast (still there at Sciacca) or non-Greek styles of monumental architecture (now vanished). They explained these sites as Daedalus' ancient handiwork, an origin which made them part of their own Greek prehistory.[12] On the south coast, between Gela and Acragas, we then find an ancient map-reference to a 'Daedalion', a 'place of Daedalus'.[13] Daedalus' engineering was even extended to Sardinia, perhaps thanks to the histories of Timaeus, a Hellenistic rationalizer in the third century BC but a western Greek by origin.[14] In Italy, however, Daedalus' role in decorating the great temple at Cumae is only Virgil's fiction, so far as present evidence goes. The first oracular temple at Cumae was Hera's, not Apollo's, and the Apollo-temple was probably not built until the sixth century BC.[15] Virgil is vague about it, and Daedalus' artwork on the doors is probably his own invention, at most imposed on stories which he had found in the learned Timaeus or in another Hellenistic source. Virgil's flight of fancy is not sound evidence for a Euboean location of Daedalus at Cumae as early as the eighth century BC.

Rather, Daedalus' roots, the sites in his main stories and his own first locations are Cretan, not Euboean. We know of historical Cretan settlers in the west, the Cretan settlers who arrived to found Gela in the 680s and helped to found Acragas, Phalaris' city, a hundred years later. They saw big non-Greek buildings among the neighbouring Sicans and Sicels and they captured some fine archaic metal objects from the nearby non-Greek sites.[16] Daedalus, they assumed, had been busy designing them and soon they helped to locate his pursuer King Minos too. In the later seventh century BC, Greeks at Selinus (Selinunte) in the far south-west of the island founded a headland settlement on their eastern borders and renamed it 'Minoa' after a place name in their own original mother-city's topography back in Greece.[17] In the early fifth century BC this 'Minoa' was then mistaken as evidence of the Cretan king Minos' presence. From debris on the site, there emerged a long-forgotten tomb, plainly, therefore, the 'tomb' of King Minos, which contained the Cretan king's very bones.[18] Such inter-connections of Cretan legend and local topography multiplied in the west, long before Timaeus and later historians helped to diffuse them across yet more sites on the island. It was, then, with Cretans, not Euboeans, that Daedalus' flight became fixed in Sicily in the seventh (not the eighth) century BC. It was a good story, and the Etruscans might have picked it up anyway, but the Cretans' support for it can only have helped its fame to spread. So we find 'Taitale' in Etruscan Italy c. 630 BC.

At the other end of the Mediterranean, it is unlikely that Daedalus owed any debt to Near Eastern myths, let alone to a myth which had been transmitted to Crete in the remote Bronze Age. Euboean travellers did not invent him, either, through their contact with the East in the eighth century BC. From Crete, Daedalus flew west, but to sites with which the later Cretan settlers in Sicily identified him from the

680s onwards. They used him to make sense of the non-Greek world which they saw around them. Cretans had not been present with the Euboeans who settled earlier at Ischia or Cumae or in east Sicily. Their travelling hero's air-miles were impressive but, on present evidence, he had not been on the first Euboeans' minds.

II

The most awesome of all Greek travelling heroes cannot fly, but he can certainly fight. He is Heracles, 'mighty, bold, lionhearted' as Homer's *Iliad* already well described him. He has an energy and range which make even Daedalus' journey seem rather parochial. Homer alludes only briefly to stories of Heracles' deeds and labours, but these allusions are proof that a wide variety of such stories was already current in Greek. He refers to Heracles' visit to Troy before the Trojan War and how he sacked the city when its king denied him his promised reward of horses. He knows how his labours arose from the jealousy of Hera. There were 'many' of them and once, at Pylos, Heracles killed Nestor's eleven brothers. Perhaps it was then, perhaps later, that at Pylos he wounded Hades 'among the dead' with a swift arrow. The story puzzled later ancient commentators, but it was probably then too that he hit the goddess Hera spectacularly in her right breast with another arrow, a barbed one. Nonetheless Heracles was still 'dearest to Zeus', although even he could not escape eventual death.[19]

'Labours' and 'might' are words which Homer already attached naturally to this hero. In Hesiod's poems, we hear more about some of these labours: Heracles kills the many-headed snaky Hydra and the lion at Nemea and, above all, kills the giant Geryon, steals his cattle 'in Erytheia' and drives them home, 'broad-faced cattle', to Tiryns in Greece.[20] To the eighth-century poets, Heracles' 'labours' were already familiar, but they were not always the labours which later sources emphasized. In art and poetry the numbers of labours continued to vary before they eventually settled at twelve.

Undoubtedly, then, travelling Euboeans knew stories of Heracles' prowess, even before Homer or Hesiod sang of them. We know of cults of Heracles on Euboea, some of which may be very old. Above all, we have a story of how he sacked the ancient city of Oechalia in Euboea itself.[21] Heracles was also part of a common stock of stories in which he showed the elements of a popular hero, voracious, hefty, a great tamer of useful animals and a great killer of wildlife which was an unusable pest and a danger. His victories were not won by magic: they relied on his courage and cunning. He had various 'addresses' in Greece, at Thebes, Aetolia and above all Argos, and some of his animal-enemies were located there too. His pre-Homeric roots went back into the 'Dark Ages' and probably, though no linguistic proof exists, into the previous Mycenaean period.[22]

Nonetheless were some of Heracles' stories adapted from stories which Greek travellers met in the Near East? There are parallels between some of Heracles' deeds and the deeds of palace-demolishing Samson (in Israel), lion-slaying, westward-travelling Gilgamesh (in Mesopotamia) and, back in the third millennium BC, the exploits of the Sumerian god Ninurta (also in Mesopotamia) against a menacing bull, a bird and much else, spoils which were brought back as trophies to Ninurta's temples. Across the centuries the old Sumerian tales about the deeds and trophies of Ninurta travelled and persisted. They became attached, we now know, to other Near Eastern gods and temples, more than a thousand years after Ninurta's heyday.[23] Greek visitors to the Levant could, then, have encountered them in the Bronze Age or afterwards, although the stories do not overlap exactly with the stories of Heracles which Greeks created. The Israelites' tales of Samson are less likely as a Greek model, because Israel was on the margins of established Greek contact. Here, above all, we risk mistaking parallel stories for causes and origins. Culture-heroes do approximately similar things in different societies, fighting against monsters and wild nature and even penetrating to the edges of the world. Heracles' animal enemies are not those of Near Eastern heroes, and the differences between theirs and his are more striking than the parallels.[24]

Heracles also laboured out west in 'neverland', in an enigmatic Erytheia, where he battled with monstrous Geryon, and in the gardens of the Hesperides, source of the golden apples. For Hesiod, Erytheia was far away by the very limits of western Ocean.[25] However, Heracles also turns up in great poetry at a specific western address, exploited in Virgil's *Aeneid*. When Aeneas visits the early site of Rome he finds its mythical king Evander, his son Pallas and the 'humble' Roman senate about their religious business: they are paying solemn honour to Heracles and the gods in a grove before the city. They 'were offering incense', Virgil tells us, 'and the warm blood (of animals) was smoking by the altars'. As King Evander explains, Heracles had once rescued Rome's early residents from a great danger, the monstrous giant ('Cacus': Bad Man) who had lived in a deep dark cave in the nearby hills and had tried to steal the cattle which Heracles was driving home to Greece from one of his labours in the west. As evening falls, Aeneas watches in awe while members of a prominent Roman family, the Potitii, come 'dressed in their customary skins, bearing torches' and make a second series of offerings at the altars. Old and young members of a Roman priestly college sing hymns of the 'glories and deeds' of Heracles: 'all the woodland rings with the clamour, and the hills resound'.[26]

This brilliant evocation of a simple Rome and its humble, impoverished senate played on the pastoral nostalgia of Virgil's Roman readers, aware of the teeming, luxurious Rome which was the wonder and curse of their own day. Virgil's scene is fiction, but it refers to a famous ancient rite. Throughout pagan Rome's history, honours were paid to Heracles at the Greatest Altar, the Ara Maxima, by a crossing-point for travellers on the River Tiber. We know of some of its rules from later sources: women could not share in the cult (a ban which is known in several other cults of Heracles).[27]

Heracles and his deeds thus span a wide horizon from east to west: in the east he was also worshipped in due course at Tyre and was even said to have visited Egypt. Although Near Eastern stories have not shaped his own, changes occur in Heracles' image and here the effects of contact between Greeks and Near Easterners can be traced more plausibly. In the later seventh century BC the Greek artists' Heracles is no longer the helmeted warrior who fights enemies with his bow. He begins to be shown wearing a lion-skin whose head is his hat and whose teeth define his hairline: most probably this lion-skin had been a dress for Near Eastern champions. So far, the earliest known example of this new style is on a metal band found in the sanctuary of Hera on Samos and dating to *c.* 630 BC.[28] By *c.* 550 BC, however, another type had emerged in stone sculpture, a youthful, unbearded god who wears a lion-skin on his back and has the lion's paws knotted on his chest. He tends to carry a club, not a bow, and to have one arm raised. This type is attested first on Cyprus and then, by extension, on the Levantine coast at the fine Phoenician site of Amrith (ancient Marathos). It is this type which was used in an early temple-sculpture of Heracles in Rome *c.* 530 BC.[29]

This new image appears to originate on Cyprus and is evidently due to contact between Greeks and a non-Greek cult on the island. The votive-sculptures from nearby Levantine Amrith, locally made *c.* 580–550 BC, are decisive evidence. The Levantines who offered them had not adopted the worship of the Greeks' Heracles. For them, their lion-clad, club-bearing figure represented a Near Eastern god, although we cannot, strictly, give him his true Phoenician name.[30] Which way, though, did the influence run? It is more likely, at present, that Cypriot and Levantine sculptors applied themes which Greeks had developed for Heracles. They used them, including the lion-skin with knotted paws, to represent a young god in their own culture. In due course other Greeks who came closely into contact with Phoenicians made another equation between their Heracles and a foreign god: this time, the equation was with Melqart. Melqart was the god of the great city of Tyre, where King Hiram, we are told, had built a temple of Melqart in the later tenth century BC. The kings of Tyre were priests of Melqart; Melqart was the 'lord' of Tyre, the god of the Tyrian citadel, 'king' (*melq*) of the 'town' (*qart*).[31] When Greeks returned to the Levant in the tenth to ninth centuries BC, Melqart's cult was already much in evidence: was Melqart equated with Heracles by the very first Greek visitors, those Euboeans whose pottery was present at Tyre by *c.* 920 BC? In their pre-literate world, evidence is necessarily lacking, but we know that the equation was made, albeit by much later Greek visitors. Herodotus accepted it as a matter of course when he visited Tyre *c.* 450 BC.[32] The precise grounds for it are still unclear to us. Unlike Heracles, Melqart was a god, not a hero, and when we see his image *c.* 850 BC on a votive block of basalt near Aleppo nothing about it would suggest Heracles to a Greek eye. Melqart's important civic role both at Tyre and in her colonies was also a weak reason for making the comparison: Heracles was not the founding-hero par excellence of early Greek settlements overseas.[33] Instead, there were surely many stories about Melqart which we do not now know, some of which must have suggested Heracles somehow to Greek visitors to Cyprus and the Levant. Stories are the likelier point of connection than images, because there was almost certainly no image of Melqart to be seen in his Tyrian temple. Instead, there were two remarkable 'pillars' (stēlai), as Herodotus explains; one was 'of refined gold, the other was of emerald which gleamed in the night'.[34] Cults of Melqart were prominent in Tyre's ancient colonies too, at Carthage and further west, at Cadiz. The cult and temple at Cadiz are known only in late sources of the Roman era, but here too there were two tall bronze pillars and no image. According to Strabo (c. 20 BC) sailors would make offerings at them after a successful journey.[35]

Despite the late date of this detailed evidence, Melqart's cult at Cadiz was very old, as old, no doubt, as the settlement itself. When Greeks ventured into the west Mediterranean in the eighth century they would encounter these cults of Tyrian Melqart and as usual they would try to make sense of what they saw. They may already have understood the god as their own Greek Heracles, and as a result Heracles' travels and labours in 'neverland' acquired precise far-western addresses. They then posed a further question: if Heracles had gone so far west, how ever did he come home to Greece? Their answers added yet more sites for Heracles' exploits, even when Melqart's presence was not there to guide them.

We can begin to trace their sitings in Greek poetry and travel-stories from the mid-sixth century BC onwards, especially those known to the forerunner of Herodotus, Hecataeus of Miletus, who told them in his *Circuit of the Earth* (c. 500 BC). The elusive Erytheia where Heracles had fought with the giant Geryon became fixed in south-west Spain by the 'boundless, silver-rooted springs of the river Tartessus', the Guadalquivir river which ran down from the mines on the 'Silver Mountain' (now the Sierra Morena).[36] From south-west Spain, therefore, Heracles was now considered to have driven off Geryon's cattle and as he took them home, his route had to loop around the Mediterranean. Near Massilia (Marseille), the plain by the River Rhône was covered with a dense array of boulders: Greek travellers explained this curious geology as the very stones which Heracles had thrown against the hostile natives when he had run out of arrows on his way home from Spain.[37] He drove the cattle, Greeks said, down through 'Italy', although the name of 'Italy' was reserved for what we now regard as southern Calabria, modern Italy's toe. Heracles was then said to have crossed into Sicily where he fought at significant points in the island's western, Phoenician zone. At Solous, west of modern Palermo, he killed the settlement's namesake, who showed himself hostile to strangers.[38] At Eryx, in the north-west, he wrestled with the local king, after betting his cattle for the king's land. On the north-west coast, Motya was the island-site of a major Phoenician settlement, only half a mile off the coast. Here, Heracles was said to have learned from the local lady 'Motya' about people who had 'stolen' his cattle. No doubt he killed these raiders too.[39]

By c. 500 BC, therefore, Heracles was being credited with overcoming enemies at major non-Greek sites on the island. Perhaps in each case a local cult of Melqart had caused Heracles' exploits to be sited at these places. These eloquent Greek stories implied that the Phoenician zone of Sicily had once been the scene of a Greek hero's victories. There were implications here for future Greek efforts at conquering the 'heritage of Heracles' but there was more to them than conquest: Heracles was also a great tamer of uncivilized nature. In Sicily, he was the hero who reshaped the landscape, cutting courses for rivers through rocks, causing hot springs to bubble or marshes to become orderly lakes.[40] We can date this important side of his career at least to the sixth century BC if we look at his similar role in northern Greece. By c. 500 BC a town called 'Heracleion' commemorated him up on the borders of Macedon and northern Thessaly just where Mount Ossa was split from Mount Olympus. The reason for the name was that thanks to Heracles, a major river there, the Peneios, was considered to have been allowed access to the Aegean sea.[41]

What, meanwhile, about the starting point of Heracles' route home from distant Spain? He had left memorials there too, the famous 'Pillars of Heracles' which are first attested for us in the west by Hecataeus, who was drawing here too on the stories of Greek travellers.[42] The site for them appears soon after in the poems of Pindar (c. 480–470 BC). For Pindar, the Pillars are the 'Gates of Gades' (Cadiz) and beyond Cadiz there is only the 'gloomy dark which

nobody may cross' (to us, the Atlantic Ocean). Other travellers, followed by Herodotus, identified them with the Straits of Gibraltar.
One pillar, they suggested, was the Rock, while the other was Ceuta
on the coast of modern Morocco. Heracles, it was said, had either
widened the straits to allow a route through to Outer Ocean or had
narrowed them so as to block out Ocean's sea-monsters.[43]

The oddity is that neither the Rock nor Ceuta looks at all like a
'pillar'. The identification of Heracles' pillars began, rather, at Cadiz
where Greek travellers found the Phoenicians' great shrine of Melqart.
We know it only from much later poetry and coin-types, but like
Melqart's parent-shrine in Tyre, it was credited with two big 'pillars'
(*stēlai*) of precious stone and a ban on women celebrants and the
offering of pigs. When Greek traders penetrated this far west and
found these pillars of Melqart, they must be the 'pillars of Heracles',
they concluded, the western limits of the known world.[44]

Were any of these early Greek travellers Euboeans? It is from the
sixth century BC that evidence for Heracles' western travels survives
for us, and by then the Greek travellers to the far west were above all
Phocaeans, Greeks from the coast of Asia Minor. Earlier Greek pottery, specifically Euboean pottery, had been reaching sites in southern
Spain and Morocco during the later eighth century, and it is wrong
to explain it all as a cargo which Phoenician seafarers, but not Greeks,
brought west.[45] There may, then, be Euboean pioneers behind these
western discoveries, people who recognized Heracles in the Melqart
whom they had met at Cyprus or Tyre and who then 'found' him
again in Carthage and with his pillars in the far west. But as yet we
cannot prove it.

What we can say is that deeds of Heracles became sited on the
western coast of Italy in the late seventh to sixth centuries BC, at or
near the sites of existing Euboean settlements. Earlier, as we shall see,
stories of the battles of Greek gods and giants were pinned down near
Naples within the horizons of the Euboean settlers: Heracles was said
to have participated in these heavenly wars.[46] By the later sixth century
BC there was a town of Herculaneum on the bay and a roadway
past the Lucrine Lake was credited to Heracles as his route. But our
evidence of these traces of the hero does not go back as yet into the
eighth century.[47]

Can we, nonetheless, credit Euboean visitors with introducing the ancient cult of Heracles in Rome which was practised at the Greatest Altar and was supposedly seen by Virgil's Aeneas? Although Roman sources later describe it as celebrated 'in the Greek rite', this Roman view of it does not mean that the cult actually originated with Greeks. Perhaps the Altar will one day turn out to have been a multi-ethnic cult-site of both Phoenician and Euboean visitors in the mid-eighth century, but as yet we do not know.[48] On present evidence we have a Heracles who travelled from east to west, but not one whose origins lie demonstrably in the east. The sites of his labours, including his Pillars, seemed to be visible in the far west Mediterranean, but if Euboeans played a role in these sitings, it is still unknown to us. Like Daedalus, Heracles validates our model of mythical travel from one end of the Mediterranean sea to the other. Through these two heroes that possibility is at least assured and exemplified.

III

Direct contact with Near Eastern languages helped to shape Greek stories of a very different type of traveller: abducted women and the men who went after them. There were good reasons why mythical travellers were almost always men: female mobility was restricted in antiquity, and a free woman could not travel alone. Exceptions, however, were heroines who eloped with a male suitor, human or divine. Only one heroine travelled far on her own and even then she travelled under duress and in disguise. She was Io of Argos, the first woman to become a real cow.

The stories of Io's travels as a cow take her from Argos to the Levant and even on to Egypt. As the ancients recognized, she was matched by another female, Europa, who travelled in the opposite direction, from the Levant to Crete. Europa travelled not as a cow but as a maiden on the back of a bull, the disguise of the god Zeus, who had desired and abducted her. Both these heroines attracted further travellers, male search parties who criss-crossed the Aegean to try to find them. These male searchers never succeeded, not even Cadmus, Europa's brother and most famous searcher. In Crete, the citizens of Gortyn claimed to have the very palm-tree under which Europa had first dismounted and bull-like Zeus had first mounted her.[49] It must have been a fascinating place for visitors.

Of these two travelling heroines, the cow-like Io is the one with local Euboean connections. In much later texts she is said to have resided on Euboea, at Argoura, even, a place which probably stood on the coast of the gulf near the former site of Lefkandi; she gave birth there.[50] However tempting it may be to make Io a myth which originated in our Euboean heartland, these Euboean links are second-ary: Io's original domicile was Argos. By origin she was the daughter of a father from the Argolid: she was believed to have been a priestess of the great Argive goddess Hera; her search party and her descendants were all Argives, and Zeus, it was said, had desired her at Argos.[51] In the fifth-century tragedy *Prometheus Bound*, Io is made to speak memorably on the dreams which had beset her, a virginal girl, and caused her to want to go out to the meadows and meet Zeus. In most versions of the story, Zeus then has sex with her, but denies the fact to his wife Hera. He breaks his vows, and as a result, the poets say, breaches of mortal lovers' vows, the 'oaths of Aphrodite', are not punishable by the Greek gods.[52] Among all these lies, Io is turned by Zeus (or Hera) into a white cow, although male vase-painters some-times show her as a bull.[53] She was tied to an olive-tree in a nearby 'grove of the Mycenaeans' where she was guarded by watchful, many-eyed Argos, at least until the god Hermes killed him. Hera then sent a notorious insect, the gadfly, which drove Io on frenzied travels through Greece and far away across the seas. In fifth-century texts, we find that Io's final destination was Egypt. Here, she was said to have given birth to Epaphus, son of Zeus, who was brought about by the stroking 'touch' of the god (*epaphē* being the Greek word for 'touching').[54] This turn to the story is manifestly later than the eighth century BC and its Euboean travellers.

In several Near Eastern poems, one of the gods mates with a hand-some cow, but Io's story is much more complex and is not Near Eastern in origin. Her disguise as a cow and its consequences are solely Greek inventions. Later artists, poets and thinkers recognized the playfulness in the story, but scholars have looked behind its developed form for a possible origin in cult and ritual. The Argive shrine of Hera was very famous and perhaps it had once had a rite involving male wearers of a bull-mask and a 'cow-faced' Hera who was perhaps impersonated by her priestess. On this view, the story of Io arose from a mimed religious ritual at Argos, to which tales of Hera's vengeance and Io's travels were later additions.[55] Argos's main temple-shrine to Hera, the Heraion, stood prominently at the east end of the Argive plain on a terraced hill which was some 400 feet high. Behind it rose a high bare mountain called Euboea, 'good for cattle'. The rites for Hera at the cult-site probably preceded the building of the terrace, which dates only to the later eighth century BC.

There were obvious word-plays here which Euboeans could turn to their advantage. The Argive hill 'Euboea' could be claimed to be their own island Euboea; Io's guardian 'Argos' could be transferred to their own town Argoura. We do not know when these transfers began, but they had made an impact on Io's genealogy as it is known to us c. 550 BC. By then Io was said to have a grandson, Abas. Abas was a name with a very strong Euboean connection (Euboeans were known as 'Abantes'). Was he inserted into Io's family by a Euboean poet or was he inserted as the Argives' response to tiresome Euboean claims to possess their own Io?[56] On the latter view, which I prefer, the Argives annexed the Euboeans' ancestor into their own ancestry and put him far down the line. If this explanation is correct, links between Io and Euboea were quite old, but were not original to Io's pedigree. We do not know if they went back to eighth-century versions of the story, but if they did, Io was a particularly relevant heroine to Euboeans when they travelled east and west.

In the west, Io turns up in Virgil's *Aeneid* as a figure who is shown in gold relief on the shield of the Italian warrior-king Turnus, a reminder that Turnus' ancestry traced mythically back to the heroes of Argos. The device is only Virgil's invention and this connection between Argos and Italy is a late fancy.[57] Otherwise, Io went no further west in legend than our Adriatic sea, between Italy and north-west Greece. Its Greek name, the 'Io-nian' sea, was traced to her presence. This derivation is explicit in *Prometheus Bound*, whose ideas of the world are much older, going back to the previous century's age of Greek travel. They may be even older still. In the early to mid-eighth century Euboeans had been active along the Adriatic coastline of north-west

Greece and in due course stories of their fellow-Euboean 'Abantes' were located inland on what travellers called the 'Mainland' (in Greek, Epeiros). But as yet no early evidence connects these Euboeans with making a link between Io and the north-west Ionian sea.[58]

Eastwards, Io's connections are more specific. Cow-shaped Io came to be located in Egypt when Greek visitors became aware of the Egyptians' own cow-horned goddess, Hathor–Isis: because of the similarity they equated this goddess with their own cow-horned Io and from the 630s onwards gave their heroine a new Nilotic resting place in Egypt. In *Prometheus Bound*, it is predicted that this Egyptian connection will have a long future: by the Nile, Io will found an 'extensive', or 'long-lasting', settlement.[59]

If Io ended up in Egypt, it was only natural to ask, once again, how she came to be there. Myths of travel abhor a vacuum, so the gaps were filled and in due course the stopping-points were written down as Io's itinerary. Stories of it take a most suggestive line. Searchers from Argos set out, we are told, to find her, led by the Argive hero Triptolemus. We would more naturally associate Triptolemus with Athens but he and his Argives passed, we are told, through Cilicia where some of them stayed to found Tarsus. Others passed on into north Syria and the valley of the Orontes, the heart of the triangle of early Greek contact. Triptolemus was eventually honoured with a hero's shrine and a yearly festival, instituted at Antioch after its foundation *c.* 300 BC. This festival was known to the geographer Strabo; it was celebrated on the slopes of Mount Kasios, the great Jebel Aqra which rises steeply above the ancient site of Al Mina.[60]

In this historic area, Io continued to activate the local residents, as we can discover from a speech in praise of Antioch by its local orator Libanius (*c.* AD 385). He describes how the Argive search party arrived on the coast, 'climbed the mountain', 'knocked on the doors' of the residents and asked for Io's whereabouts. The searchers then settled locally and founded 'Ione' beside 'the mountain', probably Mount Silpion, which stood inland near Libanius' own Antioch.[61] Another local author, the Christian John Malalas (*c.* AD 530), fills in some details. A settlement of 'Iopolis', he tells us, was indeed founded on Mount Silpion and people there 'were still called "Ionitai" by the Syrians of the region'. Once a year, the local Syrians would knock on the doors of the Hellenes in memory of the ancient searchers who had come looking for Io, the abducted girl. The door-knocking, therefore, remained a fact of the city calendar for at least two hundred years.[62]

While bound for Egypt, Io was said to have found yet another home, on the coast of Palestine. Here, the non-Greek city of Gaza issued coins which showed Io shaking hands with the city's goddess (we know of them from AD 131/2 onwards): Gaza was even said to have been called 'Ione'. Inevitably, the sea between Palestine and Egypt became known as another 'Io-nian' sea, named after Io the traveller.[63] How are we to explain these stopping-points for the abducted cow-girl and her seekers in Cilicia, north Syria and on the coastline down to Egypt? Herodotus' histories and the author of *Prometheus Bound* know that Io reached Egypt, but they say nothing of the intervening stations. However, the late sources from Antioch presume that an 'Iopolis' had existed on their nearby mountain even before Antioch was founded (*c.* 300 BC): Io's presence here is best ascribed to a linguistic muddle. In languages of the Near East, Greeks had long been called 'Iawones', or people from 'Iawan'. By a typical word-play, the Greeks, it seems, took this name to allude to Io, and so at Antioch or Gaza they located Io on her eastern travels.[64] The association persisted into the 530s AD, but when did it begin? One tempting answer is to trace it to the early Greek visitors, Euboeans of the late tenth to eighth centuries BC. They lived, after all, at Al Mina, just below the very mountain on which the cult for Io's searchers was later located. At home on Euboea they may already have been claiming Io's presence and challenging her alternative address at Argos. In the Near East, they might then believe that they had found her in all the babble about 'Iawones' with which the local inhabitants greeted them between the Cilician and the north Syrian plain: Io and her searchers then turn up at sites in this very region. It is a possible answer, but as yet there is no early evidence for it: *Prometheus Bound* ignores it, and the safer answer, at present, is to trace it to later myth-making, perhaps after Alexander's conquests, when the same name of 'Iawones' still circulated locally.

The travels of the second abducted heroine, Europa, are also best explained by confusions of language and local heritage. Already in Homer's *Iliad*, she is the daughter of 'Phoenix', the namesake, as later poets assume, of the Phoenicians. Her home, then, was a Phoenician city, usually identified as Tyre in subsequent Greek texts, from where she, too, was abducted by Zeus. He took her to Crete, where local claims to her remained very strong. Apart from the palm-tree where Zeus mounted her, her 'bones' were escorted in festivals at Gortyn and elsewhere on the island, while a spring near Gortyn commemorated the very place where she took her bath.[65] These local connections began early: Europa was already being shown on coins of Gortyn in the mid- to late fifth century BC. The tale of her seduction by Zeus existed even earlier. In his epic poem on Europa, the Corinthian poet Eumelus (arguably writing in the later eighth century BC) told how Zeus fell in love with Europa and abducted her.[66] If only we knew more about his fragmentary poem, we would be better able to follow Europa's early travels.

Instead, we have evidence for her search party, surviving from the sixth century BC onwards. The party was led from the Levant (usually from the city of Tyre) by Europa's brother Cadmus, and later sources allow us to trace its route across the Aegean. It called at the island of Rhodes, at Melos and Thera, Thasos and nearby Samothrace where, on one view, Cadmus met Harmony and married her: 'even now', the historian Ephorus remarked c. 330 BC, 'they search for Harmony in festivals on Samothrace'.[67] Most famously, Cadmus also enquired at Delphi and then founded the city of Thebes in central Greece.

The names 'Cadmus' and 'Europa' have long been connected to two word-roots in Semitic languages which were audible in the Near East: *qdm* ('east') and *ereb* ('west'). The connection has not been universally accepted, but it is attractive because basic terms of direction would be the words most likely to be known to local Greek visitors (as *rechts* and *links* are known even to Englishmen). By word-play, they suggested to the Greeks their own Cadmus (evidently 'Mr East') and their Europa (plainly, a 'Miss West'). As a result the Greek Cadmus ('Mr East') came from a Levantine address, searching for westward-travelling Europa, his sister, across the Aegean.[68] He stopped longest at Thebes, perhaps the home of an independently named Cadmus, but his route conspicuously included places where we now infer from archaeology that there was a presence of Phoenician visitors in the eighth century BC. Perhaps some oral memories of these contacts encouraged stories of Cadmus' local stops with his party of fellow-searchers. Among the searchers was 'Phoenix', the Phoenicians' Greek eponym. Cadmus also stopped in Cilicia where the coast, we have seen, was a major point of Phoenician contact: one 'Cilix' was invented as a member of the search party.[69] On the island of Samothrace, the existence of a non-Greek legendary 'Kadmilos' no doubt helped with Cadmus' location there. Eventually he and Harmony were said to have moved north-west through Greece and to have come to rest on the borders of non-Greek Illyria. In the hinterland of the Greek city-state of Epidamnus, tombs of Cadmus and Harmony were eventually believed to be sited. Through the fields of scented Illyrian iris Cadmus and Harmony were said to move 'in the shape of fearsome snakes'.[70]

What are we to make of these playful stories of travel? Neither Io nor Europa nor their searchers travelled west as well as east, to Sicily and Italy as well as to Egypt and the Levant. Possibly, our Euboeans believed that they had found their own Io among the babbling words for 'Ionian Greek' in north Syria; somebody, perhaps a Euboean, 'found' Cadmus and Europa in the two basic Near Eastern words for direction and thus gave these two heroes' travels a new orientation. The discovery of the Egyptian goddess Hathor's cow-horned images then brought cow-like Io to Egypt. Thanks to creative mistakes about foreign languages and foreign monuments there was a vast enlargement of the Greeks' 'family of peoples'. Cadmus and his kinsmen included 'Phoenix' and 'Cilix', namesakes of the Phoenicians and Cilicians; Libya and Egypt became involved in the same genealogy, while Io, as promised, turned the lands by the Nile into a long-lasting Greek settlement, if only after Alexander the Great's conquest. This mapping and genealogy nowadays tend to be credited with stark consequences for colonial power and Greek territorial claims. But they also made foreign peoples part of the Greek 'family': such people were seen as akin to the Greeks, not aliens. Greeks who devised these kinships were not defining their own Greekness by opposing foreign 'others' to themselves. They were assuming that 'others' were more like themselves than they really were.

Across the bridge of the Greek Io or Cadmus, foreign 'others' then started to present themselves eagerly as the 'same'. Non-Greek Tarsus and Gaza both claimed Io and her searchers as their Greek founders. When Alexander arrived at Sidon in 332 BC, he already found a shrine of Cadmus' father, Agenor, in the city.[71] In due course the images of Cadmus and Europa appeared competitively on the city-coins of both Tyre and Sidon. They had become yet another subject of rivalry between the two great cities in the Greek age after Alexander. By c. 200 BC, Sidon was even being represented as the mother-city of Cadmus' famous foundation in Greece, the city of Thebes. But Tyre still had a decisive card: in the second century BC, she claimed, and established, a 'kinship' directly with the Greek people of Delphi. This surprising kinship did not arise because Cadmus, that contested figure, had once consulted the Delphic oracle. It was based, as the Tyrians recorded, on a *syncrasis*, a real merger.[72] The grounds for it have not been understood, but they can only have been theatrical. In Euripides' play *The Phoenician Women*, the chorus are nobly born girls who have been sent from Tyre to Greece in order to be 'servants' at Delphi, Apollo's shrine. 'May we become mothers, may we have fine children,' they sing, rhetorically.[73] Claims to a mythical 'kinship' required the citation of evidence and some very cogent advocacy before both partners would accept it: how could the people of Delphi deny the force of what the great Euripides had written? These Tyrian girls had given birth in Greece and were indeed the Delphians' distinguished ancestors: Sidon, for once, had nothing to quote in reply.

13

A Travelling Prophet

I

Daedalus and Heracles, Io and Europa show a range of possible ways in which myths and heroes might travel with Greeks between east and west. Daedalus travelled above all with Cretans, and it is unlikely that his name derived from an earlier Greek translation of a word in a Near Eastern language, one applied to their Bronze Age god of craftsmanship, Kothar. Io and perhaps Europa gained from casual similarities, 'Io' from the Near Eastern word for 'Greeks', Europa perhaps from the word for 'west'. Heracles, the supreme traveller, owed nothing to Near Eastern words or stories, but representations of him perhaps owed something to non-Greek iconography when he was first shown wearing a lion's head and skin. He gained many new homes in the west, probably not before the seventh to sixth centuries BC, except for the furthest and most influential, his 'Pillars' in the far west. They were perhaps sited here by a travelling Euboean in the later eighth century, impressed by pillars in the temples of Melqart, the god most similar to Heracles himself.

These mythical figures were sited in new homes abroad because of the misunderstandings and inferences of visiting Greeks. Many other Greek myths would travel abroad subsequently for similar reasons: there was a pattern, and it helps to explain the sitings of the other two Greek mythical travellers who are most temptingly located in the triangle between Cyprus, Cilicia and the Levant. Both were connected with strange or monstrous animals. Perseus killed the monstrous Gorgon, from whose head, some said, the winged horse Pegasus was born. Bellerophon rode on winged Pegasus and killed the fire-breathing Chimaera, part-goat, part-lion and part-snake. Bellerophon's story first survives for us in the sixth book of Homer's *Iliad* but it is told so allusively and with such compression that longer oral versions of the story must have been known to Homer's audience. Perhaps they featured at other times in Homer's repertoire. A written pre-Homeric poem has also been suggested as a model, but it has left no trace nowadays.[1] In the *Iliad*, Bellerophon is sent east from the territory of Argos to a kingdom in Lycia in south-west Asia where he is dispatched on deadly adventures, including the killing of the fiery Chimaera. He succeeds, 'trusting in portents of the gods', as Homer mysteriously tells us but gives no further details. This silence is curious because Hesiod refers to the well-known story: Bellerophon killed the Chimaera with the help of Pegasus, the winged horse. For Hesiod, however, Pegasus' origins still floated far away in neverland. He was born from the head of the Gorgon when Perseus cut it off by the 'streams' (*pēgas*) of distant Ocean.[2] In later stories Perseus rode Pegasus far and wide and the two of them did great deeds.

After Hesiod these stories acquired specific homes on the map. Bellerophon came to be sited at Corinth, and Pegasus the winged horse became the city's emblem, eventually typifying Corinth's coins. Perseus, by contrast, belonged in the royal house of Argos. Bellerophon was eventually very popular in sculptures and on coins in Lycia, the Homeric land of his exploits. Perseus and Pegasus left a clear imprint in Caria in south-west Asia and in coastal Cilicia.[3] The Gorgon was thought to have been decapitated on a journey even further east or to have resided in the remote north African desert.

If we apply our pattern to these eastward travels, we can unravel some of the impetus behind their stopping-points. At an early date Greeks may simply have invented a winged, flying horse called Pegasus. If they needed a model for him they may have found one in objects and images derived from further east. Winged horses are known to us on Assyrian seals *c.* 1200 BC and Greeks in the Mycenaean age may have seen them in the Near East or elsewhere at second hand. Winged horses are also depicted in north Syrian art, including at Carchemish *c.* 900 BC: Greek visitors could also have seen them there, reinforcing ideas they had already had.[4] What is striking, however, is that in Hesiod (*c.* 710 BC) one function of Pegasus is to carry Zeus's lightning in heaven. In southern Cilicia we know of a local Luwian-Hittite weather-god 'Pihassassi', who is represented with thunder and lightning.[5] This god was not the origin of Pegasus: a storm-god is not the origin of a horse. However, he had a like-sounding name and Greek visitors to Cilicia may have connected their existing Pegasus with Zeus's lightning after hearing about this 'Pihassassi' and his functions and assuming, wrongly, he was their own Pegasus in a foreign land.

Bellerophon, too, may have begun as a local Greek champion, whose name meant 'killer' (-*phontes*) and was perhaps the killer first of a serpent, then of a hybrid goat-monster somewhere in 'neverland'.[6] Travellers by sea to Lycia in southern Asia and the Gulf of Antalya then became aware of an extraordinary sight in the landscape. As they rounded Cape Gelidonya, they saw the spectacle which has fascinated many sea-travellers since, a conspicuous fire which burns in the mountains beyond the coast. This fire, the Turkish *yanar*, still burns from natural gases on the slopes of Lycia's Mount Olympus. In 1902 it was visited by D. G. Hogarth, subsequently the historical adviser to Lawrence of Arabia, who describes how 'tongues of flame, spirituous, colourless, well nigh invisible in that white glare were licking the mouth of a dozen vents . . . The largest vent opens almost beneath the main group of ruins which has evidently once been a church, raised with the stones of some older building. A Greek inscription is encrusted in the blistered wall and surely some pagan temple has stood here to the Spirit of the Fire.'[7] The Christian church had been built here as a counterweight to a pagan cult-site. We now know from nearby inscriptions that it had been a sanctuary of Hephaestus, the god closely linked to fire, whose cult left a mark on many settlements in the surrounding region.[8] He was exactly the god for these flames.

The flames were 'invisible' to Hogarth by daylight, but by night, as many previous sea-travellers had attested, they are clearly visible to crews off the Lycian coast. In Semitic languages the root of the word for fire was *chmr*, resembling the Greeks' word for their goat-monster *chimaira*. This discovery may have enhanced their idea of a chimaera's nature. Mixed animal-and-human monsters are known in various combinations in sculptures, seal-stones and plaques from north Syria: a goat-headed hybrid is now known on a seal found near Adana in the Cilician plain, dated *c*. 700 BC.[9] Such foreign eastern pictures may already have helped the Greeks' imagination of the creature, but it was perhaps only after travelling along the Lycian coast that they made their hybrid goat-monster into a breather of fire too. Its name 'chimaera' seemed to be reflected in the descriptions of fellow-seafarers, Phoenicians who talked of the *chmr* along this coast. A fiery chimaera thus found its home in Lycia, before Homer's reference to it there: perhaps it was located by east Greeks who were travelling on the coast before *c.* 750 BC. On the local Mount Olympus in Lycia, it then emerged from later research inland that Bellerophon had defeated the 'fire-breather' and buried it. The 'monster' turned out to be safely underground, breathing flames and nothing more. The surrounding earth is still bare, but around it the shrubs and plants are brilliantly green, as if the chimaera's powers are strictly limited.

The two Greek travelling heroes enjoyed a vigorous local afterlife. Bellerophon became the hero of noble Lycian families inland in Lycia and took root at places which claimed to occupy the sites of his exploits in Homer. According to Homer, he then died somewhat mysteriously while 'wandering in the Aleian plain', the broad Cilician plain round Tarsus. As a result Bellerophon became sited here too by ambitious antiquarians. He had fallen from winged Pegasus and landed on Cilician soil, founding 'Tarsus' (in Greek, the sole of the foot) where his foot had first struck the ground.[10]

Perseus and Pegasus were even more widely appropriated. They became popular in coastal Caria; they penetrated Lycia; they flourished, too, in Cilicia where Tarsus was also attributed to the touch of Pegasus' foot or to the swift foot of Perseus himself. Far into the early Christian period Perseus continued to watch over Tarsus as a visiting hero, and his popularity was helped here by the competitive urges of non-Greek cities in the Cilician plain to claim Greek origins.[11] As an ancient Argive, Perseus was a prestigious ancestor. These proliferating locations belong in the rich history of local mythographers, antiquarians and scholarly poets, especially in the Hellenistic age. They took Bellerophon, Perseus and their winged horse far and wide, but like Io and Europa they were not based on an insider's knowledge of any Near Eastern myth or cult.

II

Awareness of such a myth or cult is what we want to ascribe to travelling Euboeans when they settled in the Near East in the eighth century BC, but what channels were there, we begin to wonder, through which genuine foreign knowledge could pass? In his study of wisdom which was 'alien' to Greece, Arnaldo Momigliano even diagnosed a signal 'fault of the Greeks': they were monolingual, he believed, speaking only their own language and were thus unusual because most peoples elsewhere in their world were bilingual.[12] We have seen from Greeks' Near Eastern loan-words that some of them were a little more flexible in Cilicia, Cyprus and the Levant during the tenth to eighth centuries, but our impression so far is that Greeks made little effort nonetheless and generally understood what they saw only in their own Greek terms. The underlying content was 'lost in translation'. Their example was followed by Greek successors in Egypt, who magnificently called the country's great monuments 'buns' (*pyramides*) and 'skewers' (*obeliskoi*), Greek words from which our English words for the buildings derive.

Should we think instead of Near Easterners as a possible source, people who diligently learned Greek and came west to visit parts of the Greek world, bringing 'alien' Near Eastern wisdom with them? By c. 500 BC we can detect in Greek religious practice a few ways of seeking omens or cures which derive from Near Eastern practices. These borrowings are not unduly prominent in most Greeks' ways of approaching their gods, but they had to have been borrowed directly across the language-barrier: they involved practical, working techniques.[13] Did Near Eastern religious experts travel west and pass them on, healers and diviners who came as 'migrant charismatics' to bring such skills directly in translation to the monolingual Greeks? Support for this idea has even been detected in Homer's *Odyssey* where the humble pigman Eumaeus reminds Penelope's suitors on Ithaca that 'nobody goes in person and invites a stranger from elsewhere, unless . . . he is a diviner or a healer or a carpenter or a divine singer who gives pleasure by his singing: these are the men who are invited over the boundless earth'.[14]

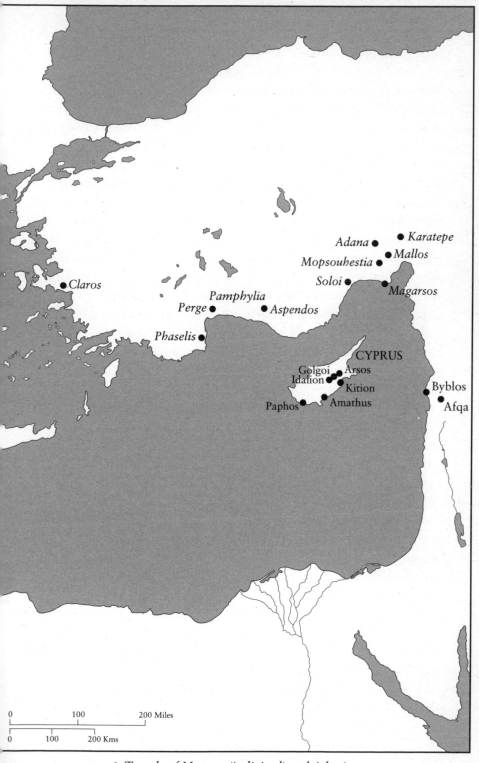

6. *Travels of Mopsus (italicized) and Adonis*

These lines of Homer, at least, are irrelevant to the argument. Eumaeus does not say that these diviners or other craftsmen are non-Greeks whom other people go all the way from Greece to invite. The mention of 'singers' implies that in Homer's mind the travelling experts here are Greeks from other Greek settlements. The Near Eastern visitors whom we infer securely from our archaeology are craftsmen whom Homer does not mention: metal-workers and jewellers who are credited with objects found in Crete and elsewhere. Champions of the influence of foreign prophets and diviners need evidence other than Homer. No travelling religious expert from the east is known to us by name in early Greek history but nonetheless 'the migrant diviners', it is suggested, 'have left their mark on mythology'. It became imprinted, on this view, at a significant point in our triangle in the east Aegean: 'Greek myth establishes a connection between Greece and Cilicia precisely around the figure of the migrant seer.'[15] If such a 'channel' existed here in real life, it would have important implications. So far from picking up stories through their own visits to the east, Euboeans and other Greeks could have received them from migrant experts who came directly to them from Cilicia. These 'migrant seers', however, have quite other roots. So far from subverting our model of Euboean travellers who went eastwards and drew their own conclusions, they are a cardinal item which reinforces it and the pattern of Greek thinking which accompanied it.

The most prominent of the migrant seers has been the most enigmatic, both for the ancients and for modern scholars. The seer Mopsus is a person whom Homeric epic never mentions, but he is connected with specific sites in southern Asia, especially Cilicia. He is connected there with other Greek seers who came to the same area, but Mopsus is the only one whose name appears to be attested in both Greek and Near Eastern languages. The impression of an underlying reality has therefore been strong.

In antiquity too, Mopsus the seer surprised scholars and historians by the number of his home addresses. In Greece itself Mopsus was at home in Thessaly where the place name Mopsion recalled his own. He was the son of Ampyx and was known as a fighter and athlete, as we can see from the earliest surviving evidence for him, inscribed on the strap of a soldier's shield, found at Olympia and dated to *c.* 600–575 BC. He was also connected with the Argonauts. He competed at the funeral-games of Jason's father; he was a Lapith who fought against the Centaurs; he acted as a seer during the Argonauts' journey, as we happen to know from the poet Pindar, *c.* 460 BC. It is only an accident of survival that no earlier evidence exists for this Thessalian hero, athlete, Lapith and seer in one.[16]

Mopsus also turns up in Asia Minor at the great oracular shrine of Claros near the Aegean coast north-west of Ephesus. Here, he was said to be the founding prophet of the sanctuary of Apollo and Artemis and his family was enhanced accordingly. At Claros, Mopsus was represented as the son of a daughter of the seer Tiresias and, some said, of Apollo himself, or at least of a marriage agreed at Delphi. This strongly oracular pedigree befitted the prophet of Claros's oracular Apollo.[17] His change of parentage and address distinguished him from Mopsus son of Ampyx in Greece, so much so that modern scholars of mythology usually identify Claros's Mopsus as a separate person.

Claros's Mopsus then turns up far further south in a most unexpected place. He is rooted on the southern coast of Asia Minor, both in cities of Pamphylia and further east in the broad Cilician plain around Tarsus and Adana.[18] He even becomes connected with north Syria and the Levant. Mopsus' fame lived on in the civic mythology of cities in Pamphylia and Cilicia and in two place names in the Cilician plain. One was Mopsoukrene, 'Mopsus' spring', where Mopsus had an oracular site. The other was the nearby Mopsouhestia, or 'Mopsus' hearth'. Its citadel is still visible at modern Misis, where it looks down on the ancient bridge across the broad Pyramus river (the Ceyhan).

Mopsus' double Asian domicile, both at Claros and near the southern coast, already puzzled the ancients. From the mid-fourth century BC onwards, we can watch intelligent Greek historians trying to make sense of his southern extension. They were not inventing or assessing a recent tradition; they were trying to smooth out the oddities in myths which went back long before their own time. The double domicile was matched by another duplicate: in both places, Mopsus became involved in a quarrel with a famous rival. At Claros he was said to have confronted another 'migrant charismatic', the famous Greek seer Calchas. Calchas had given distinguished advice to the Greeks at Troy, as described in Homer's *Iliad*, but Homer never described how Calchas then stopped at Claros on his way home. He died and was buried there, according to post-Homeric poems on the return of the various heroes from Troy. By the mid-sixth century BC evidence survives for us of the cause of his death. He had been challenged by the resident prophet Mopsus to a contest of riddling questions and answers and when he lost, he died.[19]

In southern Asia, too, Mopsus was said to have quarrelled, but this time with one of Calchas' companions. Although Homer never mentioned him, Amphilochus the Argive was also said to have taken part in the Trojan War. He started to travel home with Calchas by land and after Calchas' death he was said to have pressed on south into Cilicia. Our earliest surviving Greek source for his exploits, c. 500 BC, says that he died here at the hands of Apollo in the coastal city of Soloi. Later storytellers, however, involved Mopsus in his murder. This tradition is attested in the 450s BC and is probably even older. In its fullest form, Amphilochus is said to have entered Cilicia with Mopsus and with him to have founded the famous town of Mallos (near modern Kiziltahta) on the Pyramus river. Amphilochus then returned for a while to his home in Argos but when he came back to Cilicia, Mopsus denied him a share in the city. The pair fought a duel and killed each other, whereupon they were buried in two tombs from which neither could see the other. In antiquity these tombs were pointed out at ancient Magarsos, the modern Karatas, just by the coastline which was the scene of our 'battle of the Pyramus river' in 696 BC. The two travelling heroes had become quarrelling heroes.[20]

Mopsus' two quarrels and his two locations in Asia are most unusual: how do we explain the migrations of this 'migrant charismatic'? One influential theory has tried to link him with historical evidence: his exploits in southern Asia reflect, on this view, the deeds of a real Asian or Greek dynast who came to be remembered in later Greek myth. These theories have been built on a continuing supply of newly discovered non-Greek texts, enriched by finds made as recently as 1998. They help to explain the Greek Mopsus' travels, but how exactly do they link him to history?

In a long-known, but fragmentary, Hittite royal letter written in cuneiform script we have a reference to one 'Muksus' in connection with events in western Asia.[21] When first studied, this text was dated by scholars to *c.* 1200 BC. In 1946 a similar name was discovered in the important neo-Hittite-Luwian inscriptions at Karatepe in north-eastern Cilicia. Long bilingual inscriptions had been cut into the stone blocks of the two gateways by order of its ruler: they referred to Muksas (in Luwian-Hittite hieroglyphics) or Mps (in vowel-less Phoenician script, to be pronounced as 'Mopsu'). The name also occurs in the Phoenician inscriptions which were carved on the site's big statue of grey-black basalt, the statue of the Storm God favoured by the local ruler.[22]

These two bits of evidence were of widely separated date: Karatepe's inscriptions probably belong *c.* 700 BC. Nonetheless, with a brilliant faith in myth and history, scholars quickly connected this new evidence for Muksas (or Mopsu) with Mopsus the Greek wanderer who was said to have come south after the sack of Troy. The name 'Muksus' in the Hittite letter was even claimed to be the name of a historical Greek immigrant: the personal name 'Mo-qo-so' is known in tablets from Knossos and Pylos back in Bronze Age Greece. The geography of the movements of this 'immigrant' seemed to fit too: Karatepe's inscriptions belonged in just the area, Cilicia, to which Mopsus was said to have travelled. Best of all, the dates seemed to fall into place. When ancient scholars calculated a numerical date for the fall of Troy they placed it in a year which we would count as 1184 BC. Mopsus, then, would have wandered south in the 1180s, and wondrously, in one later Greek compilation just such a date for him survived. In *c.* AD 320 the Christian bishop Eusebius set out the parallel chronologies of biblical, Greek and Roman events. In the year 1184/3, his lists tell us, 'Mopsus reigned in Cilicia'.[23] Eusebius himself had no independent interest in the dates of remote Greek history, but he relied on the texts of earlier Greek scholars. Their work on problems of chronology drew on scholarly studies which had begun in the third century BC.

With their support, the Greek and the Hittite sources appeared to converge on the same individual and the same era: Mopsus, or Muksas, it seemed, was not 'simply a Greek fiction', but 'he is shown to have been a historical person ... he emerges as the first character from the mists of the Greek Heroic Age of whom this can be said and who can be dated independently of Greek sources'.[24] History, therefore, underlay this Greek myth, as the real Mopsus appeared to be known to Hittite contemporaries and then to have moved south, when Troy fell, to rule in Cilicia and to found a dynasty in the 1180s BC with which the rulers at Karatepe later connected themselves. The conclusion, if true, would be extremely important for the relationship between facts and myth. If Mopsus' movements are based on history, who is to say what facts may lie behind the tales of travelling Odysseus or even the myths of migrating Moses and Abraham?

These neat conclusions are too optimistic. On the Greek side, the name 'Mo-qo-so' is unlikely to have become the Muksus (or Muksas) in the two eastern texts: phonetically its likely rendering would be 'Ma-ka-sa', or Maksa. The ancient date for the fall of Troy is also irrelevant. It was the attempt of ancient scholars to fix a date for a mythical event and is evidence only of their misplaced learning. The date of 1184/3 for Mopsus' reign in Cilicia was based on this same vain calculation. Greek chronographers knew that Mopsus was said to have wandered south after the Trojan War and so they dated his southern kingdom to the year after their date for Troy's fall. Their precision began from a false premise and tried to make facts out of fictions.

On further consideration, the Hittite sources for Muksus–Muksas have become equally problematic. The Hittite letter which mentioned Muksus in western Asia has been redated by scholars before 1400 BC, about seven hundred years, then, before the mention of Muksas at Karatepe.[25] The exact date of the Karatepe inscriptions (c. 760 or 700 BC) is not crucial for the argument because they refer to the 'house' or dynasty of Muksas (Mps, in the accompanying Phoenician text). For them it was an existing entity, like the royal 'house of David' or our modern 'house of Windsor'. Its founder, Muksas ('Mopsu') thus lived earlier than c. 700, but he cannot possibly have lived and ruled near Karatepe as early as 1400 BC.

III

A historical Muksas or Mopsus, wandering and ruling in the twelfth century BC or earlier, is not the answer to the oddly widespread locations of the Greek Mopsus myths. A different approach is needed and the example of Io, Cadmus or Europa helps us to see the right way forward. The one surviving fact is that in southern Asia, a 'house of Muksas' (Mps) was indeed a reality before 700. It went back to a founder of that name who had ruled perhaps as early as the ninth or even tenth century BC. The inscriptions at Karatepe reveal that this 'house of Muksas' (Mps) ruled at Adana in the broad plains of eastern Cilicia: it is also likely to have controlled neighbouring sites, including Tarsus. The Karatepe inscriptions give the personal statements of one Azitawattas, a powerful man who connects himself with the 'house of Muksas'. He was not a member of it himself, but he acknowledges the importance of 'Awarikus', a king of Adana and a member of the 'house of Muksas' by whom he seems to have been helped to power: in the accompanying Phoenician text he is called 'Aw(a)rk(u)'.[26] Most remarkably, since 1980, at least three other local inscriptions have revealed similarly named rulers. One was found on the west slope of the Amanus mountains, the eastern border of Que, about 15 miles south-east of Karatepe (a Phoenician text also naming Aw(a)rk(u)).[27] Another lay far to the west (a Phoenician text, naming Waryk(u)) near to Rough Cilicia's boundary with Pamphylia.[28] The third is a Luwian-Hittite and Phoenician bilingual text found in 1998. It names 'Warikas' (the likeliest reading) in Luwian hieroglyphs, the grandson (in Phoenician, the 'descendant') of 'Muksas'. This bilingual text was found on the stone statue of a ruler, surely Warikas himself, sculpted as if riding in an ox-drawn chariot: it was discovered only about 20 miles south of Adana in the Cilician plain.[29] The date and exact readings of each of these texts are not certain, but they refer to closely similar names. The likeliest view is that the third, the bilingual, refers to a kinsman of the similarly named ruler attested at Karatepe. The second text, the furthest to the west, may refer to a grandson of the same name; the first, furthest to the east, refers to Karatepe's ruler himself. There may even be a fourth, north-west of the plain, but not fully published, which may mention the ruler himself too. On any view, a realm of descendants of Muksas–Mopsus is now soundly attested around Adana and is datable to the eighth century BC.

In this same eighth century, Greek pottery, as we have seen, was reaching this plain of eastern Cilicia with Greek visitors, especially with Euboeans. They were followed by Greeks who settled new towns here, especially Greeks from Rhodes who founded Soloi *c.* 700 BC on the western edge of the Cilician plain.[30] These Greek visitors, including Euboeans, found themselves in the kingdom which was known locally as the lands of the 'house of Muksas', or 'Mopsu' as Phoenicians pronounced his name. When they heard where they were, a wonderful notion dawned on them: their own hero Mopsus had been here before them. The Greek visitors did not invent a new mythical hero Mopsus in order to fit this 'Mopsu' into their own past. In their Greek myths they had such a hero already, the Mopsus who came from Greece and Claros. The names were irresistibly similar and the connection did not require great learning. Like so many Greek travellers after them, whether Herodotus or the soldiers of Alexander the Great, these Greeks in the eighth century BC made brilliant sense of what they heard abroad in terms of heroes who had travelled with them in their minds.

Some of these Greeks were Euboeans and the very place names of this kingdom made sense too. In its heartland, just to the south-east of Adana, the site of modern Misis acquired the Greek name 'Mopsouhestia', or Mopsus' hearth. It is a very curious name, but it persisted nonetheless for more than a thousand years.[31] Although it first appears for us in Greek texts of the mid-fourth century BC, its first surviving attestation is not its origin. The naming of a place after a hearth is unparalleled in Greek topography and has never yet been explained. The neo-Hittite connections of the ruling 'house of Muksas' can now provide the answer. In old Hittite, a *hesty* is a site of religious ritual, patronized by the ruling family.[32] At modern Misis, overlooking the Ceyhan river, the ruling 'house of Muksas' will have had such a *hesty* or religious centre: Greek visitors interpreted the name in Greek and called the *hesty* of Muksas 'Mopsouhestia'. This 'hearth of Mopsus' continued to glow on the Greek map throughout antiquity: its embers deserve prompt excavation.

Not far from his 'hearth' Mopsus also acquired an oracular spring, at Mopsoukrene near Mallos. We can still see why: the main feature of this site is the fine freshwater spring at modern Güzeloluk which has served through the ages as a watering place for travellers and their horses on the road southwards from Adana. In the time of Plutarch (*c.* AD 80–120) it could still confound a Roman governor who had otherwise been inclined to dismiss the claims of oracles to be speakers of the truth.[33] Before Greeks visited the site, there had probably been a simple place of divination at the local spring. Greek visitors then ascribed it to their prophetic Mopsus' care.

There was also, we now know, a familiar sound to one of the dynasty's local titles. In the bilingual inscription found south of Adana in 1998, 'Warikas' the 'grandson of Muksas' describes himself as the 'king of Hiyawa', a land of 'the plain'. The Phoenician scribes rendered this 'Hiyawa' land by their own word for Adana and its people, evidently its correct reference.[34] However, to Greek-speakers the place names had a very different resonance. They sounded just like their own 'Achaia', the land of Homer's Achaean Greeks. In earlier texts of the Bronze Age Hittite empire, an 'Ahhiyawa' people had been located somewhere west of Asia; almost certainly they were Achaean Greeks. In the ninth and eighth centuries the 'Hiyawa' land of southern Asia was quite unrelated, but the verbal resemblance caught on with Greek visitors, just as it has caught on too quickly with modern scholars since this text's recent publication. The resemblance also caught on locally. By the early fifth century, some of the Cilicians, as we know from Herodotus, had exploited the resemblance and were calling themselves 'Hypachaioi', or sub-Achaeans, in order to attach their non-Greek origins to the Greeks' own family of peoples.[35]

When a 'Mopsu' ruled in 'Hiyawa', what visiting Euboean Greek in the eighth century BC could doubt the natural inference that their own Mopsus and some Achaeans had once been there before them? The extent of the real house of the kingdom of 'Mopsu' must not be underestimated. Some of its descendants ruled in western Rough Cilicia (to judge from the recently found epigraphic evidence), but there are also signs that they had ruled even further west in adjacent Pamphylia. At Karatepe, the strong man Azitawattas refers to his dominion as far as 'the setting sun'. It may indeed have run far west, as far, even, as the fine site of Perge in Pamphylia, the 'Parha' of previous Hittite texts.[36] Here, many centuries later, Mopsus is known to us in a series of remarkable sculptures. The Hellenistic walls of the city of Perge's main gate contain niches for nine statues which date to the early second century AD: their subjects are known to us from the Greek inscriptions on their bases and derived from some spectacular antiquarian scholarship. Seven of them are mythical figures, including 'Mopsus son of Apollo from Delphi', who is one of those named as the city's founder.[37] The 'house of Muksas' had evidently ruled as far away as 'Parha' or Perge. The memory of them lived on and so either Greek visitors or Greek-speaking citizens of Perge presented their ancient historical link with Muksas (Mps) as a link with the Greek Mopsus the travelling prophet. It dignified the city in an increasingly Greek age.

At Aspendos, also in Pamphylia, the traces of Mopsus are even older. The people of this non-Greek city had the custom, foreign to Greeks, of sacrificing boars to the goddess Aphrodite. When they connected themselves to Greek culture and began to use the Greek language, they explained their practice through Greek myth. In a famous poem, the learned Greek poet Callimachus (c. 270 BC) tells how at Aspendos the hero Mopsus vowed to sacrifice to Aphrodite the first animal he encountered. He went out hunting, met a wild boar and killed it: true to his vow he began the sacrificial practice which persisted at Aspendos ever afterwards. Callimachus' explanation has been detected as far back as c. 400–350 by a brilliant use of evidence from Aspendos itself.[38] Silver coins, minted in the city, show on one side a naked horseman, armed with a javelin, on the other side a wild boar on the run. The horseman is Mopsus, out hunting in heroic nudity: the men of Aspendos were already using this mythical Greek hero to explain a barbarian aspect of their religion in Greek terms. They chose Mopsus because they could point to a local connection with him: Aspendos, too, had once been ruled by the 'house of Muksus' and its associates. We can support their belief about their past. At Karatepe, the name of the ruler Azitawattas has been convincingly linked to the pre-Greek name of the town of Aspendos itself.[39] Perhaps he came from Aspendos or perhaps he refounded it. We can, then, give credit to later Greek sources which claim that the ancient name of all Pamphylia had been 'Mopsopia', Mopsus-land.[40] There were historical reasons, too, why Greek authors attempted to link Mopsus by marriage or kinship with a mythical Pamphyle and other local namesakes along this part of the south Asian coast. We first meet these namesakes in Greek sources of the mid-fourth century BC, but they go back much earlier to the time when the local Muksas and his dynasty had ruled there, leaving a memory which needed to be explained in Greek terms. That need was first felt by Greek visitors and settlers in the eighth century BC, Euboeans and others who confronted this major coastal kingdom, a power-block which historians nowadays overlook.

The 'house of Muksas–Mopsu' may also have had an eastward extension beyond Adana and Karatepe. When Alexander the Great arrived in Cilicia in autumn 333 BC, his learned historian Callisthenes discovered that Mopsus the travelling prophet had also been active in 'Syria and Phoenicia'.[41] One reason may perhaps be that the 'house of Muksas' had ruled further east than we yet know, briefly flourishing in a part of north Syria. Other reasons are obscure to us, but we have extracts from an earlier source, the Greek-speaking Xanthus of Lydia's histories, which were written in the later fifth century BC. Xanthus wrote of 'Moxos the Lydian' with due local patriotism and connected this person with one, perhaps two, holy places in the Levant. One was Ascalon on the Phoenician coast and the other (possibly) Mabbug, a famous 'holy city' in Syria.[42] This 'Moxos the Lydian' was a local invention: his name was based on the continuing local use of the likesounding name 'Muksas' in Lydia and Anatolia, a name which even became connected with a 'Moxos-town' south-east of Lydia.[43] But the stories about his deeds at these Near Eastern cult-sites may have a historical origin. They may go back to Greek visitors' attempts to explain these places' non-Greek cult-practices in a Greek way, or even to stories which the non-Greek residents later began for the same purpose. If so, Xanthus then combined all the mentions of Mopsus' doings into one legendary story about 'Moxos': there is probably more to be discovered about the facts in Phoenicia and Syria on which his statements were based.

Whatever those facts were, they were not the deeds of a real Near Eastern 'migrant charismatic' who was bringing eastern wisdom to

the Greeks. Nor was Mopsus a Greek Aeneas who had escaped from
Troy to found a hearth and a city elsewhere. Mopsus' southern career
was the wishful interpretation of Greeks, including Euboeans, who
who were impressed by the names which locals in Cilicia told them.
These Greeks were traders, not settlers or post-Trojan warriors. It is
only a charming notion that 'Warikas', a ruler in the 'house of Mopsu',
was himself a Euboean Greek with the Greek name of Euarchos
(attested in eighth-century Euboea).[44] That derivation, sadly, is fanci-
ful: a Euboean had not carved out a kingdom for himself near Adana
and Misis. Rather, Euboeans found evidence of Mopsus when they
traded and travelled in the 'kingdom of Muksas–Mopsu' in the eighth
century BC.

To the Greeks, a verbal coincidence often seemed like a sign or an
omen. When the visiting Greeks heard locally of 'Mopsu', it would
have seemed to them like a heaven-sent omen, establishing that
Mopsus the prophet had been there before them. What, though, of
the stories which they developed about Mopsus' quarrels with other
Greek prophets? A quarrel has potential as a structural element in a
legendary story, but beneath this role there may be a historical cause:
the competing traditions of local Greek communities from c. 700 BC
onwards.

At Claros, Mopsus was said to have quarrelled with the visiting
seer Calchas. The origins of Claros's oracle are obscure, but recent
finds of pottery from renewed excavations of the site confirm that
Greek goods, and probably Greek visitors, were to be found there
already by c. 900 BC. It had a local spring and was probably a holy
site before any buildings served it. The control of Claros was soon to
be disputed between two nearby Greek settlements: Notion, which
was settled on the hill overlooking the Aegean sea, and Colophon,
which was settled inland up the river.[45]

At first, the people of Notion appear to have controlled the sanctuary. They were Aeolian Greeks by origin, a small Aeolian enclave
among the many surrounding Ionian Greek settlements along the
coast. By his origin in Thessaly, Mopsus the hero had Aeolian Greek
roots too. He was part, then, of the mythical heritage of the Aeolians
at Notion and for local reasons which are lost to us they made him
into Claros's mythical prophet. Inland from Notion, however, the

Ionians at Colophon also aspired to control the site of Claros. In the early seventh century BC their own favoured hero is known to us: men from Colophon sailed west to found a new settlement at Siris in southern Italy, and there they claimed to have the very tomb of Calchas the prophet.[46] So far from dying in a contest with Mopsus at Claros, he was said by them to be protecting their settlers in a new western home. Relations between Colophon and nearby Notion were never easy and their bitter rivalry may help to explain the story of a quarrel between the two prophets at Claros. The Aeolian Greeks at Notion had a special relationship with Aeolian Mopsus, but the Ionian Greeks at Colophon had a special relationship with Calchas. It was, then, particularly appealing for the Aeolian controllers of Claros to claim that Mopsus had outwitted Calchas and caused his death on the site. Colophon, specially close to Calchas, denied that Calchas had ever died there, but Mopsus' supremacy had already been celebrated in early Greek poetry. Although Colophon took over Claros and later reduced its old rival Notion to insignificance, the story of Mopsus' triumph could not be erased from the record.[47]

In southern Asia, Mopsus had two coastal heartlands, Pamphylia and the Cilician plain, but his relations with each of them varied. Their differing history of Greek settlement may help to explain why. The early contacts of Greeks with Pamphylia are still uncertain in the absence of adequate archaeology but we can probably discount the few late sources which allege an actual settlement there by Greeks. In Pamphylia, conspicuously, there was no tradition of a quarrel involving Mopsus. Instead, as Greek culture spread there, non-Greek settlements inland adopted Mopsus peacefully as a connection between themselves and Greek myth. The people of Aspendos, Perge and other Pamphylians used this convenient hero as a bridge between their non-Greek past and their new claims to a heroic Greek ancestry. Further west along the coastline, just before the fire-breathing Chimaera, there was a genuine Greek settlement in Lycia where Greeks from Rhodes founded Phaselis. In the Hellenistic age Greek antiquarians blended Phaselis's founders peacefully into Mopsus' family too, building on a similarity between their respective Greek names. They claimed that Phaselis's founder had been an Argive companion of Mopsus and that Mopsus' mother had prophesied their occupation of the site.[48]

In Cilicia, by contrast, Mopsus was said to have quarrelled to the death with Amphilochus the Argive. Here, the reason for the enmity may be that the traditions of two separate Greek groups of settlers collided on adjoining territory. In the eighth century BC Euboeans and other Greeks located Mopsus on the plain round Adana after encountering the local 'house of Mopsu'. By 700 BC, however, Greeks from the island of Rhodes had settled in Soloi on the coast just to the south-west of Mopsus' plain. As self-styled Argive kinsmen these Rhodians were champions of Amphilochus, the Argive travelling hero.[49] Inland on the plain, the town of Mallos followed their lead and claimed to be an Argive foundation with an oracular shrine of Amphilochus himself. This kinship distinguished them from Mopsus' nearby oracular spring at 'Mopsoukrene', their local rival. In one group of stories Mopsus then quarrelled with his rival Amphilochus and killed him. This story of a quarrel could have grown up from the competing claims of Mallos, Soloi and Mopsoukrene, local Greek communities with two different heroes as their supposed ancestors.

These competing claims extended eastwards too. In the mid-fifth century Herodotus made no mention of Mopsus, but referred to a link between the Argive Amphilochus and the Greek settlement at Posideion on the borders of Cilicia and Syria: perhaps a Rhodian Greek contingent imposed the Argive story here near the future site of Iskenderun. Later Greek scholars then asserted that Mopsus had been active further south in Syria and Phoenicia.[50] Was he, perhaps, the favoured hero of nearby Al Mina, many of whose first settlers were Euboean Greeks, familiar with their 'discovery' of Mopsus in the Cilician plain? Did Mopsus rule for Al Mina, whereas Amphilochus ruled for Posideion on the Bay of Issus? If so, the rivalry between the two prophets was replayed on north Syria's curving coastline.

What is certain, but under-appreciated, is that the local balance between these two heroes might have remained unresolved without a subsequent thunderclap: the arrival of Alexander the Great. In the late summer and autumn of 333 BC the young conqueror lay sick with a fever at Tarsus and his army delayed in Cilicia. His retained historical adviser Callisthenes had spare time meanwhile to research old problems of the country's local heroes by studying them in the field. In Alexander's company, he had travelled through Pamphylia late in the previous autumn. His rival Greek historian, Theopompus, had recently endorsed Mopsus' role in Pamphylia, but Callisthenes could now gather evidence on site. The traces of Mopsus were undeniable, so Mopsus and his followers, he decided, must have left Claros, crossed the Taurus mountains and divided themselves up. Some had stayed in Pamphylia, some in Cilicia, but others had gone on as far as Syria and Phoenicia.[51] We can now see the sound sources of his reasoning: the connections of Mopsus with Claros, his prominence at Aspendos and elsewhere in Pamphylia, the presence of the commemorative place names in Cilicia, the Greek traces in north Syria and the presence of Mps (Mopsu) in the Phoenician language which sounded so Mopsus-like to Greeks. Callisthenes had worked with his kinsman Aristotle and here, as elsewhere, he based his conclusions on evidence.

While the court historian was confirming the heritage of Mopsus, his young patron Alexander was studiously ignoring it. He visited Perge, Soloi, Aspendos and other cardinal places in Mopsus' heartland, but he is nowhere said to have honoured Mopsus himself. Instead, he did the opposite. Alexander and his Macedonian ancestors claimed to be the descendants of the revered Greek Argos. When he reached Mallos he found a place whose origins were disputed between Mopsus and Amphilochus. Artfully, the citizens emphasized their Argive ancestry by pointing to the Argive Amphilochus as their real founder. Alexander honoured Mallos for sharing his own Argive ancestors and favoured the city with financial privileges. He even sacrificed to Amphilochus as a hero. One aspiring 'Argive' thus benefited others. The 'Argive' descent of both the Macedonians and the Cilicians was highly disputed, but in 333 BC they met as kinsmen on a mythical bridge.[52]

The lesson was not lost on other cities in Mopsus' lands. Already in the fourth century BC non-Greek Aspendos had begun to emphasize her connection with Mopsus in order to explain her barbarian practices of sacrifice. In autumn 334, however, the legend of Mopsus their local boar-hunter had not saved Aspendos from Alexander's exactions. Correctly, he treated the Aspendians as a non-Greek community and punished them when they rebelled against his demands. In the decades after his death, however, Aspendos sustained a claim to a nobler origin.

We have the evidence for it at Nemea, in the territory of Argos in Greece, where fragments of a recently found Argive decree give parts of a list of communities whose claims to a kinship with Argos were honoured by the Argives themselves.[53] The decree dates to the aftermath of Alexander's reign, an era (c. 310–300 BC) which was one of continuing prestige for Argos, the supposed mother-city of the Macedonian royal family. The surviving fragments of the decree suffice to show that the list of recognized Argive kin ranged far and wide. They even included the tiny Aegean island of Seriphos: in the Greek myths Seriphos had sheltered the Argive Perseus when he was cast out as a baby from Argos's royal house. However, pride of place went to Soloi. She was recognized as an Argive city through her connections with Rhodes and the travelling hero Amphilochus. Evidently it had become important for this faraway Cilician city to have her Argive origin recognized again after Alexander's reign.[54]

Where Soloi led, other cities in and around Cilicia scrambled to follow. High on the Argive list comes no less of an intruder than Aspendos. Somehow her citizens had persuaded the Argives that they were not, after all, a barbarian community. There were very good reasons why they now pressed this claim. Anyone who had witnessed Alexander's recent favours to the self-styled 'Argive' cities in Cilicia and elsewhere knew that it paid to be seen as Argive in the new age of Macedonian kings. Despite the city's link with Mopsus, Alexander had punished Aspendos, so she dropped her emphasis on Mopsus and passed herself off as Argive instead.[55] She was remarkably successful. By the first century AD Aspendos, of non-Greek origin, appeared to be a 'foundation of the Argives' to the geographer Strabo.

From Claros to north Syria, Thessaly to Ascalon, the travels of Mopsus the hero are not evidence for a 'migrant charismatic' who was bringing wisdom from the Near East to the Greek world. They are evidence, yet again, for the flexibility of Greeks and their myths as they explained a newly found Asian kingdom, responded to civic rivalries and forged bonds of kinship between unrelated peoples. The Euboeans and other Greeks who visited the lands of the 'house of Muksas' in the eighth century did not arrive with empty minds which were waiting to be filled with Near Eastern learning. Guided by their own Greek presuppositions they drew their own conclusions and made their own misunderstandings. As a result Mopsus the mythical hero travelled, quarrelled and found a second homeland, hearth and spring. Homer's epics ignored him, but Homer's Greek contemporaries were meanwhile finding evidence of him at every turn. Mopsus then stayed in Cilicia awaiting a final discovery. In 1949 the German archaeologist Helmuth Bossert investigated the ruins of ancient Magarsos, 3 miles to the west of modern Karatas. He was much struck by the existence of two ancient burial mounds which lay near to each another, the one smaller than the other because it had been robbed. Here, he was rightly convinced, were the burial mounds ascribed to Mopsus and his enemy Amphilochus, to which the story of their quarrel had become attached.[56] They await excavation, but the heroes are indeed lying where neither can see the other, in a landscape of cotton-bushes, the modern 'white gold' of the Ceyhan river's irrigated plain.

14

Travelling Lovers

With Io or Mopsus, Europa or the fiery Chimaera we are still tracking myths which travelled to new sites through Greeks' own inferences and flexible misunderstandings. The linguistic 'fault of the Greeks' seems fertile enough, whereas an informed contact with Near Eastern stories and practice seems suggestively far from their reach. There is, however, a cult which connects more closely to genuine Near Eastern details. The cult of the Greek demigod Adonis has been repeatedly studied and reinterpreted, but its initial presence in the Greek world repays a fresh study. Its forerunners in the Near East continue to be better understood through new readings of fragmentary non-Greek evidence. The relation between this Greek cult's famous 'Orientalism' and its real Near Eastern roots has changed focus as a result. These 'roots' confronted Euboean travellers in the Levant from c. 950 BC, but the first stages of the resulting Greek cult lie somewhat later, though still in the general triangle of Cyprus, Cilicia and Phoenicia. It did not become known through 'migrant charismatics' from the east. Its development points to a human channel of contact which was most important for Euboeans too: it also has a Christian finale in this same region, the significance of which has not been understood.

Like all Greek myths, the story of Adonis survives in various versions. The names of his parents vary too but they share two constant qualities: they are not gods or demigods and at least one of them belongs in Cyprus or the nearby coastlines. Quite often, Adonis is presented as a child who was born from incest, a story which first survives for us through the poet Panyassis (c. 500 BC). In this typical version Adonis' mother was punished while still a girl with an intense sexual desire for her father. He mated with her unawares by night, but drove her out on learning what he had done. The gods concealed her as a myrrh- or spice-tree and when her bark split open after nine months her son Adonis was born.[1]

In this version Adonis' mother was named Smyrna but then became Myrrha, the world's first spice-girl. Her father was a 'king of the Assyrians' or Syrians, although others made him the king of Cyprus, Cinyras, a name known from Homer. On the fateful day of King Philip of Macedon's murder, when Alexander became king, a tragic drama about Myrrha and Cinyras is said to have been on the programme of the celebrations at the Macedonian palace: incest was about the only missing factor in the complex polygamy of Philip's own family at the time.[2] Incest, incense and an eastern parentage were fittingly exotic origins for the exotic Adonis. Sometimes he was simply called 'the eastern one' (Aous), a name which later authors then tried to fix to a mountain or river of a similar name which was connected with Cyprus. Like other stories of incest his story had a lively poetic afterlife. The tales of Adonis and Smyrna–Myrrha appealed to the poet Cinna in the age of Julius Caesar, the man whom Shakespeare later represented as torn 'for his bad verses'. Cinna, too, located Adonis in Cyprus.[3]

Adonis was such a handsome boy that Aphrodite fell in love with him. She hid him in a chest which she gave to Persephone for safe keeping but Persephone, too, fell in love and refused to give the boy back. Almost certainly this part of the story was also told by Panyassis. Zeus had to adjudge the dispute, and he ruled that Adonis should spend part of the year (some said eight months) with Aphrodite and the rest with Persephone. This judgement became connected in due course with a story of an accident. As Adonis grew up, he took to hunting, the beloved blood sport of Greek heroes, but was badly wounded by a wild boar, sent (some said) by Aphrodite's jealous lover Ares. A distraught Aphrodite searched for his body and eventually discovered it in the countryside. Flowers were said to have sprouted from the tragedy, above all blood-red anemones from Adonis' blood. Whether Adonis died out hunting or not, his fate in all stories was to move yearly between the living and the dead. As Persephone was queen of the dead, for part of the year Adonis was to stay with her in the underworld. He then returned, perhaps briefly, to Aphrodite and the world of the living. His yearly plight is best expressed in the wonderful hymn in his honour which was composed by the poet Theocritus and set in Egypt's Alexandria in the 270s BC. 'You come both here and to the underworld, so they say,' Theocritus makes his expert singer tell the audience, 'unique and alone among the demigods . . .'[4] The setting of this hymn is one of royal Alexandrian splendour, but its theology should not be discounted as a late Egyptian variation. The singer is not Egyptian herself; she is said to be repeating a widely received *muthos* ('so they say . . .'); Adonis, therefore, was generally believed to commute every year between the living and the dead.

With small variations this *muthos* is attested for us across nearly a thousand years of Greek literature from Panyassis to Christian authors. They are not 'Christianizing' the story and distorting it: with some detachment, rather, they report pagan rites and beliefs about Adonis which had persisted into the early fifth century AD. Like his parents, Adonis was not born a god: his story was embellished with heroic attributes and he was at best a demigod. Nonetheless we have scattered evidence for a cult of him, although it is nowhere sufficiently concentrated for us to be sure of its every detail in any one city at any one time. As it extends over so many centuries, scholars tend to beware of generalizing, with an apt warning that no cult is likely to have stayed unchanged in so many settings across a thousand years. However, despite the time-span, the changing contexts and the varied sites, there is a constant core, a 'typical' form which is worth bringing out.

The cult of Adonis did not belong in the calendars of public festivals in Greek cities. It was usually celebrated in households by groups of women, including courtesans, who would lament the lovely hero. They would tear their tunics and beat their bared breasts. They also engaged in some special gardening. They sowed rapidly germinating seeds of fennel, lettuce and other green herbs (but perhaps not wheat) in flowerpots or on pieces of pottery. They lamented their hero on the rooftops of houses and discarded these green pot-gardens when they marked Adonis' yearly departure for the underworld.[5] Most of our evidence is for a ritual in the heat of July, and the most vivid account of Adonis' yearly departure is once again in Theocritus' hymn. It describes how an image of Adonis lay on display in Alexandria for his female worshippers until they took it down to the sea and lamented, 'topless', his departure for the underworld.[6] Images of Adonis had been important in the cult in classical Athens too but perhaps the escort down to the sea was an Alexandrian innovation. At Alexandria, Adonis' image was perhaps thrown into the water. Elsewhere the gardens of greenery in his honour are said to have been thrown into local wells.

These female rites are remarkable, and have left a clear mark in Greek literature. We first hear a Greek lament for Adonis in verses by the poet Sappho on Lesbos *c*. 600 BC. 'Delicate Adonis is dying, Aphrodite: what are we to do?' 'Beat your breasts, girls, and tear your garments.' The poem's unusual metre is matched by its unusual form, as if a choir is lamenting the delicately lovely Adonis while a singer answers them as Aphrodite. It is the first dramatization to survive in Greek literature.[7] This bare-breasted mourning long remained customary, as we see from two neat epigrams by Dioscorides in Egypt *c*. 270 BC. He writes of two charming girls who had captivated him, one while 'beating her breasts' by Adonis' coffin, the other 'beating her milk-white breasts at Adonis' night-festival'. He represents himself as seeing them topless and willing to die ('no excuses') if one of them will do the same for him on his own voyage to the underworld. The ritual was a chance for a man to spy on a half-nude lady.[8]

This aspect of the cult helps us to understand a famous, but hitherto elusive, reference to it in Aristophanes' great comic drama *Lysistrata* (411 BC).[9] His Athenian women have taken over the city's Acropolis and a pompous, elderly Special Councillor comes to find out what is going on. He compares the trouble to women's habitual worship of 'Oriental' gods. He recalls how one Damostratus had been proposing the fateful expedition to Sicily in the public assembly in 415 BC when 'his wife' (the likeliest meaning: otherwise just 'the woman') was dancing and saying 'Woe for Adonis.' Damostratus went on with his detailed proposals but 'his wife' was 'already somewhat drunk' and said 'Beat yourselves for Adonis.' Damostratus 'urged us on forcibly' (or 'was under duress': both meanings are possible) and the result, we infer, was the expedition to Sicily, a massive Athenian disaster, on the strength of his forceful speech. Damostratus' proposals are brilliantly evoked beside the short cries of his Adonis-worshipping wife. They

are a jumble of items widely separated in time and there is no reason
to believe that any real worship of Adonis had coincided in fact with
the Sicilian debate. The comic point, however, is that this female
'wantonness' had serious effects. When 'his wife' cried 'Beat yourselves . . .', the implication to the audience is that she and her worshippers would have ripped their clothes and beaten their breasts,
'with the folds of their robes down to their ankles', as Theocritus'
hymn specifies it, 'and breasts showing'. Aristophanes means that
Damostratus saw his wife and her fellow-worshippers topless on the
roof. He had an ill-fated rush of excitement and 'spoke forcibly' (or
'under pressure'), urging the citizens into their greatest-ever disaster.

Most remarkably, these Greek rites and stories connect with vastly
older cults and stories in the Near East. 'Adonis' was modelled by
Greeks on what they saw and heard there, but we can take evidence
for it far further back than they ever knew, to songs, stories and cult
in Mesopotamian society before 2000 BC. Here the ill-fated herdsman
Dumuzi was loved and married by the goddess Inanna (Ishtar): the
Sumerian songs of their courtship are among the oldest known love
songs in the world.[10] After their union the goddess went to the lands
of the dead, apparently wishing to rule them. She failed, but escaped
on condition that she offered a substitute. As Dumuzi had not
mourned her absence, she sent demons to seize him and dispatch him
to the dead in her place. Further details continue to be recovered from
fragmentary tablets, but they correct the assumption that Dumuzi
himself died unheeded. We now know that he was spared for half of
each year while his sister went to the dead in his place. We also know
that the goddess repented of her attack on him and mourned the
absence which she had caused.[11]

The texts which survive are telling a story, not repeating the fixed
version of a single 'myth': more surprises probably remain to be found
in other versions. We know, however, from temple-texts and lists
of gods in Mesopotamia that the cult of Dumuzi was not a private
household affair. Parts of his story connected with processions of the
statue of his goddess-lover from one Mesopotamian city-temple to
another, including temples of the underworld gods.[12] There was music,
incense and lamentation in his honour, during which women beat
their breasts. A day of noisy lament for him was one of several days

in his cult, which occurred, in one known case, on several consecutive days in high summer (our late July).[13] This entire Babylonian month eventually bore his name, but there is at least one hint that locally there was worship of Dumuzi in the spring too. The cult was not only for women, but women participated and once prostitutes are specifically mentioned.[14]

The most famous modern historian of this cult is Sir James Frazer, who made it a central subject of his *Golden Bough*. For him, the extraordinarily long history of this sort of worship was best explained in terms of a persistent fact of nature. It 'explained', he believed, to primitive minds a great 'mystery', the yearly renewal of green nature in springtime.[15] When Dumuzi, or Adonis, returns to the land of the living, nature bursts into life. When he goes back to the land of the dead in mid-July the land becomes brown, parched and dying. Global warming has accentuated Frazer's explanation. However, the more we have learned from Babylonian evidence the more this explanation has been contested. Dumuzi is also linked to the sick and the dead, while Frazer knew none of the story of his love and his victimization by his goddess-lover. 'Nature' alone does not explain the cult's scope, but it should not be written out of the story. Dumuzi the herdsman was indeed mourned in high summer, the time when the herdsman's pastures, too, were brown; he came and went yearly, alternating with his sister, who was herself connected with the growing of the vine. At a date which is still disputed, he came to be related (but not equated) with young Damu, a Babylonian god of vegetation.[16] We still do not know precisely when or how Dumuzi returned yearly to the land. The one Babylonian text which mentions his reappearance is late (*c.* 700 BC), but it is almost certainly working with an earlier tradition. It assumes that Dumuzi will come again, although it does not make it clear whether he is coming only briefly during rites of lamentation or whether he is returning for a longer stay during the year.[17]

Most remarkably, this ancient cult and its stories have close similarities to the Greeks' future cult of Adonis. Dumuzi, too, came and went during the year between the lands of the living and the dead; he too was loved by a goddess and was her sexual partner: his death was mourned by her and was loudly lamented by his worshippers; women were prominent, as were incense and music; precious objects, including a bed, were displayed in his honour; July was the main month of his worship. In the Babylonian evidence, so far, we lack the 'green gardening' which is so famous in the Greeks' worship of Adonis. It was not, however, from direct contact with Babylon, let alone with these songs and worship far back in *c.* 2000–1100 BC, that the Greeks' cult took shape. It was formed later through an accessible intermediary, the Levantine Phoenician cities, places with which travelling Euboeans were familiar from *c.* 950 BC onwards.

Dumuzi's presence in these cities has to be inferred indirectly, from the Hebrew Scriptures, whose authors refer to contemporary 'heathen' practices. It is here that the green gardening is first detectable (although the reference is not undisputed). The biblical book of Isaiah (*c.* 710 BC) refers obliquely in a prophecy to what is convincingly translated as 'the planting of gardens for the lovely one' (*Na 'amin*) and the 'setting out of shoots for the foreign one' (Isaiah 17: 10–11). The 'lovely one' refers to the beloved Dumuzi, whom the Hebrew writers know as Tammuz (the West Semitic form of his name).[18] The prophet Ezekiel (*c.* 580 BC) refers with disgust to women lamenting for Tammuz by a gate of the Temple in Jerusalem. This heathen lament was the third of the 'abominations' which he claimed to have seen there in a vision.[19]

Through the Bible, Tammuz remained famous and became a resonant presence in the first book of Milton's *Paradise Lost*. In the eighth to sixth centuries BC these Hebrew references were of wider relevance. What was known as heathen practice in Jerusalem was also being practised in the Levant, especially in the coastal cities of Phoenicia. Notoriously, evidence for such cults is extremely late and is mostly concerned with worship of Adonis when the Phoenician cities had been widely exposed to Greek culture. The great city of Byblos was 'sacred to Adonis', we are told, but only by the geographer Strabo (*c.* 20 BC). Even at Byblos the existence of a pre-Greek cult has been disputed and a non-Greek recipient of it has been doubted. But we have just enough earlier evidence to refute scepticism.[20]

The most suggestive piece was first published in 1977, a Phoenician inscription on stone, found about 6 miles south of Byblos and written in a script whose form suggests a date *c.* 920–900 BC.[21] One line of it refers to the Lady of Byblos, who is known even in the Greek-speaking age as 'Balti': we also know that she was equated with the goddess Astarte–Ishtar. The previous line of the inscription refers to 'the lord' (*adon*), followed by a break in the text. The obvious supplement is Tammuz, the lord (*adon*) and loved one of Lady Astarte. The site of this recent discovery, as we shall see, is significant.

When Alexander the Great arrived and a new Greek era began, worship of the pre-Greek Tammuz was certainly rooted already in the city. It was at Byblos that a near-contemporary Greek historian located the story of Myrrha and her father, plainly because their pre-Greek models were already well known in Byblos.[22] For more details, we have to cross another five hundred years to an artful and complex Greek text, Lucian's *On the Syrian Goddess* (written in the mid-second century AD, perhaps in the early 160s).[23] Lucian claims to have learned by enquiry about the city's rites for Adonis. He also claims an eyewitness knowledge of the 'great temple' of Aphrodite in Byblos and another temple to her which was inland in the mountains.

According to Lucian, Adonis was honoured in Byblos by lamentation and breast-beating, followed by his 'sending into the air', presumably the escorting of his statue out into the open. 'On this day they tell the story that he is alive.' The women of Byblos had to shave off their hair and if they refused, according at least to Lucian, they had to stand in public for a day and have sex for a fee with strangers.[24] The 'coming alive' has been more controversial among scholars than the compulsory sex. Many scholars have seen it as a very late addition to the cult of Adonis and his forerunners, contesting the views of Frazer and *The Golden Bough*, which implicitly saw Adonis as an ancient precursor of the Christian stories of resurrection. But the oldest Sumerian stories of Dumuzi, we now know, made him commute between the lands of the living and the dead. Like Theocritus in his hymn (*c.* 270s BC), Lucian is not innovating when he reports the worshippers' claim that Adonis had 'come alive'.[25]

There was also vivid evidence in the landscape. Just to the south of Byblos runs the modern Nahr Ibrahim river, which the ancients called the 'Adonis'. Every year, Lucian tells us, its waters ran red from the mountains, signifying that Adonis had been wounded there and that the lamentation was now due. Indeed this river runs red, agitated by winds and the rain which washes red soil into its course. Travellers have often observed this staining, which occurs when the river gains water in spring. The mourning, then, was a spring event at Byblos.[26] The inscription to the Lady goddess and 'the lord' (Tammuz?) was discovered right beside this river, suggesting that its connection with them both may be as old as the tenth century BC.

Further inland, in the mountains, Lucian saw yet another ancient shrine of Aphrodite, one which we can also place exactly. At modern Afqa, the ancient Aphaca, we have the remains of ancient temples, including a shrine of Aphrodite which was rebuilt in the Roman era. The place itself has an obvious halo of sanctity, as the Nahr Ibrahim river plunges from an adjoining cliff, encouraging a green fringe of vegetation along its face and falling into a ravine below the cave. 'There is something delicious, almost intoxicating,' wrote Frazer, although he had never been there, 'in the freshness of these tumbling waters, in the sweetness and purity of the mountain air, in the vivid green of the vegetation.'[27] Two streams of water meet, one from a cave in the cliff, the other from the open mountain-face: together they flow past a levelled stone platform, the site of the main temple.

For the relevance of this site we have to look even further ahead, to Christian authors. They identify it as the very place where Tammuz died and even (less plausibly) as the place where the Lady goddess died too in her grief for him. Probably she mourned him, having 'found' him at Afqa; the site, we shall see, was indeed connected with Adonis' death and return to life. It was certainly a major centre for worshippers and it was readily integrated into Tammuz' story. The reddening of the river signified his wound; the green of Afqa, even in high summer, was the place of his 'finding' and, arguably, was a promise of his coming back to life. In Byblos the laments began in spring, but they must have culminated in a procession to this 'extramural' sanctuary, as elsewhere in the ancient world. The myth then became sited at this rare green pocket in the brown summer hinterland and, according to later Christian sources, men at Aphaca wore female clothing and women, even married women, had indiscriminate sex at the site. These practices, if true, had a symbolic value too, at least for modern interpreters. They reversed 'normal time' in transgressions which marked the occasion as a festival-suspension of everyday life.[28] Later Greek sources link the festival with the appearance of a special flaming star, as if the goddess herself was present. As elsewhere in

Syria, the worship for Tammuz–Adonis at Afqa may have occurred in the heat of July.[29]

When our Euboean travellers visited the Levant in the tenth to eighth centuries BC, this weeping for Tammuz certainly confronted them, nearly a thousand years before Lucian's claim to have seen it. Yet it was not from Byblos that Tammuz became the Greek Adonis and spread into the Aegean. His heartland, rather, was a different point in our eastern triangle: Cyprus. Again, the surviving evidence is late, no earlier (it so happens) than the Roman period, but once again our first attestation is not the proof of a practice's origin. By c. 800 BC, after all, Phoenicians had settled on the south-east coast of the island at their 'New Town' of Kition (Larnaca). They (and their women) would have brought the cult of Tammuz and Astarte with them and as they spread inland from Larnaca to Idalion, over the plain of the Mesorea and westwards towards the copper mines of Tamassos, they would have found local gods presiding over the brilliant vegetation of the Cypriot spring. At Idalion there was later to be a shrine of Adonis, based, perhaps, on a previous Phoenician cult of Tammuz. Twelve miles further east, we then find sites which became the home constituency of Adonis:[30] they can best be explained as sites attended by Greek-speaking Cypriots, adapting the cult of Tammuz which the nearby Phoenicians had brought with them.

At Golgoi, the Greek Adonis was said to have been born: one 'Golgos' was even said to have been his child from Aphrodite. At Golgoi a shrine of Aphrodite is amply attested by statuary made from the local limestone, by figurines and by the mentions of 'Aphrodite Golgaia' in inscriptions found nearby.[31] Eight miles north-east of Golgoi lies a second sanctuary, known by its modern name of Arsos. It too attracted dedications by its priestesses. Their figurines and statues match those which were found at Golgoi and although one of Arsos's local gods was Apollo, Aphrodite was plainly honoured at Arsos too, as we know from inscriptions on the site and from the types of the sanctuary's sculptures.[32]

One curious ancient text locates Aphrodite's behaviour after Adonis' death: it occurs in a collection of mythical details which was compiled from uncertain sources in the first century BC. It is remarkably specific and its underlying source has an authority that is greater than its own late date. Like other unhappy lovers, Aphrodite's first impulse, it tells us, had been to jump from the 'White Rock', but she was dissuaded by the news that her Adonis was to be found lying at the shrine of Apollo Erithios 'in Argos, a town on Cyprus'. This Argos has remained one of ancient Cyprus's unlocated sites, but the obvious answer is that it is our modern Arsos, whose name obliquely reflects its past.[33] Arsos has a sanctuary of Apollo and a very strong cult-link with Aphrodite. She was Golgoi's Aphrodite, honoured by her very same priestesses. Her worshippers, I suggest, would process out from Golgoi, Adonis' cult-centre, to 'find him' at Argos–Arsos in the shrine of Apollo, just as the goddess Aphrodite had once found him there in green nature. Just as worshippers in the Levant processed from Byblos to Tammuz' find-spot at Aphaca, so on Cyprus worshippers processed from Golgoi to nearby Argos–Arsos to 'find' Adonis, their goddess's beloved one.

There is no direct ancient evidence for this Cypriot processional route, but there is a most attractive connection. In the 270s Theocritus gives us the poetic hymn, or lament, for Adonis which is sung at his rich festival in Alexandria by a fine female singer, the unnamed 'daughter of a woman from Argos'.[34] In Greece, the ancient Argos had a place of cult for Adonis, like many other cities, but it was not at all a famous cult-centre and it had no natural connection with Egypt's Alexandria.[35] Theocritus' festival was patronized and greatly enriched by Queen Arsinoë, the wife (and sister) of the reigning king Ptolemy II. Arsinoë's strong connections with Cyprus are abundantly attested: on the island itself we have inscriptions in her honour, including some from the Mesorea plain and even from Golgoi, Adonis' legendary 'home'.[36] The expert female singer came, I suggest, from Cyprus, from the very Argos–Arsos where Adonis had been found lying. She was exactly the right accompaniment for an Adonis-festival patronized by a queen who had such close connections with the island. She sings the lament, the Greek 'Ialemos': Theocritus is presenting a Cypriot expert who has come from the heartland of Adonis' cult and lamentations. 'Lady [Aphrodite]', her song begins aptly, 'you who loved Golgoi and Idalion . . .'.

If the cult's heartland lay here on Cyprus, it was not through Euboean travellers that it spread from the Levant through the Greek

Aegean. The cult of Tammuz had confronted them on the coast, but it first passed from the Levant to Cyprus with Phoenician settlers. Their Greek-speaking Cypriot neighbours then developed a parallel cult of their own, partly by observation, partly from contact and intermarriage with Levantine women on the island, the mainstays of Tammuz. They then spread it, no doubt with their own women and daughters, through Cyprus and other Aegean islands, where we find it on Samos and on Sappho's Lesbos, like the figurines and local limestone sculptures which also spread out from Arsos and Golgoi to these places, beginning c. 600 BC.[37]

Why, though, was the Greeks' cult one of 'Adonis', not of Tammuz? His Phoenician worshippers called on their Tammuz as 'Adon' and 'Adonai', names meaning 'Lord' and 'My Lord', during the days of lamentation. Greeks heard them and as 'Tammuz' in Greek would sound most curious ('Thamouth'), the Phoenicians' Adon became the neat Greek Adonis.[38] His stories then took on elements of purely Greek style: the hunting, the romance, the bargain between the two goddess-lovers. But the cult retained much which we can match in non-Greek evidence: the female lamentation, the 'green gardening', the incense, the music, the central notion of commuting yearly between the dead and the living. Between three cultures and across two thousand years the cult would not have remained static, but the basic imprint was still unusually clear. From Greek Egypt, we have a Greek papyrus-list of a householder's expenses (c. 250 BC) which have been brilliantly explained as incurred for the worship of Adonis. Some of them are for a 'display', *deiktērion*: the Greek word and the practice have been matched exactly to the similar 'display' for Dumuzi, held centuries earlier in his old Babylonian cult.[39]

This core of cult passed to the Greeks because they observed it and learned it from participants. The choice of the name 'Adonis' was not the choice of ignorant outsiders. Their obvious informants were women, the cult's most prominent celebrants. From watching, listening and (no doubt) from sex and intermarriage with Levantines, Cypriot Greeks developed an Adonis-cult of their own. It spread from its Cypriot heartland through the rest of Cyprus, to Amathus and the great cult-centre of Aphrodite at Paphos.[40] It then appeared in due course in the west, where we now know of it at the port of Gravisca on the Etruscan-Italian coast. Here, Greeks from the east Aegean may have been its carriers: a cult-building on the site is argued to have been a special Adonis-shrine by *c.* 400 BC, whose courtyard, portico and (possibly) garden were required by the cult. There may have been similar Adonis-cults in other coastal settlements in the west, at Pyrgi or even Locri in south Italy where Aphrodite's cult was important.[41] On Sicily, the cult followed the Phoenicians' presence in the north-west sector of the island where it met and enhanced existing cults of a local Sicilian nature-hero, Daphnis. We may even have visual evidence of it. At Eryx, a Phoenician temple-city, local silver coins of the mid-fifth century BC show on one side a leaf, on the other a flower of what has been identified, optimistically, as a form of anemone, Adonis' flower. On another of the local coin-types a youth is shown before a seated lady, perhaps Adonis before his Aphrodite.[42] If this interpretation is correct, these coin-types are evidence that Adonis was worshipped here too, encouraged by the presence of Eryx's famous shrine to Astarte–Aphrodite, Adonis–Tammuz' loving goddess.

What was the great attraction in Adonis' cult which caused it to spread and persist so far and so long? As Frazer argued, it had a reference to the fertility of the natural world: the 'green gardening', above all, suggests as much. The quickly grown gardens were not left to wither as symbols of sterility. They were thrown away when Adonis returned to the dead but, as they were still green and healthy when discarded, they symbolized the fresh green growth of his brief phase among the living.[43] Eventually ancient authors give us a view of what Adonis meant but it survives only from the third century AD onwards when his cult had been explained allegorically by pagan thinkers. Without exception they present his rites as celebrations of fertility: they are a symbol, they tell us, of the fully grown fruits of the earth, in contrast to the fading flowers of spring. They do not even consider interpretations which have occurred to modern scholars, as if Adonis' women-worshippers were 'play-acting the failure of planting in order to ensure by contrast its success in reality', or even, supposedly, expressing a mocking female attitude to male sexual performance. Here, Frazer's connection with fresh growth and fertility is still relevant.[44]

Nonetheless, it does not exhaust the rites' range of meanings. They were also pre-eminently women's rites. They were not just a response to the 'special situation of Greek women seeking relief from intensive everyday pressures'.[45] They and their accompanying stories specifically presented an idealized youthful lover, to be mourned by women who lived with mundane reality: prosaic, ageing husbands of their own. Theocritus' poem, our best source, exploits exactly this contrast between the young, perfect Adonis, brightly visible, and the humdrum husbands to whom his female spectators must return.[46] Tragic love, a yearly presence and absence and a young beauty were an idealized focus for the emotions: Adonis combined an appeal to 'desperate housewives' with a relation to the growth and summer death of the green natural world.

In the early Christian period this cult of Adonis took on a new, under-emphasized significance. It came to a head in the 320s, when Constantine, the first Christian emperor, gave orders for the destruction of pagan temples at four particular places of cult in the Near East. One was in Jerusalem, on what was believed to be the site of Jesus' tomb; another was beside an ancient oak-tree at Mamre in Palestine; a third was at the harbour-town of Aigai on the Cilician coast; the fourth was at a pagan shrine in the mountainous heartland of Phoenicia.[47]

This surviving list might seem capricious, or perhaps only a small part of a wider whole, but for Christians it had a recognizable logic. 'Jesus' tomb' in Jerusalem was an obvious site for clearance. As for the oak-tree at Mamre, it was here in the book of Genesis that Abraham was said to have entertained the visiting angels. They seemed eerily to be 'now one, now three', and so Christians interpreted them as their holy Trinity, who had visited Mamre in the pre-Christian past.[48] The temple at Aigai also had a rich significance. It had recently been the residence of the pagan holy man Apollonius of Tyana, who was known for stories of his wonder-working: pagan polemicists, writing and speaking shortly before the reign of Constantine, had exalted his miracles as greater than those of Jesus.[49] As for the Phoenician shrine, Eusebius describes in a magnificent burst of rhetoric how Constantine's 'eagle eye' spied it from afar, a site off the beaten track where effeminate men dressed as women, where there was lawless concourse of the sexes, 'marriage-stealing' destruction and unmentionable practices. The site, we can see, was Aphaca where worshippers came out yearly from Byblos to honour Adonis and their Lady goddess in rites of 'social reversal'.

We can also now see the logic of Constantine's orders. At Mamre, he cleared the place where the Holy Trinity first visited mankind. In Jerusalem, he cleared the site of Jesus' tomb. At Aigai and Aphaca he attacked two sites which were central to contemporary anti-Christian polemic: the temple at Aigai where Apollonius' miracles were said to exceed Jesus' and the temple at Aphaca where Adonis' death and return countered Christian claims to a unique Resurrection. The cult of Adonis had already been used by pagans as an anti-Christian counterweight in a highly significant place. A sacred grove for 'Venus and her lover' Adonis had been planted at Bethlehem by the very cave which was supposed to have been the cave of Christ's Nativity. 'Unique and alone among the demigods', Adonis came 'both to the underworld and to the land of the living'. He had become a favourite symbol in contemporary pagan funerary art, no doubt because of his ability to return from the dead. He had not enjoyed a full resurrection because 'the fact that he had to return to some form of existence was merely necessary for creating a new opportunity to die again'.[50] But pagans, shortly before Constantine, had anticipated Sir James Frazer. By c. 300 they had been using Adonis as a counter to Christian claims of a unique triumph over death.

Armed intervention cannot eradicate a belief which extends over two thousand years. Worship at Aphaca survived Constantine, and within a hundred years Christians had to try to stop it again. The divinity of the place survived nonetheless, and Muslim visitors still leave their prayers and offerings beside the water below its cliff. Nothing, meanwhile, not even a Christian task-force, can stop the anemones on the hillsides. They flower each spring, blood-red as if from Adonis' wound, in the hills round Aphaca and the wilder parts of Cyprus. 'There yet, some say, in secret he does lie', so Spenser suggests in *The Faerie Queene*,

> Lapped in flowers and precious spicery,
> By her hid from the world, and from the skill
> Of Stygian gods, which do her love envy;
> But she herself, whenever that she will,
> Possesseth him, and of his sweetness takes her fill . . .

15

A Travelling Mountain

I

The cult of Adonis shows that a core of cult-practice and items from an ancient Near Eastern myth could indeed be encountered in our Euboean Greek travellers' eastern 'triangle' and pass across languages into Greek practice and subsequent storytelling. The transfer was not exact and the contents were not exactly researched and copied. 'Adonis' was the partial understanding of Greek outsiders who heard the cries of the worshippers of Tammuz. The core of his story of death and return became enhanced by Greeks too, who added heroic details of hunting and romance. But not everything was 'lost in translation'.

There was, therefore, a bridge across which genuine knowledge passed to Greeks. It was not some 'migrant charismatic', travelling from the Near East: it was female, the women of Phoenicia, then of Cyprus, with whom Greeks did have that informed 'intercourse' through which stories, cults and practices can pass between cultures. The rites of Tammuz, however, were unmissably public, interrupting civic life and bringing crowds out to worship at secondary shrines in the landscape. In other cases, myths of Near Eastern societies had been connected with rituals which were performed by or around a king. Among the Greeks, kingship had almost entirely vanished by the eighth century BC, except in Sparta and Cyprus. In itself, a difference of social structure would not prevent such myths from being picked up: the Greeks' myths, after all, travelled on to a second life in the very different structure of Roman society. The greater problem was accessibility, not just of language but of the rites and songs in question. It is hard to imagine that eighth-century Greek visitors to

Cilicia or the Levant were ever privileged observers of songs and rituals conducted by local non-Greek kings of the 'house of Muksas' and other dynasties.

There was, however, another bridge besides women. It was one which everyone shared and which caused myths to be told across social classes: the landscape.[1] Even now we tend to think of a landscape only as an external object, a mass of rock, soil and water which exists independently of its viewers. But nature, too, is a human invention and landscapes are creatures of culture as well as hard objects: they are given their character by human concepts. In the Near East, just as in Greece, landscapes were interpreted through myths. All visitors who arrived in these settings wanted to know why the places around them had a particular form. They would ask their local inhabitants and hear, or half-understand, their mythical explanations. The landscape affected everyone and so it was a more open bridge for myths to pass from one culture to another than the rituals around a royal court. In and around north Syria there was so much to explain and interpret. The northern and eastern coast and hinterland of our 'triangle' abound in spectacular natural landscapes: huge caves and clefts in the ground, the fast-flowing waters on the hill-site of Seleuceia (they were later said to be weeping for the Jews martyred in Greek Antioch)[2] or the sudden cliff-face, like a robbers' hideout, which rises so steeply above the Cilician plain at Anavarza, and which is the site of 'Cyinda' where Alexander the Great and his Successors understandably stored their treasure. The great chains of wooded mountains return to the coast where it bends round and Cilicia runs south into Syria. Here, we can still share the impressions which this landscape left on its Assyrian conquerors as they climbed Mount Amanus and looked westwards in wonder over the 'great sea'.

One particular mountain stands out beyond all others on this coastline, a focal point in the view both to and from north Syria, for which, as we have seen, it marks a southern boundary. Known nowadays as the Jebel Aqra, it rises to a height of c. 6,000 feet from the seashore at its foot. Its peaks are high landmarks on all the surrounding routes, whether by sea to Cyprus or by the coastal road to modern Lattakieh, north and west across the broad inland plain of the Amuq valley or up the mountain route which climbs to cross the distant 'Syrian Gates'.

This natural beacon begins with woods on its lower hills, ascends to a range of lesser peaks and ridges and then tapers finally to its highest point. In antiquity it was accurately summed up by the Roman historian Ammianus (*c.* AD 380), himself a man from the plains of Antioch beneath it: 'Wooded, and with a rounded girth it is extended on high to a great altitude.'[3] In the nineteenth century western travellers returned to climb it and they, too, were impressed by the woods which survived on the lower slopes, a mixture of oak and myrtle, birch-trees, quinces and wild pears and even the rare styrax-trees whose resin was so highly prized. Then, the mountain narrows to an alpine height: 'In April the patches of gaudy scarlet peonies alternate and are relieved by patches of yellow asphodel not far from the snowclad summit, where violets and pansies are succeeded by dark green fennel. The summit is composed of naked limestone rock . . .'[4] The woods have now been reduced by felling and the styrax-trees are gone, but above modern Bezge the track towards the summit winds sharply back on itself and the change to the grey bleakness of the upper slope becomes brutally visible. Frequently veiled in cloud, this summit causes the highest rainfall along the entire Syrian coastline. It is the focal point for the storms and the circling claps of thunder which resound along these ridges at the end of a hot summer.

Throughout antiquity the ancients acknowledged the strange genius of this place. They knew the wild animals on its wooded slopes, although characteristically they never mentioned the peonies. In the second millennium BC they already drove their flocks to its lower hills for summer pasturing and knew the mountain-range for its sources of water and its veins of precious metal.[5] They told stories of its spectacular thunderstorms and they discovered that by rising so steeply above sea level the peak offered visitors a rare opportunity: from it they could see the sunrise for about five minutes while the plains below were still in darkness.[6] It is not, then, surprising that this mountain was thought to be a seat of the gods. In late antiquity sailors and locals still called its neighbouring peak the Throne, just as it had been the 'throne' of the gods in texts which went back a thousand years into the pre-Greek past.[7]

Centuries before Homer's Olympus, the Jebel Aqra was the mountain Sapuna, the residence of Baal, one of the great gods of the

Canaanite people.[8] On its heights, as we know from texts recovered from nearby Ras Shamra (Betyllion to the later Greeks), the gods built Baal a palace of blue lapis and silver which they brought down from the clouds. The mountain itself was an object of cult and on it, too, lived the goddess Anat. In autumn, when the summer's heat breaks, the great claps of thunder echo round the neighbouring hills, lightning strikes the sea below and the waves roar in reply. Manifestly Baal is back in his mountain-palace, just as once he had returned in triumph from his victories over death (Mot) and the sea (Yamm), beating them with his two huge clubs and with his bolts of thunder and lightning.

Ras Shamra lies on the southern side of this awesome mountain and from its temple of Baal we have a fine image of Baal in action.[9] On a stone relief there, he is shown armed with his club and thunderbolt while striding forwards: a small image of the local king is shown in his protection. Below him are sculpted the outlines of four hilltops, exactly the four hills which are still visible from Ras Shamra on the Jebel Aqra's lower slopes. Below them again are shown the waves of the sea over which Baal and his weapons have been victorious. The scene of his victory was surely the sea by Ras Shamra itself at the southern foot of the mountain on which he lived. An exact local reading of this monument helps to place and explain it. The people of Ras Shamra lived just by the sea where Baal had triumphed. Each autumn, when he thundered on the mountain above them and flashed his lightning down onto the sea-swell, the stories of his triumph would reassure them that these continuing signs of power would not lead on to more wars of the world.

Even so, Baal was not the first god on this peak. Earlier settlers in north Syria, the Hurrians, had known the mountain as 'Hazzi' and had placed their own Storm God, Teshub, on the summit. Hittite rulers then took over this name for the mountain and for the weathergod on its heights. They too sang stories of his victories, including a victory over the sea by which he secured his kingship in heaven.[10] For hundreds of years, before the Greeks settled nearby, the god of the mountain had been praised on each of its sides, the north and the south side, by Hittite and by Canaanite royal singers respectively. The mountain, therefore, was an essential site for cult and prayers. On its bare summit stands a huge mound of ashes and debris, about

180 feet wide and 26 feet deep, obviously an ancient cult-site. In 1937 it was surveyed briefly before the gods intervened and storms and cold weather stopped the investigation: a Hellenistic level was reached at a depth of 6 feet but the next 20 feet plainly go down to the ninth century BC and earlier.[11] At present they are closed to further organized researches as the summit, bordering Syria, is a Turkish military zone. But one day their truth will be recovered.

This holy mountain is the barrier which split in two the Greeks' early contact with this coastline. On its northern side, by the beach at its foot, lies Al Mina, the port of call for Euboeans, Cypriots and others who came here from the early eighth century onwards. On the southern side, beyond the mountain's wall of descending ridges, lies the settlement at Ras el-Bassit, eventually to be called Posideion, where pieces of Greek pottery imply that Greek visitors had been known since c. 950 BC, but a site whose settlers and residents were Syrians and Phoenicians, not Greeks. South of it lay the White Harbour and Betyllion by the multi-cultural settlement at ancient Ugarit (Ras Shamra). Throughout antiquity, the non-Greek settlers here looked north to the same 'twin peaks' of the Jebel Aqra on the horizon, 'Mount Hazzi' and 'Mount Nanou' as the Hittite texts had called them.[12] The Hittite name persisted in neo-Hittite culture into the ninth century BC and so when Greeks settled on the north side of Mount Hazzi they continued to call its main peak 'Mount Kasios'. They gave the name of 'Antikasios' to a lower peak, probably the one which juts towards the sea south-west from the main summit.[13] Centuries later, as we have argued, Macedonians who were settled by Alexander's Successors called this stretch of coast 'Pieria', partly because the peaks of Mount Kasios suggested their own Mount Olympus to their minds. Now that we see its age-old role as the seat of the gods and their battles we can understand even more clearly why they looked at Mount Kasios in this way. It was the Olympus of the Near East.

This mountain is a beacon of ancient paganism, but it is possible to study the political history of the entire ancient world without realizing its immense significance. It will turn out to be of the greatest importance for the Greek travelling heroes who came here and for their mythical baggage. To bring out its role, we need to dwell on the later evidence for its impact.

After Alexander's conquests, when Greeks then Romans controlled this territory, they continued to be intrigued by the mountain and its god. In due course, they built a sanctuary for Zeus Kasios near the summit: the tiles, stamped with his name, were reused in the Christian buildings which were later placed on an easterly ridge of the mountain.[14] The first datable Greek reference to Zeus Kasios in north Syria belongs after Alexander's death, but here of all places it is a mistake to take our first surviving attestation of a cult as the moment of its origin.

In c. 300 BC Alexander's Successor Seleucus founded two major cities in the Amuq valley, Seleuceia on the coast and the famous Antioch in the plain inland. Before founding his coastal Seleuceia,[15] Seleucus is said to have climbed Mount Kasios (in the month of April) and sacrificed there to Zeus. An eagle, ominously, is said to have carried off part of the meat which was being sacrificed and dropped it on the coastal site opposite the mountain where there was already a settlement: Seleucus duly sited his new Seleuceia on the lower slopes of the mountains which face back southwards across the valley to the Jebel Aqra's peak. The Zeus of this separate range was called 'Zeus of the Peak'.[16] In an alternative story, however, Seleucus was said to have sacrificed to Zeus the Thunderer in the plain below and to have been guided to the new Seleuceia's site by thunder.[17] The alternative is not radically different: thunder is a sign of Zeus Kasios urging and approving too. To this day, thunder breaks out above Mount Kasios and while it rolls round the surrounding ridges it sounds in the Amuq river-plain below. These stories are known to us in authors writing long after the events of 300 BC, but the important fact is that they use earlier local sources and attach exactly to items of continuing cult in Seleucus' city Seleuceia. Coins struck there during the first century BC imitate earlier coins of the Seleucids by showing a thunderbolt, sometimes placed reverentially on a throne with a cushion.[18] Plainly it was an important item of cult in the city. In the reign of Trajan (AD 97–116) we then find coins of this thunderbolt accompanied by other coins which show a shrine of Zeus Kasios with a pointed roof, identified by its caption. An eagle, no less, stands on the roof and a holy stone object is shown inside. These two types appear together and owe their existence to an obvious event, Trajan's stay in Antioch and the Syrian plain and the saving of his life, as we shall see, by Zeus Kasios in winter AD 114/15. The late date of the coins is thus no discredit to their evidence for the nature of the cult; they were struck, surely, in 115 to honour the god who had saved the emperor. Their image of his temple was drawn from life and the eagle on top of it referred to the eagle at Seleuceia's founding-sacrifice. The stone, as we shall see, may also have had an exact reference to the god.

We can follow this cult in the personal worship of travellers of the Roman period. From Iskenderun–Alexandretta, just across the Amanus mountains, we have a significant little shrine made in lime-stone for personal worship.[19] Four pillars define it, like the four pillars round the shrine on Seleuceia's coins: inside stands a figure of the sun-god, raising his hand in blessing and surrounded by signs of the zodiac and the four winds. The shape of this entire object is a 'sacred stone', or betyl, veiled at the back and resembling the holy stone on Seleuceia's coins. The identity of its cult should not, then, be doubted. It is a worshipper's personal shrine of Zeus Kasios, combining the attributes of the god's north Syrian temple and his relation with the sun and the elements which had a particular relevance in his cult. Further east, by the Euphrates, we also have a much-discussed small altar, inscribed at the military colony of Dura by a soldier from a Roman legion which had been posted for many years in north Syria at Antioch. The altar dates from the later second century AD and is dedicated to the 'ancestral Zeus Betylos' of 'those who live by the Orontes'.[20] A betyl, or *betylos*, is a sacred stone and although the double name is not unambiguous, it ought to mean a Zeus who is worshipped 'with' a sacred stone or betyl. This soldier's legionary base was Antioch, where the most famous such Zeus was Zeus Kasios above the lower Orontes river, who was worshipped both in Seleuceia and on his mountain overlooking the river. The name 'Zeus Betylos' for him is unprecedented, but the reference was made by a foreign soldier far away who simply evoked the local Zeus near Antioch by the best-known object in his cult and imagery.

If we go back to the Hellenistic age after Alexander, the god's continuing importance is reflected in the personal names of men and women from the plain and coastline beside his mountain. They are called 'Kassio-dora' and 'Kassio-doros' ('gift of Kasios', to whom, then, one parent or both had vowed or prayed before succeeding in conceiving the child). These namesakes appear as travellers far beyond Syria in inscriptions in the Greek world, because the god's fame spread so much more widely than historical narrative allows us to see.[21] Further south on the Levantine coast, Greeks located mythical 'Kassiopeia', whose daughter, Andromeda, was exposed at Joppa to the attacks of a fearsome sea-monster. A Levantine story of a sea-monster and a woman probably underlay this tale, though it is lost to us now: Greeks perhaps modelled the name 'Kassiopeia' on the names based on 'Mount Kas(s)ios' up the coast.[22] The mountain's fame was very extensive. In an inscription recently discovered in the little coastal town of Keramos, on the south-west coast of Asia Minor, the local donor of a sundial (c. 100 BC) had its stone inscribed with Greek verses explaining that his gift would observe the 'true course of the midday, for as long as the sun shines above highest Kasios'.[23] The Jebel Aqra is not visible from Keramos but there is no need to conclude that the stone may have been transported here from a coastal town in our triangle. The author knew it as the high point for the sun at noon in the east Mediterranean. So, later, did one of the first young pupils of St Augustine, writing clumsy verses in Latin in northern Italy, months after his master's conversion to Christian celibacy.[24]

The best-attested visitors to the mountain-peak are three Roman emperors, each of whose visits illuminates the local conditions. In winter AD 114/15, the emperor Trajan was present at Antioch for a spectacular earthquake which shook the surrounding Amuq plain and fractured part of Mount Kasios itself. Trajan ascribed his own escape to a heavenly helper, evidently Zeus Kasios in person. Previously Trajan had honoured the god with a dedication of silver cups and the gilded horns of an enormous wild ox, spoils from his recent victory over the Dacians near the River Danube. These ox-horns are somewhat unusual and we should remember that way back in the Hittite Bronze Age (c. 1200 BC) the Storm God of this very mountain had already been worshipped with ox-horns.[25] The old practice may have lived on among his priests. It is from the year of Trajan's visit onwards that the coins of Seleuceia on the coast below show the rounded stone in a pillared shrine, captioned with Zeus Kasios' name. We now see why: the god had just saved his life.

When Trajan visited, he was accompanied by his adopted son Hadrian, who composed Greek verses in honour of the emperor's dedications to Zeus Kasios: aptly, he described the god as 'dark with clouds'. Nobody could have guessed that this same Hadrian, now emperor himself, would return in the year 130 and climb the mountain in the darkness of night, no doubt to witness the premature dawn at its summit. As he prepared to honour Zeus Kasios with a sacrifice, a flash of lightning is said to have killed his animal victim and the attendant who was about to slaughter it. This part of the story is probably a mischievous invention, but the author knew that the god, 'dark with clouds', was a stupendous thunderer.[26]

In spring 363 the last pagan emperor, Julian, also took the route to the bare, bleak summit, hoping to see the early dawn. The sun rose, and in 'broad daylight', so the contemporary orator Libanius assures us, Julian saw Zeus Kasios in person. So far as we know there was no personalized cult-statue of the god in Seleuceia to give him human features: perhaps, like Trajan, Julian 'saw' him as a dark-bearded figure.[27] Where such important pagans still climbed, worshipped and sensed Zeus Kasios' power, Christians badly needed their own religious counterweight. From the fifth century onwards, therefore, Mount Hazzi attracted two remarkable Christian storm troopers. First, the young Barlaam left his home in the plains below and went up to challenge the demons just below their historic seat on Mount Kasios' summit. On an eastern ridge, just above modern Bezge, he founded the least welcoming of all early Christian monasteries where the mountain reduces to bare, grey rock. He settled just by the site of the temple to Zeus at which previous Roman emperors had worshipped: perhaps it had the architecture and the sacred stone which are shown on the coins of Seleuceia across the valley. Fragments of its building were later used in the monastery which was built to commemorate him.[28] In the following century, in the 530s, Barlaam was excelled by the young Symeon from coastal Seleuceia, who showed even more stamina at a height which was no less impressive. On the hills beyond Mount Hazzi's northern slope, Symeon began a Christian life as a stationary saint on a pillar-base at the tender age of seven. Progressing ever higher, he ended by standing on the tall pillar whose base is still intact among the ruins of its surrounding Christian church.[29]

The young Symeon remained standing on a pillar here for more than forty years (until 592). As his blessing and prophecies proved their worth, they attracted important patrons, including the Byzantine emperor Maurice who built the large stone church which still stands around the pillar. The siting is extremely significant: the view through its side chapels aligns exactly with the peak of the Jebel Aqra, the demonic backdrop to Symeon's life on high. Like the elder Symeon Stylites who was his namesake and role-model,[30] the younger Symeon stood on high as an alternative Christian focus, contradicting an ancient pagan 'high place' in the mountain landscape behind him. Just below the hillside of his pillar lay the site of Sabouni, visited by Greeks in the Bronze Age and the eighth century, and on the coast below it lay the site of Al Mina, 'Potamoi Karon', the former residence of Euboean travellers. Across more than seventeen hundred years, therefore, the Jebel Aqra framed the beginning and end of pagan Greek worship in the Levant.

In the eighth century BC, Mount Kasios, its myths, its storms and gods mattered daily to the Greek contemporaries who were living in their shadow. They were a part of their mentality, part of what it meant to be a Greek on the coast of north Syria, a more important part than their Geometric pottery and *skyphoi* with semi-circles, the durable debris which survives for archaeologists and until now has dominated studies of these travellers' presence.

II

One fact is certain about Greeks' interaction with this mountain: they did not learn its name from the Phoenicians who came up to its southern side at Ras el-Bassit or passed it at sea on their way up to southern Cilicia and its plain. Phoenicians called the Jebel Aqra by the old Semitic name Saphon, which was familiar from Canaanite poems about the gods, whereas the Greeks called it Kasios. They adapted this name from the ancient name Hazzi which Hittite conquerors had picked up from Hurrian settlers in north Syria and had used in their texts between *c.* 1400 and 1200 BC. The two names diverged in their foreign impact. In the later eighth century, from the

730s onwards, Saphon is the name which the conquering Assyrians and their scribes adapted. The Greeks always held fast to Kasios and ignored Saphon.[31]

The reasons for this divergence can be explained. The Greek name 'Kasios' perhaps goes back to a contact in the Bronze Age, *c.* 1200 BC, when the neo-Hittite kings were still very powerful and Greek visitors to the nearby site at Sabouni on the Orontes heard the name 'Hazzi' from the locals. However, its survival among Greeks through the 'dark' centuries from *c.* 1150 to 950, when Greek visitors to the coast dwindled, or ceased altogether, is not attested. We should also look to the period *c.* 950–750, when Greek goods returned to the site of Ras el-Bassit near the mountain's south side and then Greeks settled Al Mina at its northern foot. We have seen how even after the old Hittite kingdom's fall, Hittite culture survived among the neighbouring kings of the north Syrian plain which lies to the Jebel Aqra's north and east. These were the years when the neo-Hittite kingdom of Patina flourished inland behind Al Mina and its capital at Kinalua on the bend of the Orontes was unscathed. The name 'Mount Kasios' prevailed because of Greek contacts on the north side of the mountain, the site, above all, of the Euboean presence at Al Mina from *c.* 780 BC onwards. By contrast, the Assyrian scribes and compilers of place names listed sites as if they were coming up northwards from the far Phoenician side of the mountain: they adopted the name 'Sapanu' from the West Semitic speakers on that part of their conquered territory.

A mountain is a static landmark, unlike a travelling hero, a Daedalus or Heracles who could find so many homes. Yet it is most remarkable how this god, and even the mountain, travelled abroad. At first their relocations were not Greek at all, but Greek travellers then followed lines which Egyptians and Levantines had already laid. The travels of Mount Kasios remind us that Greeks were only one type of traveller on these busy east Mediterranean sea-lanes.

Long before any Greeks arrived in north Syria, the god of the mountain had travelled with visitors between Egypt and the coast of the Levant. His travels went far back in time and it is not surprising to find that *c.* 1300 BC Baal Saphon, the god of the Jebel Aqra, had a temple in Egypt at Memphis.[32] When the king of Ugarit, just to the south of the mountain, wrote to the pharaoh in Egypt, he invoked his own Baal Saphon, who had a monument on the site (Ras Shamra). In the temple of Baal at Ras Shamra stood a carved representation of the god dedicated by a royal Egyptian scribe on behalf of his pharaoh, probably *c.* 1300 BC. His inscription in Egyptian hieroglyphs calls the god 'Baal Zephon'; he is invoked to give prosperity: the distinctive sandstone of this relief-sculpture had been sent to Ras Shamra all the way from Egypt. Visitors honoured the great god of the place and so, through diplomacy, trade and travel, the god entered Egypt and became known away from his mountain seat.[33]

No 'dark age' can efface a mountain and so Baal Saphon survived into the first millennium. Again, the best evidence is diplomatic. Publicly, in 677 BC, the king of Tyre invoked Baal Saphon as one of three gods who would protect his treaty with the king of Assyria: against anyone who broke it Baal Saphon would 'raise a hostile wind against your ships, to destroy your rigging and break your masts and rouse a gigantic wave at sea'.[34] The curse is a reminder that the god of the mountain was also master of the winds and sea-swells, as the old local myths had celebrated him. Those Greeks and Cypriots who had been travelling and settling on either side of the mountain since *c.* 950 BC knew exactly what this curse meant, on days when the thunderstorms rolled and lightning flashed on the peaks above them.

The god was important to individual Phoenician travellers, too. A small amulet, made of lapis lazuli, has been found recently near Tyre, inscribed with an emphatic invocation to Baal Saphon and another Baal of the mountains, the Amanus range or 'Cedar and Box-tree Mountains' which face the Jebel Aqra's north slope. This amulet is datable only by the form of its inscribed letters, which perhaps date to the sixth century BC. The owner was probably a seafarer, accustomed to travelling between Tyre, the coast of north Syria and the Bay of Issus, to whom the favours of Baal Saphon on his mountain-top and the Baal across the valley were of special importance. So he wore his blue amulet, invoking them, on a chain round his neck.[35]

Meanwhile the god of the mountain had remained important to residents in Egypt. From *c.* 600 BC onwards, evidence for his cult survives from the royal city of Memphis where Tyrians had settled up the Nile. It survives too from the eastern arm of the Nile Delta. Here, at Tell Defenneh, we have the papyrus letter of a lady who writes to another lady at Memphis concerning a financial matter. She invokes the blessing of Baal Saphon in language which implies that the god had a cult at Tell Defenneh itself. Aptly, both of the women are Phoenicians.[36] Tell Defenneh was also a home for Jewish settlers, as we know from the Hebrew Scriptures. Among them was the prophet Jeremiah in exile, and just as Levantine sailors and settlers had brought Baal Saphon and his cult to the Nile Delta, so the Israelites' contact with coastal Phoenicia had made Baal and his mountain familiar in Israel. In verses of their psalms, especially Psalm 48, and in verses of the Hebrew prophets, 'Saphon' means the 'north', as if the Jebel Aqra was a focal point for people in Israel.[37] There are even times when their praises of Yahweh and his holy mountain Sion recall the ancient Canaanite poems of praise to Baal on his north Syrian mountain-peak: Hebrew authors seem to have transposed some of the imagery which applied to the neighbouring 'heathen' gods and applied it to their own god instead.[38] Baal Saphon's impact in Israel is neatly attested by the personal name of the prophet Zephaniah, a contemporary of Jeremiah, c. 600 BC: it means 'Saphon is Yahweh'.

Jews were also aware of Baal Saphon's cult in Egypt. The prophet Jeremiah cannot have missed it during his exile at Tell Defenneh and the cult appears, famously, in the biblical story of the Exodus. This story weaves together two contradictory routes for the Israelites' return from Egypt, each of which was derived from the biblical compiler's underlying, discordant sources. One, the most famous, takes the Israelites far south through the Egyptian desert to the distant Red Sea. The other, by contrast, directs them to 'Baal Saphon' and a 'sea' to the east of it where they encamp. Probably, this route was the one given by the priestly source for our scriptural narrative, a man who was writing (in my view) in the later sixth century BC.[39]

'Baal Saphon' has been fixed here with certainty, on the Egyptian coastline just to the east of the eastern arm of the Nile Delta. On a tongue of land between the Mediterranean sea and Lake Bardawil, the promontory Ras Kasroun marks a site which was linked directly to the god.[40] The lake behind it was notoriously marshy and treacherous: it is probably the Bible's 'sea of reeds' (*yam sūf*), whose exact translation is still uncertain, although it is the 'sea' in which Pharaoh's chosen captains were drowned 'like a stone' (Exodus 15: 5). As it was a sea of 'reeds' or some other water-plant, it was a 'sea' in the sense of a freshwater lake. 'Reeds' and other water-plants will not grow in the salty Red Sea, but they will grow in Lake Bardawil, which is partly fed by freshwater sources.[41]

In a brilliant study of these biblical locations, the German scholar Otto Eissfeldt argued that there was nothing fortuitous about this siting of the pharaoh's destruction and the miracle of the Exodus: it emphasized that Yahweh was much more powerful than the local Baal Saphon, a heathen god. Certainly, the coastline by Lake Bardawil was very treacherous: in the 350s BC the marshes ruined a Persian army which invaded Egypt, and the coastline caused great problems for the young Demetrius, a flamboyant Successor of Alexander, when he and his father staged a combined land and sea attack on Egypt in 306 BC, following the 'Exodus route' in the reverse direction.[42]

After the Exodus, the next important witness to the site is Herodotus, who visited the area of Lake Bardawil in c. 440 BC. Three times he refers to 'Mount Kasios' on exactly this stretch of coast and regards it as a recognized boundary between Egypt and Syria. He also remarks on the adjacent marsh, the modern Lake Bardawil, which he calls the 'Serbonian bog': in it the monster Typhon was 'said to have been hidden'. Typhon's concealment here occurred because of his battle with Zeus: Herodotus does not happen to mention Zeus at this point, but there can be no doubt from his mention of Typhon that he associated Zeus with this Egyptian Mount Kasios and its marshland.[43]

These sitings were not the random inferences of Herodotus' own researches in the country. They were accepted facts which went back to Greek visitors before him, to Greeks who had known that Baal Saphon was worshipped in the eastern Delta and that a point on the Egyptian coast had assumed the name of the north Syrian mountain. We can be more precise about the origins of this knowledge. In the later seventh century BC, Greeks, too, had been settled at Tell Defenneh (Daphnae, as they called it) among the Jews, Phoenicians and Egyptians. Until c. 580, but not afterwards, their ships were allowed to approach Egypt by the eastern arm of the Delta.[44] The Greek knowledge of Zeus Kasios on this coastline thus arose in or before the seventh century BC through their contact with Phoenicians and Baal Saphon in and around the eastern Nile Delta. It might even go

back to eighth-century Greek visitors, coming down from Rhodes or
Al Mina in the friendly interlude of the short-lived 'Delta pharaoh'
Bocchoris. Some of them may have been Euboeans.

This second address for the god and his mountain is most remarkable. The coastline beyond the easterly arm of the Nile Delta is conspicuously flat and from the level monotony only one hill stands out
prominently, the sandy eminence of Ras Kasroun, which reaches a
height of about 300 feet above the sea. A narrow strip of land between
the sea and the lake separates it from Lake Bardawil: in the late 1960s
surveys and excavations established it as the site of Baal Saphon where
the Greeks before Herodotus had located the local Mount Kasios.
Precise distances given by later ancient geographers confirm that
'Kasion' was indeed here.[45]

Compared with the parent Mount Hazzi, this Egyptian sibling is a
very humble affair. However, the hill was important to sailors: we
can see from the Macedonians' 'reverse Exodus' into Egypt in 306 BC
that Kasion, the modern Ras Kasroun, was a landmark, but not at all
an easy anchorage. The young Demetrius and his fleet were troubled
by very rough seas off Kasion and could come no closer than half a
mile to the shore. Egyptian Kasion, therefore, looked down on a
turbulent sea, just like its Syrian prototype 'Mount Hazzi': this similarity was what encouraged the twinning of the sites. There was also
something more, lying in the lake behind. Here, as Herodotus remarks,
the fire-breathing monster Typhon was said to be located. Later Greek
authors added that his hot breath was visible beside Egypt's 'Mount
Kasios'. In the rising heat of an Egyptian morning, a haze, or at times
a damp mist, still shimmers off the lake and its adjoining marshes and
sand-dunes, as if Typhon is exhaling.[46]

Ras Kasroun, then, is a site of sadly neglected holiness, and naturally
its layers of myth were enhanced by Egyptians too. They took the
local god to be their own Horus and they equated the monster he had
beaten into the marshes with Horus' opponent Seth. By lateral thinking Greek visitors then made a similar connection to their own myths
of Zeus and Typhon. As the Greeks' prominence in Egypt increased
after Alexander's conquests, their Greek name, Kasios, became the
name for the entire eastern arm of the Nile Delta: there was even
a type of sailors' knot called the Kasiote. 'Zeus Kasios' and 'Baal

Saphon' received local dedications and at Mehamdiah (the ancient Gerra) on the west of Lake Bardawil, Baal Saphon had a small shrine.[47] Further west, on the Nile's arm, he had another, at Pelusium. We can now understand why the emperor Hadrian took such a particular interest in this area. In early 130 he arrived in Egypt from Antioch and promptly honoured the local Zeus Kasios with a new temple and cult-statue at Pelusium, 10 miles from the 'Serbonian bog'.[48] There had already been a cult of Baal Saphon here, but honours for Zeus Kasios were entirely appropriate for Hadrian, who had experienced the god's brutal power on the peak of his native Jebel Aqra in north Syria only a few months previously in the storm which was said to have killed the attendant standing beside him.

The travels of Baal Saphon and Mount Kasios are beautiful evidence of a travelling cult and its accompanying place name from one landscape to another. By c. 600 BC, perhaps even by c. 720, Greeks had added to the transpositions which Levantine visitors to Egypt had already made. The beginnings of this Greek interest are unfortunately unknown to us: Herodotus is our earliest evidence (c. 440 BC) for the existence of the Greek names 'Mount Kasios' and (by implication) 'Zeus Kasios' here in Egypt. What we cannot yet document is a role for early Euboean visitors in naming the god and the Syrian mountain and then discovering his secondary home in the Delta. He must have been very important to them, because they lived in north Syria beneath his home, and it is eminently possible that they then found his second Egyptian address. His further travels to the west are documented in the Aegean and west Mediterranean, but only from evidence which begins in the Hellenistic age after Alexander. Even then, Greek-speaking Syrians and Phoenicians were the active bearers of the god's worship, especially those whom the god continued to protect at sea. It is a sign of this power that his name is prominent on stone anchors which were dedicated by sailors in ports of Sicily and southern Spain but which do not as yet survive in examples before the third century BC. The god had kept the ship of each anchor safe at sea.[49]

So far, no such dedication has been found in the early Euboean Greek settlements of Ischia or eastern Sicily, although Euboeans sailed here, spanning the bay of Syrian Mount Kasios and the Bay of Naples. We can come no closer than Corcyra, and even here we know only of an eventual temple to Zeus Kasios on the coast. It stood, however, at the aptly named site of Cassiope on the north-east cape of the island overlooking the Vivari channel between Corcyra and the mainland and its future fine site of Butrint. Importantly, the sea here is rough and unpredictable but the cape and its channel are natural routes up the coast for sailors who are bound for the 'heel' of Italy and Otranto some 40 miles north-west across open sea. The temple stood beside the subsequent Christian church to the Virgin at Cassopitra, but we know nothing of it earlier than a coin struck in 46 BC.[50] Its established role then confronts us in a thought-provoking incident. When the vain, cruel Roman emperor Nero set off in AD 66 for his journey to win prizes as a performer and charioteer in Greece, it was on landing at Cassiope that he first performed as a singer on Greek soil. He sang a hymn, mercifully lost to us, to Zeus Kasios: he was not merely thanking the god for a safe sea-journey. The 'sun-king' Nero was singing here to the god whose mountain had such a special relationship with the rising sun.[51]

Mount Hazzi in Syria, Cape Ras Kasroun in Egypt and Cape Cassiope on Corcyra all looked over extremely treacherous coastal stretches of sea. As in the old myths in the Bronze Age, their Zeus Kasios retained an enduring role and devotion among sailors. At Corcyra we can continue to follow it in their grateful dedications, including words inscribed by a 'chief secretary of the association of athletes' when travelling west from Ephesus to Italy, thanking Zeus Kasios at Cassiope who had 'swiftly saved him, ship and all'.[52] Sailors broke into verse here in their thanks to the god of the sea and storms: they also dedicated model ships to him in gratitude. One Barbaros ('Barbarian') even dedicated two, one bigger than the other in thanks for a better voyage. 'If you grant riches too, he will hang up a ship entirely made of gold,' he adds, optimistically.[53]

In the early eighth century BC we have tracked Euboeans from the Near Eastern triangle up past Ithaca exactly to Corcyra, on which, by c. 750 BC, Eretrians among them actually settled. Others sailed on, as we have seen, across the straits to Italy, but it was through the Vivari channel, in reverse, that they will have returned with news of the new lands for the taking to their fellow-Euboeans back home. Surely these supreme sailors had already prayed in gratitude to the Zeus Kasios whom they knew so well from their beach in north Syria's Unqi. The place name Cassiope (if it existed so early) and the treacherous winds and sea would have brought him inevitably to their minds. It is, then, only an accident of survival that we have no text or dedication here from a travelling Euboean. We only know that, eventually, people here wanted to believe in the god's active presence in or before the eighth century BC. The historian Procopius in the sixth century AD describes how a ship made from white stones stood on the shore at Cassiope and bore a dedication by a merchant to 'Zeus Kasios'.[54] Some of the local people, he tells us, believed that it was the very ship on which Homer's Odysseus had been carried home to Ithaca. We know from the local dedications that it was only one more of the ships dedicated to Zeus Kasios by grateful sailors. Homer would never have claimed it: his poems, strikingly, never refer to Zeus Kasios at all.

16

The Great Castrator

This mountain, its god and their travels lie firmly within the horizon of Euboeans abroad. They lived at the mountain's foot. They coped with its storms on land and sea. They travelled west to a site on Corcyra where conditions were similar and where we know that the god of the mountain was later transposed, although we cannot yet show that they transposed him westwards in the eighth century BC. There was more to the mountain, however, than storms and winds. It was the ancient seat of the gods and of prolific stories about them. Here, at last, we can follow the Greeks as they encountered these stories in the east and then transferred items in them to new locations across their known world.

On the south side of 'Mount Hazzi', clay tablets found at Ugarit (Ras Shamra) give us fragments of ancient Canaanite myths which refer to the exploits of their god of the mountain, the lord Baal. They describe his attempt to establish his palace on the mountain's peak and the struggles with monsters and cosmic enemies which accompanied his efforts.[1] On this same mountain, the Hittites too had praised and paid cult to the established Storm God, Teshub or Tarhunta, in the Late Bronze Age (c. 1350–1200 BC). He, too, had to fight to establish his rule on Mount Hazzi: we know stories of his struggles because they survive in tablets found far away at the great Hittite palace-centre of Boghaz-Köy in central Turkey.[2] As time passed, other Levantine cultures within sight of Mount Kasios told yet more tales of the gods in its orbit. There were Phoenician stories too, but our only surviving hints of their contents lie in parts of Philo of Byblos's book on Phoenician religion. It was not compiled until c. AD 60–80 and it was composed in Greek. Although it is of uncertain authority, it drew on much earlier sources which were grounded in non-Greek traditions.[3]

Our texts of these Hittite and Canaanite stories date back at least to *c.* 1200 BC, but the stories are even older than our surviving evidence for them. If Greeks ever picked up these tales it was not by reading them in Near Eastern archives or libraries or by consulting the scribal copies which have preserved them. The scripts and written languages were mysteries to them. They had to learn them from conversation. Historians have continued to wonder about contexts in which these stories would ever have been told in public. If only we could locate one of these tales, it would be so much easier to argue how they filtered sideways, reaching others, including Greeks, on the north Syrian coast.

By a remarkable accident of survival, we have evidence for the formal telling of one group of stories in a specific place. It survives in fragmentary Hittite texts which date back to the late thirteenth century BC. As they are lists of cult-offerings, not mythical narratives, their contents are not familiar to historians of the Greeks overseas.[4] They contain lists of offerings which were to be made in honour of Mount Hazzi, the Jebel Aqra. Among the honours were the 'singing of the song of kingship' and the 'singing of the song of the sea'. These songs were not songs about a kingship exerted by Mount Hazzi itself, for which we have no evidence: they were songs of the struggle for the kingship in Heaven, the battles which left the Storm God (the Hittite Tarhunta) supreme on the mountain-top. They were sung in honour of Mount Hazzi and obviously they would be sung on Mount Hazzi itself.

This location is extremely important. Mount Hazzi rises steeply off the beach into which the Orontes river runs and dominates the view south from the two nearby Greek points of settlement by the sea: Sabouni, 3 miles inland, to which Greeks came in the Mycenaean era, and Al Mina, 'Potamoi Karon', to which they returned in the early eighth century BC. While they first visited Sabouni, there had been formal public occasions, we now see from these Hittite texts, on which the weather-god's struggles in heaven were sung on the mountain towering above them. The singing was set to music, as the Hittite word for it shows: these songs were sung as hymns, probably by choirs.⁵ The persistence of this singing is an important question, but first we need an idea of what these two songs contained. Fortunately, they resemble songs which survive in our best-known Hittite song-sequence, the one which we can reconstruct from fragmentary copies found further north at the Hittite royal capital of Boghaz-Köy.

The 'song of kingship' for Mount Hazzi was the very same song about the Storm God's kingship which we know from these sources. He (Tarhunta) had to survive the aggression of his father Kumarbi, the previous king. He then had to survive Kumarbi's attempts to dethrone him with at least three monstrous enemies deployed one after the other. The 'song of kingship' told of the battles and the 'song of the sea' told of a victory by the Storm God when water had once flooded the earth. The god of the sea had to be won over, but in the end the Storm God triumphed over his enemies. The story was set exactly by Mount Hazzi and its accompanying 'twin peaks'. It was sometimes sung as part of a ritual 'when the Storm God is brought to the mountains', no doubt to the mountains in the Jebel Aqra's range. 'The singers sing the song of the deeds of the sea, how the Storm God conquered the Sea.' This song was widely known and is cited by name in other surviving Hittite stories: parts of it have recently been recovered from fragmentary tablets too. In the orbit of Mount Hazzi it was matched by similar songs in the adjoining cultures. Fragmentary tablets from Ras Shamra on the south side of the mountain tell the story of Baal, the Canaanites' god of the mountain, and his victory over the sea-god too. This Canaanite story, told on the south side, matched the story which the Hittites were telling on the north side. There were offerings, too, to Sapanu, the mountain, just as there were offerings on the other side of it to Hazzi, its other name. They took place in the spring.⁶ There was a very good reason why such a song and a rite were common to them both. The god on Mount Hazzi, whether Baal or Tarhunta, needed to have mastered the sea which surged directly below his seat.

The Hittite 'song of kingship' begins with some gruesome episodes, but they are not as bizarre as they seem when read in isolation. In many cultures throughout the world, the prehistory of the gods is described in terms of an act of separation and a struggle for the succession to power. In these stories the first gods are Heaven and

Earth and they are believed to have been joined so tightly that all was shrouded in darkness.[7] Their joining is often described as sexual and during it there appear other gods whom they procreate. Copulating Heaven and Earth have, then, to be separated so that light can come between them. After they are separated the gods whom they have created then challenge each other in a series of family struggles. These stories are widespread across the world because mortals tend to imagine the society of the gods as a grander version of the society of rulers on earth. In kingdoms, therefore, including those of the Near East, the gods are imagined as members of a court. Their king has struggled to depose a previous king and then has to fight to retain power: the reason, ultimately, for these stories is that kings, courtiers and usurpers are recurrent items in earthly Near Eastern history. In their struggles, gods, like rulers, can be defeated, but unlike human usurpers, they can never die. As a result the tales of their succession-struggles end with the imprisonment or neutering of the losers, but never with their killing.

We can see the explanatory value of these types of story. The tales of separation explain how heaven was placed above the earth and how light originated from darkness. The tales of succession bring the gods into a hierarchy and emphasize the power of the victor, the ruling god, in the tellers' own times. Both these types of story are known to us from fragmentary Hittite texts although the separation of Heaven and Earth is less well known because it survives only in a passing reference in the few texts which we have. Once upon a time, we learn, Heaven and Earth had been cut apart with a 'copper cutter', probably a toothed saw, which was then preserved in an ancestral storehouse. Later, the Storm God and the other gods were reminded of this ancient weapon's existence when they took refuge on Mount Hazzi, the Jebel Aqra, during a crisis. They were being threatened by a fast-growing monster of stone and they used the 'copper cutter' to destroy it beside the Jebel Aqra's seashore.[8]

The struggles for succession in the Hittite heaven are known in more detail through fragmentary texts whose scope and sequence continue to be clarified by modern scholarship. Four gods succeeded each other, the fourth of whom was Tarhunta the Storm God, the reigning lord on Mount Hazzi. The Storm God then had to preserve his rule against various challengers whom his predecessor, Kumarbi, fathered against him. Kumarbi had been the third ruler in the Hittite series: he was the son of the first ruling god and had served the second, Anu (Heaven), as a cupbearer at court. Kumarbi's own succession had been a grim occasion.[9] He had fought Anu and after a long struggle he had forced him to take flight: as Anu flew up to the sky, Kumarbi pulled him down and bit off his private parts with his teeth. Anu warned him that his mouthful of manhood would impregnate him with three dreadful gods: Kumarbi spat out as much as he could, but he could not expel everything. Anu's sperm became 'mixed in his stomach, just as bronze (is mixed) from copper and tin'. So a child was conceived inside him and began to try to come out. Kumarbi asked for this child to be given to him so that he could destroy it: the text is fragmentary, but we know that Kumarbi says: 'Give me my [so]n, I will eat [h]im.' This child is Tarhunta the Storm God: fragmentarily, we read, '. . . Tarhunta, I want to eat; I will crush (him)'. Kumarbi takes up something 'to eat', but it is a hard stone which hurts his teeth. He begins to cry out. The stone is then set aside and is to be given a name (which we cannot translate) and to be paid cult, one sort of cult for the rich, another for the poor. Then, and only then, does the Storm God, his son, emerge from inside him.

The surviving words of this part of Kumarbi's song are so important for Greek historians because they resemble a very famous episode in Greek myth. It is first known to us in the elegant poem the *Theogony*, which Hesiod composed *c.* 715–705 BC. As Hesiod tells it, the story combines elements of both a separation and a succession.[10] The Greek Heaven and Earth are the first generation of gods, but father Heaven persists in making love to mother Earth and refuses to allow any of her children to be born. In pain, Earth contrives to make a great sickle and then calls on her unborn sons for help. One of them, Cronos, volunteers.

In Hesiod's poem, the union of Heaven and Earth is not continuous and so daytime already exists in the intervals while the pair are apart: the separation has begun, but it is not total. When Heaven next 'came to mother Earth, bringing dark night' as Hesiod skilfully expresses it, he lay on her and began his all-night sexual marathon. But Cronos was waiting in ambush and when Heaven was in place, he took the sharp-toothed sickle in his hand and swiped from behind at his father's sexual parts. He 'mowed them off vigorously' and threw them away behind him. Furies, Giants and nymphs sprouted from the drops of blood which hit the ground, but the parts themselves were thrown into the sea. White foam, or *aphros*, spread out from them and gave birth to the Greek goddess of love, *aphro-dite*. She was spawned from Heaven's foaming DNA.

After this act of castration Cronos ruled as King Cronos in place of his neutered father.[11] He married his sister Rhea and he too fathered children. He devoured each one, fearing the warning of his parents that one of them would one day rule in his place: it was this episode in the story that stood on the bowl which was ingeniously faked for Phalaris in Sicily and falsely inscribed to suggest it was Daedalus' work. The story was indeed a very old one. Eventually Rhea contrived to hide her youngest son, Zeus, and gave Cronos a stone to swallow instead of the child. Cronos vomited the stone, but Zeus grew up in safe keeping at a distance. Zeus then released the Titans, who had been born to Heaven and Earth before Heaven's castration. With the Titans' help he deposed Cronos and began to rule in heaven.

The story we meet in Hesiod's poem has an evident resemblance to the old Hittite story of kingship, although the correspondence is not complete. In the Greek story, there are three successive generations of gods (Heaven, Cronos, Zeus), whereas the Hittite songs tell of four. In the Hittite story, but not the Greek, these successors in heaven are from two separate branches of the family line. In the Greek story there is not the same emphasis on a succession of kings, which the Hittite songs describe as happening every 'nine years'. In the Greek story, Cronos swipes with a sickle and parts Heaven and Earth. In the Hittite stories, Heaven and Earth were parted with a 'copper cutter' but Kumarbi is not said to have done the cutting himself. Instead he attacks Anu (Heaven) later and castrates him with his teeth. He impregnates himself in the process. In the Greek story, Cronos does not bite Heaven: he castrates him with a sickle and is the first to be called a king. A goddess, Aphrodite, is born from Heaven's sperm and Cronos then has children by impregnating his wife Rhea in the usual way. However, the three gods in the Greek story of succession match the second, third and fourth gods in the Hittite sequence and there are at least eight other conspicuous similarities between the two stories, including the substitution of a stone for an unborn son. When the Hittite tablets began to be studied in the 1930s, a resemblance was already evident. Improved knowledge of the Hittite texts has made the resemblance very much stronger: no specialist who has kept up with the subject would now contest it.[12]

The case for the stories' relationship does not depend on our two surviving written sources, as if one of them must have been the direct source of the other. More than five hundred years separate Hesiod from our texts of the Hittite song and in neither case are we reading the one and only version of the myth. Hesiod was telling a story which was already older in Greek than his own adornment of it, and our text of the Hittite song had itself been copied from an older tablet. Our single surviving text of it cannot have defined every subsequent Hittite telling of the story, either in 1200 BC or later: Hittites, indeed, did not treat texts which they borrowed from others as canonical, or allow them to inhibit their own versions of the story. There will have been other Greek and Hittite versions, now lost to us, and they may have been even closer to each other. As time passed they may also have amalgamated more details from similar stories in neighbouring cultures. If we work backwards from the Greek story which had taken shape by c. 710 BC, 'we begin to hear a many-voiced interplay . . .', as a great connoisseur has suggested, 'all of which seems to have some connection with Hesiod'.[13]

Behind this 'many-voiced interplay', however, one human fact is certain: at some point, somewhere, particular Greeks talked to people in the Levant, heard their stories and wove them into their own stories of their gods. This 'interplay' had several phases, and both parties to it should be allowed to contribute. Greeks surely did not arrive in the east in the Mycenaean age with empty minds on these topics. Tales of a separation of Heaven and Earth are widespread in many cultures, including cultures which cannot have influenced each other directly. The Greeks, then, may have had their own independent stories of a succession of gods in heaven and may already have believed that Heaven ruled, then Cronos, then Zeus. On arriving in the east they would realize that there was a fortuitous convergence between their existing stories and the stories of people they met there. Greeks did not adopt the cruel story of castration in order to fill a vacuum: they took it over because it amplified their existing stories of the gods' struggles. We can even suspect how some of this amplification took root. When Greeks heard the Hittite stories about Kumarbi, they heard (almost certainly) that he was a god of corn and the corn-harvest.[14] So, in their own stories, was Cronos, one of whose roles was to be a god of the harvest.[15] It was easier, then, for them to credit Cronos with deeds which their foreign informants ascribed to Kumarbi. One of these deeds was the emasculation of Heaven with a bite of the teeth. However, there was also a Hittite story of the parting of Heaven from Earth with a 'cutter', a weapon fit for the Greek Cronos.[16] The castration was therefore ascribed by Greeks to a cutting swipe with a sickle, not a crude bite. As a harvester, Cronos was some-times imagined to carry a cutter for reaping. How better for him to have separated his father Heaven from mother Earth than by castrating him with his personal type of cutter, a harvest-sickle?

The influence of Near Eastern stories on the Greek story in Hesiod is evident, but the date of this influence remains very controversial. Scholars have tended to pose a choice, either an influence in the Late Bronze Age (c. 1200 BC) or one in the eighth century BC, much nearer to Hesiod's own time. The early date has a decided aptness. The Hittites' 'song of kingship' was indeed being sung c. 1200 BC in honour of Mount Hazzi and it could have been encountered then by Greek visitors from Crete or Cyprus or further afield when they visited the coastline near that very mountain and settled at Sabouni just opposite it on the Orontes river. However, we need not think of only one contact behind what we now read in Hesiod's Greek and we should not polarize the question as if only the thirteenth or the eighth century BC is possible. An earlier contact in the thirteenth century may have left its mark on Greek stories about the gods which then lived on for the next three or four hundred years, passed on by word of mouth. These half-remembered tales were then greatly confirmed when Greeks returned and settled once again on the Levantine coast at Al Mina beside Mount Hazzi. This settlement was an eighth-century event, not far from Hesiod's lifetime. Although Euboean goods, and probably Euboean Greeks too, had been finding their way to the Levant since the tenth century BC, a knowledge of the struggles on the mountain required Greeks to be living directly beside it and wanting to understand its gods' stories. During the first phase of Greek visiting, not settlement, we have suggested that the coast of Unqi and the Orontes river were not a main destination of Cypriot Greeks or Phoenicians. We should think, rather, of an initial Bronze Age encounter, confirmed by Greeks from Euboea when they established a firm presence on the north side of Mount Hazzi. That establishment, our Al Mina, occurred in the early eighth century BC.

At that date Mount Hazzi still soared above the plain and, as we have seen in some detail, a neo-Hittite culture persisted in the north Syrian kingdom of Patina (Unqi) and its capital of Kinalua (Tell Tayinat) inland. So, surely, did the singing of the 'song of kingship' in the mountain's honour, on the mountain itself. After all, the mountain was still the same potent and dominating force in people's lives. Whether or not any Greeks went up onto its slopes to hear such songs and to ask what they meant, their neighbours, not least their local women, would know about these performances and could pass on the ancient stories to their enquiring Greek visitors on the beach below. They were sure to be asked, because the gods of the mountain affected everyone, whatever language they spoke. When tremendous thunder rolled off the mountain, the lightning flashed and the sea began to swell off Al Mina's beach, any Greek would wish to know the divinities of the place. They would ask their neighbours, their co-residents and sometimes their bed-mates and learn the stories which the landscape and songs 'of the sea' and 'of kingship' on Mount Hazzi had kept alive. Our two channels of transmission of genuine Near Eastern knowledge, women and the landscape, here combine as one.

Can we add further arguments for the date when Greeks' stories about the gods' struggles were intensified by this sort of contact? The story which we now read in Hesiod contains two particular hints. In Homer's epics and Hesiod's poem, Cronos is called by the epithet *ankulomētēs*, a word which means 'crooked-counselling'. In fact, Cronos was not characterized by acts which were particularly devious. It looks as if his adjective has changed from the older and apt *ankulamētēs*, meaning the 'crooked reaper' with a crooked sickle.[17] This older word for 'reaping' contained the meaning around which the Near Eastern story of Kumarbi had converged with the Greeks' stories about Cronos, but it had started to fade from memory for poets in Hesiod's active lifetime. The convergence, then, between Cronos and Kumarbi has to have occurred some while before *c.* 720 BC.

There is a second hint which points to a date after *c.* 1200 BC, perhaps *c.* 900–780, involving a separate Greek zone from the Euboean presence at Al Mina. Unlike the Hittite story, Hesiod's story brings in the goddess of sexual love, Aphrodite, and describes how she was born, a 'birth of Venus', from Heaven's scattered male parts. Why ever was Aphrodite brought into the older succession story at all? She had an important cult at Paphos on Cyprus, where her worship may even have originated for the Greeks.[18] She had another cult on the island of Cythera off southern Greece. According to Hesiod, the male 'foam' from which she was born floated first to Cythera, then eastwards to Paphos on Cyprus. He was imagining its progress from a vantage-point in Greece, whereas in real life Aphrodite may have travelled from the eastern 'triangle' westwards to the Greek mainland. Nonetheless Hesiod assumes that it was on the west coast of Cyprus, at or near Paphos, that Aphrodite first emerged onto the land and 'grass grew beneath her slender feet'.[19]

Perhaps, then, Greeks who worshipped Aphrodite at Paphos in Cyprus first attached their goddess's birth to an older 'succession' tale of the gods which was known to them from north Syria's coast. At Paphos, Aphrodite's cult was directly connected with the Near East: the historian Herodotus inferred that it derived from worship of the goddess Astarte at Ascalon on the Levantine coast.[20] Had, then, Astarte's Phoenicians also picked up the old Hittite 'song of kingship' on this coastline and attached their own goddess to its tale of castration too? The one surviving source for Phoenician interest in the story is the late *Phoenician History* of Philo of Byblos. He tells in Greek how the Phoenician god El 'ambushed his father Heaven and castrated him near the spring and rivers ... and the blood from his genitals dripped into the spring and waters of the rivers, and until this day the place is shown'.[21] In Philo's history, El (Cronos) was the founder of the 'first city', Byblos. As a man of Byblos, Philo would not omit a chance to emphasize his city's antiquity. But the 'red rivers', once again, are the Nahr Ibrahim and its tributaries in Byblos's hinterland. We do not know how far back this location of the dreadful deed went (it might have been invented long after Hesiod's time), but it does at least show that a tale of castration was not impossible in Phoenician storytelling.

On Cyprus, priests and worshippers of Aphrodite–Astarte linked their goddess with the 'song of kingship' as sung on Mount Hazzi, the Jebel Aqra. Whether Phoenicians had already made this connection in their own homeland we cannot now say, but at Cythera and Paphos the story was told in a milieu where the two peoples, Greek and Phoenician, met. This meeting was not obviously one in the Bronze Age when Aphrodite and her cult were formed. It sits better in the eleventh to early eighth centuries, when Phoenicians were visiting Old Paphos and then settling on Cyprus and when Cypriots were aware of the seat of the stories, Mount Hazzi and its surrounding region, which they visited by sea. Their own great goddess Aphrodite could be worked into the story, which gained from the Cypriots' ingenious retelling. Their version is a mythical pair to the fine 'black-on-red' glazed jugs and pottery which were innovations of this same fertile period in Cypriot history. In Greek the story was retold with a well-omened pun: *aphros* ('male foam') caused Aphro-dite's birth.

In the early eighth century Euboeans below Mount Hazzi encountered the local story afresh for themselves, probably without the 'birth of Venus': that part of the story flourished on Cyprus, where, as casual visitors, some of them might have heard it too. What mattered, first of all, was the basic story of succession in heaven. Scholarly concern to establish one date for the Greeks' appropriation of the Hittite story has caused a simpler question to be ignored: whatever became of the story's main agent, the sickle? It was, after all, the most memorable item in the story which the Greeks developed. Inquisitive Greek minds might well wonder about its whereabouts. We happen to know that in the oldest Hittite story, the cutter was kept respectfully near the mountain after the parting of Heaven and Earth, and was available for use in a second round of battles. This repeated use of it did not pass into the Greek story as told by Hesiod. Since antiquity the question of the sickle's whereabouts has not been posed, but enough survives in later, localized Greek texts to give exact answers. The main answer is an eighth-century one, confirming that the story of the god's castration was particularly fresh and lively at that time.

On the fully developed Greek map, various promontories became known as Drepanon, the Greek word for a sickle.[22] They had a distinctive, hooked outline, and among them there was one on the west coast of Cyprus, another on the south shore of the Sea of Marmara (south-east of modern Istanbul), another on the coast of Achaea, overlooking the Gulf of Corinth, another in north-western Sicily where the ancient name Drepanon survives as the modern Trapani. The attachment of myths to place names continued to exercise authors throughout antiquity and so it might seem impossible to trace such locations back into the eighth century BC. At one sickle-shaped site, however, the connections between place and object are impeccably early.

By the Straits of Messina, between Sicily and Italy, Greeks settled on what is nowadays the Sicilian site of Messina at a date probably *c.* 730–720 BC. Our most authoritative source for this settlement is the historian Thucydides (writing about it *c.* 410 BC), who tells us that the place was at first called 'Zancle' after its existing name among the Sicels who lived there. In the Sicels' language *zancle* meant a 'sickle', a name with an obvious relevance. The settlement lay beside a natural harbour which was defended by a hooked, sickle-shaped promontory. We meet this aspect of the site on the coins which Greeks later struck for their settlement: on them the harbour appears with a dolphin and the caption 'DANK(LE)'.[23] At the site itself the vista from its sickle-shaped point still runs east across the narrows to Italy: 'Messina now is a modern city with a few medieval buildings surviving,' wrote Sicily's historian, E. A. Freeman, even before the earthquake of 1908 destroyed the town. 'The Greek lives only in the witness which the view still gives to his skill in choosing the position of his cities.'[24]

At this sickle-shaped settlement there was something more. We know it from the poetry of the learned Alexandrian Callimachus (*c.* 270 BC) in which he set out to answer a curious fact about the city's origins: why was no individual founder bidden by name to attend the 'founder's feast' at Zancle? In the second book of his famous erudite poem *On Origins* he remarked, in brilliant verse, how all the cities in Sicily had feasts for named founders: he purported to put the peculiar problem of Zancle to one of the Muses herself. Clio, the Muse of history, answered him and 'amazed' him: Zancle had had two founders, who had quarrelled while founding their city.[25] They had asked Apollo (presumably at Delphi) which of them should be the true founder, but they were told that neither of them could be. So on the days of Zancle's 'founder's feast' the presiding magistrates invite no founder by name. In the course of this dazzling answer Callimachus' Muse of history evoked the first Greek founders of Zancle and their actions on the site: 'The founders placed wooden towers,' the Muse tells us, 'strengthened with battlements, around the sickle of Cronos for, there, the sickle with which he sheared off his father's parts has been hidden in a hollow under the ground.' Callimachus' local knowledge was very well founded. As elsewhere, it was based on the researches of Aristotle and his pupils, who probably included a 'Constitution of the Zancleans' among the 158 local 'constitutions' which they compiled c. 330 BC.[26] These works were based on local evidence and in this case they would reflect what the people of Zancle themselves affirmed. Their city's special relationship with Cronos can be confirmed from neglected evidence which is much earlier than Aristotle's writings. In 648 BC Zancle founded a secondary settlement at Himera, to the west of their own, on the coast of Sicily below Monte San Calogero. Alone of the Greek settlements in Sicily, Himera showed the god Cronos on its silver coinage, a fact which is known to us from surviving coins struck c. 410 BC.[27] Cronos is not usually worshipped in a Greek city's cults and his prominence on Himera's coinage is exceptional. The reason for it is simple: the cult had derived from Himera's mother-city Zancle, so closely connected with Cronos. The coinage allows us to take this connection back to the mid-seventh century BC when Himera was first founded from Zancle. Zancle was already a 'Cronos-centre', because of the discovery which local tradition later passed to Aristotle's pupils and thence to Callimachus. The awesome 'sickle of Cronos' was to be found on the site.

The exact date of Zancle's own foundation in the eight century BC is not given by Thucydides, our one reliable textual source. It is disputed nowadays between archaeologists and historians.[28] Archaeologists point to contemporary evidence, to a very few fragments of Greek pottery on the site which match eighth-century pottery from Pithecussae. Zancle, they argue, was founded from Ischia–Pithecussae and as its site on the straits between Sicily and Italy was so strategic for Greek travellers, it might even have been founded *c.* 770–760 BC, soon after the settlement on Ischia itself. According to Thucydides, however, the settlement began with 'robber-pirates' from Italian Cumae, the Greek settlement opposite Ischia which had been founded from that island perhaps *c.* 750 BC.[29] 'Later' they were joined by a 'crowd from Chalcis and the rest of Euboea' who shared in the land. As a result the site had two founders, Perieres from Cumae (specifically, the Italian Cumae) and Crataemenes from Chalcis. He seems to mean that Perieres had led the 'robber-pirates', whereas Crataemenes led the crowd who 'came later'. We cannot square him with our archaeologists' dating from pottery and their proposal that the settlement was made from Ischia.

Thucydides does not consider Zancle to be the first Greek settlement in Sicily, an event he places in 735 BC: he cannot, therefore, have thought of Zancle as founded *c.* 760. Either we believe him or we believe an interpretation of a tiny proportion of the pottery on the site: his detailed authority is preferable, but the decision is not crucial for the trail we are tracing. On either view Zancle was founded by Euboean Greeks, whether as early as 770–760 or else, much more probably, *c.* 730–720.

With the help of Callimachus' poem we can enter into these Euboeans' supreme discovery. Their founders put 'towers, strengthened with battlements, around the sickle of Cronos', either around its revered site or more probably as walls round the city or its central point. Within them the sickle lay beneath the ground: symbols of these towers, four of them, have even been detected on the city's later coinage. To my eye they are not obviously towers, but the rest of the story is specific. 'There', Callimachus' speaker, the Muse Clio, tells us, 'it has been hidden in a "hollow" (*gypē*) under the ground.'[30] The rare Greek word *gypē* means a hollow, but not necessarily a natural cave. Who, then, had 'hidden' it there? Surely the founders themselves: they must have seen the object in order to identify it, because the locals, the non-Greek Sicels, would never have mentioned Cronos, a Greek god, and identified the sickle as his. Sicels, I suggest, showed to the Euboean founders a revered ancient sickle, one of the historic relics on their site: the founding Euboeans then put it in a special 'hollow', perhaps a specially dug pit, within the city's inner wall. It was an ancient sickle, perhaps one which some Sicels (or even the Euboean founders) had recently dug up. Did it show any signs of bloodstains and, as Hesiod's poetry later claimed, was it a right-handed sickle with very sharp teeth? It was so very venerable that perhaps it had come to the site as an import from far away. Here there is a fine possibility: was it one of those bronze sickles with tube-shaped handles which reached the west Mediterranean and are best known to us on Sardinia, although their ultimate origin was the distant British Isles?[31] Was the sickle which was believed to have castrated Heaven in fact a sickle from Britain, perhaps specifically one from East Anglia or an Essex sickle 'with sharp teeth'? Whatever the object's origins, the Euboean founders interpreted it, like archaeologists, in terms of knowledge which they already had. They had talked a little to the Sicels and had established, perhaps with difficulty, that the name of their site meant 'sickle'. They then saw a special sickle and linked it with their stories of the gods. It seemed like a heaven-sent omen: they had found the Great Castrator. They laid it respectfully in their new city's centre beneath the ground.

These Greek settlers at Zancle were exactly the right people to detect Cronos' hand on an ancient sickle's handle. If we believe the archaeologists, they were Euboeans straight from Ischia: if we prefer Thucydides, Perieres and his men from Cumae were Euboeans by descent, settlers who had moved to Cumae c. 750 BC from the Euboeans' first settlement at Pithecussae. As we know from the goods which continued to reach Ischia and be placed in its settlers' graves, they and their families included Euboeans who had close contacts with the Near East, with Cilicia, north Syria and the Levant. As for the co-founder Crataemenes, he and his fellow-Euboeans came from the homeland of these pioneers, the island of Euboea, whose goods and persons had been reaching Cyprus and Tarsus, Al Mina and points on the coast of the Levant since the tenth century BC. In this Near Eastern milieu, on Cyprus and below Mount Hazzi, Euboeans, our travelling heroes, had encountered the stories of Heaven's emasculation and the ancient 'cutter' which had separated Heaven and Earth: they had heard, too, from Cypriots here and on Cyprus of the birth of Aphrodite from the scattered DNA of the god. These stories, therefore, were very vivid in their minds. When they and their kinsmen travelled westwards they took these stories with them, singing them just as their neighbours and bed-mates in Unqi had sung the 'song of kingship in heaven' on Mount Hazzi itself. In the west they were ripe for yet more evidence, and on the straits at Zancle they found it: the very sickle itself. These Euboeans beautifully conform to our hopes of them: they found in the west something which they had learned about so vividly through their recent contacts with the east: unlike Io or Cadmus, Adonis, Mopsus or Zeus Kasios, the 'sickle of Cronos' is an incontestable example of a story which travelled from east to west with our travelling heroes, Euboean Greeks. It travelled in the eighth century, either in 770–760 BC when Al Mina was still young or (following Thucydides' belief) in c. 730–720 when the eastern links with the west were still strong, as proven by the objects laid then in Euboeans' contemporary graves on Ischia.

The discovery at Zancle requires us to look more closely at some of the other sites which are connected with a sickle on the Greek map. Only a few of them are linked to myths of the gods in our surviving Greek evidence, which includes many localized texts and images on coins. On the southern coastline of the Sea of Marmara, on the Gulf of Izmit, there is an appropriately shaped promontory near modern Hersek which for Greeks became the site of Drepanon, a sickle. Nowadays the promontory is a deserted stretch of marshland but in antiquity it was a natural landmark for sailors, a crossing-point for the gulf and a marker for the river-route, now silted, which ran inland. This 'Drepanon' did lie on sea-routes of early Greek visitors but there was no association with Cronos here and his castrator.[32]

On the sea-route from mainland Greece to the west, two sickle-shaped points are more suggestive. Near Argyra on the coast of Achaea, the cape near Bolina was known to the traveller Pausanias (c. AD 150) as the site from which 'Cronos' sickle' was thrown into the sea.[33] The cape is a natural landmark for sea-travellers in the Gulf of Corinth and it may well be that the connection between the sickle-cape and Cronos occurred to early Euboean travellers as they headed west along the gulf as early as the eighth century BC. If the sickle had entered the sea here, was it ever washed up and if so where was it? They travelled westwards, wondering about these questions:

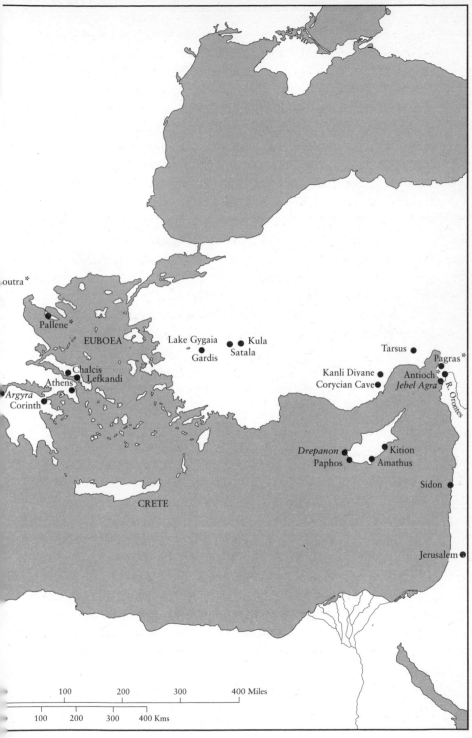

7. *Cronos' sickle (italicized), Typhon and the Giants (asterisked): east*

8. Cronos' sickle (italicized), Typhon and the Giants (asterisked): west

on their coastal route to the west lay an island with very strong sickle-connections, Corcyra, the modern Corfu.

Like Zancle, Corcyra had a suggestive pre-Greek name whose root *krk* underlay the Greek 'Kerkura'. It has been explained as meaning a sickle, no less, in the local pre-Greek language.[34] In due course a sickle was indeed believed to have been buried beneath the island. It was mentioned by Aristotle and his researchers who were drawing on local information, but for them it was the 'sickle of Demeter', goddess of the harvest. The island was exceptionally fertile and this explanation did it justice. As the Aristotelians had located the sickle of Cronos at Zancle further west, they had to make the 'sickle' of Corcyra into something else, Demeter's relic.[35]

Their theory was not the only one. According to the historian Timaeus (active *c.* 320–265 BC) Corcyra's sickle was nothing less than the 'sickle of Cronos' itself.[36] He was a scholarly man, but there were local reasons which might have distorted his view here. Timaeus was a citizen of Tauromenium in Sicily (the modern Taormina), the neighbouring Greek city to Zancle. As a matter of civic rivalry he might have denied his neighbours' greatest treasure and located it across the sea on Corcyra instead. However, he had good grounds for his Corcyran location. In the wake of Homer's *Odyssey* the people of Corcyra claimed that their island was the legendary Phaeacia which Odysseus had visited. By 500 BC, we know that one Greek writer on myths was claiming that the Phaeacians, so 'close to the gods', had been born from the very blood which had spurted from Heaven's castration.[37] The Corcyraeans, therefore, were the children of Cronos' 'mowing' with his sickle and no doubt they would like to claim that they owned the tool, too.

Might the sickle have had two early addresses, thereby justifying both Aristotle's and Timaeus' statements? By *c.* 750 BC Greeks had settled on Corcyra: here, too, they were Euboeans. Like the Euboeans who settled at Zancle, they learned from the locals that their island-location was called 'sickle'. Corcyra's settlers were Euboeans from Eretria, whereas Zancle's settlers included Euboeans from Chalcis, Eretria's neighbour and intensely hostile rival. The men of Chalcis claimed to have found Cronos' sickle at Zancle, but the sickle may already have been claimed by their enemies, the men of Eretria on

Corcyra. Euboean Greeks, however, were not the only people travelling the Mediterranean who knew a story of castration in heaven. Phoenicians knew it too, people who lived and travelled in Mount Hazzi's orbit, and they too journeyed west from the same Levantine coast. While Euboeans claimed that they had found the sickle in the west, did Phoenician travellers, perhaps, claim that they had found it themselves?

Like these travellers we should begin by visiting Cyprus. On the western coastline of the island lies a promontory known in antiquity as Drepanon which juts, sickle-shaped, into the sea.[38] Some 30 miles to the south-east of it, also near this coast, lies Old Paphos, the seat of the famous cult of Aphrodite whom the Phoenicians worshipped as Astarte. As Hesiod charmingly reminds us, she first set foot on land near Paphos, and the archaeologist J. L. Myres has described how he witnessed an 'emergence' here in progress in the winter of 1913. The south-west wind, he saw, forced two breakers to collide off the coast: 'When the angle of impact is about 90°,' he wrote, 'the "break" is both concentrated within a small width of swell, and very violent, so that the breaker shoots up in a column like a water-spout, 10–15 feet high, and falls back in an outward cascade of foam which may be carried some feet to leeward by the wind. It looks exactly like a human figure literally "rising from the sea" and spreading long hair and dripping arms. In December 1913 Mr. Markides and I watched this effect recurring every few minutes, for over half an hour . . .'[39] It still recurs on this same coast, as it surely recurred in the years from 1200 to 750 BC: priests of Astarte–Aphrodite in her nearby shrine at Paphos would have observed the same phenomenon. Here was the goddess's approach-route: might they also claim that the emasculating instrument, the sickle of Cronos, which caused her birth from father Heaven had been cast into the sea at Drepanon (Sickle), the aptly named promontory which lies only some 30 miles up the Cypriot coast?

On Phoenician routes to the west this sickle had a further site. In north-west Sicily near modern Trapani, Astarte–Aphrodite had a cult-site as famous as Paphos, ancient Eryx (now Erice), whose steep cliff was graced by her distinctive temple. Here, Phoenician settlers founded a cult of Astarte which Greeks understood in due course as a cult of their own Aphrodite, perhaps adding a cult for Adonis too.

In antiquity, modern Trapani was ancient Drepanon, a place with another sickle-shaped harbour which earned it its name. Not until the 270s BC do we happen to have evidence of anything more, but it is preserved for us by the erudite Greek poet Lycophron.[40] He refers at Eryx to the 'leap of Cronos' sickle': he must be referring to the 'leap' of the sickle as it was thrown from the cliff of Eryx into the sea which lies off Drepanon's sickle-shaped promontory exactly below the cliff. Like all the learning in Lycophron's cryptic poem this 'leap' is likely to go back to very much older Greek sources than Lycophron himself: behind them, in turn, may lie a story begun by Phoenicians. They, too, had adapted the legend of the separation of Heaven and Earth from their neighbours in the Levant. In the west, the Phoenician priests of the goddess Astarte at Eryx may have capitalized on the existence of a sickle-shaped settlement, Drepanon, which lay on the seashore beneath their goddess's shrine. In their separate sphere they may have started a story which Euboean Greeks had also started in theirs.

At Trapani or on Cyprus, there is a risk of ascribing too great an antiquity to later antiquarians' stories. At Zancle, however, the finding of Cronos' sickle is firmly fixed as an event of the later eighth century. It allows us to correct a subsequent Greek's perplexity. In the second century AD the traveller Pausanias remarked about the legends of Cronos that 'long ago those Greeks who were thought to be wise spoke their saying in riddling allegories and not directly at face value: I therefore inferred that the things said about Cronos were a sort of wisdom of the ancient Greeks'.[41] Pausanias was mistaken. The stories were not allegories: they were imports, taken into Greek culture by Greeks' contacts with specific places and other cultures. They were not taken up in connection with a cult or a religious ritual nor were they wisdom acquired from 'migrant Eastern charismatics' coming to Greece. They were acquired because they amplified stories which Greek visitors already knew and because they made sense of specific landscapes in which Greeks came to live. From Mount Hazzi to the Straits of Messina, the myth travelled specifically with Euboean Greeks in the eighth century who applied it to new objects and new places which it seemed to explain. These Euboeans applied what they heard in the east to what they encountered in the west, true travelling heroes in the age of Homer. But Homer's epic poems do not even mention these myths and locations which were so much to the forefront of Euboeans' minds.

Nowadays, our 'Birth of Aphrodite' is imagined through Botticelli's image of a goddess drifting to the seashore among a swirl of roses. The painter derived this image from vernacular Italian sources, not directly from the ancient Greek stories of Cronos' vigorous, right-handed swipe.[42] But the sea still foams in an 'outward cascade' off the coast below Cypriot Paphos and stands in crests on the straits by Messina where Cronos' sickle was reverently buried beneath the ground. Further north, beyond the classical world, stories of the separation of Heaven and Earth continued to be told far and wide, even among the distant Eskimos. In the polar regions darkness envelops the earth in winter with only the briefest chink of daylight. When Captain Peary discovered the Greenland Eskimos, they were amazed to meet a stranger from the world beyond. The rest of the world, they told him, is lying in darkness and only here, in our fragment of winter daylight, has human life survived. In their northern darkness, Heaven's separation from Earth seems far from complete, as if Cronos did not cut quite enough from his father before the sickle was thrown away.

17

Travelling Monsters

I

The Greeks who encountered these stories in and around Mount Kasios reacted to them in a typically Greek way. They did not ascribe them to a newly discovered god, 'Kumarbios' or 'Tarrhuntas'. They credited them to their own Zeus. They added a local adjective to Zeus's name, making a 'Zeus Kasios' who had a particular relevance to storms and rough seas, just as he had in his north Syrian home. They credited tales of Kumarbi to their own Cronos and tales of Tarhunta to their own ruling weather-god, Zeus.

Both these responses were characteristically Greek and, later, Roman too. We can compare the naming of Zeus Kasios with the later, exemplary transfer of another neo-Hittite cult into the Graeco-Roman world. The neo-Hittite weather-god had an active shrine and cult up in the mountains of Syrian Commagene at ancient Doliche, modern Tell Dülük. Not even a venturesome Euboean went up so far north and discovered it. The cult persisted, ignored by the great waves of Alexander and Graeco-Roman history, but it was then encountered by Roman soldiers, perhaps first by soldiers serving in the region in the 70s AD. Soldiers, then and later, helped to spread the cult. They identified this weather-god as Jupiter 'Dolichenus', giving him an adjective of place.[1] They then took over his imagery in exact detail. We see the god in the Roman west on monuments which are some of our best images of a neo-Hittite god: he retains the characteristic pigtail and belted skirt, a double-headed axe in one hand, a thunderbolt in the other. He is particularly worshipped by soldiers in the Roman world and he retains his role as a god with power over mining and metals. He is the pair to 'Zeus Kasios', but unfortunately we have no early images of that Zeus in Euboean company when he, too, would have worn his neo-Hittite dress.

Euboeans also equated the gods of the ancient 'song of kingship' with their own Cronos and Zeus. In my view they already had an old story of their gods' succession which helped them make this transfer, but behind it lay a constant Greek belief, one which we know best in Herodotus, the great Greek traveller and enquirer. For Herodotus, in general the 'gods are the same everywhere' and when confronted with cults and names abroad his instinct is to 'read' them as his own Greek gods: 'the power of attraction was greater than the power of repulsion'. So it was already for our Euboeans, even when faced with the repulsive details of the Great Castrator. It is a persistent Greek attitude, of which they are the first known example. Their encounters with foreigners were not coloured by the belief that such people's religion was false and inferior, the belief that tinges Christians, Muslims, Hindus or atheists nowadays.

Once made, the equation with a Greek god could be usefully applied elsewhere. Through Greeks' direct contact with the Near Eastern stories Cronos came to be credited with devouring his own children. When Euboeans travelled to Tyre or Amathus, Carthage or Sulcis, they too discovered that Phoenicians offered infants to their gods. They were not wrong in this perception, although Near Eastern archaeologists have sometimes wished they were: Greeks identified the receiving god of this cult (Baal Hammon, in particular) as Cronos, their only god with a history of consuming babies.[2] Romans later equated him with their Cronos-equivalent, Saturn. One side of Saturn and Cronos had been agrarian, festive and tinged with a 'golden age'. Greek contact with the Near East brought a darker element into his story which helped, however, to translate what Phoenicians did.[3] Cronos retained this grim usefulness, which became attached to one side of his myth and personality: it is the reason why some of the warlike, ferocious gods in western Asia were later interpreted as Cronos too.[4]

In the old Hittite story, Kumarbi had eaten his children, but then he was given a stone instead. Our one text of this episode is still fragmentary, but its scholars infer that Kumarbi threw the stone away, ordering it (perhaps) to be named and apparently to be preserved and paid cult.[5] There is a widespread history of 'sacred' stones in Syrian and Levantine religion and we are far from sure which of them was worshipped, which symbolized a god or how their public received them. However, Kumarbi's stone was set up somewhere in honour, and one natural guess is that it was set up on or near Mount Hazzi, the seat of the Storm God, whose life it had helped to save. There is, then, an obvious possibility. Coins from Seleucus' city in the plain below Mount Hazzi show a prominent conical stone in a pillared shrine which is captioned 'Zeus Kasios' and topped by the eagle which was so important for the god and his role in founding the city.[6] This stone is not obviously symbolizing a mountain. It is better understood as a symbol, or attribute, of the god himself. It may then be an image of the ancient stone which Kumarbi had tried to eat instead of Tarhunta–Zeus, thereby saving his son's life. Perhaps an image of the stone stood in a temple to him down in Seleucus' city, but it is much more attractive to see the captioned shrine as the shrine up on Mount Kasios itself, the Jebel Aqra, which lay in the city's territory. Perhaps, as in the ancient myth, a stone was preserved there, at least until Christian monks turned the site into a monastery.[7]

In the Greek world, as we shall see, such a stone had an exact and instructive eighth-century location. Meanwhile there are subsequent threads in the 'song of kingship' which need to be tracked. The struggles among the gods on the Jebel Aqra did not end with the castration of Heaven, the ancient sky-god. The victor Kumarbi was then deposed by his own son, the child whom he had tried to devour. This son was the god of storms and weather. From his seat on the mountain he then had to survive enemies whom the older gods raised up against him. Kumarbi fathered several monsters to challenge him, including a snaky monster followed by a gigantic monster of stone.

Meanwhile on the south side of the Jebel Aqra there were old Canaanite stories of the Storm God's triumph over a snaky monster too. He was 'Ltn' ('Litanu' or 'Lotan'), 'the coiling serpent, the tyrant of seven heads'. We know about him from fragmentary tablets found at Ras Shamra which date to the thirteenth century BC, but we can be sure that his story continued to be told in the Levant in the ninth and eighth centuries. It left a mark then on the contemporary prophets and psalmists, who can still be read in the Hebrew Scriptures.[8] Just as

Baal had defeated snaky 'Litanu', so Yahweh was said to have bound snaky 'Leviathan'. Once again Israel's Yahweh was credited with deeds like those of his neighbouring heathen gods. On his holy mountain Sion he had prevailed over 'the dragon and the sea', just as Baal had prevailed over a dragon on his holy mountain Sapanu, the Jebel Aqra. Hebrew prophets and psalmists continued to exploit the theme of this victory. Optimists even saw it as the prelude, or prequel, to Yahweh's victory over all the foreign oppressors of Israel.

That sequel has yet to happen, but back in the eighth century BC these stories could influence Israel because they were still being told in the nearby Phoenician cities. They were alive, then, when Greeks traded and settled in or near these cities: the Greeks, too, developed stories of their ruling god's triumphs. In them, their Storm God Zeus overthrows the very father Cronos who had tried to devour him as a baby. Zeus then has to survive counter-attacks from rivals, including a snaky monster Typhon. When we first meet Typhon in any detail, he has a part in Hesiod's poem the *Theogony* (c. 715–705 BC).[9] On his first appearance in it he is 'terrible, insolent and lawless', the monster, 'they say', who mated with Echidna ('Miss Viper'), a virgin at the time. Echidna lived far away 'beneath the earth in Arima'. Here, Hesiod knows of the same mysterious location as Homer and like Homer he presents his knowledge of Typhon as hearsay. Much later in the poem Typhon appears in more detail and fights a dreadful combat of his own. Now we learn that he is the youngest child of mother Earth. A hundred snake's-heads grow from his shoulders whose tongues flicker and whose eyes flash fire. These heads make all sorts of noises, sometimes emitting sounds which the gods could understand, sometimes sounding like an animal, a bull or a lion or a pack of young hounds. Zeus fought this polyphonic monster with his weapons of thunder and lightning causing the 'whole earth and heaven to seethe'. He scorched Typhon's snaky heads, 'lashed' him and threw him, shattered, to the ground.

It is arguable whether this fuller second description of Typhon and his battle featured in Hesiod's original poem or not, but for the moment the important point is that these Greek stories inarguably match details of the stories of combat and snaky battles in the earlier Hittite stories. In Homer's *Iliad*, too, Zeus 'lashes' Typhon, and, by philological argument, this precise wording has been taken back to a supposed Indo-European origin and then traced forwards through a range of subsidiary languages.[10] Even if true, this type of linguistic conjecture does not explain when and where the Hittite and the Greek stories came into contact and took on a similar content. Their similarities are very striking. Like Kumarbi, the Greek Cronos eats his children; like the Storm God, Zeus escapes and overthrows his father. Like the Storm God, Zeus then has to contend with a snaky monster whom he beats and 'lashes' as his captive. Like the far-flung sickle of Cronos, the battles and travails of Typhon are subjects for a historical and topographical treatment: the results bring them exactly into the horizons of travelling Euboeans.

II

We happen to have three different stories of the contests of the Hittite Storm God and a snaky opponent. Two are extremely old and are known only in a single text from *c.* 1250 BC which ascribes them to one Kella, the priest of the 'storm-god of Nerik'. The other, the 'song of Hedammu', began, like so much else, as an older story which the Hittites took over. Its context among Hittite songs has gradually become clearer to us.

Kella the storytelling priest told how the Storm God was once defeated by a hostile snake.[11] The Storm God summoned the other gods for advice, with the result that the goddess Inara prepared a feast with copious wine and other drink. She enlisted a mortal helper, who insisted on sleeping with her as a price for his help: she then dressed up and lured the serpent from his hole by inviting him to eat and drink at her banquet. The serpent and his children ate and swelled up; they were unable to return to the hole and so the goddess's mortal helper tied up the serpent and the Storm God slaughtered him. The story went on to tell how the goddess installed her helper in a high-rise house on a rock but that he caught sight of his wife and children from her skyscraper and longed to go home. Thereupon the goddess killed him. The boundaries between gods and mortals, the story implies, are not to be transgressed, not even by sexual passion.

In the second story, the serpent began by defeating the Storm God, whereupon he stole the god's heart and eyes. The Storm God married a poor man's daughter and fathered a son. He waited and in due course this son married the serpent's daughter. The son then asked his new family to give him his father's heart and eyes: he received them and returned them to the Storm God. The Storm God then went down to the sea again and killed both the serpent and his own son, who had been obliged to fight on the side of his family-by-marriage.

These two tautly narrated stories of serpent-wars are rich in word-play and in wider references to aspects of Hittite culture. The second story exploits a pattern of Hittite marriage, whereby a son-in-law asks for a price from his new bridal family (in this case he asks for his father's heart and eyes) and, on payment, joins his bride's family and deserts his own. The first story is explicitly linked to the role of the king in the important *purulli* festival: 'Let the land grow and thrive and let the land be protected,' participants declared, 'and when it grows and thrives they perform the festival of *purulli*.' Almost nothing else is known of this festival except that it coincided with a renewal of growth in nature, perhaps in autumn, and honoured the all-important waters and rivers on which that growth depends.[12]

The topography of the two stories is different. The *purulli* festival, we are told, commemorated the entrusting to the king of underground waters, apparently a 'river of the watery abyss' which descends to the underworld.[13] The first of the two stories places the Storm God's battle at Kiskilussa, a place name which scholars locate in northern Anatolia near the Kizil Irmak river, about 40 miles inland from the southern coastline of the Black Sea. In the second story, however, the Storm God is fighting 'by the sea'. This sea could be our Black Sea north of Kiskilussa, but the story could also have travelled southwards as Hittite rule extended there too. Then the 'sea' would be the Mediterranean sea off Cilicia, the Kizzuwatna of Hittite topography.

These stories are extremely old, existing long before our Euboeans reached Cilicia and north Syria, but we have artistic evidence that stories of snaky combat persisted into neo-Hittite times too. At Malatya in north Syria a stone relief in the local ruler's Lion Gate shows two figures confronting a snake-monster. One of them, armed with a lance, is a god and the other is his helper. Objects from the sky are shown striking the monster's body and may well be thunderbolts, the god's weapon. This battle between a god and a snake-monster shows that stories of the combat had lived into the neo-Hittite era: the sculpture is dated by its scholars to the tenth century BC.[14] It brings these tales of combat close to the time when Greeks were among the visitors to Cilicia, north Syria and their coast.

We also have a third Hittite story, which is separate from the two told long ago by Kella the priest.[15] The essence of it is that the storm-god Teshub confronted a snaky monster called Hedammu which the previous king in heaven, Kumarbi, had raised against him by fathering it on a daughter of the sea-god. Once again he was eventually saved by the loyal goddess Inara. This time she lured the snake-monster from the sea, charmed him with music, plied him with drink and appeared naked before him, exciting him sexually. Our text of the story unfortunately breaks off here, but we know that Hedammu was then defeated by the weather-god: perhaps he was thrown into the sea. As his next move, Kumarbi chose to send a monster of stone to do battle; we now see why. Unlike the snake it would be unmoved by drink and sex.

For some while scholars did not realize that the surviving fragments of this story belonged among the stories of the other succession-struggles between the gods in the Hittite heaven. In fact, Hedammu was one story in this same group and belonged, therefore, in that very 'song of kingship' which we have found to have been sung in honour of Mount Hazzi, the Jebel Aqra. The text's surviving fragments have been rearranged to give a significant gain to our knowledge. At the beginning of Hedammu's story, a god, surely Kumarbi himself, declares: '[I come] from the mountain 'Mountain'; [I raised] a dragon.'[16] This 'Mountain' is none other than Mount Hazzi, the Jebel Aqra. The story of Hedammu was not only sung by choirs on the mountain's lower slopes: it was set on and around Mount Hazzi itself. The sea from which the snake-monster came and into which (no doubt) it was thrown was the sea below Mount Hazzi, either the sea at the mountain's base or the sea on the side of our 'triangle' which runs across from Cyprus to Cilicia. At the foot of this very mountain Euboean travellers settled and on this same gulf of the sea they travelled to the kingdom in southern Cilicia which they equated, optimistically, with their very own Greek prophet Mopsus.

Most remarkably, clear echoes of these three old Hittite stories survive in out-of-the-way late Greek sources, somehow resonating across as much as 1,500 years. Three particular texts have long been seen to be relevant. One is an erudite poem on fishing by Oppian (c. AD 180); another, the first two books of a long, learned and highly rhetorical epic about Dionysus by Nonnus, a Christian and a 'wandering poet' who travelled from his home in Egypt in the early fifth century AD (c. 430). The third is a prose 'library' of mythological Greek stories falsely ascribed to the scholarly Apollodorus of Athens but actually written in the first or second century AD. These sources may seem obscure supports for arguments about the eighth century BC, but they have particular aspects which make them more valuable on these topics. Oppian lived in south Cilicia, close to the very coast-line which looks across to Cyprus or south-east to the Jebel Aqra: he knew the shore, its myths and its topography from personal experience.[17] Nonnus used earlier sources, mostly lost to us, but he also travelled through Syria and into Asia Minor, visiting some of the cities whose local myths he versified and researched on his travels. 'He was not shut up in the one Library at Alexandria', his great expert, Louis Robert, well understood, 'in order to write at random, aiming to produce piles of papyrus before they were then clumsily integrated into the plan of a new epic about Dionysus. He was a traveller, giving "recitals" of his works', often in the very cities which his poem honoured and dignified.[18] As for the prose book of myths, a brilliant study of its section on Zeus and Typhon has established that an earlier Greek hexameter poem underlies its wording. It was probably a learned poem of the Hellenistic age and as such would have drawn on earlier sources.[19]

Each of the three sources, then, has much more authority than the late date of their authors suggests. When Oppian alludes to the war of Zeus and Typhon, he describes how Typhon was lured by a banquet (a 'fish-picnic') and came out of his capacious pit to eat on the sea-shore: Zeus blasted him there with thunder and lightning and beat his heads on the rocks. The luring of the snake-monster by a banquet goes back to one of the two old Hittite tales which were combined and told by Kella the priest *c.* 1250 BC.[20] Nonnus, by contrast, describes gigantic 'Star Wars' between Zeus and Typhon in which Typhon steals the storm-god's thunderbolts and lightning and also takes away his sinews. He hides them in a cave by the sea, but he is then enchanted by the power of music, played to him by the hero Cadmus. He hands over the sinews and falls into a musical trance, whereupon Cadmus reclaims Zeus's thunder and lightning too. Battles with Zeus ensue in which Nonnus excellently describes the gigantic size and dangerousness of the monster Typhon, who is covered not even to the waist when he stands armed with cliffs and mountains, challenging heaven, in the waves of the Aegean sea. The music in his story recalls the music which charmed Hedammu in the old Hittite song; the encounter, like Hedammu's, is also by the seashore; the theft of Zeus's sinews recalls the theft of the Storm God's 'heart and eyes' in the Hittite song too.[21]

The relation between the two types of stolen items is clearer in the third version, the prose book of myths. The gigantic Typhon's head, we are told, brushed the stars; his hands spread to the east and west and a hundred dragon's-heads grew from each of them; from his thighs downwards he was made of hissing vipers. Zeus attacked him with thunderbolts and at close quarters with an 'adamantine sickle'. He chased him precisely to Mount Kasios, the Jebel Aqra, but Typhon overcame him, seized the sickle and cut out his sinews. He took them away to the seashore in Cilicia, wrapped them in a bearskin and gave them to the she-dragon Delphyne. She guarded them in a cave, but the god Hermes and goat-Pan recovered them, and fitted them back onto Zeus. They enabled him to return in his chariot and blast and batter Typhon to defeat. Again, the Hittite echoes here are clear: the setting on Mount Kasios, the theft of the sinews (in Hittite, the 'heart and eyes'), the use of the 'adamantine sickle' (surely the same sickle which had castrated Heaven and which the Hittite gods were to use in their next round of cosmic battles). The name Delphyne is unique in Greek myths but it can be given a Hittite derivation. The bearskin is unique too. Nonnus, perhaps, has made one theft into two, the 'sinews' being symbols of thunder and lightning, although he passed over their theft on Mount Hazzi and their cutting by the ancient weapon.

These stories share the same location: the seashore of Cilicia where
a cave contained the stolen sinews and a 'capacious pit' held the
monster himself. In Homer, however, we hear of a different name,
'Arima' or 'the Arimoi', where Typhon is still being lashed: in Hesiod
it is the place where his snaky mate Echidna lives. So we return to the
problem with which this book began: where are these 'Arimoi' or
'Arima', a people or a place where the ground shakes mightily just as
the ground once resounded beneath the feet of the advancing Greek
army as battle began at Troy? The ancients themselves were uncertain;
moderns have differed, or multiplied opinions. But the question can
now be answered, squarely in the horizon of Euboean travelling
heroes.

III

We have already met one resting place for Typhon in our study of the
travelling Mount Kasios. On the eastern arm of the Nile Delta, Typhon
was said to have been 'hidden' by the victorious Zeus in Egypt. Beside
Lake Bardawil, the surrounding marsh is the famous 'Serbonian bog',
where the battered monster lay defeated and his hot breath is still
faint but visible in the midday heat-haze above the ground. This
Egyptian resting place for him was already known to Herodotus, but
it goes back much earlier to Greek visitors to this arm of the Delta
before c. 580 BC. It has an important implication. Those Greeks who
believed it had already associated the struggles of Zeus and Typhon
with the real Mount Kasios, the parent of this Egyptian hillock, the
true Mount Hazzi on the north Syrian coast. When they found a
second 'Mount Kasios' in Egypt they readily located Typhon there
too, as part of its 'Kasian' ambience. They were encouraged, no doubt,
by the Egyptians' stories which told of a fight between the gods and
the turbulent, disruptive Seth, a Typhon-like enemy.

This Egyptian resting place, however, was never connected with
'Arima'. This silence is notable because such a range of sites was
eventually linked with the name. The candidates are short-listed by
the geographer Strabo (c. 20 BC), who could no longer choose between
them: Lydia, Syria, Cilicia, and even Sicily and the west. These ancient

theories have been dismissed as 'evidently the product of learned speculation' or as 'des créations plus ou moins artificielles'.[22] But they were not made at random. They never included Lake Bardawil, the Egyptian bog where Typhon still breathed. In fact, each of them makes excellent sense when considered in terms of its landscape.

We can trace the location in Lydia back to the mid-fifth century BC. It was then that the local historian, Xanthus of Lydia, placed a king Arimous in the region called Burnt Lydia where he must have ruled over so-called 'Arimoi'. In due course ancient scholars even adjusted their texts of Homer's *Iliad* to place the Arimoi near Sardis 'because the place is wooded and struck by lightning'.[23] Indeed it is, because the plain east of Sardis soon starts to show the black, scorched scars of volcanic eruptions. On its north-east edge the aptly named Burnt Lydia begins, leading on to the village of Kula where the black cones of dead volcanoes loom large in the landscape. In the 1820s William Arundell travelled here in search of the 'seven Christian churches of Asia' cited in the biblical book of Revelation. Instead he found a landscape scarred by the wrath of God. 'Ascending the mountain', he wrote, 'and looking back on Koolah, the view was extraordinary . . . the lava rock range looked like the blackness of a burnt forest or as if the waves of the ocean in a violent gale had suddenly been vitrified, the colour black instead of green, the same striking contrast with the houses and minarets and trees while over the volcanic mountain rose the full moon, giving from some atmospheric cause a most lurid light.'[24] How better could the ancients explain this landscape than as the site of the battle between Zeus and fire-breathing Typhon?

In Nonnus' erudite poem (*c.* AD 430) the details are even more exact because they are drawn from his own local researches and from earlier sources now lost to us. At Lydian 'Statala', he tells us, Typhon belched out fire and smoke when struck by Zeus's thunderbolt. He burnt the land until a priest of Lydian Zeus left his nearby temple and halted the monster with two powerful words: 'stop, you wretch' (*stēthi, talan*). The blazing monster halted. This rare local myth has been brilliantly explained by its connoisseur, Louis Robert.[25] 'Statala' is the ancient Satala, the modern Adali-Karata, which lies on the western edge of Burnt Lydia's volcanic outreach. Down the nearby river-valley had come a great outflow of lava from the volcanic crater of the Kaplan Alan, which lies 10 miles away to the east, the burnt landscape whose slopes are now 'wooded' as the ancient scholars recognized when changing their texts of Homer. One long tongue of this lava poured amazingly far down the valley and stopped precisely at ancient Satala on the edge of the plain of Sardis. Surely, its future onlookers thought, a hero had stopped it. Below volcanic Mount Etna in Sicily the brave Christian St Agatha would supposedly cut off her breasts and throw them to an advancing flood of lava so as to halt it before it scorched her town of Catania. At Satala, however, a pagan male priest of Zeus halted the lava with words, not breasts: '*Stā, talan*', two Greek words which explained the origin of the place name 'Statala'. The landscape and the place name gave rise to this memorable rationalization.

To the west of Satala lay something else, the gloomy lair of Typhon's concubine Echidna ('Miss Viper'). To the north of Sardis stretches the great 'Salisbury Plain' of Lydian burial mounds, huge man-made tumuli which once contained the Lydian kings. On the northern edge of this plain the ground turns into a swampy lake, Lake Gygaia or Koloe (the modern Mermere Gölü). Water-birds, including cranes, and clouds of mosquitoes still gather on this melancholy stretch of water which is thickly covered with great clumps of reeds. The reeds even form into small islands which can be made to move: in antiquity these 'dancing' reeds, a valuable resource, were honoured with a yearly festival. The lake was always extremely rich in fish and even now a few fishing-boats are kept on its shallows. But this gloomy swamp had a grimmer resident, Echidna herself.[26] To the east, in Burnt Lydia, flaming Typhon had scorched the landscape. In Lake Gygaia his Echidna lived on in the swamp.

Myths about the two of them made brilliant sense of two eerie Lydian landscapes and as a result the 'Arima' of Homer and Hesiod was interpreted as a people ('Arimoi') and given an inland home beyond Sardis. This home was not 'the product of learned speculation'. It was the conclusion of people who had travelled, looked at the landscape and been justly terrified.[27] But it was not Homer's location for Typhon's 'lashing': the monster was not still being beaten there. Only later did Xanthus, himself from Lydia, advance this local candidate for Typhon's 'Arimoi'.

As Mount Kasios was such a scene of battles with ancient 'dragons of the sea', north Syria may seem a much more promising candidate for Arima's true location. However, it was not seriously argued, so far as we know, until *c.* 100 BC, and then only by Posidonius, a man from Syrian Apamea. He had various arguments apart, perhaps, from local pride.[28] The 'Arimoi' were surely Aramaeans, the people in northern Syria whose Aramaic language continued to be widely spoken. 'Typhon', he claimed, was the ancient name of north Syria's Orontes river: it had been cut out of the landscape by Typhon the monster when he was struck by Zeus and burrowed underground to escape.[29]

Each of these arguments had evidence to support it. From the lower slopes of the Jebel Aqra the serpentine course of the Orontes river is still visible as it snakes away through its clearly cut bed. It became known as 'the Serpent' in Greek, perhaps because of its shape rather than because of any non-Greek evidence that the river was associated with battles between the weather-god and his snaky enemy.[30] In Assyrian texts of the eighth and seventh centuries BC the 'land of Aram' is indeed described as 'the land A-ri-mi' and its people are known as A-ra-me.[31] However, the names which royal Assyrian scribes used did not influence Greek visitors to this region. Greeks always talked of 'Mount Kasios', from 'Hazzi', not Saphon from the Assyrians' *sa-pu-na*. They never met the Assyrians' writers: the Greeks' 'Arima' began with a short 'ă' in quantity, not the long vowel-sound of the Assyrians' A-ra-me. Strabo did refer to a holy cave on Mount Kasios, but the only local candidates for the cave in question have no connection with a snake-monster.[32] At most, our later Greek sources listed some preliminary struggles with Typhon in this area. He severed Zeus's sinews, we hear, on Mount Kasios: in the ancient stories he had been battered in or near the adjoining sea, so he might have snaked away to escape the onslaught. Had he cut the river-bed of the Orontes beyond the mountain and then disappeared like its river into its underground channels? But he was not still being 'lashed' there in his lair, nor was the viper Echidna anywhere near him.

The Aramaeans, then, are a false trail. Strabo's third candidate, Cilicia, is also in the Cilician-Levantine triangle but it is very much more promising. In the early fifth century BC Pindar described the lair which 'nurtured Typhon' as the 'highly celebrated Cilician cave': it was presumably there, as we know in a fragment of one of his lost poems, that he claimed that 'once, among the Arimoi', Zeus had battered Typhon, the monster with 'fifty' heads.[33] If this cave was 'highly celebrated' for Pindar's audience, its location in Cilicia was older than his lifetime. It also persisted locally. A hundred and forty years after Pindar we can follow it with the help of Callisthenes, the historical adviser of Alexander the Great.

According to Callisthenes, 'the Arimoi are located by the Corycian cave near Calycadnus and the promontory of Sarpedon: the neighbouring mountains are called "Arima"'.[34] Callisthenes' conclusion was not the guess of an armchair scholar. In the autumn of 333 BC he had ample opportunity to pursue his researches by fieldwork in Cilicia while his king Alexander lay sick at Tarsus. He had a scholarly interest in Homeric questions; he had worked with Aristotle on a text of the *Iliad* for his royal patron, the same Alexander whom the world of the Homeric hero inspired and fascinated. Callisthenes had checked and explained the diverse evidence along this coastline for Mopsus the prophet and his complex wanderings. Of course, as a lover of Homer he also wanted to solve the vexed location of the Arimoi and Typhon's 'lashing' in the second book of the *Iliad*.

From two separate angles his location of the site near the coast of southern Cilicia can be shown to be anything but 'learned speculation'. In Hittite treaties of the Bronze Age we have the place name 'Arimmatta', which lies north, however, of Callisthenes' location, being sited in the mountains up near modern Konya. It might, however, have been applied further south at a second site with similar distinctive features to the northern one.[35] We also have the separate Hittite place name 'Erimma', which certainly lay in Cilicia. 'Erimma' is mentioned in connection with the boundary running between the Hittite empire and its adjacent Cilician kingdom. One part of this boundary was set to run along what must be the Lamos river 'towards the sea'. Callisthenes' site for the 'Arima' mountains lies precisely near this Lamos river and although the location of 'Erimma' is not wholly certain in the treaty, it is an old Hittite name, probably one from the very area to which Callisthenes refers.[36] Once again, therefore, a place name in southern Cilicia lived on from the old Hittite past: in 333 BC the locals in Cilicia told Alexander's historian of this 'Arima', an age-old point of reference. There is also the evidence of the Cilician landscape itself. Near the Calycadnus river, about 10 miles east of Seleuceia (the modern Silifke) and scarcely a mile inland from the sea, the ground collapses into two dramatic ravines, which are known nowadays in Turkish as 'Heaven' and 'Hell'.[37] The local limestone has been loosened by an underlying river, resulting in a 'cave lying open with eaten-away rocks' as the Roman poet Lucan (*c.* AD 60) correctly described its nature. The smaller of the two ravines (Hell) is inaccessible, but the larger (Heaven) used to have a rough path (nowadays, sadly, replaced by a long flight of modern steps) which descended to the floor some 200 feet below its rim. In the shade of the cliffs grew one of nature's great prizes: saffron crocuses, which were widely believed to be the finest in the world. In the mid-second century AD the doctor Galen even recorded how he went in person down into the abyss to inspect the crocuses 'exactly'. They did not impress him, he said, as especially fine crocuses or as strongly scented ones, but despite Galen the orange stigmata of their flowers remained an invaluable source of scent, dye and spices. These 'Corycian crocuses' continued to command the highest prices in lists of goods and customs-dues as late as *c.* AD 400.[38]

The Corycian crocuses grew, accessibly, by the Corycian cave, the exact site mentioned by Pindar and Callisthenes. They had vanished, however, when the gorge was rediscovered for western scholarship by the Russian traveller Tchihatchev on 30 June 1853. The scholarly Theodore Bent then revisited it in 1890 and found precisely the 'encircling eyebrow of a cliff' which Strabo had mentioned and the thick undergrowth kept 'fresh and green' by the shade of the great rocks. 'This brushwood is now very thick,' Bent reported, 'and far more luxuriant than it is ever found on the upper and more exposed plateau. Here, too, are many pomegranates, the fruit of which the nomads come to gather in late summer . . .' Bent checked for the crocus, 'but we could find no trace of it now, though it is common enough in the surounding district'.[39]

A cave on the floor of this ravine is noted in our fullest ancient description of the site, given by the minor ancient geographer Pomponius Mela (*c.* AD 50).[40] His Latin draws on others' first-hand reports of the place, but he notes, correctly, the thick vegetation of the main chasm. He adds that a 'low cave' opens off its floor. Inside it, he says, runs an underground river which gives off echoes of a strange divine music: this river, the ancient Aous, still flows beyond human reach, running south-westwards for about a mile to the bay now known in Turkish as 'Sweet Water'.[41] In late antiquity the river supplied a fine bathhouse here which was adorned with a mosaic floor of the Three Graces. It flowed on under the shore, as it still does, emerging in the open sea and accounting for the strange sight of cattle being watered among the salt waves: they are taken to drink the river's fresh water where it bubbles up. In antiquity this Aous river (the 'eastern one') was believed to run on under the sea and rise, some 40 miles away, in Cyprus, where there was a similarly named Aous river too. The bad Roman poet Cinna connected Adonis, son of an 'eastern' Aous, with this Cypriot river, but he certainly did not locate Adonis at the Corycian cave or among its crocuses.[42]

The cave's associations were very different. In due course a temple was built at its very entrance, probably in the third century BC, and was dedicated to the gods, formalizing offerings which had no doubt been paid there for many years. On the wall of the cave one visitor, c. AD 200, arranged for the inscription of some apt Greek verses: 'Before entering the broad recess in the depths of the earth in Arima, where the echoing Aous disappears with voiceless streams, I, Eupaphis, propitiated Pan and Hermes . . .'[43] One pilgrim among many over the years, Eupaphis accepted that the site of the cave lay in elusive 'Arima'. He also accepted that Pan and Hermes were the relevant local divinities. The reason is beautifully clear to us. The goat-god Pan and Hermes are exactly the gods whom Oppian and our prose book of Greek myths, with its earlier poetic source, had specified as Zeus's helpers in the recovery of Zeus's stolen sinews. In this very cave 'in Arima', therefore, Typhon had hidden the parts which he had cut from Zeus with the sickle and wrapped in a protective bearskin. Hermes and Pan had then recovered them from the abyss.

This site, the 'Corycian cave', is thus the site of a truly alarming pre-Christian myth. We can understand why a pagan temple, apparently to Zeus, was built so far down inside this gorge, right by the cave's entrance. In inscriptions found at the nearby settlement of Corycos, Zeus is specifically entitled the 'Zeus of Victory', referring to his victory, therefore, in the war with Typhon.[44] We can also understand why the temple by the cave was laboriously replaced with a Christian church, which reused its stones and pillars *c*. AD 500. The church is the most deliberate Christian counterweight to an old pagan holy place. It, too, was set very far down the gorge, on the floor of the steep chasm where it would cancel out the demonic presences in the cave beyond: goat-Pan, Hermes and the snaky Typhon. When Gertrude Bell reclaimed knowledge of this church for scholarship in 1906, she found it had been dedicated to the Virgin Mary.[45]

Like Adonis' Aphaca, this natural sanctuary is still a place for prayers: Turkish visitors tie strips of cloth on the bushes to mark their requests for blessings. However, the low entrance to the river-cave was not the recognized entrance to Typhon's own lair. Here, Pomponius Mela is decisive: 'There is a narrow mouth, extremely cramped, as those who have tried it have reported, which is therefore steeped in continual darkness and never easy to see through . . . but it is memorable both in nature and in myth, because it is the lair of Typhon and also because it kills at once whatever is thrown into it . . .'[46] This 'narrow mouth' is not the cave on the floor of Heaven's ravine nor is it in the more northerly ravine now known as Hell. Until recently boys on the site would take willing visitors to a small hole in the ground about 300 yards to the west of the main ravine down which we could climb into exactly the cramped darkness which Mela describes. A pathway runs here through rocks and stalactites in a narrow cavern while the sound of the Aous river, no longer 'voiceless', echoes eerily with Mela's 'divine music' along the cleft. The deadliness of the fumes was an ancient exaggeration, but no visitor can mistake the sinister darkness of Typhon's true lair.

The 'Corycian cave' is mentioned in our ancient histories of Alexander while Alexander lay sick in Cilicia and his army had to wait in the autumn months of 333 BC. In these months, while the saffron crocus was in flower, Callisthenes, like Galen after him, had perhaps gone on a personal visit to the ravine.[47] Perhaps he had stood by the cave's opening, like Eupaphis and the church-builders, Gertrude Bell and another historian of Alexander (myself) many centuries after him. Perhaps, like Mela's informants, he had seen the nearby chasm in which Typhon was said to have lain.

Not long after Callisthenes' researches a temple was built near the upper rim of the main ravine (Heaven), on whose walls were inscribed names, over time, of the cult's yearly priests. The temple, manifestly, was a temple to the god Hermes and perhaps to his helper Pan, the two gods who had recovered Zeus's sinews from the cave below. Several of the priests' names are based on Hermes' own, but even more of them are based on pre-Greek roots which go back to the Luwian language of the late Hittite period.[48] Quite a few of them are based on the name of the Hittite god of deer and flocks ('Runza' or 'Runt'), the god whom Greeks understood as Pan. The priests' names thus reflect precisely the importance of Pan and Hermes, the gods whom they served in their temple's cult.

This cult helps to explain the knowledge surviving as late as *c.* AD 180 in Oppian's poem on fishing. Oppian describes himself as the 'giver of delight and singer of hymns at the shrines of Hermes in Cilicia'. These 'shrines', we now realize, include the shrine of Hermes at the chasm of the Corycian cave, one of several in this area. Here, Oppian had performed hymns, singing, no doubt, of the god's saving role against the snaky menace of Typhon. He told a story which had traces of the old Hittite songs because the outline of those songs had lived on in this former centre of neo-Hittite culture. He also knew the existence of traces of Zeus's battles along the coastline. He tells how the god beat Typhon's 'hundred heads' on the rocks and 'even now, tawny banks along the seashore are red with the blood of the struggles with Typhon'.[49] These 'banks' are tawny stone cliffs, not banks of soft sand: 5 miles to the north-east of the Corycian cave, at Kanytelleis in the territory of ancient Elaioussa, another huge ravine plunges deep into the ground, known nowadays as Kanli Divane (meaning in Turkish, 'the crazy place of blood'). There is no cave or underground river here, but the tawny face of its rock is marked with conspicuous streaks of red. From the fifth century AD onwards Christians built no fewer than four basilica-churches by the rim of this ravine, which plunges down to a depth of 200 feet. No text survives to explain this surge of new Christian building, but pagan buildings had existed on this site at least since the third century BC, including another temple deep down, it seems, on the ravine's floor.[50] At this ravine, I suggest, the cluster of Christian buildings was another counterweight, designed to cancel the marks of Typhon's demonic blood on the cliff below and the existence of a cult of Zeus beside or inside the ravine itself. The red on the rock face could be reinterpreted in Christian terms as the bloodstains of legendary Christian martyrs, acceptable heroes in this old pagan place. From these stories, perhaps, the Turkish name developed: it refers to a belief that condemned criminals were once thrown to wild animals in the deep ravine.

When did Greeks first encounter the cave, its pre-Greek place name (Erimma or Arimmatta) and the traces of old Hittite stories about these snake-wars? Their knowledge went back before Pindar and surely it went back to the eighth century BC when Greeks from Euboea and elsewhere were visiting southern Cilicia, discovering the long-lost traces of Mopsus and visiting the region's ancient sites. On the river they found the religious centre, or *hesty*, of Muksas and called it 'Mopsus' hearth'. On the coast, near Corycos, they visited the awesome ravines and heard the place name 'Arima'. They also heard the stories of serpent-wars which linked up with stories which they had already heard at Mount Kasios across the bay. Among the songs which were sung on that mountain was the song of the monstrous serpent Hedammu and his wars with the Storm God. Up on the mountain, the Storm God had lost his sinews to the snake and now, in Cilician 'Arima' itself, Greek visitors learned where those sinews had been hidden and where the snaky monster had had its lair. But the site also had an obvious significance for Hittite religion and its accompanying songs. 'Let the land grow and thrive and let the land be protected . . .': at the ancient *purulli* festival the Hittite kings of the past had been entrusted with a 'river of the watery abyss' which descended to the world below. The rites may even have been celebrated at a specially built sacred pool and pit at one of their ancient palace-sites.[51] Hittite kings had ruled in Bronze Age Cilicia and after their empire's fall *c.* 1200 BC some of their culture had survived into the neo-Hittite age of the tenth to eighth centuries BC. If the ruling 'house of Muksas' had maintained the ancient *purulli* festival of the past, there was one 'watery abyss' above all others and one supreme 'descending river' in their south Cilician kingdom: they were the Corycian cave at 'Arima' and the Aous river which ran away into its depths. Perhaps the name Arimmatta had been applied to the site, transposed from the Arimmatta with a similar watery abyss which existed further to the north-west. No evidence survives, as yet, of late Hittite activity on the unexcavated site, but at the old *purulli* festival the songs which were recited were the songs of the Storm God and his serpent-wars. They had been sung, I suggest, for ruling members of the 'house of Muksas' who left their *hesty* at Misis and came down for continuing *purulli* festivals at the Corycian cave.[52] Their continuing cult-performance explains how the old Hittite stories lived on to confront Greek visitors who passed them, in turn, into later Greek poetry. Cult, ritual and the landscape had kept these themes alive for centuries, until Euboeans and other Greek visitors heard about them on site in the eighth century BC.

In Greek the snake-monster became 'Typhon', a name of uncertain derivation. 'Typhon' did not derive from the Phoenicians' name 'Saphon' for the Jebel Aqra mountain: a mountain, anyway, is not an apt origin for a snake. Perhaps, as Posidonius claimed, the nearby Orontes river had had a suggestive earlier name now lost to us, but the likelier guess, despite the short 'ŭ' of his name, is that 'typhon' derived from the Greeks' own *tūphōn*, their 'smoking' and 'smouldering', like the 'smoking' monster whom Zeus set on fire. The change in the 'u'-sound was perhaps more easily made during a transfer between two Greek words.[53] At Arima, Greek visitors then saw this monster's watery cave and, like subsequent travellers, stared down into the nearby cleft where the 'divine music' of the Aous river sounded underground. Manifestly it was Typhon's ancient lair, the scene of the Storm God's victory. But one question remained: where was the serpent nowadays? Some said he had been vanquished in the sea; others, that his bloodstains were visible on the nearby cliffs. But others, as Homer knew, said that Zeus, even now, was 'lashing' him from time to time while the ground above him shook. This 'lashing' cannot be by the Cilician shore. Its abysses and the Corycian cave are the results of erosion, not of earthquakes. The ground hardly shakes here and the Aous river, running out to sea, was a 'voiceless stream' to later pilgrims. The monster and his viperous mate had certainly lived here once, but to explain the continuing lashing and shaking yet another location is needed. It belongs at the heart of our Euboeans' travels, supporting the view that it was they who first discovered

Typhon in the cave and on great Mount Hazzi as they travelled to and fro between north Syria and the Cilician shore.

IV

Far from Syria, far from Cilicia, Strabo knew a fourth location: there were those who placed Typhon in the west, under the island of Pithecussae, no less. The location is known to go back to the writings of Pherecydes of Athens (fifth century BC) but he was only reporting an older tradition.[54] It was already known to Pindar in 470 BC and he exploits it in the wonderful ode, our First Pythian, which he composed for the Sicilian tyrant Hieron. 'The sea-fencing cliffs off Cumae and the island of Sicily weigh on his shaggy chest', the chest of 'hundred-headed Typhon', who lies buried beneath the earth. These cliffs are not cliffs 'above' Cumae, as translators tend to imply: Cumae's site includes its steep acropolis, the coastline's one high point. They are the cliffs 'off' it, the island-cliffs of Ischia, to a poet who imagines himself looking up from Sicily towards them.[55] They include the 'cliff' of Ischia's Monte Vico, the acropolis-hill on which the first Euboeans settled.

Why was Typhon located out here? The answer, again, is geological. On Ischia the hot breath of Typhon still penetrates the island's soil, whether in the hot smoking springs on the beach of Marina dei Maronti or in the nearby Cavascura river, which runs steaming from the rocks to the mud-baths and springs of Casamicciola on the island's northern coast. The entire region is scarred with the marks of the earth's thin or punctured crust. To the south-east of Cumae lie the sulphurous 'Phlegraean Fields', which still hiss with hot vapours at the site of the modern Solfatara. On the coastline beyond Naples Mount Vesuvius smokes and boils from its volcanic crater. The first Greek settlers lived with evidence of Typhon all around them in the landscape. They even experienced him at his worst. Strabo records how in due course they were driven off Ischia by 'earthquakes and eruptions of fire, sea and hot waters'. The volcanic history of the island is still not exactly dated, but archaeologists have found layers of volcanic dust and pebbles above the eighth-century levels of the recently identified Greek site at Punta Chiarito on the island's south coast.[56]

We know precisely who these first settlers were. They were Euboeans from Chalcis and Eretria, arriving c. 770 BC. They or their friends also knew from first-hand experience Al Mina and the bay across to southern Cilicia. Like their Euboean cups and pottery they had reached Al Mina below Mount Kasios and like the 'lyre-player' seals with which they and their children were carefully buried on Ischia they knew southern Cilicia, their source, and its rule by the 'house of Muksas' or 'Mopsus'. On and around Mount Kasios they had heard songs about the Storm God's slaying of a serpent-monster. At the Cilician cave in 'Arima', they had seen where the serpent had had his lair. They had even seen the bloodstains of his battering against the nearby Cilician cliffs. Now in the west they saw and heard him being 'lashed' beneath the earth, hissing, flaming and occasionally turning and tossing in the volcanic chambers beneath Ischia.

There was another good reason for their discovery: as at Zancle, home of the 'sickle', it was supported by language. The first settlers called Ischia Pithecussae, the enigmatic 'Monkey Island', on which, though now lost to us, monkeys had lived and caught their attention. The island was not named at random. Here too the Greek settlers had asked for the local name, and from nearby Etruscans they learned it. Etruscans had a name for the island which meant, according to Greek sources, 'monkey': the Greeks, therefore, called it 'Monkey Island' too. Our understanding of the Etruscan language is still slight, but its experts accept the word in question, transmitted by Strabo's sources and later Greek lexicographers, though not as yet found in an original Etruscan text. The word could hardly have been more significant: Arima.[57]

It was not just a coincidence; it seemed an omen from the gods. In Cilicia, at one place called Arima, Euboeans had found Typhon's lair. Under Ischia, at another Arima, Euboeans had now found where Zeus was still 'lashing' him in punishment. From the moment they settled on the island, Typhon's presence was visible, in the black lava-rock at Zaro, in the clouds of vapour at the island's hot springs, in the rumblings which were already audible even before the monster tossed stupendously and showered the island again with volcanic fallout.

Within forty years Euboeans also settled on the east coast of Sicily, arriving first at Naxos, then at Leontini in the mid-730s BC. Every day here their view to the horizon was marked by the smoking cone of snow-capped Etna, another stupendous volcano. On Etna's slopes the ground was burnt to cinders and even the bushes of its distinctive broom-trees had been blackened. Here fire-breathing Typhon had been battered one last time before being imprisoned for 'lashing'.[58] He was lying there too underground, pinned down by a mountain on his body. He was, after all, enormous, the physical match for any known giant. In the west he lay flat and extended, tossing and turning under Ischia, writhing in north-east Sicily, and seething offshore in the Lipari islands off Sicily's north coast. Far from his Cilician cave he was being 'lashed' here by Zeus, pinned down in the second 'Arima'.

These perceptions were first worked out by Euboeans between c. 770 and 730 BC and from their lateral thinking Pindar, three hundred years later, constructed the opening of his magnificent poem. He knew the fame of the Cilician cave which Euboeans had discovered, the cave which 'nursed Typhon among the Arimoi'. He knew that Zeus had bound Typhon beneath the earth, from the islands off Cumae to Mount Etna, his 'heavenward column'. He also knew facts of the landscape. He knew the snow on the peak of Etna, 'nurse of the sharp snow throughout the year'. He knew how an eruption 'belches out purest streams of unapproachable fire' and hurls rocks as far as the sea, which Pindar then lands in the water with a fine poetic crash. He knew that Etna's peaks are 'dark-leaved' because they are so blackened with lava and cinders, colouring their special vegetation.[59] In the 470s Pindar was writing his poem for Hieron, who had founded a new town of Etna just beneath the mountain. Pindar knew what the local Greeks said about their strange landscape but his perceptions are so exact that he had surely witnessed Typhon in action 'pricked by his rocky lair'. In the 470s Etna had burst into a volcanic eruption, and Pindar was out in the west at his patron's request. 'Il est permis de penser', concludes Jacqueline Duchemin, the connoisseur of Pindar and his sources, 'que le poète, avec ses hôtes, a fait lui-même l'excursion et qui'il s'est avancé peut-être à la rencontre de la lave brûlante.'[60]

Unlike the priest in Burnt Lydia he did not halt the lava with his words. Instead, Pindar was effusing in the wake of others' white-hot theories, the theories of travelling Euboeans who had understood their western landscapes through what they had seen and heard in the east. From one Arima to the other, it was they who had first grasped the truth about Typhon, brilliantly piecing together the clues of landscape and place names and local stories which went back to the old Hittite songs of kingship and the sea.

18

Base-camp to Battlefield

When Typhon was found to be pinned below the western landscape, his cave in Cilicia became his former lair, the place which had nursed him. We can understand, then, why the poet Nonnus (c. AD 430) makes the victorious Zeus tell Typhon, 'I will build for you, you utter wretch, a cenotaph', an empty tomb. On it he would engrave, 'This is the monument of earth-born Typhon, who once lashed the heaven with rocks but was burned up by heavenly fire.'[1] The right place for this cenotaph is the Corycian cave at the first of the two Arimas, in Cilicia, where guides, perhaps, told visitors what Nonnus duly reports. Typhon's relocation, however, was only part of a wider Euboean pattern of thought. In the succession-struggles in heaven he was not the only opponent of the gods to be defeated and buried far away. There had been others almost as monstrous: their bodies encouraged Euboeans to one final burst of brilliant lateral thinking.

In the Greek stories Zeus had also had to fight the Titans, children (like Cronos) of Earth and Heaven who had been banished beneath the earth. To defeat them he released other children of mother Earth, the fearsome Hundred Handers, of whom Briareus was one. In some versions Briareus was the best rewarded and so he ended up with a home in the sea.[2] Seafaring Euboeans were more than familiar with Briareus: they localized him on their island: they even had cults of him.[3] When we find Briareus as the first name linked with the 'Pillars' which stood out in the far west, pillars which later became the Pillars of Heracles, the location has puzzled literary scholars: 'what a god of the Aegean sea . . . has to do with the far west is hard to see . . .'[4] It is not so hard if we attach it to our Euboean trail: an early Euboean traveller may have named the Pillars after a familiar figure in

Euboeans' minds.[5] By the mid-third century BC we find Briareus named as a monster who is pinned beneath Etna and who helps to cause its eruptions. Perhaps here too it was a Euboean settled nearby who added this hundred-handed monster to the team with Typhon beneath the volcano.[6]

Just as Hundred Handers were not Titans, so Titans were not strictly Giants. They were easily confused, because both were the children of mother Earth: Giants were said to have been born from the blood of Heaven's castration which fell onto the earth below: they had even been born in full armour, ready to fight. Obviously, Giants were physically huge and in some later versions they were credited with snaky feet. Like Titans, they tried to assault the gods' home of Mount Olympus but after a cosmic battle they were defeated and killed.[7]

We know of an early poem on the battle of the Titans but we do not happen to know of an early battle of the Giants.[8] No doubt one existed, helping to sort out the details of the war and the catalogue of Giants, which runs even in modern scholarship to more than fifty names.[9] Among the most famous were Porphyrion, Alcyoneus and Enceladus, huge beings who were characterized by insolence and lawlessness. In Homer's *Odyssey* there is a brief hint of Giants in the prehistory of happy Phaeacia: they were a 'wild tribe', ruled by unruly Eurymedon, whose daughter was the Phaeacian king Alcinous' grandmother.[10] Giants are mortal, it seems, for Homer, and not born from gods. We do not happen to have images of the Giants on Greek pottery until the early sixth century BC,[11] but in the related battles of Titans the early Greek poets' imagination seems to us most filmic and most akin to our 'special effects'. The same, surely, was true of the battles of Giants, who then left a major mark on temple-sculptures, one which we see best in a great moment in Euripides' play *Ion*. The chorus of fifteen women look up at the sculptures on Apollo's temple at Delphi, which they are visiting, and pick out the figures whom they see, the 'rout' of the Giants by the gods. Athena fights one, Zeus another: 'What about this? A flaming thunderbolt in the hands of Zeus?' 'I see it: he is scorching awesome Mimas [another Giant] with fire.'[12] These battles symbolized the victory of order over wild lawlessness, a theme which was exploited by tyrants, kings and cities.

The comic poet Aristophanes, typically, turned it round, making the victorious gods 'boastful' too. However, it was a myth which he could take for granted in his audience's knowledge, and, on one modern view, he exploited the familiar form of a 'battle of Giants' in his own political comedy.[13] Above all the myth is brilliantly evoked by Plato in his philosophical dialogue *The Sophist*. He sets up an argument between the holders of two different views about the real world, calling them 'giants' and by implication, 'gods'. 'Giants' are those who believe that only material things exist, things which can be touched, whereas 'gods' are not brutal materialists: in the argument, even the 'Giants' soon divide into the 'reformed' and the 'unreformed', as they still do in our day.[14] As Plato and Aristophanes show, the story was there in people's minds, but like our films of 'Star Wars', its graphic battles began to strike educated people as rather ridiculous. By the second century AD, to dream of the battle of Giants, the tireless dream-interpreter Artemidorus tells us, would be to dream of an 'obsolete thing, full of nonsense' and would only signify that events would turn out contrary to the dreamer's expectations.[15]

Despite the intellectuals, individual Giants were not obsolete: they continued to be fixed to particular places. Giant-like figures were said to be hidden beneath the sea, subdued there by the sea-god Poseidon, or by particular narrows and capes on important sea-routes.[16] Some of them were linked to Euboea. Two such 'Giants', Orion and Peloros, were then sited on either side of the straits between Sicily and Italy, a heartland of Euboean travel and settlement. The evidence for these sitings is late, but they may well have been made by Euboeans in the eighth century, carrying memories of their Giant-like figures to the west.[17] In the east, meanwhile, a whole cluster of genuine Giants were said to have been at home in our 'triangle'. A Giant Adanos was said to have lived in Cilicia at age-old Adana, a central site in the kingdom of the 'house of Muksas'. Another, Pagras, had lived in the mountains named after him where the road from the Bay of Issus descends from the Amanus mountains and the Syrian Gates to the plain of Unqi. In the plain itself there was even a Giant called Orontes after the local river.[18]

At one level we can begin to understand these Near Eastern locations of Giants if we remember that there were famous Near Eastern stories about Giants of superhuman size. We know them best in the biblical book of Genesis, where the Giants, like most lesser men since, 'lusted after the daughters of men'. There were said to be Giants in the Promised Land and we also have to reckon with big prodigies like the king of Bashan, Og.[19] The Giants were only one group among the many superhumans whose stories circulated in Near Eastern cultures. Once again Greek visitors could hear tales of them, especially as they were not floating legends. Giants had left specific, physical relics.

In some places Giants were seen to have scattered huge boulders, markers of their ancient battlegrounds or even of their graves. Unlike a creature as vast and monstrous as Typhon, Giants also appeared to have left their decomposed bodies in the ground.[20] In favoured areas of the ancient world, especially on plains, in caves and river-valleys, the corpses of previous inhabitants lay just below the surface of the soil.[21] Nobody in antiquity, not even a Greek thinking laterally, ever suggested that species of big animals had once lived on earth and become extinct. When their bones and entire skeletons were brought to the surface by floods and earthquakes, they seemed unbelievably big. They were the bones, obviously, of superhumans and of creatures who had fought in the myths. We have already seen how at 'Utterly Bloody' on Samos people looked at the red earth and saw bones big enough to be Dionysus' elephants in their heroic, tusking battle against the Amazons. It was not a bad guess about the bones of an elephantine mammoth. However, they were only one gigantic relic in a much wider network. Its scope has been brilliantly analysed by Adrienne Mayor in her recent study of the 'first fossil-hunters'. Using ancient texts about the discoveries of bones and our modern archaeologists' reports of dinosaur-discoveries, she has even drawn for us 'Maps of the Giants' across the Mediterranean and the Near East.

We can add more items to her list and then focus it on our eighth century BC. No such bones are described in antiquity in the soil of Euboea itself, although they have been excavated at two main points on the island, but if we look east we find relevant outliers which were known to the ancients. In the plain of Unqi, in north Syria, Alexander's Successor Seleucus was believed in local stories to have found the bodies of Giants who had once lived near his newly founded city. 'Two miles from Antioch,' the chronicler John Malalas, a man from

7. The bay at modern Koumi, near ancient Cumae on Euboea, looking across towards Scyros.

The extinct volcano at Mount Oxylithi, Euboea, on whose slopes the vineyards grew until 1910.

19. The famous Cesnola krater, or mixing-bowl, standing at just under four feet. It was exported to Kourion on Cyprus and is almost certainly a Euboean work, *c.* 750 BC. The very fine pattern shows grazing horses, its painter's distinctive theme, waterbirds and two goats on their hind legs on either side of a 'Tree of Life' pattern. The motifs were widely imitated and the painter arguably originated in Chalcis.

20. Pendent semi-circle decoration on a Euboean skyphos (*left*), *c.* 770 BC, and birds in rectangular panels on an Attic skyphos (*right*), *c.* 750 BC, both imported to Cyprus.

21. Pottery fragment with incised lettering, on the borders of Greek and Near Eastern scripts, from the sanctuary of Apollo Daphnephoros at Eretria, *c.* 750 BC.

22. Kadmos from Phoenicia giving the alphabet to the Greeks. Bronze coin of Tyre, from the reign of the Roman emperor Philip the Arab, 249–244 BC.

23. The Nora Stone, with a Phoenician inscription, Sardinia, perhaps *c.* 800 BC. The text was discovered in the late eighteenth century and is the oldest Phoenician inscription so far known on Sardinia. It mentions Sardinia, the god PMY, who is known at Kition on Cyprus, and possibly the elusive Tarshish, probably modern Huelva in south-west Spain.

24. View of Pithecussae, the modern Ischia.

25. The site of Al Mina, excavated by Leonard Woolley, in modern Turkey, being examined by Sir John Boardman, its greatest modern interpreter.

26. Ivories of Levantine craftsmanship supporting the arms of the throne from Tomb 79 at Salamis, Cyprus, late eighth century BC.

27. Aerial view of the acropolis and seaside site of Cumae, beside the bay of Naples, Italy.

28. View of the Jebel Aqra, or Mount Casios, along the shore by Al Mina, seen from the site of Seleuceia in Pieria.

29. Stele showing the Storm God Baal standing on the mountain-peaks of the Jebel Aqra range and holding the local king protectively, from Ras-Shamra, formerly Ugarit, c. 1320–1260 BC.

30. Originally called *The Giant*, now known as *The Colossus*, by Goya, before 1812. This is our finest image of a Giant overshadowing the world, as the ancients will have imagined one. The figure has been explained as standing for Napoleon, or the Spanish Inquisition, or Spain, or, more plausibly, for the giant evoked in a Basque poem of 1808 arriving to defeat Napoleon's troops in the Peninsular War, a type of belief which the ancients, too, could accommodate in their world.

31. Zeus throwing his lightning at Typhon. Chalcidian hydria, by the Typhon Painter, *c.* 550 BC.

32. Entrance to the Corycian Cave, once the lair of Typhon, with the later Christian church to the Virgin Mary cancelling him out since the fifth century AD.

33. *Saturn Devours his Child*, by Goya, 1820–23, ultimately derived from Hesiod's verses about Cronos. Saturn's erect penis has been painted out by later hands. The child seems from its body-shape to be a girl. One of the Black Paintings in Goya's Farmhouse of the Deaf (the Quinta del Sordo, near Madrid).

34. Gigantic tusks of a mammoth, the biggest known in Europe, with Evangelia Tsoukala and her team, their excavators at Milia, near Grevena, Macedon, north Greece.

the city in question, tells us, 'there is a place which has the bodies of men stoned by the wrath of the gods. Even now [*c.* AD 530], they call them "Giants". One Pagras lived in this land and was a Giant. He was thunderbolted by fire. So it is clear that the people of Antioch in Syria live in the land of the Giants.'[22] In north Syria, Adrienne Mayor reminds us, there are still patches of 'burning earth', or combusible lignite, 'and large fossil remains': the combination was the supreme proof of Giants' presence.[23] There were also the bones of huge animals and the big teeth of hippopotamuses, one of which ended up in the shrine at coastal Tell Sukas, visited by Greeks in the sixth century BC, and bits of elephants like the shoulder-bone from Unqi which reappeared for us a mere three thousand years later.[24] In the river-bed of the Orontes, during the reign of the Roman emperor Lucius Verus (AD 161–9), an enormous skeleton was revealed when the river's course 'split', probably when it was diverted artificially. The onlookers sent envoys to the famous oracle-shrine of Apollo at Claros to ask the god what they had found. He told them (through his human prophet) that the skeleton belonged to the Giant Orontes, who was connected, he said, with India.[25] Even the gods endorsed the reading of big bones as bits of Giants.

Giants, an insolent tribe, had challenged Zeus and the gods: where, then, were their battlegrounds and base-camp? The most famous answer for the battleground lay in western Italy on the smouldering Phlegraean Fields. The battleground lies just inland by the north-west curve of the Bay of Naples, where there were evident reasons for its location. The landscape is still volcanic and in the Phlegraean Fields the crust of the earth is remarkably thin. All visitors to the modern Solfatara recognize Strabo's impression of the region: 'a foul smell, full of sulphur and fire and hot springs'. The scorched, hissing ground here looks like the final scene in a prehistoric epic of the wars of the world. Strabo duly explains it by the 'wounds of the thunderbolted Giants which pour out streams of fire and water'.[26] In 1776, when Sir William Hamilton described it, he remarked how 'the hollow sound produced by throwing a heavy stone on the plain of the crater of Solfaterra seems to indicate that it is supported by a sort of arched natural vault and one is induced to think that there is a pool of water beneath this vault which boils by the heat of a subterranean fire still deeper'.[27] For the ancients this 'fire' was the fire of smouldering Giants and the 'water' was the blood of their wounds.

There were also the bones of Giants who had been killed in combat with the gods. We are fortunate to have a great survey of heroes' and Giants' relics which was composed in Greek by Philostratus soon after AD 217: it drew on earlier sources, hearsay and his own experience.[28] The Neapolitans, he tells us, have made a 'wonder' out of the bones of Alcyoneus, a prime member of our modern Catalogue of Giants, one who was the oldest (some said) of the entire family and a captain in the Giants' wars against the gods. The people of Naples say 'that many of the Giants have been cast down there and that Vesuvius smokes on top of them'.[29] Indeed they did, because we know quite separately that in August AD 79, when the volcano blackened the sky and destroyed Pompeii, 'there were those who thought that the Giants were rising to revolt, for many of their forms were visible in the smoke and besides, a sound of trumpets could be heard . . .'[30]

Bones of Alcyoneus and his army continued to turn up from the region's shallow crust and its Pleistocene prehistory. In the late fifteenth century, perhaps in the 1480s, the Renaissance humanist and antiquarian, the celebrated Giulio Pomponio Leto (1428–97), came down from Rome to the Phlegraean Fields and visited ancient Puteoli (Pozzuoli: Rione Terra) in the heartland of the Giants.[31] He was the founder of the Roman Academy, the circle for lovers of the classical world; he called himself its Pontifex Maximus, or High Priest; he was imprisoned briefly by the suspicious Pope; he had travelled with fellow Academy members to the Christian catacombs on the outskirts of Rome where, below ground, he and his friends wrote graffiti on the walls, still visible, which commemorated their visits to bones they believed to be those of the martyrs. We now know that he left a longer and grander Latin graffito on the site of Puteoli's Christian church of San Procolo. In 2003 Francesco Pisano published his brilliant discovery in Naples of the text of Pomponio Leto's inscription, preserved in a German scholar's re-edition of the *Small Book of Wonders of the Civic Community of Puteoli and Neighbouring Places*, first published in Latin in 1475, the first public guidebook in Italy. Pomponius Leto, we now know, wrote competent Latin elegiac verse on 'the bones of the giants which are visible at Puteoli'. He struck the right note of wonder. 'Whoever you are who comes, stupefied, to the bones of the Giants, learn why they have been piled beneath Etruscan soil.' His explanation was classically accurate, as befitted the High Priest of classical learning. Heracles had driven off the 'noxious crowd' of Giants from the hill and citadel of Puteoli, the one which we, too, can visit. He had been returning home with his 'captive herd', the cattle which he had captured in faraway Spain. Some of the opposing Giants had escaped to Otranto, others to the Etruscans. Others had been killed on the spot. 'Therefore kind posterity preserves the huge bodies and bears witness of such ancestors to the world.'

In the late fifteenth century, therefore, Pomponius, the 'Pontifex Maximus', had seen gigantic bones and marvelled at them by the church of San Procolo in Puteoli. Just as he had written graffiti beside the human bones in Christian catacombs, so now he wrote an explanation for tourists of the Giants' bones at Puteoli and had it inscribed on, or near, stone blocks by the main church. The bones may have been known already to the ancients: the church of San Procolo stands on a venerable pre-Christian site and reused the stonework of the Temple of Augustus which had been built there in the early first century AD.[32] Alternatively, the bones were discoveries which had been made more recently by farmers and travellers in the dinosaur-ridden Phlegraean Fields.

Pomponius's classical learning is notable, as we should expect from the founder of the Roman Academy. Heracles' involvement in the Bay of Naples battle was widely attested but the detachment of a cohort of Giants to Otranto was a rarer item. Pomponius had met it, we shall see, in the geographer Strabo. In the following century such a reading of big bones began to become controversial, as we can infer from discussions of the bones which were displayed locally in the gardens of a great palace built by the Spanish nobleman Pietro di Toledo. During the huge eruptions of Vesuvius in 1538 the old stories of the Giants, Typhon and their battles had sprung to educated minds. The bones in di Toledo's palace may have been exposed during these upheavals, but learned opinion was changing and in the seventeenth century the connection with Giants was controversial: critics now dismissed them as the bones of whales.[33]

The Otranto cohort, nonetheless, was still perceptible. Strabo describes for us how they had taken refuge at the small town of Leuca, about 85 miles by sea from Tarentum, on the southern tip of Italy's heel. Mother Earth had enveloped them there in a water-spring which was 'foul-smelling' from the 'ichor' of the Giants' bodies, what we would call sulphur.[34] This cohort of survivors were the 'Leuternian Giants'. Strabo's source was probably the learned Timaeus, himself from the Greek West: 'Leuca' lay on the tip of the heel of Italy, by the modern site of Sta Maria da Leuca and its caves, including a 'Cave of the Giants', with deposits of prehistoric bones, including bits of rhinoceros.[35] Here, too, foul-smelling sulphurous springs and big prehistoric bones coexisted and testified to the Giants' presence.

Traces of the last battle were also alleged, inevitably, in the far west near Tartessus (up the Rio Tinto beyond Huelva).[36] Sicily, too, was fertile dinosaur-territory, well into the seventeenth century, but it was perhaps only the fine imagination of the late Roman poet Claudian to locate the 'gaping jaws and prodigious skins' of the Giants among thick trees in a forest near Etna's summit where their 'faces, fixed in the trees, still threaten cruelly'. There is no sign of them nowadays among the oaks and broom-trees.[37] A much better known location lay in northern Greece on the most westerly of the three prongs of the Chalcidic peninsula, the one whose west coast looks across to south-east Macedon.

In antiquity Pallene on the southern sector of this peninsula was also known as 'Phlegra', as Herodotus had already discovered.[38] This transfer of the name from Italy is most remarkable. The peninsula is not volcanic. There is not even a decent mountain, a fact which has perplexed our great connoisseur of Giants in Greek poetry, Francis Vian: nowhere, he rightly protested, is this 'Phlegra' more than 1,000 feet high.[39] The ancients, however, were sure that it was a base for Giants. In the third century AD the geographer Solinus was quite explicit: at Pallene 'traces of the Giants' destruction continue to be seen to this day when torrents swell with rain and excess water breaks their banks and floods their fields. They say that even now in clefts and ravines people discover bones of immeasurable enormity.' In the early third century, too, Philostratus was even more sure of the facts: 'In Pallene, which the poets name Phlegra, the earth contains many such bodies of Giants who once camped there and many are revealed by storms and earthquakes. Not even a shepherd can be cheerful about that place when the ghosts clatter beneath it, the ones which are mad there.'[40]

Since 1994 we have at last understood what the ancients meant. When the road through Pallene began to be relaid through the hills of Mount Kassandra, three enormous teeth were unearthed by one of the Greek workmen, G. Miteloudis, near the modern village of Aghia Paraskevi. The teeth belonged to cousins of our elephants which had once stood some 15 feet high: 'The traditional homeland of the mythical Giants turns out to be the old stomping-ground of the stupendous *Deinotherium giganteum*.'[41] Here too the geology helped to confirm them. The teeth were found in deep beds of sand, near hot, sulphurous springs which are one of the village's local assets. Further north, where the hills and woods begin, excavations between 1998 and 2007 have turned up bones of giraffes and mastodons and the jawbones of prehistoric monkeys, among many other species. They were found on the peninsula's east-facing side, near the coast, and in 2002–4 yet more mastodon bones were found at nearby Fourka, just inland from the west-facing coast.[42] We now have a 'triangle' of prehistoric sites with copious bones on the southern part of the Pallene peninsula. There are no scorched plains in the vicinity except for the pine-trees near modern Peukochora, burned by forest fires in summer. The hills by Aghia Paraskevi are green and wooded and roll peacefully on down to the sea on the south coast of the peninsula, but there is no doubt now why already before 480 BC Greeks had transferred the name of Phlegra to this place. As in the western Phlegraean Fields they had found bones of a brood of Giants at sites on the southward end of the peninsula: there were even some similar hot springs, smelling of sulphur. They explained the two locations sensibly. In the west, Phlegra was the battlefield of the Giants' war with the gods: Zeus had scorched it with thunderbolts and it was still steaming and smelling from the dead and wounded. In northern Greece, Phlegra–Pallene was the Giants' base-camp where they had bred and gathered, preparing for their big fight. Some of them had died there too and their bones and steaming presence were still visible.

The Pallene Giants also had some outliers. Our lists of ancient Giants need to include spectacular evidence, word of which reached post-classical Europe in late autumn 1691. Eighteen miles from Thessalonica, at a village called Cailloubella, the skeleton of a 'Giant' was discovered and carefully verified by order of the French consul. The skull was found intact with a tooth which weighed 15 pounds: the arm-bone was enormously thick.[43] The find was the talk of Paris in an age when the historicity of Giants was becoming ever more controversial.[44] Who could deny this latest example, though nobody thought to connect it with the ancient Phlegra and its base-camp? Giants in this plain had been readily accessible to early Greek settlers, traders and visitors at sites near the coast of the Thermaic Gulf. Further inland the ancients also placed the awesome 'Almops', whose traces have been restored to us since 1990. Up in the Barnous mountains north-west of the Macedonian capital of Pella, a series of 'bearcaves' have been explored at Loutra, yielding big bones of the cave-bear, a leopard and other large mammals. Along the bottom of the gorge runs the 'Hot River' (Thermopotamos), linking the finds of big prehistoric animals with hot springs and here too with steaming 'evidence' of Giants buried underground.[45] Since 1990, the western kin of 'Almops' have also been located at Macedonian sites near modern Grevena. They include the skeleton of a straight-tusked elephant and at Milia, about 10 miles to the north, the spectacular tusks of mammoths, including a pair of tusks, found in 2007, which rank as the longest so far known in the world.[46] If the ancients had been aware of them, they would have had to locate a war of Giants and elephants in this upper hill-kingdom, source of some of Alexander's most notorious officers and infantry.

The lands which became the Macedon of Philip and Alexander were underpinned by famous Giants, clustered in base-camp and scattered along a trail through the river-plains and mountains to the west and north-west.[47] Nonetheless, in antiquity, the claims of the two Phlegras, one in north Greece, one in Italy, were eventually contested by other candidates. An alternative battlefield was claimed in Arcadia: Arcadian evidence confronted the travelling Pausanias when he visited the sites while compiling his 'guidebook' in the second century AD. The earth was said to smoulder near Megalopolis: in its temple of Asclepius, Pausanias saw the huge bones of a Giant, the very one, he was told, who had helped to protect mother Rhea against child-consuming Cronos when she arrived in Arcadia with the infant Zeus in her arms.[48] There was excellent local evidence for this story. Bones of all sorts of prehistoric animals had been found in the ground, and near Megalopolis itself there were mines of lignite. Nowadays they belong to a Greek power-company: as Adrienne Mayor observes, 'these same combustible lignite deposits', formerly the graves of smouldering Giants, 'provide modern Greeks with electricity'.[49]

Arcadia was a strident alternative, but how do we explain the two separate Phlegras in Italy and northern Greece and the ancient perceptions which underlay them? The answer is beautifully clear: they go back to our travelling heroes, Euboeans of the eighth century who had spanned all the links in the chain.[50] Like their pottery, they had already visited the coastal plain near modern Thessalonica where we still find outlying corpses of Giants and where the French consul's informant in 1691 saw one with his own eyes. Above all, on the northern peninsula of Pallene their pottery had long been reaching coastal sites, including Scione on the sea by the Phlegra caches of dinosaurs. By the 730s BC they had settled at Mende by the long, magnificent beach which sweeps along the coastline just to the west of the Giants' base-camp near modern Aghia Paraskevi.[51] They had walked a few miles inland from their acropolis-site at Vigla and had looked and marvelled at the local bones and bits of skeletons of an 'immeasurable enormity'. They also saw Giants' hot, gasping breath coming up in the nearby sulphur-springs. There had been Euboean contact with the bay here for some two centuries, before a formal foundation of Mende which was later dated c. 730 BC. The founders were Euboean Eretrians.

Like their famous wine, their kinsmen and their drinking-cups, Eretrians from Mende travelled widely: no doubt they sometimes travelled with Euboeans from their common home, going west up the coast of Greece to Corcyra where fellow-Eretrians had settled since c. 750 BC and across the open sea to the heel of Italy at modern Otranto and on down the coast of the Salento peninsula to Leuca, the tip of Italy's heel. Here too on the modern Punta Ristola, at the western edge of Leuca's bay, there were caves with apparent bones of Giants and, just inland, another sulphurous, evil-smelling spring in which fugitive Giants, plainly, were sweating from wounds sustained in their battle further west. Scenting Giants, Euboean sailors travelled on round Italy's toe, up through the straits to the Bay of Naples and to the site of their settlement at Cumae (perhaps first settled in *c.* 750 BC). Just to the east of its territory lay the crowning evidence, the sulphurous thunderbolted landscape of the Phlegraean Fields. It was still steaming from Zeus's weapons and the Giants buried beneath it. Offshore, meanwhile, on Ischia lay monstrous Typhon, tossing and turning under punishment and stretching as far as Sicilian Etna. The entire volcanic landscape made sense in terms of the wars of the gods.

Some of these same Euboean travellers had gone east to our Cypro-Levantine triangle, to the plain of Cilicia which later claimed to have Giants and to the mouth of the Orontes river where workmen would later find the body of another Giant, from India. In this region they would travel up from the plain of Unqi to the Syrian Gates and then down on the further side of the pass to their Posideion on the Bay of Issus. As their road left the plain of Unqi for the Cedar and Box-tree Mountains, it passed by 'Pahri' and its outlying rocks, the Pagras of Greek topographers, by the 'Pagric Mountains'. Here, even in *c.* 300 BC, Seleucus was believed to have found the bodies of Pagras the Giant and other Giants killed by the gods. Their bones were visible, just as such bones would have been visible to Euboeans and their fellow-travellers on this land-route in the eighth century BC.

Across the Mediterranean these Euboeans made brilliant sense of the enormous bones they found. Giants had once ruled and fought in Syria, as Near Eastern stories said; they had gathered in base-camp on Pallene's peninsula; they had fought the gods and died or been buried in the Phlegraean Fields near Naples: a cohort had escaped, though wounded, and was hidden, still sweating, in the foul-smelling water by Leuca on the heel of Italy.

Euboeans were 'stupefied', no doubt, by these traces of Giants: how did they relate them to their own times? Centuries later the erudite Pliny the Elder was to argue from such huge bones that men were becoming smaller as the conflagration of the world was approaching and 'consuming' the former abundance of men's 'seed'.[52] His view was supported by St Augustine, himself a great believer in Giants' relics: he had been to inspect a Giant's tooth, he tells us, which was as big as a hundred normal teeth, and had been found near Utica, that ancient Phoenician foundation of the ninth to eighth centuries BC.[53] There was also a scriptural complication, words falsely ascribed to the biblical Ezra. The Lord God, their author wrongly claimed, told Ezra to ponder the consequences of women who gave birth in their later age. 'Ask a woman that beareth children and she shall tell thee . . . They that be born in the strength of youth are of one fashion and they that are born in the time of age, when the womb faileth, are otherwise. Consider therefore thou also, how that ye are less of stature than those that were before you.' In our ageing world, future children would be even smaller, 'born to a creature [the world] which is past the strength of youth'.[54] Biblical biology is at its mistaken best here, refuted daily by late-bearing females and their chunky babies in the modern West. In the fifteenth century, however, Christian observers reached another sombre conclusion: plainly men's seed had become cooler and much less plentiful, because the seed that fathered such huge Giants in the past must have been abundant and hot.[55] Nobody discussed whether women were also contracting and narrowing.

Euboeans were not yet troubled by thoughts of an ageing world or fears that their sperm was cooling and dwindling. The Giants, they believed, had been born from superhuman seed: it had dropped to earth in the blood of castrated Heaven. Humans could not hope to compete with a heavenly emission. Subsequently there had been an age of heroes, as Euboeans knew from their poets, when men were bigger and stronger and 'not as mortals nowadays'. In the days of the Trojan War there had been gods too, who were found to be at least 700 yards long when wounded on earth.[56] But they belonged to a separate age: their existence was not evidence that post-heroic mortals were becoming smaller by the year. There was no problem, either, about the precise age in which each individual Giant had lived, whether before or after the Flood. For Christians, it was a crucial question. As Scripture showed, the antediluvian Giants were the real monsters, brutal, tyrannical and (on biblical evidence) extremely keen on sodomy. There was only one virtuous pre-Flood Giant: Noah. After the Flood, Giants reappeared, but they were smaller and more moderate Giants like the biblical king Og.[57]

Lacking Scripture and its problems, Euboeans were not bothered by the type of Giant they found. In one titanic lifetime, from the 780s to the 720s BC, they had discovered what none of the other mainland Greeks knew. They had located in the New West what they had (re)learned in the Old East, transferring items in myth from one end of their world to the other. No autochthonous, stay-at-home Athenian, no eastward-looking lord of Miletus, no horse-riding squire of Thessaly knew any of what they had heard and seen, from the ancient songs on Mount Hazzi to the long-lost lands of Mopsus, from one Arima and Phlegra to the other across the swelling sea. The gods had fought and won victories where only these Euboeans knew, connoisseurs of the trail of the succession-struggles in heaven. But those years were also formative years for the masterpieces of Greek poetry, the epics of Homer and the near-contemporary poems by Hesiod. What the Euboeans had discovered relates differently to the horizons of each of these poems: it is to them, finally, we need to return and add one final relic to the Euboeans' trail across their world.

PART FOUR

Just So Stories

I trust that the reader ... will by now be persuaded of the general thesis that Greek poetry from Hesiod and Homer down to Pindar and Aeschylus is pervaded by influences from West Asiatic literature and religious thought and that this was not the consequence of a single focused burst of radiation but reflects an ongoing process over a broad front.

M. L. West, *The East Face of Helicon* (1997)

> ... as imagination bodies forth
> The forms of things unknown, the poet's pen
> Turns them to shapes, and gives to airy nothing
> A local habitation and a name.

William Shakespeare,
A Midsummer Night's Dream, v. i. 7

Except the blind forces of Nature, nothing moves in this world which is not Greek in its origin.

Sir Henry Maine, *Village Communities* (1875)

19

Homeric Horizons

We can at last understand the echoing sound of the Greek army's feet in Homer's *Iliad* as they first advance across the plain of Troy. It was not like a sound from Syria, as if Homer meant 'Aramaeans' by his puzzling Arimoi: Zeus was not lashing the monster Typhon in a lair under Unqi's ground. It was not like a sound among people called Arimoi: it was like a sound 'in Arima', a place. The sound was not in Cilician Arima because the cave there was empty and, as pilgrims found, its underground river was 'voiceless'. Typhon had moved elsewhere. It was a sound off the Bay of Naples, echoing on the island which Etruscans called Arim(a), their Monkey Island, which we now know as Ischia. When Homer reached for a simile to make the sound of his Greek army vivid to us, he reached far away to the western extremity of the Greeks' settled world. The sound was thunderous and a worldwide comparison did it justice. When the *Iliad*'s fighting is about to begin, an Italian landscape is cited to catch the sound of it.

Despite the perplexity of many of the ancients, the sound was not lost on all of them. Gratifyingly, Virgil retained an inherited hint of the truth. In the ninth book of his *Aeneid*, the rampaging hero Turnus spears to death a fearsome Trojan who falls with such a crash that the earth groans and his huge shield thunders over him like a clash of rocks which causes the 'Euboic' shore off the Bay of Naples to clamour and sends tremors to the 'hard bed, Inarime, laid at Zeus's command on Typhon'. 'Inarime' here is Ischia–Pithecussae: the name had been used by an earlier Greek poet who had turned the old Etruscan-based name 'Arima' into a feminine Greek proper name Arimē and prefixed it, as in Homer's original simile, with the Greek word *ein*, meaning 'in'. Poetically, the island was given the metrical name 'Einarime' by a correct transposition of Homer's elusive 'ein Arimois' to its site. The name then puzzled Latin-speaking authors but appealed to Virgil as a poetic title for Ischia in the forced rhetorical passage in which he tries to use a resonance of Homer to evoke his hero's deeds of war.[1]

We can also appreciate an unnoticed element in the *Iliad*'s own momentum. Before referring us to faraway Arima, Homer has already compared the sound of the advancing Greeks to something else, the noise of birds in the 'Asian meadow', the 'geese and cranes and long-necked swans' who settle with such a clamour.[2] He begins by referring us eastwards, to the meadow which is our first surviving use of the word 'Asian' in history or literature. After his Catalogue of the Greek ships he resumes his comparisons and now refers us westwards, to the furthest Greek settlement on an island off the coast of Italy. First east, then west, but in both there is a 'crash'. In Arima the ground seems to thunder from chastised Typhon but in that haunting 'Asian meadow' the birds cause a similar din. It was best understood by the Homeric enthusiast MacLair Boraston, who heard the very 'crash' of Homer's verb from birds which were alighting in India in February 1906: 'To say the meadow "crashed" were modesty; but "crash" is the only word. It was a sound in which there were many parts, each flung down, as it were, to ring like metal and smash like glass, a sound that leaped along the nerves and seemed to touch a spring that set free impulses belonging to a time when man himself was more intimately a part of that Nature he now stands aside to contemplate. *Smaragei de te leimōn*.'[3]

Does Homer's western simile help us to date his *Iliad*? On Ischia, Strabo tells us, the Euboean settlers were 'later' driven out by 'earthquakes and eruptions of fire, sea and hot water'. We do not know the date of this upheaval, although at Punta Chiarito we have those layers of black volcanic dust in a level of the site which archaeologists date to the 'late eighth century BC'. From evidence in and around the San Montano cemetery, the 'Euboean period of Pithekoussai . . . is taken to end around 700 BC'.[4] Is this 'end' the date of Strabo's eruption and should we thus date Homer's *Iliad* after 700 BC? The eruption, however, is not what Homer is describing. The ground 'groaned' beneath the Greeks as if under angry Zeus, 'whenever he lashes the ground around Typhoeus'. It is an intermittent process, rather than the crash of a sudden volcanic upheaval. By Monte Vico, as elsewhere on Ischia, rumblings can still be heard from time to time beneath the earth while steam comes up through the island's hot springs. Homer has heard reports of this ominous pre-seismic rumbling, but not of a final stupendous eruption. It is the rumble which fits the sound of the Greeks as their feet strike the ground, not the outburst of a volcano with which their tramping could not be fairly compared.

If there is a date here, it is a date before 700 BC while Typhon was still fretting but not trying to break out. He is not with his mate Miss Viper: he is alone in his bed, so 'they say'. 'They say' is rarely used in Homer's epics and sometimes, as nineteenth-century commentators realized, the phrase applies merely to 'a thing universally admitted', the pre-eminent power of Zeus or the fact that Olympus is the gods' home.[5] Homer also uses it elsewhere 'of things well known, and indeed to emphasise the fact that they *are* well known', but when used for the distant Ischia the sense is more 'men say, and they are surely right' about a faraway land. Later in the poem, at a great moment, Achilles reminds King Priam about Niobe, 'all tears' for her dead children, 'on Sipylus, where they say . . .' Nowadays the supposed stone image of Niobe on Sipylus is correctly identified with a rock-cut Hittite (or pre-Hittite) monument on the mountain near modern Manisa, by the road inland towards Sardis.[6] At this point too, 'they say' refers to hearsay, in Homer's view to correct hearsay but not quite with the 'authority of tradition'.[7] Just as 'they say' heightens the faraway nature of Sipylus, so it heightens that of Arima earlier in the poem.

We shall return to the question of the date and sources of this hearsay. It is important, first, to look for the eastward horizons of Homer's epics and then to set them beside the trail of travel and lateral thinking which we have identified for real Greeks in the eighth century, above all Euboeans. Their focal points are somewhat different.

II

For action in Homer's south-east Aegean, the place to visit is a lowly hut on the south of Ithaca (our modern Ithaki), the scene, nonetheless, of two unforgettable tales of travel.[8] In the *Odyssey*, noble Odysseus returns in humble rags, the king in disguise at the hut of his slave Eumaeus, keeper of the royal pigs. The conventions of hospitality delay their personal histories, but then at last they speak. On two successive nights the king and the pigman talk after dinner, telling stories of their previous lives.

Odysseus begins, concealing his true identity by claiming to have been born a bastard, the son of rich Castor and a slave-concubine on the island of Crete. When Castor died, so he says, his legitimate sons cast lots to divide their inheritance (the usual Greek practice) but they gave the bastard very little and only a small place in which to live. He was a strong warrior, however, and so he won a wife from a rich family. 'Work in the fields was not to my liking, nor care of the household which brings up fine children': instead he liked 'oared ships and wars and polished spears and arrows'. A true Cretan captain at arms, he fought on nine lucrative campaigns and then shared the command of Cretan troops in the Trojan War. Returning to Crete, 'I stayed only a month, taking pleasure in my children, my wife and my possessions.' No family man, he was reclaimed by war and adventure. He raised a band of like-minded companions and after feasting and honouring the gods they all sailed south to Egypt.[9]

With a following wind they reached the 'fair-flowing Aigyptos' (our Nile Delta) 'on the fifth day'. While the son of Castor sent out scouts, his men 'gave way to insolence' and started to ravage the land without orders, killing Egyptian men and carrying off their women and children. The local people heard the shouting and at dawn came out to fight, turning the Greek raiders to flight (which was caused by Zeus, Odysseus says). When many of them had been killed, the 'son of Castor' resorted to one last appeal. He was not responsible for his men's misdeeds, so he took off his helmet and dropped his spear and shield: he approached the chariot of the Egyptian king and 'took hold of his knees and kissed them'. It was a classic act of Greek supplication, or *hiketeia*.[10]

The self-abasement of the Cretan was extreme and occurred in very hostile circumstances: Homer ascribes the sudden idea of it to Zeus. The Egyptian king accepted, and restrained his hostile subjects because he respected 'the anger of Zeus the god of strangers'. On both sides more than human calculations were involved. As the 'son of Castor' was both a stranger and a suppliant, he combined two related categories which Homer's epics connect with protection from the gods. Knowing the 'rules' of *hiketeia*, the Egyptian king set him in his chariot and took him, weeping, to his home where he gave him a role of honour in his social group. The Cretan thus stayed in Egypt and received 'many gifts' from the Egyptians. They were not being naive or trusting foreigners too much. They gave gifts because their king had recognized his suppliant as an honoured guest.

Seven years passed and then a man from Phoenicia arrived in Egypt, a 'deceitful grasping man who was already the cause of much harm to others'. He even deceived the son of Castor, or so deceitful Odysseus' story pretends. He persuaded him to go back to his home in Phoenicia and after a year put the Cretan on board a ship for Libya, pretending that together they would 'ship a cargo' but really intending to sell the Cretan as a slave for an enormous price. The wind blew them smoothly to Crete but changed course and smashed the boat in a tempest. The son of Castor (Odysseus claims) escaped with Zeus's help by floating on the ship's wrecked mast for 'nine days' until he reached dry land. The local king took him in and even told him how he had recently entertained 'Odysseus', showing him the treasure of 'bronze, gold and much-worked iron' which the great hero would soon be bringing home. He put the Cretan on a ship, so the real Odysseus claims, which would take him towards Ithaca and again, the crew tried to enslave him. They put him, supposedly, in rags (hence the rags which Eumaeus could see on his visitor), tied him up and beached their ship for a while in Ithaca. Again the gods intervened: they undid the Cretan's bonds, hid him on land from his captors and brought him to Eumaeus' hut.

Odysseus' story is an excellent instance of how a Greek tale involves the gods throughout its narrative: they are honoured before leaving Crete; they account for sudden turns of events, the running away, the risking of supplication, the onset of a storm. They free a captive from his bonds 'easily' and keep him safe from his persecutors, centuries before Euripides' lines in his play *The Bacchae* on Dionysus' escape from prison or the Christian Acts of the Apostles story of Peter's similar rescue by an angel. Odysseus' story is told with unquestioning assurance that the gods explain and enhance the adventures. The same assurance comes naturally to the next Greek teller of a military man's tale in Asian lands some three centuries later, Xenophon the Athenian.[11] From Homer to Xenophon, the pupil of Socrates, this way of telling brings us close to how Greeks understood their world. It also characterized Greeks in the eighth century BC.

On two more occasions Odysseus tells yet more lies in which he alleges that he is a Cretan, once to his protecting goddess Athena, herself in disguise, and once to one of his wife's suitors in his own halls. Why does he choose this particular 'origin'? 'Wide Crete', that long island, is a land in the *Odyssey* of 'ninety cities' and a multi-lingual mixture of five peoples. In the *Iliad*'s Catalogue, seven Cretan towns are named (Crete is now an island of 'a hundred cities') and, although Homer's knowledge of names is precise, the aura of Crete is the aura of an unusual place which lies beyond the daily knowledge of people like Eumaeus on distant Ithaca.[12] As in later Greek impressions of it, distant Crete is a place where warriors are strong and military adventurers proliferate, but the poet's knowledge of it is not due to remote Bronze Age tradition, surviving from a past *c.* 1300 BC. It fits more readily in the ninth to eighth centuries and once, indeed, the mists clear and Homer gives us a much more focused view. Earlier in the *Odyssey* he has made the elderly Nestor describe how the hero Menelaus and his Greek ships were blown by a storm to Crete on their journey home from Troy.[13] They came to 'where the Cydonians dwelt round the streams of the Iardanos river', a point which we would place near modern Chania on the island's north-west coast. But then they met a 'smooth rock, going steeply down into the sea' on the 'borders of Gortyn on the misty deep'. The direction has changed now to the south and south-west coast of Crete: the south wind, we are told, drives the 'great waves against a headland on the left towards Phaistos' and a 'small rock holds back the great waves'. There, the storm-driven ships were dashed on the reefs, but the men escaped death.

Even in late antiquity there were commentators who considered Homer's precise topography here to be connected to 'true history'. In 1928, Sir Arthur Evans, excavator of the Cretan palaces and connoisseur of the island, published his first-hand knowledge of the Cretan shoreline.[14] Evans followed an earlier suggestion, made in 1896, and pointed out a jutting 'headland of white rock' exactly on the shoreline between the territories of Gortyn and Phaistos of which it is the 'natural boundary'. It forms 'the first real shelter for ships coming round the south-western cape of Crete in a southerly gale'. Phaistos lies only 4 miles away by land: on its 'left' towards Phaistos, just as Homer says, there is the island of Paxamidi, 'shaped like a couchant Sphinx' about 7 miles offshore and then a reef called the 'Papadoplaka' (the 'Priest's Slab') which breaks any big wave ('pushing it back', in Homer's words) before it reaches the shore. The reef has sunk down nowadays as the sea level has risen since antiquity. It was also bigger in the eighth century BC than it is nowadays: German pilots used it for bombing practice in the 1940s.

By the shore Evans already found abundant pottery and recognized this bay as a major shelter which was used from the Minoan period (c. 1400 BC) to the later Greek centuries (c. 600 BC). Since 1976 American archaeologists have dug the area at modern Kommos and revealed buildings, pottery and sanctuaries of local, Phoenician and Greek visitors in three main phases before 600 BC.[15] The reef, the Priest's Slab, appears to have been linked to the shoreline by a sand-spit and could give shelter to ships which escaped being driven onto its rocks. The site's later name in Greek antiquity was almost certainly Amyclaion: the name reflects a link with Amyclae, an important place in Menelaus' Spartan homeland. If Amyclaion was the eventual ancient name of Kommos, it shows that the ancients, too, connected the site with Menelaus. Presumably, they did so after Homer and his story of Menelaus' Cretan shipwreck.[16]

Homer seems to approach this shore from the south-west, although Menelaus' ships should be coming to it from the north. There are imprecisions, but when he turns to describing the coast in the storm, the fit is generally so good that he is evidently describing this very bay.[17] Either he or his immediate predecessors knew it from first-hand reports. They had heard of it from sea-travellers who were going past south-west Crete and for whom the rest of inland Crete was a dimly known place, as it is to Homer himself. This knowledge was knowledge of only a small part of the island's shoreline and is perhaps most likely to have entered Homer's epic tradition *c.* 800–730 BC. It is consistent with such a date that it came in through Greeks, not through Phoenicians, whose language and perceptions have not marked its details at all.

As for the trip to Egypt, it too is intended to be exotic, something by which Eumaeus will be 'stirred'. Homer shows no clear knowledge of the place. Egypt (*Aigyptos*) is his name for the River Nile. He imagines, simply, that the people share common ground with Greeks. The local king obeys the Greek rules of a Greek 'game' of supplication because he fears a Greek god, Zeus the god of strangers. Nonetheless, Odysseus' long false tale resembles a historical novel rather than a fairy-tale legend. It uses a precise framework with elements which we can connect with Homer's own (eighth-century) range. His Phoenicians include a visitor to Egypt: in the ninth to mid-seventh centuries especially, we can trace such Phoenician visitors, both by their pottery and as the carriers of Egyptianizing goods across the Mediterranean or the shippers of wine and other cargoes by sea from their coastal cities to the Nile Delta.[18] When Phoenicians founded their settlements in north Africa, including Auza (*c.* 880–850 BC) and Carthage (on present evidence, *c.* 800–760) they took cargoes between their home cities and Libya, like Homer's mendacious Phoenician trader.[19] On their route west they passed, as he did, by Crete, touching at Kommos where the American excavators have found a sanctuary which was visited by passing Phoenicians from *c.* 900 BC: they then constructed a small shrine there in their own style *c.* 800 BC, placing Egyptian figurines on it.[20] On the northern side of Crete, at Knossos, archaeologists have found a bronze bowl of tenth-century origin, made by a Cypriot and inscribed by a Phoenician with words which have been read as referring to a previous dedication of the bowl to Amon, an Egyptian god. This much-travelled object ended up in a Cretan Greek's grave with Greek pottery which dates to the ninth century BC.[21] It touches on three of the points in Odysseus' story: Crete, Phoenicia and (possibly) Egypt. So does the shrine built at Kommos *c.* 800 BC, whose debris suggests 'a port of call where Cretans, central Greeks, probably other Greeks, perhaps even Phoenicians, lied to each other over wine and limpets'.[22] Mendacious Odysseus would have been in his element.

A similar framework recurs twice in the poem when Odysseus is again telling lies.[23] When he tries to deceive the disguised Athena, he assumes that Crete is an island which faraway Phoenicians would credibly visit too: we know that it was, from *c.* 900 BC onwards. When he tells another lying tale to one of his wife's suitors in his own hall, he pretends to have been a rich man, one who had fallen in with 'roving pirates' and accompanied them, again, to the 'Aigyptos river', a 'long journey'.[24] Once again Greek visitors began to kill and raid without their leader's orders but the nearby Egyptians armed themselves and hit back. Once again the gods guided the story and once again it was Zeus who put panic into the hearts of Greek men. Many of them were killed, others were put to work as slaves, but the rich Greek was given to a 'guest-friend' of his captors, Dmētor (the Tamer), who 'ruled in might over Cyprus'. A Cypriot is indeed a likely visitor, as the island's south coast is an accessible starting point for a voyage to Egypt: 'guest-friendship' between a Cypriot Greek and an Egyptian is not implausible. The setting of this raid, too, is the Nile Delta and the victim a local king. Local rulers in the Nile Delta were a feature of the history of Egypt in the ninth and eighth centuries BC. As we have seen, the Greeks' later praises of one such king, 'Bocchoris', imply that, somehow, a Greek had been in close contact or favour with this Egyptian ruler (a Delta king in the 720s BC). Whether Homer anticipated such a contact in his stories, or reflected this one, we cannot be sure. Elsewhere in the *Odyssey*, he takes us yet again to Egypt and in his mirage of the country and its culture he gives one credibly Egyptian name ('Thon').[25] He also credits the visiting Helen with a plausible Egyptian item, a powerful drug (the drugs of Egypt were also esteemed by later Greek doctors). After these traces of reality his mirage returns. Thon's wife has a purely Greek name and Helen, he tells us, has been given presents by women in Egypt, including a metal workbasket on a metal stand with wheels. We know from archaeology that such stands were made, not in Egypt, but in Cyprus or the Levant from where they were sometimes brought across to Greeks, including Euboeans in tenth-century Lefkandi.[26]

Such contacts as there are between Odysseus' plausible stories and our archaeology are best placed in the ninth and eighth centuries BC: a Phoenician trading a cargo to Libya earlier than *c.* 880 would somewhat surprise us. Naturally this framework does not date the poet himself. At any time between *c.* 880 and *c.* 620 BC he could have composed these plausible fictions by using Greek hearsay from his own or a recent generation: local rulers in the Nile Delta could have remained an item in Greek travellers' memoirs even after the change to a single major dynasty in Egypt *c.* 665 BC. But on one point Homer is particularly true to our eighth-century evidence. Twice, his Greek visitors to Egypt start killing and seizing slaves after arriving by sea. In the Levant, from Tyre to Cilicia, eight-century Ionian Greeks, we have seen, were doing exactly this. 'The Ionians have arrived,' as the Assyrian man on the spot wrote in *c.* 730; they were already a familiar hazard. What afflicted the Levant in the mid-eighth century afflicts Egypt in Homer's fiction. A mid-eighth-century base for it is the most attractive guess.

The most important gain here, even for historians, is a sense of the subtlety of Homer's art. In recent Greek rural societies, lying has sometimes seemed an acceptable form of self-assertion: the context in which Odysseus lies is somewhat different to our own.[27] It is also brilliantly constructed. In Eumaeus' hut, Odysseus the master tells lies, whereas Eumaeus, the slave, follows on by telling a true story. Odysseus' lies include travels to Crete, the Levant and Egypt which are plausible in the real eighth-century world. Eumaeus believes these lies, not because he is awed by the military prowess and man-slaying feats of his informant, but because of a typical Homeric movement of the heart and soul: 'Indeed, you stirred my spirit deeply, telling each of your sufferings and your wanderings.' Humble Eumaeus is touched and believes all the lies, except for the one truth which Odysseus tells, that Odysseus is nearby and will soon come home.

There may even be more of a game between the poet and his audience. The nucleus of the story told by the 'son of Castor' is a journey from Crete to Ithaca. It claims knowledge that the real Odysseus has returned to Ithaca's nearby land of Thesprotia. Is Homer playing here with previous stories of Odysseus' return home, but giving them to his own Odysseus as part of a lying story?[28] This analysis has always had its attractions: if so, an older, simpler tale of Odysseus' return has been sidelined by Homer into a false story, whereas his new story of the hero's return has been enhanced with stories from a fantasy world. These fantastic stories are the ones which Odysseus tells to the idyllic Phaeacians, a mythical audience. They hear the great tales of his adventures with the Cyclops, the Lotus-Eaters, the Sirens and many more, all of which they believed, although the tales are impossible, set outside the real world. Eumaeus, by contrast, believes a false story which is a mixture of eighth-century plausibility and the older story of Odysseus' route home. In games of truth and falsehood Homer was already a master-player.

III

On the following evening it is Eumaeus the pigman's turn to tell his story. 'Let the two of us drink and feast in this hut and take pleasure in each other's bitter troubles while we remember them: after the event a man finds pleasure in his troubles if he has suffered much and wandered far ...' Eumaeus, so wise, warns that it will be a long sleepless night.[29]

He was born, he explains, on a wondrous isle called Syrie where nobody suffered in old age but the god Apollo would send them all to a gentle death. This island of blessed euthanasia had two cities, over which his father, 'like the immortal gods', ruled as king. When princely Eumaeus was a little boy, seafaring Phoenicians arrived, 'grasping men' once more, whose dark ship brought 'countless trinkets'. In his father's house worked a 'fine, big Phoenician slave-girl, skilled at glorious handiwork', who looked after the young Eumaeus, but one day one of the Phoenicians had sex with her by the hollow ship when she had gone out to wash the clothes: 'Making love', Eumaeus wisely observes, 'leads astray the minds of young women even if they are good workers.' The slave-girl explained after the act that she too was Phoenician by origin, the daughter of noble Arybas of Sidon, a man who was 'overpoweringly rich'. In her youth she had been captured by raiders, 'Taphians', who had seized her and sold her away from her Phoenician family. Her Phoenician seducer promised to take her home, and so she made his colleagues swear an oath and agree to a secret plan. She would bring a reward for her transport, 'as much gold as comes to hand', and something else too, 'the son of my noble master whom I tend, such an artful one (*kerdaleos toios*) who runs with me whenever I go out'. This little boy was Eumaeus.

For a whole year the Phoenician visitors exchanged the goods from their ship and then, on their final visit, they sent one of their company to the palace with a necklace of gold strung with beads of amber. The queen and her slave-maids handled and admired it: Homer's image is a fine one, a mistress and her slaves united in feminine wonder at a piece of jewellery. Meanwhile the Phoenician nurse slipped away. She took several gold cups from the table where the king and his councillors had been feasting. She also took the trusting young Eumaeus, who was at her side. They put to sea on the Phoenicians' ship but on the seventh day the nurse died and was thrown overboard to the 'seals and fishes'. Storm-winds then blew the ship away to Ithaca where the distressed young Eumaeus was sold for a fine price. But he was bought by Odysseus' father, a master who showed a neglected Homeric virtue, 'kindliness'.[30]

Homer never describes a character who changes from good to bad: the Phoenician nurse is a slave who misbehaves only for temporary reasons, first sex, then an offer of transport back to her home and freedom. Unlike Odysseus' story, Eumaeus' story does not involve the gods in its main events: they intervene only when bringing his nurse to her death and sending the storm-winds at sea. But once again the people in this story live at risk from raiders, although this time they are Phoenicians, not Greeks.

Eumaeus' home, Syrie, is an idyllic island which neither we nor Homer can place in the real world. Nonetheless Phoenician traders came to visit it bringing trinkets in their dark ships, just like the Phoenician jewellery or the ostrich-eggs, the rare shells and metal bowls which we find in cemeteries on a few of the Greek Aegean islands and ascribe to skilled Phoenician craftsmen and the transporters of their objects, whether Phoenicians or not. We even have amber-like beads for necklaces from sites on Crete or in the Levant. They are just the goods for Phoenicians to bring, for reasons which even Homer and his tradition probably did not know. Real amber, from the northern Baltic, had reached a few Greek sites in the distant Mycenaean age, but there was also 'false' amber, traceable to a 'Lebanese fossilized resin': examples of it survive from the ninth to seventh centuries at Phoenician sites within easy reach of Sidon, the home of Homer's Phoenicians:[31] it derived from particular trees, the liquidambars in the Levant. Other trinkets of Levantine origin had also been reaching Greek sites from the tenth century BC onwards and, as we have seen, are best known to us at places on Crete and coastal Euboea. Homer's image of Phoenician visitors fits comfortably with this evidence, which expands in the ninth and eighth centuries BC and implies that real Phoenicians' routes ran up to the north Aegean or out further west.

In the same words as Eumaeus earlier, Odysseus admits to being deeply moved. This time there are no lies and there is a socially significant truth: loyal Eumaeus, a slave by necessity, turns out to be nobly born after all, a king's son. As for his home, Syrie is in faraway neverland, but the travels in the story have a connection with realities. As always, Homer's only named Phoenician city is Sidon, 'rich in bronze', but not because Sidon is a distant echo of the reality of the long-lost Mycenaean age.[32] Rather, Sidon's importance in the ninth and eighth centuries BC is underestimated in our modern histories, which centre on Tyre instead.[33] Not until 677 BC was Sidon sacked by the Assyrians. Again, it is easier (but not obligatory) to place Homer's focus on this rich and famous city before it had been sacked in the real world.

The *Iliad* and *Odyssey* amplify these themes elsewhere. To Sidon (not Tyre) go Menelaus when returning from Troy and Paris when eloping with fair-haired Helen; Sidon is always a rich place for Homer, a source of superb textiles (brought to Troy by Paris) or silver and silver-gilt bowls adorned with gold. In the Greek world we find such Phoenician bowls in graves and sanctuaries, bronze bowls for the most part but decorated with well-worked figures: silver bowls are known too, in Cyprus or in the further 'Italian' west.[34] Like Sidon, Egypt too is a land of great riches. Thebes, a city, is full of treasures, a few of which were given to the visiting Helen and Menelaus. 'Thebes' is a Greek name for the place, but it was probably based on a word heard in Egypt itself: it was quite rich enough in the ninth or eighth centuries BC for rumours about this ancient centre to have reached a Greek visitor to the Delta at that time.[35] However, beyond these generalized riches and these bowls of magnified splendour, Homer gives no impression of these cultures' profound difference from the Greeks' own. His Egyptian kings behave like noble Greeks and one has a Greek name: so do all their wives. His Phoenician kings have Greek names only (Arybas or 'Phaidimos', Mr Bright). They give gifts to noble visitors, as do Homer's well-behaved Greek heroes.

In the tenth to eighth centuries there were Greeks in the real world who knew so much more about such peoples and a further 'triangle' on the eastern map. They were Euboeans from Chalcis and Lefkandi, then Chalcis and Eretria who went with their cargoes to kingdoms on Cyprus which Homer omits, Amathus or Salamis or Kourion, founded after the heroic Bronze Age. They also went to Cilicia, the kingdom of Mopsus–Muksas, to north Syria, Mount Hazzi and places from Ras el-Bassit to Tyre and even Gaza. At Al Mina, perhaps even briefly at Tyre, they settled and interacted with real north Syrians and Phoenicians. None of these places turns up in Homeric epic. At them they spoke to local inhabitants in their non-Greek languages; sometimes they made love to their women; they adopted their units of precious metal and their words for luxuries, incense or scents; they enlarged their view of the gods by hearing the tales of battles and succession in the locals' heaven. They knew far more than 'Sidon' and south-west Crete and people called 'Tamer' and 'Mr Bright'. These Euboeans had a knowledge of lands, cultures and languages on which Homer, their contemporary, never drew, not even for his original similes or tales where he was most free to invent.

20

The View from Ascra

I

Homer's poems are reticent about the places and peoples among whom contemporary Euboeans moved. They are equally reticent, as we shall now discover, about their mythical discoveries from east to west. At most they lie in the epics' background: more often they are absent altogether.

The bones and battlefield of the Giants had been a major Euboean discovery, east, north and west. In the epics it is striking that Homer gives none of their locations and that he does not even give details of a battle of Giants and gods. He mentions that the Giants had once been close to the gods, who had even moved among them openly. However, these Giants had been a 'wild tribe' and their king Eurymedon had 'destroyed' them and destroyed himself: we are not told when or how.[1] When Homer presents briefly his own battle of the gods in the war for Troy, he describes their vast size and overwhelming combat, but he nowhere compares them with Giants. Titans, rather, seem to be in his mind's eye. The episode is the least successful in his entire poem, as if this sort of enlarged combat with 'special effects' did not come easily to his genius. He nowhere refers to the Giants' bones or battlefield and never mentions their base-camp.

Sometimes his gods are called the 'Heavenly Ones' (*Ouraniones*), perhaps in the sense of 'descendants of father Heaven'.[2] There is no mention, however, of the sexual embrace of Heaven and mother Earth or their forcible separation. Instead our primeval parents are watery, very different to Earth and Sky. They are Ocean and mother Tethys. Ultimately they derive from stories further east, from the Babylonians'

349

Epic of Creation, whose mother, Tiamat, was the watery sea and whose name, sometimes written as 'Tawtu', became Tethys in Greek.[3] She remained a rare and undeveloped goddess for the Greeks. In Homer, the old Babylonian story of creation has fallen far into the background. Instead Ocean and Tethys are a long-married couple who have quarrelled and no longer make love. In an exquisite touch Homer makes the goddess Hera pretend that she is going off to try to reconcile them. Their original Near Eastern role has been brilliantly transposed. After so many years together, even our world's first parents are in need of marriage counselling.[4]

'Creation' does not interest Homer at all, and as for the prehistory of his universe it was not neo-Hittite or north Syrian in origin. Their dire stories are nowhere mentioned. There is no castration of copulating Heaven. There is not even a hint of a sharp-toothed sickle. Cronos, the son who used it, is 'crooked-counselling' (*ankulomētēs*), although he shows no sign of devious thinking. Originally he had been 'crooked-reaping' (*ankulamētēs*), armed with his great castrator, but his adjective then changed as his act receded into the background, and for Homer and his teachers his counsel became crooked instead of his weapon. Nothing is said about Heaven's blood or sperm and nothing is said to have been born from it, no Furies, no Giants, not even Aphrodite the goddess of love. The mother of Homer's Aphrodite is the child of mother Dione, an ancient name whose root meant 'Mrs Sky'. She is a genuine mother, not a scattering of *aphros* or male 'foam'.

There have been unforgettable quarrels in Homer's heaven and there are frequent threats of yet more to come. Hephaestus, the lame god, has been thrown out by his mother in her disgust at his being disabled. There is even a threat that Zeus will challenge and beat all the gods in a tug-of-war conducted with his primeval 'golden rope'.[5] But notoriously there have been no castrations, no children devoured by Cronos, no stone consumed as a substitute. Down in the underworld, Cronos now sits with the Titans. Zeus has defeated him, but the poet gives no gory details of the war.[6]

Does he avoid such gruesome stories because of his epic's fine sense of propriety? Some of this avoidance goes back into his particular poetic tradition: Homer inherited Cronos the 'crooked-counselling', not 'crooked-reaping', and Dione as Aphrodite's mother. Elsewhere, however, Homer has not sanitized his gods so that they do not quarrel, fight or make love indecorously among themselves. It seems, then, that he has simply not mentioned one cluster of old stories.

He has not mentioned others on our trail, either. Mopsus' main career was as a post-Iliadic wanderer but he might perhaps have earned a mention in one or other list of names. Adonis might perhaps have appeared in a simile and so might Io. These absences might all be fortuitous, but Homer's topography also provokes thought. His Cilicians have been transferred to live up nearer Troy. Once, he alludes to the Aleian plain but only as part of a hero's vague wandering. There is not a hint of Mount Kasios and its god, its storms and dangers for sailors in Syria or Egypt. It is not that Homer lacks or avoids exact topographic details beyond his poems' main focus. In the twentieth book of the *Iliad*, Achilles rebounds from a challenge to the Trojan Aeneas and kills Iphition, the son of a nymph. 'Lie there,' he tells him, 'most violent of men . . . though your family is by the Gygaean lake where your father's estate is, by the fishy Hyllus and the eddying Hermus.' Here a modern critic has discerned Achilles' 'tendency to invoke distant places and resounding names . . . far removed from the battle-ground of Troy', but in fact the places are remarkably exact.[7] The 'Gygaean lake' is the gloomy Mermere Gölü in ancient Lydia with its reeds, its swampy surrounds and its water-birds just north of the burial mounds of the Lydian kings. The 'eddying' Hermus is the river which cuts through the Lydian plain to the south of it, 'turbulent and raving' as travellers have found it since to be. It is the source, even the direct source, of the lake which lies just to the north. The Hyllus river is the modern Cam Çay, defining the plain which runs north from the Gygaean lake. Its own upper course is more complex and one nearby branch of it may even have run down south into the lake's northern shore.[8] The lake, to this day, is famously 'fishy': so is the Hyllus river exactly on the northern plain beyond the lake with which Homer links it.[9] The lake is the furthest point east in Asia to which Homer refers, but he or his tradition evokes it exactly with its place name and its two nearby rivers, north and south, one of them correctly called 'fishy', a quality ascribed to no other river in his epics. But there was something else about the lake too, as we happen to know from Greek sources in the fifth century BC: Echidna, or 'Miss Viper', lived there, the mate of Typhon, who, on one view, had been scorched to death in nearby Burnt Lydia just beyond Homer's view.[10] But here and elsewhere in his poems Homer never mentions her.

Silence does not entail Homer's own ignorance, but if we are to think of him living, composing and performing in one particular place, we might expect him to mention myths, mythical people and places which were especially vivid to his audience there. All of these omitted myths and places were vivid to Euboeans who were travelling on the one 'hotline' between Greeks and the Near East which we can follow in eighth-century evidence. To a minority of modern scholarly readers it is Homer, however, who owes an important debt to the Near East; on one view, it may even be 'a greater challenge to isolate and appreciate what is Greek in Homeric poetry than to enumerate its foreign sources'.[11] Most of us find the challenge to lie in exactly the opposite direction, unless we somehow believe 'the probability is that "Homer" was not the name of a historical Greek poet, but the imaginary ancestor of the "Homeridai". The question is then how the Homeridai got their name . . . it is conceivable that [they] correspond . . . to a Phoenician prototype *bᵉnē' ōmerīm, "sons of speakers", that is, tale-tellers as a professional class.'[12] It remains much more conceivable that they were the self-styled followers, perhaps even the family, of Homer the greatest Greek poet.

Nonetheless, did Homer himself have a 'hotline' connected to contemporary poets in Near Eastern cultures? One has been claimed to run directly from his *Iliad* to Assyrian court poets in the seventh (not eighth) century BC.[13] Even if we believe its unlikely dating, the 'hotline' turns out to be a wrong number. Its supporters appeal to the washing-away of the *Iliad*'s poetic wall before the Greek camp at Troy, as if this event is closely paralleled by an Assyrian description of King Sennacherib's 'destruction' of Babylon in 689 BC which Homer therefore knew.[14] However, Homer's gods are to wash the Greeks' wall into the sea by sending torrential rains and by diverting the local rivers. Conversely, Sennacherib claims that he threw walls, temples and towers of Babylon into the canals, some of which he dug out for the purpose. Earth from the city was then carried down into the sea: 'I dissolved [the city-gate and the site of the gods' houses] in the waters and turned it into a flood-plain.' Apart from his exaggerations Sennacherib did not claim to use heavy rain. He claimed to flatten the buildings and only then to throw them into the canals. Homer's gods, by contrast, will use storms and rivers to break down the wall and wash it utterly away (and thereby explain why it is no longer visible). Homer owes no debt here to Assyrian court-sources.

Lists of such 'parallels' between Homer and bits of Near Eastern poems in Near Eastern languages do not entail contact between them. Even if they did, in what sense would Homer's own poems then be 'eastern'?[15] When, too, did such 'imports' belong? Were they acquired much earlier in the poetic tradition which Homer learned, and, if so, are he or his audiences still aware of them? Or are they contemporary 'neo-Oriental' borrowings and, if so, do he and his audience feel them still to have an exotic tone? The points at issue are not the place and personal names which Homer's epics contain when their plots dwell on events in Asia itself. The Greek name 'Ilion' (Troy) indeed derives from the city's Luwian name in the Bronze Age.[16] The *Iliad* also includes deeds of Lycians from south-west Asia, people with names like Pandaros or Lycaon or Sarpedon, all of which can be traced back to local Lycian names in the Luwian language. These heroes' names may go back to early contacts between Greeks and Lycia (called 'Lukka'), perhaps even as early as the Late Bronze Age (*c.* 1300–1200 BC).[17] Such parallel names say nothing about the transfer of eastern poetic themes, let alone of eastern poetry contemporary with Homer himself. To find such transfers scholars look above all to the Babylonian poem *Gilgamesh*. Many believe (though I do not) that there is at least one echo of *Gilgamesh* in the *Iliad*, when Homer describes Achilles' mourning over the dead body of his beloved Patroclus.[18] The motif in question occurs in only one tablet of our various tablets of the Gilgamesh story, but it is not a late eighth- (or seventh-) century BC addition to an older whole.[19] If there was a debt to the Gilgamesh story here, it could go back to a contact made five centuries or more before Homer. He himself could be quite unaware of it.

The most plausible eastern parallels cluster round the goddess Aphrodite. In the *Iliad*'s fourteenth book she gives Hera erotic items of beauty, including a strap to be criss-crossed and worn running between her heavenly breasts: like this strap, the verses may indeed have had an eastern flavour for their audience.[20] In the fifth book of the *Iliad* Aphrodite takes refuge in heaven, complaining of her wounding by the rough male heroes in battle. This scene of the wounding goddess of love complaining of her own wounds is paralleled, perhaps significantly, in earlier Babylonian poetry.[21] Such a clustering of eastern items round Aphrodite is suggestive. The goddess, at home on Cyprus, was believed by the Greeks themselves to have an eastern connection in her cult. She is the goddess to whom we would most expect 'eastern' motifs to be applied.

One passing allusion to Tethys and two short scenes with Aphrodite do not make Homer's epics part of the contemporary Near East. Parallels may arise between them for quite other reasons than verbal contact. In the fifteenth book of the *Iliad* Poseidon recalls how Zeus and the gods once cast lots for their respective kingdoms. In the old Babylonian *Story of Mankind* the gods also cast lots for their kingdom: 'There is hardly another passage in Homer', Walter Burkert has written, favouring eastern influences, 'which comes so close to being a translation of an Akkadian epic.'[22] So near, and yet so far: it is not just that we now know the story was translated into Hittite, reaching western Asia in the Late Bronze Age. It need not be the source of Homer's divine lottery at all. By far the most powerful source for Homer's description of the relations of gods with men and with each other is sociological: Homer has made 'the gods men', as the ancients observed, but above all because the social relations of his mortal world have been projected onto the relations imagined between the gods in heaven. The gods' company is a magnification of the social world which Homer and his oral predecessors knew and absorbed in real life. The gods are aristocrats enlarged: they tend to treat mortals as aristocrats treat the lower classes. Like aristocrats they value 'honour'; they 'give to the one who gives to them', but like aristocrats they do not always give in return; like aristocrats, too, they have their favourites and also their loves. On earth, Greek sons divided their inherited property by casting lots for separate shares of it. In heaven, therefore, the gods do the same, without any need for a Babylonian 'influence'. On earth, Greek aristocrats met in a council or a 'gathering' (assembly): in heaven, therefore, Greek gods do the same. It is irrelevant whether or not the gods of Near Eastern sources also met in assemblies and councils. The Homeric imagination of the supernatural arises from earthly Greek society, as experienced in a largely pre-literate age. It does not rest on foreign borrowing.

Theories of Homer's borrowings from eastern texts raise practical problems, too, above all the problem of the texts' accessibility. In the eighth century Greeks did not read the cuneiform scripts which expressed Assyrian, Hittite or Babylonian lore: they had no more idea of their contents than did the soldiers and the scholar Callisthenes with Alexander the Great in the same area four centuries later. As we have repeatedly illustrated, they listened, spoke and sometimes constructively misunderstood. Strikingly, Homer happens to ignore particular misunderstandings of Greek travellers in his time. We have traced the inferences of Euboeans from Mount Hazzi to Monkey Island, but every single one of them is missing from Homer's epics, as is their main 'triangle' of contact with Cyprus, Cilicia and the Levant. Yet on one recent view, the *Odyssey*, at least, is a Euboean poem, composed by an epic poet in Euboea. Nothing in its dialect and language requires us to believe this origin and its silence about the Euboeans' eastern and western discoveries points to the opposite conclusion. In the seventh book of the *Odyssey*, the poet simply refers famously to Euboea by name: Alcinous, king of the happy Phaeacians, promises his guest Odysseus that his men will row him to his 'country and house and wherever else is dear to you, even if it is much further away than Euboea. Those of our people who saw Euboea when they were carrying fair-haired Rhadamanthys to see Tityos the son of earth say it is the furthest away of places.'[23] 'Where else', the great expert Martin West has asked, 'would a poet be likely to imagine *Euboea* as the Phaeacians' furthest horizon', unless he himself was a singer on and from Euboea?[24] In the fantasy-journeys of Phaeacians, we might reply, any place name might crop up from the real Greek world. But there is another, compelling alternative.

Already in the sixth to fifth centuries BC, if not earlier, there were those who linked the poet Homer with Chios in the east Aegean off the coast of Asia Minor. We know of a family clan of Homeridai on Chios, 'descendants of Homer', who are mentioned in a sixth-century text and attested in a list inscribed on marble *c.* 300 BC, found on

Chios as recently as 2002.[25] We also know of Homeridai, 'singers of stitched songs', who performed the Homeric poems and were perhaps the same family clan: they are attested in our surviving evidence c. 460 BC.[26] No other island is known to have had Homeridai, a point which Chiotes later pressed in their claims to have been the poet's compatriots. The claims of the clan and the singers might be false, but they existed within two centuries of Homer's (probable) lifetime. For a Chiote, the *Odyssey*'s lines about Euboea were very close to home. In the mid-fifth century BC the erudite, amiable Ion of Chios wrote a text on 'Chios's Foundation'. One group of its early settlers, he said, were Cretans, others were 'Abantes from Euboea', followed in the next generation by more Euboeans, this time from Histiaea on the island's north-west coast, who came 'in accordance with an oracle from Delphi'.[27] Ion knew local traditions about his Chios which we do not and these early settlers deserve to be taken seriously. There was a neatness, then, for Homer on Chios to refer before a Chiote audience to Euboea, one of their own homelands, as the furthest point in the world. Chiote expatriates would enjoy this allusion to their former home as if it was so very far away. It was a particularly neat allusion because for some of Homer's Chiote audience, Euboea was nothing of the sort. It was visible on clear days from hills in the south of Chios. On one such hill lies the 'hall' at Emporio, one of the sites where it has been suggested Homer performed. It is tempting to imagine the poet turning away from his audience here and pointing with one hand as he sings his verses in which Alcinous calls Euboea the furthest place on earth. With a gesture, he indicates it.

Other people on Chios are worth considering too. Ion refers to Cretan settlers, a claim which suggests that families of Cretan origin still lived on his home island. We have seen, too, the historical genealogy of Ion's near-contemporary on Chios, Heropythos, who listed his ancestry back to one 'Kyprios' in c. 880–860 BC. In the *Odyssey* and the *Iliad*, both Crete and Cyprus are described with touches of precision, but not always with accuracy. Crete is 'hundred-citied' or 'ninety-citied', with a cave near Amnisos and a mixture of polyglot people who were divided into three, as they were indeed divided in their Dorian tribes.[28] There are also the cliff and coastline to which Menelaus' ships were driven by the storm-wind and which fit with so many details on the coast by modern Kommos and its ancient sanctuary for travellers.

On Cyprus there is no such precise sense of place, but Paphos and Aphrodite's cult are mentioned and, although kings are named with vague Greek names, Cinyras of Paphos is specifically said to have given an exotic breastplate to King Agamemnon.[29] Its description suggests a breastplate of Near Eastern style but Homer's knowledge of the island itself is limited. Many sources have been suggested for his knowledge nonetheless, originating long before Homer himself or even in his own experience: 'though unlikely to have been a Cypriot himself,' Martin West has proposed, he 'may have visited the island or had some contact there'. The reason, he thinks, lies in the mention of Cinyras of Paphos although 'he is not a man of arms and does not belong in the world of Agamemnon. The poet has introduced him gratuitously, presumably to humour Cypriot friends.'[30] The hints of local Cypriot knowledge here are much more tenuous than Homer's precise details about a place, our Kommos, on Crete.[31] However, both can be accommodated to a Homer on Chios where there were Chiotes who had Cretan connections and Cypriots also resided.

In the *Odyssey*, Nestor describes the Greek captains' deliberations about their route home from Troy with a rare exactness: they wondered whether to go past the north of Chios to the island of Psyria (modern Psyra), or to turn down the inland channel between Chios and 'windy Mimas' on the Asian coast and then south of Chios and on from there.[32] The two routes are exact, as any Chiote would know. Chiotes, however, were probably not those in Homer 'who say' about Typhon's lair 'in Arima'. Some east Greek pottery and items have indeed been found in Pithecussae's graves from the later eighth century BC, but the source of Typhon's lashing here was ultimately the island's Euboean contingent.[33] By *c.* 730 some of them on Ischia knew Homer's *Iliad*, on a defensible reading of the inscription on 'Nestor's cup'. Homer had fans on Ischia, any of whom might have told him or an east Greek friend about the local rumblings of Typhon. Alternatively the reports of Typhon that originated with Euboeans on the island reached Homer at second or third hand. Similar reports, from a similar ultimate source, had reached him about wondrous Libya, which Euboeans, again, had been visiting at least since 760 BC. The details about the coast of Crete at Kommos could come from someone, ultimately, who had travelled west on the 'fast lane' by sea from the Levant. In the eighth century, from *c.* 800 to 725, Greek pottery from one of the buildings at Kommos on Crete includes 'a number of . . . vases [which] will have had a Euboean, Cycladic or east Greek origin', pieces whose carriers were within Homer's orbit at first or second hand.[34] Those who incline to a touch of Spanish colour in the setting of the *Odyssey*'s underworld can trace it to a similar source, to Euboeans or those to whom they talked, as Euboean pottery had been reaching south-west Spain, initially *c.* 850 BC but in greater quantity *c.* 750–700, surely with Euboean carriers.[35]

However, where Euboeans could be precise, Homer was vague. What Euboeans had found about the gods and their wars, Homer omitted entirely. This pattern becomes more sharply focused if we look for it in his near-contemporary, the poet Hesiod, too.

II

Whatever the view from Chios or the nature of the island's Greek population and its Homerids, nobody knows where Homer lived or whether there was one Homer for the *Iliad*, another for the *Odyssey*. His poems' exact descriptions of place are not only Chiote ones: we can only make informed guesses about them, mine being a single Homer on Chios. With Hesiod, we are certain. He is the first literary personality in the world and at first sight his home is unexpected.[36] Hesiod tells us that he lived in little Ascra, a 'wretched village, bad in winter, foul in summer, good at no time'. Ascra lies in Boeotia on the east side of Mount Helicon where the site has now been rediscovered. Its modern surveyors consider it 'a delightful site with as pleasant and refreshing a situation a Greek city could have',[37] but Hesiod had to live there and they did not.

For his family, Ascra was a second-best. Hesiod describes how his father used to 'sail in ships, lacking a noble livelihood'. He lived over at Aeolian Cyme, not the Cyme in Italy or Euboea, but the Cyme which was an Aeolian Greek settlement in north-west Asia Minor. He came west to Ascra 'fleeing evil poverty in his dark ship'. Hesiod presents his father as engaged in trade in order to make a living, but failing and being forced to come across to Greece. He 'settled near Helicon', coming there for what was probably the first time in his life.[38] His journey from east to west ran in exactly the opposite direction to the journeys which we have been studying and it ended at a place we would never consider. Nonetheless, it is the one eighth-century journey which is described by a first-hand source.

Even in Ascra, Hesiod was adept at the traditional diction, metre and style of hexameter verse. He had listened to and studied with oral masters who are now lost to us, reminding us how many practitioners of this poetry have disappeared from the eighth-century record. He presents himself as reluctant to travel by sea and in his *Works and Days* he speaks with the voice of a resolute small farmer. Yet his other surviving poem, his *Theogony* or *Generations of the Gods*, is full of wide-ranging detail. Ascra lies far off our travelling Euboeans' trail, but the *Theogony* is the poem which most coincides with it.

Unlike Homer, Hesiod alludes in detail to many of the stories which we have tracked. He dwells on the separation of Heaven while embracing mother Earth. He describes Heaven's castration by Cronos, the sickle, the shower of fertile blood and white male foam and the consequent birth of Aphrodite. He describes the tricking of the cannibal Cronos by the gift of a stone and the saving of his newborn son Zeus. He describes Cronos' overthrow and Zeus's rule. There are no battles with Giants, but there is a decidedly filmic battle between Zeus and the Titans. There is also a final battle between Zeus and the many-headed Typhon. On his first appearance in the poem, Typhon is dwelling 'in Arima, so they say', a reference which matches the Homeric tradition. On his second appearance, near the end of the poem, he is the monstrous opponent of Zeus who is battered into defeat and scorched into submission but is the source, nonetheless, of hostile winds at sea.[39]

However did a man from 'wretched' Ascra know this particular cluster of succession stories, one which Homer's epics had omitted at almost every point? One source might be his father, a much-travelled man whose influence has been detected in Hesiod's verses about seafaring and even in his remarkable hymn to the goddess Hecate, a 'personal god' for Hesiod and his family, one who may have been picked up on their father's travels.[40] Yet a father 'fleeing poverty' in Cyme in north-west Asia was also not directly on the travellers' trail which ran from Unqi to Ischia. Did Hesiod's local poetic teachers pass the backbone of his *Theogony* on to him? The poem takes 'Chasm' (in Greek, *Chaos*) as its starting-point and is not concerned with the question of its first creation. What concerns Hesiod, rather, is procreation. In Greek, *Chaos* is neuter, but Hesiod then follows on with two words for darkness, one masculine, one feminine. So they mate, as their gender allows, and other gendered pairs follow. His poem then teems with details of subsequent families of the gods and with divine personifications of the powers and forces in our lives. Hesiod's mind and inheritance are very fertile. In the view of Paul Veyne, considering whether Greeks believed in their myths, 'Hesiod knows that we will take him at his word, and he treats himself as he will be treated: he is the first to believe everything which enters his head.'[41] But it 'entered his head', Hesiod tells us, with special authority, the authority of the Muses, whom he represents as having appeared to him in a vision and having told him that they, his superiors, know how to speak 'many plausible falsehoods but, when we wish, to utter things that are true'. The implication is not that the poem which follows may be partly fiction and partly true, as if the Muses told him 'to give his imagination rein, and among his hypotheses some would be true'.[42] It is that his song, the Muses' song, will be true because the Muses, his superiors, 'wish it'. In heaven, as Hesiod begins by telling us, the Muses themselves sing a song about the 'children of Heaven and Earth', the gods and much else: the themes of the song resemble much that Hesiod himself then sings. He set out to sing what the Muses sang too, but to our eye, not his, it was grouped round a backbone of stories derived ultimately from the Near East.

Apart from the Muses, 'whose sweet voice flows timelessly from their lips', Hesiod needed earthly informants for these stories. His local poetic teachers are unlikely to be his source: as Homeric epic implies, tales of Cronos and his bad habits were not prominent in the main epic tradition by which such teachers were formed. We must look, instead, for Hesiod's own travels. His poems attest two, both of which are relevant. One was to the 'dells of Parnassus', the site of the Delphic oracle. Hesiod was daring to sing about the generations of the gods and any such person would understandably go up to ask the gods' own spokesmen, the priests at eighth-century Delphi, for an authoritative view of the subject. He was told of one item there, a local relic, a great 'sign and wonder'.[43] If we consider who these Delphic priests were, we can recognize how much else he will have learned.

We have one account of the origins of Delphi's priesthood, memorably described in a hexameter hymn in honour of Delphic Apollo. This hymn was composed c. 580–570 BC, perhaps exactly in 582 for the Pythian Games at Delphi, to judge from its internal references to the site and its priesthood's history.[44] It describes in unforgettable detail how Apollo chose his first priests: Apollo had observed a 'swift ship', the poet tells us, 'on the wine-dark sea; in it there were many fine men, Cretans from Minos' city of Knossos'. These Cretans were travelling 'on business' in their dark ships to sandy Pylos, but Apollo jumped into it in the shape of a dolphin, 'big and fearsome' ('Delphinios' was one of his cult-names).[45] He prevented the ship from landing at Pylos and guided it along the sea to Crisa off the Gulf of Corinth, where he revealed himself in a shower of sparks. He explained his identity to the terrified Cretans and told them to eat, then to follow him up to the 'place where you will have a rich temple'. So they made offerings to the gods, ate and followed Apollo as he played 'delightfully' on the lyre and 'stepped high': the Cretans 'danced in time and followed, singing "Iē Paiēon", like the paeans of the Cretans in whose breasts the divine Muse has placed honey-voiced singing'. They arrived at Delphi; Apollo showed them his temple and 'their hearts were stirred within them'.

These Cretans, the poet tells us, are men 'who make holy offerings to their god and announce the rulings of Apollo of the golden sword, whatever he says when he gives oracles from the bay-trees in the dells of Parnassus'.[46] This poem was a hymn sung to honour Delphic Apollo, evidently at Delphi itself. It was explicit before an audience who knew the local traditions: 'If the (Delphic) Hymn to Apollo conveys a historical message, it is above all that there were once Cretan priests at Delphi.'[47]

Apollo's oracle was a recent venture at Delphi: it seems to have begun *c.* 825–800 BC, about a century before Hesiod's visit. On Crete we can point to flourishing local cults of Apollo, including cults of Apollo 'Delphinios'; Crete had a long history of tripods, items which were to be prominent in the Delphic cult, and it also had paeans, or distinctively metrical songs, the type of song which Delphic Apollo is said to have incorporated into his own worship.[48] Archaeologically, Cretan bronzes have been found at Delphi from the eighth century onwards, accompanied by Cretan sculptures until *c.* 620–600 BC.[49] Dedications at the site cannot establish the identity of its priest-hood, but for once we have an explicit text to set beside archaeo-logical evidence. The hymn explains what this evidence cannot: Delphi's Apollo was served by Cretans and the oracle was instituted by Cretans who had come west. Perhaps they were not 'on business' when they came to the site by Parnassus, but they were the originators of its cult.

A century or so later, when Hesiod visited Delphi, Apollo was being served by Cretans of the second or third generation. What stories did they tell him about the birth of the gods? Here, we can be specific, thanks to a reference by Hesiod himself. In the 'dells of Parnassus', he tells us, Zeus had fixed a 'sign henceforwards, a wonder for mortal men'. It was a stone, but an extremely special one: the very stone which Zeus's mother had given to father Cronos, the one which he had eaten instead of the baby Zeus and which he had 'vomited up'. The last to be swallowed, it was the first to come up. Last in, first out, it was on show at Delphi, *c.* 710 BC.[50]

This stone belongs at the very heart of the ancient stories of the gods' struggles in heaven, the stories which we have traced to their Near Eastern origins on and around Mount Hazzi. The Cretans who showed off this holy relic knew the accompanying stories which were its context, the very ones which Hesiod's poem has immortalized. We can put this knowledge in a historical milieu. Archaeologically, their home island of Crete shows a clear, close contact with imports from Cyprus, especially *c.* 850–750. Their home site of Knossos is well excavated and there too the Cypriot contact is evident in pottery, bowls and metalwork.[51] The succession-struggles in the old Hittite heaven were connected in a Greek context with the 'birth of Aphro-dite', the product of Heaven's castration. This Aphrodite was Cyprus's

Aphrodite: it was on Cyprus that her birth had been blended into the older story which had come to Cypriots from the Levant. There were Phoenicians, too, on Cyprus and there were Phoenician objects, Phoenician visitors and perhaps a few Phoenician residents at Knossos and other parts of Crete. But Phoenician storytelling was not needed to bring the story on to Crete. Through their Cypriot contacts, the Cretans at Knossos received the story of the struggles and births of the gods in Greek. It had floated across from Cyprus like their imports of Cypriot goods and it was present on Crete in the age when the first priests at Delphi were growing up. They were men from Knossos itself.

Just as Cypriot Greeks had already worked details of their Aphrodite's birth into this song of succession-struggles, so Cretan Greeks then worked in their local details of the birth of Zeus. In Hesiod's version, the baby Zeus is taken away by mother Rhea to be 'reared and nursed in broad Crete'. The details are remarkably specific: she took him in 'the dark night' first of all to Lyktos and hid him in a 'cave, hard to approach, on the thickly wooded Aegean mountain'. There he grew up and returned to overthrow Cronos, 'as was fated'.[52]

The sacred caves on Crete are famous, attracting worshippers for more than a thousand years before Hesiod's poem. We are still not sure which cave is the cave at Lyktos and one answer is that Hesiod himself was unaware too. In later Greek sources *lyktos/lyttos* was explained as a word meaning 'high up': Hesiod may have taken a Cretan word for 'high' to be a place name near the cave.[53] 'High up', the cave was surely the great Zeus-cave on Mount Ida, the place of arduous mountain-pilgrimage where excavations, as we have seen, show the exceptional quantity of precious offerings made in the ninth to eighth centuries BC. It was there that the energetic Couretes were said to have danced and clashed their shields in order to conceal the baby Zeus's crying. This legend attaches to dances which were performed in the local cult at the cave. It is from the Zeus-cave that we have the impressive bronze shields for ceremonial use, including those which were adapted from north Syrian styles. We even have that eastern-style 'gong' of Greek workmanship which could be struck to sound out in the ritual dancing.[54]

Just as the Cretan craftsmen of these shields drew on a Near Eastern style and adapted it in a Greek way, so Cretan storytellers of the local birth of Zeus worked their Cretan story into the old Near Eastern framework about the cannibal Cronos which had reached them from Cyprus. Their local Cretan tale was fitted into the older succession story.[55] The controlling city of the Ida cave was probably Knossos, home of the first priests at Delphi; the enlarged story then passed to the new Delphic shrine in the company of these Knossians. Through them, in the later eighth century, it became known to Hesiod. We know that it was told at the Delphi which he visited, and the story of Cronos' stone presupposed the other stories of succession-struggles among the gods. Despite Hesiod's credit to the Muses whom he met on Mount Helicon, his greater debt was to Cretans, the priests on Delphi's nearby Parnassus.[56]

He saw for himself the very stone, 'a wonder for mortal men'; no doubt the Cretans took him out and showed it proudly to him on the hillside. He heard the stories which are now the backbone of his poem; he then took his poem away to perform at a competition. In his other surviving poem, *Works and Days*, Hesiod tells us how, once, he risked a sea-crossing. He went off to sing at the funeral-games of Amphidamas where 'many prizes were announced by the sons of that brave man'.[57] Hesiod won the prize for poetry, a tripod with fine handles, and dedicated it on Mount Helicon where the Muses had first inspired him. His winning poem, as modern scholars have inferred, was therefore his other surviving work, the *Theogony*, the one whose verses credit it to the Muses on Helicon. They were the proper recipients of his prize-tripod because it was their *Theogony* poem which had won it.

The site of the victory helps to explain it. The contest was held at Chalcis, before the very lords of Euboea's greatest city-state whom we have followed along their trail from east to west. Hesiod performed for them, the 'boy from Ascra', but nonetheless he sang the very stories which made up the bulk of the Euboeans' own worldwide discoveries. He had learned them quite separately, from Cretans at Delphi; the Cretans had learned them from Cyprus; Cypriots had learned them ultimately from north Syria where the 'songs of kingship' were sung in honour of Mount Hazzi. Far from Ascra, meanwhile, Hesiod's Euboean hearers had already learned these stories for themselves, on Cyprus and at the foot of Mount Hazzi where they and their fathers had visited and settled at Al Mina–Potamoi Karon. Unlike Hesiod and his Delphic informants they had then discovered these stories' cardinal items far away in the west. Later Greek fiction, c. 400 BC, claimed that Homer and Hesiod had competed together in the games for Amphidamas on Euboea and that Hesiod had won the prize. Poetically, it should have been no contest, but if Homer had ever come to Chalcis, on this one occasion, before such an audience, even he might not have been the victor.

It is possible that Hesiod gained even more than a prize-tripod. After telling of Zeus's wars with the Titans and the extremities of the world where they lived, Hesiod's poem returns to Typhon, whom he has mentioned nearly five hundred hexameter verses earlier. This time his story is much more detailed. Typhon is the child of mother Earth and Tartarus, the 'underworld'. He opposes Zeus's rule, hissing and howling variously through his hundred snaky heads. If Zeus had not marshalled his thunder and lightning Typhon would have become the 'king of mortals and immortals' instead. The earth shook; the land and sea seethed; Hades trembled and so did Cronos and the Titans inside it. But Zeus burnt the monster and beat him until he collapsed and fell flaming in the mountain-dells. The earth there burned with unbelievable heat: 'vexed in his heart' Zeus threw the scorched Typhon into the underworld.[58]

Critics and readers have often felt this powerful episode to be an afterthought to the main poem, added, perhaps, and not composed by Hesiod himself. It seems, on this reading, to be tacked on after the battle of Zeus and the Titans, whose general structure it matches.[59] It might even belong with a modern view of 'the archaic mode of thought ... [which] does not deal with an object once and for all, thereafter simply discarding it; rather, its habit is to circle around its object, in order to inspect it from changing viewpoints'.[60] Hesiod, on this view, is a poet of 'multiple approaches', and his two references to Typhon in the same poem are an example of his 'circling round'.

The explanation may be less an 'archaic mode' of thinking and viewing than a straightforward matter of sources. The fuller treatment of Typhon may be Hesiod's own addition to his poem after his victory at Euboean Chalcis. It was not from a second visit to Delphi that he learned these further details. We can see from our hymn to Delphic Apollo that the Typhon story developed differently there. At Delphi, Typhon was eventually said to be the child of the goddess Hera, not, as in Hesiod, the child of mother Earth. By verbal analogy Typhon also became merged there with Delphi's own snake-monster Python, whom Delphic Apollo slew.[61] This Delphic version is not Hesiod's at all. From later sources we know of a local 'Typhon-hill' in Boeotia, but we do not know that it existed in Hesiod's time.[62] Nothing in his story is connected to such a place. There was a simpler, much more accessible source for his details about the monster: the Euboeans for whom he sang at Chalcis. In the eighth century they had tracked Typhon from one end of the Mediterranean to another. They gave Hesiod his prize and with it, I suggest, another story to add to his winning poem.

The story's particular location and even its imagery support this suggestion. According to Hesiod, 'flames rushed from the stricken Typhon in the mountain-glens of steep Aïdna . . .' This place name should not be put in brackets as if it has been jumbled unintelligibly by copyists of Hesiod's text: it is his own attempt to render 'Aïtna', the Etna of which he had heard for the first time from informants.[63] They were Euboean informants at Chalcis, people who knew from their own travels what Hesiod did not, that Typhon was still writhing under western Etna, the mountain whose smoking craters crowned the view from their Euboean settlements on Sicily's coast. As Typhon fell, he burnt the woods, those thickets of oak and chestnut and wiry broom-trees which still run up to the charred slopes of Etna's volcanic ash. Euboeans had seen them and reasoned that the earth here, as Hesiod describes it, had 'burnt with incredible heat'. It had melted, even, like tin when heated by skilled craftsmen or like iron which melts by fire in mountain-woods. Hesiod's similes were the perfect similes for Euboeans to have visualized, people who heated iron and tin with wood-fires and bellows on the hill-slopes of Typhon's Ischia or in their settlements in Etna's orbit.

To Chalcis, Hesiod brought a poem with a backbone of wars in heaven which he had learned from Cretan priests at Delphi. From Chalcis, he returned with a prize-tripod and another episode of heavenly war to add to what he had sung. This second Typhon was a new approach, not the 'multiple approach' of an archaic, circling mind. Typhon, he had discovered, was the source of fierce, stormy winds at sea. No sailor himself, Hesiod can only have heard this connection from others who were. They were the members of his Euboean audience who had travelled the seas off Ischia and Etna where Typhon was stretched out in punishment, exhaling and causing the storm-winds for the sailors who passed over his imprisoned body.

The *Theogony* is considered by many nowadays to be the most Orientalizing of our early Greek poems, with a backbone whose ultimate origin is Near Eastern. There was, however, no 'hotline' between Hesiod here and a source in a non-Greek language: the relevant message from such eastern hotlines had already been adjusted by Greeks long before his lifetime, first on Cyprus, then on Crete, from where Cretans from Knossos carried it west to Delphi. There was no eastern 'hotline', either, for Hesiod's second poem, *Works and Days*, although its existence has so often been postulated. When Hesiod gives us a version of human history, he 'sums it up' for us, he tells us, and presents it as a story of five succeeding ages.[64] The first was an age of gold, the second of silver, the third of bronze. Then there was the age of the heroes, and now it is the grim age of iron in which Hesiod lives. This sequence of deteriorating ages is linked to deteriorating metals and to an increasing impact of old age on each era's inhabitants. In due course a similar sequence of metal ages is attested in an Iranian pattern, devised by Zoroastrians, from whose milieu it then appears in the biblical book of Daniel (*c.* 160 BC): has Hesiod therefore derived his idea of it from the east? These eastern sources date long after Hesiod's lifetime. The Iranian source has been traced back only as far as the aftermath of Alexander's conquests, an event which it presupposes: those conquests were four hundred years after Hesiod.[65] This Iranian idea was then picked up and written down by a Jew, whereupon the author of the book of Daniel drew on it as an existing source: the book of Daniel was compiled more than a century and a half after Alexander. The only way to credit Hesiod personally with a Near Eastern source for his metal ages is to invent an older source, now lost to us, a Babylonian one perhaps, which eventually passed eastwards to Iran but first came westwards into Hesiod's orbit. However, no such Babylonian prototype is known to us. The simpler view is that Hesiod inherited a Greek story. The sequence of metals from gold to iron was a sequence very easily seen and applied in poetry by a Greek in the 'iron age'. Another Greek, perhaps Hesiod himself, then inserted a fifth age, the age of the all-important Greek heroes. This basic Greek scheme then travelled eastwards with Greeks *c.* 330–300 BC and influenced Iranian storytelling in the wake of the turbulent conquests of Alexander the Great.[66]

Works and Days has been compared with many other such Near Eastern 'parallels', but in Hesiod's own time there is no evident Near Eastern contact behind any of them: they are casual similarities.[67] There is only one such eastern contact in his poetry, the one behind his *Theogony*, but it reached him at two removes after two Greek adaptations, one by Greek Cypriots, another by Greek Cretans. By the time that Hesiod met these stories they were not obviously 'eastern' for him at all. They were the wisdom of Apollo's Greek priests who were serving a Greek god. Hesiod's 'Near Eastern' stories simply derived from his own two journeys in central Greece, one on foot to Delphi, the other, a very short boat-trip across to Long Island, Euboea.

Euboeans, however, had already made one of these journeys on their own account. They, too, had boated across and gone up to Delphi, perhaps passing through Boeotia, perhaps through Corinthian territory. We know that they had already consulted Delphic Apollo about their plan to found a Sicilian settlement in 734 BC.[68] This visit, made before Hesiod's poem, was unlikely to have been Euboeans' first to the Delphic site and it was by no means to be their last. Like Hesiod, Euboeans had looked around. They had surely been shown the priests' great 'sign and wonder', the very stone which mother Rhea had given to the child-eating Cronos. It fitted so excitingly into the trail which they had already tracked from east to west. On the mountain-slopes above Al Mina they had heard the stories of Heaven's castration, the child-eating Kumarbi and the struggles of Tarhunta the Storm God by which he imposed and maintained his rule. On Cyprus they had learned how Aphrodite had been born from Heaven's castrated parts. Independently, Eretrian Euboeans on Corcyra and Chalcidian Euboeans at Zancle had found the very sickle which had once parted Heaven from Earth. In Cilicia, at the first Arima, they had seen the old lair of the weather-god's snaky enemy. On Pithecussae, the second Arima, they had heard and seen where that snaky enemy Typhon was being lashed by Zeus. Typhon extended south to Etna and agitated the intervening sea with hostile winds when he exhaled: he also sent up smoke and fire from the mountain which pinned down a part of his body. Behind their settlement at Cumae on the Bay of Naples Euboeans had found the smouldering, sulphuric landscape of the Giants' last stand. In northern Greece, just inland from their settlement at Mende, they had seen the very bones of the Giants in the base-camp where they had gathered to fight their war. At Delphi they then found the final piece in their lateral thinking across the world: the very stone which Cronos had swallowed instead of Zeus. Near Mount Hazzi, above their home at Al Mina, they had heard the local story of Kumarbi's similar deception. Perhaps they did not yet know what we know from an old Hittite text, that Kumarbi had ordered the stone to be set up and paid cult. Perhaps they also did not know what we have inferred, that the stone in the story, the sacred stone which was later shown in its shrine for Zeus Kasios on Seleuceia's coins, was high up on the mountain-top itself. Instead, Euboeans came west and saw its double at Delphi, a stone with a hole for its anointing, as the travelling Pausanias was to describe it some nine centuries later, just like a 'sacred' stone or betyl in the Near East.[69] The Cretans pointed this wonder of a relic out to them, but they had no need to repeat its accompanying story. Their visitors knew it even better than they did.

From Unqi to Ischia, the Euboeans thus found the four crucial items in the ancient stories of succession in heaven. Perhaps when they found the Great Castrator at Zancle they had sent to Delphi to ask for confirmation: we know that Zancle's two Euboean founders sent an envoy to Apollo (surely Delphian Apollo) about which of them should take priority.[70] If they asked the god about their sickle too, Delphic Apollo would have supported their inference: he was only as wise as his priests, Cretan immigrants, for whom the tales of the Great Castrator were part of their mental inheritance. Then, for the funeral-games for Amphidamas at a date between c. 710 and 705 BC, the 'boy from Ascra' came over from Boeotia to Chalcis with a poem whose backbone matched the Euboeans' trail and expressed it in neat hexameter verse. He did not know the whole story. His poem had no wars with the Giants, no fully developed story of Typhon, but the prize was a foregone conclusion.

2 1

Just So Stories

I

The great Greek poets of the eighth century did not owe a debt to contemporary Near Eastern texts.[1] They were not the beneficiaries of 'migrant charismatics' or foreign poets who had come west, let alone of eastern 'defectors' from the Assyrian conquests in the Near East. Their poems' major 'eastern' debt was to a technique adapted by other Greeks, the alphabet. Neither Homer nor (possibly) Hesiod depended on the new alphabetic writing in order to compose his hexameters. The *Iliad* and *Odyssey* were essentially oral poems, the last in the 'oral phase', but the new 'Phoenician letters' enabled both poets' works to be written down, arguably as dictated versions, and thus survive.[2]

In the later eighth and especially seventh centuries BC mainland Greek painters would begin to represent monsters and lion-like or snaky figures on Greek pottery in a new 'Orientalizing' phase.[3] They used the impetus of figures seen on Near Eastern objects and imports to help them to represent figures which existed in Greek myths. They were not copying eastern prototypes exactly so as to bring new non-Greek imports into Greek stories. They were Orientalizing in the full sense, using eastern details in a free way without asserting their underlying meaning, like our painters of Chinese cups for export or makers of furniture in a chinoiserie style. Perhaps for their viewers, such paintings had an exotic eastern feel which evoked a faraway eastern world of unknown animals and legendary monsters. It may be tempting to think that these Greek painters were only following what travellers and storytellers had already done some sixty years earlier, as if the word, here too, preceded the image in early Greek culture. However, Euboeans were not Orientalizing when they amplified the Greek tales of struggles and successions in heaven. They were adding details, they believed, which were told in the east about their same gods and which were supported by the landscape from Syria to Italy. They were not exotic: they were true.

Nonetheless, Near Eastern writers, the Greek poets and their Euboean contemporaries shared a more general way of thinking, one which is visible in the best-known religious text of the eighth-century Near East. Neither culture derived it from the other. It was not Orientalizing. It was a parallel way of making sense of the eighth-century world.

The Euboeans' mythical thinking was a reasoned attempt to explain and understand. There was no opposition in it between 'myth' and 'reason'. When they relocated myths and interpreted objects and landscapes in mythical terms, they did so on the strength of evidence which they had seen, heard and creatively misunderstood. Sometimes they reasoned from analogy, especially from verbal analogy. In southern Asia, Muksas–Mopsu was the very Mopsus whom they knew already: his religious *hesty* must be their Greek *hestia*, or hearth. They were impressed by identical place names, the Luwian-Hittite Erimma or Arimmatta in Cilicia and the Etruscans' Arim(a) out in the west. They encountered these similarities as Greeks in a culture in which like-sounding words were taken to be omens, good signs from the gods. They were not just playing with puns.

They also inferred the origins of this or that from its name or physical appearance. In Greek literature and religious writings we know this practice as 'aetiology', the telling of a story of how something came to be, what we know nowadays as a 'just so story'.[4] The origin described in the story might be the origin of a name or a religious practice, a settlement or a people, a social custom, an object or even a feature of the visible world. The just so story tends to be a story of mythical origins: it does not describe any of its subject's history or subsequent development over time. Aetiology typifies so many of the Greeks' hymns to their gods, the stories they tell about their festivals and rituals, the foundation-myths of their cities and their explanations of place names and landscapes connected with their god and his cult. In the eighth century BC, throughout the Greek world, choirs were already singing hymns to their gods and in them, as later, they too would have been telling stories of the 'origin' of this or that practice or monument in honour of the god whom they celebrated. Likewise, the Cretans at Delphi told a just so story about their wondrous stone, a story which made it the western world's first holy relic. However, the first known Greek authors of aetiologies are travelling Euboeans, from *c.* 780 to 720 BC. Hitherto unrecognized, they stand at the head of a centuries-long sequence of Greek aetiological poems and travel texts, ethnography and antiquarian writings which use just so stories as an appropriate part of their genres.

At Corcyra and Zancle, these Euboeans heard that the pre-Greek place name meant 'sickle'. Which sickle, then, was it? Surely, they reasoned, it was the 'sickle of Cronos', the Great Castrator. On Ischia, they saw clouds of hot steam coming up through the crust of the earth: they heard subterranean, pre-seismic rumbling and on nearby Sicily they saw Etna smoking and flaming. What were they? Their origin was Typhon, who had been transferred from one Arima to another and was the continuing victim of punishment by Zeus. In the plain of Unqi, the Chalcidic peninsula of Pallene and the Bay of Naples, they saw vast bones, the debris of dinosaurs, which lay on or near the surface of the earth. Why were they so big? They were bones of the Giants. Why, then, was the ground by the Bay of Naples so scorched and steaming and why did a spring near the tip of Italy's heel smell so sulphurous and foul? The Giants had fought there and lost to the gods. Beneath the ground their wounds were oozing.

Once again Homer stands apart. Conspicuously there are no such just so stories in his epics. When the legendary Phaeacians return from transporting Odysseus, their ship is turned to stone by the sea-god Poseidon. The very ship was later claimed to be visible in the harbour at Corcyra, a self-styled candidate for the Phaeacians' mythical island. In the *Odyssey*, this miracle is not linked to the future, to explain a Corcyrean landscape which is said to be visible 'even now': instead, it is said to conform to an ancient prophecy, looking backwards, not forwards, in the poem's horizons.[5] In Hesiod, by contrast, just so stories proliferate. They explain particular names, the names of the Titans or Pegasus or Aphrodite, who was born from *aphros*, father Heaven's foam. They also explain social practices: how mankind received fire, why only the fat and the bones are offered when animals are killed for the gods, how diseases and troubles entered man's life (they were released on the all-male world by the first woman, heedless Pandora).[6] Here, too, Hesiod and his prize-giving Euboeans shared a similar way of looking at the world.

Aetiologies were a very much older feature of Near Eastern texts, and in the eighth century BC they were teeming in one of the texts which underlies our edited book of Genesis. Far from Hesiod, far from these Euboeans' trail, a way of thinking in terms of origins characterized the Genesis author whom biblical scholars now know as the Yahwist, J. His (not, surely, her) date and place remain disputed, but a widely defended view, which I share, is that J lived and wrote in Jerusalem in the southern kingdom of Judah and that his career belonged in the mid- to late eighth century BC, while the northern kingdom of Israel still existed and thus before 720 BC.[7] If so, J is the exact contemporary of the travelling Euboeans and a slightly older contemporary of Hesiod, although he was wholly unknown to them both.

In J's contributions to the book of Genesis there is the same concern to show the origins of names and places and peoples. Sometimes these origins are secondary to their accompanying story. The siting of Jacob's vision of the ladder to heaven at Bethel (meaning 'house of God') is perhaps an example. So is 'Babel', the place of 'confusion', where God scattered the peoples of the world and 'confused' their speech into separate languages.[8] These names' explanations are parts of the story, but they did not cause the entire story to arise. There would probably have been a story anyway of Jacob's dream or of the origin of multi-lingual man. Sometimes, however, the story's existence depends solely on the origin behind it.[9] The need for mankind to labour accounts for the story of the expulsion of Adam and Eve from Eden. The names of particular wells in the desert account for the story that Isaac had dug them out on his travels.[10]

Like Hesiod, J tells just so stories to account for social practices: why men do not speak the same language, or why the pharaoh of Egypt, after Joseph's advice, still takes a fifth of the harvest in his country.[11] There are even scriptural just so stories for antique objects and the smouldering landscape. Just as the Euboeans looked in wonder at an ancient sickle which they discovered in Sicily, so Jews looked in wonder at primitive cutlery and tried to explain it. In the book of Joshua, the Lord God tells Joshua to 'make thee sharp knives and circumcise the people of Israel': during their years of wandering in the wilderness their men had escaped the operation. So Joshua ordered a mass circumcision at the place which is now called Gilgal, a name meaning 'rolling away', like the rolling back of their foreskins.[12] The place name was not solely responsible for the story. In our Greek text of it, translated from a fuller Hebrew text now lost to us, we are told that, when Joshua died, the very knives used in this surgery were buried in his grave at Timnath-serah and 'remained there unto this day'. Indeed they did: the site was eventually explored and 'the discovery in 1870 of Stone Age artefacts at Timnath-Serah, the burial-place of Moses' successor [Joshua], give us a clue to the origins of this tale'.[13] Stone knives from the distant past had been found near the presumed site of Joshua's grave and had intrigued their ancient discoverers. What was their 'origin'? Why, they must be the very knives with which Joshua had ordered the returning male Israelites to be made into proper Jews.

There are no biblical tales of the bones of Giants, but there is the tantalizing report of Og of Bashan's gigantic bed: it was a bed of iron, 'nine cubits long and four cubits wide'. It must, then, have been visible somewhere, perhaps as a platform in the rocks: 'is it not in Rabbah', the book of Deuteronomy insists, 'among the children of Ammon?'[14] There was also a famous scorched landscape near the Dead Sea which J had already pondered, the site of ruined Sodom and Gomorrah. Whatever had caused this landscape's destruction? A story of origin arose to explain it. The landscape was a witness to God's wrath, but why had God been so angry? Because the men of Sodom had been exceptionally sinful. What, then, had been their sin? It must have been sodomy, and not just sodomy but an attempt to force this practice on unwilling strangers. Who were those strangers? They were not any old visitors; they were messengers, surely, of God with whom the men of Sodom had clamoured to have sex.[15] The just so story points to different emphases in Greek and Israelite culture. Euboeans explained a burnt landscape by Zeus's battering of a cosmic monster and his thunderbolting of insolent Giants. J, their contemporary, explained such a landscape in terms of God's punishment of mortals for attempted male sex with an angel. A visiting Greek god, a Zeus with his male 'catamite' Ganymede or an Apollo with his beloved Hyacinthos, would not have been so shocked by the attempt.

From Zancle to Timnath-serah, from the Bay of Naples to Sodom, eighth-century men explained oddities they found in the landscape by inventing just so stories. In scriptural sources those oddities were said to be persisting 'even unto this day'. Euboeans, too, had had a sense of the prehistory of what they saw, believing them to be items which were persisting from an earlier phase of Zeus's rule. It is only the accident of survival that not until the 'Homeric' hymn to Hermes (perhaps c. 500 BC) do we first meet the phrase 'as still nowadays', the phrase which marks out later Greek aetiologies, including those which occurred to the travelling soldier Xenophon as he invented stories of origins ('still so, even now') for customs and styles of dress which he had seen personally in the east during his campaigns in the Persian empire.[16]

The same personal inquiry or *historiē*, the same appeal to evidence, the same trust in like-sounding names and places were to characterize stories told about foreign items to Herodotus, the 'father of history', c. 450–430 BC.[17] But this type of Greek story had a longer, unrecognized Greek ancestry, stretching back to Euboeans who had applied its way of thinking across the Mediterranean in an age when aetiology was a way of understanding the world from Ischia to Sodom, from Pallene to the 'cities of the plain'. This way of thinking was to have a long Greek afterlife, above all in Greek ethnography and subsequent travellers' tales. Significantly, Herodotus did not construct such just so stories himself. When he included them, it was only on the authority of some of his informants. Some of the tales they told him were tales of origins whose setting was mythical, like the trail which Euboeans traced from east to west. It was not from this trail that history took its origin. They were not tales of a chain of events, extending in explanatory sequences through time.[18] Just so stories about origins are not the origin of history, of the telling and writing what really happened, and why.

II

'I wish I was here, or I wish I was there': no Greek minds in the age of Homer had travelled further than eighth-century Euboeans' but their trail of myths and travel from east to west was a feature only of their lifetimes. After 700 BC the west was no longer so new to the Greeks and the settlers in it did not come with Near Eastern contacts, stories and women still fresh in their company. In the later eighth century BC, while Sargon was building his palaces and garden, Euboea's two main city-states, Chalcis and Eretria, fought long and hard, unknown to him, and weakened themselves in the major war on their island's Lelantine plain. In 696 BC Sennacherib's Assyrians defeated the ships of Euboeans and other 'Ionian Greeks' at the battle of the Pyramus river. The Euboean pre-eminence at Al Mina declined and never again were Greek founders in the west to be those who were leaders in the east. The freshness of such contacts had gone, until Alexander extended them into yet more eastern worlds. On the lower slopes of Mount Kasios, cult was still paid, but only to the Greek hero Triptolemus, located there as a 'searcher' for the legendary Io. Like her, he was a Greek imposition on a landscape which had formerly been ruled by a very different god.

In this one eighth century, just so stories and lateral thinking had been possible for particular Greeks, the contemporaries of our great Greek epic poems. A rare life was therefore possible, rarer than a life with Isaiah in Israel or with Phoenicians travelling from Tyre to Huelva or even the planters of King Sargon's Garden Mound. It suggests a final just so story of its own under the care of the goddess Hera in flight.[19]

A Hipposthenes could have been born then, around 750 BC, to a Euboean father and a non-Greek mother on the site of Mende up in northern Greece, in land which, centuries later, would be filled with Macedonian settlers, the contemporaries of Alexander the Great. As a boy he would learn to sing and play music, dance and ride and begin to use a sword. He would go inland on walks to Pallene to see the vast bones of the Giants, evident relics of their heavenly wars. But then his father Dorippos died and, just as Homer's Andromache had feared so poignantly for her child, Hector's son, in the *Iliad*,

Hipposthenes was 'pushed away' from the banquets and dinners by boys still more fortunate than himself and sent packing, a wanderer, to his father's mother's kin at Chalcis on Euboea.

When he had grown up, in the apsidally shaped house of Hippochares his uncle, he was consigned, as an outsider, to a boat which was to carry wine and oil to his Euboean kin on Chios. It was there, after selling the cargo, that he sat with his family for two successive nights and heard the elderly Homer singing an epic of Odysseus in the megaron hall on the hill at Emporio, pointing with his hand to Euboea across the sea when his Alcinous described it as the furthest point on earth.

He made new guest-friends from Chios who gave him gifts in Homeric style, on the strength of hearing Homer himself. Hipposthenes then travelled on to Cyprus, to the harbour and royal acropolis at Amathus, where he first saw 'purple-people', Phoenicians from the Levant. Curious, he sailed on east with the next Euboean ship which visited, carrying the simple, two-handled drinking-cup which his uncle Hippochares had told him to treasure always, a cup with a bird painted near the rim of its brown-orange clay. From Amathus, in less than a day, the boat with the wind behind it put in on the shore of Unqi, at the 'royal storehouse' by the Orontes river where yet more wine was unloaded, greetings were exchanged and Hipposthenes was left to fend for himself in the settlement.

He worked the land and he helped with the horses. In the spring he rowed out on piratical raids against the passing Phoenicians and in the summer he joined the troops who fought for Assyria on the route to Hamath. In the autumn he bought fourteen-year-old Anas from his proceeds of the spoils. He made love with her on the seashore and whenever he left on horseback, driving herds of horses to Kinalua and its court inland, she would call him her Master of the Animals and laughingly hold her breasts like the bronze ladies, attendants of the goddess Ishtar, on the brow-band of his horse's harness, trophies from his raids inland. When he returned she would lie with him and tell him stories of how her family had once been kings of Carchemish but Assyrians had sold her mother into slavery at Kinalua on the Orontes, whence she had been brought for sale at Ahta by the sea. On stormy nights she told him the stories of the gods on the mountain

Hazzi beneath which they lay. She had sung them in choirs as a girl on the hill-slopes, the 'song of kingship' and the 'song of the sea'. They were stories of the battles by which Tarhunta–Zeus had come to reign in heaven and of the Great Castrator which had once parted Heaven from Earth, in a way (she promised) in which she would never part him from her.

Sometimes they travelled for a day to the foot of the Box-tree Mountain where bones as big as those of Pallene's Giants caused Hipposthenes, too, to tell stories of his own. They went down to Greek Posideion on the bay and, by boat, across to the Pyramus river, to a land whose family of kings seemed to be the 'sons of Mopsus' and where Anas learned of the rituals which were still performed at a ravine in Arima by the sea. They went down to its awesome cave in autumn, past the flowering saffron crocuses, to see for themselves the lair of the monster in the local songs.

In the next year self-satisfied Assyrian officers arrived on the shore of Unqi and started to talk of 'assessment' and demand payments from what they called the king's 'karu(n)'. Anas and Hipposthenes decided to leave, following reports of a new home in the west where the people were less aggressive, where wine and oil were readily sold for metals and anyone with skilled, deft fingers could twist and sell gold and silver for *kerdos*, gain. In the spring, while the cries for 'Adonai/Adonis' were being heard in the city of Byblos, they took a Phoenician ship westwards, in return for rowing and payment. They passed the south-west corner of Crete and beached in the bay where 'a small rock holds back the great waves' from the protected beach. They went up to the little shrine where they drank wine and poured libations, the Phoenicians to Melqart, the Greeks to Poseidon. They then risked the open sea to Cythera and up to the Ionian islands to Ithaca (not Cephallenia), the home of Odysseus and the suitors of whom Homer had once sung.

It was Hipposthenes' turn now to tell Anas stories, the stories of Eumaeus and Penelope, while they waited and traded their Near Eastern finger-rings and seals. Like Homer, he amazed her with tales of a neverland beyond, of the Cyclopes and Circe who once turned men into swine. They took a passage into the world beyond them with the next Euboean crew who were travelling north to Corcyra, across to Italy and Sicily and on through the straits to the bay, our Bay of Naples. At Cumae they stopped and sold Anas' jewellery to the strange Wild Men who came down from the Tiber valley. They bought a plot of land and a horse: they went over to Monkey Island and heard the restless, rumbling Typhon in his second Arima; beyond Cumae they saw the scorched landscape with yet more debris of the Giants. It was here that Anas give birth to a son, Chairippos, who died while still an infant after only three months. They took a spare wine-jar from a batch sent over from Ischia, knocked a hole in its side and inserted their baby's small body. On it Anas laid the lyre-player seal she had been given in Cilicia, the 'land of Mopsus', an amulet against evil spirits as her own north Syrian mother had taught her. They put the jar in a grave and Hipposthenes laid his 'one-bird' cup beside it, a tribute to the life which his son would never grow to enjoy.

A cloud lay over Cumae now, and in the following spring Hipposthenes took his Anas off to see Euboea, knowing he could sell the rings of her gold-working and the studded iron belts and helmets which he had looted from Etruscan war-bands in the west. On the straits between Italy and Sicily they stopped at Zancle with thoughts of Odysseus and monstrous Scylla and Charybdis on their minds. A Chalcidian cousin of Hipposthenes had led the Euboean settlers and it was he in person who showed them the site's most holy relic, the Great Castrator in its pit protected by wooden towers and walls. Returning to the Gulf of Corinth they went up to Delphi to dedicate one of the Etruscan helmets in return for their safe journey. At Delphi they saw the missing link in Anas' stories, the stone which had once been consumed by Kumarbi–Cronos, and as they looked in amazement they heard the Cretic rhythm of Apollo's Cretan priests and their chants of 'Iē Paiēon'.

From Delphi they returned home, across the swirling currents of the narrow Euripus channel to Chalcis where the morale of the fighters was high and 'one last push' was expected to end the Lelantine war by Hippion (the month of July). First, there were the funeral-games for Hipposthenes' young cousin Amphidamas, killed in the recent sea-battle in the gulf. There was a poetic contest in his honour, and Hipposthenes shouted with the best of them for a prize for the 'boy from Ascra', Hesiod, and his poem which brought order and hexameter poetry into so much which he and Anas had seen and discussed in the past six years.

The day after, it was back to the battlefield, with Hipposthenes mounted on his fiery horse Phosphoros, his bronze north Syrian harness fixed for him by Anas, his long hair flowing from the back of his head in true Abantic fashion and a fine Chalcidian sword in his hand. He rode into battle, reliving the valour of an epic hero, no longer the sailor but the warrior in combat. He died, killed by an illicit Eretrian archer, but his life had combined ideals of the *Iliad* and the *Odyssey*, uniting valour and cunning, shown in combat and journeys by sea.

His companions brought his body home and Anas and his female kin began to mourn him for fourteen days. On the eighth day of distress, Anas died too. The two of them were buried, she in a pit-grave with her family's antique pendant from Carchemish around her neck, he, after cremation, in two cauldrons of bronze with his bones wrapped in purple cloth and his horse Phosphoros killed and buried in a pit beside him. They lie, as yet unfound, by the East Gate of Chalcis which leads out onto the Lelantine plain.

'If, indeed, he was ever so . . .', as Homer's Helen and Priam remark so poignantly of their lost loved ones. '*Ei pot' eēn ge . . .*', as if the past might be an illusion. But Hipposthenes' life was a possible life, not a 'buried life', one in which new worlds seemed to open and attest to the stories of the heavenly past, a life indeed, not 'life, as it were . . .'

The Dating of Homer

An eighth-century date for Homer is, I think, the most widely held. In 1966 M. L. West championed the priority of Hesiod, on whom he had written a commentary, and since then he has continued to publish arguments for putting Homer in the first half of the seventh century BC. In 1976 W. Burkert supported such a dating from the mention of Egyptian Thebes in *Iliad* Book 9 in an article which proved influential (for instance, on R. G. Osborne, *Greece in the Making* (1996), 159) but is no longer convincing (my Chapter 19 n. 35, with bibliography attacking it from two different directions). In passing or at length, a seventh-century Homer has been proposed by a few scholars since: they are listed by M. L. West, 'Iliad and *Aethiopis*', CQ 53 (2003), 12 n. 56 ('as many lines of evidence indicate and many modern scholars agree'). Bibliography and arguments for such a dating are advanced accessibly by H. J. van Wees, 'Homer and Early Greece', in Irene J. F. de Jong (ed.), *Homer: Critical Assessments*, vol. 2 (1999), 1–32.

I certainly do not believe them. My arguments for an eighth-century Homer include the following. (i) Nestor's cup on Ischia presupposes Nestor's cup in the *Iliad*, which existed, therefore, before c. 740 BC. Seventh-century Homerists, naturally, do not accept this natural inference (van Wees, 'Homer and Early Greece', 5). (ii) I accept the linguistic analysis of R. Janko, *Homer, Hesiod and the Hymns* (1982), which convincingly places the Homeric epics before Hesiod. Janko's suggested dates may be too precise, but the sequence stands up and requires Homer to belong in the eighth century as Hesiod belongs in the late eighth century, c. 710–700 BC. I accept that Amphidamas at *Works and Days* 654–6 did indeed die in the Lelantine War and that that war was a late eighth-century event. The case was well set out by A. Blakeway, 'The Date of Archilochus', in C. Bailey *et al.* (eds.), *Greek Poetry and Life: Essays Presented to Gilbert Murray* ... (1936), 47–9, and although it has been amplified, contested and despaired of so often, nothing written since persuades me that it is wrong. I accept that Amphidamas did die in the

War, as Plut., *Mor.* 153F eventually implies from earlier sources. Of course seventh-century Homerists see their need to contest the war, the link with Amphidamas and Janko's datings, but they do not persuade me. Their need will ensure that such arguments continue to appear.

(iii) When orally-composed poems are set in an earlier age, their composers tend not to succeed in excluding altogether anachronisms from, or near to, their own lifetime. For example, Homer does not exclude three (Doric, post-Trojan War) tribes on his Rhodes: *Iliad* 2.668. It is interesting to consider a rather different example from more recent times. There was elaborate anachronism in the orally composed Cretan 'epic' of the capture of the German general Kreipe by Paddy Leigh Fermor and his associates on 27 April 1944. It is memorably discussed by J. A. Notopoulos, 'The Genesis of an Oral Heroic Poem', *GRBS* 3 (1960), 135–44. Admittedly, the plot and date encouraged it, but 'the oral tradition adjusts itself to deal with the contemporary'. Homer, however, does succeed in excluding hoplite warfare altogether, a major change of the early seventh century BC: J. Latacz, *Kampfparänese, Kampfdarstellung und Kampfwirklichkeit in der Ilias* ... (1977) fails in the attempt to countenance a 'hoplite Homer'. He was accessibly answered by H. van Wees, 'The Homeric Way of War: The *Iliad* and the Hoplite Phalanx', *G&R* (1994), 1–18 and 131–55, though van Wees also tries to maintain an early seventh-century date for Homer. Homer succeeded in excluding all traces of hoplite warfare because he composed before it existed.

(iv) The *Odyssey* is the later of the two epics, a fact neatly presented by R. B. Rutherford, 'From the *Iliad* to the *Odyssey*', *BICS* 38 (1991), 37–54. Even so, it reflects 'the exploration and not the colonization of the West': I cite here the acute summary and discussion by O. Murray, 'Omero e l'etnografia', *Kokalos*, 34–5 (1988–9), 1–17, at 11. As he rightly sees, Odysseus' contacts with faraway peoples are not 'those of a "culture-hero" who is anticipating the future Greek expansion'. Verses such as Hom., *Od.* 9.110–30 do not alter this point, nor does Hom., *Od.* 7.43–5 on the Phaeacians' town, which merely projects what Homer imagined from his own home region. L. H. Jeffery, *Archaic States of Greece* (1976), 50–51, claims wrongly that the 'extended descriptions of natural scenery in the *Odyssey* . . . [in foreign lands] are one of the debts of literature to the colonial movement'. They are a debt to an earlier generation, the 'travelling heroes' of my Chapter 8. From the mid-730s onwards Greek settlements proliferated in Sicily and elsewhere: I find it more plausible to place the *Odyssey* before this rush began. A date for it *c.* 760–740 BC means that the poet was composing in the age of Pithecussae and Cumae, but not much else, in the faraway west. The 'pre-settlement' tone of Odysseus' travels fits very easily then. It is quite different from the tone of the next travelling 'culture-hero', Heracles, in the seventh to sixth centuries BC (my pp. 207–9, with notes), an age of widespread Greek settlement.

(v) I cannot place Homer's serene acceptance of aristocratic rule after the shock dealt to it by the first tyrannies in the Greek world in the early 650s BC.

(vi) Our earliest datable Greek inscription is still c. 750 BC, but the Greek alphabet existed earlier, as evidence from Gabii to Gordion now implies: my p. 33 and nn. 11–12; p. 71 and n. 83. Those who agree that Homer was aware of writing and/or that writing preserved his epics can date him in the mid- to later eighth century without too much difficulty.

(vii) Archaeologists continue to discuss items in the poems' material culture as if they can set a 'terminus' after which Homer composed. A very thorough survey of this approach and some of its items is given by J. P. Crielaard, 'Homer, History and Archaeology: Some Remarks on the Date of the Homeric World', in J. P. Crielaard (ed.), *Homeric Questions* (1995), 201–88. We disagree on the implications of writing, colonization and 'cult statues' and on a date for Homer 'somewhere in the seventh century BC' (p. 274). Individual such items, whether the Gorgon on Agamemnon's shield (Hom., *Il.* 11.36) or Odysseus' brooch (Hom., *Od.* 19.226–31), are not firm dating-points. Our archaeological record is so very far from definitive: Gorgons were depicted before 700 BC, but are merely not yet known on a shield before 650 BC. Furthermore, items may have been inserted by later singers into earlier wholes. On other grounds, too, M. I. Finley, *The World of Odysseus* (1979, rev. edn.), 149, rightly insists 'no argument may legitimately be drawn from a single line or passage or usage'. Hom., *Il.* 9.404–5 refers to 'such things as the stone threshold of Apollo' contains at rocky Delphi. The 'threshold' implies a temple and the context implies riches. C. A. Morgan, *Athletes and Oracles* (1977), 132, 'can find no convincing evidence for temple construction in the sanctuary area at Delphi before the mid-seventh century at the earliest'. Even if her controversial view were to be correct, the lines in *Iliad* Book 9 can be understood as a later addition without damaging the surrounding sense of 9.403 and 406.

(viii) My discussion of *Iliad* Book 2's '*Ein arimois . . .*' in my Chapters 17 and 19 proposes an individual 'terminus' *before* which Homer composed (the big volcanic eruption on Ischia), not (like archaeological objects) *after* which a verse existed. This terminus is c. 700 BC.

(ix) The ancients' dates for Homer, long after his lifetime, are too high. Herodotus (2.53) knows he is arguing against higher dates than the one he gives, what we calculate as c. 850 BC. We might argue here that he has reckoned '400' years from ten forty-year generations, which should be scaled down, amounting only to 330–350 years: he would then place Homer on our calculation c. 790–760 BC, pretty close to my preferred date. He does not, however, imagine a *seventh*-century Homer, nor (I think) do any others in his mind. If Homer lived in the early seventh century it is surprising that the ancients remembered nothing correctly about his dating or career. H. van Wees, 'Homer and Early Greece', 9 and nn. 23–6, correctly observes that Terpander, just such an early seventh-century poet, was convincingly remembered for performing at the Karneia festival in Sparta in 676 BC: one 'fragment' fits that, famously well (Plut., *Vit. Lyc.* 21.4). Van Wees does not observe that no such 'career knowledge' was preserved about Homer. It did not survive, because he belonged to an earlier era than Terpander.

(x) I am in a minority, perhaps of one, in dating Archilochus c. 740–680 BC, contrary to F. Jacoby, 'The Date of Archilochus', CQ 35 (1941), 97– 109, whose assault on views he found in Oxford is not convincing. Nothing so far known by Archilochus shows that he was writing with knowledge of Homer, but I find his 'tone' easier to place if the epics already existed.

(xi) First, the *Iliad*, then the *Odyssey* were composed, I believe, c. 760–740 BC, probably by one and the same Homer, not two separate poets. This date of composition naturally does not exclude the probability of a few later insertions into the poems we now read. I do not, however, accept two more extreme views of their 'world' and their 'evolution'. Finley, *The World of Odysseus*, 49, proposed 'pinning down the world of Odysseus to the tenth and ninth centuries before Christ'. 'The poet', he claims, 'transmitted his inherited background materials with a deceptively cool precision', partly because they were 'built so much from formulas'. In fact, Homeric 'formulas' do not preserve social values, practices and 'institutions', items which Finley wished to locate c. 950–800 BC. 'Formulas' describe the sea or the dawn or things like horses, items which exist at any period. Alternatively, other scholars are attracted by a slowly evolving epic, even a sort of 'people's Homer'. R. Seaford, *Reciprocity and Ritual* (1994) is an accessible representative of this view, with the further belief that the *Iliad* and *Odyssey* predominated 'over other possible versions of themselves and over the epic cycle' because of 'their exceptional embodiment of the aspirations of the early polis' (pp. 153–4). I cannot see this 'exceptional embodiment' in our *Iliad* nor, apart from the problem of its ending, can I see that our *Odyssey* evolved into its (unified) plot. Neither poem has been seriously shaped by the early to mid-sixth century BC.

The majority view, an *Iliad* and *Odyssey* of the later eighth century BC, is upheld well by I. Morris, 'The Use and Abuse of Homer', *Cl.Ant.* 5 (1986), 81–138.

Notes

ABBREVIATIONS

The ancient sources are mostly identified in S. Hornblower and A. Spawforth (eds.), *The Oxford Classical Dictionary*, 3rd edn. (1996). Modern journals are mostly identified by the abbreviations listed in *L'Année Philologique* (2005), which is available online at http://www.annee-philologique.com.

FGrH   F. Jacoby, *Fragmente der griechischen Historiker* (1923–)
IG   *Inscriptiones Graecae* (1873–)
LIMC   *Lexicon Iconographicum Mythologiae Classicae* (1981–)
RE   A. Pauly, G. Wissowa and W. Kroll, *Real-Encyclopädie d. klassischen Altertumswissenschaft* (1893–)
SEG   *Supplementum epigraphicum Graecum* (1923–)

CHAPTER I

1. Hom., *Il.* 15.79–83; Williams (1993), 179 n. 30; I used these lines to begin lectures in the USA in 1992/3: they are used as an epigraph by Dougherty (2001).
2. Hom., *Il.* 15.170, and Janko (1994), 237, on parallels to travelling 'like a thought'.
3. Sharples (1983), 1–7; Gaskin (1990), 1–15; Williams (1993), 21–58.
4. Morris (1987); Morris (1998), 21–36; Morris (2000), 257–306, for more ideas; Osborne (2004), 87–102, at 91–2, for a survey; de Polignac (2006), 203–24; Burkert (1992C), 533–51, a brilliant overview.
5. Tandy (1997); Hanson (1995).
6. Finley (1956), 140.
7. Popham, Sackett and Themelis (1980), appendix C by J. H. Musgrave, 439.

8. Ridgway (1992), 48.

9. Triantaphyllou (1999), 353–64, at 363.

10. Hom., *Od.* 20.383.

11. Bremmer (1987), 156–71, at 161.

12. Finley (1981), 157–71, at 161.

13. Majno (1975) is excellent here; Robertson (2002), 103–10.

14. Hom., *Il.* 11.265–6; see now Holmes (2007), 45–84.

15. Hom., *Il.* 13.599; Majno (1975), 143.

16. Hom., *Il.* 11.618–44; Ridgway (1997), 325–44.

17. Hom., *Il.* 11.740.

18. Hom., *Od.* 4.220–24.

19. Hom., *Od.* 10.302–6; Scarborough (1991), 138–72, esp. 139 and 141 n. 5. 'Moly' was certainly not our *Galanthus* (snowdrop). ·

20. Kourou (1988), 314–24; on Crete, Coldstream (1979A), 257–63.

21. Curt. 5.2.11.

22. Faure (1987); Panayota (2003), plates 130–33 on women buying scent.

23. Hes., *Op.* 70–95; Hes., *Theog.* 585–602.

24. Zimmerman (1989); Langdon (1993), 51–2, 60–66, 75–6, 81, 103–9, 176–7, 213–22, 225–31, with excellent bibliography; Zaphiropoulou (1999) for a cavalry battle on Paros; Morgan (2001), 195–227, esp. 200–202 and 215–18; Rolley (2007), 63–70.

25. Hom., *Il.* 15.679–84 and *Od.* 5.371; Hom., *Il.* 10.513 is less certain; Lorimer (1950), 504 n. 2.

26. Langdon (1993), 64–6; Hom., *Il.* 15.679–84, has one rider jumping across four horses, but it is decidedly similar. Was this Attic cup showing something Homeric, I cannot help wondering?

27. Athenagoras, *Leg.* 17.3: his source is unknown. Lubtchansky (2005), 1, also cites this neglected passage.

28. Himmelmann (1990), esp. 32, which I follow, despite Schmölder-Veit (2005), 29–42, at 34; Böhm (1990) and (2003), 363–70 on the Near Eastern figures. I am particularly grateful to Dr Annette Haug for detailed help with this vexed question.

29. Ahlberg (1971) for the change; Himmelmann (2000), 253–323, at 298; Osborne (1997), 504–28.

30. *IG* 7.52, with McDonnell (1991), 183 n. 2.

31. Thuc. 1.6.5 and McDonnell (1991), 182–93, with full bibliography and a slightly different conclusion from mine.

CHAPTER 2

Most (but not all) of the cultures I touch on here are discussed in detail in *The Cambridge Ancient History*, 2nd edn., vols. 3/1 and 3/2, edited by John Boardman, I. E. S. Edwards, N. G. L. Hammond *et al.* (1982 and 1991). The latest of many exhibition catalogues on the Phoenicians and their western contacts is *La Méditerrannée des phéniciens de Tyr à Carthage* (2007), a magnificent work which cites the previous major exhibitions and gives further scholarly references, especially to works on Phoenician craftsmanship which my notes to this chapter presuppose.

1. Bickerman (1980), 75–9.
2. Rawson (1996), 113 and 123–4.
3. Thapar (2000), 119.
4. Grenet (2005), 29–51, an excellent study, esp. 47 nn. 3–4.
5. Radner (2003), 37–64.
6. Tadmor (1994), 232–7 and 269–73.
7. Luckenbill (1927), vol. 2, p. 84, with Limet (1992), 37–55.
8. Meiggs (1982), 74–81.
9. Tadmor (1994), 105, translating Iran Stele II B 18–24.
10. Ponchi (1991).
11. 2 Kings 18: 34 with Hawkins (2004), 151–64; Gonçalves (1986) is fundamental, with Tadmor (1994), 273–82; Kuhrt (2002), 13–34.
12. Tadmor (1994), 81, translating Annals 23, lines 17–18; Oded (1979) on deportations.
13. Taşyürek (1975), 169–80.
14. Tadmor (1994), 177; Cogan (1974), 48–58.
15. Daniel 3: 1, where I think that the gold statue of Tiglath Pileser underlies the story, transposed to Nebuchadnezzar near Babylon.
16. Bickerman (1986), 282–98, esp. 290–91.
17. Dalley (1985), 31–48.
18. Bickerman (1988), 9–12; Becking (1992).
19. Gonçalves (1986), 110.
20. Isaiah 7: 14; and Caird (1980), 78–9, for a clear exposition.
21. Translation given in Kuhrt (1995), 629–31; Cannuyer (1995), 43–58, for contents.
22. Frame (1999), 31–57, and Redford (1999), 58–60, despite whom I opt for the simpler conclusion, that Shebitku (who handed over Yamani of

Ashdod) ruled *c*. 715–695 BC, and Shabaku (who killed 'Bocchoris') ruled *c*. 730–715 BC, replacing Bocchoris in the (early?) 720s.

23. Oded (1974), 38–49; Kestemont (1983), 53–78, esp. 71; Tadmor (1994), 171 n. 16, however, for huge payments from Tyre.

24. Baurain (1986), 7–28, and Markoe (2005) for the names and identities; Niemeyer (2000), 89–115, with relevant bibliography; Lipinski (2004), 267–336, an admirable survey.

25. 1 Kings 9: 11; Briend and Humbert (1980).

26. Culican (1986), 549–69, though the lily in question is not the 'Martagon' (550); Caubet and Poplin (1987), 273–301, at 300, on elephant-ivory 'brusquement utilisé'; Caubet, Fontan, Herrmann and le Meaux (2007), 205–15, a brilliant survey; on purple, Doumet (2004), 38–49.

27. Bordreuil (2007), 72–83, a lucid summary; for the increasing use of writing in eighth-century South Arabia, which my 'China to Cadiz' omits, Caubet and Gadja (2003), 1220–38.

28. Bikai (1983), 396–402.

29. Yon (1987), 357–74, esp. 366–7; Lipinski (1983), 209–34, with bibliography, although I do not accept his conclusion.

30. Text in Lipinski (2004), 46–9: I differ about the 'Carthage' in question and the attempted link with Hiram of Tyre, not Sidon. Katzenstein (1973) admits to a bias towards Tyre, eclipsing Sidon.

31. Bikai (2004), 302–11.

32. Joseph., *AJ* 8.324 = Menander, *FGrH* 783, F3, for Auza; Docter, Niemeyer, Nijboer and van der Pflicht (2005), 557–77, on Carthage.

33. Bafico, Oggiano, Ridgway and Garbini (1997), 47–54; Ridgway (2006), 239–52.

34. Van Berchem (1967), 307–38, a chain of brilliant speculation.

35. Walbank (1957), 665–9; Feeney (2007), 86–100.

36. Sagona (2002), 24–39; Lipinski (2004), 375–80, with due caution about an early phase.

37. Aubet (2001), 305–37, with map on 306.

38. Arruda (1999–2000), esp. 185–218; Habibi (1992), 145–53, esp. 151, and Lopez Pardo (2005), 46–60, esp. 49 n. 16; El Khayari (2007), 294–5, is important.

39. Diod. Sic. 5.22; Timaeus in Plin., *HN* 4.104; Penhallurick (1986); Cunliffe (1988).

40. Nuttall (2007), 300 and 303.

41. Frankenstein (1979), 263–94.

42. Brown (1960), 97–102; Markoe (1998), 233–41, suggests iron was imported from Crete, but 235 n. 5 also cites local iron in the Lebanon; Morris

(1992), 132, over-emphasizes iron, I think, as a Phoenician import: Ezekiel 27: 12 cites iron as only one item from Tarshish.

43. Markoe (1992–3), 11–31; Ezekiel 27: 12 cites tin from Tarshish too.

44. Ps.-Arist., *Mir. ausc.* 844ᵃ18; Gill (1988), 1–12.

45. Gonzalez de Canales, Serrano and Llompart (2006), 13–30.

46. 1 Kings 10: 22, with Lipinski (2004), 225 and 226–65, for the controversies; Ezekiel 27: 12 and 27: 25, though later in date.

47. Ezekiel 27: 12; Diakonoff (1992), 168–93, a fundamental study.

48. Caubet (1983), 193–8; Savio (2004).

49. Gras (1989), 128–47.

50. Loud and Altman (1938); Caubet (1995); Reade (1995), 225–51.

51. Luckenbill (1927), vol. 2, p. 42; for his predecessor in *c.* 880–860 BC, who was 'gathering fruit continuously like a squirrel', the excellent text in Wiseman (1984), 37–43.

52. Parpola (1995), 47–77, a fine study; Fontan (2004), 456–63.

53. Stronach (1990), 171–80, at 172–3; Karmel Thomason (2001), 63–96; I thus reject Wiseman (1983), 137–44, at 138 n. 21: 'KUR.Hamani could equally well refer to the Elamite region.'

54. Fuchs (1994), 340–41, text 37B.

55. Damerji (1995), 1–83.

56. Prag (1989), 159–66, with the (still controversial) redating summarized in Brixhe (2004), 271–89.

CHAPTER 3

The connections between Greeks and others in the Mediterranean are excellently illustrated through the essays and catalogue of objects co-ordinated as part of the Cultural Olympiad in 2003: N. C. Stampolidis (ed.), *Sea Routes . . . from Sidon to Huelva: Interconnections in the Mediterranean, 16th–6th c. BC* (2003). W. Burkert, *Die orientalische Epoche in der griechischen Religion und Literatur* (1984), remains a brilliantly concise and adventurous study of the possible impact of Near Eastern events, texts and images on the Greeks: the title of the English translation, *The Orientalizing Revolution* (1992), is a little misleading. T. J. Dunbabin, *The Greeks and their Eastern Neighbours* (1957), is a brilliant pair to it whose interest is enhanced by the passage of time. Ian Morris, *Archaeology as Cultural History* (2000), advances bold interpretations of the diffusion of myths, the so-called 'Dark Ages' and the arrival of writing. The essays in S. Deger-Jalkotzy and I. S. Lemos (eds.), *Ancient Greece: From the Mycenaean Palaces to the Age of*

Homer (2006), give an invaluable, up-to-date regional view. The art of the Greek eighth century is memorably discussed by N. Himmelmann, *Reading Greek Art* (1998), accessible now in English. There are still many penetrating observations on art and crafts in L. H. Jeffery, *Archaic States of Greece* (1976), a tribute to the sharp eye of the great expert on early Greek inscriptions and the alphabet.

1. Fuchs (1994), 440, with references; Stylianou (1989), 8–15, is important; Lipinski (2004), 51–4; Na'aman (1998), 239–47; Yon and Malbran-Labat (1995), 159–79, are decisive on the stele's original siting.
2. Stylianou (1989), 8–15.
3. Fuchs (1994), 440, with references.
4. Fuchs (1994), 319, lines 117–19; Elayi and Cavigneaux (1979), 59–75.
5. Parker (2000), 69–77, with bibliography: the translation is contested at minor points. Mark (2005), 104–14, importantly challenges van Doorninck (1982), 277–86, and the theory that Greek ships had rams by *c.* 900 BC.
6. Fuchs (1998), 124–31, with bibliography, but not the new evidence about Egyptian pharaohs' dates.
7. Brinkman (1989), 53–71, has led the sceptics; but Rollinger (1997), 167–72, is one of those still rightly unconvinced.
8. Buchner and Ridgway (1993), 378–82; Ridgway (1999B), 143–52, wrote unaware of the new evidence bearing on Bocchoris' dates in Egypt.
9. Hdt. 2.44; 6.46–7; Lipinski (2004) is still cautious about dating.
10. Boardman (1999C), 54–94, a masterly survey; Winter (1976), 1–22, and Gubel (1987), 20–34, on ivories, with my Chap. 2 n. 26 above.
11. Johnston (2003), 263–76, summarizes the present position; Ruijgh (1997), 553–603, a longer overview.
12. Brixhe (2004), 271–89, with excellent bibliography.
13. Powell (1991) vigorously enlarges Wade-Gery (1952), 11–14, but like the contributors to the review in the *Cambridge Archaeological Journal*, 2 (1992), 115–26, I cannot believe him.
14. Csapo (2005), excellent on modern theories of 'myth'; Hansen (1997), 463–88, on folk tale.
15. Antonaccio (1995A); Morris (1988), 750–61, and (2000), 267–73; Kistler (1998).
16. Demand (2004), 61–84; Forrest (2000), 280–92; Morris (1987); Malkin (1987), 261–2, for various views.
17. Parker (1996), 28 and n. 65, on early calendars; Forrest (1957), 160–75; Parke (1967) and (1985), on oracles; Burkert (1992C), 533–51, on religion.
18. West (1997), 61–106.

19. Culican (1986), 581–614, on the 'Huntsman's Day' narrative and much else of fundamental importance; Hermary (1992), 129–38, not all of which I believe; Hom., *Il.* 18.570–72, the Linus song.

20. Hainsworth (1991), a fundamental study among many.

21. Graziosi (2002), 20–124.

22. Mitchell (1990), 183–93, at 184–5, for such days at Hadrianic Oenoanda.

23. Hom., *Od.* 17.518–20.

24. Janko (1998), 1–13, my preferred view, perhaps with a touch of writing helping an 'orally derived' whole, as in Foley (2002) and Dowden (1996), 47–61; Kullmann (1984), 307–23, and West (2003B), 1–14, esp. 1–14, (2001), 10–11, and (2003A), 479–88, believe in a literate, textually composing Homer: sadly, I cannot.

25. Hom., *Od.* 6.112–32; Verg., *G.* 2.88–9, with Mynors' note *ad loc.*; Lib., *Or.* 11.236; *Ep.* 1257; and Julian., *Ep.* 58, 401A (written to Libanius!); Ps.-Julian., *Ep.* 80.

26. West (2003A), 479–88, for brilliant surgery which I do not think to be necessary; de Romilly (1995), 103–13, on Homeric gardens.

27. Gould (2001), 239–40.

28. Malkin (1998), with full bibliography; Bérard (1957), still a fine collection of sources; I do not count the 'Ionian Migrators' as 'returning heroes'.

29. Hom., *Il.* 2.455–79.

30. Wiegand and Schrader (1904), 12–13, on similar flocks in the delta of the nearby Maeander river in early 1898: P. J. Thonemann alerted me to this.

31. Hom., *Il.* 2.780–85.

CHAPTER 4

The fundamental studies on early Greek items in the Near East are by J. N. Coldstream, especially his 'Exchanges between Phoenicians and Early Greeks', *National Museum News, Beirut*, 11 (2002), with an acutely chosen bibliography. Joanna Luke, *Ports of Trade: Al Mina and Geometric Greek Pottery in the Levant* (2003), contains very helpful lists, but more has turned up already and a pendent semi-circle *skyphos* is announced near Pella in the Decapolis east of the Jordan: see the intervention by L. Nigro in *Mediterranea: Quaderni di archeologia etrusco-italica* (2005), 647. I hesitate, therefore, to link 'phases' of such imports into the Levant with local phases of change in Euboea and elsewhere. This approach has been taken in very different styles by Irene S. Lemos, 'The Changing Relationship of the Euboeans and the

East', in Alexandra Villing (ed.), *The Greeks in the East* (2005), 53–60, and Ian Morris, 'Negotiated Peripherality in Iron Age Greece: Accepting and Resisting the East', in P. N. Kardulias (ed.), *World Systems Theory in Practice: Leadership, Production and Exchange* (1993), 63–84. Recent finds of Euboean pottery at Sidon are not yet published but will surely fill out the picture.

On the Lefkandi connection, the excavator M. Popham gave a groundbreaking lecture in Oxford which was a cardinal point in my re-thinking of Chapters 4–7 of this book. It appeared as 'Precolonization: Early Greek Contact with the East', in G. R. Tsetskhladze and F. de Angelis (eds.), *The Archaeology of Greek Colonisation: Essays Dedicated to Sir John Boardman* (1994), 11–34. The site was then further illuminated by I. S. Lemos in *The Protogeometric Aegean* (2002), which is basic to my chapter. Like her, I was inspired by V. R. Desborough's ideas on a 'ceramic *koinē*' between Euboea, Thessaly and relevant islands, set out in his essay in F. Emmison and Roy Stephens (eds.), *Tribute to an Antiquary: Essays Presented to Mark Fitch by Some of his Friends* (1976), 25–40. Typically, he was kind enough to give me a copy in typescript when I first joined him as a Fellow of New College, Oxford in autumn 1977.

1. Malkin (2003), 153–70, esp. 156, on 'social and religious modalities of collective memory'. For sceptical rejection, which I do not share, Osborne (1998), 251–69.

2. Hom., *Od.* 14.290–97; 15.417.

3. Hom., *Od.* 13.272, not exploited by Winter (1995), 247–72.

4. Hom., *Od.* 15.417.

5. Hom., *Il.* 23.743–7; Crielaard (2003), 49–62, an important study: for a similar travelling object in the Levant, see catalogue entry no. 163 in *La Méditerranée des phéniciens* (2007), 340.

6. Snodgrass (1998) for the debate; Himmelmann (1998), 67–102, brilliant on narrative art in general; Coldstream (1991), 37–56.

7. Papadopoulos (2005), p. 577.

8. Karageorghis (2002B), 115–41, surveying this debated question.

9. Fantalkin (2001), 117–25; Coldstream (2003A), 247–58; Finkelstein (2004), 181–8; Gilboa, Sharon and Zorn (2004), 32–59.

10. Munger (2003), 66–82, and Gilboa, Sharon and Zorn (2004), 32–59.

11. Catling (1998), 365–78.

12. Lemos (2002), 197–212.

13. Gilboa (1999), 109–39.

14. Coldstream (1998A), 303–10.

15. Schreiber (2003), an exceptional study, convincingly challenging the proposed 'Phoenician' origin and Aegean factories of 'black-on-red'.

16. Coldstream (1998B), 353–60, at 357–9, and (2003A), 247–58.

17. Bonatz (1998), 211–29.

18. Kopcke (2002), 109–17, on Tell Hadar; Bonatz (1998), 214–15: 'a date at the beginning of Protogeometric, i.e. shortly after 1050 BC, best paralleled in the fill of the Toumba building, Lefkandi II.1.23 and plate 49, 166–7'. The piece was found in 'Iron IB Level 7C', which could stretch on from the mid-eleventh to the mid-tenth centuries. Level 8 is dated, tentatively, c. 1050 BC (p. 137). The parallel piece at the Toumba belongs c. 960–950 BC. Bonatz suggests that the Syria piece is Argive, a prototype for a similar Argive import at Lefkandi. The piece is fragmentary and not distinctive, but I incline to an Attic-Euboean origin, c. 960 BC, as at Lefkandi too.

19. Courbin (1993), 95–114, esp. 104.

20. Coldstream (2003A), 247–58, at 253.

21. Coldstream, with Bikai (1988), 35–44; Coldstream (1989), 90–96.

22. Popham, Sackett and Themelis (1980); Lemos (2002); Lemos, *Archaeological Reports*, 52 (2006–7), 38–40, on the settlement which Dr Lemos and her expert team kindly showed me in 2007.

23. Popham, Sackett and Themelis (1980), 423–7, for a survey. The main candidates now are: (i) Argoura (Knoepfler 1981, 289–329; opposed well by Bérard 1985, 268–75); (ii) Lelanton (G. L. Huxley, as suggested to Jeffery, 1976, 69); (iii) Oichalia (Forrest, Boardman and many others: certainly wrong, as it was in 'District 5' of the territory on the north-east-facing coast: map in Knoepfler 1997, 402–3: was it Viglatoura, perhaps?); (iv) 'Old Eretria' (not Strabo's, however, at 10.1.10; Mazarakis Ainian 1987, 3–23, summarizes the long doxography and the case against); (v) We do not know (though Lefkandiots afforced the (new?) Eretria c. 850–800, to the east of them).

24. Summarized in Lemos (2002), 226–7; the first 'eastern' jug was in Skoubris T.48, in Lefkandi I.347–8, plate 270.

25. Summarized, with big bibliography, in Lemos (2002), 161–8. The suggestion that the knife might signify the lady's role as a priestess is mine.

26. The apt phrase is Peter Brown's (1977) in a later context.

27. Hom., *Il.* 23.165–83. I cannot agree with Poplin (1995), 253–66, that at 23.172 Achilles is 'groaning' at the need to kill horses, whose presence on the pyre is therefore skated over quickly by the poet. '*Megala stenachizōn*' is a formulaic phrase. The 'groaning' is for Patroclus and the sad occasion. If Poplin really believes that five living horses can be put on a bonfire, I would need ('groaning greatly') to see him do it.

28. Hom., *Il.* 6.419–20; *Il.* 23.786; *Il.* 7.87–91.

29. Frederiksen (1979), 277–311, at 294, for this good phrase.

30. Lemos (2002), 140–46 and 216–17, for a survey.

31. Blome (1984), 9–21; Antonaccio (1995B), 5–28, not always accurate about the site; West (1997), 398.

32. Crielaard (1998), 187–205, at 189; Rizza (1979), 194–7; Reese (1995), 35–42; Hadjisavvas, *BCH* 124 (2000), 697.

33. For example, Coldstream (2002), 15–32, at 19, and (2003B), 36–8.

34. Carter (1998), 172–7, on the little jugs which she considers to be Egyptian 'antiques' and possibly brought over in the tenth century from the Levant.

35. Lemos (2002), 165, on T.39, with Coldstream (2002), 15–32, at 21–2.

36. Lemos (2007A), 275–80.

37. Popham and Lemos (1999), 151–7: a forthcoming study by J. H. Kroll shows, importantly, that the weights in this grave are local and varied: they are not Near Eastern, a point supporting Lemos (2003), 187–96.

38. Lemos (2005), 53–60, at 56, suggested a decline in Euboean imports to the east *c.* 900–850 BC, but the recent finds at Tel Rehov suggest caution, still, about any 'gap'.

39. Coldstream (1979B), 255–69, and (1995A), 187–214; Crielaard (1999), 261–90, esp. fig. 2; Lemos and Hatcher (1991), 197–208.

40. Coldstream and Mazar (2003), 29–48.

41. Dorsey (1991); Schreiber (2003), 78–80.

42. Bikai (1987A) and (1987B), 125–8.

43. Bikai (1987C), 1–19; Masson and Sznycer (1972), 13–20, on the inscription.

44. Joseph., *AJ* 8.146 and *Ap.* 1.118, have a splendid textual problem in their manuscripts. I follow von Gutschmid in reading *itukaiois*, therefore 'Utica', and not the (emended) *Kitiois*. The problem is clearly and correctly set out by Bikai (1992), 241–8.

45. Coldstream (1969), 1–8; Steph. Byz. s.v. Melos; Hdt. 1.105, 2.44, 4.747, 6.47.

46. Coldstream (2003B), 70–71; Blandin (2007), vol. 1, pp. 90–91.

47. Coldstream (2007), 135–9, for the changing debate; I disagree with him about the implications of the Near Eastern seals in some of the women's graves; for slave-jewellers, Meiggs-Lewis, *GHI* 79. A47 and p. 247; Hyp., *C. Athenog.* 23–5.

48. Mazarakis Ainian (2002), 149–78, and (2007).

49. Van de Moortel and Zachou (2003–4), 39–48; *Archaeological Reports*, 53 (2006–7), 40–41.

50. A huge bibliography, surveyed (with an independent viewpoint) by Papa-

dopoulos (2005), 580–88; note also E. Scarlatidou and W. Constantinidou, *AEMTh*. 17 (2003), 213–21, on Gonna, about 7 miles south of Thessalonica; M. Tiverios, H. Manakidou, ibid., 195–9, on Kabournaki, and M. Tiverios, S. Gimatzidis, *AEMTh*. 16 (2002), 223–33.

51. Vokotopoulou (1996), 319–28.

52. Carington-Smith and Vokotopoulou (1992), 495–502; Papadopoulos (2005), 589–90, refers to Orientalia, not yet published, 'some of which were thought to be Phoenician'.

53. I reject Hammond (1995), 307–15, and his attempts to place the '*chalkidikon genos*' of Hdt. 7.185 and 8.127 back in the early post-Mycenaean period. My arguments are more or less those of Mele (1998), 217–28, at 221–4.

54. Thuc. 4.110.1 means that Torone is a Chalcidian-Euboean settlement: I agree with Hornblower (1997), 177–86. Knoepfler (1990), 99–115, is important on the calendar (despite Papadopoulos 2005, 587–8), but I hesitate to track it back here into the early 'Dark Ages'. Vokotopoulou (1996), 319–28, is also still fundamental.

55. Coldstream (1996), 133–45, with esp. 142 on the oldest MG II *krater*, on T.Pyre 14; perhaps later texts linking Attica and Euboea are a memory of this, not just of Athens' fifth-century 'empire'; Pind., *Pae.* 5; Ps.-Scymn. 571–7; Strabo 10.1.8.

56. Coldstream (1995C), 391–405; Liston and Papadopoulos (2006), 7–38; Morris and Papadopoulos (2004), 225–42.

57. Coldstream (2003B), 79–81; the 'Isis' figurine cannot now be a main argument that those ladies were priestesses of Demeter. They may have been, but similar figurines occur in Lefkandi Toumba burials, not obviously with priestesses.

58. Coldstream (1982A), 261–75, is no longer convincing here.

59. Ion of Chios, *FGrH* 392, F1–3; Lemos (2002), 240, and items exhibited in the island's Archaeological Museum.

60. Paus. 7.5.5–8, with Graham (1978), 61–98, esp. 90–91. There is a '*chalcitis*', too, in Paus. 7.5.12 and at least by 340 BC a 'harbour of the Chalcidians' in H. Engelmann and R. Merkelbach (eds.), *Die Inscriften von Erythrai und Klazomenai*, vol. 1 (1972), nos. 41 and 151.

61. Crielaard (1993), 139–46, and (2006), 271–97, also discusses this well.

62. Blandin (2007), vol. 1, pp. 90–91, 101–7, 109–22, with bibliography.

63. Crielaard (2002), 239–96.

64. Coldstream (1983), 201–7.

65. Crielaard (1999), 261–90.

66. Ezekiel 27: 13; Diakonoff (1992), 168–93, at 185.

67. Riis (1970), 164.

68. Themelis (1980), 78–102; Schmid (1999), 273–93, esp. 278 n. 21 and 283 n. 48.

69. Theophr., *De Odor.* 28.

70. Schreiber (2003), 65–73; Faure (1987).

71. Hom., *Il.* 2.537; Thgn. 784 and 892; Walker (2004), 14 and n. 48, quoting Hiller von Gaertringen, *A Lexicon of Greek Personal Names*, vol. 1 (1987), 347, for *oinos*-names at Eretria, but note also ibid., vol. 3/B (2004), 321–2, for Thessaly.

72. Leake (1835), 253: 'The chief produce of the island is wine; from Cumae and Kastrevala alone, 20,000 barrels of 54 okes are sent to Smyrna and the Black Sea'; Robert (1978A), 535–8, alerted me to this. For the volcano, Philippson (1951), 615–22, with repeated stress on the area's fruits, crops and fine vineyards (615). I am extremely grateful to Sylvian Fachard for taking me to the region and sharing his detailed knowledge of it.

73. Brodersen (2001), 25–8, with earlier bibliography. However, (i) Steph. Byz. sometimes errs but he depends on informed, if varied, Hellenistic sources; Fraser (1996), 3–6, for a summary; Whitehead (1994), 98–124, discusses errors, but a total invention of a place is another matter; (ii) I cannot evade Strabo 5.4.3., as Brodersen has to: see my Chap. 9 n. 37 below; (iii) Scymnus 238 is not evidence for a first foundation of Italian Cumae by Aeolian Cumae: see my Chap. 9 n. 37 below. Ancient Cumae lies somewhere near modern Koumi, perhaps on or near one of the local Mycenaean sites overlooking Stomio Bay.

74. Sapouna-Sakellaraki (1997), 35–42, and (2002), 117–49; Lemos and Hatcher (1986), 323–37.

75. Ezekiel 27: 18–19; Millard (1962), 201–3, though he wrongly places Helbun about 15 miles north-east of Hama, following A. Musil, *Palmyrena* (1928), 230–33. Dussaud (1927), 265–7, is preferable: he cites later testimony to fine grapes here (287), and notes that locals, according to al Bosrani, sold snow, serving it in the shops and even transporting it as far as Cairo in times without fridges.

76. Coldstream (1979B), 253–69, and (1995A), 187–214; Crielaard (1999), 261–90.

77. Murray (1995), 33–43, without, however, the important Pryor (1988), esp. 6–7, 94–6, 116–17 for what I discuss.

78. Ibn Jubayr (trans. 1952), 326–7.

79. Dem. 56.20, trusted (unwisely) by Casson (1988), 271 n. 3; contrast, however, Tammuz (2006), 145–62.

80. Crielaard (2000A), 51–63.

81. 2 Samuel 8: 18, 15: 18, 20: 7, 20: 23; 1 Kings 1: 38; Burkert (1992A), 25, with proper caution.

82. Wade-Gery (1952), 8–9 and 92: 'The inscription makes it clear that Kyprios is intended as a person, not as an ethnic qualifying Eldios.' I agree, having seen a squeeze copy with W. G. Forrest and the text in the Chios Museum, *pace* West (1997), 620.

83. Johnston (2003), 263–76, for the present position; among the vast bibliography see especially Powell (1991), Brixhe (2004), 271–300, and my Chap. 8 nn. 48–9.

84. Marek (1993), 27–44; I doubt Csapo (2000), 105–7, who favours multiple origins; Dr P. Haarer suggested to me a possible origin on board ship; Aupert (2003), 107–21, for early inscriptions from Amathus, so far no earlier than the sixth century BC.

85. Burkert (1992A), 29, and (2004), 19.

CHAPTER 5

The complex history and archaeology of Cyprus in this general period is brilliantly surveyed by V. Karageorghis, *Early Cyprus* (2002), a book for specialists and non-specialists, with excellent illustrations and many penetrating comments on recent theories and discoveries about the island's past; O. Casabonne, *La Cilicie dans l'époque achéménide* (2004), is a very full study of the geography and topography; Claude Mutafian, *La Cilicie au carrefour des empires*, vols. 1–2 (1988), is a clear and penetrating study by a former *normalien*; J. D. Hawkins, *Corpus of Hieroglyphic Luwian Inscriptions*, vols. 1/1 and 1/2 (2000), is the masterpiece among recent studies touching on this area; A. M. Jasink, 'I greci in Cilicia nel periodo neo-assirio', *Mesopotamia*, 24 (1989), 117–26, is a recent, brief survey of the Assyrian evidence for this region and the gaps in our knowledge.

1. Hom., *Od.* 17.443; Hom., *Il.* 11.20; Baurain (1980), 277–308; Ribichini (1982), 479–500; West (1997), 57.

2. Iacovou (2005), 17–44; Iacovou (2006), 315–36.

3. Iacovou (2002), 101–22; Petit (1999), 108–20.

4. Chrestou (1998), 207–16, and esp. the discussion by Karageorghis and others, 229–320: 'I put "*tophet*" in inverted commas' (230).

5. Yon (1992A), 301–6, and (1999), 17–33; Coldstream (1986), 321–9, esp. 326–7; Karageorghis (1977), 61–4, for five fragments, Euboean to my eye, from pieces found at Kition, dating to SPG-MGI.

6. Karageorghis (1967–78) and (2002A), 19–29; despite Coldstream (2003B), 349–50, who still emphasizes the *combination* of so many 'Homeric' features.

7. Gjerstad (1979), 89–93.

8. Coldstream (1983), 201–7, and (1986), 321–9, at 326–7, noting parallels with Amathus T.194 and elsewhere; Crielaard (1993), 139–46.

9. Coldstream (1979B), 253–69.

10. Gisler (1995), 11–95; Coldstream (1994B), 77–86; Chrestou (1996), 165–82, important on the origin of Cesnola's so-called 'Kourion Treasure', now in the Metropolitan Museum; Marankou (2000), on its 'excavator'.

11. Coldstream (1994A), 155–9.

12. Xen., *An.* 1.2.22; Dagron and Feissel (1987), no. 109, pp. 188–9.

13. Dio Chrys., *Or.* 34.21.

14. Ozbayogou (2003), 159–72, at 165–71.

15. Robert (1963), 22–7, and Casabonne (2004), 32–3, on buffaloes; 1 Kings 10: 28 and Hdt. 3.90 on horses; Casabonne (2004), 34 and n. 91, on 'Sizzu' as a 'land of horses'.

16. Hom., *Il.* 6.201.

17. Strabo 13.1.60–62; 14.4.1, with Leaf (1923), 305–16; Dupont-Sommer and Robert (1964), 52–3, with notes.

18. Bing (1973), 346–90, but Diod. Sic. 18.62.2; 19.56.5; and 20.108.2 all make topographic sense if Cyinda is Anavarza. It explains, too, why the treasurer Harpalus was lodged at nearby Tarsus in Theopompus, *FGrH* 115, F254A–B; at 14.5.10, Strabo's *'hyperkeitai'* is inaccurate, as often in his work.

19. See Chap. 13, pp. 229–33.

20. Casabonne (2004), 79; Tac., *Hist.* 2.3; Apollod., *Bibl.* 3.14.3; Fourrier (2003), 79–91, is too sceptical about the pottery.

21. Houwink ten Cate (1961), 127 and 130, for names; Kammenhuber (1990), 188–95, with bibliography.

22. Hawkins (2000), 3; Hawkins (1986), 363–76.

23. Tekoglu and Lemaire (2000), 961–1006, with bibliography and lists of the inscriptions at 992 nn. 59–63 and 1006 nn. 108–9.

24. Lemaire (1983), 9–19.

25. Hawkins (2000), 44, preferable to the earlier dating still canvassed by Lipinski (2004), 116–19; Röllig (1999), 50–81; Bron (1979).

26. Winter (1979), 115–52, at 138–9.

27. Sinclair (1990), vol. 4, pp. 277–82, a clear summary.

28. Çambel (1999), 20–23 and frontispiece, and plates 32–3.

29. Hawkins (2000), 53; Hawkins (1980), 213–25, and (1989), 189–98.

30. Mellink (1950), 141–59, at 144.

31. Dio Chrys., *Or.* 35.1–2; Bing (1971), 99–109, was even inclined, wrongly, to accept Tarsus as a colony of Lindos.

32. Strabo 14.5.8; Pompon. Mela 1.77, with Hind (1999), 77–84.

33. Arslan (2003), 258–61, for excavations so far.

34. Casabonne (2004), 41–2 and n. 114; 80–81.

35. Hom., *Il.* 23.186; it helps to explain Ar., *Lys.* 944 (the *rhodion muron* there is a typical *funerary* oil).

36. Dr M. Rix confirmed this to me from his own field work; twice-flowerers in Verg., *G.* 4.119, with R. A. B. Mynors' *Commentary*, 274, unconvincingly considering it 'probably a poetical expression for an unusually long season'.

37. Ridgway (1992), 60–63, for the type.

38. Arr., *Anab.* 2.5.9.

39. Hdt. 3.91.7.

40. Hodos (2000), 145–53.

41. Sinclair (1990), vol. 4, pp. 309–11, on the 'Little Gate', *portella*, here; in antiquity, Xen., *An.* 1.4.9; Callisth., *FGrH* 124, F35; Hammond (1994), 15–26.

42. Hdt. 3.91.1, with Asheri (1990), 304–7, on the value of the list.

43. *RE*, vol. 22/1 (1953), 421–6, s.v. 'Poseidion'.

44. Xen., *An.* 1.4.6; Arr., *Anab.* 2.6.2.

45. Sinclair (1990), vol. 4, pp. 309–12.

46. Pind., *Ol.* 7.19; Thuc. 7.57.6.

47. *IG* 12.9, 1189, 20–29; Vokotopoulou (1996), 319–28, esp. 326: 'holy places of Poseidon, or Poseideia, which the Eretrians used to found on the coast close to their colonies'.

48. Heidel (1953), 117–88, at 146–51.

49. Abydenos, *FGrH* 685, F5(6), who quotes what 'he says', that is Sennacherib's own text, surely known in Greek through Berossos; Berossos, *FGrH* 680, F7 c.31, known from Alex. Polyhistor.

50. Arr., *Anab.* 2.5.3; Casabonne (2004), 122–3.

51. Abydenos, *FGrH* 685, F5; I disagree with Momigliano (1934), 412–16.

52. Dalley (1999), 73–81, at 76.

53. Niebuhr already proposed to read 'Athene', rightly, in Abydenos, *FGrH* 685, F5(6). The problem of the 'temple' is wholly misunderstood by Burstein (1978), 24, his F2A and F28.

54. Arr., *Anab.* 2.5.1; Robert (1951), 256–9.

55. Houghton (1984), 99–110, esp. 102 and plates 12–13.

56. Arr., *Anab.* 2.5–2.7; Lane Fox (1973), 162–72.

CHAPTER 6

E. Lipinski, *Itineraria Phoenicia* (2004), deals in full with the main 'Phoenician' coast, and C. Doumet-Serhal (ed.), *A Decade of Archaeology and History in the Lebanon* (2004), has magnificent photographs of major sites and much else. The short chapters on 'Les Sites' in *La Méditerranée des phéniciens de Tyr à Carthage* (2007), 267–76, are importantly up to date with recent bibliographies. D. Bonatz, 'Some Considerations on the Material Culture of Colonial Syria in the Iron Age', *EVO* 16 (1993), 123–57, has much of relevance, but he does not distinguish correctly between 'Posideion' and Ras el-Bassit at this date and his sections on Al Mina are now out of date.

1. Bordreuil (1988), 301–14, esp. 310–11, for a *'par 'ar Hmn'* which I would explain as Pahri-Pagras at the foot of the Amanus range; Spuler, in RE, vol. 18 (1942), 9311; Sinclair (1990), vol. 4, pp. 266–71.
2. Bell (1928), 336.
3. Key Fowden (1999), 2.
4. Seyrig (1970), 290–311, at 297–8.
5. Waldbaum (1994), 55–8; Luke (2003), 34 n. 85, thinks the Ekron sherd 'may have been part of a fill'.
6. Schreiber (2003), 160–62; Herrea Gonzalez and Balensi (1986), 159–71.
7. Coldstream (2003A), 247–58.
8. Coldstream and Mazar (2003), 29–48 and figs. 7–8.
9. Amos 6: 4 ff., with the important notes in Wolff (1973), 273–5, the essential guide; Eissfeldt (1966), 165–76, on party words.
10. Kelso (1948), 22–3, with fig. 2 showing handles, although Honeyman (1939), 76–90, at 82, denied them on Hebrew cups. I hesitate to accept the evidence of a modern 'survival' presented in Sukenik (1940), 59–61, although Prausnitz (1966), 177–88, approves it as explaining Jael's 'lordly dish' at Judges 5: 25. His supposed Phoenician 'kraters' are, strictly, amphorae.
11. Boardman (2002B), 1–16, at 8–10; Isaiah 1: 22.
12. Saidah (1977), 135–46; Courbin (1977), 147–57, suggested an Argive origin, but Attic looks more likely; Bordreuil (1977A), 159–61.
13. Stager (2003), 233–48, an essential study.
14. Diod. Sic. 14.97.
15. Kroll (2003), 313–24, an excellent study.
16. Luke (2003), 33.
17. Frost (2001), 61–74; Raban (1998), 428–38.

18. Riis (1988), 315–24.
19. Riis (1970), 44–73.
20. Perreault (1993), 59–83, at 72–7; Boardman (2006B), 507–34, at 522; 'some features of a Greek temple, without quite being one'. The tiles and the Greek inscription 'might attest no more than literate and accomplished slaves'. Bonatz (1993), 123–57, at 132–3.
21. Yon (2006).
22. Yon (2000), 2.
23. Stucky (1983); Lagarce and Lagarce (1995), 141–54.
24. Jo. Malalas, *Chron.* 11.3 (ed. J. Thurn, 2000, 205); Frost (2001), 61–74.
25. Na'aman (2004A), 33–9; I disagree with his suggested translation as 'Cape of the Tyrians', and I follow von Soldt (2005), 159. I also disagree with his location for it.
26. Courbin (1986), 175–204; Courbin (1990), 503–9.
27. Dionys. Per. 914–16, on '*Posideia erga*', i.e. Ras el-Bassit; Diod. Sic. 34/5 F28; Le Rider (1986), 393–408.
28. Courbin (1978), 48–62, on the medieval names; 'Pollcinum, Pomcin, Pocin' derive, I suggest, from the Greek *Polichnion*, a 'settlement', not from the much earlier Posideion.
29. Courbin (1986), 175–204, but I reject his identification on 187–8; Luke (2003), 32–3 and 36, for a list of finds.
30. Seyrig (1970), 290–311, at 297–8 (important).
31. *Stadiasmos Maris Magni*, 140–49, esp. 145; compare Ps.-Arist., *On Winds* 973^a/15.
32. Dussaud (1927), 413–39, is still excellent; Strabo 16.2.8 on the 'nymphaion'.
33. Seyrig (1970), 290–311, at 302–3; App., *Syr.* 63; Polyb. 5.58.4; Diod. Sic. 19.79; Dussaud (1927), n. 7; T. Reinach, *Journal des Savants* (1905), 556, called it the 'Ptolemaic Calais', very aptly.
34. 1 Kings 10: 28.
35. Ezekiel 27: 14.
36. Yenar (2005) for regional survey.
37. Reese, in Moorey (1999), 118; Caubet and Poplin (1987), 273–301.
38. Moorey (1999), 115: 'it probably survived into the Iron Age.'
39. Fuchs (1994), 325, line 230, an important bit of evidence.
40. Grayson (1991), 217–18.
41. Hawkins (2000A), 400–405.
42. Lipinski (2000).
43. Lemaire (1977), 27–40, for Luwian names in Phoenician seal-inscriptions there; Melchert (2003) for local Luwian studies.

44. Hawkins (2000A).

45. Lemaire (2001), 185–91.

46. Hawkins (2000B), 400–401; Hawkins (1980), 213–25; Hawkins (1989), 188–97; Bonatz (2000).

47. Kohlmeyer (2001) and Hawkins (2000), 361–424.

48. Assaf (1990); Alexander (2002), 11–20; Zimansky (2002), 177–92.

49. Jasink (1995), with map on p. 142; Hutter (1996), 116–22.

50. Hawkins (2000), 576.

51. Mazzoni (1994), 319–39, and (1995), 181–91.

52. Hawkins, Hattin-Pattin, *Reallexikon der Assyriologie*, vol. 4, pp. 160–62.

53. Hawkins, Kinalua, *Reallexikon der Assyriologie*, vol. 5, pp. 597–8; against Harrison, I agree with Hawkins (2000).

54. Seyrig (1970), 290–311, at 298: 'encore de nos jours fort dangereuse', whereas Woolley (1953), 20, calls it 'one of the few harbours on this rocky and inhospitable coast, a sheltered roadstead amply sufficient for the little ships of the ancient world'. Holleaux (1942), 281–309, and Pamir (2006), 535–43, at 536 n. 5, on ancient and more recent navigability.

55. Grayson (1996), 17.

CHAPTER 7

Al Mina has sprung back into controversy but the studies by Boardman (2002A) and (2005) show that it has not all been without good effect. The chronology of the site (and my next two chapters) are partly linked with the vexed chronology of particular cups, the Euboean pendent semi-circle *skyphoi* ('pss'). Heroic work was done on them by R. A. Kearsley, *The Pendent Semi-circle Skyphos . . .*, BICS Supplement 44 (1989), and also 'The Greek Geometric Wares from Al Mina Levels 10–8 . . .', *Med. Arch.* 8 (1995), 7–81, trying to work out an orderly sequence, but her chronology is no longer convincing and it is important that I have not followed it here or in the west. Among the objections to it are the following: (i) She did not draw on the growing body of evidence from Lefkandi: M. R. Popham and I. Lemos review her schema from that angle especially in *Gnomon* (1992), 152–5. (ii) The growing body of evidence from Eretria does not fit her schema, either, and its classifiers there, especially C. Léderrey, explain to me that they have many pieces whose shapes and contexts do not fit the schema or the chronology of Kearsley's work. So they have abandoned her datings and her 'Type 6', and started again with a chronology which will appear in one of the Swiss School's *Eretria* volumes. (iii) Kearsley's chronology tends to bring down the foundation 'date' of Al Mina to the 730s BC (she suggests a link with Greek 'mercenaries' there after the main Assyrian conquest of 738 BC). There was, however, older Greek material on the site. Her Al Mina would then become a much later foundation than everybody's foundation of Pithecussae (except that of K. de Vries: see notes to my Chap. 8 below). I cannot possibly believe that. (iv) Her schema conflicts with those (which are too low, if anything) in Iron Age coastal Italian sites at Veii and especially Pontecagnano, on which see the important judgements of N. Kourou, in G. Bartoloni and F. Delpino (eds.), *Oriente e occidente: metodi e discipline a confronto*, Mediterranea: quaderni di archeologia etrusco-italica, 1 (2005), 497–515, at 500–502: Kearsley Type 6 *skyphoi* 'should be dated to the period 770–750 BC', he concludes, 'as suggested by the Al Mina material too'. (v) Her schema is also at odds with recent finds at Huelva: 'Type 6' fragments there occur with Phoenician and other Greek material dating *c.* 800–750 BC. In short, her important work is not valid for dating and its typology is not a secure guide. Nonetheless, as a major publication, it is still (understandably) being applied to Euboean finds, especially in Italy, but it should be dropped there too.

My suggestion that '*Potamoi/u Karon*' is a Greek attempt to render a non-Greek name matches a suggestion about the later '*Koilē* Syria' which had previously caused so many theories in studies of Alexander and his Successors. M. Sartre, 'La Syrie creuse n'existe pas', in P. L. Gatier *et al.*, *Géographie historique au proche-orient* (1988), 15–40, correctly revived the explanation of A. Schalit in 1954: '*Koilē*' is a Greek transcription of the Aramaic *kul* ('all', 'the entire'). The crux at Arr., *Anab.* 2.13.7, is solved: Alexander appoints a satrap of 'All Syria', a previous entity. I suggest the Greeks' '*Karon*' is a similar rendering of non-Greek *karu*.

1. Woolley (1953), 19.

2. Boardman (2005), 278–91; Woolley (1937), 1–15; Woolley (1938), 1–30, 153–70; Robertson (1940), 3–21.

3. Woolley (1953), 178; Pamir (2006), 535–43, revisiting the site.

4. Woolley (1953), 192.

5. Poulsen (1912), 57–9, 74–82, 109–18; Homann-Wedeking (1950), 19–21.

6. Boardman (1957), 1–29.

7. Boardman (1990A), 169–90; Boardman (1999A), 135–61; Boardman (2002A), 315–31, with full bibliographies of the views he counters, also set out in Lehmann (2005), 61–92; he updates Kearsley (1995), 7–81, whose chronology I do not accept.

8. Boardman (2005), 284, suggests that the use of rectangular 'bricks' implies

Greeks; however, Haines (1970), 45 and plate 117D, shows both square and rectangular bricks in the non-Greek buildings at Tell Tayinat.

9. Luke (2003), with bibliography.

10. Tadmor (1994), Stele IIB, lines 12–13 on p. 105. I had noticed this before reading Zadok (1996), 11–13, who noticed it too. Boardman (2002A), 315–31, at 328, doubts it, but S. Dalley (whom he acknowledges at n. 28) was not so sceptical when we looked at the full context again.

11. Diod. Sic. 19.79.6: one manuscript reads '*potamou*', perhaps correctly: 'Trading Post of the River [Orontes]' fits rather nicely. Dussaud (1927), 419, wrongly emends to '*Potamous Hydaton*', which is Seleuceia-in-Pieria.

12. Zadok (2005), 76–107, with 80–95, a fine study of Carians in Babylon.

13. Before the new Tiglath Pileser text, '*karun*' had been proposed by M. Astour, and reasserted by him in a letter to J. Elayi (1987), 249–66, at 263–4. S. Dalley doubts his attempted explanation of *Potamoi* by a putative Akkadian *putamu*: the name will have arisen later in the neo-Assyrian period. Greeks, I suggest, took over the word *karu* only, to which they added their own Greek *potamoi*, or better still *potamou*, giving the meaning 'Trading Post of the River'. The words *bit karani* are also applied to Gaza and the Phoenician cities in the Assyrian texts: they do not mean that each place so called by Assyrians is Phoenician.

14. Saggs (2001), 166–7, on text ND 2737; despite Na'aman (2004B), 69–70, the place is not Ras el-Bassit, whose eighth/seventh-century Greek contact was minimal. The site was not a Greek settlement (see my Chap. 6 nn. 28–9 above).

15. Boardman (2002A), 315–31, at 323, for this much-discussed question: 'the Red Slip of Al Mina is most probably local.' So far as I can judge, the picture changes from Level 8 onwards, but, at first, only marginally (from the published material): Lehmann (2005), 83–4, is the most important summary so far. The 'Red Slip' at issue is not the 'Samaria Ware' which Bikai, in Coldstream with Bikai (1988), 37, summarized elsewhere: 'there is no doubt in this writer's mind that what was once called "Samaria Ware" is properly "Phoenician Fine Ware".' Boardman (2005), 278–91, at 285, insists: 'the few other finds in the early levels seem wholly Syrian-Assyrian in origin. I know not one piece which could be proved Phoenician.' Of course, the later levels, from 7 up, tell a different story (Level 3 had bronze coins from Arados), but they belong much later in very different circumstances.

16. Descoeudres (1978), 7–19, esp. no. 6 and p. 12. The table compiled by Boardman (2002A), 315–31, at 321, includes a tiny proportion of 'East Greek' before 750 BC.

17. Coldstream (2002), 15–32, at 17 n. 58, diagnoses *JHS* 60 (1940), 3, fig. 1, no. 1 as Attic MGI. Boardman (2005), 278–91, at 288, suggests the

chronology may indeed need to be raised and if so 'it relieves the odd situation of finding Euboean latest SPG pss cups being succeeded abruptly or even overlapping with production of pure LG skyphoi with quite different shapes and decoration'. Boardman (2002A), 315–31, at 327 n. 5, records his find on the site of a piece of a closed vase 'which should be 9th c. at least'. Descoeudres (2002), 49–72, has a useful table of the various dates proposed for the settlement's origins since 1938, but his insistence on p. 51 is certainly not cogent, that 'thus, the date of 770–750 BC for the first settlement at Al Mina can now be considered as established beyond reasonable doubt, and will, hopefully, be adopted in due course across the Divide' (his term for the discussions since 1986).

18. Donbaz (1990), 5–24; Ponchi (1991); Puech (1992), 311–34; Lipinski (2000), 215; Hawkins (1995A), 87–101, at 96, suspects the stele is a *'pierre errante'*.

19. Tadmor (1994), 56–8 and 186–7.

20. McEwan (1937), 8–16, at fig.10.

21. Woolley (1953), 182, made bold use of Jo. Malalas, *Chron.* 8.15, on Kasos and Cretans, Amyke and Cypriots. Compare, earlier, Lib., *Or.* 11 (*Antiochikos*), 52–5 and 91; Steph. Byz., *Ethnika* (ed. Meinecke, 1849, 364), s.v. 'Kasos', quotes the Kasos mentioned at Hom., *Il.* 2.676, and links 'Mount Kasios', the Jebel Aqra above Al Mina, to his name. There were earlier Hellenistic ethnographers behind this link, but Stampolidis (2003), 47–79, at 52, actually believes the link was with Kasos, the island off Crete. Like 'Amyke' (for the Amuq plain) the name 'Kasos' is simply an eponym, brought into the story because of the existing Mount Kasios in north Syria.

22. Kearsley (1999), 109–34; Boardman (2002A), 315–31, at 319; Descoeudres (2002), 49–72, at 58.

23. Luke (2003) proposes this theory.

24. Luke (2003), 44, with bibliography.

25. Boardman (2002B), 1–16, emphasizes the presence of 'handles', but the *skyphoi* of this phase are not cups with pronounced feet.

26. Kearsley (1999), 109–34, proposes this theory.

27. Fuchs (1994), 325, lines 250–52.

28. Yu Treister (1995), 159–78.

29. Seyrig (1970), 290–311, at 298 and n. 1, is an important corrective.

30. Tadmor (1994), 57, Annals 25, line 10: 'all types of herbs'.

31. Braun (1982), 25, on *ku-mi-no, sa-sa-ma, krokos, kasia* and so forth; Amigues (2007), 261–318, for the balsam-trees.

32. Lipinski (2000), 35–7, 51–4 (I do not accept the link with our Arimoi, however); Fuchs (1994), 423.

33. Boardman (1990B), 1–17, esp. 10: 'the whole production might easily have been contained in a single sack'; Boardman and Buchner (1966), 1–62, esp. 61, on their non-Greek craftsmen, but 'there were Greeks at Tarsus who could have helped on their way the many seals which passed to the West'; Huber (2003), 61, and especially Lemos (2002), 123–30, at 126, for Euboean finds; Poncy, Casabonne et al. (2001), 9–38, esp. 11, for origins of the stone.

34. Momigliano (1975A), 7–8.

35. Braun (1982), 1–31, at 28: 'most Semitic loan-words in Greek attest trading contacts only.' Burkert (1992A), 33–40, inclines to a wider range of such words.

36. On loan-interest, Hudson (1992), 128–43, perhaps rightly; Szemerenyi (1974), 144–57, with 150 ('agapē') and 155–6 ('kibdēlos').

37. Boardman (1999B); Böhm (2003), 363–70; Kunze (1931).

38. Lebessi (1975), 169–76, at 173; Kotsonas (2006), 147–72.

39. Kantor (1962), 93–117, full of Near Eastern details; Kyrieleis and Röllig (1998), 37–75; Jantzen (1972), 58–62; Charbonnet (1986), 117–56; Held (2000), 131–4; see also now Luraghi (2006), 21–47, esp. 38–42.

40. Eph'al and Naveh (1989), 192–200; Bron and Lemaire (1989), 35–44.

41. Güterbock (1983), 155–64.

42. Lipinski (2000), 376–90, for the campaigns.

43. Lipinski (1994), 92–3, and (2000), 388–9; it went to Arslan Tash, for which see Thureau-Dangin et al. (1931).

44. Dussaud (1927), 232 and 434.

45. Charbonnet (1986), 117–56, for details.

46. Hdt. 5.99.

47. Hom., Il. 4.141–5.

48. Frézouls (1988), 15–40.

49. Ptol., Geog. 5.14.9, is simply wrong when he limits Pieria to the Amanus mountains.

50. Abel (1933), 147–58, esp. 155: 'les colons retrouveraient aussi en quelque sorte la physionomie du pays qu'ils avaient quitté.'

51. Bell (1928), 335 and 329 (the 'Bay of Naples').

CHAPTER 8

The basic study is now B. d'Agostino, 'The First Greeks in Italy', in G. R. Tsetskhladze (ed.), *Greek Colonisation: An Account of Greek Colonies and Other Settlements Overseas*, vol. 1 (2006), 201–38. The main Greek evidence in this chapter is inevitably ceramic only, about fifty bits of pottery (cups, mostly) and thus no more than in the Near East in Chapter 4, down to *c.* 800 BC. There is not even the evidence of Lefkandi's Toumba graves to compare with it, *c.* 800–760 BC. But I believe this pottery is a chance survivor, indicating other, bigger, exchanges, and in Italy too, if it is found in a tomb, it is an indicator of the dead person's foreign Greek contacts.

An unresolved issue is the Early Iron Age chronology in Italy and adjacent regions. One view is that the most widely used schema should go 'up' by at least fifty years. The answers are not yet evident, but if the higher chronology prevails, the dates of the deposition of some of the Greek pottery in Italy which I discuss will go up well in advance of the settlement of Pithecussae. This dating suits the argument of this chapter very well. The main lines of the debate are set out in Gilda Bartoloni and Filippo Delpino, 'Oriente e occidente: metodi e discipline a confronto', in *Mediterranea . . . Quaderni di archeologia etrusco-italica*, 1 (2005), 497–660. Also in this volume, I have profited especially from Nota Kourou on the Greek imports (497–576), A. J. Nijboer on the dating problems of the Iron Age (527–56) and Massimo Botto on the dating of Phoenician settlement ('colonizzazione') in the central and west Mediterranean (579–630). The general discussions (631–50) are extremely helpful.

I have ignored the high dating for the inscribed 'Nora Fragment' on Sardinia, repeatedly urged by F. M. Cross but well re-examined by E. Lipinski, 'The Nora Fragment', *Mediterraneo antico*, 2 (1999), 667–71: 'it confirms the Phoenician presence in Sardinia in the late ninth century, but it cannot be used as evidence that the Phoenicians were on the island in the 11th century BC.'

On the Greek side, I have not accepted Kearsley's chronology of Euboean pendent semi-circle *skyphoi* although it remains current in most publications of 'western' material. My reasons are given in the introduction to the notes to Chapter 7 above. I accept, however, *c.* 780–760 BC as cardinal dates for the one-bird *skyphoi* (late Attic MG II to LG I), brilliantly advanced by J. N. Coldstream, 'Some Problems of Eighth-century Pottery in the West, Seen from the Greek Angle', in *La Céramique grecque ou de tradition grecque au VIIIe siècle en Italie centrale et méridionale*, Cahiers du Centre Jean Bérard, 3 (1982B), 24–7, subsequently confirmed with a Euboean origin by A. Andreiomenou, 'Skyphoi de l'atelier de Chalcis', *BCH* 108 (1984), 37–69, figs. 23–6. I hesitate to call the type 'exclusively from Chalcis', because there are a few examples at Eretria. Importantly there is an (unpublished) 'one-bird' *skyphos* fragment from Al Mina now in Cambridge: Coldstream, op. cit., 25. It resembles others from Veii. As for the chevron *skyphoi*, Coldstream, op. cit., 22–4, set the terms of the debate, but again the pattern is now known at

Chalcis too (Andreiomenou, op. cit., 37–69). The pattern is important in the west, but since Coldstream, op. cit., 22, pendent semicircle *skyphoi* (except on Pithecussae) are better known there too.

Uncertainties of dating mean that I have not dwelt on other Euboean pottery fragments in other parts of west Italy, which are probably datable *c.* 740–700 BC and thus after the first contacts in this chapter. For examples in Sabine country, see A. Guidi, 'Cures Sabini', in G. Bartoloni, *Le necropoli arcaiche di Veio* (1997), 237–8. For others at Tarquinia, M. Bonghi Jovine and C. Chiaramata Trere, *Tarquinia: Testimonianze archeologiche e ricon-struzione storica . . .* , vol. 3 (1997), 371–89. I cannot judge links even further north, but H. V. Herrmann in *ASAA* 45 (1983), 271–94, esp. 281, argues that Etruscan-'Villanovan' items at Olympia include items also known from northern Italy, up to the Alps.

1. Hom., *Od.* 24.207–13.
2. Hom., *Od.* 24.387–90 and 366.
3. Hom., *Od.* 20.383.
4. Hom., *Od.* 24.303–7.
5. Hom., *Od.* 4.85–90; Dickie (1995), 29–56, at 44–5.
6. Hom., *Od.* 18.295–7.
7. Hom., *Od.* 1.52–3.
8. Pompon. Mela 3.8.
9. Hom., *Od.* 10.510–15, with Breglia Pulci Doria (1998), 323–36, and Antonelli (1995), 203–22, for other western-Italian theories, and West (2005), 39–64, at 55, for a Bosporan theory without, it seems, a fiery river.
10. Schulten (1922), 90.
11. Fear (1992), 19–26, at 26.
12. Tylecote (1984), 115–62, at 122–3, 129–30.
13. Køllund (1992–3), 201–14.
14. Lo Schiavo (2000), 141–58.
15. Matthäus (2000C), 41–76, esp. 64–9 and 64 n. 45's bibliography; Matthäus (2001), 153–214.
16. Eder (2006), 549–80, at 568–70; Karageorghis and Lo Schiavo (1989), 15–29; Almagro-Gorbea (2001), 239–70, at 242–3, suspects the spit is Cypriot.
17. Crielaard (1998), 187–204; Almagro-Gorbea (2001), 239–70, an important study from the west.
18. Pacciarelli (1999); De Salvia (1999), 213–17; Mercuri (2004), 291–2, on (probably) Phoenician bowls in Calabria.
19. Lipinski (1999), 667–81, on the date (*c.* 800 BC) of the 'Nora Fragment'.

On the Nora Stone, Lipinski (2004), 234–46, rejecting Cross (1992), 13–19, although his own translation of lines 5–7 is speculative; the text may mention PMY, a god known at Kition and thus a Cypriot link; Bernardini (1996), 535–45, for other early Phoenician traces on Sardinia.

20. Bafico, Oggiano, Ridgway and Garbini (1997), 45–54; Ridgway (2006), 239–52.

21. Ps.-Arist., *Mir. ausc.* 838^{b}20; Paus. 10.17.1.

22. Malkin (1998), 64–7; Ps.-Scymn. 442–3, with Malkin (1998), 78–80, and Hammond (1998), 393–9, at 398, on Eretrians who 'probably occupied the tip of the peninsula at Buthrotum on the Albanian coast so that they controlled the Corfu Channel'.

23. Malkin (1998), 70–72; Morgan (1988), 313–38.

24. D'Andria (1990), 281–90, and (1997), 457–508.

25. Descoeudres (1996–7), 207–31; F. Trucco and L. Vagnetti (2001), 290–91, for LG pottery later up near Sybaris.

26. Snodgrass (2000), 171–8.

27. Vosa (1978), 104–10.

28. Lo Schiavo (1994), 61–82.

29. Douglas (1928), 308, on the 'enchantment of the straits of Messina when under certain conditions of weather, phantasmagoric palaces of wondrous shape are cast upon the waters – not mirrored, but standing upright, tangible, as it were; yet diaphanous as a veil of gauze'.

30. Bailo Modesti (1998), 367–75; Gastaldi (1994), 49–60; Kourou (2005), 497–515.

31. Brandt, Jarva and Fischer Hansen (1997), 219–31; Ridgway, Boitani and Derius (1985), 139–50.

32. Boitani (2005), 319–32.

33. La Rocca (1974–5), 86–103; La Rocca (1982), 45–54.

34. Verg., *Aen.* 8.95–6.

35. Ross Holloway (1994), 44–6, 68–80, for a survey.

36. Camporeale (1997), 197–9; Livy 1.14–15; Dion. Hal., *Ant. Rom.* 2.55; Plut., *Vit. Rom.* 25; Giovannini (1985), 373–87.

37. Markoe (1992), 61–84, at 71.

38. Naso (2000), 193–208.

39. Gras (1976), 341–69; d'Agostino (2004), 236, on the lagoon at Pontecagnano as a pirate-harbour; Strabo 6.2.2, citing Ephorus, for '*ta lēstēria*' of Etruscans near Sicily before *c.* 740 BC.

40. Cygielman and Paganini (2002), 387–410, on Sardinians; Markoe (1992–3), 11–32, esp. 18, on the ostrich-eggs in Vetulonia T. VII (*c.* 750–720 BC).

41. Ps.-Arist., *Mir. Ausc.* 837^{b}30; Serv., *ad Verg. Aen.* 10.172: first a founda-

tion from Corsica, then from Volterra. Camporeale (2004), 29, on iron and Populonia.

42. Delpino (1997), 185–96; Bartoloni (2006), 375–82, and Botto (2000), 63–98, remind us of Phoenician wine-imports too.

43. Ridgway (1997), 325–44; Moretti Sgubini (2004), 150–65, adds an earlier grater in a tomb at Vulci *c.* 730–720 BC.

44. D'Agostino (2004), 236–51.

45. Gras (1981), 318–26, on the absence of Greek items from the main Etruscan metal-zones.

46. Ampolo (1997), 211–17; Ridgway (1996), 87–97; Bitti Sestieri (2000), 28–9, against the brilliant theories of Peruzzi (1992A), 459–68.

47. Dion. Hal., *Ant. Rom.* 1.84.5; Plut., *Vit. Rom.* 6.2; Plut., *Mor.* 320; Steph. Byz., s.v. 'Tabioi'; Ampolo (1997), 211–17, on the connection's late origin.

48. Colonna (2005), 478–83; the burial might even be pre-800 BC (484), with Bitti Sestieri also intervening at 485–7.

49. Bitti Sestieri (2000), 28–9.

CHAPTER 9

The dating of Pithecussae's foundation has long been fixed at *c.* 770–760 BC by the heroic excavators of the site, especially G. Buchner. Arguments were elegantly set out by M. W. Frederiksen (1984), 62–4, and afforced by a very few of the further pieces discussed by Coldstream, 'Euboean Geometric Imports from the Acropolis at Pithekoussai', *ABSA* 90 (1995), 251–67. Nonetheless, K. de Vries, 'Eighth Century Corinthian Pottery Evidence for the Dates of Greek Settlement in the West', in Charles K. Williams II and Nancy Bookidis (eds.), *Corinth*, vol. 20: *Corinth the Centenary, 1896–1996* (2003), 141–56, has mounted an interesting challenge from Corinthian evidence, trying to down-date Pithecussae to the 730s. He compares chevron cups and Thapsos cups on the island with examples found in wells in Corinth. The attempted revision is not convincing. We are still left with MG II fragments to explain on Ischia; he does not engage with the arguments Frederiksen advanced even before the discovery of these MG II pieces; he does not discuss the Aetos 666 cups dated to Ithacan contexts; he ignores Cumae; he is too confident from one (distant) counter-example that Ischia's 'one-bird *skyphoi*' should come down into the 730s BC. He also compares Ischian evidence from graves which are not those of the first settlers with Corinthian evidence of the 730s–720s, an unilluminating match. I am not alone in rejecting his suggestion. Suppose it were true: then, there would be settlements in Sicily perhaps before Pithecussae; there might be a wave of settlers for Pithecussae in the first boats fleeing Assyrian control at Al Mina in the 730s; everything would become compressed in c. 735–720 BC. My 'trail' of myths and objects could live with the schema, although there would be quite a gap between Pithecussae and the first Euboean cups arriving c. 800 BC in coastal Italy. But I am not alone in thinking it wrong.

The scale of the settlement is also uncertain. I incline to a very low figure: I. Morris, 'The Absolute Chronology of the Greek Colonies in Sicily', *Acta Arch.* 67 (1996), 57, suggested 4,000–5,000; R. Osborne, *Greece in the Making, 1200–479 BC* (1996), 114, writes of '5–10,000 within a generation'.

The basic studies of G. Buchner and D. Ridgway, *Pithekoussai*, vol. 1 (1993), and the good short survey by D. Ridgway, *The First Western Greeks* (1992), reviewed by Ridgway with hindsight, in D. Ridgway, F. Serra Ridgway, *et al.* (eds.), *Ancient Italy in its Mediterranean Setting: Studies in Honour of Ellen Macnamara* (2000), 179–91. G. Buchner and B. d'Agostino, 'La "Stipe dei Cavalli" di Pitecusa', *AMSMG* 3 (1995), 9–100, is an essential complement, as is A. Bartonek and G. Buchner, 'Die ältesten griechischen Inschriften von Pithekoussai', *Die Sprache*, 37 (1995), 129–231.

1. Braccesi (1993), 11–23.
2. Dougherty (2001), 149–50, for a possible 'Euboean' *Odyssey*, which I reject: see my Chap. 20 below.
3. Strabo 5.4.9; Livy 8.22.6, with Oakley (1998), 628–38, for the long bibliography and the controversies.
4. Hansen (2006), 1–39, esp. 33–4: he opts for Pithecussae as a *polis*.
5. Frederiksen (1984), 68.
6. Xenagoras, *FGrH* 240, F28B; Lycoph., *Alex.* 691–3; Ovid, *Met.* 14.90; I reject Pliny and follow his 'aliqui' at *HN* 3.82; Peruzzi (1992B), 115–26, at 123 n. 18, suggests the plural refers to the archipelago. I hope that someone will eventually sort out the origins of the many Greek island names in *-oussai* and trace them to particular Greeks; I cannot do it myself, but for the debate see Garus Alonso (1996), 105–24.
7. Strabo 13.4.6; Serv., *ad Verg. Aen.* 9.712; Hesych., s.v. 'Arimoi'.
8. Peruzzi (1992), 115–26, with Gras (1994), 127–33, but see Coldstream (2000), 92–8, at 94 with n. 40.
9. Xenagoras, *FGrH* 240, F28; Lycoph., *Alex.* 691–3.
10. Coldstream (1995B), 251–67, esp. 266; de Vries (2003), 141–56, at 147, for further pieces and a discussion which fails to eliminate their early dating.
11. Strabo 5.4.9; Buchner (1979), 129–44, at 136.
12. Petacco (2003), 37–70, is important.

13. Cantarella and de Francesco (2001), 37–54.

14. Mazzella (1593), 22, credits a discovery of alum and sulphur on Ischia to Bartholomeus Perdicus, from Genoa, in 1465.

15. Plin., *HN* 35.184; Diod. Sic. 5.10; Strabo 6.2.10.

16. Strabo 5.4.9; Buchner (1979), 136, for the text; Mureddu (1972), 407–9, argued for *chruseia* as 'oreficerie', but this sense is not assured by the texts he cites.

17. Ridgway (1992), 91 and 99–100.

18. Buchner (1979), 129–44.

19. Thuc. 6.2.6.

20. Justin, *Epit.* 18.5; Scheid and Svenbro (1985), 328–42.

21. Kourou (2002), 89–114, esp. 93.

22. Feeney (2007), 98, with J. C. Quinn also suggesting a Carthaginian 'source', on different grounds from mine.

23. Docter, Niemeyer, Nijboer and van der Pflicht (2005), 557–77, on bones.

24. Kourou (2002), 89–114, is a fundamental survey; on the 'Cintas Chapel', actually a part of the tophet, Gras, Rouillard and Teixidor (1995), 272–82, and on its local pottery, Briese (1998), 419–52.

25. Ridgway (1999A), 301–8.

26. Ps.-Scylax, *Periplus* 111; Lipinski (2004), 338, with full bibliography; Braun (2004), 287–348, esp. 330–33, a brilliant study; Treidler (1959), 257–83; Gras (1990), 87–93; Boardman (2006A), 195–200; Kourou (2002), 89–114, at 100 n. 70, an unpublished LG import at Utica.

27. Braun (2004), 331–2, esp. n. 77.

28. Diod. Sic. 20.58.2–5.

29. Rightly stressed by Boardman (2006A), 195–200, at 197.

30. Hom., *Od.* 4.85–90 and 18.295–6; Dickie (1995), 29–56, at 44–5.

31. Aubet (2001), 237–42; Fletcher (2006), 173–94.

32. Aubet (2001), 231–4: she cites the island settlements of Arwad and Tyre as predecessors, but why, then, wait till *c.* 725 BC to replicate them in this zone of the Phoenician presence? I prefer Pithecussae as a local model, if one was needed.

33. Boardman (2004), 149–62, at 155–60.

34. Albore Livadie (1986), 189–205, at 202–4.

35. D'Agostino (1999), 207–27, for the finds and the problem; Frederiksen (1984), 61–2, for the earlier state of the question.

36. Morhange *et al.* (2002), 153–66, canvass a harbour on the north, but I still incline to Frederiksen (1984), 70–71.

37. Strabo 5.4.4, with Livy 6.22.5–6 and Frederiksen (1984), 59–61; I reject the suggestion that the participating 'Kyme' is the Kyme in Aeolia; if Ps.-Scymn.

236 is Ephoran (Jacoby prints it as 70 F134B), that discredits its favour for Aeolic Kyme still more (Ephoran patriotism will have distorted the truth). Even then, Ps.-Scymn. only mentions 'Aeolians' as a second phase of settlers after Chalcidians ('*proteron* . . .', '*eita* . . .'). So I disagree with Mele (1979), 28–9.

38. Coldstream (1995B), 251–67, at 252 n. 1, and, for examples, Buchner and Ridgway (1993), 700.

39. Frederiksen (1984), 69.

40. Buchner (1953–4), 37–55, esp. 52–4 (suggesting a race); Coldstream (1981), 241–9; Payne (1940), 147–8, for the similar pose on LPC pottery, but not later; for Greek riding's influence, Lubtchansky (2005), 38–41.

41. Plin., *HN* 19.11.

42. Niemeyer (1990), 469–89.

43. Neeft (1989), 59–65 and 309.

44. Kourou (1988), 314–24.

45. Ridgway (1992), 62 and fig. 12.

46. De Salvia (1978), 1005; Boardman (1994), 95–100; Ridgway (2000), 235–43.

47. Coldstream (1993), 89–107; Shepherd (1999), 268–300, is good on the evidence from Syracuse, but for Ischia the older view, to my mind, still stands.

48. Colonna (1995), 325–42.

49. D'Agostino (2006A), 201–37, at 219; d'Agostino (1994), 19–27.

50. D'Agostino (2003), 75–84.

51. Docter (2000), 135–48.

52. Docter (2000), 135–48, with Aubet (2006), 35–47, at 46.

53. Tronchetti (2000), 346–51; Bernardini (1991), 613–73; Kourou (2002), 89–114.

54. Strabo 5.4.9; Walker (2004), 142, thinks that the Eretrians stayed, but expelled the Chalcidians to Cumae. Pithecussae's subsequent 'Chalcidian' tradition is against him.

55. Buchner (1982A), 275–88; d'Agostino (1999), 207–27, esp. 213–17.

56. D'Agostino (1994–5), 9–100, for the possible shrines; Coldstream (1998A), 303–10, and (2006), 49–56, on plates. See my Chap. 11 nn. 4–5, for stars.

57. Buchner (1982B), 277–306, still, I think, the right line of approach.

58. Ridgway (1992), 60–61.

59. Ridgway (2000), 235–43.

60. Lemos, *Archaeological Reports*, 52 (2005–6), 63.

61. In essence, I agree with Murray (1994), 47–54; bibliography in Buchner and Ridgway (1993), 751–8, with the early note, too, by Page (1956), 95–7.

62. Peters (1998), 584–600; Hansen (1976), 25–53.

63. Blandin (2000), 134–46, and exhibits in the permanent display in Thessaloniki Archaeological Museum, eleventh–eighth centuries BC.

64. Murray (1994), 47–54.

65. Powell (1991), 163–7; also Watkins (1976), 25–40.

66. Ridgway (1992), 50.

67. Markoe (1985), and (1992–3), 11–32.

68. Canciani (1974–5), 84, with Buchner (1979), 129–44, at 142: it was 'associated with an unusual footed cup, also Euboean'.

69. De Simone (1972), 490–521; Colonna (1973), 132–50.

70. Doubted by Haynes (2000), 60–61, but accepted by de Simone (1995), 283–90, at 287.

71. Maggiani (1972), 183–7.

72. Ridgway (1997), 325–44, and now Moretti Sgubini (2004), 150–65.

73. Emiliozzi (2001), 315–34.

74. Frederiksen (1979), 277–311, at 290, on 'Rutile Hipucrate'; Coldstream (1993), 89–107.

75. Bagnasco Gianni (1999), 85–106.

76. Hesych., s.v. 'chalkidizein'; Plut., *Mor.* 761A; Hdt. 1.135, on Persians; de Simone (1970), 311–30, includes 'katmite' in his invaluable list; Ath. 13.601E–F, on Ganymede at Chalcis.

77. Buchner (1979), 129–44, at 130–33, important for dating; Frederiksen (1979), 277–311, at 290–92: 'essentially Greek ... established beyond reasonable doubt', despite renewed doubts by Guzzo (2000), 135–47, who also notes the two horse-bits at 139 and 141.

78. Crielaard (2000B), 499–506, at 502–3: for the silver thread, compare Bedini (1975), 370–92, at 380, on T.132 at Castel di Decima and perhaps T.68B, at 348–9.

79. Huber (2003), 129–33, on Eretrian ladies' clothes, perhaps in a ritual context; compare Blandin (2007), vol. 2, plate 198. Coldstream (2000), 92–8, at 94 n. 48 and fig. 8, admires the 'full, flounced skirt, recalling representations in the Late Bronze Age', more 'retro', then, than dowdy.

CHAPTER 10

J. N. Coldstream, 'Greeks and Phoenicians in the Aegean', in H. G. Niemeyer (ed.), *Phönizier im Westen* (1982), 261–72, was a landmark for precise contextualized examples of Phoenician impact in the Greek world. It is instructive how some of its main suggestions now need revision, about jewellery, for instance, or Phoenician 'factories' of 'black-on-red' in the Aegean. J. P. Crielaard, 'How the West was Won: Euboeans *vs.* Phoenicians', *HBA* 19–20 (1992–3), 235–62, suggested 'considerable differences in socio-economic organization' (246). In Phoenician cities, 'trade was probably organized through mercantile "firms" of specialist traders, which were possibly kinship-based groups, which could be extended by the incorporation of slave or other dependent labour'. I do not think we yet understand the words and texts which may bear on this question. There is a great danger of anachronistic, or partisan, translations. Socially, phratries in the archaic Greek *poleis* might be not so dissimilar groups. I doubt if Greek traders were less 'flexible' than those in a Phoenician (royal) city. My Chapters 9 and 10 also aim to blur the impression of a 'race' or a 'contest' between the two peoples in Crielaard's striking title: his winners, incidentally, are Euboeans.

Fascination with Phoenicians and all the exhibitions about them tend to pass over the travels of 'Levantine', non-Phoenician objects, east and west. M. Cristofani, 'Un' iscrizione cuneiforme su un vaso bronzeo di una tomba di Faleri', *Stud. Etr.* 39 (1971), 315–25, publishes such an item, deposed *c.* 650–600 BC at Montanaro. Above all, A. Onasoglou, 'Hoi geometrikoi taphoi tēs Traganas stēn anatolikē Lokrida', *AD* 35 (1981), 1–57, publishes a bronze bowl inscribed with the name 'Muwazi' (a former owner) which is north Syrian, in a lady's grave *c.* 800–750 BC. These circulating objects probably travelled by sea with Greeks (not north Syrians) in the 'Euboean orbit'. Tragana is near Opuntian Locris, a reminder that a 'penumbra' of north Syrian imports also spread onto the nearby coastline, across from Euboea. But Euboea was the centre: I do not accept the radical proposals of J. K. Papadopoulos, 'Phantom Euboeans', *JMA* 10 (1997), 191–219, which have been very widely answered and are therefore omitted in my text.

1. Hom., *Il.* 2.536–41; Walker (2004), 43–6.
2. Buchner (1979), 138; compare Kahil (1980), 525–31, at 530: 'sans aucun doute . . . les Eubéens furent les maîtres du commerce et des échanges . . .'
3. Hdt. 2.44, 6.46–7; des Courtils, Kozelj and Muller (1982), 409–17.
4. Hdt. 1.105.3, Paus. 3.23.1, with J. G. Frazer's note.
5. D'Agostino (2006B), 57–69, is now fundamental.
6. D'Agostino (2006B), 57–69, at 61, on Tomb 82; Eretrian-Euboean pottery was diagnosed, too, in the cemetery at Exochi near Lindos by Boardman, *AJA* 63 (1959), 398–9.
7. Schreiber (2003), 221–80, is now fundamental on the (non-Phoenician) origins of 'black-on-red' and its examples on Cos and Rhodes.
8. Coldstream (1969), 1–8; Zenon, ap. Diod. Sic. 5.58.2.

9. Shaw and Shaw (2000), 12–24, 92–3, 105, 302–11, 698–700.

10. Matthäus (1998), 127–58.

11. Kourou and Karetsou (1998), 243–54.

12. Matthäus (2000B), 517–49; Matthäus (2000A), 267–80; Coldstream (2003B), 401–3, for important details.

13. Kunze (1931); Hoffman (1997), a full study.

14. Matthäus (1999), 255–60, but Burkert (2003), 135–53, suggests other origins.

15. Kondoleon (1965), 1–45, and Walker (2004), 141–82, give Eretria the first prize, unconvincingly; Bakhuizen (1976), 78 ff., gives it to Chalcis.

16. Thuc. 1.15 implies the date c. 705 BC; an earlier good overview still in Jeffery (1976), 63–70, though she was too negative about eighth-century Chalcidic allies; Parker (1997) and Hall (2007) do not succeed in advancing the subject. I must admit to dating Archilochus, too, c. 740–680 BC, despite the counterblast by Jacoby, and so Archilochus F3 West is, to my mind, contemporary with the war. Theognis 891–4 certainly does not refer to the war: the verses imply social *stasis*, which I connect with Periander and Potidaea, as does Wade-Gery (1952), 61. We are certainly not dealing with a 'Hundred Years [Lelantine] War'.

17. Ducrey, Fachard *et al.* (2004) is excellent; Walker (2004), 73–140; Mazarakis Ainian (1987), 3–24, and the bibliography in Blandin (2007), vol. 1, pp. 15–20, which I have used and presuppose.

18. Close-Brooks (1967), 22–4, and Christiansen (2000), 1–17, on P. D. Bröndsted and the Villanovan belt he bought in Euboea and sold to the Bibliothèque Nationale in Paris. There are a few western items in the 'aire sacrificielle' of Artemis, discussed in Huber (2003), 172–4.

19. Huber (2003), 170–72, with glass 'birds', lyre-player seals and scarabs all together here. Kahil (1980), 525–31, tentatively proposed a small cult-site of Astarte–Aphrodite too, but the suggestion is not sound: Blandin (2007), vol. 1, pp. 38–9, for a refutation.

20. Le Rider and Verdan (2002), 133–52.

21. Kenzelmann Pfyffer, Theurillat and Verdan (2005), 51–82, with Wachter, ibid., 84–6. For no. 66 (pp. 76–7 and n. 69) they suggest cautiously 'un communicant de passage à Érétrie?', whereas I would think of an Eretrian in my Cilician-north Syrian triangle, c. 800–780 BC.

22. Johnston and Andriomenou (1989), 217–20, with *SEG* 47.1963, and West (1994), 9–15, at 12, wondering if the graffito is magic and claims the 'power to deal with feminine bad temper'. Regretfully, I cannot believe her.

23. Details in Ducrey, Fachard *et al.* (2004); on the Eretrian cemeteries, Crielaard (2007), 169–88, importantly.

24. Coldstream (1994B), 77–86; Gisler (1995), 11–95, but Coldstream (2003B), 388, now inclines to an origin at Chalcis.

25. Crielaard (1990), 1–12, at 4–19; Csapo *et al.* (2000), 109–10; I think, too, of the Macedonians' use of double axes out hunting, in *JHS* 85 (1965), plate 20, 2.

26. Preliminary publication by A. Psalti, who kindly showed me fuller details at the Eretria Museum.

27. Sapouna-Sakellaraki (2002), 117–49; Strabo 10.1.10.

28. Plut., *Mor.* 392A–B, with Thuc. 6.3.2, Hammond (1995), 307–15, at 314–15, and Hatzopoulos, *BCH* 114 (1990), 639–68.

29. Mazarakis Ainian (2002), 149–78, for a summary and Mazarakis Ainian (2007) for relations with Euboea; Robert (1960A), 195 n. 2, for rivalries over Oropos persisting into the tenth century AD.

30. Mazarakis Ainian (1998), 179–215, esp. 210; Hom., *Il.* 2.948; Strabo 9.4.4; Arist. F613 (Rose). At Thuc. 2.23.3 we should probably read '*peraikè*' not '*graikè*': for the controversy, S. Hornblower, *Comm. on Thuc.* (1991), 218–19. In general, Schachter (2003), 45–74, at 46–9.

31. Fowler (1998), 1–19, esp. 14–15: 'it would have been very easy for the Pythia to greet her southern enquirers as "Sons of the Hellenes" '; Hall (2002), 125–53, although a role for Olympia belongs later, surely.

32. Arist., *Mete.* 352ᵃ33; on the 'downgrading' of '*Graikoi*' (and *Makedones*) as descendants of Deucalion's daughters (not sons), Fowler (1998), 14–15; for the mentions of Graikoi in the Hesiodic Catalogue, M. L. West (1985), 54, and, with a different emphasis, Osborne (2005), 5–24, at 8–9. On [H]ellōpia-Hellopes around Dodona and also in Euboea, Hdt. 8.23, Strabo 10.1.3–4; on *Helloi-Selloi* at Dodona, Hesiod F240 (M.–W.).

CHAPTER 11

The localization of myths, and the travels and western destinations of the heroes, are subjects extensively treated by Italian scholars with a command of rare ancient commentators and scholiasts and a faith in their historical value which I cannot claim to match. The excellent study of Andrea Debiasi, *L'epica perduta: Eumelo, il ciclo, l'occidente* (2004), is particularly impor-tant, with a valuable bibliography of the many Italian studies on similar themes, several of which bear on those in this part of my book. I have not dwelt on the obvious later example, the Hesperides and the Isles of the Blessed, as they are excellently discussed by V. Manfredi, *Le Isole Fortunate: topografia di un mito* (1993). The Euboeans' mental cargo is discussed well but differently, by L. Antonelli, 'Sulle nave degli Eubei', *Hesperià*, 5 (1995), 11–24.

1. Hom., *Od.* 9.322, the mast; Mark (2005) is an excellent study of the many vexed questions about Homeric shipbuilding and seafaring and a source of clear, usually convincing, answers.

2. Wallinga (1993), 33–65, is important, especially on the *eikosoros* and the (probable) changes in the eighth century; Mark (2005), 50–69, on sewn or 'laced joinery' and 143–5 on rowing which, I think, he underestimates: nobody wants to row far in a strong headwind.

3. Hom., *Od.* 12.286–90.

4. Coldstream and Huxley (1991), 221–4; Monti (1998–9), 115–32, a very valuable article.

5. Szemerenyi (1962), 19–20.

6. Hom., *Od.* 12.95–7.

7. Vermeule (1979), 179; Papadopoulos and Ruscillo (2002), 187–227.

8. Graham (2001), 327–48, at 347.

9. Hom., *Od.* 1.430–33.

10. Hom., *Od.* 17.248–50.

11. Hes., *Op.* 633–9.

12. Crielaard (1994), 45–53, for the Euboean social context.

13. Hes., *Op.* 493; Burkert (2003), 135–53, for an 'Oriental' origin which I cannot quite believe.

14. Frederiksen, *Archaeological Reports* for 1976–7, 59; Blazquez (1983), 213–28, excellent on musical instruments in the far west.

15. Erskine (2001), 140–41, for sources; Kleibrink (2006), pp. x–xi, with her further bibliography, brilliantly connecting the Epeios legend with the timber temples and fine carpentry of the local Oenotrians. Unlike her I still doubt that this '*nostos*-legend' began pre-720 BC.

16. Dunbabin (1948A), 1–18, esp. 11–18, is still fundamental.

17. Gjerstad (1944), 107–23, for sources and Iacovou (1999), 1–28, at 11–13, for recent discussion; Mitford (1971), nos. 89, 104 with 25, 65 and 66, on Perseus in Cyprus: I do not think these mythical links were started as early as the eleventh century BC.

18. Malkin (1998), 94–119, a brilliantly clear interpretation; Malkin (1999), 243–61, on Odysseus the 'protocolonisateur'.

19. Despite Malkin (1998), 118–19, I prefer the local theory which he discusses at 112–14.

20. Malkin and Fichman (1987), 250–58, excellent on Hom., *Od.* 3.153–85. On Ithaca, Paizis-Danias (2006) is magisterial.

21. Bérard (1957) gives all the sources; Hardie (1969), 14–33, at 15 n. 5 (Circeii) and 22 (Baiae/Baios); West (2005), 39–64, for quite a different orientation.

22. Hes., *Theog.* 1015–18, with West (1966), 435–6, with whose literary (not historical) reasons I agree; Jameson and Malkin (1998), 477–86, publish Latinos in a Greek inscription datable *c.* 550–500 BC, but unlike them I do not think it changes the eighth-century Hesiod and his poem.

23. Wiseman (1995), 47–8, unwisely uses Nonnus (*c.* AD 430) to decode the original Ps.-Hesiodic reference (*c.* 600 BC), in *Theog.* 1015–18.

24. Livy 1.56.2 with R. M. Ogilvie's comments; Polyb. 3.22.11, with F. W. Walbank's comments; Strabo 5.3.6.

25. West (2005), 39–64, in every sense a tour de force.

26. Hom., *Il.* 7.467–9, knows this.

27. Morgan (1994), 105–42, esp. 135–42, on possible contributions by Eumelus, and especially West (2002), 109–34, at 118–28.

28. West (1985), 145–54; Coldstream (2003B), 146–56.

29. Chares, *FGrH* 125, F5.

30. Boyce (1955), 463–77, with the bibliography.

31. Gera (1993), 221–44, on Panthea; Plut., *Vit. Alex.* 23.9–10; Arr., *Anab.* 4.19.5, on Roxane and Darius' wife.

32. Arr., *Anab.* 5.3.2, with A. B. Bosworth's comments (1995), 213–17.

33. Strabo 11.14.12–14.

34. Herzfeld (1968), 334; Lane Fox (1973), 296.

35. Bernard (1997), 131–216, a superb study; Ptol., *Geog.* 6.10.3.

36. Arr., *Anab.* 6.24.2–3. For similar alleged input, Arr., *Anab.* 7.20.3–5, on Icaros island (now Failaka), whose name derived from a Greek version of eastern 'Akarun'. Strabo (16.3.4) also says the inhabitants of what must be Tylos claim that 'Tyros'/Tyre is their colony: compare Hdt. 7.89. Again, 'the inhabitants' may be an exaggeration. The source is probably Androsthenes, Alexander's sea-captain, and the (over-)interpretation is his, based on the similarity of Greek names. See also now Bernard (1995), 353–408, at 393, for much more, brilliantly, on this.

37. Bickerman (1952), 65–81, at 76.

38. Nonnus, *Dion.* 13.468–70, with Robert (1958), 137–44, at 139–41.

39. Eur., *Bacch.* 13–22 and 566–75, for Macedonian context; Bosworth (1996A), 140–66, for Dionysus and Alexander.

40. Curt. 7.9.11; Plin., *HN* 6.49; Bosworth (1995), 31.

41. Arr., *Anab.* 5.1–2, with Bosworth (1995), 200–207.

42. Arr., *Anab.* 5.2.5–6, with Bosworth (1995), 204, on Arr., *Ind.* 1.4–5. For the different case, a Persian who perhaps did know Greek, see Arr., *Ind.* 37.2–4, and Strabo 16.3.5–7, with Bosworth (1996B), 66–70: I still wonder

if the Persian's 'information' is only another exaggeration by Nearchus, as in *Anab.* 6.24.2.

43. Arr., *Anab.* 5.2.2, where my emphasis would be slightly different from that of Bosworth (1996B), 122.

44. Holdich (1910), 132–3.

45. Holdich (1910), 134.

46. Arr., *Anab.* 7.13.

47. Xen., *An.* 4.4.16; Lane Fox (2004), 184–214, at 187 n. 11; Strabo 11.5.2 (Theophanes); Plut., *Vit. Pomp.* 35.3; Robert (1980), 192–201, on the territory.

48. Callisth., *FGrH* 124, F34, surely genuine; variant versions in Arr., *Anab.* 2.4.3; Aristob., *FGrH* 139, F9 and elsewhere.

49. I extend Dalley (2003), 171–89, at 186–7, to Assyrian monuments too.

50. Wörrle (1998), 77–83; *SEG* 48.1561 (with good notes on the name 'Hellaphilos', not irrelevant to my Chap. 13 n. 55 below); Isoc., *Euag.* 49–50.

51. Malkin (1994), 181–7, for sources.

52. Plut., *Vit. Sert.* 9.3–4.

53. Plin., *HN* 5.2–3; Strabo 17.3.8; Roller (2003), 54 and 154.

54. Ath. 5.221 C–E.

55. Mayor (2000), 121–6.

56. Mayor (2000) is brilliant, here; see my Chapter 18; Debiasi (2004), 81–98; de Polignac (1998), 23–30, though I am unsure, still, about Hera's early role in the west.

57. Plut., *Quaest. Graec.* 56; Mayor (2000), 91–3, which I quote.

58. Valenza Mele (1979), 19–51; Chap. 18 below.

59. Hom., *Od.* 1.351–2.

CHAPTER 12

I have chosen myths which have been tentatively linked already to Euboeans and so I can economize somewhat on detailed references. The ways in to them are their *LIMC* entries, vols. 3/1, 313–21 (on Daidalos), 4/1, 728–838 (by J. Boardman and others, on Herakles), 4/1, 76–92 (by M. Robertson, on Europa) and 5/1, 661–76 (on Io). Morris (1992) is very wide-ranging and thought-provoking. Its underlying theories, however, are unconvincing, that Daidalos was formed through contact with the Levant (no Greek ever says so in a surviving text: contrast Cadmus; also, see my n. 5 below) and that the Athenians then 'kidnapped' this figure of Levantine origin and promoted him as an Athenian figure in their own great fifth century BC (this argument is mainly based on silence before the fifth century). The collection by C. Bonnet and C. Jourdain-Annequin (eds.), *Héraclès: d'une rive à l'autre de la Méditerranée . . .* (1992), has articles of direct relevance to my theme. Mitchell (2001), 339–52, connects Io and Euboeans in a rather different way without my eastern horizon. West (1997), 442–72, is a clear summary of the case for an eastern element in the names of Io and Europa and a wide-ranging tour of conjectures about Heracles.

1. Green (2004), 40–46, excellent on the flight-plan and 'eponymous association': I think it accounts for Daedalus in or near Euboea.
2. Hom., *Il.* 18.590–92.
3. Verg., *Aen.* 6.14–64; much elaboration in Zevi (1995), 178–92. I do not think Daedalus' presence here is by transfer from the eponymous Cumae in Euboea, attractively proposed by Green (2004), 45.
4. Ridgway (1994), 69–76.
5. Morris (1992), 85 and 97–8, a brilliant attempt to derive the name 'Daidalos' (she renders him as 'Mr Skilful') from the Ugaritic craft-god 'Kothar wa hasis', whose adjectival 'hasis' she renders as 'wise' or 'cunning'. She thinks a Greek translated this 'hasis' and through 'transmission by a calque' came up with the Greek 'Daidalos'. I think the names do not quite overlap in meaning and I hesitate to accept this.
6. Bendall (2007), 17; I am grateful to her for expert caution about the meaning of this place name. Morris (1992), 76–7, also warns about jumping to a link here with our Daedalus.
7. Simon (2004), 419–32, at 422, contests Morris (1992), 257–268 and 386, who claims that Athenians 'kidnapped' Cretan Daedalus despite his (supposed) Levantine origin. I, too, doubt Morris's theory.
8. Best in Simon (1995), 407–13, and (2004), 419–32.
9. Paus. 8.46.2, 9.40.3–4; Dunbabin (1948B), 318; Morris (1992), 199.
10. Higbie (2003), 33, on the Chronicle 27, with commentary at 109–11.
11. Hdt. 7.169–71.
12. Diod. Sic. 4.78.
13. Perhaps at Palma: Dunbabin (1948B), 138, with Morris (1992), 201 n. 22.
14. Diod. Sic. 4.30; in general, Pearson (1975), 171–95, esp. 182–3, an excellent study.
15. Frederiksen (1984), 75, rightly, with the important 83 n. 152 against attempts to give the early credit to Hera.
16. We can compare 'Epeios the Trojan carpenter' at Lagaria, explaining the excellent local Oenotrian wood-working: see my Chap. 11 n. 15. Morris

(1992), 204–11, tries to involve Phoenicians rather too widely in pre-Greek settlements in Sicily.

17. Dunbabin (1948A), 1–18, at 7–9, on 'Minoa': he wonders if the name had a Megarian ultimate origin (8), my own view (Thuc. 3.51). He adds, 'no one would now regard Minoa as a Phoenician name', but Morris (1992), 208–9, tries to revive it: the later signs, pots and so forth of Punic origin prove nothing. Plut., *Vit. Dion.* 25.6–7, for Carthaginians there, later.

18. Diod. Sic. 4.79.

19. Baurain (1992), 67–109, at 73, listing all the passages in Homer; Hom., *Il.* 5.392, for the wounding of Hera.

20. Hes., *Theog.* 290–92.

21. Easterling (1982), 15, and the (lost) *Capture of Oechalia*; Hom., *Il.* 2.730; Strabo 10.1.10.

22. Burkert (1998), 11–26, at 18–19.

23. Burkert (1992B), 111–27; Nergal is obviously important, here; Annus (2002).

24. Boardman (1998), 27–36.

25. Hes., *Theog.* 290–94.

26. Verg., *Aen.* 8.280–305.

27. Macrob., *Sat.* 3.6.12–17, citing Varro and others; also 1.12.28; Plut., *Quaest. Rom.* 60, with H. J. Rose's notes; Sabbatucci (1992), 353–6, for problems of origins.

28. Brize (1985), 53–90, plates 15–24: an important discovery.

29. Jourdain-Annequin (1992) is very important.

30. Jourdain-Annequin (1992) and Yon (1992B), 145–63, at 150–54, on 'le jeune dieu/homme au lion' on Cyprus and at Amrith. It is clearly wrong to call him 'Melqart' as he has such a different iconography.

31. Bonnet (1988), 97–9.

32. Hdt. 2.44. It is guaranteed in Greek inscriptions much later; Yon (1992B), 158, and Fraser (1970), 31–6, on Heracleides names from Kition, with a bilingual text of Heracleides–'bdlmlqart' *c.* 200 BC. But this is only an accident of survival in the light of Herodotus and others.

33. Bonnet (1988), fig. 6 (the image) and 399–409, but the 'colonizing' Heracles is only a sixth-century BC phenomenon in Greek sources and I doubt this aspect of him led to the association with Melqart.

34. Hdt. 2.44, with A. B. Lloyd's comments, ad loc.; Bonnet (1988), 233–6.

35. Diod. Sic. 5.20; Sil., *Pun.* 3.31–2.

36. Braun (2004), 287–348, at 287–303, is now fundamental; Stesich., *Geryoneis* F184; Strabo 3.2.11.

37. Aesch., F199, with Plin., *HN* 21.57 and Braun (2004), 287–348, at 299.

38. Hecat., *FGrH* 1, F77.

39. Phot., *Bibl.* 142B; Hecat., *FGrH* 1, F76.

40. Diod. Sic. 4.24.1. for Heracles' favours near Leontini which included the great lake, the Arabs' Biviere, drained later by Mussolini. It has needed a Borghese, a lady, to make a great garden there in Heracles' wake since the 1960s.

41. Ps.-Scyl. 66; Damastes, *FGrH* 5, F4.

42. Hecat., *FGrH* 1, FF39, 41 and 35b.

43. Pind., *Nem.* 4.111; Braun (2004), 287–348, at 301–2, with Diod. Sic. 4.18.4–5.

44. Strabo 3.5.5–6, with Braun (2004), 287–348, at 302.

45. Chap. n.

46. Valenza Mele (1979), 19–51.

47. Hardie (1969), 14–33, at 17 n. 12, rightly dating the roadway after the foundation of Dicaearchia (*c.* 525 BC).

48. Sabbatucci (1992), 353–6.

49. Theophr., *Hist. pl.* 1.9.5: I say 'where' because the text says 'epi' (surely 'by', not 'in'), yet Plin., *HN* 12.11, says 'under' ('sub'). Le Rider (1966), 14 n. 1, for the controversy; van Effenterre (1961), 544–68, at 564 n. 8.

50. Mitchell (2001), 339–52, is important here; Steph. Byz., s.v. 'Argoura'.

51. West (1985), 144–54, and Dowden (1989), 118–21, and (1992), 77, are decisive here.

52. [Aesch.], *PV* 645–57; Hes., F124 (West–Merkelbach).

53. Moret (1990), 3–26.

54. Aesch., *Supp.* 45; 313–15; 535; 1066, and West (1997), 443–5, for all sorts of their possible parallels; I agree that Jeremiah 46: 20 is only a coincidence.

55. Dowden (1989), 117–46, at 134, and (1992), 108–9; West (1997), 443.

56. Mitchell (2001), 339–52, at 345–8, with an interpretation which differs from mine.

57. Verg., *Aen.* 7. 789–92.

58. [Aesch.], *PV* 840–41; Mitchell (2001), 339–52, at 341–4, though the link with Dodona is rather different; Bonnafé (1991), 133–93, is good on Io's route in this play.

59. Hdt. 2.41.2; [Aesch.], *PV* 814–15, where 'makran' is explained by 774 and 853; Asheri (2001), 27–38.

60. Strabo 16.2.5.

61. Lib., *Or.* 11.44–52.

62. Jo. Malalas, *Chron.* 2.29.

63. Eustath. on Dionys. Per. 92.

64. Burkert (1992A), 160 n. 18.

65. Ath. 15.678B; van Effenterre (1961), 544–68, at 564–5 n. 9.

66. Paus. 9.5.8 and West (2002), 109–34, at 126–8.

67. Ephorus, *FGrH* 70, F120.

68. West (1997), 448–50, for the suggestion made first in 1646; I do not believe his own 'Phoenician' theory (450).

69. Hdt. 7.91, for Cilix; Steph. Byz. is rich in local legends of this sort: s.v. 'Itanos', 'Cythera', 'Melos'; Bunnens (1979), 258–61.

70. Callim. F11 and Nonnus, *Dion.* 44.113–18; Ap. Rhod. 4.516–18.

71. Arr., *Anab.* 2.24.2; Eur., *Phoen.* 291, for the *syngeneia*; Bickerman (1939), 91–9, brilliantly on Sidon's view of it.

72. Pomtow (1918), 26–8, at 26, and corrections by Wilhelm (1974), 76–9.

73. Eur., *Phoen.* 1060–61; I have written at more length on this in an article 'The First Hellenistic Man', to appear in 2008–9.

CHAPTER 13

The Near Eastern sources known up to 1990 are excellently surveyed and discussed by J. Vanschoonwinkel, 'Mopsos: Légendes et réalité', *Hethitica*, 10 (1990), 185–211. In 1950 even M. J. Mellink, in *BO* 3 (1950), 149, was caught up in excitement about a Bronze Age Mopsus: 'it is not difficult', she wrote, 'to predict what Mopsus's pottery looked like', envisioning typical LM III C pots as known in Cilicia. In fact, none existed. From the other pole of interpretation F. Prinz (1979, see below) concluded (25 n. 23) that 'to identify MPS/Mks [known at Karatepe] with the Mopsus of Greek legend is wholly perverse'. But I equate the two again here, albeit in a different way. The nearest I have since found to it is R. Baldriga, 'Mopso tra oriente e Grecia: Storia di un personaggio di frontiera', *QUEC* 46 (1994), 35–71, but he is wrong about the role of 'Callinus' and wrong about Mopsus at Ascalon too.

The new Cilician inscriptions have been exciting. It is now believed that the Phoenician text of a trilingual inscription on a damaged relief of the Storm God, found in 1986 at Ivriz near Konya, north-west of the south Cilician plain, mentions Wrk/(A)warikku, possibly *c.* 730 BC. The initial publication was by Dinçol (1994), 117–28, and we wait for more detail on this member of the 'house of Mopsu/Mopsos'. I am most grateful to H. C. Melchert for his philological expertise on the names involved. He kindly sent me a copy of a conference paper (to appear) by N. Oettinger on 'The Seer Mopsos (Muksas) as a Historical Figure', which concludes that in him 'a ruler of the "Dark Ages" becomes historically manifest. Maybe he was part of the Sea Peoples'. From classicists I expect works on 'Writing the Bronze

Age: Cultural Poetics, Social Memory and Reception', equating the deceptive 'Hiyawa' with Achaeans. But this chapter aims to refute them in advance.

1. Frei (1993), 39–65; Hom., *Il.* 6.155–205.
2. Hes., *Theog.* 285–6.
3. Robert (1977), 88–132, at 112; Jameson (1990), 213–23, for the Argive origin.
4. Dunbabin (1953), 1164–84; Haas (1994), 326, plates 53A–B.
5. Already suggested by Bossert (1952–3), 293–339, at 333; Frei (1993), 39–65, at 48–9, and now Hutter (1995), 79–98.
6. Katz (1998), 317–34, especially 325–6, for '[B]ellerophontes' as a snake-killer.
7. Hogarth (1910), 111; Malten (1925), 121–60.
8. Lalaguë-Dulac (2002), 129–61, esp. 130.
9. Casabonne and Porcher (2003), 131–40, at 131–3; Amandry (1948), 1–11, on fire-breathing monsters; Dunbabin (1953), 1164–84, still valuable on hybrid animal-monsters.
10. The earliest *surviving* text linking the chimaera and the Lycian 'fire' is Ctesias, *FGrH* 688, F45. Steph. Byz., s.v. 'Tarsos'; Dionys. Per. 868–70.
11. Robert (1977), 88–132; Dio Chrys., *Or.* 33.1 and 47; Piérart (1992), 223–44.
12. Momigliano (1975B), 9–19.
13. Burkert (1992A), 46–52 and 75–9.
14. Hom., *Od.* 17.383–5.
15. Burkert (1992A), 52.
16. *LIMC*, vol. 6/1 (1992), 650–52, with evidence for 'Mopsos I'. Ap. Rhod. 1.1086, Paus. 5.17.10 and *LIMC*, vol. 6/1, 652 no. 6 (from Olympia); Hes., [*Sc.*] 191; Pind., *Pyth.* 4.189–91; Strabo 9.5.22.
17. Strabo 14.4.3; Paus. 7.3.2; Pompon. Mela 1.88; Scheer (1993), 164–8.
18. Strabo 14.4.3 where 'Callisthenes' is the correct reading, not 'Callinos', as has been established by the palimpsest text in Aly (1956), column iii.32 and p. 206. This cardinal point, repeatedly overlooked (e.g. Scheer, 1993, 177), is also seen by M. L. West in his edition of *Iambi et Elegi Graeci*, vol. 2 (1992), 50; also, as a source, Steph. Byz., s.v. 'Pamphylia'.
19. Prinz (1974), 23–4, is excellent here; also Parke (1985), 113–21.
20. *LIMC*, vol. 1, 713–19; Hes. F279, on a death at Soloi, killed by Apollo; Strabo 14.5.16 cites Sophocles; Lycoph., *Alex.* 444.
21. Goetze (1968), 36–7 and 140; KUB 14, 1 reverse 75.
22. Hawkins (2000), 45–70, and Çambel (1999), 62–88; Bron (1979).
23. Euseb., *Chron.*, ap. Jerome (ed. R. Helm, 1984, 60): 'Mopsus regnauit in

Cilicia a quo Mopsicrenae et Mopsistae.' The underlying (Hellenistic) source took 1184 BC as the date of Troy's fall. Jerome–Eusebius adopts the alternative '1182 BC', giving the impression (wrongly) that Mopsus' Cilician kingdom began *before* Troy fell.

24. Barnett (1953), 140–43; compare *CAH*, vol. 2/2 (1975), 363–6.

25. Otten (1969), 32–3; rightly dating this text before 1420 BC.

26. Hawkins (2000), 49: column II.7–11; in his 'Karatepe 3' (89) he is called '[M]ukatalas' son'.

27. Lemaire (1983), 9–19.

28. Mosca and Russell (1987), 1–28.

29. Tekoglu and Lemaire (2000), 961–1006, esp. 973–4 n. 6; Dinçol (1994), 117–28, reporting 'the Ivriz text'.

30. Arr., *Anab.* 1.26.4; Ps.-Scymn. 75; Polyb. 21.24; Strabo 14.667 and 671; Stroud (1984), 193–216, at 195 line 7.

31. Theopomp., *FGrH* 115, F103; Bossert (1957–8), 186–9, 461–3 and plate 22, arguing that it is 'Pahri'.

32. Gurney (1976), 38–43.

33. Plut., *De def. orac.* 434D; Bossert (1950A), 122–5, with Abbildung 1, showing the spring.

34. Tekoglu and Lemaire (2000), 961–1006, at 968 paragraphs I, II, III and VII with 106; Brixhe (1976), 147–8 and 191, has an optimism about the Greek language in eighth-century BC Pamphylia which I reject. The allegations of 'Argive' origins there are all much later in date and tendentious.

35. Hdt. 7.91; Casabonne (1999), 69–88, at 71; Lebrun and de Vos (2006), 45–64, at 47–9, incline, wrongly, to the identification.

36. Otten (1988), 61–2.

37. Weiss (1984), 179–207, at 181–2. Scheer (1993), 187–98: the Magnificent Seven include Calchas, too, as a founder for whom Hdt. 7.91 is the source. They also include 'Rixos': attempts to identify him with '[A]warikus' would be excessive; Scheer (1993), 196, notes the oddity of this person, however. 'Rhakios' is an even less plausible '[A]warikus' in Greek: Scheer (1993), 182–7, for his Greek origins.

38. Robert (1960A), 177–88, brilliant on Callim., *Aet.* F200A, with Pfeiffer (1949), 198. Brixhe (1976), 194–5, proposes a date after 400 BC, perhaps even 300 BC.

39. Houwink ten Cate (1961), 44–77, suggested a link between Azitawattas and 'Estwedus' (Aspendos). I doubt the link with Sanduarri proposed by Winter (1979), 115–52, at 146.

40. Theopomp., *FGrH* 115, F103; Plin., *HN* 5.96; Scholiast on Dionys. Per. 850.

41. Callisthenes (not Callinus) in Strabo 14.4.3.

42. Xanthus, *FGrH* 765, F17A, and Nic. Dam., *FGrH* 90, F16; Lightfoot (2003), 65 and n. 166.

43. Bérard (1891), 556–62, a Moxoupolis in Cabalis, which has been linked with Lydia, although it is far from Sardis; *Suda*, s.v. 'Moxos Lydos'; Houwink ten Cate (1961), 46, is not convincing.

44. Lipinski (2004), 116–30, especially 119–22; H. C. Melchert has kindly confirmed to me the philological obstacles to this connection.

45. Gauthier (2003), 61–100; Piérart (1984), 161–71, on Notion as 'Colophon-on-Sea'.

46. Lycoph., *Alex.* 1047; Malkin (1998), 226–31.

47. Mopsus (surely from Claros) and Torrebus (for Lake Karios) on coins of Hierapolis in Phrygia in the second century AD: Robert (1982), 334–57, at 346–7; J. and L. Robert, *Bull. Épig.* (1967), 582 and Robert (1962), 314–16.

48. Philostephanus, in Athen. 7.297F–298A; Prinz (1979), 28–30.

49. Stroud (1984), 193–216, at 195 line 7; Polyb. 21.24; Strabo 14.667 and 671.

50. Callisth., ap. Strabo 14.4.3.

51. Theopomp., *FGrH* 115, F103; Callisth., in Strabo 14.4.4.

52. Arr., *Anab.* 2.5.8–9.

53. Stroud (1984), 193–216; the decree belongs in the context, I think, of Argos's symbolic prominence in the new Argive-Argead era of Macedonian successor 'kings'; I am tempted to connect it with the marriage at Argos of Demetrius and Pyrrhus' sister Deidameia in 303 BC. Asian cities in the Antigonid sphere might well like to link themselves with Argos, the Macedonian 'mother-city', recently in the news after this Antigonid wedding: Plut., *Vit. Dem.* 25.

54. *IG* 4.480; Stroud (1984), 193–216, at 215–16, not, however, explaining the link with Perseus' infancy.

55. Arr., *Anab.* 1.26.2–27.4; Strabo 14.667C; Eustath., on Dionys. Per. 852.

56. Lycoph., *Alex.* 444; Bossert (1950A), 122–5.

CHAPTER 14

Adonis has been massively studied by many scholars and I refer only to the clear and very valuable summary of his death and return in Mettinger (2001), 113–54, with a history of interpretation which has somewhat escaped recent classical scholarship. M. M. Fritz (2003) is a major work of value on the Mesopotamian background until the Assyrian era and I have been much helped by it. Burkert (1979), 105–111, has superb endnotes and is a master-piece of concise insight. At 107 he remarks of Adonis on Cyprus that 'prob-ably matters were still more complicated than we suspect'. No doubt they were, but I stand by the local Cypriot connection I construct here, though the evidence is late and indirect. One approach is to emphasize flexibility, invented 'tradition' and change at every turn, hidden from us across two thousand years of cult. In this case I am more impressed by strong continuity which is not just an antiquarian illusion.

1. Apollod., *Bibl.* 3.14.4, with further sources cited by J. G. Frazer in the Loeb edn. of Apollodorus (1921), vol. 2, pp. 84–7.
2. Frazer, op. cit., 84 n. 1, with Suet., *Calig.* 57.9, and Joseph., *AJ* 19.94–5.
3. Parthenius F29, with Lightfoot (1999), 181–5; Zoilus, *FGrH* 758, F9; Catull. 95.5–6 and Wiseman (1974), 49.
4. Apollod., *Bibl.* 3.14.4, probably using Panyassis throughout; Ribichini (1981), 148–9, on Greek heroic elements; Theoc., *Id.* 15.153–6, with Gow (1950), 265.
5. Origen, *Sel. in Ezech.* 8.12 = *PG* 13.797–800; Jerome, *Expl. in Ezech.* III, 8.14 = *PL* 25.82–3; Will (1975), 93–105, tried to dismiss them as late 'Christianizing' readings of the cult, but I entirely agree with Mettinger (2001), 130: 'nothing in these passages indicates that they contain a Christian misreading of the pagan material.'
6. Atallah (1966) with Weill (1966), 644–98, and (1970), 591–3; on the gardens, still Sulze (1926), 44–50, and (1928), 72–91; on the probable use of corn, Atallah (1966), 211–13; Baudy (1986) is wonderfully down to earth (*Samenprüfung*) but not the answer; Detienne (1970) is wayward and best left to one side. On the date, Cumont (1932), 257–64, and (1935), 46–50; I discount Ar., *Lys.* 387 ff. and therefore Dillon (2003), 1–16; 'topless', Theoc., *Id.* 15.134–5, with Gow's notes on the fall of the dress, but not on the breasts (except their dative case).
7. Sappho F140A (Campbell); Seaford (1994), 279–80, is excellent, here.
8. Dioscor. in *Anth. Pal.* 5.53 and 5.193, with Theoc., *Id.* 15.135: 'stēthesi phainomenois'.
9. Ar., *Lys.* 387–95, with Plut., *Vit. Alc.* 18.2–3 and *Vit. Nic.* 13.7. So much is merged impossibly here (the 'Zacynthian hoplites' of Thuc. 7.31.2) and the context suits a totally inaccurate account by the (pompous) Proboulos. I thus disagree with Dover-Andrewes, *HCT*, vol. 4 (1970), 223–4; the lines do *not* show that the Adonia really coincided with this assembly in (?) late spring. The Plutarch passages are secondary.
10. Sefati (1998) and Fritz (2003), for evidence.

11. Kramer (1966), 31, and Alster (1996), 1–18, thereby refuting the lucid scepticism of Gurney (1962), 147–60.

12. Richter (1999), 133; Kutscher (1990), 29–44; Matsushima (1993), 209–19; Buccellati (1982), 3–7.

13. George (2003), 834.

14. Fritz (2003), 339–41, on dates; 354–9, women; 105–6, prostitutes.

15. Frazer (1913), 3.

16. Mettinger (2001), 141–3; Fritz (2003), 361–8.

17. Fritz (2003), 104–6, with bibliography on 'Ishtar's Descent' and its final surviving lines.

18. Mettinger (2001), 125–8, a lucid summary; Ribichini (1981), 94–8, contested the reference to Tammuz, I think wrongly.

19. Fritz (2003), esp. 354–9.

20. Strabo 16.2.18, with a cautious Millar (1993), 275–8; contrast, rightly, Ribichini (1981), 145–59.

21. Bordreuil (1977B), 23–7, a very important study; Mettinger (2001), 140–41.

22. Cleitarchus, *FGrH* 137, F3.

23. Luc., *Syr. D.*, superbly studied by Lightfoot (2003).

24. Luc., *Syr. D.* 6.

25. Theoc., *Id.* 15.135–6, and Lightfoot (2003), 319–26, admirably, on Luc., *Syr. D.* 6.

26. Luc., *Syr. D.* 8, with Lightfoot (2003), 316–18, on the date.

27. Frazer (1913), 28; Ribichini (1981), 159–63; I am very grateful to Matthew Nicholls for careful drawings and photographs of the site.

28. Melito of Sardis, *Apology* 5, an important text here; Lipinski (1995), 104–6.

29. Cumont (1935), 46–50.

30. Gaber (1994), 161–4; no early archaic finds have been made here.

31. Steph. Byz., s.v. 'Golgoi'; Lycoph., *Alex.* 589; Paus. 8.5.2 (implying a very old shrine there); Hermary (2004), 47–68, an excellent study; Connelly (1988), 75–7; Karageorghis (2000), 106–33, 708–20 and 406–30, for superb pictures.

32. Hermary (2004), 47–68, at 51–2, with Text 68 in Connelly (1988), 17–20.

33. Ptol. Chennos, in Phot., *Bibl.* 190; Menardos (1908), 133–7, which I owe to Connelly (1988), 17, and her advice. I merely differ from Menardos by deriving modern Arsos directly from the (lost) ancient Argos without the detour through ancient *alsos* which he proposed (234).

34. Theoc., *Id.* 15.97, with the Scholiast: 'adēlon tis hē poiētria autē'; Gow, commenting, correctly insists 'Argeia' is an ethnic.

35. Paus. 2.20.6 (an *oikēma* for Adonis, only).

36. Hermary (2004), 47–68, at 56 (very important, including her cult in Golgoi, surely in the Aphrodite temple); Anastassiades (1998), 129–40, for more texts; Hermary (2004), 58, on the new early Ptolemaic division of the territory, making a ' "district" placé sous la protection d'Aphrodite' in which 'Golgoi joue désormais un rôle non négligeable'. I link this new role and new district to Ptolemy II, reflecting the importance of Queen Arsinoë; Reed (2000), 319–51, pursues a different line.

37. Schmidt (1968), 54, and Connelly (1988), 18–19.

38. Eissfeldt (1970); Mettinger (2001), 124–7 and 140–41.

39. *Pap. Petrie* 3.142, with the bold tour de force of Glotz (1920), 169–222; Gow (1950), 262–4; Stol (1988), 127–8, and esp. Scurlock (1991), 3.

40. Paus. 9.41.2, a *hieron archaion*; Steph. Byz., s.v. 'Amathous'; Pirenne-Delforge (1994), 331–2 and 363–6, stresses that evidence of Adonis on Cyprus only goes back to Roman-period texts, but not that those texts already remark that some of the shrines are 'ancient'.

41. Torelli (1997), 233–91; Müller (2000), 26–41, arguing that Phoenicians brought 'Adonis' to Sicily; Balduin (1997), 107–37, a trace there.

42. Lee (1999), 1–31, where I struggle to recognize even a Pulsatilla, the wrong flower, strictly, as the Adonis anemone should be the scarlet *Anemone coronaria*; sadly I cannot recognize it, either, in the sculpted crowns of the Cypriot priestesses in Cassimatis (1982), 156–63, although their flowers include narcissi.

43. Mettinger (2001), 146–8, trying to distinguish 'death and sterility' in the gardens in Greece from 'green' ones in the Levant: I disagree. I also distinguish (as many do not) the 'short-lived' gardens from gardens which were allowed to wither *before* being thrown out: the latter are implied, but not until Julian, *Caesars* 329C–D, a late and stylized passage.

44. Porphyry, on Euseb., *Praep. evang.* 3.11.12, is important. He contrasts Attis, a symbol of flowers which bloom before fruiting, and Adonis, who represents the 'cutting of completed fruits'. Compare Amm. Marc. 22.9.15. Porphyry is not a literary fantasist on these cults. Burkert (1979), 107; Winkler (1990), 188–204, quite unsustainable.

45. Burkert (1979), 107: he also sees the lament as partly 'counteracting the guilt of success in playacting catastrophe in order to avert it' (121). I disagree.

46. Also seen by Davies (1999), 152–7: the 'gap between the ideal and the mundane, the elevated and the trivial'. Fritz (2003), 354–9, on Dumuzi–Tammuz and, independently, female 'Sehnsucht nach der Ideal'.

47. Euseb., *Vit. Const.* 3.55–6; Euseb., *Triac.* 8.4–6, exaggerated into a total

'spying' operation against all caves and shrines in Euseb., *Vit. Const.* 3.57.4, with Barnes (1981), 390 n. 20, for more. I am not discussing the ban on prostitution at Heliopolis, however.

48. Genesis 18: 1–33, a great episode; Miller (1984).

49. Philostr., *VA* 1.7; Euseb., *C. Hieroclem, passim*; Dagron and Feissel (1987), 137–41, on the important verses inscribed on an architrave in this general period at Mopsuhestia, as they verify (140), not actually at Aigai itself. But they testify to Apollonius' local fame.

50. Jerome, *Ep.* 58.3; Paulinus, *Epist.* 31.3 (blaming Hadrian); Koortbojian (1995), 49–62; Versnel (1993), 154.

CHAPTER 15

The material here is less familiar to classical historians, but is excellently discussed in scattered non-classical publications to which I am greatly indebted, although I add, I hope, a few extras to them. The studies cited below by C. Bonnet (1987), W. Fauth (1990) and K. Koch (1993) are particularly helpful. The article by P. Chuvin and J. Yoyotte (1986) is especially valuable for the contributions by L. Robert. I have gained above all from the local knowledge and linguistic expertise of P. Bordreuil in his studies which I cite. W. Djobadze (1986) is the indispensable hero of archaeology on the mountain, but not, as yet, of the ash-altar on the very summit which I was able to see briefly in 1997 in its militarized zone. Earlier studies of the Graeco-Roman evidence by A. Salač, 'Zeus Kasios', *BCH* 46 (1922), 160–89, and A. B. Cook, *Zeus*, vol. 2 (1925), 981–6, were valuable, but did not go back into the non-Greek roots or forward into Christian antiquity. In my view, the mountain's district 'Kassiotis' solves simply and neatly the problem of the enigmatic 'Alexandreia hē kabiōsa' or 'Kabissos', lengthily discussed, without a solution, by P. M. Fraser, *Cities of Alexander the Great* (1996), 21–3. The corruption of the name is very slight: 'Kassios' or perhaps 'Kassiotē/-tis' (my n. 29). It then neatly matches, and explains, the 'Alexandreia hē Kasos' in the *Chronicon Paschale* which Fraser relates only to the island 'Kasos' off Crete (contrast my Chap. 7 n. 21 for 'Kasos' as the eponym of Mount Kasios). This solution is not unimportant. It would restore an alleged Alexandria to the Orontes plain (below Mount Kasios) as a 'rival' or counterweight to the great Seleucid Antioch. It would thus fit well with the (still controversial) theory of Fraser that the fictitious Alexandrias in these lists were Ptolemaic fabrications created in order to diminish the Seleucid achievement. One of the big gaps in this theory is the absence of evidence for a counterweight to the Seleucids' great Antioch: 'Alexandreia hē Kasos/ Kassiotē' fills it very well.

1. Buxton (1992), 1–15.
2. 'Potamoi Hydatōn', predecessor of Seleuceia, surely explains Chuvin (1988), 99–110, at 108 n. 19, and Jo. Malalas, *Chron.* 8.207.
3. Amm. Marc. 22.14.4.
4. Barker (1853), 273, and Amigues (2007), 261–318, on plants; Djobadze (1986), fundamental for the setting.
5. Bordreuil (1990), 257–67.
6. Ainsworth (1838), 305, calculated the mountain's height with his barometer by climbing it and checking with Lieutenant Eden, RN, stationed at its foot; for problems with the barometer, however, pp. 10–11.
7. *Stadiasmos Maris Magni*, 143, and Dussaud (1927), 421.
8. Kapelrud (1952), 56–9; Koch (1993), 171–224, at 185–97.
9. Bordreuil (1991), 17–27, a brilliant study.
10. Rutherford (2001B), 598–609.
11. Schaeffer (1938), 323–7, and the superb plate 36.
12. Bordreuil (1989A), 273–4, and (1989B), 275–9; Koch (1993), 171–224, at 199–207.
13. Strabo 16.2.8.
14. Seyrig in Djobadze (1986), 203, with his 4–5.
15. Seyrig (1939), 296–301, and *Antiquités syriennes*, vol. 3 (1946), pp. v–vi, with a significant correction. Chuvin (1988), 99–110.
16. Polyb. 5.58; *OGIS* 245.
17. Seyrig, *Antiquités syriennes*, vol. 3 (1946), 28 n. 4.
18. Butcher (2004), 413–25.
19. Seyrig (1963), 17–19.
20. Seyrig (1933), 68–71, much discussed by Millar (1993), 1–15, but not with the (to my mind) likely connection to Zeus Kasios: Seyrig (1963), 19, was also cautious.
21. Robert (1963), 179 n. 9, (1969), 1583, and in *Études déliennes*, *BCH* Suppl. 1 (1973), 442–3. We can compare the names Kasiodoros and Kasios in *A Lexicon of Greek Personal Names*, vol. 2, giving three Antiochenes, an Apamean and a Milesian in Athens; Seyrig (1963), 31 no. 34, has a Barsephones; Bordreuil (1989A), 274 n. 41, has an Ali Nanu; Zadok (1978), 59, has a Harusapanu. 'Orophoric' mountain names here are ancient and long-lived: Richter (1998A), 125–34, esp. 129–30, on earlier 'Hazzi'-based names.
22. J. C. Balty in *LIMC*, vol. 8/1, 666–70, summarizes the problems well; the main sources are Nonnus, *Dion.* 25.135, 33.296, 41.236; Balty (1981),

95–106, and Daszewski (1986), 454–70, exploit a mosaic in Paphos; Bowersock (1990), 51, slips slightly, concluding 'the victory of Cassiopeia represents the triumph of the gods associated in particular with Cassios, the Mons Cassios in Lebanon [*sic*]', but the general link is probably correct.

23. Varinlioglu (1986), 23–4: however, (i) 'akrotatou' rules out his preference for the (flat) Kasion in Egypt. The reference is to north Syria; (ii) 'isamēria' is not the equinox, but a day with equal halves, divided by the sun above Mount Kasios at midday.

24. Augustine, *Ep.* 26.

25. *Anth. Pal.* 6.332; Arr., *Parth.* F36A; Dio Cass. 68.25.5.

26. Haas (1982), 117, on offerings of ox-horns; *Hist. Aug., Vit. Hadr.* 14.3 (a suspect part, however, of this variable Life); Dio Cass. 69.2.1; Birley (1997), 230.

27. Amm. Marc. 22.14.4; Julian., *Mis.* 361D, and especially Lib., *Or.* 18.172, claiming a sighting 'in broad daylight'.

28. Peeters (1909), 805–13; Djobadze (1986), 5–6 and 203.

29. Van den Ven (1962), esp. 200*–211* and the valuable map at the end of vol. 2. At vol. 2, p. 139 n. 2, I disagree about the topography of the 'pleura kassyotē'. It lay, surely, at the Jebel Aqra.

30. Brown (1995), 66, a cardinal insight: 'Symeon stood on the limestone ridge as a highly personalised challenge to the ancient pilgrimage site on the top of Sheikh Barakat.' My point is that 'Symeon the Younger', his avowed imitator, did the same with Mount Kasios, a point missed, however, by Van den Ven, vol. 1, pp. 170*–177*.

31. Bonnet (1987), 101–43, esp. 102–12; Koch (1993), 171–224, at 199–211.

32. Fauth (1990), 105–18, at 116–17.

33. Yon (1991), 284–8; Eissfeldt (1968), 53–7; Koch (1993), 171–224, at 185–9; Fauth (1990), 105–18, at 117, on the iconography (it does not show Seth).

34. Luckenbill, vol. 2 (1927), no. 587.

35. Bordreuil (1986), 82–6.

36. Aimé-Giron (1940), 433–60; Bonnet (1987), 101–43, at 121–2 n. 113.

37. Psalm 48: 1–2; Koch (1993), 171–224, at 173–82.

38. Bonnet (1987), 101–43, at 115–16, on Psalm 89: 13–14; for a later replacement of Yahweh by Baal (taking his revenge?), Nims and Steiner (1983), 261–74.

39. Exodus 14: 2; Numbers 33: 7; Lane Fox (1991), 78–80, with bibliography.

40. Chuvin and Yoyotte (1986), 41–63, at 42; Fauth (1990), 105–18, at 110–18; above all, Verreth (2000), 471–87.

41. Verreth (2000), 471–87, for the problem; Cazelles (1955), 321–64, and Dothan (1969), 135–6, for differing views on it.

42. Eissfeldt (1932), still a classic; Diod. Sic. 16.45.5 and 20.74.2–3, with 1.30.4–9.

43. Hdt. 2.6 and 3.5.

44. Hdt. 2.179.

45. Verreth (2000), 471–87, for full details.

46. Plut., *Vit. Ant.* 3.5–6.

47. *Suda*, s.v. 'Kasiotikē amma'.

48. Chuvin and Yoyotte (1986), 41–63, at 50–51; Birley (1997), 235–7.

49. Chuvin and Yoyotte (1986), 41–63, at 59–61.

50. J. and L. Robert, *Bull. Épig.* (1972), no. 223; Kostoglou-Despini (1971), 202–6; Plin., *HN* 4.19.

51. Suet., *Ner.* 22.

52. *IG* 9.1 (2001), 845; the bibliography on 842–7 is all relevant.

53. *IG* 9.1 (2001), 844.

54. Procop., *Goth.* 4.22.25–9.

CHAPTER 16

I have not included three traces of Cronos in the eastern 'triangle' which I discuss because they are not directly connected with the Euboean trail of this chapter. However, they support Cronos' local 'image'. One is found at the future Flaviopolis (near modern Kadirli) in the north-east of the Cilician plain up the Pyramus river in the general area of the lands formerly ruled from Karatepe. Coins there show a veiled Cronos with a sickle, discussed by L. Robert in *La Déesse de Hierapolis Castabala* (1964), 25–6: they are surely an echo of the old themes of the 'song of kingship' and allude to Cronos–Kumarbi's role in it. For the same reason coin-images of Cronos continued to appear in south-west Cilicia near the Corycian cave, noticed by T. S. MacKay, *ANRW* 18/3 (1990), 2102–3. Down in Phoenician Arados, Cronos is also honoured, probably because of his congruence with Phoenician stories of their gods: L. Robert discusses him and his grim over-tones in his *Opera Minora Selecta*, vol. 1 (1969), 601–3, 'le grand dieu phénicien mangeur des enfants'. A district of the city was even named after him.

On the dominant 'golden age' aspects of Greek Cronos, not relevant to my chapter, W. Burkert, 'Kroniafeste und ihr altorientalische Hintergrund', in his *Kleine Schriften*, vol. 2 (2003), pp. 154–71, wonders if festivals of Cronos were spread in the eighth century BC on an axis through Naxos, Samos and Colophon. Plato played from time to time with this alternative 'golden age' Cronos (most brilliantly in the *Statesman* 271–4). The most memorable allegory of Cronos and the grim succession stories occurs in his (neo-) Platonist followers, brilliantly explained by P. Hadot, 'Ouranos, Kronos and Zeus in Plotinus' *Treatise Against the Gnostics*', in H. J. Blumenthal and R. A. Markus (eds.), *Neoplatonism and Early Christian Thought: Essays in Honour of A. H. Armstrong* (1981), 124–36. I am glad to be able to omit the Cronos sections of the text in the Derveni Papyrus, columns 13–15. Despite earlier vivid claims that it described Zeus swallowing Cronos' penis (a novel twist to 'Sex and Succession'), it is now clear that the true text was less dramatic and had no such meaning: T. Kouromenos *et al.*, *The Derveni Papyrus* (2006), 133–4, and the comments on 25–8.

1. Gibson (1978) and, above all, Smith (1994), especially 1–116.
2. Haas (2006), 130–76, is now fundamental, replacing even the invaluable English translation by Hoffner (1998). Of course, these stories had an even earlier Hurrian life, but I have omitted it, for simplicity's sake.
3. Barr (1974), 17–68, is still indispensable; Edwards (1991), 213–20.
4. Rutherford (2001B), 598–609, is essential; Haas (2006), 151–2 and 212–13; Akdojan and Wilhelm (2003), 214–31, esp. at 223–7, for the Hurrian background and offerings, too, to the nearby peak of 'Mount Nanos' in the Jebel Aqra's range.
5. Rutherford (2001B), 598–609, establishes this point.
6. Smith (1994), esp. 63–9, doubting previous theories of a 'seasonal' connection; the local weather does make me suspect one, as it does, too, Yon (1989), 461–6. De Moor (1970), 302–27, at 306, even suggests a continuity of spring rites, extending to those in Jo. Malalas, *Chron.* 198.22.
7. Staudacher (1942); West (1966), 212–13.
8. Haas (2006), 170–72, for the well-known text.
9. Haas (2006), 134–40, esp. 139, for the latest translation.
10. Hes., *Theog.* 154–210 and 453–506, with West's fine commentary.
11. Hes., *Theog.* 476.
12. Güterbock (1946) saw the detailed overlap; Osborne (1996), 142–3, incidentally, does not engage with the Hittite texts as they are now more fully understood.
13. Burkert (1987), 10–40, at 22.
14. Haas (2006), 133: Kumarbi as 'Gerstengott'.
15. Nilsson (1951), 122–4, though opposed by West, on Hes., *Theog.* 205.
16. There are many sickle-like cutters in Near Eastern imagery and stories

too: Bordreuil and Pardee (1993), 63–70, and especially Sahin (1999), 165–76, 'der Gott mit der Sichel'.

17. Hainsworth (1993), 65, on Hom., *Il.* 9.37.

18. Karageorghis (2003), 353–61, and also Karageorghis and Karageorghis (2002), 263–82, postulating a 'birth' from Athart–Astarte, becoming 'Aphtos, then Aphrodite' in Greek. I accept this origin.

19. Hes., *Theog.* 192–5.

20. Hdt. 1.105.

21. Philo, *FGrH* 790, F2, 29.

22. *RE*, vol. 5/2 (1905), 1698; Leake (1830), 414: 'the name was often applied by the ancients to low, sandy promontories which, by the action of currents in the sea upon the deposits of rivers, assume the form of a *drepanon*, or sickle.'

23. Thuc. 6.4.5; coins in Robinson (1946), 13–20, nos. 24–7, struck on a Euboic-Chalcidian standard.

24. Freeman (1891), 390.

25. Callim., *Aet.* F43, 57–75, with Pfeiffer (1949), and his exhaustive notes.

26. Fraser, vol. 1 (1972), and vol. 2 (1972), 1071 nn. 348–9, for this source. Ehlers (1933) did not engage with it, or with the high authority of the Aristotelian local sources; nor does Massimilla (1996), 339–48, still thinking that Callimachus 'invented' the Cronos-story at Zancle.

27. *LIMC*, vol. 6/1 (1992), 143–4; Ciaceri (1911), 66–76, is excellent here.

28. Vallet (1958), 59, the 'problem'; d'Agostino (2006A), 201–37, at 221: 'in truth [*sic*] the enterprise must have originated with Pithekoussai when Cumae did not exist'; Antonelli (1996), 315–25; Consola Langher (1996), 377–415.

29. Thuc. 6.4.5, specifying 'Kumē en Opikiai' as the first founder ('archēn') and the 'Euboian crowd' as later back-up ('husteron'). Its foundation is later than the 'first' Naxos, emphasized at 6.3.1. I reject the later Diod. Sic. 13.59, Ps.-Scymn. 283–6, and, in Sicily, Strabo 6.268, which lack Thucydides' (undented) authority.

30. Callimachus' 'mowing' echoes Archil. F138B; Hesych., s.v. 'gypas'.

31. See Chap. 8 n. 17 above on 'Essex castrators'.

32. Steph. Byz., s.v. 'Drepanē'; W. Rugé, in *RE*, vol. 5/2, 1698; Mango (1994), 143–58; Vianu (2004), 78–86.

33. Paus. 7.23.4, with the acute Leake (1830), 414, and Philippson, in *RE*, vol. 5/2, 1698.

34. Hammond (1967), 418 n. 1.

35. Arist., F512 (Rose); Callim., *Aet.* F14.

36. Scholiast on Ap. Rhod., *Argon.* 4.984 ff.; Vian (1981), vol. 3, pp. 29–37,

on Apollonius Rhodius archly reacting to Callimachus' location of the sickle; Antonelli (2000).

37. Acusil., *FGrH* 2, F4; Alcaeus F441 (Campbell) would, if correct, take the idea back to *c.* 600 BC.

38. Ptol., *Geog.* 5.14.1; Hogarth (1889), 10–19; Bakirtzis (1995), 247–53.

39. Myres (1940–45), 99.

40. Lycoph., *Alex.* 869, with the Paraphrasis (P) and in E. Scheer (ed.), Lycophron, *Alexandra*, vol. 1 (1881), 75, and the Scholiast on Lycoph., *Alex.* 972.

41. Paus. 8.8.3; compare Plato, *Resp.* 377e–78a.

42. Wind (1968), 128–37. I do not think that Botticelli owed any direct debt to the high theorizing of Ficino. Politian, *Giostra* 1.99, is nearer his level, and in the right milieu; for Politian's learning, including Hesiod and Nonnus, Vian (2005A), 609–20, a fine study; on the roses, Wind (1968), 137 n. 27, without wondering what type of rose they are. The answer is probably a variety of *Rosa damascena*, current in the garden of the Villa Medici, at Fiesole (Galletti, 1986, 50–90, suggested 'alba incarnata', a name which is no longer in botanical use, but is nowadays our 'Great Maiden's Blush'; it is too double a rose to be Botticelli's). As for the shell, it would be lovely to accept its identification with the 'fossilised sea-shells' which occur on Venus' island of Cythera. They are strikingly similar, but despite Tsoukala (2001), 277–301, at 288–9, I cannot believe that Botticelli knew this directly.

CHAPTER 17

Nobody, I think, has fully untangled Typhon before, but I was glad to find so much on the Cilician location in Houwink ten Cate (1961). It was particularly gratifying on a visit to the recently opened Archaeological Museum on Ischia in 1999 to meet by chance on the steps Professor Giovanni Castagna, who kindly presented me with the most recent number of *La Rassegna d'Ischia*, 20/1 (June 1999), containing his article 'Pithekoussai "Testa di Ponte" del mito di Tifeo in Occidente', 3–10, the nearest I had read to some of the views on Typhon which I brought with me. At home, in the benighted Cotswolds, such local *Rassegne* would merely contain articles on sheep-tracks and mullioned windows. It is a tribute to the persistent local patriotism and antiquarianism of these Italian regions. There may be more such local understanding in the books of S. Di Meglio, *Ischia, storia e leggenda* (1961) and *I toponimi greco-latini dell'isola d'Ischia* (1960), unavailable in Britain.

Typhon is the ultimate origin of our 'typhoon', as is brilliantly explained by Bonnet (1987), 101–43, at 138 n. 222, with bibliography and a tour via the Far East.

1. Merlat (1960), 1–98; Vanel (1965); Speidel (1978), 3 n. 1, importantly corrected by Seyrig, *Syria*, 47 (1970), 93 n. 4; Hörig (1984), 2131–79.
2. Versnel (1993), 90–135, at 101–2; Leglay (1966).
3. Versnel (1993), 90–135, detects a fruitful 'inconsistency'; I explain it, rather, by historical accretions to Cronos (originally a 'golden age' god) who also became a child-eater (through Kumarbi). Through this side of his persona, he was then the god who could explain the horrible non-Greek behaviour in the Phoenician world or the warlike cults in Anatolia. In the main Greek world, this horrible Cronos was not cultically prominent.
4. Robert (1978B), 3–48, a brilliant digression on peripheral cults of Cronos and Cronos the Titan as a 'founder' on the rocky Lycian heights of Tlos.
5. Haas (2002), 230–37, argues for the stone being set up and worshipped at Bronze Age Ebla. Even if so, other cults elsewhere would always be possible.
6. Butcher (2004), 413–25.
7. Djobadze (1986).
8. Day (1985), for a survey.
9. Hes., *Theog.* 304–7 and 820–81.
10. Watkins (1992), 319–35, more briefly than Watkins (1995); Katz (1998), 317–34, is full of interest.
11. Hoffner (1998), 10–14; Beckman (1982), 11–15; Haas (2006), 97–103, with more bibliography.
12. Haas (1994), 696–747.
13. Gordon (1967–9), 70–82.
14. Delaporte (1940), plate 22; Houston Smith (1965), 253–60.
15. Siegelova (1971), a groundbreaking study; Haas (2006), 153–6; Haas, Salvini *et al.* (2004), vol. 1, p. 19.
16. Houwink ten Cate (1991), 83–148, esp. 117–19, a fine study to which I owe much.
17. Oppian, *Hal.* 3.7–8 and 3.208–9; Houwink ten Cate (1961), 207 and n. 2.
18. Nonnus, *Dion.* 1.137–2.712; Robert (1977), 88–132, at 113 n. 129, a classic which unfortunately left no mark on Hopkinson (1994).
19. Apollod., *Bibl.* 1.6.3, with Zuntz (1951), 12–35, esp. 31 n. 142, another neglected classic.
20. Oppian echoes Hittite Version 1, while Apollod. and Nonnus echo Hittite 2, as explained in Houwink ten Cate (1961), 209.
21. Vian (1978), 157–72, a brilliant overview of Nonnus. Nonnus' Cadmus

is traceable to a source, Pisander of Laranda F15 (Hutsch), but I also think there is a toponymic relevance: see n. 27 below.

22. Strabo 13.4.6; West (1966), 251; Vian (1960), 19–38, at 20; compare G. S. Kirk, *The Iliad: A Commentary, Books 1–4* (1985), 243: 'it is clear that ancient critics did not know which particular region this signified.' By Chap. 19 nn. 1–2 below, my readers, I trust, will know better.

23. Xanthos, *FGrH* 765 F13; Strabo 13.4.6, with West (1966), 250–51.

24. Arundell (1828), 262, which I owe to the brilliant pages in Robert (1962), 287–317, at 304–5 n. 1, on the 'Pays brulé': his own photographs show it in plates 27–8.

25. Nonnus, *Dion.* 13.474–87, with Robert (1963), 297–312, and Robert (1958), 37–44.

26. Hdt. 1.93; Lycoph., *Alex.* 1353; above all, Robert (1982), 334–57.

27. Arundell (1828), 260: 'I was much struck, I might almost say horror-struck.' I am also awestruck by Vian (1978), 157–72, on the digression suddenly inserted by Nonnus in *Dion.* 1.153: Vian acutely sees a separate local source-tradition and endorses the location of its cave, smoking and white-topped, with Hierapolis (modern Pammukale); note, too, Nonnus calls it the 'Mygdonian Gorge' and equates the general area with Phrygia. Cadmus' role can, I think, be related to the local river Cadmos, the origin, therefore, of his presence in this episode (the Cadmos mountains nearby are also relevant). Pisander of Laranda certainly involved him, and may be the entire source, but Nonnus draws on Xanthus of Lydia elsewhere and I wonder if Xanthus is not the original source of this 'Lydian-Phrygian' episode too. Vian, commenting on Nonnus, *Dion.* 1.153 (Budé edn., 144 n. 153), is a starting-point for study of this typical Nonnian enigma.

28. Strabo 16.4.27: Arima is 'tēn Surian autēn'.

29. Strabo 13.4.6 and 16.2.7; Scholiast on Hom., *Il.* 2.783.

30. Strabo 16.2.7; Jo. Malalas, *Chron.* 7.83C.

31. Bonnet (1987), 101–43, at 133–4; Tadmor (1994), 294; Fuchs (1994), 422.

32. Strabo 16.2.8, the 'spēlaion to hieron', for which see Dussaud (1927), 425. It needs an archaeologist.

33. Pind. F93; Pind., *Pyth.* 1.17 and esp. 8.16.

34. Callisthenes, *FGrH* 124, F33.

35. A clue to the name's Hittite overtones, perhaps, in Otten (1988), column 1, 24–6: an Arimmatta is linked there to a 'watery abyss', for which see Gordon (1967–9), 70–82, and above all Hawkins (1995B), 45, brilliantly decoding the Hittites' interest in the big sacred pool and pit (route) to the underworld at their complex at Hattusa. This is not Callisthenes' Arima (which is far south, by the coast), but I wonder, or even suspect, that the

same 'Arima' name may have been applied there too because of its remarkable natural 'watery abyss'.

36. Garstang and Gurney (1959), 54, lines 40–48 of the Sanassura Treaty. I am grateful to O. R. Gurney for pursuing in detail the suggestion I put to him, one of the last such ever. He (not I) observed that Forlanini (1988), 145, had raised it, albeit in general terms. Casabonne (2004), 71 n. 243, considers 'Erimma' as Callisthenes' 'Arima' to be 'une hypothèse sujette à caution' because the boundary given in the Sanassura Treaty is 'Lamiya', in his view the place Lamos, not the Lamos river. If 'Erimma' lies by the Corycian cave, he finds it hard that it is given by this treaty to 'Kizzuwatna' on the other (east) side of the boundary-line. Boundaries are not always logical, and in my view it shows the value the Hittites placed on this site with its 'watery abyss' and so, against geographic logic, they kept it. O. R. Gurney was still willing to accept the identification, on less elaborate grounds. The area needs prolonged excavation, after survey again around the cave's well-known site. I believe it contains (neo-)Hittite evidence.

37. Keil and Wilhelm (1931), 214–18, well worth enjoying. Bent (1891), 206–24; MacKay (1990), 2045–2129, a good survey with bibliography and the cave's discovery at 2104 n. 239.

38. Lucan, *BC* 3.226; Strabo 14.5.5 ('krokos aristē'); Dioscor., *Mat. Med.* 1.26 ('krokos kratistos'); Galen, *On Antidotes* 1.14 (he inspected it 'akribōs'); also, interestingly, the tireless Dionys. Per. 387; prices in Dagron and Feissel (1987), 175, and, above all, Robert (1960B), 334–5 nn. 2–4, a tour de force. Ironically, in view of the 'hunt' for the cave, V. Langlois presented the winner, Tchihatchev, with a saffron crocus, but from the wrong Cilician ravine: Robert (1976), 190–91 and n. 42.

39. Bent (1891), 206–24, at 213.

40. Pompon. Mela 1.13; Bent (1891), 206–24, at 214.

41. Bent (1891), 206–24, at 212, J. and L. Robert, *Bull. Épig.* (1974), 612.

42. Parth. F29, with Lightfoot (1999), 181–5. On Cinna, see Catull. 95.5, discussed remarkably by Leigh (1994), 181–95, who is unfortunately indifferent to the cave and its topography: it has nothing to do with Adonis or Virgil's Old Man of Tarentum.

43. Wrongly copied as 'Zeu Paphie' by Bent, but corrected by Heberdey and Wilhelm (1896), 154.

44. Solin., *Coll. Rer. Mirab.* (ed. Mommsen), section 38.3 (pp. 162–3), gives a remarkably good description of the cave; I believe him, therefore, when he adds 'in eo sacrum Iovis est fanum'; Dagron and Feissel (1987), 44–5 nos. 16 and 17, for Zeus Epineikios honoured nearby. Houwink ten Cate (1961), 212–13, for the various honours locally for Hermes, too.

45. Feld and Weber (1968), 254–67; MacKay (1990), 2045–2129, at 2105–8; Keil and Wilhelm (1931), 214–19 with plates 50–54; Bell (1906), 7–36, at 30–31.

46. Pompon. Mela 1.13; Keil and Wilhelm (1931), 214–19; Casabonne and Porcher (2003), 131–40, at 131–2, with a diagram.

47. Callisth., *FGrH* 124, F33, shows he talked to locals; Curt. 3.4.10 where the cave (with crocuses) and other sites 'monstrabantur', perhaps by local informants as recorded in an Alexander-historian, not just in Curtius' own rhetoric.

48. Houwink ten Cate (1961), 212–13, with 130–31.

49. Oppian, *Hal.* 3.7–14; Dagron and Feissel (1987), 45 n. 5, on his local origins; Oppian, *Hal.* 3.24–5, on bloodstains.

50. Gough (1976), 435; MacKay (1990), 2045–2129, at 2085–6. At the pre-Christian tower by the ravine, one priest was 'Teucer son of Tarkyaris': his patronym derives ultimately from Tarhunta the Storm God.

51. Imitating Hawkins (1995B), 45, and his sacred pool.

52. Houwink ten Cate (1961), 212, catches the right tone: 'there is a strong argument in favour of the Illuyankas myth being the cult-myth of Corycus.' He wrote, however, before the Hedammu story, an even better candidate, was known.

53. Bonnet (1987), 101–43, at 132–43, but I doubt her derivation of the name from the mountain. The Semitic root *sp‘*- on her p. 136 is more promising (Houwink ten Cate, 1961, 210 n. 7, also endorsed a Phoenician origin for the name).

54. Strabo 13.4.6; Fowler (2000), 307; Pherecydes F54, with a possible detour through the Caucasus.

55. Pind., *Pyth.* 1.16–19; for my translation here of 'hyper', compare, for example, Thuc. 8.95.5.

56. De Caro and Gialanella (1998), 337–53; Albore Livadie (1986), 189–205, at 202–4.

57. Strabo 13.4.6; Hesych., s.v. 'Arimos'; Serv., *ad Verg. Aen.* 9.712; Bonfante and Bonfante (2000), 71 and 124 n. 35. I cannot agree with the derivation from 'pithoi' ('Vaseburgh') preferred by Ridgway (1992), 36. I also reject the 'explanations' given by Cerchiai (1996), 141–50.

58. Pind., *Ol.* 4.6–7; *Pyth.* 1.19–20 and F92.

59. Pind., *Pyth.* 1.16–17 ('pote'), 19–24 and 28 ('melamphyllais').

60. Duchemin (1956), 150–53, calls Pindar a 'témoin oculaire' and compares his poem with the eruption of 8 July 1955. I quote Duchemin (1995), 49–67, at 54–5.

CHAPTER 18

The identity of Giants' bones is brilliantly pursued by Adrienne Mayor (2000), though without Euboeans and an eighth-century trail. In Macedon, Greece, my researches on the ground have been fortified by help from Professor Evangelia Tsoukala of Aristotle University, Thessaloniki and her scientific researches which have had such brilliant results. In myth and poetry, the studies by F. Vian (1952 and 2005) rise to the challenge of the subject. O. Waser's remarkable article 'Giganten' in *RE Suppl.* 3 (1918), 655–759, is a superb collection of evidence. My trail connects the pieces available, from prehistoric teeth to fragments of Greek poets, in a new way.

1. Nonnus, *Dion.* 2.628–30; Vian (1978), 157–72, at 159, thinks aptly of local guides pointing out this monument.
2. West (1966) on Hes., *Theog.* 149 and 817–19; Scholiast on Ap. Rhod., *Argon.* 1.1165, is especially important, also citing Ion and Eumelus, on whom see West (2002), 109–34 at 111–12.
3. Solin. 11.16; Scholiast on Ap. Rhod., *Argon.* 1.1165; Steph. Byz., s.v. 'Karystos'; Hesych., s.v. 'Titanida'.
4. Ael., *VH* 5.3; Arist. F678 (Rose); Parth. F31; I quote Lightfoot (1999), 192.
5. Mele (1981), 138–9; Gras (1992), 27–44, at 34–5.
6. Callim., *Hymn* 4.143; Vian (2005B), 192–203; another gigantic Aigaion had a 'tomb' at the mouth of the Rhyndacos river in Mysia, for which see Ap. Rhod. 1.1165 and Vian, *Notice* in the Budé edn., vol. 1, pp. 28–31; on the landscape, but not the tomb, Robert (1980), 89–98.
7. Vian (1952B), 20–29 and 169–74; Hes., *Theog.* 185–6.
8. Solin. 11.16 calls Euboea 'almost wholly the land of Titans'. West (2002), 109–34, at 117 n. 36.
9. Waser (1918), 655–759, at 737–59, a remarkable work. So is Vian, *LIMC*, vol. 4/1 (1988), 191–270, esp. 268–9, partly based on Waser.
10. Hom., *Od.* 7.56–60 and 204–6; 10.120–22.
11. Vian, in *LIMC*, vol. 4/1 (1988), 210–11.
12. Eur., *Ion* 215–18.
13. Ar., *Av.* 823–5 and 1249–52, with Dunbar (1995), 7–9 and ad locc.; Bowie (1993), 58–66, rather adventurously on Ar., *Eq.*
14. Plato, *Soph.* 246–8.
15. Artem. 4.47.
16. Vian (1944), 97–117, and (1952A), 129–55.

17. Camassa (1986), 133–62; Strabo 1.2.12–17; 6.1.5.
18. Eust., on Dionys. Per. 919; Paus. 8.29.4; Waser (1918), 655–759, at 751–2.
19. Genesis 6: 1–4; Numbers 13: 33; Deuteronomy 3: 11.
20. Robert (1960), 313 n. 2, on coins of Acmoneia and Brouzos showing Zeus with two Giants, explained by Robert in terms of two local mountains which show a 'stream' of big boulders (the work of Giants); for these, Philippson (1911), 75–6.
21. Mayor (2000), a brilliant book to which I owe much.
22. Jo. Malalas, *Chron.* 8.16.
23. Mayor (2000), 198.
24. Riis (1970), 85–6; Moorey (1999), 118.
25. Paus. 8.29.4; Jones (2000), 476–81, for dating.
26. Strabo 5.4.6.
27. Hamilton (1776), 68.
28. Philostr., *Her.* 8. 15; Jones (2001), 141–9.
29. Waser (1918), 655–759, at 738–9.
30. Dio Cass. 66.23.1; compare 66.22.2.
31. Pisano (2003), a splendid study.
32. Frederiksen (1984), 354.
33. Schnapper (1986), 177–200, another brilliant study; de Toleto (1539).
34. Strabo 6.3.5; Pisano (2003), 40; Ps.-Arist., *Mir. ausc.* 97: 'the smell is so bad that the sea is not navigable'; Lycoph., *Alex.* 1356–8; Timaeus underlies them, as Geffcken (1892), 15, also saw.
35. Cremonesi (1978), 9–10; Blanc (1958–61), 308–13.
36. Just., *Epit.* 44.4.1; Paus. 10.4.6.
37. Claud., *De Rapt. Proserp.* 3.332–50.
38. Hdt. 7.123; Apollod., *Bibl.* 1.6.1; Lycoph., *Alex.* 1404–8.
39. Vian (1952B), 180; 226 ('aucune trace de manifestations volcaniques').
40. Solin. 9.6; Philostr., *Her.* 10.28.
41. Tsoukala and Melentis (1994), 633–40: I am so grateful to E. Tsoukala for all her help with her remarkable discoveries which underlies nn. 42, 45, 46 and 47 below. I quote Mayor (2000).
42. Tsoukala and Bartsiokas (in press), kindly sent in proof to me.
43. Comiers (1692), 82–131, a remarkable contribution: the giant is mentioned by Schnapper (1986), 177–200, at 188–9.
44. Schnapper (1986), 177–200.
45. Tsoukala (2003), in full colour.
46. Tsoukala (2007), again in colour; Tsoukala and Lister (1998), 117–39, a straight-tusked elephant, and Tsoukala (2000), 165–91, a mammoth.
47. Tsoukala (1992), 79–92, with helpful distribution map.

48. Paus. 8.29.1 and 8.32.5, with Frazer (1898).
49. Mayor (2000), 99 and 298 nn. 36–7.
50. Already guessed, but at the wrong date, by Vian (1952B), 221: 'les colons eubéens, après l'avoir localisé en Chalcidique, l'ont transplanté aussi à Cumes dès la fin du VIème siècle?' My role is to remove his question mark and change his 'VI' to 'VIII'.
51. Vokotopoulou (1996), 319–28; Hammond (1998), 393–9.
52. Plin., *HN* 7.73.
53. August., *De civ. D.* 15.9.
54. 4 Ezra 5: 2.
55. Céard (1978), 37–76, a fascinating study.
56. Hom., *Il.* 21.407.
57. Deuteronomy 3: 11.

CHAPTER 19

Odysseus' lying Cretan tales have been much discussed. A historically plaus-ible context is emphasized by T. F. R. G. Braun, 'The Greeks in Egypt', in *Cambridge Ancient History*, vol. 3/3 (1982), 32–56. I differ from the pre-cision of W. Burkert, 'Der *Odyssee*-Dichter und Kreta', in his *Kleine Schriften*, vol. 1 (2001), 127–37, who considers (133) that the 'lying tales of Odysseus, in so far as they show reality, fit through and through in the years between 738 and 664 BC'. The limits are rather more widely spaced, I believe.

1. Verg., *Aen.* 9.708–16; Ravaglioli (1985), 932; Hardie (1994), 224–5, is only rather general.
2. Hom., *Il.* 2.460–63.
3. MacLair Boraston (1911), 216–50, at 249–50.
4. Gialanella (1996), 251–68; Ridgway (1992).
5. Hom., *Il.* 19.96 and 416, with W. Leaf's excellent comments.
6. Hom., *Il.* 24.615; Paus. 1.21.3; André Salvini and Salvini (1996), 7–20, with 9 n. 14 on the modern impostor, now shown locally.
7. Stinton (1976), 60–89, esp. 65: such a phrase 'frequently introduces mythi-cal *exempla*, the point being to invoke the authority of tradition'.
8. Hom., *Od.* 14.191–362, 15.389–484; Paizis-Danias (2006), 11–96.
9. Hom., *Od.* 14.199–245.
10. Hom., *Od.* 14.257–84; Gould (1973), 74–103, esp. 95.
11. Acts 12: 7 and Eur., *Bacch.* 442–7, with Celsus, in Orig., *C. Cels.* 2.34; Parker (2004), 131–53.

12. Hom., *Od.* 19.172–80; Hom., *Il.* 2.645–9; Burkert (2001), 127–37; compare Hom., *Od.* 19.188.

13. Hom., *Od.* 3.291–300.

14. Evans (1928), 88–92.

15. Shaw (2006), an excellent summary of the major excavation-volumes, esp. Shaw and Shaw (2000); for the sand-spit and a possible (later?) sea-wall, Shaw (2006), 55 and 57.

16. Shaw and Shaw (2000), 709–11 and 728 nn. 62–8; Amyclaion is also the suggestion of A. Chaniotis with Steph. Byz., s.v. 'Amyclaion', to support it; Kitchell (1979–80), 129–34, has refuted the supposed city-name 'Lisse'.

17. Shaw (2006), 51, on 'the largest waves . . . built up by an onshore west wind, usually during the winter months': the Notos at *Od.* 3.295 is not, strictly, a due-west wind. Heubeck, West and Hainsworth (1988), 179, are not accurate in implying that the 'Komo' location requires Homer's 'smooth rock', 'cape' on the left and 'small rock' to be all one and the same.

18. Gubel (2007), 111–17.

19. Aubet (2001).

20. Shaw (2000), 1107–19; Shaw (2006), 139–40 (important additions).

21. Lipinski (2004), 182–4, for an Egyptian reading of the text, a rather bold one.

22. Csapo (1991), 211–16, at 215.

23. Hom., *Od.* 13.256–86, 17.415–44.

24. Hom., *Od.* 17.420–44, with Emlyn-Jones (1986), 1–10, esp. 7–9, on the changes in the 'pattern' to suit the speaker's social context.

25. Hom., *Od.* 4.228–32.

26. Hom., *Od.* 4.124–30, with Coldstream (1998C), 5–19, at 11 and 14 n. 63, on a similarity between Penelope's throne and one from Nimrud, and a (questionable) tracing of its creator's name, Ikmalios, to a Phoenician origin; better still, compare Karageorghis (2002B), 164, with fig. 341 from Salamis, T. 49.

27. Walcot (1977), 1–19.

28. Danek (1998), with bibliography.

29. Hom., *Od.* 15.397–487.

30. Hom., *Od.* 14.139, 15.490. 'Ēpios' is not discussed by Finley (1956), 136–57, among Homeric 'morals and values'.

31. Moorey (1999), 79–81; Todd (1993), 236–48, at 236; Schaeffer (1939), 99–100, on 'amber' beads at Ugarit; Beck (1979), 15–17.

32. Lorimer (1950), 67, rightly rejected by Dunbabin (1957), 35 n. 2, but I cannot follow him in explaining Homer's usage by biblical 'parallels' as if Tyre and Sidon are interchangeable.

33. Katzenstein (1973) was openly partisan about Tyre; Lipinski (2004), 17–36, and Fletcher (2004), 51–77, for elements in favour of Sidon.

34. Markoe (1985). Some of these bowls may be made by Cypriots, others by 'north Syrians'.

35. Vandorpe (1995), 203–39, at 211 n. 52, on the name 'Thebes'; Burkert (1976), 5–21, has been influential on supporters of a seventh-century Homer, but I do not believe it, nor (the author kindly tells me) does he any longer. Kelly (2006), 321–33, revives the case that Hom., *Il.* 9.381–4, is based on the Late Bronze Age.

CHAPTER 20

For a different view of Homer and his 'debt' to the 'Oriental' sources, M. L. West, *The East Face of Helicon* (1997), is essential. Its chapter on Hesiod (276–333) amplifies West's brilliant commentaries on the *Theogony* (1966) and the *Works and Days* (1978). I can only offer a different emphasis, one which impressed me before finding that P. Walcot, *Hesiod and the Near East* (1966), had ended by considering Euboean connections, albeit with a different range of Near Eastern sources and in a different way. W. Burkert, *Babylon, Memphis, Persepolis* (2004), gives an admirably concise account of the main 'contacts' currently upheld by scholars between Homer and items in Near Eastern texts.

Froma I. Zeitlin, 'Apollo and Dionyos: Starting from Birth', in H. E. J. Horstmanshoff, H. W. Singer *et al.* (eds.), *Kykeon: Studies in Honour of H. S. Versnel* (2002), 209, differs totally from me about Delphi's claims to what she (mis)describes as Cronos' 'obstetrical feat': she sees 'an attempt to transform Delphi into a place of male maternity, especially considering the name Delphi itself as related to the word for "womb" (as are dolphins who figure in the Homeric Hymn)'. Actually, Cronos vomited up the stone.

1. Hom., *Od.* 7.54–63, 7.206, 10.120.

2. Hom., *Il.* 5.898, with Kirk's comments.

3. Burkert (1992A), 92–3.

4. Hom., *Il.* 14.200–10.

5. Hom., *Il.* 1.590–94, 18.395–9; the rope, at 8.19–27.

6. Hom., *Il.* 5.898, with G. S. Kirk, *The Iliad: A Commentary* (1990), 3: 'references to Kronos imprisoned below the earth show the Homeric tradition to have been aware of the Succession-myth describing the violent displacement of the first generation of gods'. Aware, yes – Hom., *Il.* 8.479–81 or 14.279 – but not explicit about it or emphatic about any of it.

7. Hom., *Il.* 20.385–92; Griffin (1986), 31–57, at 53.

8. Philippson (1911), 11–12, and Robert (1982), 334–57 at 341.

9. Radet (1893), 13: 'très poissoneux', and Philippson (1911), 11 and also 12: after an hour's walk north to the 'Kum Tschai', he found a crystal-clear stream and spring 'in dem zahlreiche Fische spielen'. The naming and course of the upper Cam Çay is a complex matter, hinted at by the *Barrington Atlas*, map 56, and I cannot pursue it here.

10. Chap. 17 n. 26.

11. Morris (1997), 595–623, at 623.

12. West (1997), 622–3.

13. West (1997).

14. Hom., *Il.* 7.445–63: West (1995), 203–19, and (1997), 377–80. When he asks 'where did the poet of the *Iliad* get the idea of diverting rivers against a wall to wash it away? This could never be a natural idea in Greece', he overlooks Xen., *Hell.* 5.2.4–7, where Agesilaus, at Mantinea, had not been reading Assyrian sources. For his other ('Eastern') example, the blocking of rivers with corpses, see the (Greek) Ptolemy, in Arr., *Anab.* 2.11.8.

15. Osborne (1993), 231–7, a very acute critique.

16. Högemann (2000), 183–98, with much else too which I do not believe; Latacz (2002), 98 and 146.

17. Raimond (2007), 143–62, at 144–5, for a summary of this debated topic; Mellink (1995), 33–43.

18. Hom., *Il.* 18.316–23, with West (1997), 334–47, esp. 341–2, and even Griffin (1992), 189–211.

19. George, *CR* 50 (2000), 103–6, an important review.

20. Hom., *Il.* 14.188–223, with Richardson (1987), 125–32, and on her 'sexy brassière' (R. Janko, *The Iliad: A Commentary, 13–16* (1994), 185) see Bonner (1949), 1–6, an excellent insight.

21. Hom., *Il.* 5.318–430; Burkert (1992A), 96–8.

22. Hom., *Il.* 15.187–95; Burkert (1992A), 90–91.

23. Hom., *Od.* 7.321–6.

24. West (1988), 151–72, at 172: 'the *Odyssey* might be a Euboean poem . . . But the poet of the *Iliad*, to all appearances, lived in Asia Minor.' Dougherty (2001), 148–51, follows suit, claiming 'the Phaeacians offer the Euboeans a model to think with' (151). Firmly against West, Cassio (1998), 11–22.

25. Acousilaos, *FGrH* 2, F2: Hellanicus 4, F20 and now Malouchou (2006), 81–90, with a careful discussion; the approach and conclusion of West (1999), 364–82, were wondrously different.

26. Pind., *Nem.* 2.1–2; Plato, *Phdr.* 252B, *Ion* 530D, *Resp.* 599E; Isoc.,

Helen 65; Hippostratus, *FGrH* 568, F5, identifies the *genos* as the singers of Homer's poetry '*ek diadochēs*'.

27. Ion, *FGrH* 392, F1.

28. Burkert (2001), 127–37; Hom., *Il.* 2.649, *Od.* 19.172–7, 19.188 and 18.177; West (1981), 169–75, for another possible 'Cretan version'.

29. Hom., *Il.* 11.19–28, with Richardson (1987), 125–32.

30. West (1997), 628–9.

31. Karageorghis (2006), 665–75, on the precise word '*allothrooi*' if (but only if) the 'Temesa' in Hom., *Od.* 1.183–4, alludes to Tamassos on Cyprus.

32. Hom., *Od.* 3.169–75.

33. T.397, for instance, in Pithekoussai 1.429.

34. Johnston (2000), 189–226, at 224; Coldstream and MacDonald (1997), 191–245, at 235.

35. Dominguez and Sanchez (2001), 12 ff., and esp. 88, where I do not accept the (widespread) view that 'Greek artefacts dating to the 8th c. . . . certainly were brought in Phoenician cargoes . . . and are evidence of Phoenician, not Greek, trade'. At Toscanos, we even have locally imitated Euboean ceramics, not for non-Greek use surely.

36. Wade-Gery (1958), still classic; Edwards (2004) is also to the point: I too have envisaged Ascra as 'autonomous' (67), a minority view.

37. Hes., *Op.* 640; Wallace (1974), 5–24, esp. 8.

38. Hes., *Op.* 633–40: I take '*nassato*' to mean 'he settled' and, despite G. L. Huxley, *CR* (2005), 201, I think Wade-Gery (1958), 5, thought so too when writing he 'returned' to Boeotia.

39. Hes., *Theog.* 306 and 820–80.

40. West (1966), 90: the *Hymn to Hecate* (Hes., *Theog.* 411–52) is a counter to extravagant talk of 'Greek religion as *polis*-religion'. No cults of Hecate are attested, even later, in Boeotian *poleis*. Strauss Clay (2003), 138, even thinks the hymn attests 'to the poet's understanding of [Hecate's] critical mediating function'.

41. Burkert (2005), 3–20, on the gendering of the first pairs; Veyne (1983), 28–9.

42. West (1966), 161–2, is still fundamental on Hes., *Theog.* 26–8, against views like Wade-Gery's (1958), 7; Hes., *Theog.* 33–51, for the Muses' own song.

43. Hes., *Theog.* 497–500.

44. West (2003A), 9–12, a lucid summary of the date; I still incline to the brilliant core of Forrest (1956), 33–52; Chappell (2006), 331–48, surveys the theories, but is too negative at 332–4; at 334 n. 3 Forrest dates the hymn after the institution of chariot-racing at the Pythia in 582 BC; I prefer 582 BC

itself and thus explain *Hymn. Hom. Ap.* 270–71, with the clear hint that Telphusa is being deceitful at 375–81. Cassola (1975), 97–104, lists much more bibliography, none of which alters this cardinal point; Malkin (2000), 69–77, is positive about the poem but does not discuss the Cretans.

45. *Hymn. Hom. Ap.* 388–520, a marvellous passage; Philippe (2005), 241–54, on 'Delphinios'.

46. *Hymn. Hom. Ap.* 392–6.

47. Huxley (1975), 119–24, at 122. Predictably, the archaeologically focused Morgan (1990), 145–6, runs out at this fence: 'the presence of Cretans accords with the demands of sanctuary politics'! Contrast, rightly, Forrest (1956), 33–52.

48. Jeffery (1976), 191–2, a neat summary; Huxley (1975), 119–24. Rutherford (2001A), 24–5 and 205–7; Forrest (1957), 160–75, on the origins of the cult.

49. Rolley (1977), esp. 145–6. Only secondarily was the name Crisa linked to Crete–Cressa: Servius, *ad Verg. Aen.* 3.32, is not primary evidence; Kolk (1963), 34 n. 33.

50. Hes., *Theog.* 497–500.

51. Coldstream (1979A), 257–63.

52. Hes., *Theog.* 477–82.

53. Steph. Byz., s.v. 'Lyktos'; A. Chaniotis kindly helped me here; West (1966), 297–8, for other possibilities, to me less convincing.

54. Matthäus (2000B), 517–49; Hoffmann (1998); Matthäus (2000A), 267–80; Coldstream (2003), 401–3; Kunze (1931); Hoffman (1997).

55. West (1966), 290–93, saw it as 'an account deriving from Minoan Crete' reconciled by 'the Greek theogonic tradition'. I would minimize the Minoan influence.

56. West (1978), 30, touches on this possibility, albeit more generally; compare West (1997), 627.

57. Hes., *Op.* 654–7.

58. Hes., *Theog.* 820–80, esp. 868.

59. West (1966), 379–83, a brilliant presentation; I also agree with West (1966), 397–9, on the poem's ending; Kelly (2007), 371–402, does not persuade me at all.

60. Rowe (1983), 124–35.

61. *Hymn. Hom. Ap.* 305–74; I disagree with West (2003A), 11–12, that this episode is due to Cynaethus, honouring Hera, who was linked to Samos and his patron Polycrates. I regard it simply as a Delphic episode, originating there and annexing the Typhon-story into its own Python legend.

62. Hes., [*Sc.*] 32.

63. Hes., *Theog.* 860, suspected, however, by West (1966), 393: there did not need to be a full eruption, as West implies, for Typhon to be sited under Etna. He sends up smoke and noise very often: they sufficed.

64. Hes., *Op.* 106–201, with West (1978), 173–7; despite Sourvinou-Inwood (1997), 1–22, I think there is overall deterioration from age to age.

65. Daniel 2: 38–45; Boyce (1984), 68–85; Potter (1994), 188; Koenen (1994), 1–34, at 11–13, a major study.

66. Bickerman (1988), 24–5, on one reworking at this time.

67. West (1997), 306–33, for a brilliant array of parallel passages.

68. Thuc. 6.3.1, surely Delphic Apollo, not Delos's.

69. Paus. 10.24.6; Hes., *Theog.* 498–500; West (1997), 294–5.

70. Callim., *Aet.* F43, 74–8 on (Delphic) Apollo; the 'boy from Ascra' is my forerunner of that 'boy from Stratford' who rounds off Nuttall (2007), 383, so memorably; for (later) Homeric traces on Euboea, Debiasi (2001), 9–36.

CHAPTER 21

1. 'Contemporary' is above all my point here. West (1997) distinguishes Oriental and 'neo-Oriental' and (except for Aphrodite, perhaps) it is the latter category I struggle to see in Homer. Burkert (2004), 31, thinks 'Tethys' was borrowed after the Bronze Age, but we do not know when. Koenen (1994), 23, argues more cautiously for a 'broad cultural matrix', and even a structure, shared with Egyptian and other texts, but considers it far from 'contemporary', though he accepts that other details may have arrived later (25–6).

2. Perennially controversial, of course: I incline to Janko (1998), 1–13, and Hainsworth (1991), 11–42, but nonetheless with a hint of text (did Homer note down a main plot?) to satisfy Dowden (1996), 47–61, but not the fully literate view of West (2003B), 1–14, esp. 14.

3. Rasmussen (1991), 57–78, for beginnings.

4. Kirk (1972), 83–102, among very many; Calame (1996), likewise.

5. Hom., *Od.* 13.162–83, esp. 172–8, with *Od.* 8.564–70.

6. Hes., *Theog.* 209, 197–200, 282–3; *Op.* 50–105; *Theog.* 521–616. J. L. Lightfoot kindly points out to me the frequent aetiological element in Hesiodic fragments: FF71, 125, 188A, 226.

7. Lane Fox (1991), 58–9, with bibliography; Fichtner (1956), 372–96, on name-aetiologies in J; Golka (1976–7), 410–28, and (1977), 36–47.

8. Genesis 28: 19 and 11: 9, with Westermann (1984), commentary: he is resistant to the frequently obvious inference that the aetiology gave rise to the entire story being told. Gunkel (1964) is still fundamental on this matter.

9. An 'aetiological narrative' is distinct from a narrative which also includes an aetiology – for instance Genesis 35: 20 on Rachel's grave: Rachel died anyway, but an existing place gave (probably) the further embellishment, that Jacob 'set up a pillar'.

10. Genesis 26: 18–33.

11. Genesis 47: 26.

12. Joshua 5: 2–9.

13. Lane Fox (1991), 229–30, using Bickerman (1988), 179, quoted here too; for 'cult-aetiologies' in the Old Testament, Soggin (1960), 341–7, at 341.

14. Deuteronomy 3: 11.

15. Genesis 19: 6–19, 29: Westermann (1985), 297, remarkably claims that 'the attempt to explain Genesis 19 as an etiological narrative' is misguided: rather, he thinks, the essence is 'the experience of a catastrophe'. But the origin of this episode is not explained by an 'essence' distilled by an empathetic modern reader.

16. Childs (1963), 279–92, for the biblical examples; *Hymn. Hom. Herm.* 125; Lane Fox (2004), 184–214, at 212–14.

17. Hdt. 3.48 may be an example; Pagels (1927) looks for others, but they are embedded in tales told to Herodotus by oral sources. Hdt. 5.88–9 has an aetiological element (5.88), but it is also a complex chain of (alleged) historical causes.

18. Van Seters (1992), 28–32, well stresses the need to distinguish between a historian searching for '*aitiai*' and what *we* call 'aetiology'. Van Groningen (1953), 26, was wrong to describe the 'flourishing historical science of Herodotus' as 'particularly rich in aetiological elements'.

19. My Euboeans' (significant) names are chosen from a good stable, the excellent equine list in Bechtel (1900), 326–31; 'Anas' is in Hawkins (2000), 96: 'my beloved wife', at Carchemish. The Chalcidian month of Hippion is discussed by Knoepfler (1989), at 39–59; 'Phosphoros' is a horse-name in the excellent list in Toynbee (1948), 24–37, esp. 26–33. Hipposthenes showed Homeric 'manliness' (*ēnoreē*), not 'excessive manliness' (*agēnoriē*), so as to please Graziosi and Haubold (2003), 60–76. 'Buried lives' are derived from Matthew Arnold's poem and 'Life, as it were', from the end of Henry James's *Washington Square*.

Hipposthenes, Anas and Phosphoros lie buried, in my view, beneath the car park of the Green Land *phytorio* (Plant Centre) on the road out from Chalkis to Eretria.

Bibliography

Abel, F. M. (1933), 'Oronte et Litani', *Jo. of Pal. Or. Soc.* 13: 147–58.

Ahlberg, G. (1971), Prothesis *and* Ekphora *in Greek Geometric Art.*

Aimé Giron, N. (1987), 'Ba'al Saphon et les dieux de Tahpanhes dans un nouveau papyrus phénicien', *ASAE* 40: 433–60.

Ainsworth, W. (1838), *Researches in Assyria, Babylonia and Chaldaea.*

Akdojan, R., and Wilhelm, G. (2003), 'Hethitische und hurritische Keilschrifttafeln aus dem Besitz für anatolische Kultur in Ankara', *Zts. für Assyr.* 93: 214–31.

Albore Livadie, C. (1986), 'Considerations sur l'homme préhistorique et son environnement dans le territoire phlégréen', in his *Tremblements de terre: éruptions volcaniques et vie des hommes dans la Campanie antique,* 189–205.

Alexander, R. L. (2002), 'The Storm God at 'Ain Dara', in R. A. Yener and H. A. Hoffner (eds.), *Recent Developments in Hittite Archaeology and History: Papers in Memory of Hans G. Güterbock,* 11–20.

Almagro-Gorbea, M. (2001), 'Cyprus, Phoenicia and Iberia: From "Precolonization" to Colonization in the "Far West"', in L. Bonfante and V. Karageorghis (eds.), *Italy and Cyprus in Antiquity: 1500–450 BC,* 239–70.

Alster, B. (1996), 'Inanna Repenting: The Conclusion of Inanna's Descent', *Acta Sumerologica (Japan)* 18: 1–18.

Aly, W. (1956), *De Strabonis Codice Rescripto.*

Amandry, P. (1948), 'Pyrpnoos Chimaira', in *Mélanges O. Picard,* vol. 1, *RA* 29–32: 1–11.

Amigues, S. (2007), 'Le Styrax et ses usages antiques', *JS:* 261–318.

Ampolo, C. (1997), 'L'interpretazione storica della più antica iscrizione del Lazio', in G. Bartoloni (ed.), *Le necropoli arcaiche di Veio,* 211–17.

Anastassiades, A. (1998), 'Arsinoēs Philadelphou: Aspects of a Specific Cult on Cyprus', *RDAC:* 129–40.

André Salvini, B., and Salvini, M. (1996), 'Nouvelles considérations sur le relief rupestre de la prétendue "Niobe" du mont Sipyle', in H. Gasche and B. Hrovda (eds.), *Collectanea Orientalia: histoire, arts de l'espace et industrie de la terre. Études offertes en hommage à Agnes Spycket*, 7–20.

Annus, A. (2002), *The God Ninurta in the Mythology and Royal Ideology of Ancient Mesopotamia.*

Antonaccio, C. (1995A), *An Archaeology of Ancestors: Tomb Cult and Hero Cult in Early Greece.*

Antonaccio, C. (1995B), 'Lefkandi and Homer', in O. Andersen and M. Dickie (eds.), *Homer's World: Fiction, Tradition and Reality*, 5–28.

Antonelli, L. (1995), 'Le localizzazioni della Nekyia di Odisseo: un itinerario sulle tracce degli Eubei', *Hesperià*, 5: 203–22.

Antonelli, L. (1996), 'La falce di Crono: considerazioni sulla prima fondazione di Zancle', *Kokalos* 42: 313–35.

Antonelli, L. (2000), *Kerkyraika: ricerche su Corcira alto-arcaica tra Ionia e Adriatico.*

Arruda, A. M. (1999–2000), *Los fenicios en Portugal.*

Arslan, N. (2003), 'Zur Frage der Kolonisation Kilikiens anhand der griechischen Importkeramik', in B. Schmaltz and M. Söldner (eds.), *Griechische Keramik in kulturellen Kontext*, 258–61.

Arundell, W. (1828), *A Visit to the Seven Churches of Asia.*

Asheri, D. (1990), *Erodoto*, vol. 3.

Asheri, D. (2001), 'La *makra apoikia* di Io in Egitto', in S. Bianchetti *et al.* (eds.), *Poikilma: studi in onore di Michele R. Cataudella*, 27–38.

Assaf, Ali Abu (1990), *Der Tempel von Ain Dara.*

Atallah, W. (1966), *Adonis dans la littérature et l'art grecs.*

Aubet, M. E. (2006), 'Burial, Symbols and Mortuary Practices in a Phoenician Tomb', in E. Herring, I. Lemos *et al.* (eds.), *Across Frontiers: Etruscans, Greeks, Phoenicians and Cypriots. Studies in Honour of D. Ridgway and F. R. Serra Ridgway*, 35–47.

Aubet, M. M. (2001), *The Phoenicians and the West.*

Aupert, P. (2003), 'Le Dépot archaïque du rempart nord d'Amathonte II: les premières inscriptions grecques alphabétiques d'Amathonte', *BCH* 127: 107–21.

Bafico, S., Oggiano, I., Ridgway, D., and Garbini, G. (1997), 'Fenici e indigeni a Sant' Imbenia (Alghero)', in P. Bernardini, R. D'Oriano and P. G. Spanu (eds.), *Phoinikes B Shrdn: i fenici in Sardegna*, 45–54.

Bagnasco Gianni, G. (1999), 'L'acquisizione della scrittura in Etruria: materiali a confronto per la ricostruzione del quadro storico e culturale', in G. Bagnasco Gianni and F. Cordano (eds.), *Scritture mediterranee tra il IX e il VII secolo a. C.*, 85–106.

453

Bailo Modesti, G. (1998), 'Coppe a semicercli penduli dalle necropoli di Pontecagnano', in M. Bats and B. d'Agostino (eds.), *Euboica: l'Eubea e la presenza euboica in Calcidica e in occidente*, 367–75.

Bakhuizen, S. L. (1976), *Chalcis-in-Euboea: Iron and Chalcidians Abroad*.

Bakirtzis, C. (1995), 'The Role of Cyprus in the Grain Supply of Constantinople', in V. Karageorghis and D. Michaelides (eds.), *Cyprus and the Sea*, 247–53.

Balduin, L. (1997), 'Nakome: il sito e la sua storia', *Patavium* 5: 107–37.

Balty, J. C. (1981), 'Une version orientale méconnue du mythe de Cassiopée', in *Mythologie gréco-romaine, mythologies périphériques*, Colloques internationaux du CNRS, 593, 95–106.

Barker, W. B. (1853), *Lares and Penates*.

Barnes, T. D. (1981), *Constantine and Eusebius*.

Barnett, R. D. (1953), 'Mopsos', *JHS* 73: 140–43.

Barr, J. (1974), 'Philo of Byblos and his "Phoenician History"', *BJRL* 57: 17–68.

Bartoloni, G. (2006), 'Vino fenicio, coppe greche', in E. Herring, I. Lemos *et al.* (eds.), *Across Frontiers: Etruscans, Greeks, Phoenicians and Cypriots. Studies in Honour of D. Ridgway and F. R. Serra Ridgway*, 375–82.

Baudy, G. J. (1986), *Adonisgärten: Studien zur antiken Samensymbolik*.

Baurain, C. (1980), 'Kinyras, la fin de l'âge de bronze à Chypre et la tradition antique', *BCH* 104: 277–308.

Baurain, C. (1986), 'Portée chronologique et géographique du terme "phénicien"', in E. Lipinski (ed.), *Studia Phoenicia*, 4: 7–28.

Baurain, C. (1992), 'Héraclès dans l'épopée homérique', in C. Bonnet and C. Jourdain-Annequin (eds.), *Héraclès: d'une rive à l'autre de la Méditerrannée. Bilan et perspectives*, 67–109.

Bechtel, F. (1900), 'Das Wort "Hippos" in den eretrischen Personennamen', *Hermes*, 35: 326–31.

Beck, C. W. (1979), 'Appendix: Analysis of an Assyrian Amber Statuette', *Occasional Papers on the Near East* 1: 15–17.

Becking, B. (1992), *The Fall of Samaria: A Historical and Archaeological Study*.

Beckman, G. (1982), 'The Anatolian Myth of Illuyanka', *JANES* 14: 11–15.

Bedini, A. (1975), 'Castel di Decima: la necropoli arcaica', *Notizie degli Scavi*, 29: 370–92.

Bell, G. (1906), 'Notes on a Journey through Cilicia and Lycaonia, Part II', *Rev. Arch.*: 7–36.

Bell, G. (1928), *The Desert and the Sown*.

Bendall, L. M. (2007), *Economics of Religion in the Mycenaean World: Resources Dedicated to Religion in the Mycenaean Palace Economy*.

Bent, J. (1891), 'A Journey in Cilicia Tracheia', *JHS* 12: 206–24.

Bérard, C. (1985), 'Argoura fut-elle la capitale des futurs érétriens?', *MH* 42: 268–75.

Bérard, J. (1957), *La Colonisation grecque de l'Italie méridionale et de la Sicile*, 2nd edition.

Bérard, V. (1891), 'Inscriptions d'Asie mineure', *BCH* 15: 538–62.

Bernard, P. (1995), 'Légendes de fondations hellénistiques (Apamée sur l'Oronte) et paysage et toponymie dans le proche-orient hellénisé', *Topoi* 5: 353–408.

Bernard, P. (1997), 'Les Origines thessaliennes de l'Armenie vues par deux historiens thessaliens de la génération d'Alexandre', in P. Briant (ed.), *Topoi supplément*, 1:131–216.

Bernardini, P. (1991), 'Un insediamento fenicio a Sulci nella seconda metà dell' VIII sec. a. C.', in *Atti del III Congresso Internazionale di studi fenici e punici*, vol. 2: 663–73.

Bernardini, P. (1996), 'Le origini della presenza fenicia in Sardegna: tipologie di insediamento e cronologia', in E. Acquaro (ed.), *Alle soglie della classicità . . . studi in onore di Sabatino Moscati*, 535–45.

Bickerman, E. (1939), 'Sur une inscription grecque de Sidon', in *Mélanges syriens offerts à René Dussaud*, vol. 1: 91–9.

Bickerman, E. J. (1952), '*Origines Gentium*', *CP* 47: 65–81.

Bickerman, E. J. (1980), *Chronology of the Ancient World*.

Bickerman, E. J. (1986), *Studies in Jewish and Christian History*, part 3.

Bickerman, E. J. (1988), *The Jews in the Greek Age*.

Bierling, M. P. (ed.) (2002), *The Phoenicians in Spain*.

Bikai, P. M. (1983), 'The Imports from the East – Appendix II', in V. Karageorghis (ed.), *Palaepaphos-Skales: An Iron Age Cemetery in Cyprus*, 396–406.

Bikai, P. M. (1987A), *The Phoenician Pottery of Cyprus*.

Bikai, P. M. (1987B), 'Trade Networks in the Early Iron Age: The Phoenicians at Palaepaphos', in B. W. Rupp (ed.), *Western Cyprus: Connections*, 125–8.

Bikai, P. M. (1987C), 'The Phoenician Pottery', in V. Karageorghis, O. Picard and C. Tytgat (eds.), *La Nécropole d'Amathunte Tombes 110–385*, 1–19.

Bikai, P. M. (1992), 'Cyprus and Phoenicia: Literary Evidence for the Early Iron Age', in G. K. Ioannides (ed.), *Studies in Honour of Vassos Karageorghis*, vol. 1: 241–8.

Bikai, P. M. (2004), 'Phoenician Ceramics from the Greek Sanctuary', in J. W. Shaw (ed.), *Kommos*, 4/1: 302–11.

Bing, J. (1971), 'Tarsus: A Forgotten Colony of Lindos', *JNES* 30: 99–109.

Bing, J. (1973), 'A Further Note on Cyinda-*Kundi*', *Historia*, 22: 346–90.

Birley, A. R. (1997), *Hadrian: The Restless Emperor*.

Bitti Sestieri, A. M. (2000), 'The Reconstruction of Italian Protohistory', in D. Ridgway, F. Serra Ridgway *et al.* (eds.), *Ancient Italy in its Mediterranean Setting: Studies in Honour of Ellen Macnamara*, 28–9.

Blanc, A. C. (1958–61), 'Industria musteriana su calcare e su valve di Meretrix Chione associata con fossili di Elefante . . . in nuovi giacimenti costieri del Capo di Leuca', *Quaternaria*, 5: 308–13.

Blandin, B. (2000), 'Une tombe du IXème siècle av. J. C. à Érétrie', *AK* 43: 134–46.

Blandin, B. (2007), *Eretria XVII: les pratiques funéraires d'époque géométrique à Érétrie*, vols. 1–2.

Blazquez, J. M. (1983), 'Las liras de las estelas Hispanas de finales de la Edad del Bronce', *AEA* 56: 213–28.

Blome, P. (1984), 'Lefkandi und Homer', *WJA* 10: 9–21.

Boardman, J. (1957), 'Early Euboean Pottery and History', *ABSA* 52: 1–29.

Boardman, J. (1990A), 'Al Mina and History', *OJA* 9: 169–90.

Boardman, J. (1990B), 'The Lyre-player Group of Seals: An Encore', *JDAI Arch. Anz.*: 1–17.

Boardman, J. (1994), 'Orientalia and Orientals on Ischia', in B. d'Agostino and D. Ridgway (eds.), *Apoikia: scritti in onore di Giorgio Buchner*, AION, vol. 1: 95–100.

Boardman, J. (1998), 'Herakles' Monsters: Indigenous or Oriental?', in C. Bonnet, C. Jourdain-Annequin and V. Pirenne-Delforge (eds.), *Le Bestiaire d'Héraclès*, Kernos Supplement 7: 27–36.

Boardman, J. (1999A), 'The Excavated History of Al Mina', in G. R. Tsetskhladze (ed.), *Ancient Greeks West and East*, 135–61.

Boardman, J. (1999B) *The Greeks Overseas*, 4th edition.

Boardman, J. (2002A), 'Al Mina: The Study of a Site', *AWE* 1: 315–31.

Boardman, J. (2002B), 'Greeks and Syria: Pots and People', in G. R. Tsetskhladze and A. M. Snodgrass (eds.), *Greek Settlements in the Eastern Mediterranean and the Black Sea*, 1–16.

Boardman, J. (2004), 'Copies of Pottery: By and For Whom?', in K. Lomas (ed.), *Greek Identity in the Western Mediterranean: Papers in Honour of Brian Shefton*, 149–62.

Boardman, J. (2005), 'Al Mina: Notes and Queries', *AWE* 4: 278–91.

Boardman, J. (2006A), 'Early Euboean Settlements in the Carthage Area', *OJA* 25: 195–200.

Boardman, J. (2006B), 'Greeks in the East Mediterranean, South Anatolia,

Syria, Egypt', in G. R. Tsetskhladze (ed.), *Greek Colonisation: An Account of Greek Colonies and Other Settlements Overseas*, vol. 1: 507–34.

Boardman, J., and Buchner, G. (1966), 'Seals from Ischia and the Lyre-player Group', *JDAI* 81: 1–62.

Böhm, S. (1990), *Die nackte Göttin: Zur Ikonographie und Deutung unbekleideter weiblicher Figuren in frühgriechischen Kunst*.

Böhm, S. (2003), 'The "Naked Goddess" in Early Greek Art: An Orientalizing Theme *par excellence*', in N. Stampolidis and V. Karageorghis (eds.), *Ploes . . . Sea Routes . . . Interconnections in the Mediterranean, 16th–6th c. BC*, 363–70.

Boitani, F. (2005), 'Le più antiche ceramiche greche e di tipo greco a Veio', in G. Bartoloni and F. Delpino (eds.), *Oriente e occidente: metodi e discipline a confronto*, Mediterranea: quaderni di archeologia etrusco-italica, 1: 319–32.

Bonatz, D. (1993), 'Some Considerations on the Material Culture of Coastal Syria in the Iron Age', *EVO* 16: 123–57.

Bonatz, D. (1998), 'Imported Pottery', in S. M. Cecchini and S. Mazzoni (eds.), *Tel Afis (Siria): scavi sull' acropoli, 1988–1992*, 211–29.

Bonatz, D. (2000), *Das syro-hethitische Grabdenkmal: Untersuchung zur Entstehung einer neuer Bildgattung in der Eisenzeit im nord-syrisch-südestanatolischen Raum*.

Bonfante, G., and Bonfante, L. (2002), *The Etruscan Language: An Introduction*, 2nd edition.

Bonnafé, A. (1991), 'L'Itinéraire d'Io dans le *Prométhée*', *JS*: 133–93.

Bonner, C. (1949), 'A *kestos himas* and the Saltire of Aphrodite', *AJP* 70: 1–6.

Bonnet, C. (1987), 'Typhon et Baal Saphon', in E. Lipinski (ed.), *Studia Phoenicia*, 5: 101–43.

Bonnet, C. (1988), *Melqart: cultes et mythes de l'Héraclès tyrien en Méditerranée*.

Bordreuil, P. (1977A), 'Épigraphie d'amphore phénicienne du 9 c. BC', *Berytus*, 25: 159–61.

Bordreuil, P. (1977B), 'Une inscription phénicienne champlevée des environs de Byblos', *Semitica*, 27: 23–7.

Bordreuil, P. (1986), 'Nouveaux documents religieux phéniciens II', in E. Lipinski (ed.), *Studia Phoenicia*, 4: 82–6.

Bordreuil, P. (1988), 'Du Carmel à l'Amanus: notes de toponymie phénicienne', in P.-L. Gatier, B. Helly and J.-P. Rey-Coquais (eds.), *Géographie historique au proche orient*, 301–14.

Bordreuil, P. (1989A), 'La Topographie économique de l'Ougarit', *Syria*, 66: 273–4.

Bordreuil, P. (1989B), 'La Citadelle sainte du Mont Nanou', *Syria*, 66: 275–9.

Bordreuil, P. (1990), 'La Déesse Anat et les sources de Sapon', in B. Geyer (ed.), *Techniques et pratiques hydro-agricoles et traditionelles en domaine irrigué*, 257–67.

Bordreuil, P. (1991), 'Recherches ougaritiques I: où Baal a-t-il remporté la victoire contre Yam?', *Semitica*, 40: 17–27.

Bordreuil, P. (2007), 'L'Alphabet phénicien: legs, héritages, adaptation, diffusion, transmission', in E. Fontan and H. le Meaux (eds.), *La Méditerranée des phéniciens de Tyr à Carthage: catalogue*, 72–83.

Bordreuil, P., and Pardee, D. (1993), 'Le Combat de Ba'alu avec Yammu d'après les textes Ougaritiques', *MARI* 7: 63–70.

Bossert, H. T. (1950A), 'Reisen in Kilikien', *Orientalia*, 19: 122–5.

Bossert, H. T. (1950B), 'Vorbericht über die archäologische Untersuchung von Karataş', *Belleten*, 14: 664–6.

Bossert, H. T. (1952–3), 'Die phönikisch-hethitischen Bilinguen vom Karatepe', *Jahrb. für kleinasiatische Forschung* 2: 293–339.

Bossert, H. T. (1957–8), 'Misis', *A. f. O.* 18: 186–9 and 461–3.

Bosworth, A. B. (1995), *A Historical Commentary on Arrian's History of Alexander*, vol. 2.

Bosworth, A. B. (1996A), 'Alexander, Euripides and Dionysus: The Motivation for Apotheosis', in R. W. Wallace and E. M. Harris (eds.), *Transitions to Empire*, 140–66.

Bosworth, A. B. (1996B), *Alexander and the East.*

Botto, M. (2000), 'Tripodi siriani e tripodi fenici dal Latium Vetus e dall'Etruria meridionale', in P. Bartoloni and L. Campanella (eds.), *La ceramica fenicia di Sardegna: dati, problematiche, confronti*, 63–98.

Bowersock, G. W. (1990), *Hellenism in Late Antiquity.*

Bowie, A. M. (1993), *Aristophanes: Myth, Ritual and Comedy.*

Boyce, M. (1955), 'Zariadres and Zarir', *BSOAS* 17: 463–77.

Boyce, M. (1984), 'On the Antiquity of Zoroastrian Apocalyptic', *BSOAS* 47: 68–85.

Braccesi, L. (1993), 'Gli eubei e la geografia dell'Odissea', *Hesperià*, 3: 11–23.

Brandt, J. R., Jarva, E. and Fischer Hansen, T. (1997), 'Ceramica di origine e di imitazione greca a Ficana nell'VIII sec. a.c.', in G. Bartoloni (ed.), *Le necropoli arcaiche di Veio*, 219–31.

Braun, T. (2004), 'Hecataeus' Knowledge of the Western Mediterranean', in K. Lomas (ed.), *Greek Identity in the Western Mediterranean: Papers in Honour of Brian Shefton*, 287–348.

Braun, T. F. R. G. (1982), 'The Greeks in the Near East', in J. Boardman and N. G. L. Hammond (eds.), *Cambridge Ancient History*, 2nd edition, volume 3/3: 1–31.

Breglia Pulci Doria, L. (1998), 'I cimmeri a Cuma', in M. Bats and B. d' Agostino (eds.), *Euboica: l'Eubea e la presenza euboica in Calcidica e in occidente*, 323–36.

Bremmer, J. (1987), 'The Old Women of Ancient Greece', in J. Blok and P. Mason (eds.), *Sexual Asymmetry: Studies in Ancient Society*, 191–213.

Briend, J., and Humbert, J. B. (1980), *Tell Kheisan (1971–6): une cité phénicienne en Galilée*.

Briese, C. (1998), 'Die Chapelle Cintas: das Gründungsdepot Karthagos oder eine Bestattung der Gründungsgeneration', in R. Rolle, K. Schmidt and R. F. Docter (eds.), *Archäologische Studien in Kontaktzonen der antiken Welt*, 419–52.

Brinkman, J. A. (1989), 'The Akkadian Words for "Ionia" and "Ionian"', in R. F. Sutton (ed.), *Daidalikon: Studies in Memory of Raymond V. Schoder, S.J.*, 53–71.

Brixhe, C. (1976), *Le Dialecte grec de Pamphylie*.

Brixhe, C. (2004), 'Nouvelle chronologie anatolienne et date d'élaboration des alphabets grec et phrygien', *CRAI*: 271–89.

Brize, P. (1985), 'Samos und Stesichoros zu einem früharchäischen Bronzeblech', *MDAI(A)* 100: 53–90.

Brodersen, K. (2001), 'The Urban Myth of Euboian Cyme', *AHB* 15: 25–8.

Bron, F. (1979), *Recherches sur les inscriptions phéniciennes de Karatepe*.

Bron, F., and Lemaire, A. (1989), 'Les Inscriptions araméennes de Hazael', *RA* 83: 35–44.

Brown, P. R. L. (1977), *Relics and Social Status in the Age of Gregory of Tours*.

Brown, P. R. L. (1995), *Authority and the Sacred: Aspects of the Christianisation of the Roman World*.

Brown, W. L. (1960), *The Etruscan Lion*.

Buccellati, G. (1982), 'The Descent of Inanna as a Ritual Journey to Kutha?', *Syro-Mesopotamian Studies*, 4: 3–7.

Buchner, G. (1953–4), 'Figürlich-bemalte spätgeometrische Vasen', *MDAI(R)* 60–61: 37–55.

Buchner, G. (1977), 'Nuovi aspetti e problemi posti dagli scavi di Pitecusa con particolari considerazioni sulle oreficiere di stile orientalizzante antico', in *Contributions à l'étude de la société et de la colonisation eubéennes*, Cahiers du Centre Jean Bérard, 1: 59–86.

Buchner, G. (1979), 'Early Orientalizing: Aspects of the Euboean Connection', in D. Ridgway and F. R. Serra Ridgway (eds.), *Italy before the Romans*, 129–44.

Buchner, G. (1982A), 'Articolazione sociale, differenze di rituale e composizione dei corredi nella necropoli di Pithecusa', in G. Gnoli and J. P. Vernant (eds.), *La Mort, les morts dans les sociétés anciennes*, 275–88.

Buchner, G. (1982B), 'Die Beziehungen zwischen der euboischen Kolonie Pithekoussai auf der Insel Ischia und dem nordwestsemitischen Mittelmeerraum in der zweiten Hälfte des 8. Jhdt. v. Chr.', in H. G. Niemeyer (ed.), *Phönizier im Westen*, 277–306.

Buchner, G. (1986), 'Eruzioni vulcaniche e fenomeni vulcano-tettonici di età preistorica e storica nell'isola d'Ischia', in C. Albore Livadie, *Tremblements de terre: éruptions volcaniques et vie des hommes dans la Campanie antique*, 145–88.

Buchner, G., and Ridgway, D. (1993), *Pithekoussai*, vol. 1.

Bunnens, G. (1979), *L'Expansion phénicienne en Méditerranée*.

Burkert, W. (1976), 'Die hunderttorige Theben und die Datierung der *Ilias*', WS 89: 5–21.

Burkert, W. (1979), *Structure and History in Greek Mythology and Ritual*.

Burkert, W. (1987), 'Oriental and Greek Mythology: The Meeting of Parallels', in J. Bremmer (ed.), *Interpretations of Greek Mythology*, 10–40.

Burkert, W. (1992A), *The Orientalizing Revolution*.

Burkert, W. (1992B), 'Eracle e gli altri eroi culturali del vicino Oriente', in C. Bonnet and C. Jourdain-Annequin (eds.), *Héraclès: d'une rive à l'autre de la Méditerrannée. Bilan et perspectives*, 111–27.

Burkert, W. (1992C), 'The Formation of Greek Religion at the Close of the Dark Ages', SIFC 10: 533–51.

Burkert, W. (1998), 'Héraclès et les animaux: perspectives préhistoriques et pressions historiques', in C. Bonnet, C. Jourdain-Annequin and V. Pirenne-Delforge (eds.), *Le Bestiaire d'Héraclès*, Kernos Supplement, 7: 11–26.

Burkert, W. (2001), 'Der *Odyssee*-Dichter und Kreta', in his *Kleine Schriften*, vol. 1: *Homerica*, 127–37.

Burkert, W. (2003), 'Lescha-Liškah: Sakrale Gastlichkeit zwischen Palästina und Griechenland', in his *Kleine Schriften*, vol. 2: *Orientalia*, 135–53.

Burkert, W. (2004), *Babylon, Memphis, Persepolis: Eastern Contexts of Greek Culture*.

Burkert, W. (2005), 'Hesiod in Context: Abstractions and Divinities in an Aegean-Eastern *Koinē*', in E. Stafford and J. Herrin (eds.), *Personifications in the Greek World: From Antiquity to Byzantium*, 3–20.

Burstein, S. M. (1978), *The Babyloniaca of Berossus*.

Butcher, K. (2004), *Coinage in Roman Syria: Northern Syria 64BC–AD253*.

Buxton, R. G. A. (1992), 'Imaginary Greek Mountains', *JHS* 112: 1–15.

Caird, G. B. (1980), *The Language and Imagery of the Bible*.

Calame, C. (1996), *Thésée et l'imaginaire athénien: légende et culte en Grèce classique.*

Camassa, G. (1986), 'I culti dell'area dello Stretto', *Atti Convegno Taranto,* 26: 133–62.

Çambel, H. (1999), *Corpus of Hieroglyphic Luwian Inscriptions,* vol. 2: *Karatepe-Arslantaş.*

Camporeale, G. (1997), 'Il sale e i primordi di Veio', in G. Bartoloni (ed.), *Le necropoli arcaiche di Veio,* 197–9.

Camporeale, G. (2004), *The Etruscans outside Etruria.*

Canciani, L. (1974–5), 'Un biconico dipinto da Vulci', *Dialoghi di Archeologia,* 8: 84.

Cannuyer, Chr. (1995), 'À propos du code d'honneur de la guerre dans la stèle triomphale de Piye', in Chr. Cannuyer, J. Ried and A. van Tongerloo (eds.), *Guerre et paix: War and Peace,* 43–58.

Cantarella, F., and de Francesco, S. (2001), 'Il più probabile ruolo del Punto Chiarito di Ischia sino alla metà del V. sec. A.C.: una posizione della pirateria di Pithekussai', *Orbis Terrarum,* 7: 37–54.

Carington-Smith, J., and Vocotopoulou, J. (1992), 'Excavation at Koukos, Sykia', *AEMTh* 6: 495–502.

Carter, J. B. (1998), 'Egyptian Bronze Jugs from Crete and Lefkandi', *JHS* 118: 172–7.

Casabonne, O. (1999), 'Notes ciliciennes', *Anatolia Antiqua,* 7: 69–88.

Casabonne, O. (2004), *La Cilicie de l'époque achéménide.*

Casabonne, O., and Porcher, A. (2003), 'Notes ciliciennes', *Anatolia Antiqua,* 11: 131–40.

Cassimatis, H. (1982), 'À propos de couronnes sur les têtes masculines en calcaire de Chypre', *RDAC:* 156–63.

Cassio, A. C. (1998), 'La cultura euboica e lo sviluppo dell'epica greca', in M. Bats and B. d'Agostino (eds.), *Euboica: l'Eubea e la presenza euboica in Calcidica e in occidente,* 11–22.

Cassola, F. (1975), *Inni omerici.*

Casson, L. (1988), *Ships and Seamanship in the Ancient World.*

Catling, R. W. V. (1998), 'Exports of Attic Protogeometric Pottery and their Identification by Non-analytical Means', *ABSA* 93: 365–78.

Caubet, A. (1983), 'Les œufs d'autruche au proche-orient ancien', *RDAC:* 193–8.

Caubet, A. (ed.) (1995), *Khorsabad: le palais de Sargon II., roi d'Assyrie.*

Caubet, A., Fontan, E., Herrmann, G., and le Meaux, H. (2007), 'The Age of Ivory', in E. Fontan and H. le Meaux (eds.), *La Méditerrannée des phéniciens de Tyr à Carthage: catalogue,* 205–15.

Caubet, A., and Gadja, I. (2003), 'Deux autels en bronze provenant de l'Arabie méridionale', *CRAI*: 1220–38.

Caubet, A., and Poplin, F. (1987), 'Les Objets de matière dure animale: étude du matériau', in M. Yon (ed.), *Le Centre de la ville: Ras Shamra-Ougarit III*, 273–301.

Cazelles, H. (1955), 'Les Localisations de l'Exode et la critique littéraire', *Rev. Bibl.* 62: 321–64.

Céard, J. (1978), 'La Querelle des Géants et la jeunesse du monde', *Journal of Mediev. and Renaiss. Studies*, 8: 37–76.

Cerchiai, L. (1996), 'Le scimmie, i giganti e Tifeo: appunti sui nomi dell'Ischia', in L. B. Pulci Doria (ed.), *L'incidenza dell'antico: studi in memoria di Ettore Lepore*, vol. 2: 141–50.

Chappell, M. (2006), 'Delphi and the *Homeric Hymn to Apollo*', *CQ* 56: 331–48.

Charbonnet, A. (1986), 'Le Dieu aux lions d'Érétrie', *AION* 8: 117–56.

Childs, B. S. (1963), 'A Study of the Formula "Until this Day"', *JBL* 82: 279–92.

Chrestou, D. (1996), *Kypro-archaikē Marmiakē Taphikē Architektonikē*.

Chrestou, D. (1998), 'Cremation in the Western Necropolis of Crete', in V. Karageorghis and N. Stampolidis (eds.), *Eastern Mediterranean Networks: Cyprus-Dodecanese-Crete, 16th–6th Century BC*, 207–15.

Christiansen, J. (2000), *The Rediscovery of Greece: Denmark and Greece in the Nineteenth Century*.

Chuvin, P. (1988), 'Les Fondations syriennes de Séleucos Nicator dans la *Chronique* de Jean Malalas', in P. L. Gatier, B. Helly and J.-P. Rey-Coquais (eds.), *Géographie historique au proche orient*, 99–110.

Chuvin, P., and Yoyotte, J. (1986), 'Documents relatifs au culte pélusien de Zeus Casios', *Rev. Arch.*: 41–63.

Ciaceri, E. (1911), *Culti e miti nella storia dell'antica Sicilia*.

Close Brooks, J. (1967), 'A Villanovan Bronze Belt from Euboea', *BICS* 14: 22–4.

Cogan, M. (1974), *Imperialism and Religion: Assyria, Judah and Israel in the Eighth and Seventh Centuries BC*.

Coldstream, J. N. (1969), 'The Phoenicians at Ialysos', *BICS* 16: 1–8.

Coldstream, J. N. (1979A), 'Some Cypriot Traits in Cretan Pottery, c. 950–700BC', in V. Karageorghis (ed.), *The Relations between Cyprus and Crete, c. 2000–500BC*, 257–63.

Coldstream, J. N. (1979B), 'Geometric Skyphoi in Cyprus', *RDAC*, 253–69.

Coldstream, J. N. (1981), 'Some Peculiarities of the Euboean and Geometric Figured Style', *ASAt* 59: 241–9.

Coldstream, J. N. (1982A), 'Greek and Phoenicians in the Aegean', in H. G. Niemeyer (ed.), *Phönizier im Westen*, 261–75.

Coldstream, J. N. (1982B), 'Some Problems of Eighth-century Pottery in the West Seen from the Greek Angle', in *La Céramique grecque ou de tradition grecque au VIIIème siècle en Italie centrale et méridionale*, Cahiers du Centre Jean Bérard, 3: 21–37.

Coldstream, J. N. (1983), 'Gift Exchange in the Eighth Century BC', in R. Hägg (ed.), *The Greek Renaissance of the Eighth Century BC*, 201–7.

Coldstream, J. N. (1986), 'Kition and Amathus: Some Reflections on their Westward Links', in V. Karageorghis (ed.), *Cyprus between the Orient and the Occident*, 321–9.

Coldstream, J. N. (1989), 'Early Greek Visitors to Cyprus and the Eastern Mediterranean', in V. Tatton-Brown (ed.), *Cyprus and the East Mediterranean in the Iron Age*, 90–96.

Coldstream, J. N. (1991), 'The Geometric Style: Birth of the Picture', in T. Rasmussen and N. Spivey (eds.), *Looking at Greek Vases*, 37–56.

Coldstream, J. N. (1993), 'Mixed Marriages at the Frontiers of the Early Greek World', *OJA* 12: 89–107.

Coldstream, J. N. (1994A), 'A Figured Attic Geometric *Kantharos* from Kition', *RDAC*: 155–9.

Coldstream, J. N. (1994B), 'Pithekoussai, Cyprus and the Cesnola Painter', in B. d'Agostino and D. Ridgway (eds.), *Apoikia: scritti in onore di Giorgio Buchner*, AION, vol. 1: 77–86.

Coldstream, J. N. (1995A), 'Amathus Tomb 194: The Greek Pottery Imports', *RDAC*: 187–214.

Coldstream, J. N. (1995B), 'Euboean Geometric Imports from the Acropolis at Pithekoussai', *ABSA* 90: 251–67.

Coldstream, J. N. (1995C), 'The Rich Lady of the Areopagus and her Contemporaries', *Hesperia*, 64: 391–403.

Coldstream, J. N. (1996), 'Knossos and Lefkandi: The Attic Connections', in D. Evely, I. G. Lemos and S. Sheratt (eds.), *Minotaur and Centaur: Studies in the Archaeology of Crete and Euboea, Presented to Mervyn Popham*, 133–45.

Coldstream, J. N. (1998A), 'Drinking and Eating in Euboean Pithekoussai', in M. Bats and B. d'Agostino (eds.), *Euboica: l'Eubea e la presenza euboica in Calcidica e in occidente*, 303–10.

Coldstream, J. N. (1998B), 'The First Exchanges between Euboeans and Phoenicians: Who Took the Initiative?', in S. Gitin, A. Mazar and E. Stern (eds.), *Mediterranean People in Transition: Thirteenth to Early Tenth Century BCE*, 353–60.

Coldstream, J. N. (1998C), *Light from Cyprus on the Greek 'Dark Age'?*

Coldstream, J. N. (2000), 'Some Unusual Geometric Scenes from Euboean Pithekoussai', in I. Berlingò, H. Blanck *et al.* (eds.), *Damarato: studi di antichità classica offerti a Paola Pelagatti*, 92–8.

Coldstream, J. N. (2002), 'Exchanges between Phoenicians and Early Greeks', *National Museum News, Beirut*, 11: 15–32.

Coldstream, J. N. (2003A), 'Some Aegean Reactions to the Chronological Debate in the Southern Levant', *Tel Aviv*, 30: 247–58.

Coldstream, J. N. (2003B), *Geometric Greece*.

Coldstream, J. N. (2006), 'Other People's Pots: Ceramic Borrowings between the Early Greeks and Levantines', in E. Herring, I. Lemos *et al.* (eds.), *Across Frontiers: Etruscans, Greeks, Phoenicians and Cypriots. Studies in Honour of D. Ridgway and F. R. Serra Ridgway*, 49–56.

Coldstream, J. N. (2007), 'Foreigners at Lefkandi?', in A. Mazarakis Ainian (ed.), *Oropos and Euboea in the Early Iron Age*, 135–9.

Coldstream, J. N., with Bikai, P. M. (1988), 'Early Greek Pottery in Tyre and Cyprus: Some Preliminary Considerations', *RDAC*, 1988.2: 35–44.

Coldstream, J. N., and Huxley, G. L. (1991), 'An Astronomical Graffito from Pithekoussai', *PP* 51: 221–4.

Coldstream, J. N., and MacDonald, C. F. (1997), 'Knossos: Area of South-west Houses, Early Hellenic Occupation', *ABSA* 92: 191–245.

Coldstream, J. N., and Mazar, A. (2003), 'Greek Pottery from Tel Rehov and Iron Age Chronology', *IEJ* 53, 29–48.

Colonna, G. (1973), 'Nomi etruschi di vasi', *AC* 25–6: 132–50.

Colonna, G. (1995), 'Etruschi a Pitecusa nell'orientalizzante antico', in A. Storchi Marino (ed.), *L'incidenza dell'antico: studi in memoria di Ettore Lepore*, 1.325–42.

Colonna, G. (2005), intervention in discussion in G. Bartoloni and F. Delpino (eds.), *Oriente e occidente: metodi e discipline a confronto*, Mediterranea: quaderni di archeologia etrusco-italica, 1: 478–83.

Comiers, C. (1692), 'Histoire générale des Géants', in *Mercure Galant*, March 1692: 82–131.

Connelly, J. B. (1988), *Votive Sculpture of Hellenistic Cyprus*.

Consola Langher, S. (1996), 'Zankle in età arcaica e classica', in S. Consola Langher (ed.), *Siracusa e la Sicilia greca tra età arcaica ed alto ellenismo*, 377–415.

Courbin, P. (1977), 'Une pyxis géométrique argienne au Liban', *Berytus*, 25: 147–57.

Courbin, P. (1978), 'A-t-on retrouvé l'antique Posideion à Ras el-Bassit?', *Archeologia*, 116: 48–62.

Courbin, P. (1986), 'Bassit', *Syria*, 63: 175–204.

Courbin, P. (1990), 'Bassit-Posideion in the Early Iron Age', in J.-P. Descoeudres (ed.), *Greek Colonists and Native Populations*, 503–9.

Courbin, P. (1993), 'Fragments d'amphores protogéométriques grecques à Bassit (Syrie)', *Hesperia*, 62: 95–114.

Cremonesi, G. (1978), 'Introduzione', in *Leuca*, 9–10.

Crielaard, J. P. (1990), 'Some Euboean and Related Pottery in Amsterdam', *Babesch*, 65: 1–12.

Crielaard, J. P. (1993), 'The Social Organization of Euboean Trade with the Eastern Mediterranean during the 10th to the 8th centuries BC', *Pharos: Journal of the Netherlands Institute in Athens*, 1: 139–46.

Crielaard, J. P. (1994), 'Nausikleitē Euboia: Socio-economic Aspects of Euboian Trade and Colonization', *Archeion Euboikōn Meletōn*, 30: 45–53.

Crielaard, J. P. (1998), 'Surfing on the Mediterranean Web: Long Distance Communication during the Eleventh and Tenth Centuries BC', in V. Karageorghis and N. Stampolidis (eds.), *Eastern Mediterranean Networks: Cyprus-Dodecanese-Crete, 16th–6th Century BC*, 187–205.

Crielaard, J. P. (1999), 'Early Iron Age Pottery in Cyprus and North Syria: A Consumption-oriented Approach', in J. P. Crielaard, V. Stissi and G. J. van Wijngaarden, *The Complex Past of Pottery*, 261–90.

Crielaard, J. P. (2000A), 'Homeric and Mycenaean Long Distance Contacts: Discrepancies in the Evidence', *Babesch*, 75: 51–63.

Crielaard, J. P. (2000B), 'Honour and Value as Discourse for Early Greek Colonization (8th–7th Centuries BC)', in F. Krinzinger (ed.), *Die Ägäis und das westliche Mittelmeer*, 499–506.

Crielaard, J. P. (2002), 'Past or Present? Epic Poetry, Aristocratic Self-promotion and the Concept of Time in the 8th and 7th Centuries BC', in F. Montanari (ed.), *Omero tremila anni dopo*, 239–95.

Crielaard, J. P. (2003), 'The Cultural Biography of Material Goods in Homer's Epics', *GAIA: Revue interdisciplinaire sur la Grèce archaique*, 7: 49–62.

Crielaard, J. P. (2006), '*Basileis* at Sea: Elites and External Contacts in the Euboean Gulf Regions from the End of the Bronze Age to the Beginning of the Iron Age', in S. Deger-Jalkotzy and I. S. Lemos (eds.), *Ancient Greece: From the Mycenaean Palaces to the Age of Homer*, 271–97.

Crielaard, J. P. (2007), 'Eretria's West Cemetery Revisited', in A. Mazarakis Ainian (ed.), *Oropos and Euboea in the Early Iron Age*, 169–88.

Cross, F. M. (1972), 'An Interpretation of the Nora Stone', *BASOR* 208: 13–19.

Csapo, E. (1991), 'An International Community of Traders in Late 8th–7th Century BC Kommos in Southern Crete', *ZPE* 88: 211–16.

Csapo, E. (2000), 'The Iron Age Inscriptions', in J. W. Shaw (ed.), *Kommos*, vol. 4/1: 105–7.

Csapo, E. (2005), *Theories of Mythology*.

Csapo, E., *et al.* (2000), 'Catalogue of Iron Age Inscriptions', in J. W. Shaw (ed.), *Kommos*, vol. 4/1: 109–10.

Culican, W. (1986), *Opera Selecta: From Tyre to Tartessos*.

Cumont, F. (1932), 'Adonis et Sirius', in *Mélanges Gustave Glotz*, vol. 1: 257–64.

Cumont, F. (1935), 'Adonis et Canicule', *Syria*, 16: 46–50.

Cunliffe, B. W. (1988), *Mount Batten, Plymouth: A Prehistoric and Roman Port*.

Cygielman, M., and Pagnini, L. (2002), 'Presenze sarde a Vetulonia: alcune considerazioni', in O. Paoletti (ed.), *Etruria e Sardegna tra l'età del bronzo finale e l'arcaismo*, 387–410.

D'Agostino, B. (1994), 'Pithekoussai: una *apoikia* di tipo particulare', *AION* 1: 19–27.

D'Agostino, B. (1994–5), 'La "Stipe dei Cavalli" di Pitecussa', *AMSMG* 3: 9–100.

D'Agostino, B. (1999), 'Euboean Colonisation in the Gulf of Naples', in G. R. Tsetskhladze (ed.), *Ancient Greeks West and East*, 207–27.

D'Agostino, B. (2003), 'Scrittura e artigiani sulla rotta per l'Occidente', in S. Marchesini and P. Poccetti (eds.), *Linguistica e storia: scritti in onore di Carlo de Simone*, 75–84.

D'Agostino, B. (2004), 'The Etruscans in Campania', in G. Camporeale, *The Etruscans outside Etruria*, 236–51.

D'Agostino, B. (2006A), 'The First Greeks in Italy', in G. R. Tsetskhladze (ed.), *Greek Colonisation: An Account of Greek Colonies and Other Settlements Overseas*, vol. 1: 201–37.

D'Agostino, B. (2006B), 'Funerary Customs and Society on Rhodes in the Geometric Period: Some Observations', in E. Herring, I. Lemos *et al.* (eds.), *Across Frontiers: Etruscans, Greeks, Phoenicians and Cypriots. Studies in Honour of D. Ridgway and F. R. Serra Ridgway*, 57–69.

D'Andria, F. (1990), 'Greek Influence in the Adriatic: Fifty Years after Beaumont', in J.-P. Descoeudres (ed.), *Greek Colonists and Native Populations*, 281–90.

D'Andria, F. (1997), 'Corinto e l'Occidente: la costa adriatica', in *Corinto e l'occidente: atti del 34° Convegno di studi sulla Magna Grecia, Taranto (1995)*, 457–508.

Dagron, G., and Feissel, D. (1987), *Inscriptions de Cilicie*.

Dalley, S. (1985), 'Foreign Chariots and Cavalry in the Assyrian Armies of Tiglath-Pileser III and Sargon II', *Iraq*, 47: 31–48.

Dalley, S. (1999), 'Sennacherib and Tarsus', *AS* 49: 73–81.

Dalley, S. (2003), 'Why Did Herodotus not Mention the Hanging Gardens of Babylon?', in P. Derow and R. Parker (eds.), *Herodotus and his World*, 171–89.

Damerji, M. S. B. (1995), 'Gräber assyrischer Königinnen aus Nimrud', *JRGZM* 45: 1–83.

Danek, G. (1998), *Epos und Zitat: Studien zu den Quellen der* Odyssee.

Daszewski, W. A. (1986), 'Cassiopeia in Paphos – a Levantine Going West', in V. Karageorghis (ed.), *Cyprus between the Orient and the Occident*, 454–70.

Davies, M. (1999), 'Theocritus' Adoniazusae', *G&R* 42: 152–7.

Day, J. (1985), *God's Conflict with the Dragon and the Sea: Echoes of a Canaanite Myth in the Old Testament*.

De Caro, S., and Gialanella, C. (1998), 'Novità pitecusane: l'insediamento di Punta Chiarito a Forio d'Ischia', in M. Bats and B. d'Agostino (eds.), *Euboica: l'Eubea e la presenza euboica in Calcidica e in occidente*, 337–53.

De Moor, J. C. (1970), 'Studies in the New Alphabetic Texts from Ras Shamra, II', *UF* 2: 302–27.

De Polignac, F. (1998), 'Navigations et fondations: Héra et les eubéens de l'Égée à l'Occident', in M. Bats and B. d'Agostino (eds.), *Euboica: l'Eubea et la presenza euboica in Calcidica e in occidente*, 23–30.

De Polignac, F. (2006), 'Analyse de l'espace et urbanisations en Grèce archaïque: quelques pistes de recherches récentes', *REA* 108: 203–24.

De Romilly, J. (1995), 'Trois jardins paradisiaques dans l'*Odyssée*', in her *Rencontres avec la Grèce antique: 15 études et conférences*.

De Salvia, F. (1978), 'Un ruolo apotropaico dello scarabeo egizio', in M. B. de Boer and T. A. Edridge (eds.), *Hommages à M. J. Vermaseren*, vol. 3: 1005.

De Salvia, F. (1999), 'Gli *Aegyptiaca* di Torre Galli', in M. Pacciarelli, *Torre Galli: la necropoli della prima età del Ferro (Scavi Paolo Orsi 1922–3)*, 213–17.

De Simone, C. (1970), *Die griechischen Entlehnungen im Etruskischen*, vol. 2.

De Simone, C. (1972), 'Per la storia degli imprestiti greci in etrusco', in *ANRW*, vol. 1/2: 490–521.

De Simone, C. (1995), 'Le più antiche relazioni greco-etrusche alla luce dei dati linguistici', in A. Storchi Marino (ed.), *L'incidenza dell'antico: studi in memoria di Ettore Lepore*, vol. 1: 283–90.

De Toleto, P. G. (1539), *Ragionamento del terremoto del Nuovo Monte: del aprimento di Terra in Pozulo nel anno 1538 e de la significatione d'essi.*

De Vries, K. (2003), 'Eight Century Corinthian Pottery Evidence for the Dates of Greek Settlement in the West', in C. K. Williams II and N. Bookidis (eds.), *Corinth*, vol. 20: *Corinth the Centenary, 1896–1996*, 141–56.

Debiasi, A. (2001), 'Variazioni sul nome di Omero', *Hesperià* 14: 9–36.

Delaporte, L. (1940), *Malatya: Arslan Tepe*, vol. 1.

Delpino, F. (1997), 'I greci in Etruria prima della colonizzazione euboica: ancora su crateri, vino, vite e pennati nell'Italia centrale protostorica', in G. Bartoloni (ed.), *Le necropoli arcaiche di Veio*, 185–96.

Demand, N. (2004), 'Models in Greek History: The Question of the Origins of the *Polis*', *AHB* 18: 61–84.

Des Courtils, J., Kozelj, T., and Muller, A. (1982), 'Des mines d'or à Thasos', *BCH* 106: 409–17.

Descoeudres, J.-P. (1978), 'Euboeans in Australia', in J.-P. Descoeudres *et al.*, *Eretria: fouilles et recherches*, vol. 6: 7–19.

Descoeudres, J.-P. (1996–7), 'The *Chiusa* at the *Masseria del Fano* in Salento', *Med. Arch.* 9/10: 207–31.

Descoeudres, J.-P. (2002), 'Al Mina across the Great Divide', *JMA* 15: 49–72.

Detienne, M. (1970), *The Gardens of Adonis*, English translation.

Diakonoff, I. M. (1992), 'The Naval Power and Trade of Tyre: Introductory Remarks', *IEJ* 42: 168–93.

Dickie, M. (1995), 'The Geography of Homer's World', in O. Andersen and M. Dickie (eds.), *Homer's World: Fiction, Tradition and Reality*, 29–56.

Dillon, M. P. J. (2003), 'Woe for Adonis – but in Spring, not Summer', *Hermes*, 131: 1–16.

Dinçol, B. (1994), 'New Archaeological and Epigraphical Finds from Ivriz: A Preliminary Report', *Tel Aviv*, 21: 117–28.

Djobadze, W. (1986), *Archaeological Investigations in the Region West of Antioch and the Orontes.*

Docter, R. F. (2000), 'Pottery, Graves and Ritual I: Phoenicians of the First Generation in Pithekoussai', in P. Bartoloni and L. Campanella (eds.), *La ceramica fenicia di Sardegna: dati, problematiche, confronti*, 135–48.

Docter, R. F., Niemeyer, H. G., Nijboer, A. J., and van der Pflicht, H. (2005), 'Radiocarbon Dates of Animal Bones in the Earliest Levels of Carthage', in G. Bartoloni and F. Delpino (eds.), *Oriente e occidente: metodi e discipline a confronto*, Mediterranea: quaderni di archeologia etrusco-italica, 1: 557–77.

Dominguez, A. J., and Sanchez, C. (2001), *Greek Pottery from the Iberian Peninsula.*

Donbaz, V. (1990), 'Two Neo-Assyrian Stelae in the Antakya and Kahraman-maras Museum', *Annual Review of the Royal Inscriptions of Mesopotamia Project*, 8: 5–24.

Dorsey, D. A. (1991), *The Roads and Highways of Ancient Israel*.

Dothan, M. (1969), 'Archaeological Survey of Mount Casius and its Vicinity', *Eretz Israel*, 9: 135–6.

Dougherty, C. (2001), *The Raft of Odysseus*.

Douglas, N. (1928), *Old Calabria*.

Doumet, J. (2004), 'Ancient Purple Dyeing by Extraction of the Colour from Murex . . .', in C. Doumet-Serhal (ed.), *A Decade of Archaeology and History in the Lebanon*, 38–49.

Dowden, K. (1989), *Death and the Maiden*.

Dowden, K. (1992), *The Uses of Greek Mythology*.

Dowden, K. (1996), 'Homer's Sense of Text', *JHS* 116: 47–61.

Duchemin, J. (1956), *Pindare, poète et prophète*.

Duchemin, J. (1995), 'Le Captif de l'Etna: Typhée, "frère de Prométhée"', in her *Mythes grecques et sources orientales*, 49–67.

Ducrey, P., Fachard, S., *et al*. (2004), *Archaic Eretria*.

Dunbabin, T. J. (1948A), 'Minos and Daidalos in Sicily', *PBSR* 16: 1–18.

Dunbabin, T. J. (1948B), *The Western Greeks*.

Dunbabin, T. J. (1953), 'Bellerophon, Heracles and the Chimaera', in G. E. Mylonas (ed.), *Studies Presented to D. M. Robinson . . .*, vol. 2: 1164–84.

Dunbabin, T. J. (1957), *The Greeks and their Eastern Neighbours*.

Dunbar, N. (1995), *Aristophanes: Birds*.

Dupont-Sommer, A., and Robert, L. (1964), *La Déesse de Hierapolis, Castabala, Cilicie*.

Dussaud, R. (1927), *Topographie historique de la Syrie antique et médiévale*.

Easterling, P. E. (1982), *Sophocles: Trachiniae*.

Eder, B. (2006), 'The World of Telemachus: Western Greece 1200–700 BC', in S. Deger-Jalkotzy and I. S. Lemos (eds.), *Ancient Greece: From the Mycenaean Palaces to the Age of Homer*, 549–80.

Edwards, A. T. (2004), *Hesiod's Ascra*.

Edwards, M. J. (1991), 'Philo or Sanchuniathon? A Phoenician Cosmogony', *CQ* 41: 213–20.

Ehlers, W. (1933), *Die Grundung von Zankle in den* Aitia *des Kallimachos*.

Eissfeldt, O. (1932), *Baal Zaphon, Zeus Kasios und der Durchzeug der Israeliten durchs Meer*.

Eissfeldt, O. (1966), 'Etymologische und archäologische Erklärung alttesta-mentlicher Wörter', *J. Ant.* 5: 165–76.

Eissfeldt, O. (1968), 'Ba'al Saphon von Ugarit and Amon von Ägypten', in his *Kleine Schriften*, vol. 4: 53–7.

Eissfeldt, O. (1970), *Adonis und Adonaj*.

El Khayari, A. (2007), 'Le Maroc', in E. Fontan and H. le Méaux (eds.), *La Méditerrannée des phéniciens de Tyr à Carthage: catalogue*, 294–5.

Elayi, J. (1987), 'Al Mina sur l'Oronte a l'époque perse', in E. Lipinski (ed.), *Studia Phoenicia*, 5: 249–66.

Elayi, J., and Cavigneaux, A. (1979), 'Sargon II et les ioniens', *Oriens Antiquus*, 18: 59–75.

Emiliozzi, A. (2001), 'Technical Problems Concerning Orientalizing Vehicles in Cyprus and Etruria', in L. Bonfante and V. Karageorghis (eds.), *Italy and Cyprus in Antiquity: 1500–450 BC*, 315–34.

Emlyn-Jones, C. (1986), 'True and Lying Tales in the *Odyssey*', *G&R* 33: 1–10.

Eph'al, I., and Naveh, J. (1989), 'Hazael's Booty Inscriptions', *IEJ* 39: 192–200.

Erskine, A. (2001), *Troy between Greece and Rome*.

Evans, A. J. (1928), *The Palace of Minos*, vol. 2.

Fantalkin, A. (2001), 'Low Chronology and Greek Protogeometric and Geometric Pottery in the Southern Levant', *Levant*, 33: 117–25.

Faure, P. (1987), *Parfums et aromates de l'antiquité*.

Fauth, W. (1990), 'Das Kasiongebirge und Zeus Kasios: Die antike Tradition und ihre vorderorientalischen Grundlagen', *UF* 22: 105–18.

Fear, A. T. (1992), 'Odysseus and Spain', *Prometheus*, 18: 19–26.

Feeney, D. C. (2007), *Caesar's Calendar*.

Feld, O., and Weber, H. (1968), 'Tempel und Kirche über der korykischen Grotte', *Ist. Mitt.* 17: 254–67.

Fichtner, J. (1956), 'Die etymologische Ätiologie in den Namengebungen der geschichtlichen Bücher des alten Testaments', *VT* 4: 372–96.

Finkelstein, I. (2004), 'Tel Rehov and Iron Age Chronology', *Levant*, 36: 181–8.

Finley, M. I. (1956), *The World of Odysseus*, revised edition.

Finley, M. I. (1981), 'The Elderly in Classical Antiquity', *G&R* 28: 156–71.

Fletcher, R. (2006), 'The Cultural Biography of a Phoenician Mushroom-lipped Jug', *OJA* 25: 173–94.

Foley, J. M. (2002), *How to Read an Oral Poem*.

Fontan, E. (2004), 'La Frise du transport du bois du palais de Sargon II. à Khorsabad', in C. Doumet-Serhal (ed.), *A Decade of Archaeology and History in the Lebanon*, 456–63.

Forlanini, G. (1988), 'La regione del Tauro nei testi hittiti', *VO* 8: 145.

Forrest, W. G. (1956), 'The First Sacred War', *BCH* 80: 33–52.

Forrest, W. G. (1957), 'Colonization and the Rise of Delphi', *Historia*, 6: 160–75.

Forrest, W. G. (2000), 'The pre-*Polis Polis*', in R. Brock and S. Hodkinson (eds.), *Alternatives to Athens*, 280–92.

Fourrier, S. (2003), 'Cyprus and Cilicia in the Iron Age', *Olba*, 7: 79–91.

Fowler, R. L. (1998), 'Genealogical Thinking: Hesiod's *Catalogue* and the Creation of the Hellenes', *PCPS* 44: 1–19.

Fowler, R. L. (2000), *Early Greek Mythography*, vol. 1.

Frame, G. (1999), 'The Inscription of Sargon at Tang-i-Var', *Orientalia*, 68: 31–57.

Frankenstein, S. (1979), 'The Phoenicians in the Far West', in M. T. Larsen (ed.), *Power and Propaganda: A Symposium on Ancient Empires. Mesopotamia*, vol. 7: 263–94.

Fraser, P. M. (1970), 'Greek-Phoenician Bilingual Inscriptions from Rhodes', *ABSA* 65: 31–6.

Fraser, P. M. (1972), *Ptolemaic Alexandria*, vols. 1–3.

Fraser, P. M. (1996), *Cities of Alexander the Great*.

Frazer, J. G. (1898), *Pausanias' Description of Greece*, vol. 4.

Frazer, J. G. (1913), *The Golden Bough*, vol. 4: 1.

Frederiksen, M. W. (1979), 'The Etruscans in Campania', in D. Ridgway and F. R. Serra Ridgway (eds.), *Italy before the Romans*, 277–311.

Frederiksen, M. W. (1984), *Campania*.

Freeman, E. A. (1891), *History of Sicily*, vol. 1.

Frei, P. (1993), 'Die Bellerophontessage und das Alte Testament', in B. Janowski, K. Koch and G. Wilhelm (eds.), *Religionsgeschichtliche Beziehungen zwischen Kleinasien, Nordsyrien und der Alte Testament*, 39–65.

Frézouls, E. (1988), 'Fondations et refondations dans l'orient syrien: problème d'identification et d'interpretation', in P.-L. Gatier, B. Helly, J.-P. Rey-Coquais (eds.), *Géographie historique au proche-orient*, 15–40.

Fritz, M. M. (2003), '... *und weinten um Tammuz': die Götter Dumuzi-Ama'usumgal'anna und Damu*.

Frost, H. (2001), 'Two Cypriot Anchors', in L. Bonfante and V. Karageorghis (eds.), *Italy and Cyprus in Antiquity: 1500–450 BC*, 61–74.

Fuchs, A. (1994), *Die Inschriften Sargons II aus Khorsabad*.

Fuchs, A. (1998), *Die Annalen des Jahres 711 v. Chr.: nach Prismenfragmenten aus Nineve und Assur*.

Gaber, P. (1994), 'In Search of Adonis', in F. Vandenabeele and R. Laffineur (eds.), *Cypriote Stone Sculpture*, 161–4.

Galletti, G. (1996), 'Una committenza medicea poco nota: Giovanni di

Cosimo e il giardino di villa Medici', in C. Acidini Luchinat (ed.), *Giardini Medicei del Quattrocento*, 50–90.

Garstang, J., and Gurney, O. R. (1959), *The Geography of the Hittite Empire*.

Garus Alonso, J. L. (1996), 'Estudios sopra Toponimia Griego en el Mediterraneo Occidental: nombres en -oussa', *Complutum*, 7: 105–24.

Gaskin, R. (1990), 'Do Homeric Heroes Make Real Decisions?', *CQ* 40: 1–15.

Gastaldi, P. (1994), 'Struttura sociale e rapporti nel IX sec. a.c.', in *La presenza etrusca nella Campania meridionale*, Biblioteca degli studi etruschi, 28: 49–60.

Gauthier, P. (2003), 'Le Decret de Colophon ancienne en l'honneur du thessalien Asandros et la sympolitie entre les deux Colophons', *JS*: 61–100.

Geffcken, J. (1892), *Timaios Geographie des Westens*.

George, A. R. (2003), *The Babylonian Gilgamesh Epic*.

Gera, D. L. (1993), *Xenophon's Cyropaedia: Style, Genre and Literary Technique*.

Gibson, J. C. L. (1978), *Canaanite Myths and Legends*.

Gilboa, A. (1999), 'The View from the East: Tel Dor and the Earliest Cypro-Geometric Exports to the Levant', in M. Iacovou and D. Michaelides (eds.), *Cyprus and the Historicity of the Geometric Horizon*, 109–39.

Gilboa, A., Sharon, I., and Zorn, J. (2004), 'Dor and Iron Age Chronology: Scarabs, Ceramic Sequence and 14C', *Tel Aviv*, 31: 32–59.

Gill, D. W. J. (1988), 'Silver Anchors and Cargoes of Oil: Some Observations on Phoenician Trade in the Western Mediterranean', *PBSR* 56: 1–12.

Giovannini, A. (1985), 'Le Sel et la fortune de Rome', *Athenaeum*, 63: 373–87.

Gisler, J.-R. (1995), 'Érétrie et le peintre de Cesnola', *Archaiognosia*, 8: 11–95.

Gjerstad, E. (1944), 'The Colonization of Cyprus in Greek Legend', *Opuscula Archaeologica*, 3: 107–23.

Gjerstad, E. (1979), 'A Cypriot Greek Royal Marriage in the Eighth Century BC', in V. Karageorghis *et al.* (eds.), *Studies Presented in Memory of Porphyrios Dikaios*, 89–93.

Glotz, G. (1920), 'Les Fêtes d'Adonis sous Ptolémée II', *REG* 33: 169–222.

Goetze, A. (1968), *Madduwattas*.

Golka, F. W. (1976–7), 'The Aetiologies in the Old Testament', *VT* 26: 410–28 and 27: 36–47.

Gonçalves, F. J. (1986), *L'Expédition de Sennacherib dans la littérature hébraïque ancienne*.

Gonzalez de Canales, F., Serrano, L., and Llompart, J. (2006), 'The Precolonial Phoenician Emporium at Huelva in 900–770BC', *Babesch*, 81: 13–30.

Gordon, E. L. (1967–9), 'The Meaning of the Ideogram KASKAL.KUR = Underground Water-course', *JCS* 21: 70–82.

Gough, M. (1976), 'Kanli Divane', in R. Stillwell (ed.), *The Princeton Encyclopaedia of Classical Sites*, 435.

Gould, J. (2001), *Myth, Ritual, Memory and Exchange*.

Gould, J. P. (1973), 'Hiketeia', *JHS* 93: 74–103.

Gow, A. S. F. (1950), *Theocritus*, vol. 2.

Graham, A. J. (1978), 'The Foundation of Thasos', *ABSA* 73: 61–98.

Graham, A. J. (2001), 'Religion, Women and Greek Colonization', in his *Collected Papers on Greek Colonization*, 327–48.

Gras, M. (1976), 'La Piraterie tyrrhénienne en mer Egée: mythe ou réalité?', in *Mélanges offerts à Jacques Heurgon*, 341–69.

Gras, M. (1981), 'L'Etruria mineraria', in *Atti del XII Convegno di studi etruschi e italici*, 318–26.

Gras, M. (1989), *L'Univers phénicien*.

Gras, M. (1990), 'Les Eubéens et la Tunisie', *Bulletin des travaux de l'Institut National du Patrimoine, comptes rendus, Tunisie*, 5: 87–93.

Gras, M. (1992), 'Le Mémoire de Lixus...'; in *Lixus: actes du colloque ... 8–11 novembre 1989*, Collection de l'École Française de Rome, 166: 27–44.

Gras, M. (1994), 'Pithécusses: de l'étymologie à l'histoire', in B. d'Agostino and D. Ridgway (eds.), *Apoikia: scritti in onore di Giorgio Buchner*, AION, 1: 127–33.

Gras, M., Rouillard, P., and Teixidor, J. (1995), *L'Univers phénicien*.

Grayson, A. K. (1991), *Assyrian Rulers of the Early First Millennium BC*, vol. 1: *(1114–859 BC)*.

Grayson, A. K. (1996), *Assyrian Rulers of the Early First Millennium BC*, vol. 2: *(858–745 BC)*.

Graziosi, B. (2002), *Inventing Homer*.

Graziosi, B., and Haubold, J. (2003), 'Homeric Masculinity: *Ēnoreē* and *Agēnoriē*', *JHS* 123: 60–76.

Green, P. (2004), *From Ikaria to the Stars*.

Grenet, F. (2005), 'An Archaeologist's Approach to Avestan Geography', in V. Sarkosh Curtis and S. Stewart (eds.), *Birth of the Persian Empire*, 29–51.

Griffin, J. (1986), 'Homeric Words and Speakers', *JHS* 106: 31–57.

Griffin, J. (1992), 'Theocritus, the *Iliad* and the East', *AJP* 113: 189–211.

Gubel, E. (1987), *Phoenician Furniture*.

Gubel, E. (2007), 'La Glyptique phénicienne', in E. Fontan and H. le Meaux (eds.), *La Méditerranée des phéniciens de Tyr à Carthage: catalogue*, 194–7.

Gunkel, H. (1964), *The Legends of Genesis*, English translation.

Gurney, O. R. (1962), 'Tammuz Reconsidered: Some Recent Developments', *JSS* 7: 147–60.

Gurney, O. R. (1976), *Some Aspects of the Hittite Religion*.

Güterbock, H. G. (1946), *Kumarbi: Mythen von churritischen Kronos aus den hethitischen Fragmenten zusammengestellt, übersetzt und erklärt*.

Güterbock, H. G. (1983), 'A Hurro-Hittite Hymn to Ishtar', *JAOS* 103: 155–64.

Guzzo, P. G. (2000), 'La Tomba 104 Artiaco di Cuma o sia dell'ambiguità del segno', in I. Berlingò, H. Blanck *et al.* (eds.), *Damarato: studi di antichità classica offerti a Paola Pelagatti*, 92–8.

Haas, V. (1982), *Hethitische Berggötter und hurritische Steindämonen*.

Haas, V. (1994), *Geschichte der hethitische Religion*.

Haas, V. (2002), 'Der Schicksalsstein: Beobachtungen zu *K.Bo.* 32.10', *AOF* 29: 230–37.

Haas, V. (2006), *Die hethitische Literatur*.

Haas, V., Salvini, M., *et al.* (2000), *Corpus der hurritischen Sprachendenkmäler*.

Habibi, M. (1992), 'La Céramique à englobe rouge phénicien de Lixus', in *Lixus: actes du colloque . . . 8–11 novembre 1989*, Collection de l'École Française de Rome, 166: 145–53.

Haines, R. C. (1970), *Excavations in the Plain of Antioch*, vol. 2.

Hainsworth, J. B. (1991), *The Idea of Epic*.

Hainsworth, J. B. (1993), *The Iliad: A Commentary*, Books 9–12.

Hall, J. M. (2002), *Hellenicity*.

Hall, J. M. (2007), *A History of the Archaic Greek World*, c. 1200–479BCE.

Hamilton, W. (1776), *Campi Phlegraei: Observations on the Volcanoes of the Two Sicilies*.

Hammond, N. G. L. (1967), *Epirus*.

Hammond, N. G. L. (1994), 'One or Two Passes at the Cilicia-Syria Border?', *Anc. World*, 25: 15–26.

Hammond, N. G. L. (1995), 'The Chalcidians and "Apollonia of the Thraceward Ionians"', *ABSA* 90: 307–15.

Hammond, N. G. L. (1998), 'Eretria's Colonies in the Area of the Thermaic Gulf', *ABSA* 93: 393–9.

Hansen, M. H. (2006), 'Emporion: A Study in the Use and Meaning of the Term in the Archaic and Classical Periods', in G. R. Tsetskhladze (ed.), *Greek Colonisation: An Account of Greek Colonies and Other Settlements Overseas*, vol. 1: 1–39.

Hansen, P. A. (1976), 'Pithecusan Humour: The Interpretation of Nestor's Cup Reconsidered', *Glotta*, 54: 25–53.

Hansen, W. (1997), 'Homer and the Folktale', in I. Morris and B. Powell (eds.), *A New Companion to Homer*, 463–88.

Hanson, V. D. (1995), *The Other Greeks: The Family Farm and the Agrarian Roots of Western Civilization*.

Hardie, C. G. (1969), 'The Great Antrum at Baiae', *PBSR* 37: 14–33.

Hardie, P. (ed.) (1994), *Virgil*: Aeneid *Book IX*.

Hawkins, J. D. (1980), 'Late Hittite Funerary Monuments', in B. Alster (ed.), *Death in Mesopotamia*, 213–25.

Hawkins, J. D. (1986), 'Writing in Anatolia', *World Archaeology*, 17: 363–76.

Hawkins, J. D. (1989), 'More Late Hittite Funerary Monuments', in K. Emre *et al.* (eds.), *Anatolia and the Ancient Near East: Studies in Honour of Tahsin Ozgüe*, 188–97.

Hawkins, J. D. (1995A), 'The Political Geography of North Syria and Southeast Anatolia in the Neo-Assyrian Period', in M. Liverani (ed.), *Neo-Assyrian Geography*, 87–101.

Hawkins, J. D. (1995B), *The Hieroglyphic Inscriptions of the Sacred Pool Complex at Hattusa (Südburg)*.

Hawkins, J. D. (2000A), *Corpus of Hieroglyphic Luwian Inscriptions*, vol. 1: *Inscriptions of the Iron Age*, part 1.

Hawkins, J. D. (2000B), *Corpus of Hieroglyphic Luwian Inscriptions*, vol. 1: *Inscriptions of the Iron Age*, part 2.

Hawkins, J. D. (2004), 'The New Sargon Stele from Hama', in G. Frame (ed.), *From the Upper Sea to the Lower Sea: Studies on the History of Assyria and Babylonia in Honour of A. K. Grayson*, 151–64.

Haynes, S. (2000), *Etruscan Civilization: A Cultural Study*.

Heberdey, R., and Wilhelm, A. (1896), *Reisen in Kilikien*.

Heidel, A. (1953), 'The Octagonal Sennacherib Prism in the Iraq Museum', *Sumer*, 9: 117–88.

Held, W. (2000), *Das Heiligtum der Athena in Milet*.

Hermary, A. (1992), 'Quelques remarques sur les origines proche-orientales de l'iconographie d'Héraclès', in C. Bonnet and C. Jourdain-Annequin (eds.), *Héraclès: d'une rive à l'autre de la Méditerranée. Bilan et perspectives*, 129–38.

Hermary, A. (2004), 'Autour de Golgoi: les cités de la Mesaoria aux époques hellénistique et romaine', *CCEC* 34: 47–68.

Herrera Gonzalez, M. D., and Balensi, J. (1986), 'More about the Greek Geometric Pottery at Tell Abu Hawam', *Levant*: 159–71.

Herzfeld, E. (1968), *The Persian Empire*.

Heubeck, A., West, S., and Hainsworth, J. B. (1988), *A Commentary on Homer's* Odyssey, vol. 1.

Higbie, C. (2003), *The Lindian Chronicle and the Greek Creation of their Past*.

Himmelmann, N. (1990), *Ideale Nacktheit in der griechischen Kunst*.

Himmelmann, N. (1998), *Reading Greek Art*, English translation.

Himmelmann, N. (2000), 'Klassische Archäologie: kritische Anmerkungen zur Methode', *JDAI* 115: 253–323.

Hind, J. (1999), 'Pomponius Mela on Colonies in West and East', in G. R. Tsetskhladze (ed.), *Ancient Greeks West and East*, 77–84.

Hodos, T. (2000), 'Kinet Hüyük and Al Mina: A New View on Old Relationships', in G. R. Tsetskhladze, A. J. N. W. Prag and A. M. Snodgrass (eds.), *Periplous: Papers on Classical Art and Archaeology Presented to Sir John Boardman*, 145–53.

Hoffman, G. L., (1997), *Imports and Immigrants: Near Eastern Contacts with Early Iron Age Crete*.

Hoffner, H. A. (1998), *Hittite Myths*, 3rd edition.

Hogarth, D. (1889), *Devia Cypria*.

Hogarth, D. G. (1910), *Accidents of an Antiquary's Life*.

Högemann, P. (2000), 'Zum Iliasdichter – ein anatolischer Standpunkt', *Studia Troica*, 10: 183–98.

Holdich, T. (1910), *The Gates of India*.

Holleaux, M. (1942), 'Les Guerres syriennes: le papyrus de Gourub', in his *Études d'épigraphie et d'histoire grecque*, vol. 3: 281–309.

Holmes, B. (2007), 'The *Iliad*'s Economy of Pain', *TAPA* 137: 45–84.

Homann-Wedeking, E. (1950), *Die Anfänge der griechischen Grossplastik*.

Honeyman, A. M. (1939), 'The Pottery Vessels of the Old Testament', *PEQ*: 76–90.

Hopkinson, N. (ed.) (1994), *Studies in the* Dionysiaca *of Nonnus*.

Hörig, M. (1984), 'Iupiter Dolichenus', *ANRW*, vol. 17/4: 2131–79.

Hornblower, S. (1997), 'Thucydides and Chalcidic Torone', *OJA* 16: 177–86.

Houghton, A. (1984), 'The Seleucid Mint of Mallus and the Cult Figure of Athena Magarsia', in A. Houghton, S. Hester *et al.*, *Festschrift für/Studies in Honour of Leo Mildenburg*, 99–110.

Houston Smith, R. (1965), 'Un cylindre syrien représentant Baal', *Syria*, 42: 253–60.

Houwink ten Cate, Ph. H. J. (1961), *The Luwian Population Groups of Lycia and Cilicia Aspera during the Hellenistic Period*.

Houwink ten Cate, Ph. H. J. (1991), 'The Hittite Storm God: His Role and his Rule according to Cuneiform Sources', in D. J. W. Meijer (ed.), *Natural Phenomena: Their Meaning, Depiction and Description in the Ancient Near East*, 83–148.

Huber, S. (2003), *L'Aire sacrificielle au nord du sanctuaire d'Apollon Daphnephoros . . ., Eretria 14*.

Hudson, M. (1992), 'Did the Phoenicians Introduce the Idea of Interest to Greece and Italy – and if So, When?', in G. Kopcke and I. Tokumaru (eds.), *Greece between East and West, 10th to 8th Centuries BC*, 128–43.

Hutter, M. (1995), 'Der luwische Wettergott *pihaššašši* und der griechische Pegasos', in Chr. Zinko (ed.), *Studia Onomastica et Indogermanica . . . Festschrift für Fritz Lochner von Hüttenbach zum 65. Geburtstag*, 79–98.

Hutter, M., (1996), 'Die Ineinanderfliessen von luwischen und aramäischen religiösen Vorstellungen in Nordsyrien', in P. W. Haider (ed.), *Religionsgeschichte Syriens: von der Frühzeit bis zur Gegenwart*, 116–22.

Huxley, G. L. (1975), 'Cretan *Paiawones*', *GRBS* 16: 119–24.

Iacovou, M. (1999), 'The Greek Exodus to Cyprus: The Antiquity of Hellenism', *MHR* 14: 1–28.

Iacovou, M. (2002), 'Amathous: An Early Iron Age Polity in Cyprus. The Chronology of its Foundation', *RDAC*: 101–22.

Iacovou, M. (2005), 'The Early Iron Age Urban Forms of Cyprus', in R. Osborne and B. W. Cunliffe (eds.), *Mediterranean Urbanization 800–600BC*, 17–44.

Iacovou, M. (2006), 'From the Mycenaean Qa-Si-Re-U to the Cypriote Pa-Si-Le-Wo-Se: The *Basileus* in the Kingdom of Cyprus', in S. Deger-Jalkotzy and I. S. Lemos (eds.), *Ancient Greece: From the Mycenaean Palaces to the Age of Homer*, 315–36.

Jameson, M. H. (1990), 'Perseus the Hero of Mykenai', in R. Hägg and C. Nordquist (eds.), *Celebrations of Death and Divinity in the Bronze Age Argolid*, 213–23.

Jameson, M. H., and Malkin, I. (1998), 'Latinos and the Greeks', *Athenaeum*: 477–86.

Janko, R. (1994), *The Iliad: A Commentary*, vol. 4: Books 13–16.

Janko, R. (1998), 'The Homeric Poems as Oral Dictated Texts', *CQ* 48: 1–13.

Jantzen, U. (1972), *Ägyptische und orientalische Bronzen aus dem Heraion von Samos*.

Jasink, A. M. (1995), *Gli stati neo-ittiti: analisi delle fonti scritti e sintesi storica*.

Jeffery, L. H. (1976), *Archaic States of Greece*.

Johnston, A. W. (2000), 'Building Z at Kommos: an 8th c. Pottery Sequence', *Hesperia*, 69: 189–226.

Johnston, A. W. (2003), 'The Alphabet', in N. Stampolidis and V. Kara-georghis (eds.), *Ploes ... Sea Routes ... Interconnections in the Mediter-ranean, 16th–6th c. BC*, 263–76.

Johnston, A. W., and Andriomenou, A. (1989), 'A Geometric Graffito from Eretria', *ABSA* 84: 217–20.

Jones, C. P. (2000), 'The Emperor and the Giant', *CP* 95: 476–81.

Jones, C. P. (2001), 'Philostratus' *Heroikos* and its Setting in Reality', *JHS* 121: 141–9.

Jourdain-Annequin, C. (1992), *Héraclès-Melqart à Amrith: recherches icono-graphiques*.

Kahil, L. (1980), 'Contribution à l'étude de l'Érétrie géométrique', in *Hē Stēlē ... Tomos eis Mnēmēn Nikolaou Kontoleontos*, 525–31.

Kammelhuber, A. (1990), 'Marduk und Santa in der hellenistischen Über-lieferung des 2. Jhdt. v. Chr.', *Orientalia*, 59: 188–95.

Kantor, H. (1962), 'A Bronze Plaque with Relief Decoration from Tell Tainat', *JNES* 21: 93–117.

Kapelrud, A. S. (1952), *Baal in the Ras Shamra Texts*.

Karageorghis, J. (2003), 'The Goddess of Cyprus between the Orient and the Occident', in N. Stampolidis and V. Karageorghis (eds.), *Ploes ... Sea Routes ... Interconnections in the Mediterranean, 16th–6th c. BC*, 353–61.

Karageorghis, J., and Karageorghis, V. (2002), 'The Great Goddess of Cyprus or the Genesis of Aphrodite in Cyprus', in S. Parpola and R. M. Whiting (eds.), *Sex and Gender in the Ancient Near East: Proceedings of the 47th Rencontre assyriologique internationale*, 263–82.

Karageorghis, V. (1967–78), *Excavations in the Necropolis at Salamis*.

Karageorghis, V. (1977), 'Pottery from Kition', in E. Gjerstad (ed.), *Greek Geometric and Archaic Pottery Found in Cyprus*, 61–4.

Karageorghis, V. (2000), *Ancient Art from Cyprus: The Cesnola Collection*.

Karageorghis, V. (2002A), 'La Nécropole "royale" de Salamine: quarante ans après', *CCEC* 32: 19–29.

Karageorghis, V. (2002B), *Early Cyprus*.

Karageorghis, V. (2006), 'Homeric Cyprus', in S. Deger-Jalkotzy and I. S. Lemos (eds.), *Ancient Greece: From the Mycenaean Palaces to the Age of Homer*, 665–75.

Karageorghis, V., and Lo Schiavo, F. (1989), 'A West Mediterranean Obelos from Amathus', *RSF* 17: 15–29.

Karmel Thomason, A. (2001), 'Representations of the North Syrian Land-scape in Neo-Assyrian Art', *BASOR* 323: 63–96.

Katz, J. (1998), 'How to Be a Dragon in Indo-European ...', in J. Jasanoff,

H. C. Melchert and L. Oliver (eds.), *Mìr Curad: Studies in Honor of Calvert Watkins*, 317–34.

Katzenstein, H. J. (1973), *The History of Tyre from the Beginning of the Second Millenium BCE to the Fall of the Neo-Babylonian Empire in 538 BC*.

Kearsley, R. A. (1995), 'The Greek Geometric Wares from Al Mina Levels 10–8 and Associated Pottery', *Med. Arch.* 8: 7–81.

Kearsley, R. A. (1999), 'Greeks Overseas in the Eighth Century BC: Euboeans, Al Mina and Assyrian Imperialism', in G. R. Tsetskhladze (ed.), *Ancient Greeks West and East*, 109–34.

Keil, J., and Wilhelm, A. (1931), *Denkmäler aus rauhen Kilikien*, MAMA, vol. 3.

Kelly, A. (2006), 'Homer and History: *Iliad* 9, 381–4', *Mnemosyne*, 59: 321–33.

Kelly, A. (2007), 'How to End an Orally-Derived Epic Poem', *TAPA* 137: 371–402.

Kelso, J. L. (1948), 'The Ceramic Vocabulary of the Old Testament', *BASOR Supplementary Studies*, 5–6: 22–3.

Kenzelmann Pfyffer, A., Theurillat, Th., and Verdan, S. (2005), 'Graffiti d'époque géométrique provenant du sanctuaire d'Apollon Daphnéphoros à Érétrie', *ZPE* 151: 51–82.

Kestemont, G. (1983), 'Tyr et les assyriens', in E. Gubel *et al.* (eds.), *Redt Tyrus – sauvons Tyr*, Studia Phoenicia, vol. 1: 53–78.

Key Fowden, E. (1999), *The Barbarian Plain: Saint Sergius between Rome and Iran*.

Kirk, G. S. (1972), 'Aetiology, Ritual, Charter: Three Equivocal Terms in the Study of Myth', *YCS* 22: 83–102.

Kistler, E. (1998), *Die 'Opferinne-Zeremonie': Bankettideologie am Grab, Orientalisierung und Formierung einer Adelsgesellschaft in Athen*.

Kitchell, K. (1979–80), 'Aipeia: A False City of Crete', *CJ* 75: 129–34.

Kleibrink, M. (2006), *Oenotrians at Lagaria near Sybaris*.

Knoepfler, D. (1981), 'Argoura: un toponyme eubéen dans la meidienne de Démosthène', *BCH* 105: 289–329.

Knoepfler, D. (1989), 'Le Calendrier des Chalcidiens de Thrace: essai de mise au point sur la liste et l'ordre des mois eubéens', *JS*: 23–59.

Knoepfler, D. (1990), 'The Calendar of Olynthus and the Origins of the Chalcidians in Thrace', in J.-P. Descoeudres (ed.), *Eumousia: Ceramic and Iconographic Studies in Honour of Alexander Cambitoglou*, 99–115.

Knoepfler, D. (1997), 'Le Territoire d'Érétrie et l'organisation politique de la cité (dēmoi, chōroi, phylai)', in M. H. Hansen (ed.), *The Polis as an Urban Centre and as a Political Community: Acts of the Copenhagen Polis Centre*, vol. 4: 352–449.

Koch, K. (1993), 'Hazzi-Safon-Kasion', in B. Jankowski, K. Koch and G. Wilhelm (eds.), *Religionsgeschichtliche Beziehungen zwischen Kleinasien, Nordsyrien und der Alte Testament*, 171–224.

Koenen, L. (1994), 'Greece, the Near East and Egypt: Cyclical Destruction in Hesiod and the Catalogue of Women', *TAPA* 12: 1–34.

Kohlmeyer, K. (2001), *Der Tempel des Wettergottes von Aleppo*.

Kolk, D. (1963), *Der pythische Apollonhymnos als aitiologische Dichtung*.

Køllund, M. (1992–3), 'Sea and Sardinia', *HBA* 19–20: 201–14.

Kondoleon, N. (1965), 'Hoi Aeinautai tēs Eretrias', *AE* 1963: 1–45.

Koortbojian, M. (1995), *Myth, Meaning and Memory on Roman Sarcophagi*.

Kopcke, G. (2002), '1000 BCE? 900 BCE? A Greek Vase from Lake Galilee', in E. Ehrenberg (ed.), *Leaving No Stones Unturned: Essays on the Ancient Near East and Egypt in Honour of Donald P. Hansen*, 109–17.

Kostoglou-Despini, K. (1971), 'Anaskaphē eis Kassiopēn Kerkuras', *Athens Annals of Archaeology*, 4: 202–6.

Kotsonas, A. (2006), 'Wealth and Status in Iron Age Knossos', *OJA* 25: 147–72.

Kourou, N. (1988), 'Handmade Pottery and Trade: The Case of the "Argive Monochrome" Ware', in J. Christiansen and T. Melander (eds.), *Proceedings of the Third Symposium on Ancient Greek and Related Pottery, Copenhagen, 1987*, 314–24.

Kourou, N. (2002), 'Phéniciens, chypriotes, eubéens et la fondation de Carthage', *CCEC* 32: 89–114.

Kourou, N. (2005), 'Early Iron Age Greek Imports in Italy', in G. Bartoloni and F. Delpino (eds.), *Oriente e occidente: metodi e discipline a confronto*, Mediterranea: quaderni di archeologia etrusco-italica, 1: 497–515.

Kourou, N., and Karetsou, A. (1998), 'An Enigmatic Stone from Knossos: A Re-used Cippus?', in V. Karageorghis and N. Stampolidis (eds.), *Eastern Mediterranean Networks: Cyprus-Dodecanese-Crete, 16th–6th Century, BC*, 243–54.

Kramer, S. N. (1966), 'Annual Resurrection: An Important Correction to "Inanna's Descent"', *BASOR* 183: 31.

Kroll, J. (2003), 'Weights, Bullion Currency and Coinage . . .', in N. Stampolidis and V. Karageorghis (eds.), *Ploes . . . Sea Routes . . . Interconnections in the Mediterranean, 16th–6th c. BC*, 313–24.

Kron, U. (1998), 'Sickles in Greek Sanctuaries: Votives and Cultic Instruments', in R. Hägg (ed.), *Ancient Greek Cult Practice from the Archaeological Evidence*, 187–216.

Kuhrt, A. (1995), *The Ancient Near East, c. 3000–330 BC*.

Kuhrt, A. (2002), 'Sennacherib's Siege of Jerusalem', in A. K. Bowman, H. M. Cotton *et al.* (eds.), *Representations of Empire*, PBA 114: 13–34.

Kullmann, W. (1984), 'Oral Poetry Theory and Neoanalysis: Homeric Research', *GRBS* 25: 307–23.

Kunze, E. (1931), *Kretische Bronze-reliefs*.

Kutscher, R. (1990), 'The Cult of Dumuzi/Tammuz', in J. Klein and A. Skaist (eds.), *Bar-Ilan Studies in Assyriology Dedicated to Pinhas Artzi*, 29–44.

Kyrieleis, H., and Röllig, W. (1998), 'Ein altorientalischer Pferdeschmuck aus dem Heraion von Samos', *MDAI(A)* 103: 37–75.

La Rocca, E. (1974–5), 'Due tombe dell'Esquilino: alcune novità sul commercio euboico in Italia centrale nell' VIII sec. a. C.', *Dialoghi di archeologia*, 8: 86–103.

La Rocca, E. (1982), 'Ceramica d'importazione greca dell' VIII sec. A. C. a Sant'Omobono: un aspetto delle origini di Roma', in *La Céramique grecque ou de tradition grecque au VIIIème siècle en Italie centrale et méridionale*, Cahiers du Centre Jean Bérard, 3: 45–54.

Lagarce, J., and Lagarce, E. (1995), 'Ras ibn Hani au Bronze Récent', in M. Yon, M. Sznycer and P. Bordreuil (eds.), *Le Pays d'Ougarit autour de 1200 av. J-C.*, Ras Shamra-Ougarit, vol. 11: 141–54.

Lalaguë-Dulac, S. (2002), 'La Chimère, un lieu du culte original pour le dieu Héphaistos', *Hethitica*, 15: 129–61.

Lane Fox, R. (1973), *Alexander the Great*.

Lane Fox, R. J. (1991), *The Unauthorized Version*.

Lane Fox, R. (2004), 'Sex, Gender and the Other in Xenophon's *Anabasis*', in R. Lane Fox (ed.), *The Long March: Xenophon and the Ten Thousand*, 184–214.

Lanfranchi, G. B., Roaf, M., and Rollinger, R. (2003), *Continuity of Empire: Assyria, Media, Persia*.

Langdon, S. H. (ed.) (1993), *From Pasture to Polis*.

Latacz, J. (2002), *Troia und Homer: der Weg der Lösung eines alten Rätsel*.

Le Rider, G. (1966), *Monnaies crétoises du Ve. au Ier. siècle av. J.-C.*

Le Rider, G. (1986), 'Les Monnaies de la fouille de Bassit', *BCH* 110: 393–408.

Le Rider, G., and Verdan, S. (2002), 'La Trouvaille d'Érétrie: réserve d'un orfèvre ou dépot monétaire', *AK* 45: 133–52.

Leaf, W. (1923), *Strabo on the Troad*.

Leake, W. M. (1830), *Travels in the Morea*, vol. 3.

Leake, W. M. (1835), *Travels in Northern Greece*, vol. 2.

Lebessi, A. (1975), 'The Fortetsa Gold Rings', *ABSA* 70: 169–76.

Lebrun, R., and de Vos, J. (2006), 'À propos de l'inscription bilingue de l'ensemble sculpturel de Çineköy', *Anatolia Antiqua*, 14: 45–64.

Lee, I. (1999), 'The Flower of Adonis at Eryx', *NC* 159: 1–31.

Leglay, M. (1966), *Saturne africain*.

Lehmann, G. (2005), 'Al Mina and the East', in A. Villing (ed.), *The Greeks in the East*, 61–92.

Leigh, M. (1994), 'Servius on Virgil's *Senex Corycius*: New Evidence', *MD* 33: 181–95.

Lemaire, A. (1977), 'Essai sur cinq sceaux phéniciens', *Semitica*, 27: 27–40.

Lemaire, A. (1983), 'L'Inscription phénicienne de Hassan-Beyli reconsiderée', *RSF* 11: 9–19.

Lemaire, A. (2001), 'Les Languages du royaume de Sam'al aux IX–VIII s. av. J.-C. et leurs relations avec le royaume de Que', in E. Jean, A. Dincol *et al.* (eds.), *La Cilicie: espaces et pouvoirs locaux*, 185–91.

Lemos, I. S. (2002), *The Protogeometric Aegean*.

Lemos, I. S. (2003), 'Craftsmen, Traders and Some Wives in Early Iron Age Greece', in N. Stampolidis and V. Karageorghis (eds.), *Ploes . . . Sea Routes . . . Interconnections in the Mediterranean, 16th–6th c. BC*, 187–96.

Lemos, I. S. (2005), 'The Changing Relationship of the Euboeans and the East', in A. Villing (ed.), *The Greeks in the East*, 53–60.

Lemos, I. S. (2007A), '*Epei pore muria hedna . . . (Iliad* 22.472): Homeric Reflections in Early Iron Age Elite Burials', in E. Alram-Stern and G. Nightingale (eds.), *Keimelion: Elitenbildung und elitärer Konsum von der mykenischen Palastzeit bis zur homerischen Epoche*, 275–80.

Lemos, I. S. (2007B), 'Recent Archaeological Work on Xeropolis Lefkandi: A Preliminary Report', in A. Mazarakis Ainian (ed.), *Oropos and Euboea in the Early Iron Age*, 123–30.

Lemos, I. S., and Hatcher, H. (1986), 'Protogeometric Skyros and Euboea', *OJA* 5: 323–37.

Lemos, I. S., and Hatcher, H. (1991), 'Early Greek Vases in Cyprus: Euboean and Attic', *OJA* 10: 197–208.

Lightfoot, J. L. (1999), *Parthenius of Nicaea*.

Lightfoot, J. L. (2003), *Lucian, On the Syrian Goddess*.

Limet, H. (1992), 'Le Cheval dans le proche-orient ancien', in L. Bodson (ed.), *Contributions à l'histoire de la domestication*, 37–55.

Lipinski, E. (1983), 'La Carthage de Chypre', in E. Gubel *et al.* (eds.), *Redt Tyrus – sauvons Tyr*, Studia Phoenicia, vol. 1: 209–34.

Lipinski, E. (1994), *Studies in Aramaic Inscriptions and Onomastics*, vol. 2.

Lipinski, E. (1995), *Dieux et déesses de l'univers phénicien et punique*.

Lipinski, E. (1999), 'The Nora Fragment', *Mediterraneo antico*, 2: 667–71.

Lipinski, E. (2000), *The Aramaeans: Their Ancient History, Culture and Religion*.

Lipinski, E. (2004), *Itineraria Phoenicia*.

Liston, M. A., and Papadopoulos, J. K. (2006), 'The "Rich Athenian Lady" Was Pregnant: The Anthropology of a Geometric Tomb Revisited', *Hesperia*, 73: 7–38.

Lo Schiavo, F. (1994), 'Bronzi nuragici nelle tombe della prima età del ferro di Pontecagnano', in *La presenza etrusca nella Campania meridionale*, Biblioteca degli studi etruschi 28: 61–82.

Lo Schiavo, F. (2000), 'Sea and Sardinia: Nuragic Bronze Boats', in D. Ridgway, F. Serra Ridgway *et al.* (eds.), *Ancient Italy in its Mediterranean Setting: Studies in Honour of Ellen Macnamara*, 141–58.

Lopez Pardo, F. (2005), 'Inscripción fenicia arcaica de Lixus', *Madr. Mitt.* 46: 46–60.

Lorimer, H. L. (1950), *Homer and the Monuments.*

Loud, G., and Altman, C. B. (1938), *Khorsabad Part II: The Citadel and the Town.*

Lubtchansky, N. (2005), *Le Cavalier tyrrhénien: représentations équestres dans l'Italie archaïque.*

Luke, J. (2003), *Ports of Trade: Al Mina and Geometric Greek Pottery in the Levant.*

Luraghi, N. (2006), 'Traders, Pirates, Warriors: The Proto-History of Greek Mercenary Soldiers in the Eastern Mediterranean', *Phoenix*, 60: 21–47.

McDonnell, M. (1991), 'The Introduction of Athletic Nudity: Thucydides, Plato, and the Vases', *JHS* 111: 182–93.

McEwan, C. W. (1937), 'The Syrian Expedition of the Oriental Institute of the University of Chicago', *AJA* 41: 8–16.

MacKay, T. S. (1990), 'The Major Sanctuaries of Pamphylia and Cilicia', *ANRW*, vol. 18/3: 2045–2129.

MacLair Boraston, J. (1911), 'The Birds of Homer', *JHS* 31: 216–50.

Maggiani, A. (1972), 'Aska eleivana', *SE* 40: 183–7.

Majno, G. (1975), *The Healing Hand: Man and Wound in the Ancient World.*

Malkin, I. (1987), *Religion and Colonization in Ancient Greece.*

Malkin, I. (1994), *Myth and Territory in the Spartan Mediterranean.*

Malkin, I. (1998), *The Returns of Odysseus.*

Malkin, I. (1999), 'Ul sse protocolonisateur', *Mediterr. Ant.* 2: 243–61.

Malkin, I. (2000), 'La Fondation d'une colonie apollonienne: Delphes et l'*Hymne homérique à Apollon*', in A. Jacquemin (ed.), *Delphes cent ans après la grande fouille: essai de bilan . . .*, BCH supplément 36: 69–77.

Malkin, I. (2003), ' "Tradition" in Herodotus: The Founding of Cyrene', in P. Derow and R. Parker (eds.), *Herodotus and his World*, 153–70.

Malkin, I., and Fichmann, A. (1987), 'Homer, *Odyssey* III, 153–85: A Maritime Commentary', *MHR* 2: 250–58.

Malouchou, G. E. (2006), 'Nea epigraphē genōa', in G. E. Malouchou and A. P. Matthaiou (eds.), *Chiakon symposion eis mnēmēn W. G. Forrest*, 81–90.

Malten, L. (1925), 'Bellerophontes', *JDAI* 40: 121–60.

Mango, C. (1994), 'The Empress Helena, Hellenopolis, Pylae', *Travaux et mémoires*, 12: 143–58.

Marankou, A. (2000), *The Consul Luigi Palma di Cesnola, 1832–1904: Life and Deeds*.

Marek, C. (1993), 'Euboia und die Entstehung der Alphabetenschrift bei den Griechen', *Klio*, 75: 27–44.

Mark, S. (2005), *Homeric Seafaring*.

Markoe, G. E. (1985), *Phoenician Bronze and Silver Bowls from Cyprus*.

Markoe, G. E. (1992), 'In Pursuit of Metal: Phoenicians and Greeks in Italy', in G. Kopcke and I. Tokumaru (eds.), *Greece between East and West, 10th to 8th Centuries BC*, 61–84.

Markoe, G. E. (1992–3), 'In Pursuit of Silver: Phoenicians in Central Italy', *HBA* 19–20: 11–32.

Markoe, G. E. (1998), 'The Phoenicians on Crete: Transit Trade and the Search for Ores', in V. Karageorghis and N. Stampolidis (eds.), *Eastern Mediterranean Networks: Cyprus-Dodecanese-Crete, 16th–6th Century BC*, 233–41.

Markoe, G. E. (2005), *The Phoenicians*.

Massimilla, G. (1996), *Callimaco: Aitia libri primo e secondo*.

Masson, O., and Sznycer, M. (1972), *Recherches sur les phéniciens à Chypre*.

Matsushima, E. (1993), 'Divine Statues in Mesopotamia: Their Fashioning, Clothing and Interaction with the Society', in E. Matsushima (ed.), *Official Cult and Popular Religion in the Ancient Near East*, 209–19.

Matthäus, H. (1998), 'Cyprus and Crete in the Early First Millennium BC', in V. Karageorghis and N. Stampolidis (eds.), *Eastern Mediterranean Networks: Cyprus-Dodecanese-Crete, 16th–6th Century BC*, 127–58.

Matthäus, H. (1999), 'The Greek Symposium and the Near East: Chronology and the Mechanisms of Cultural Transfer', in R. F. Docter and E. M. Moorman (eds.), *Proceedings of the XV International Congress of Classical Archaeology, July 1998*: 225–60.

Matthäus, H. (2000A), 'Crete and the Near East during the First Millennium BC: New Investigations of the Bronze Finds from Idean Cave', in *Pepragmena 8 Diethnous Krētologikou Synedriou*, A2: 267–80.

Matthäus, H. (2000B), 'Die idaische-Zeus-Grotte auf Kreta, Griechenland und der vordere Orient im frühen Jahrtausend v. Chr.', *JDAI Arch. Anz.*: 517–49.

Matthäus, H. (2000C), 'Die Rolle Zyperns und Sardiniens im mittelmeerischen Interaktionsprozess während des späten zweiten und frühen ersten Jhdt. v. Chr.', in F. Prayon and W. Röllig (eds.), *Der Orient im Etrurien*, 41–76.

Matthäus, H. (2001), 'Studies on the Interrelations of Cyprus and Italy during the 11th to 9th Centuries BC: A Pan-Mediterranean Perspective', in L. Bonfante and V. Karageorghis (eds.), *Italy and Cyprus in Antiquity: 1500–450 BC*, 153–214.

Mayor, A. (2000), *The First Fossil Hunters: Palaeontology in Greek and Roman Times*.

Mazarakis Ainian, A. (1987), 'Geometric Eretria', *AK* 30: 3–24.

Mazarakis Ainian, A. (1998), 'Oropos in the Early Iron Age', in M. Bats and B. d'Agostino (eds.), *Euboica: l'Eubea e la presenza euboica in Calcidica e in occidente*, 179–215.

Mazarakis Ainian, A. (2002), 'Recent Excavations at Oropos (Northern Attica)', in M. Stamatopoulou and M. Yeroulanou (eds.), *Excavating Classical Culture: Recent Archaeological Discoveries in Greece*, 149–78.

Mazarakis Ainian, A. (2007), *Oropos and Euboea in the Early Iron Age*.

Mazzella, S. (1593), *Opusculum De Balneis Puteolorum, Baiarum et Pithecussarum*.

Mazzoni, S. (1994), 'Aramaean and Luwian New Foundations', in S. Mazzoni (ed.), *'Nuove' fondazioni del vicino oriente antico: realtà e ideologia*, 319–39.

Mazzoni, S. (1995), 'Settlement Pattern and New Urbanization in Syria at the Time of the Assyrian Conquest', in M. Liverani (ed.), *Neo-Assyrian Geography*, 181–91.

Meiggs, R. (1982), *Trees and Timber in the Ancient Mediterranean World*.

Melchert, H. C. (ed.) (2003), *The Luwians*.

Mele, A. (1979), *Il commercio greco arcaico: Prexis ed Emporie*.

Mele, A. (1981), 'Intervention', in *Nouvelle contribution à l'étude de la société et de la colonisation eubéennes*, Cahiers du Centre Jean Bérard, 6: 138–9.

Mele, A. (1998), 'Calcidica e calcidesi: considerazioni sulla tradizione', in M. Bats and B. d'Agostino (eds.), *Euboica: l'Eubea e la presenza euboica in Calcidica e in occidente*, 217–28.

Mellink, M. J. (1950), 'Karatepe: More Light on the Dark Ages', *BO* 3: 141–59.

Mellink, M. (1995), 'Homer, Lycia and Lukka', in J. B. Carter and S. P. Morris (eds.), *The Ages of Homer*, 33–43.

Menardos, S. (1908), 'Where Did Aphrodite Find the Body of Adonis?', *JHS* 28: 133–7.

Mercuri, L. (2004), *Eubéens en Calabre à l'époque archaïque.*

Merlat, P. (1960), *Jupiter Dolichenus.*

Mettinger, T. (2001), *The Riddle of Resurrection.*

Millar, F. G. B. (1993), *The Roman Near East.*

Millard, A. R. (1962), 'Ezekiel 27.19: The Wine Trade of Damascus', *JSS* 7: 201–3.

Miller, W. T. (1984), *Mysterious Encounters at Mamre and Jabbok.*

Misilaidou-Despotidou, V. (2001), 'Mia Nea Epigraphē apo tou Aphytou', in *Panellēnio Synedrio Epigraphikēs, Thessalonikē, 22–3 Oktovriou 1999*, 79–90.

Mitchell, L. G. (2001), 'Euboean Io', *CQ* 51: 339–52.

Mitchell, S. (1990), 'Festivals, Games and Civic Life in Roman Asia Minor', *JRS* 80: 183–93.

Mitford, T. B. (1971), *The Inscriptions of Kourion.*

Momigliano, A. (1934), 'Su una battaglia tra assiri e greci', *Athenaeum*, NS 12: 412–16.

Momigliano, A. (1975A), *Alien Wisdom: The Limits of Hellenisation.*

Momigliano, A. (1975B), 'The Fault of the Greeks', *Daedalus*, 104: 9–19.

Monti, P. (1998–9), 'Homeric Tradition in the Mediterranean Navigation of the Pithekoussans', *Talanta*, 30–31: 115–32.

Moorey, P. R. S. (1999), *Ancient Mesopotamian Materials and Industries: The Archaeological Evidence.*

Moret, J.-M. (1990), 'Io Apotauromenē', *Rev. Arch.*: 3–26.

Moretti Sgubini, A. M. (2004), 'Vulci: la tomba del guerriero della Pelledraro', in *Scavi nello scavo: gli etruschi non visti*, 150–65.

Morgan, C. A. (1988), 'Corinth, the Corinthian Gulf and Western Greece during the Eighth Century BC', *ABSA* 83: 313–38.

Morgan, C. A. (1990), *Athletes and Oracles: The Transformation of Olympia and Delphi in the Eighth Century BC.*

Morgan, C. A. (1994), 'The Evolution of a Sacral "Landscape": Isthmia, Perachora and the Early Corinthian State', in S. E. Alcock and R. G. Osborne (eds.), *Placing the Gods*, 105–42.

Morgan, C. A. (2001), 'Figurative Iconography from Corinth, Ithaka, and Pithekoussai: Aetos 600 Reconsidered', *ABSA* 96: 195–227.

Morhange, C., *et al.* (2002), 'Il problema della localizzazione del porto antico di Cuma: nuovi metodi e risultati preliminari', in B. d'Agostino and A. d'Andrea (eds.), *Cuma: nuove forme di intervento per lo studio del sito antico*, 153–66.

Morris, I. (1987), *Burial and Ancient Society: The Rise of the Greek City-state*.

Morris, I. (1988), 'Tomb Cult and the Greek Renaissance', *Antiquity*, 62: 750–61.

Morris, I. (1998), 'Burial and Society after Ten Years', in S. Marchegay, M.-T. le Dinahet and J.-F. Salles (eds.), *Nécropoles et pouvoir*, 21–36.

Morris, I. (2000), *Archaeology as Cultural History*.

Morris, S. P. (1992), *Daidalos and the Origins of Greek Art*.

Morris, S. P., and Papadopoulos, J. K. (2004), 'Of Granaries and Games: Egyptian Stowaways in an Athenian Chest', in A. P. Chapin (ed.), *Charis: Essays in Honor of Sara A. Immerwahr*, Hesperia Supplement, 33: 225–42.

Mosca, P. G., and Russell, J. (1987), 'A Phoenician Inscription from Cebel Ires Dagi in Rough Cilicia', *Epigr. Anat.* 9: 1–28.

Moscati Castelnuovo, L. (1989), *Siris: tradizione storiografica e momenti della storia di una città della Magna Grecia*.

Müller, H. P. (2000), 'Daphnis: ein Doppelgänger des Gottes Adonis', *ZPDV* 116: 26–41.

Munger, S. (2003), 'Egyptian Stamp-seal Amulets and their Implications for the Chronology of the Early Iron Age', *Tel Aviv*, 30: 66–82.

Mureddu, P. (1972), 'Chruseia a Pithecussai', *PP* 27: 407–9.

Murray, O. (1994), 'Nestor's Cup and the Origins of the Greek *Symposion*', in B. d'Agostino and D. Ridgway (eds.), *Apoikia: scritti in onore di Giorgio Buchner*, AION, vol. 1: 47–54.

Murray, W. M. (1995), 'Ancient Sailing Winds in the Eastern Mediterranean: The Case for Cyprus', in V. Karageorghis and D. Michaelides (eds.), *Cyprus and the Sea*, 33–43.

Myres, J. L. (1940–45), 'Aphrodite Anadyomene', *ABSA* 41: 99.

Na'aman N. (1998), 'Sargon II and the Rebellion of the Cypriot Kings against Shilta of Tyre', *Orientalia*, 67: 239–47.

Na'aman, N. (2004A), 'Ra'shu, Re'si-ṣurri and the Ancient Name of Ras ibn Hani', *BASOR* 334: 33–9.

Na'aman, N. (2004B), 'Re'si-suri and Yauna in a Neo-Assyrian Letter (ND 2737)', *Nouvelles assyriologiques brèves et utilitaires* = *NABU* 3: 69–70.

Naso, A. (2000), 'Etruscan and Italian Artefacts from the Aegean', in D. Ridgway, F. Serra Ridgway *et al.* (eds.), *Ancient Italy in its Mediterranean Setting: Studies in Honour of Ellen Macnamara*, 193–208.

Neeft, C. W. (1989), *Protocorinthian Subgeometric Aryballoi*.

Niemeyer, H. G. (1990), 'The Phoenicians in the Mediterranean: A Non-Greek Model for Expansion and Settlement in Antiquity', in J.-P. Descoeudres (ed.), *Greek Colonists and Native Populations*, 469–89.

Niemeyer, H. G. (2000), 'The Early Phoenician City-states on the Mediter-ranean: Archaeological Elements for their Description', in M. H. Hansen (ed.), *A Comparative Study of Thirty City-state Cultures*, 89–115.

Nijboer, A. J., and van der Pflicht, J. (2006), 'An Interpretation of the Radiocarbon Determinations of the Oldest Indigenous-Phoenician Stratum Thus Far Excavated at Huelva, Tartessos (South West Spain)', *Babesch*, 81: 31–6.

Nilsson, M. P. (1951), 'The Sickle of Cronos', *ABSA* 46: 122–4.

Nims, C. F., and Steiner, R. C. (1983), 'A Paganized Version of Ps. 20, 2–6 from the Aramaic Text in Demotic Script', *JAOS* 103: 261–74.

Nuttall, A. D. (2007), *Shakespeare the Thinker*.

Oakley, S. (1998), *A Commentary on Livy, Books VI–X*.

Oded, B. (1974), 'The Phoenician Cities and the Assyrian Empire in the Time of Tiglath-Pileser III', *ZPDV* 90: 38–49.

Oded, B. (1979), *Mass Deportations and Deportees in the Neo-Assyrian Empire*.

Osborne, R. G. (1993), 'A la grecque . . .', *JMA* 6: 231–7.

Osborne, R. G. (1996), *Greece in the Making, 1200–479 BC*.

Osborne, R. G. (1997), 'Heroic Nakedness and Greek Art', *Gender and History*, 9: 504–28.

Osborne, R. G. (1998), 'Early Greek Colonization', in N. Fisher and H. van Wees (eds.), *Archaic Greece: New Approaches and New Evidence*, 251–69.

Osborne, R. G. (2004), 'Greek Archaeology: A Summary of Recent Work', *AJA* 108: 87–102.

Osborne, R. G. (2005), 'Ordering Women in Hesiod's *Catalogue*', in R. Hunter (ed.), *The Hesiodic* Catalogue of Women, 5–24.

Otten, H. (1969), *Sprachliche Stellung und Datierung des Madduwatta-Textes*.

Otten, H. (1988), *Die Bronzetafel aus Bogazköy: ein Staatsvertrag Tuthaliyas IV*.

Ozbayoglou, E. (2003), 'Notes on Natural Resources of Cilicia', *Olba*, 8: 159–71.

Pacciarelli, M. (1999), *Torre Galli: le necropoli della prima età del Ferro (Scavi Paolo Orsi 1922–3)*.

Page, D. L. (1956), 'Greek Verses from the Eighth Century BC', *CR* 6: 95–7.

Pagels, K. A. (1927), *Die Bedeutung des ätiologischen Moments für Herodots Geschichtschreibung*, Diss. Berlin.

Paizis-Danias, D. I. (2006), *Homer's Ithaca on Cephallenia? Facts and Fancies in the History of an Idea*, Ithacan Friends of Homer Association.

Pamir, H. (2006), 'Al Mina and Sabuniye in the Orontes Delta: The Sites', in

G. R. Tsetskhladze (ed.), *Greek Colonisation: An Account of Greek Colonies and Other Settlements Overseas*, vol. 1: 535–43.

Panayota, B. (2003), *La Laine et le parfum: epinetra et alabastres, forme, iconographie et fonction*.

Papadopoulos, J. K. (2005), *The Early Iron Age Cemetery at Torone*, vol. 1.

Papadopoulos, J. K., and Ruscillo, D. (2002), 'A *Ketos* in Early Athens: An Archaeology of Whales and Sea Monsters in the Greek World', *AJA* 106: 187–227.

Parke, H. W. (1967), *Oracles of Zeus*.

Parke, H. W. (1985), *The Oracles of Apollo in Asia Minor*.

Parker, B. J. (2000), 'The Earliest Known Reference to the Ionians in the Cuneiform Sources', *AHB* 14: 69–77.

Parker, R. (2004), 'One Man's Piety: The Religious Dimension of the *Anabasis*', in R. Lane Fox (ed.), *The Long March: Xenophon and the Ten Thousand*, 131–53.

Parker, R. C. T. (1996), *Athenian Religion: A History*.

Parker, V. (1997), *Untersuchungen zum lelantischen Krieg und verwandte Problemen der frühgriechischen Geschichte*.

Parpola, S. (1995), 'The Construction of Dur-Sarrukin in the Assyrian Royal Correspondence', in A. Caubet (ed.), *Khorsabad, le palais de Sargon II., roi d'Assyrie*, 47–77.

Payne, H. (1940), *Perachora*, vol. 1.

Pearson, L. (1975), 'Myth and *archaeologia* in Italy and Sicily in Timaeus and his Predecessors', *YCS* 24: 171–95.

Peeters, P. (1909), 'S. Barlaam du Mont Kasios', *MUSJ* 3: 805–13.

Penhallurick, R. D. (1986), *Tin in Antiquity: Its Mining and Trade in the Ancient World with Particular Reference to Cornwall*.

Perrault, J.-Y. (1993), 'Les Emporia grecs du Levant: mythe ou réalité?', in A. Bresson and P. Rouillard (eds.), *L'Emporion . . .*, 59–83.

Peruzzi, E. (1992A), 'Cultura greca a Gabii nel secolo VIII a.C.', *PP* 47: 459–68.

Peruzzi, E. (1992B), 'Le scimmie di Pitecussa', *PP* 47: 115–26.

Petacco, L. (2003), 'Anfore fenicie, anfore pithecusane, anfore etrusche: considerazioni sul modello "tirrenico"', *Miscellanea etrusco-italica*, 3: 37–70.

Peters, M. (1998), 'Homerisches und Unhomerisches bei Homer und auf dem Nestorbechen', in J. Jasanoff, H. C. Melchert and L. Oliver (eds.), *Mìr Curad: Studies in Honor of Calvert Watkins*, 584–600.

Petit, T. (1999), 'Eteocypriot Myth and Amathusian Reality', *JMA* 12: 108–20.

Pfeiffer, R. (1949), *Callimachus*, vol. 1.

Philippe, A.-L. (2005), 'L'Épithète Delphinios', in N. Belayche, P. Brulé *et al.* (eds.), *Nommer les dieux: théonymes, épithètes, épiclèses dans l'antiquité*, 241–54.

Philippson, A. (1911), *Reisen und Forschungen in westlichen Kleinasien*, Petermanns Mitteilungen, Ergänzungsheft 172.

Philippson, A. (1951), *Die griechischen Landschaften: eine Landeskunde*, vol. 1, part 2.

Piérart, M. (1984), 'Deux notes sur la politique d'Athènes en Mer Egée (478–5)', *BCH* 108: 161–71.

Piérart, M. (1992), 'Les Honneurs de Persée et d'Héraclès', in C. Bonnet and C. Jourdain-Annequin (eds.), *Héraclès: d'une rive à l'autre de la Méditerranée. Bilan et perspectives*, 223–44.

Pirenne-Delforge, V. (1994), *L'Aphrodite grecque.*

Pisano, F. (2003), *Le ossa dei giganti della Rocca di Pozzuoli.*

Pisano, G. (1999), 'Remarks on Trade in Luxury Goods in the West Mediterranean', in G. Pisano (ed.), *Phoenicians and Carthaginians in the West Mediterranean*, 15–30.

Pomtow, H. (1918), 'Neue delphische Inschriften', *Klio*, 15: 26–8.

Ponchi, S. (1991), *L'Assiria e gli stati transeufratici nella prima metà dell' VIII sec. a.C.*

Poncy, H., Casabonne, D., *et al.* (2001), 'Sceaux du muse d'Adana . . .', *Anatolia Antiqua*, 9: 9–38.

Popham, M. R., and Lemos, I. S. (1999), 'A Euboean Warrior Trader', *OJA* 14: 151–7.

Popham, M. R., Sackett, L. H., and Themelis, P. G. (eds.) (1980), *Lefkandi*, vol. 1: *The Iron Age.*

Poplin, F. (1995), 'L'Homme et l'animal dans le bûcher de Patroklos', in L. Chaia (ed.), *L'Animal dans l'espace humain*, Anthropozoologica, 21: 253–66.

Potter, D. S. (1994), *Prophets and Emperors.*

Poulsen, F. (1912), *Der Orient und der frühgriechische Kunst.*

Powell, B. (1991), *Homer and the Origin of the Greek Alphabet.*

Prag, A. J. N. W. (1989), 'Reconstructing King Midas: A First Report', *AS* 29: 159–66.

Prausnitz, M. W. (1966), 'A Phoenician Krater from Akhziz', *Or. Ant.* 5: 177–88.

Prinz, F. (1979), *Gründungsmythen und Sagenchronologie.*

Pryor, J. H. (1988), *Geography, Technology and War: Studies in the Maritime History of the Mediterranean, 649–1571.*

Puech, E. (1992), 'La Stèle de Bar Hadad a Melqart et les rois d'Arpad', *Rev. Bibl.* 99: 311–34.

Raban, A. (1998), 'Near Eastern Harbours: 13th–7th c. BC', in S. Gitin, A. Mazar and E. Stern (eds.), *Mediterranean People in Transition ... Papers of First International Symposium held by the Ph. and M. Berman Center for Biblical Archaeology in Honour of T. Dothan*, 428–38.

Radet, G. (1893), *La Lydie et le monde grec aux temps des Mermnades.*

Radner, K. (2003), 'An Assyrian View on the Medes', in G. B. Lanfranchi, M. Roaf and R. Rollinger (eds.), *Continuity of Empire: Assyria, Media, Persia*, 37–64.

Raimond, E. A. (2007), 'Hellenization and Lycian Cults during the Achaemenid Period', in C. J. Tuplin (ed.), *Persian Responses*, 143–62.

Rasmussen, T. (1991), 'Corinth and the Orientalizing Phenomenon', in T. Rasmussen and N. Spivey (eds.), *Looking at Greek Vases*, 57–78.

Ravaglioli, S. (1985), 'Inarime', in *Enciclopedia Virgiliana*, vol. 2: 932.

Rawson, J. (ed.) (1996), *Mysteries of Ancient China.*

Reade, J. (1995), 'The Khorsabad Glazed Bricks and their Symbolism', in A. Caubet (ed.), *Khorsabad, le palais de Sargon II., roi d'Assyrie*, 225–51.

Redford, D. B. (1999), 'A Note on the Chronology of Dynasty 25 and the Inscription of Sargon at Tang-i-Var', *Orientalia*, 68: 58–60.

Reed, J. O. (2000), 'Arsinoe and Adonis: The Poetics of Ptolemaic Imperialism', *TAPA* 130: 319–51.

Reese, D. (1995), 'Equid Sacrifice and Burial in Greece and Cyprus, an Addendum', *JPR* 9: 35–42.

Ribichini, S. (1981), *Adonis: aspetti 'orientali' di un mito greco.*

Ribichini, S. (1982), 'Kinyras di Cipro', in V. Lanternari, M. Massenzio and D. Sabbatucci (eds.), *Studi in Memoria di Angelo Brelich*, 479–500.

Richardson, N. J. (1987), 'Homeric Cyprus', in *The Civilizations of the Aegean and their Diffusion in Cyprus and the Eastern Mediterranean, 2000–600 BC*, 125–32.

Richter, T. (1998), 'Anmerkungen zu den hurritischen Personnamen', in D. I. Owen and G. Wilhelm (eds.), *Studies on the Civilization and Culture of Nuzi and the Hurrians*, 125–34.

Richter, T. (1999), *Untersuchungen zu den lokalen Panthea Süd- und Mittel-babyloniens in altbabylonischer Zeit.*

Ridgway, D. (1992), *The First Western Greeks.*

Ridgway, D. (1994), 'Daidalos and Pithekoussai', in B. d'Agostino and D. Ridgway (eds.), *Apoikia: scritti in onore di Giorgio Buchner*, AION, vol. 1, 69–76.

Ridgway, D. (1996), 'Greek Letters at Osteria dell'Osa', *O. Rom.* 20: 87–97.

Ridgway, D. (1997), 'Nestor's Cup and the Etruscans', *OJA* 16: 325–44.

Ridgway, D. (1999A), 'The Carthaginian Connection: A View from San Montano', in R. Rolle, K. Schmidt and R. F. Docter (eds.), *Archäologische Studien in Kontaktzonen der antiken Welt*, 301–8.

Ridgway, D. (1999B), 'The Rehabilitation of Bocchoris', *JEA* 85: 143–52.

Ridgway, D. (2000), 'Seals, Scarabs and People in Pithekoussai I', in G. R. Tsetskhladze, A. J. N. W. Prag and A. M. Snodgrass (eds.), *Periplous: Papers on Classical Art and Archaeology Presented to Sir John Boardman*, 235–43.

Ridgway, D. (2006), 'Early Greek Imports in Sardinia', in G. R. Tsetskhladze (ed.), *Greek Colonisation: An Account of Greek Colonies and Other settlements Overseas*, vol. 1: 239–52.

Ridgway, D., Boitani, F., and Derius, A. (1985), 'Provenance and Firing Techniques of Geometric Pottery from Veii', *ABSA* 80: 139–50.

Riis, P. J. (1970), *Sūkās I, the North-east Sanctuary and the First Settling of Greeks in Syria and Phoenicia*.

Riis, P. J. (1988), 'Quelques problèmes de la topographie phénicienne, Usnu, Paltos, Palleta et les ports de la région', in P.-L. Gatier, B. Helly and J.-P. Rey-Coquais (eds.), *Géographie historique au proche-orient*, 315–324.

Rizza, G. (1979), 'Tombes de chevaux', in V. Karageorghis (ed.), *The Relations between Cyprus and Crete, c. 2000–500 BC*, 194–7.

Robert, L. (1951), 'Contribution à la topographie de villes de l'Asie Mineure méridionale', *CRAI*: 256–9.

Robert, L. (1958), 'Philologie et géographie I. Satala de Lydie, Kérassai et Nonnos, *Dionysiaques* XIII', *Anatolia*, 3: 137–44.

Robert, L. (1960A), 'Monnaies et divinités d'Aspendos', *Hellenica*, 11–12: 177–88.

Robert, L. (1960B), 'Recherches épigraphiques', *REA* 62: 334–5.

Robert, L. (1962), *Villes d'Asie Mineure*.

Robert, L. (1963), *Noms indigènes dans l'Asie Mineure gréco-romaine*.

Robert, L. (1969), *Opera Minora Selecta*, vol. 3.

Robert, L. (1976), 'Une inscription agonistique attribuée à Corycos en Cilicie' *RPh* 50: 177–92.

Robert, L. (1977), 'Documents d'Asie Mineure', *BCH* 101: 88–132.

Robert, L. (1978A), 'Documents d'Asie Mineure', *BCH* 102: 535–8.

Robert, L. (1978B), 'Les Conquêtes du dynaste lycien Arbinas', *JS*: 3–48.

Robert, L. (1980), *À travers l'Asie Mineure*.

Robert, L. (1982), 'Documents d'Asie Mineure', *BCH* 106: 334–57.

Robertson, C. (2002), 'Wounds and Wounding in the *Iliad*', *AHB* 16: 103–10.

Robertson, C. M. (1940), 'The Excavation at Al Mina, Sueidia IV', *JHS* 60: 3–21.

Robinson, E. S. G. (1946), 'Rhegion, Zankle-Messana and the Samians', *JHS* 66: 13–20.

Roller, D. W. (2003), *The World of Juba II and Kleopatra Selene.*

Rolley, C. (1977), *Les Trepieds à cuve clouée*, Fouilles de Delphes, 5/3.

Rolley, C. (2007), 'Techniques, travail: la naissance des styles à l'époque géométrique', *Pallas*, 73: 63–70.

Röllig, W. (1999), 'Appendix 1. The Phoenician Inscriptions', in H. Çambel (ed.), *Corpus of Hieroglyphic Luwian Inscriptions*, vol. 2: *Karatepe-Arslantaş*, 50–81.

Rollinger, R. (1997), 'Zur Bezeichnung von "Griechen" in Keilschrifttexten', *Revue assyriologique et d'archéologie orientale*, 91: 167–72.

Ross Holloway, R. (1994), *The Archaeology of Early Rome and Latium.*

Rowe, C. J. (1983), '"Archaic Thought" in Hesiod', *JHS* 103: 124–35.

Ruijgh, C. J. (1997), 'La Date de la création de l'alphabet grec et celle de l'épopée homérique', *BO* 54: 533–603.

Rutherford, I. (2001A), *Pindar's Paeans.*

Rutherford, I. (2001B), 'The Song of the Sea', *Studien zu den Boghaz-Köy-Texten*, 45: 598–609.

Sabbatucci, D. (1992), 'Ercole e la fondazione del culto dell'Ara Massima', in C. Bonnet and C. Jourdain-Annequin (eds.), *Héraclès: d'une rive à l'autre de la Méditerrannée. Bilan et perspectives*, 353–6.

Saggs, H. (2001), *The Nimrud Letters, 1952.*

Sagona, C. (2002), *The Archaeology of Punic Malta.*

Sahin, M. (1999), 'Neue Beobachtungen zum Felsrelief von Ivriz, Konya: nicht in den Krieg, sondern zu Ernte. Der Gott mit der Sichel', *AS* 49: 165–76.

Saidah, R. (1977), 'Une tombe de l'âge du fer à Tambourit (Sidon)', *Berytus*, 25: 135–46.

Sapouna-Sakellaraki, E. (1997), 'A Geometric Electrum Band from a Tomb in Skyros', in O. Palagia (ed.), *Greek Offerings: Essays on Greek Art in Honour of John Boardman*, 35–42.

Sapouna-Sakellaraki, E. (2002), 'Skyros in the Early Iron Age: New Evidence', in M. Stamatopoulou and M. Yeroulanou (eds.), *Excavating Classical Culture: Recent Archaeological Discoveries in Greece*, 117–49.

Savio, G. (2004), *Le uova di struzzo dipinte nella cultura punica.*

Scarborough, J. (1991), 'The Pharmacology of Sacred Plants, Herbs and Roots', in C. A. Faraone and D. Obbink (eds.), Magika Hiera: *Ancient Greek Magic and Religion*, 138–72.

Schachter, A. (2003), 'Tanagra: The Geographical and Historical Context,

Part One', *Pharos: Journal of the Netherlands Institute in Athens*, 11: 45–74.

Schaeffer, C. F. A. (1938), 'Les Fouilles de Ras Shamra-Ugarit: 9. campagne. Fouilles sur le sommet du Djebel Akra et aux ruines du couvent de S. Barlaam', *Syria*, 19: 323–7.

Schaeffer, C. F. A. (1939), *Ugaritica*, vol. 1.

Scheer, T. J. (1993), *Mythische Vorväter: zur Bedeutung griechischer Heroen- mythen im Selbstverständnis kleinasiatischer Städte.*

Scheid, J., and Svenbro, J. (1985), 'Byrsa: la ruse d'Elissa et la fondation de Carthage', *Annales*, 40/2: 328–42.

Schmid, S. G. (1999), 'Decline or Prosperity at Roman Eretria?', *JRA* 12: 273–93.

Schmidt, G. (1968), *Samos VII: kyprische Bildwerke aus dem Heraion von Samos.*

Schmölder-Veit, A. (2005), 'Kleider machen Frauen? Griechische Frauendar- stellung des 8. Jhdt. v. Chr.', in N. Sojc (ed.), *Neue Fragen, neue Antworten: antike Kunst als Thema der Gender Studies*, 29–42.

Schnapper, A. (1986), 'Persistance des géants', *Annales, ESC* 41: 177–200.

Schreiber, N. (2003), *The Cypro-Phoenician Pottery of the Iron Age.*

Schulten, A. (1922), *Fontes Hispaniae Antiquae*, vol. 1.

Scurlock, J. A. (1991), '*Taklimtu*: A Display of the Grave Goods?', *Nouvelles assyriologiques brèves et utilitaires = NABU*, 1: 3.

Seaford, R. (1994), *Reciprocity and Ritual.*

Sefati, Y. (1998), *Love Songs in Sumerian Literature.*

Seyrig, H. (1933), in P. V. Baur, M. I. Rostovtzeff and A. R. Bellinger (eds.), *The Excavations at Dura Europos: Fourth Season. Preliminary Report*, 68–71.

Seyrig, H. (1939), 'À propos du culte de Zeus à Seleucie', *Syria*, 20: 296–301.

Seyrig, H. (1963), 'Antiquités syriennes 82, une idole Bétylique', *Syria*, 40: 17–19.

Seyrig, H. (1970), 'Antiquités Syriennes, 92. Seleucos I et la fondation de la monarchie syrienne', *Syria*, 47: 290–311.

Sharples, R. W. (1983), ' "But Why Does My Spirit Speak With Me Thus?" Homeric Decision Making', *G&R* 30: 1–7.

Shaw, J. W. (2000), 'The Phoenician Shrine, *ca.* 800 BC, at Kommos in Crete', in *Actas del IV congreso internacional de studios fenicios y punicos*, 1107–19.

Shaw, J. W. (2006), *Kommos: A Minoan Harbor Town and Greek Sanctuary in Southern Crete.*

Shaw, J. W., and Shaw, M. C. (2000), *Kommos IV: The Greek Sanctuary*, part 1.

Shepherd, G. (1999), 'Fibulae and Females: Intermarriage in the Western Greek Colonies and the Evidence from the Cemeteries', in G. R. Tset-skhladze (ed.), *Ancient Greeks West and East*, 268–300.

Siegelova, J. (1971), *Appu-Märchen und Hedammu-Mythos*.

Simon, E. (1995), 'Early Images of Daidalos in Flight', in J. B. Carter and S. P. Morris (eds.), *The Ages of Homer*, 407–13.

Simon, E. (2004), 'Daidalos-Taitale-Daedalus: neues zu einem wohl-bekannten Mythos', *AA*: 419–32.

Sinclair, T. A. (1990), *Eastern Turkey: An Architectural and Archaeological Survey*, vols. 1–4.

Smith, M. S. (1994), *The Ugaritic Baal Cycle*, vol. 1, Supplement to Vetus Testamentum, 55.

Snodgrass, A. M. (1998), *Homer and the Artists: Text and Picture in Early Greek Art*.

Snodgrass, A. M. (2000), 'Prehistoric Italy: A View from the Sea', in D. Ridgway, F. Serra Ridgway *et al.* (eds.), *Ancient Italy in its Mediter-ranean Setting: Studies in Honour of Ellen Macnamara*, 171–8.

Soggin, J. A. (1960), 'Kultätiologische Sagen und Katachese im Hexateuch', *VT* 10: 341–7.

Sourvinou-Inwood, C. (1997), 'The Hesiodic Myth of the Five Races', in O. Palagia (ed.), *Greek Offerings: Essays on Greek Art in Honour of John Boardman*, 1–21.

Speidel, M. P. (1978), *The Religion of the Roman Army*.

Stager, L. E. (2003), 'Phoenician Shipwrecks in the Deep Sea', in N. Stampol-idis and V. Karageorghis (eds.), *Ploes . . . Sea Routes . . . Interconnections in the Mediterranean, 16th–6th c. BC*, 233–48.

Stampolidis, N. C. (2003), 'A Summary Glance at the Mediterranean in the Early Iron Age', in N. C. Stampolidis (ed.), *Sea Routes . . . from Sidon to Huelva: Interconnections in the Mediterranean, 16th–6th c. BC*, 47–79.

Staudacher, W. (1942), *Die Trennung von Himmel und Erde*.

Stinton, T. C. W. (1976), 'Si credere dignum est . . .', *PCPS* 202: 60–89.

Stol, M. (1988), 'Greek *Deikterion*: The Lying-in-state of Adonis', in J. H. Kamstra *et al.* (eds.), *Funerary Symbols and Religion: Festschrift for H. van Voss*, 127–8.

Strauss Clay, J. (2003), *Hesiod's Cosmos*.

Stronach, D. (1990), 'The Garden as a Political Statement: Some Case-studies from the Near East in the First Millenium BC', *Bull. of the Asia Institute*, 4: 171–80.

Stroud, R. S. (1984), 'An Argive Decree from Nemea concerning Aspendos', *Hesperia*, 83: 193–216.

Stucky, R. (1983), *Ras Shamra – Leukos-Limen* (1983).

Stylianou, P. J. (1989), *The Age of the Kingdoms: A Political History of Cyprus in the Archaic and Classical Periods.*

Sukenik, E. L. (1940), 'Note on a Pottery Vessel of the Old Testament', *PEQ*: 159–61.

Sulze, H. (1926), 'Adōnidos Kēpoi I', *Angelos*, 2: 44–50.

Sulze, H. (1928), 'Adōnidos Kēpoi II', *Angelos*, 3: 72–91.

Szemerenyi, O. (1962), *Trends and Tasks in Comparative Philology.*

Szemerenyi, O. (1974), 'The Origins of the Greek Lexicon: *ex Oriente Lux*', *JHS* 94: 144–57.

Tadmor, H. (1994), *Inscriptions of Tiglath-Pileser III, King of Assyria.*

Tammuz, O. (2006), '*Mare clausum*? Sailing Seasons in the Mediterranean in Early Antiquity', *MHR* 20: 145–62.

Tandy, D. W. (1997), *Warriors into Traders: The Power of the Market in Early Greece.*

Taşyürek, O. A. (1975), 'Some New Assyrian Rock-reliefs in Turkey', *AS* 25: 169–80.

Tekoglu, R., and Lemaire, A. (2000), 'La Bilingue royale louvite-phénicienne de Cineköy', *CRAI*: 961–1006.

Thapar, R. (2000), *Early India from the Origins to AD 1300.*

Themelis, P. (1980), 'Anaskaphē Eretrias', *PAE for 1978*: 78–102.

Thureau-Dangin, F., *et al.* (1931), *Arslan Tash.*

Todd, J. M. (1993), 'The Continuity of Amber Artifacts in Ancient Palestine: From the Bronze Age to the Byzantine Era', in C. W. Beck and J. Bouzek, *Amber in Archaeology: Proceedings of the Second International Conference on Amber in Archaeology*, 236–48.

Torelli, M. (1997), 'Les Adonies de Gravisca, archéologie d'une fête', in F. Gaultier and D. Briquel (eds.), *Les Plus Religieux des hommes: état de la recherche sur la religion étrusque*, 233–91.

Toynbee, J. M. C. (1948), 'Beasts and their Names in the Roman Empire', *PBSR* 16: 24–37.

Treidler, H. (1959), 'Eine alte ionische Handelskolonisation in numidischen Afrika', *Historia*, 8: 257–83.

Triantaphyllou, S. (1999), 'An Early Iron Age Cemetery in Ancient Pydna, Pieria: What Do the Bones Tell Us?', *ABSA* 93: 353–64.

Tronchetti, C. (2000), 'Importazioni e imitazioni nella Sardegna fenicia', in

P. Bartoloni and L. Campanella (eds.), *La ceramica fenicia di Sardegna: dati, problematiche, confronti*, 346–51.

Trucco, F., and Vagnetti, L. (2001), *Torre Mordillo 1987–90: le relazioni egee di una comunità protostorica della Sibaritide.*

Tsoukala, E. S. (1992), 'Quaternary Faunas of Greece', *Courier Forsch.-Inst. Seckenberg*, 153: 79–92.

Tsoukala, E. S. (2000), 'Remains of a Pleiocene *Mammut borsoni* ... from Milia (Grevena, W. Macedonia, Greece)', *Ann. Paléontol.* 86: 165–91.

Tsoukala, E. S. (2001), 'Les Faunes quaternaires des îles grecques', *Bull. de la soc. des sciences historiques et naturelles de la Corse*, 696–7: 277–303.

Tsoukala, E. S. (2003), *Hē Pella kai hē Palaiontologia: Hē Arkouda tōn Spēlaiōn stēn Periochē tēs Almōpias.*

Tsoukala, E. S. (2007), *Ta Grevena kai hē Palaiontologia to kunēgi tōn elephantōn tou parelthontos*, 2nd edition.

Tsoukala, E. S., and Bartsiokas, A. (in press), 'New *Mesopithecus pentelicus* specimens from Kryopigi, Macedonia, Greece', *Journal of Human Evolution.*

Tsoukala, E. S., and Lister, A. (1998), 'Remains of a Straight-tusked Elephant, ESR Dated to Oxygen Isotope Stage 6 from Grevena', *Bolletino della Società Paleontologica Italiana*, 37: 117–39.

Tsoukala, E. S., and Melentis, J. (1994), '*Deinotherium giganteum* KAUP (*Proboscidea*) from Kassandra Peninsula', *Geobios*, 27: 633–40.

Tuplin, C. (2004), 'Medes in Media, Mesopotamia, Anatolia', *AWE* 3: 223–51.

Tylecote, R. F. (1984), 'Copper and Bronze Metallurgy in Sardinia', in M. S. Balmuth and R. J. Rowland, *Studies in Sardinian Archaeology*, vol. 1: 115–62.

Valenza Mele, N. (1979), 'Eracle euboico a Cuma: la gigantomachia e la Via Heraclea', in *Recherches sur les cultes grecs en l'occident*, Cahiers du Centre Jean Bérard, 19–51.

Vallet, G. (1958), *Rhégion et Zancle.*

Van Berchem, D. (1967), 'Sanctuaires d'Hercule-Melqart III, Rome', *Syria*, 44: 307–38.

Van de Moortel, A., and Zachou, E. (2003–4), '2004 Excavations at Mitrou, East Locris', *Aegean Archaeology*, 7: 39–48.

Van den Ven, P. (1962), *La Vie ancienne de S. Syméon Stylite le Jeune*, vols. 1–2.

Van Doorninck, F. H. (1982), 'Protogeometric Longships and the Introduction of the Ram', *IJNA* 11: 277–86.

Van Effenterre, H. (1961), 'Pierres inscrites de Dréros', *BCH* 85: 544–68.

Van Groningen, B. (1953), *In the Grip of the Past*.

Van Seters, J. (1972), *Prologue to History*.

Vandorpe, K. (1995), 'City of Many a Gate, Harbour for Many a Rebel', in S. P. Vleeming (ed.), *Hundred Gated Thebes*, 203–39.

Vanel, A. (1965), *L'Iconographie du dieu de l'orage dans le proche-orient jusqu'au VIII. s. a.C.*

Vanschoonwinkel, J. (1990), 'Mopsos: légendes et réalité', *Hethitica*, 10: 185–211.

Varinlioglou, E. (1986), *Die Inschriften von Keramos*.

Vermeule, E. (1979), *Aspects of Death in Early Greek Art and Poetry*.

Verreth, H. (2000), 'Lake Serbonis and Sabkhat Bardawil in the Northern Sinai', in L. Mooren (ed.), *Politics, Administration and Society in the Hellenistic and Roman World*, 471–87.

Versnel, H. S. (1993), 'Kronos and the Kronia', in his *Transition and Reversal in Myth and Ritual*, 90–135.

Veyne, P. (1983), *Did the Greeks Believe in their Myths?*

Vian, F. (1944), 'Les Géants de la mer', *Rev. Arch.* 2: 97–117.

Vian, F. (1952A), 'Génies des passes et des défilés', *Rev. Arch.* 39: 129–55.

Vian, F. (1952B), *La Guerre des Géants*.

Vian, F. (1960), 'Le Mythe de Typhée', in O. Eissfeldt *et al.*, *Éléments orientaux dans la religion grecque*, Colloque de Strasbourg, 22–24 mai 1958, 19–38.

Vian, F. (1978), 'Mythologie scolaire et mythologie érudite dans les *Dionysiaques* de Nonnos', *Prometheus*, 4: 157–72.

Vian, F. (1981), *Apollonios de Rhodes, Argonautica III*, Budé edition.

Vian, F. (2005A), 'Ange Politien: lecteur des poètes grecques', in his *L'Épopée posthomérique: receuil des études*, 609–20.

Vian, F. (2005B), 'Le Syncrétisme et l'évolution de la gigantomachie', in his *L'Épopée posthomérique: recueil des études*, 192–203.

Vianu, M. A. (2004), 'Présence nord-syrienne et chypriote en Mer Noire', *AWE* 3: 78–86.

Vokotopoulou, J. (1996), 'Cities and Sanctuaries of the Archaic Period in Chalkidike', *ABSA* 91: 319–28.

Vokotopoulou, J., and Christidis, A.-P. (1995), 'A Cypriot Graffito on an SOS Amphora from Mende, Chalcidice', *Kadmos*, 34: 5–12.

Von Soldt, W. H. (2005), *The Topography of the City State of Ugarit*.

Vosa, G. (1978), 'Le necropoli della valle del Marcellino presso Villasmundo', *Cronache di archeologia*, 17: 104–10.

Wade-Gery, H. T. (1952), *The Poet of the* Iliad.

Wade-Gery, H. T. (1958), 'Hesiod', in his *Essays in Greek History*, 1–15.

Walbank, F. W. (1957), *A Historical Commentary on Polybius*.

Walcot, P. (1977), 'Odysseus and the Art of Lying', *Ancient Society*, 8: 1–19.

Waldbaum, J. C. (1994), 'Early Greek Contacts with the Southern Levant', *BASOR* 293: 55–8.

Walker, K. G. (2004), *Archaic Eretria: A Political and Social History from the Earliest Times to 490 BC*.

Wallace, P. W. (1974), 'Hesiod and the Valley of the Muses', *GRBS* 15: 5–24.

Wallinga, H. T. (1993), *Ships and Sea-power before the Great Persian War*.

Waser, O. (1918), 'Giganten', *RE* Suppl. 3: 655–759.

Watkins, C. (1976), 'Observations on the "Nestor's Cup" Inscription', *HSCP* 80: 25–40.

Watkins, C. (1992), 'Le Dragon hittite Illuyankas et le géant grec Typhoeus', *CRAI*: 319–35.

Watkins, C. (1995), *How to Kill a Dragon: Aspects of Indo-European Poetics*.

Weill, N. (1966), 'Adōniazousai ou les femmes sur le toit', *BCH* 90: 644–98.

Weill, N. (1970), 'La Fête d'Adonis dans la *Samienne* de Ménandre', *BCH* 94: 591–3.

Weiss, P. (1984), 'Lebendiger Mythos', *WJ* 10: 179–207.

West, M. L. (1966), *Hesiod: Theogony*.

West, M. L. (1978), *Hesiod: Works and Days*.

West, M. L. (1985), *The Hesiodic Catalogue of Women*.

West, M. L. (1988), 'The Rise of the Greek Epic', *JHS* 108: 151–72.

West, M. L. (1995), 'The Date of the *Iliad*', *MH* 52: 203–19.

West, M. L. (1997), *The East Face of Helicon: West Asiatic Elements in Greek Poetry and Myth*.

West, M. L. (1999), 'The Invention of Homer', *CQ* 49: 364–82.

West, M. L. (2000), 'The Gardens of Alcinous and the Oral Dictated Text Theory', *Acta Acad. Scient. Hung.* 40: 479–88.

West, M. L. (2002), '"Eumelos": A Corinthian Epic Cycle?', *JHS* 122: 109–34.

West, M. L. (2003A), *Homeric Hymns, Homeric Apocrypha, Lives of Homer*.

West, M. L. (2003B) '*Iliad* and *Aethiopis*', *CQ* 33: 1–14.

West, M. L. (2005), '*Odyssey* and *Argonautica*', *CQ* 55: 39–64.

West, S. R. (1981), 'An Alternative *Nostos* for Odysseus', *LCM* 6: 169–75.

West, S. R. (1994), 'Nestor's Bewitching Cup', *ZPE* 104: 9–15.

Westermann, C. (1984), *Genesis, 1–11*, English translation.

Westermann, C. (1985), *Genesis, 12–36*, English translation.

Whitehead, D. (1994), 'Site Classification and Reliability in Stephanus of

Byzantium', in D. Whitehead (ed.), *From Political Architecture to Stephanus Byzantius*, 98–124.

Wiegand, T., and Schrader, H. (1904), *Priene*.

Wilhelm, A. (1974), *Akademieschriften zur griechischen Inschriftenkunde*, vol. 2.

Will, E. (1975), 'Le Rituel des Adonies', *Syria*, 52: 93–105.

Williams, B. (1993), *Shame and Necessity*.

Wind, E. (1968), *Pagan Mysteries in the Renaissance*.

Winkler, J. J. (1990), *The Constraints of Desire*.

Winter, I. J. (1976), 'Phoenician and North Syrian Ivory Carving in Historical Context', *Iraq*, 38: 1–22.

Winter, I. J. (1979), 'On the Problems of Karatepe: The Reliefs and their Context', *AS* 29: 115–52.

Winter, I. J. (1995), 'Homer's Phoenicians: History, Ethnography or Literary Trope?' in J. B. Carter and S. P. Morris (eds.), *The Ages of Homer*, 247–72.

Wiseman, D. J. (1983), 'Mesopotamian Gardens', *AS* 33: 137–44.

Wiseman, D. J. (1984), 'Palace- and Temple-gardens in the Ancient Near East', in HIH Prince Takahito Mihasa (ed.), *Monarchies and Socio-religious Traditions in the Ancient Near East*, 37–43.

Wiseman, T. P. (1974), *Cinna the Poet and Other Roman Essays*.

Wiseman, T. P. (1995), *Remus: A Roman Myth*.

Wolff, H. W. (1973), *Joel and Amos: A Commentary*.

Woolley, L. (1937), 'Excavations near Antioch in 1936', *AJ* 16: 1–15.

Woolley, L. (1938), 'The Excavation at Al Mina, Sueidia', *JHS* 58: 1–30 and 153–70.

Woolley, L. (1953), *A Forgotten Kingdom*.

Wörrle, M. (1998), 'Leben und Sterben wie ein Fürst: Überlegungen zu den Inschriften eines neuen Dynastengrabes in Lykien', *Chiron*, 28: 77–83.

Yenar, K. A. (ed.) (2005), *The Amuq Valley Regional Project*, vol. 1.

Yon, M. (1987), 'Le Royaume de Kition', in E. Lipinski (ed.), *Studia Phoenicia*, vol. 5: 357–74.

Yon, M. (1989), 'Shr Mt: la chaleur de mot', *UF* 21: 461–6.

Yon, M. (1991), 'Arts et industrie de la pierre', in M. Yon (ed.), *Ras-Shamra-Ougarit*, vol. 6: 284–8.

Yon, M. (1991), 'El: père des dieux', *Mém. et. Mon. Piot.* 71: 1–19.

Yon, M. (1992A), 'The Goddess of the Salt Lake', *Kypriakai Spoudai*, 54–5: 301–6.

Yon, M. (1992B), 'Héraclès à Chypre', in C. Bonnet and C. Jourdain-Annequin (eds.), *Héraclès: d'une rive à l'autre de la Méditerrannée. Bilan et perspectives*, 145–63.

Yon, M. (1999), 'Salamis and Kition in the 11th–9th c. BC: Cultural Homogeneity or Divergence?', in M. Iacovou and D. Michaelides (eds.), *Cyprus and the Historicity of the Geometric Horizon*, 17–33.

Yon, M. (2000), in M. Yon, V. Karageorghis and N. Hirschfeld (eds.), *Céramiques mycéniennes d'Ougarit*, 2.

Yon, M. (2006), *The City of Ugarit at Ras Shamra*, new edition, English translation.

Yon, M., and Malbran-Labat, F. (1995), 'La Stèle de Sargon II à Chypre', in A. Caubet (ed.), *Khorsabad, le palais de Sargon II., roi d'Assyrie*, 159–79.

Yu Treister, M. (1995), 'North Syrian Metalworkers in Archaic Greek Settlements?', *OJA* 14: 159–78.

Zadok, R. (1978), 'Phoenicians, Philistines and Moabites in Mesopotamia', *BASOR* 230: 59.

Zadok, R. (1996), 'Geographical and Onomastic Remarks', *Nouvelles assyriologiques brèves et utilitaires = NABU* 1: 11–13.

Zadok, R. (2005), 'On Anatolians, Greeks and Egyptians in Chaldaean and Achaemenid Babylon', *IEJ* 32: 76–107.

Zaphiropoulou, Ph., (1999), 'I due "Polyandria" dell'antica necropoli di Paros', *AION* 6: 13–24.

Zevi, F. (1995), 'Gli eubei a Cuma: Dedalo e l'*Eneide*', *RFIC* 123: 178–92.

Zimansky, P. (2002), 'The Hittites and 'Ain Dara', in R. A. Yener and H. A. Hoffner (eds.), *Recent Developments in Hittite Archaeology and History: Papers in Memory of Hans G. Güterbock*, 177–92.

Zimmerman, J.-L. (1989), *Les Chevaux dans l'art géométrique grec*.

Zuntz, G. (1951), 'On the Etymology of the Name Sappho', *MH* 8: 12–35.

List of Illustrations

1. Face reconstruction of the skull found in the mound at Gordion, tentatively identified as Gordios, father of King Midas, and dated to the early eighth century BC. (Manchester Museum, Photo: John Prag)

2. Ivory Sphinx of Phoenician workmanship, eighth century BC. (Louvre Museum, Paris)

3. The Garden Mound at Khorsabad, recalling the Amanus Mountains. Drawing of a bas-relief of the late eighth century BC. (After P. Botta/M. E. Flandin, *Monuments de Niniveh*, 1849–59)

4. The flight of King Luli of Tyre from the Assyrians in 701 BC. Drawing from a relief fragment from the palace of Sennacherib in Nineveh. (After A. H. Layard, *Illustrations of the Monuments of Nineveh*, 1849)

5. Silver-gilt Cypro-Phoenician bowl found in Praeneste, Italy, early seventh century BC (Villa Giulia, Rome)

6. Idaean cave on Crete, before the recent excavations, site of rituals and rich dedications in honour of Zeus, who was protected here as a baby from his devouring father, Cronos. (Photo: G. Sakellarakis)

7. Horses decorating the lid of an Attic geometric jar, or pyxis, eighth century BC. (Houston Museum of Fine Arts, Texas; gift of Mrs Annette Finnigan)

8. Attic Geometric cup depicting riders on horseback, eighth century BC. (Los Angeles County Museum of Art, Hans Cohn Collection)

9. Ostrich-egg decorated with incised ornaments and birds, from Montaldo di Castro, Italy, *c.* 650 BC. (Villa Giulia, Rome)

10. Bronze cauldron with griffins and sirens on an iron tripod, from a tomb in Salamis, Cyprus, late eighth century BC. (Cyprus Museum, Nicosia)

11. A statue of Herakles–Melkart, found in Idalion, Cyprus, 490–470 BC. (Cyprus Museum, Nicosia)

12. Daedalus the craftsman working on a wing, cornelian ringstone, probably third century BC. (Danicourt Collection, Péronne)

13. The hero Mopsus hunting a wild boar, silver drachma of Aspendos,

Pamphylia, *c.* 400–360 BC. (Private collection, ex Frank Sternberg Auction; Photo: CNG)

14. Perseus rescuing Andromeda from the sea-monster (Ketos), Corinthian amphora, first half of the sixth century BC. (Altes Museum, Berlin, Photo: R. Bishkek)

15. Aphrodite and Adonis attended by Eros. Attic red-figure squat lekythos, *c.* 410 BC. (Louvre Museum, Photo: J. Jastrow)

16. Storm God from Karatepe, basalt sculpture, *c.* 700 BC. (Photo: R. Guenay)

17. Bay near modern Koumi, near ancient Cumae on Euboea, looking across towards Scyros. (Photo: S. Fachard)

18. The extinct volcano at Mount Oxylithi, Euboea, on whose slopes the vineyards grew until 1910. (Photo: S. Fachard)

19. The famous Cesnola krater, or mixing-bowl, exported to Kourion on Cyprus, almost certainly a Euboean work, *c.* 750 BC. (Metropolitan Museum of Art, New York.)

20. Pendent semi-circle decoration on a Euboean skyphos, *c.* 770 BC, and birds in rectangula panels on an Attic skyphos, *c.* 750 BC, both imported to Cyprus. (Ashmolean Museum, Oxford)

21. Pottery fragment with incised lettering, on the borders of Greek and Near Eastern scripts, from the sanctuary of Apollo Daphnephoros at Eretria, *c.* 750 BC. (Photo: Swiss School of Archaeology)

22. Cadmos from Phoenicia giving the alphabet to the Greeks, bronze coin of Tyre, from the reign of the Roman emperor Philip the Arab, 244–249 BC. (Bibliothèque nationale de France, Paris)

23. The Nora Stone, with a Phoenician inscription, Sardinia, perhaps *c.* 800 BC. (Museo Archeologico Nazionale, Cagliari, Sardinia)

24. View of Pithecussae, the modern Ischia (Photo: S. Lucia)

25. The site of Al Mina, excavated by Leonard Woolley, in modern Turkey, being examined by Sir John Boardman, its greatest modern interpreter (Photo: M.-H. Gates).

26. Ivories of Levantine craftsmanship supporting the arms of the throne from Tomb 79 at Salamis, Cyprus, late eighth century BC. (Cyprus Museum, Nicosia)

27. Aerial view of the acropolis and seaside site of Cumae, beside the bay of Naples, Italy. (Photo: I. Romina)

28. View of the Jebel Aqra, or Mount Casios, along the shore by Al Mina, seen from the site of Seleuceia in Pieria. (Photo: R. Lane Fox)

29. Stele showing the Storm God Baal, from Ras-Shamra, formerly Ugarit, *c.* 1320–1260 BC. (Louvre Museum, Paris)

30. *The Giant*, now known as *The Colossus*, by Goya, before 1812. (Museo del Prado, Madrid)

31. Zeus throwing his lightning at Typhon. Chalcidian hydria by the Typhon Painter, *c.* 550 BC. (Louvre Museum, Paris, Photo: B. Saint-Pol)

32. Entrance to the Corycian Cave, once the lair of Typhon, with the later Christian church to the Virgin Mary cancelling him out since the fifth century AD. (Photo: M. Finke)

33. *Saturn Devours his Child* by Goya, *c.* 1819–23. (Museo del Prado, Madrid)

34. Gigantic tusks of a mammoth, the biggest known in Europe, with Evangelia Tsoukala and her team, their excavators at Milia, near Grevena, Macedon, north Greece. (Artistotle University, Thessalonica, Photo: Prof. E. Tsoukala)

p. 72 A chariot frieze decorating the neck of a Geometric amphora found in a pit in the west sector of the Eretria excavation, *c.* 740 BC. (Eretria Apotheke)

p. 161 Alphabetic inscription on Nestor's cup, *c.* 740 BC, from Ischia. Found in the grave of a young boy in the San Montano cemetery. (Villa Arbusto, Lacco Ameno, Ischia)

p. 172 Lyre-player seal, showing a standing lyre player and beneath the lyre a six-pointed star and a small bird set to the side, *c.* 730 BC. (Drawing: J. Boardman)

Index

Abantes, on Euboea, 162; kinsmen of
  Io, 212–13; 356, 380
Acco, 21, 47, 91
Acragas, 200, 202
Adana, called Danuna, 79; and Mopsus,
  225; and 'Awarikus', 229
Adonis, 240–54, 255; and Cypriot
  Aous, 310; not in Homer, 351; and
  Hipposthenes, 378
aetiology, 371–6
Afqa, and Adonis, 249–50
Agatha, cuts off breasts and halts lava,
  306
Aghia Paraskevi, and Pallene Giants,
  327, 329
Agrios, among Etruscans, 183
Ahta, perhaps Al Mina, 106, 377
Aidna, as Etna in Hesiod, 366
Ain Dara, 101
Al Mina, 104–20, 139, 259, 265, 365
Alcyoneus, a Giant captain, 320, 324
Aleppo, 98, 100–101
Alexander, avoiding smell of dead, 9;
  route into Syria, 84; and Mallos, 83,
  87–8, 237; locating myths in East,
  185–92; and Dionysus, 188–91; and
  war-elephants, 194–5; in Cilicia,
  236–8, 308, 311; no foreign
  languages, 355
Alexandria, and cult of Adonis, 243
Almops, a Giant in Macedon, 328
alphabet, invention and use, 33–4; 71–2
Amanus, 'Mountains of Box-trees', 17,
  80, 89, 99, 100, 109, 256, 266
Amarynthos, on Euboea, 170
Amathus, pottery imports, 53, 61, 88,
  377; and winds, 69; and alphabet,

perhaps, 71; site and history, 73; and
  Sardinia, 126; and Hipposthenes,
  377
Amazons, and Alexander's army, 191
amber, and resins, 346–7
Ammianus, describes Jebel Aqra, 256
Amos, and partying, 92
Amphidamas, on Euboea, 364–5, 379
Amphilochus, travelling hero, 83, 85,
  165; and Calchas, 226, 236
Amrith, and Heracles' iconography, 206
Amyclaion, probably Kommos on Crete,
  341
Anas, mates with Hipposthenes, 337–80
Anavarza, ancient Anazarbus, 79, 256
Anemones, and Adonis, 241; discovered
  at Eryx, 252
Antaeus, his 'corpse', 193
Antioch, 89, 91; and Io, 213
Aous, Cilician river, 310–11; its 'divine
  music', 314; 'voiceless', 314
Aphrodite, and Adonis, 241–2; birth of,
  278, 359–72; in Homer, 353–4;
  reaching Cyprus, 292–4; in Hesiod,
  359, 372
Apollo, at Delphi, 35, 361–2, 366,
  368–9
Apollodorus, pseudonym of author on
  myths, 302–3
Apollonius of Tyana, at Aigai, 253
Arachosia, the Kandahar site, 16
Aramaeans, 100–101, 114, 307
Argos, and Amphilochus, 83, 85, 165;
  and orientalizing heroes, 184; and Io,
  211–12; and Hera, 212; and Cilician
  cities, 237–8
Argoura, and Io on Euboea, 217

'Arima-Arimoi', in Homer, 41, 114, and in Hesiod, 304; in Lydia, 306; in Syria, 307; in Cilicia, 308–9, 313; on Ischia, 316–17, 335; 368, 371

Arimmatta, Hittite place name, 308, 313–14, 371

Aristophanes, and Adonis, 243–4; and Giants, 321

Armenians, and Jason, 186–7

Arnold, Matthew, and 'grave Tyrian trader', 150–51

Arpad, 18, 100; and Al Mina, 109–10

Arundell, William, on Turkish volcanoes, 305

Arwad, 21, 47, 91, 95

Arybas, in Homer's Sidon, 345

Ascalon, 69, 91, 93; and 'Moxos', 233

Ascra, 358

Ashdod, and Yamani, perhaps a Greek, 31

'Asian Meadow', in Homer, 40–41, 336

Aspendos, and Mopsus, 232, 235; and Alexander, 237

Assyrian kings, and Medes, 17; and Urartu, 17; and Unqi, 100–102

Atalia, queen with Sargon, 28

Athenians, female burials and Lefkandi, 63; pots at Salamis on Cyprus, 75; and Daedalus, 197

Augustine, pupil of, 262; and Giants' teeth, 330

Auza, in Libya, 22, 25, 147, 342

Avesta, 'beautiful' places, 16

Azitawattas, at Karatepe, 231–2; linked to Aspendos, 232

Baal, on Jebel Aqra, 258; at Memphis, 265–6; in Israel, 267; in Nile Delta, 268–9

Babel, 373

Bahrain, 17

Baios, supposedly founds Baiae, 183

Baken-Renef, Pharaoh ('Bocchoris'), 32; scarab at Ischia, 32, 155, 343

Balkh-Bactra, a 'beautiful' place, 16

Bardawil, Lake and Zeus Kasios, 268–9; shrine at, 270; and Typhon, 304

Barlaam, stormtrooper on Jebel Aqra, 263

Bell, Gertrude, on 'Mount Cassius' and its shore, 120; at Corycian Cave, 311

Bent, Theodore, on crocuses and Corycian Cave, 309

Berkeley, Bishop, concerning Ischia, 151

Berossus, Babylonian historian, 86

Bethlehem, and Adonis, 254

Betyllion, or Ras Shamra, 96–7, 258–9

Beylan Pass, 80

Bikni, Mount, 16

'black-on-red', pottery from Cyprus, 52

Boardman, Sir John, on Euboean pottery at Al Mina, 105

'Bocchoris', Greek name for Baken-Renef, 32; seal on Ischia, 32, 152, 155; 343

Boraston, MacLair, and 'crashing' birds, 336

Briareus, and Euboeans, 195, 319–20

Byblos, and Tammuz-Adonis, 246–7, 378

Cadiz, and Phoenicians, 24; and Heracles, 207–9

Cadmus, searching for Europa, 210

Cailloubella, and Giants, 328

Callimachus, poetry on Mopsus, 232; on sickle of Cronos, 284–5

Callisthenes, historical adviser with Alexander, 192; and Mopsus, 232, 236; and Arima, 308; and Corycian Cave, 311; no foreign languages, 355

Calycadnus, and nearby cave, 308–9

Carthage, 22, 23; and Greek residents, 94; and the Dido story, 144; its foundation, 145

Cassiope, on Corcyra, dedications at, 271–2

Castor, son of, invented by Homer's Odysseus, 338–9

Catania, saved by mastectomy, 306

Celenderis, 82

Cerveteri, pottery showing 'Taitale', 200

Chalcidic Peninsula, and Lefkandi, 61

Chalcis, 53, 75, 168–9; dominates in West by 730 BC, 154; and homosexuality, 168; and sickle of Cronos, 291–2; and Hesiod, 364–6; 369; and Hipposthenes, 379

Chalos river, or Afrin, 101

Chares, and Persian legend, 185–6

Chimaira, and Bellerophon, 220; in Lycia, 220–21

Chios, and Euboea, 63–4, 70–71, 356, 376

chronology, of 'dark ages', 50–51, 129–30

Cilicia, 77–88; its shores, 78, 99, 113; roses, 82–3; eponym 'Cilix', 216; and Perseus with Pegasus, 219

Cinyras, in Homer, 75, 357; and King Philip, 241

Circeii, and 'Circe', 183–4

Claros, oracle and Mospus, 225–6; and Colophon, 235

Colophon, and Claros, 234; and Calchas, 235

Constantine, attacking pagan cult-sites, 253–4

Corcyra, 130, 154, 175; and Zeus Kasios, 270–72; and sickles of gods, 291–2; and *Odyssey*, 372; 378

Cordelia, in eighth century BC, 24

Corinth, goods in Corcyra and southeast Italy, 130–31; on Ischia, 151–4; annexing myths and heroes, 184

Cornwall, alleged links with Phoenicians, 24

Corycian Cave, in Cilicia, 308–12

Crete, and King David, 70; bronze shields, 116, 363–4, and Phoenicians, 166–7; and Ida Cave, 167, 363–4; 'orientalizing', 166–8; and Minos, 201; and Homer, 338–43; and Delphi, 360–62, 372; and Cyprus, 362–3

Cronos, castrates Heaven, 277–8; his stories expand, 279–80, 296–7, 362–4; eats children, 296; and Homer, 350–51; and stone, 368

crusaders, and sea-winds, 69

Cumae, in west Italy, 148–50, 152; Euboean burial, 160; and Daedalus, 198; temples, 202; 379

Cumae, on Euboea, 67, 142

Cyprus, 'seven kings' and Sargon, 30; pottery in eleventh and tenth centuries BC, 51–2; and Lefkandi, 55, 57; and Sardinia, 126–7; and west Italy, 132; and Heracles, 206; and Adonis, 249–51, 254

Cythera, and Aphrodite, 282–3

Daedalus, 197–203

Daniel, and golden image, 19; and ages of metal, 367

'Dark Ages', dissipated by travelling pottery, 50–51

David, King, and bodyguards, 70

Delphi, oracle at, 35; and Cretans, 201, 361–2; akin to Sidon, 217; 379

Delphyne, Typhon's helper, 303

Demavend, Mount, 16

Demetrius, son of Antigonus, and Egypt, 269

dinosaurs, bones and myths, 194, 322–30

Dionysus, eastern travels and origins, 188–91

Dioscorides, and topless Adonis-worshippers, 243

Dodona, oracle at, 35, 172

Doliche, 295

Domuztepe, 80–81

Dor, tenth century BC Greek cup, 53

Drepanon, place name, 284; on Sea of Marmara, 288; on Gulf of Corinth, 288; on Sicily, 292–3

Dumuzi, 244–6

Dur Sarrukin, 'Sargon's Citadel', 27–8

Echidna, Typhon's mate, 304; her name, 306

Egypt, in eighth century BC, 20–21, 31, 47–8; and Greeks, 32; and Lefkandi, 58; and Phoenician ships, 93; and Ischia, 155–6; in Homer, 338–9, 342–4

elephants, in north Syria, 99, 120; in Morocco, 194; bones on Samos, 194–5

Eleutherna, and Phoenician grave-markers, 166

Emporio, and Homer, 356, 377

Epeios, travelling carpenter, 160

Ephorus, on Europa, 215

Eretria, and Lefkandi, 53; scents, 66; on Ischia, 138–9; expelled from West, 154; and Milesians, 164; contacts, east and west, 169–70; only sex and horses, 171; founds Methone, 171; claims to sickle of Cronos, 291–2; illicit archer, 380

'Erimma', Hittite place-name, 308

Eryx, and perhaps Adonis, 252
Eryx, and the Great Castrator, 293
Eskimoes, and darkness, 294
Essex, and the Great Castrator, 286
Etruscans, and Phoenicians, 23, 24, 159; and Greek sanctuaries, 134; and Elba, 134; and metals, 134; and Greek imports, 135–6, 159–60; big settlements, 135; 'orientalizing' imports, 159; and Euboean craftsmen, 159–60; and Greek sex, 160
Euboea and Euboeans, Gulf of, 53–4; numbers abroad, 168; and Chalcidic north, 62–3, 168, 321–32; and Chios, 63–4, 70–71; 356, 376; as sailors, 175–80; scale of trading, 70; pottery abroad, 53–70, 74–7, 83, 95–8, 129–34, 138–60, 153; at Posideion, 85; and Philistines, 91; at Al Mina, 105, 108–10, 111, 113–14, 120, 139, 259, 265; and horses, 113, 150, 159–60, 380; horse-harness, 115, 118, 377; perhaps at Oricos, 130; in Sicily and west Italy, 129–34; at Rome, 133; on Ischia, 138–60, 355, 379; on Tunisian coast, 145–7; at Cumae, 148–50, 159–61, 379; in Homeric 'neverland', 183–4; and myths, 195–6; and Heracles, 209–10; and Io, 214; perhaps locating Mopsus, 233, 236; perhaps locating Zeus Kasios, 271–2; and Great Castrator, 285–92; and foreign gods, 296; and Typhon, 314, 316, 366; and Giants, 327, 329–32; and *Odyssey*, 355; and Delphi, 368–9
Eumaeus, in *Odyssey*, on poetry, 37; on experts from afar, 222–3; with Odysseus, 338; on early life, 345–7
Eumelus, on Europa, 215
Eupaphis, inscribed verses at Corycian Cave, 310
Europa, travelling heroine, 210; mounted by Zeus, 211; and Cadmus, 215–16
Eurybates, and dark skin, 127, 147
Eurycleia, slave, but not concubine, of Laertes, 177
Eusebius, gives 'date' for Mopsus, 227–8

Evans, Sir Arthur, and Homer on Crete, 341–2
Exodus, route by Nile Delta, 267, 269
Ezekiel, and Tyre's imports, 26, 66, 68; and Cilician horses, 99
Ezra, Fourth Book of, on shrinking babies, 331

Ficana, and Euboean pottery, 132–3
Fourka, near Mende, and Giants, 327
Frazer, Sir James, 245, 252

Gabii, early inscription, 136–7
Ganymede, in Eretria and at Chalcis, 160, 375
Gaza, and Assyrian images, 18; as 'Io-ne', 214
Geryon, his cattle and Heracles, 207
Giants, 320–32, 349, 369, 374
Gilgamesh, and Homer, 353
Golgoi, and Adonis, 249–50
Gordios, father of Midas, skull, 29
Gorgon, sighted in desert, 194; killed by Perseus, 219
Gortyn, scene of Zeus's sex with Europa, 211; bones of Europa, 215; and Homer, 340–41
Graia, 171–2
Gravisca, and Adonis, 251–2
'Greatest Altar', in Rome, 205, 210
Gygaea, Lake, home of Echidna, 306; 351–2

Hadad, Storm God in Syria, 117
Hadrian, on Jebel Aqra, 263; at Pelusium, 270
Hamath, 18, 100
Hamilton, Sir William, and the Solfatara, 323
Hazael, of Damascus, and horse-harness, 116–17
Hazzi, Mount, the Jebel Aqra, 258–9, 273–5, 283, 286; and Hedammu, 301; and Typhon, 303, 364
'Heaven and Hell', ravines in Cilicia, 309
Hecataeus, of Miletus, his *Circuit of the Earth* and north Africa, 145; and Heracles, 207–8
Hector, and Homeric burials, 56, 82
Hedammu, Hittite serpent, 301

Helbon, and Syrian wine, 67
Helen, and drugs, 8; elopes to Sidon, 47,
   in Egypt, 347–8
Hellenes, and Delphi, 172
Hera, on Euboea and perhaps Ischia,
   178; and Euboeans' travels, 195;
   Homeric breast-straps, 353–4
Heracles, and Antaeus, 193; as
   travelling hero, 203–10; on Euboea,
   203–4; on Sicily, 208; his pillars in
   the West, 208–9
Hermes, fights Typhon, 310, 312
Hermopolis, captured by Piye, 20
Hermus, river in Lydia, 351
hero-cults, at old mounds, 35
Herodotus, and Posideion, 84; and
   Kasion in Egypt, 268; and aetiology,
   375
Heropythos, genealogy, 70, 356
Hesiod, sexist grumbling, 9; date of, 36;
   Theogony ends before lines on Circe's
   children, 182–3; stories of Cronos,
   271–81, 359; birth of Aphrodite,
   278–9, 282; and Typhon, 298, 359,
   365–6; poems' sources, 358–69; and
   Hecate, 359–60; his Theogony and
   the Muses, 360; and Delphi, 361–4;
   and his prize, 379–80
Hezekiah, king of Judah, 20
Hilakku, 'rough Cilicia', 79
Himera, and the cult of Cronos, 285
Hippocles, at Cumae, 149
hippopotamus, in north Syria, 99, 323
Hipposthenes, living life to the full,
   376–80
Hiram, king of Tyre, 26, 58
Histiaea, and wine, 67
'Hiyawa', not Achaeans, 231
Hogarth, D. G., and Lycian fire, 220
Holdich, Sir Thomas, tracking
   Dionysus, 189–91
Homer, psychology of heroes, 3–4; and
   slavery, 6; and wounds, 7; pain relief,
   8; (probable) date, 36–7 and
   appendix; (possible) performance-
   context, 37–8; and his 'Garden of
   Alcinous', 38–9; similes for Greeks'
   advance, 40–41; place-names and
   travel-tales, 46–7, 77, 338–44,
   351–2; objects' travels and
   archaeology, 48; and Cilicians, 78,

351; and Carian or Lydian women,
   119; and West, 121–4, 131, 335–6;
   and Ischia, 158; and Heracles, 203;
   and Typhoeus-Typhon, 298–9,
   335; and Giants, 320, 349; and
   Odysseus' lying tales, 338–44; and
   Eumaeus, 344–7; and 'Near East',
   352–5; and Crete, 340–42, 356–7;
   and Cyprus, 73, 357; and Chios,
   356–8; and absence of aetiologies,
   372
Homeridai, on Chios, 355–6
horses, in eighth century BC art and
   society, 10; origin of drawing, 10;
   and Piye in Egypt, 20; buried at
   Lefkandi, Cyprus, Crete, 57–8;
   winged, at Carchemish, 219; and
   Hipposthenes, 379–80
Hoshea, king of Israel, 19
Huelva, and Phoenicians, 25–6; and
   Euboean goods, 26; and Odyssey,
   124

Ia', Assyrian name for Ionians, 30
Ialysos, and Phoenicians, 166
Iamani, perhaps Greek, usurping power
   at Ashdod, 31
Iatnana, Assyrian name for Cyprus, 30
Ibn Jubayr, on winds, 69
Ida, cave, 167–8, 363–4
Illubru, 85
Imm, in north Syria, 118
Immanuel, 20
Inanna, loves Dumuzi, 244
Inarime, 355–6
Ingira, also Anchiale, 82, 86
Io, as a cow, 210; her travels, 210–14
Ion, of Chios, 356
Ionians, raiders and Sargon, 30–31
'Iopolis', in north Syria, 213
Iphition, from Gygaean Lake, 351
Isaiah, prophecies, 20; lips and coal, 29
Ischia, San Montano cemeteries, 6, 140,
   153; and Euboeans, 138–60; and
   gold items, 143–4; 'multicultural',
   within limits, 151–5; eruption on,
   336–7
Iskenderun, in Cilicia, 85, 87, 89; and
   Zeus Kasios, 261
Israel, kingdom of, 19
Ithaca, caves and Odysseus, 181–2

J, Jahwist in *Genesis*, 373
Jacob, and aetiology, 373
Jason, and travelling myths, 184, 187
Jebel Aqra 91, 99; and metals, 112; and Io, 213; and gods, 255–72; and songs, 274–5, 297, 301
John Malalas, on Io in Syria, 213–14; on Giants in Syria, 322–3
Joseph, and aetiology, 373
Joshua, and his knives, 374
Julian, on Jebel Aqra, 263
Julius Caesar, and locals' stories, 187–8

Kanli Divane, ravine, 312
Karabur, Assyrian rock carvings, 18
Karatepe, 80–81; and 'lyre-player' seals, 115; and 'Muksas', 227, 229; and Azitawattas, 231–2
Kassiopeia, and sea-monster, 262
Kassios-names, 261–2
Kella, priest at Hittite Nerik, 299
Keramos, and Zeus Kasios, 262
Kerethites, and King David, 70
Khaldeh, 93
Kinalua, or Tell Tayinat, 100–101, 109, 111, 265, 376–7
Kinet Hüyük, perhaps Issus, 83
Kinyras, 73, 357
Kirua, a rebel, 85
Kition, as Qart Hadasht, 22; Sargon's stele, 30; and Euboean pots, 59, 77; site and history 73–4
Kizzuwatna, 80
Knossos, Phoenician letters on a bowl, 166, 342; and Daedalus, 198–9; and Delphi, 361–2; and Ida, 364
Kokalos, 197, 200
Kommos, traders' stop-over, 166; and Homer, 341–3, 358
Kothar, 199
Koukos, and Euboeans, 62
Koumi, and Euboean wine, 67–8; 142
Kourion, 'Cesnola' krater, 75, 170; and Perseus, 181
Kumarbi, god, 275; eats children, 277, 299; and harvest, 280; matches Greek Cronos, 280–82; and stone, 296–7; and Hedammu, 301, 368
Kundu, name for Cyinda, 79

Lamos, river, 79, 308
Latinos, among Etruscans, 183
Lear, king in eighth century BC, 24
Lefkandi, cemeteries and dead, 6; Toumba and building, 55–9; and Homer, 56–7; and Athens, 63; not Phoenician, 63; and Chios, 64; after 820 BC, 74, 157, 168
Lelantine War, on Euboea, 169
Leto, Pomponio, and old bones, 324–5
Leuca, 326
Leuternians, 326
Libya, and Homer, 122–3; and Phoenicians, 344
life-expectancy, ancient, 6
Lindos, Chronicle of, 200
Lisbon, and Phoenicians, 24; and Homer, 124
Lotan, Leviathan, 297
Loutra, and Macedonian prehistoric animals, 328
Lucan, poetry on Corycian Cave, 309
Lucian, on Adonis, 247–8
Luoyang, 13
Luwian, language, 80, 100–101, 220, 227, 353, 371
Lycians, in Homer, 353
Lyktos-Lyttos, on Crete, 363
lyre-player seals, 114–15, 139; on Ischia, 155–6, 316

Macedonians, in north Syria, 119–20; and Giants, 328
Magarsos, coins, site and temple, 87–8; tombs, including Mopsus', 239
Malatya, and snake-monster, 300
Mallos, 83, 85, 87–8; and Amphilochus, 226, 236; and Alexander, 237
Mamre, and angels, 253
Marius, and a Gorgon, 194
Masefield, John, and Phoenicians, 151
Massilia, near Heracles's 'boulders', 207–8
Mayor, Adrienne, her study of fossils and Giants, 322, 329
Medea, 'Metaia' in Etruria, 200
Medes, and towns, 16; and horses, 16–17
Megiddo, 91
Melqart, as Tyre's 'Heracles', 206–7
Mende, and Euboeans, 62, 168, 329, 369, 376

Menelaus, in Libya, 122–3; off Crete, 340–42; in Egypt, 347–8

Messapians, hostile to foreign settlers, 131

metals, on Cyprus, Sardinia and in Africa and South Spain, 25; in south Cilicia, 82; ages of metals in Hesiod, 367–8

Methone, and Euboeans, 171

migrant seers or charismatics, 224–6, 238

Miletus and Milesians, receiving horse-harness, 118, 164

Milia, and a mammoth in Macedon, 328

Minos, 197, 201–2; and Minoa, 202; 361

Mita, the Greeks' king Midas, 29; and alphabetic script, 33

Miteloudis, G., a finder of Giants' teeth, 327

Mitrou, and Euboea, 62

monkeys, and Ischia, 141, 316; and Tunisia, 146–7

Mopsouhestia, 225; name's origin, 230, 313

Mopsoukrene, 'Mopsus' spring', 225, 231, 236

Mopsus, his travels, 224–39; not in Homer, 351

Mount Batten, and metal-trading, 24

Muksas, 'house of', 79, 81, 313–14, 315, 371

Muksus, in Hittite letter, 226–7

muthoi, as 'myths' and their diffusion, 34–6, 179–85, 222, 255–6

Myres, J. L., sees Aphrodite, 292

Myriandros, 84

Myrrha, spice-girl, and Adonis, 241; and king Philip II, 241

mythical heroes, their travels, 180–85

nakedness, in eighth century BC art, 11; in early athletics, 11

Nanou, peak of Jebel Aqra range, 259

Naples, and Giants, 324

Nemea, and inscribed list of 'Argive' kin, 238

'Nestor's Cup', on Ischia, 157–8, 357

Nineveh, 28, 110

Ninurta, parallels with Heracles's exploits, 204

Niobe, 'all tears', 337

Noah, virtuous, no sodomite, 331

Nonnus, Christian poet, on Typhon, 302–3, 319; and Statala, 305–6

Nora, and Phoenician inscribed stone, 128

Notion, and Claros and Mopsus, 234–5; 'kills' Calchas, 235

Odysseus, love for Penelope, 10; seamanship of, 176; caves on Ithaca, 181–2; lying tales, 338–45; and Eumaeus, 338, 344–7

Oechalia, in Euboea, 204

Og, king, 331, 374

Olympic Games, and nudity, 11; dating, 13

opium, ancients' use of, 8–9

Oppian, poet, on Typhon, 302, 310, 312

orientalizing, and Phoenicians, 27; and Greeks, 240–41, 370–71

Orion, and Euboeans, 195; 327

Orontes, river, 91, 99, 101–2; and Al Mina, 103, 106, 109; and Hazael, 117; and Macedonians, 119–20; its serpentine bed, 307; and Giants, 321

Oropos, and Eretria, 62, 171; and purple-dye, 66; in Graia, 171–2

Orsippus, a Megarian nude runner, 11

ostrich eggs, 27, 346

Otranto, and Giants, 325–6

Oxylithos, Mount, on Euboea, and volcanic soil, 67

Pagras, 89, 330; a Giant, 321

Pahri, perhaps modern Misis, 79, 225

Pallene, peninsula, 327, 376

Paltos, and Euboean pottery, 95

Pamphylia, and Mopsus, 233, 235

Pan, fights Typhon, 310, 312

Panaima, and bones on Samos, 194–5

Pandora, 5; releases troubles for men, 374

Panyassis, poetry on Adonis, 240–41

Paphos, on Cyprus, and birth of Aphrodite, 282–3; and arrival of Aphrodite, 292; 294

Patroclus, Homeric funeral, 56

Pausanias, allegorizes Cronos-stories, 293; on Giants in Arcadia, 328–9

Peary, Captain, and Greenland, 294
Pegasus, 218–19; and Cilician 'namesake', 220; and aetiology, 372
Peloros, a Giant on Straits of Sicily, 321
Perge, 'Parha' in Hittite, 232; and the 'Magnificent Seven' statues, 232
Perseus, at Kourion, 181; and Gorgon, 193; as travelling hero, 218–21
Phalaris, of Acragas, 200–201
Phaselis, later linked with Mopsus, 235
Philistines, and King David, 70; and Greek pottery, 91
Philo, of Byblos, 273–4; and castration-story, 282–3
Phlegra, and volcanic sites, 315, 323, 329, 330; on Chalcidic peninsula, 326–8; 329
Phoenicians, name 21; territories, 21; luxuries, 21; and stars, 176; literacy of, 21–2, 71; on Cyprus, 22, 60, 292; and Greeks, 33; on Crete, 22, 47, 166–8, 341–2; on Sardinia, 22, 128; in west Italy, 23, 127–9, 131–7, 156, 159; at Rome, possibly, 23; on Malta, 23; on Motya, 148; in Spain, at Malaga, 23; on south coast, 23; and metals, 25, 26, 60, 80–81, 134–5, 159; and Europa, 216; and dedications at Greek sites, 32–3; poems and myths, 36–7, 246–51, 267, 273–4, 282–3; in Homer, 47–78, 339–44, 345–8; and Egypt, 27, 93, 267–8, 342; on Rhodes at Ialysos, 60, 166; Melos, Thera and Cythera, 60; ships and cargoes, 93, 143, 345–8; and Ischia, 153, 156; and sickles, 293; and Kommos, 341–2
Pieria, in north Syria, 119, 258; in Macedon, 119
Pindar, and Pillars in west, 208; on Cilician cave and 'Arima', 307–8; on Typhon in west, 315; his effusions on Etna, 316–18
Pithekoussai, off Italy, 140–44, 176–7; in Tunisia, 146–7; and Daedalus, 198–9; and volcanic features, 315, 336; and Typhon, 315–17
Piye, king in Egypt, 20, 29
Plato, on gods and Giants, 321
Pliny the Elder, and dwindling seed, 330

Pomponius Mela, accurate about Corycian Cave, 309–10
Pontecagnano, 132, 141
Poseidonius, and Arimoi, 307
Posideion, 84, 88, 330; a second, later one at Ras el-Bassit, 97–8, 258
Potamoi Karon, probably Al Mina, 106–7, 139–40
pottery, absence of figurative art, 48; historical value, 48–50, 163; networks in Aegean, 51–2; use and carriers in Levant, 59–61, 68, 79, 91, 95–8; as gifts, 65, 75, 159, 170; trading, 65–6, 75, 91–2, 93–4; important finds at Al Mina, 104–6, 108, 109–11; early renewed contact with Italy and West, 126–33, 135; alphabetic inscriptions on, 137–8, 157, 170; important finds on Ischia, 141–3, 151–5; at Cumae, 148–50; at Carthage, 145; on Rhodes, 166; sex and horses on pottery, 170
Prometheus, his myths' locations, 186–7
Ptolemy I, ravages Al Mina, 107
Purulli festival, 300; 313–14
Puteoli, and Giants, 324–5
Pydna, 6
Pyramus, river in Cilicia, 80, 98, 225, 239
Python, at Delphi, 366

Que, Assyrian name for Cilicia, and Greek raids, 30–31; boundaries, 80; 85, 99

Ras el-Bassit, and Greek pottery, 52; as 'Cape of the Rocks', 97; as a later Posideion, 97–8, 106, 259
Ras ibn Hani, and the 'White Harbour', 96
Ras Kasroun, lake and Zeus Kasios, 267–9
Ras Shamra, or Ugarit, 96–7
Remus, 23; at school, 137
Rhodes, and Phoenicians, 60; and roses, 82, 155; and sea-routes, 69; Pottery abroad, 79, 82, 152, 155, 157–8; and Argos, 85; perhaps at Posideion, 85; in c. 850–700 BC, 165–6; and Soloi, 155, 230
Rio Tinto, and Odyssey, 124

Rome, and Phoenicians, 23; 'origins' of, 23; and Euboean pots, 133; and salt-flats, 133
Romulus, 23; at school, 137
Runza, or Hittite Runt, 312

Sabouni, near Al Mina, 104, 264, 274
saffron crocus, 113, 309
Salamis, Cyprus, royal burials, 74; pottery in tombs, 74–5
Samaria, and Assyrians, 19; and Greek pottery, 91–2, 98
Samaritans, worshipping Yahweh, 19
Samos, sanctuary of Hera and Eastern dedications, 32; pottery abroad, 82; and at Al Mina, 108; and horse-harness, 118, 164; and Chalcis, 164; and bones at Panaima, 194–5
Samson, similar to Heracles, 204
Sandon, god in Cilicia, 80
Sant' Imbenia, on Sardinia, 128–9, 132
Saphon, the Jebel Aqra, 264–5; in Israel, 267; in Egypt, 270; and Typhon
Sappho, and Adonis, 243, 251
Sapuna, the Jebel Aqra, 257–8
Sardara, and Cypriot bronzes, 125–6
Sardinia, and Phoenicians, 22, 127–9; exports in West, 126–7; and Cyprus, 127
Sargon, king and garden, 27–8, 85
Sariseki, 83
Saturn, eats children, 296
Saurias, of Samos, 'inventor' of drawing, 10
scent, ancient uses, 9, 82, 155
Scyros, and Euboeans, 67–8, 171
Seleuceia, in north Syria, 98; and martyred Jews, 256; founding of, 260
Seleucus, his capital, 98; 260; and Giants, 322
Semiramis, in Makran desert, 187
Sennacherib, king, 86–7, and his monuments, 192–3; destruction of Babylon, 352–3; 376
'Serbonian Bog', 270, 304
Sertorius, finds a Giant, 193–4
Shalmaneser III, conquers north Syria, 102
Sicels, and Laertes in Homer, 121–2, 131
Sicily, and Daedalus, 200–202; and

Heracles, 208; and Adonis, 252; and Typhon, 317, 366, 372
Sidon, and Kition, 22; rivalry with Tyre, 22; only Phoenician city in Homer, 47, 346–7; pottery-kilns, 93; claims to Cadmus, 217; and Delphi, 217
Sindos, near Thessalonica, and Euboean goods, 62
Sipylus, and Niobe, 337
Sodom, and aetiology, 374–5
Solfatara, crater of, 323–4
Solinus, on Giants, 326
Soloi, and metals, 82; and Argos, 238
Spain, and Phoenicians, 23–6, 127
Statala, and Typhon, 305–6
Suksu, Tell Sukas, 95–6
Sulcis, on Sardinia, 147–8; and Euboean pottery, 153
Symeon the Younger, pillar-saint, 263–4
Syrian Gates, 84

Tammuz, in Jerusalem, 246; in Byblos, 246; at Afqa, 248; on Cyprus, 249; as 'Adon', 251, 255
Tarentum, in 706 BC, 164
Tarhunta, storm god, 273, 276–7, 368
Tarshish, at Huelva, 26
Tarsus, called Tarzu, 79, 192; and Pegasus, 221; and Perseus, 221
Tel Rehov, and Greek pottery, 59, 91
Tell abu Hawam, 91, 98
Tell Afis, find of Greek pottery fragments, 52
Tell Defenneh, papyrus-letter at, 266–7
Tell Hadar, find of Greek pottery fragments, 52
Tell Sukas, 95–6; 323
Tell Tayinat, and land routes, 112–13
Tethys, in Homer, 350
Thasos, island and Phoenicians, 32, 165
Thebes, in Egypt and Homer, 347–8
Theocritus, and Adonis, 242
Theopompus, and Mopsus, 237
Thesprotia, and Odysseus, 344
Thon, Egyptian in Homer, 343
Thucydides, and athletic nudity, 11; and Euboean settlement, 162; and Zancle, 285–6
Tiglath Pileser III, king 17–18; at Gaza, 19; pressure on Phoenicians, 24, 26; conquers in Syria, 117

Timaeus, 201; and sickle of Cronos, 291

Timnath Serah, and Joshua, 374

Titans, 200, 319–20, 349–50, 359; aetiology, 372

Titans, in Homer, 349–50

Di Toledo, Pietro, and Giants, 325

Torone, and Euboeans, 62

Torre Galli, in Calabria, 128, 156

Toscanos, in Spain, and Euboean pottery, 148

'Town of Iauna', probably Al Mina, 107

Trajan, in Syria, 97, 260–61; and Zeus Kasios, 260–63

Trapani, and Cronos' sickle, 292–3

'Travelling heroes', returning in legend from Troy, 38, 180–81; in real life, tenth to eighth century BC, 40

Triptolemus, travelling hero, 213, 376

Tunisia, and Euboeans, 145–7

Tutammu, king of Kinalua in 740 BC, 110, 113

Typhon, in Lake Bardawil, 268; fighting Zeus, 298–318; in West, 317, 330, 335, 366, 372; in Hesiod, 365–6; and Hipposthenes, 379

Tyre, and colonies; and Greek pottery, 68–9, 93, 94–5; winds at sea, 69–70; imports of horses, 99; and Cadmus, 217; and Baal Saphon, 266

Unqi, in north Syria, 17, 18, 101–2, 321, 323, 330, 372

Utica, and Phoenicians, 145; and a Giant, 330

Vedas, and Indian society, 16

Virgil, and Daedalus, 198; and Heracles in Rome, 205; and Turnus with Io, 212

Volterra, founds Populonia, 134

Warikas, ruler near Adana, 229; and 'Hiyawa', 231; not a Euboean 'Euarchos', 234

Woolley, Leonard, digs at Al Mina, 103–4, 110; on warrior-traders, 112

Xanthus, of Lydia, on travelling 'Moxos', 233; on 'Arimous' and Typhon, 305

Xenophon, in Cilician Plain, 78; route into Syria, 83–4; gods in his narrative, 340; and aetiology, 375

Xi'an, old capital of Zhou, 16

Yaba, wife of Tiglath Pileser III, her burial, 28

Yahweh, and Baal, 267; and 'dragon of the sea', 298; punishes gross sodomy, 374–5

Zancle, and sickles, 284–7, 379

Zariadres-Zarir, and Persian legends, 185–6

Zeus, and Cronos, 278–9, 362; on Crete, 363–5; and Typhon, 298–317, 365

Zeus Betylos, probably Zeus Kasios, 261

Zeus Kasios, 260–72; in Egypt and western Mediterranean, 270–71; 295

'Zeus of Victory', in south Cilicia, 310–11

Zhou, ruling in China before 771 BC, 13

Zincirli, languages at, 101

Zoroastrians, and ages of metals, 367